REGIMENTAL RECORDS
OF THE
ROYAL WELCH FUSILIERS

THE WAR MEMORIAL, WREXHAM.

[*Frontispiece*

REGIMENTAL RECORDS

OF THE

ROYAL WELCH FUSILIERS

(LATE THE 23RD FOOT)

COMPILED BY

MAJOR C. H. DUDLEY WARD, D.S.O., M.C.
(LATE WELSH GUARDS)

VOL. III
1914—1918
FRANCE AND FLANDERS

The Naval & Military Press Ltd

Reproduced by kind permission of the Regimental Trustees

Published by

The Naval & Military Press Ltd

Unit 10, Ridgewood Industrial Park,

Uckfield, East Sussex,

TN22 5QE England

Tel: +44 (0) 1825 749494

Fax: +44 (0) 1825 765701

www.naval-military-press.com

© The Naval & Military Press Ltd 2005

CONTENTS

I.

II.

THE SHOCK.

1914

CONTENTS

III.

OFFENSIVE OPERATIONS: FIRST PERIOD.

1915

IV.

OFFENSIVE OPERATIONS: SECOND PERIOD.

1916–1917

V.

OFFENSIVE OPERATIONS: THIRD PERIOD.

1917

VI.

DEFENSIVE OPERATIONS.

1918

VII.

PURSUIT OF THE ENEMY.

1918

LIST OF ILLUSTRATIONS

xi

LIST OF MAPS

EXPLANATION OF DIVISIONAL SIGNS USED ON MAPS

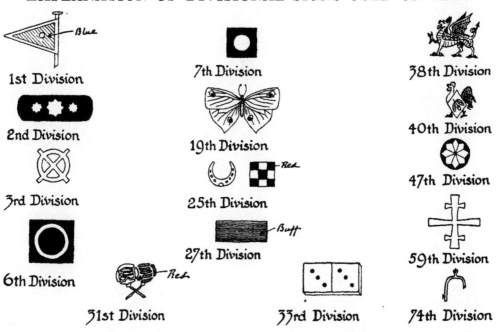

I

REGIMENTAL RECORDS OF THE ROYAL WELCH FUSILIERS

REGIMENTAL RECORDS OF THE ROYAL WELCH FUSILIERS

THERE had never, since the days of Cardwell, been such a thorough over-hauling of our military system as occurred between the end of the South African War and 1914. We had engaged in many wars, but had, apparently, not been prepared for any. There had been periods of panic, when it was believed that a foreign host would descend on the marshes of Kent, when Ballot Acts were put into force, and citizens armed themselves, sometimes with ridicule, and prepared to repel the invaders. Even in the winning of those continents which now form part of the British Empire there was no prepared military organisation for conquest ; those were the acts of adventurers with, at best, the half-hearted approval of the State.

The British citizen has hugged the idea that the sea, being a British element, and perhaps the Fleet, would protect the country from invasion and, maybe, the Colonies from seizure. Can one date the Blue-water School from the loss of Calais by Bloody Mary, when the Kingdom ceased to be continental and became insular, and any renown which England may have possessed for military organisation vanished ? It marks the commencement of that parsimonious system, inaugurated by good Queen Bess, which has found such favour ever since.

During the last century there was a vague guiding principle that India required a certain number of troops ; and there was an established custom of sending small bodies of troops to foreign stations. The Army, existing because it was there, and reluctantly paid for, carried out these duties ; but no one thought sufficiently of the matter to make arrangements which would enable the Army to take the field, either at home or abroad, until a Committee was formed to consider the matter in 1886.

It was then that Lord Wolseley, for the first time, asked the pertinent question of the Government, " What duties is the Army expected to perform ? "

In reply to this embarrassing query, Mr. Stanhope, Secretary of State, declared that the objects of our military organisation were : (1) the effective support of the civil power in the United Kingdom ; (2) to find the number of men for India which had been fixed and arranged with the Government of India ; (3) to find garrisons for all our fortresses and coaling-stations at home and abroad, and to maintain those garrisons at all times at the strength fixed for a peace or war footing ; (4) to be able to mobilise rapidly for Home defence two army corps of Regular troops, and one partly composed of Regulars and partly of Militia ; (5) to organise the military forces of the Crown not allotted to army corps, or garrisons, for the defence of London, and for the defence of mercantile ports ; (6) subject to the foregoing considerations, to aim at being able, in case of necessity, to send abroad two army corps, with cavalry division and line of communication.

"But," he continued, "it will be distinctly understood that the possibility of the employment of an army corps [1] in the field of any European war is sufficiently improbable to make it the primary duty of the military authorities to organise our forces efficiently for the defence of this country."

Everyone then went to sleep, until the South African War revealed the perilous nature of our military organisation, and a situation, *inter alia*, that at one time practically the whole of the Regular Army was in South Africa and India, and the Government, in a panic, created Royal Reserve regiments !

"It would be a national misfortune," said Lord Lansdowne, Secretary of State for War, "were it to become known that after our first army corps had left these shores we could produce only thirty-six battalions, with nothing behind them but a number of partially trained Militia battalions, and the men who had been discarded by the Regular battalions. . . ."

Mr. Stanhope's two army corps did not exist.

The war was followed, as is usually the case, by an inquiry into the misdemeanours of the War Office. The edifice, which was in Pall Mall, has since been pulled down, together with the organisation.

The Royal Commission of inquiry was under the chairmanship of Lord Elgin, and had, as members, Lord Esher, Sir George Taubman Goldie, Sir Henry Norman, Sir John Hopkins, Sir George Edge, Sir John Jackson, Lord Strathcona (representing Canada), and Sir Frederick Matthew Darley (representing New South Wales). The publication of their report created a sensation which was diligently fanned by His Majesty's Opposition. The shaft of ridicule was not spared. "While Mr. Brodrick (Secretary of State) occupies himself with the fifteenth alteration of a piece of braid

[1] An army corps was then three divisions ; a division was a total force of 11,000.

or the quality of a General's cock feathers, he can have no time to see that the sighting of rifles is correct, the transport in working order, the reserve of boots adequate, or details of that sort ! '' (Press.)   '' He has tinkered with buttons, caps, and shoulder-straps.   He has evoked a paper scheme of army corps quite unsuited to our national circumstances, and ruinously costly.   But that is all ! '' (Press.)

In spite of the indignation created, there was a real danger that the question of Army reform might be shelved, or some patchwork scheme introduced and accepted through waning of interest.   The country was passing through a phase of political reaction.   There were, as subjects for oratory, Education, the Fiscal Question, and the employment of Chinese in South Africa ; and the country was being asked to remember the scandals of the war rather than consider the reorganisation of the forces of the Crown.   But, behind all this turmoil, there were a few people who, indifferent to all the misrepresentations of political controversy and determined to solve the problem of the Army, were absorbed in constructive effort.

'' One of the main difficulties,'' Sir Douglas Haig wrote,[1] '' seems to be the want of continuity in ideas and direction at Headquarters.   Schemes seem to be hastily taken up, without due consideration of what the ultimate effect will be, and then quickly another scheme is started to cover the shortcomings of the former one, so that we have confusion worse confounded.''

King Edward sought to induce Lord Esher, who had indicated certain far-reaching reforms in his note to the Royal Commission Report, to take the office of Secretary of State for War.   In a characteristic reply Lord Esher presented '' his humble duty, and begs to say that, the more he reflects the more certain he is that he cannot successfully, and to the satisfaction of your Majesty, become connected with any political party, and take over the highest political affairs.

'' He is deeply grateful to your Majesty, but he knows his own limitations, and he feels sure that his abilities and training are not such as to qualify him for high office, and especially for political controversy.''

To Mr. Balfour, Lord Esher wrote bluntly : '' Political office is abhorrent to me, and I have not the qualifications for it ; but if you think it right to adopt the plan of appointing, under your supervision and that of the Secretary of State, a board of three, of whom I shall be the chairman, to carry out W.O. reorganisation, I will do all in my power to help you.   This is a very difficult piece of work and I feel I could do it.''

[1] *Esher Correspondence.*

At this time Mr. Arnold-Forster succeeded Mr. Brodrick as Secretary of State for War, and commenced producing schemes of reform which were used by his political opponents as so much ammunition.

WAR OFFICE RECONSTRUCTION.

The reformers had in mind not so much the evolving of new ideas as the application of old and sound ones. An " Imperial Committee of Defence " existed in the time of Cromwell as an idea which was given effect, and it was this old idea they were pressing, for a start.

" If Arnold-Forster is wise, he will bury his memoranda for the present, and he will throw all his energies into the creation of a department for the Defence Committee (we will not call it a General Staff) and a War Office Council as an executive authority. . . . My suggestion to you comes to this, do not let Arnold-Forster be in a hurry. Brodrick created six beautiful army corps on paper. Let his colleague beware ! " [1]

Eventually the definite step was taken of appointing a Committee of Three—Lord Esher, Sir John Fisher, and Sir George Clarke—under the name of the War Office Reconstruction Committee. The report they tendered was a remarkable and far-reaching document, containing a revolutionary scheme of decentralisation. It was the basis of the 1914 system.

Counsel and action, however, did not go together. Ideas were diffused. Lord Roberts would say no more than that he could not say whether the changes advocated would improve matters, but " of this I am quite sure, that the system now in force could not continue." Lord Wolseley evidently did not understand the proposals, and repeated what has, no doubt, been said since Monck made the civilian William Clarke Secretary at War : " We have for the last forty years or more, contrary to the practice of every other European nation, striven to govern the Army by politicians. Why not, as an experiment, try to govern it by a soldier ? "

Mr. Arnold-Forster, who received the report with ill-grace, was absorbed in his own schemes, which included a general reduction of battalions and the splitting of the Regular Army into two parts with distinct conditions of service. The component parts of our land forces would have been, under his schemes, a Foreign Service Army, a Home Service Army, the Militia, the Yeomanry, the Volunteers, and, possibly, at the tail end, Rifle Clubs, in which Lord Roberts was beginning to take an interest.

Whatever merits his schemes may have contained, such an arrangement could not have stood the test of war.

[1] *Esher Correspondence* : E. to Prime Minister.

But, under Mr. Arnold-Forster's regime, certain of the proposals of the Committee of Three were put into execution : the Commander-in-Chief (Lord Roberts) disappeared,[1] the Army Council was recognised as a permanent body, and there was a tentative tinkering with administrative districts and commands. But at the same time there was a threat to commence sweeping units away.

QUESTIONS OF ARMY REORGANISATION.

Lord Esher wrote urgently to Mr. Balfour that the adoption of a part of his Committee's scheme would not compensate for the loss " of the one successful coup St. John [Brodrick] effected, which was an army corps, fully equipped for war, officered and trained by the men who would command it in the field. The old fallacy which you see cropping up in the letters of Knox and Halliburton, etc., was the counting of heads—the numerical standard applied to organisation. The question of how many men now at Aldershot you can put in the field is not of vital importance. The real point is how many cadres you can put in the field. Mobilisation will give you the men, but it will not give you divisional commanders and their staffs, brigadiers and their staffs, cavalry commanders and their staffs, infantry commanders and their staffs, and batteries of artillery, trained and exercised together, under a General who knows his officers and whose officers know him."

The Defence Committee then examined the scheme, and Lord Esher sent a report of its proceedings to the King :

" The Committee has been presided over by Mr. Balfour, and in his absence by Lord Esher. On every occasion Lord Roberts has been present, and has taken the greatest interest in the subject.

" Mr. Arnold-Forster's scheme has been found unsuitable to the requirements of India, both in peace and war. It is impracticable in some of its most important particulars. These observations refer more especially to the plan of splitting up the Army into two portions, and largely reducing the cadres of the Regular Army. On the other hand, there are portions of the scheme, relating to large depôts, and the grouping of regiments for certain purposes, and lowering the establishments of regiments at home, which can be usefully carried out.

" Mr. Arnold-Forster's scheme, taken as a whole, gave the Committee

---

[1] It was said that Lord Roberts found on his writing-table a curt note of dismissal, for which the Committee of Three was held responsible. This is not true. He was in the confidence of the Committee, and well aware of their intentions and what they were pressing for. The letter—and something of the sort was written—was not inspired or seen by any of the Committee. Of this I have Lord Esher's assurance.—C. H. D. W.

the impression of having been thought out by him with a view to the requirements of peace rather than of war. To do him justice, he complained that the purposes for which the Army was required have never been made clear to him.

" Mr. Balfour, after long inquiries by the Defence Committee, and very full correspondence with Lord Kitchener, has now laid down the requirements of India in the event of war with Russia on the North-west Frontier. . . . Mr. Balfour has placed it on record that in approaching all questions of Army reform the primary consideration is to meet the eventualities of a war with Russia on the frontiers of India. . . ."

The original question asked by Lord Wolseley was now answered in an unequivocal way.   It was assumed that the Army was not to be organised for the defence of these shores ; in Sir John Fisher's words, " Home defence is adequately provided for by the Fleet " : but the Army was intended to take the field at any threatened point where the interests of the Empire were imperilled, and especially on the North-west Frontier of India.

Peace strategy must inevitably be a changing thing. After careful examination of motives, military and naval dispositions, secret reports, possibilities and probabilities arising from treaty obligations, or any other cause, the Defence Committee could, in the summer of 1905, find no indication of a European War in which Great Britain might become involved. The Indian Empire was the only danger-spot, and Russia the enemy.

Within a few months the Committee was considering the startling possibility of Germany as an enemy ! [1]

In the midst of a perfect Babel of oratory, with the taxation of bread, the Chinese coolie, and the Army all mixed up in delightful confusion, Mr. Balfour resigned office.

The position then stood : The Committee of Imperial Defence had been established definitely, and continuity recognised ; it had laid down certain great principles on which to base Army reform. The post of Commander-in-Chief had been abolished. The Army Council had been established, and the reconstruction scheme for the War Office accepted, though it was not in full working order. A commencement had been made with the General Staff ; one might say it was in being. The main sphere of uncertainty lay in the reduction of units or establishment ; the retention or abolition of the Militia ; the future of the Volunteers ; and generally

---

[1] The Kaiser's attitude during the South African War may be said to have roused the suspicions of some people, but there was a considerable party which did not approve of the Home Government's policy from the date of the Jameson Raid, and they found a ready excuse for the Emperor's friendliness towards the President of the South African Republic. But any *war* suspicion coincided with, and was swamped by, the greater certainty of commercial war.

a scheme which would provide a second line and at the same time be capable of expansion to the needs of a war of the first magnitude.

As many people expressed it, it was to find a substitute for conscription.

THE MODEL ARMY.

King Edward once remarked that the happiest efforts of each Secretary of State were usually the abolition of his predecessor's reforms.

Sir Henry Campbell-Bannerman's Government, with Mr. Haldane as Secretary of State for War, was looked upon as a Little England Government with a mild spice of Liberal Imperialism. They were pledged to economy—they were also pledged to efficiency—but the fatal word " economy," applied to the Army, was feared to be a substitute for destruction. No one doubted that they would scrap the work of Mr. Brodrick and Mr. Arnold-Forster, and reduce the Army to impotence as a fighting force.

The military world was despondent. Within fifty years there had been four distinct military policies : the policy of Palmerston, with its coast fortifications, which cost £7,420,000, and was useless ; the eight Army Corps scheme of 1875 ; the Defence scheme of 1889, with its London defences—a total waste of money ; and the six Army Corps scheme of Mr. Brodrick in 1901. What would be the next ?

The history of the British Army shows that military organisation has always depended on a territorial system of recruiting and, more or less, of administration. " We take the territorial arrangements of regiments established in 1873 as the basis of our scheme," said the Committee of Three. Mr. Haldane turned to the origin of this idea for his conception of a National Army, which would have the Regular Army as a spearhead, or Striking Force.

Queen Elizabeth had to face a military crisis, and she was a ruler whose financial principles were of a parsimonious nature. She directed that in each county a convenient number of men should be chosen " meet to be sorted in bands, and to be trained and exercised in such sort as may be reasonably borne by a common charge on the whole county." This order was the origin of the trained bands, or local Militia regiments.

These regiments met once a month, during the summer, and learned to drink rather than drill—with the exception of the City of London.

When civil war broke out, both the Royalists and Parliamentarians found the trained bands outside London useless. " The county levies were ready enough to fight in defence of their own homes, but were unwilling to move far from them. . . . The Parliament tried to meet it [the difficulty] by the establishment of associations of counties, which were virtually military districts, and did something, though not much, to widen the narrow sympathies of the militiamen." (Fortescue.)   Each county had its garrisons raised by the County Committee, and each group of Associated Counties had each their major-general and Field Army.   So Mr. Haldane visualised a National Army which should be formed of the people and managed by specially organised local associations—in fact a new Model Army !

It might be called, Mr. Haldane suggested, the Territorial Army.

In the matter of home defence, Mr. Haldane once more laid down the principle that the Navy must be recognised as a complete guarantee against invasion.   The Territorial Army should be regarded rather as a latent source of strength, which would have to be gradually developed during the progress of war, than as an active force which would be immediately available at the commencement of hostilities.

The possibilities of the Associations which were to raise this force were great.   They should, Mr. Haldane thought, be the means of awakening throughout the country a healthy interest in all that appertained to the Army.   At first they would have to concentrate their energies on the organisation of the Territorial Army, and on the training of its personnel ; and it was only necessary to emphasise the advisability of entrusting to them the management of all funds expended on the Territorial Army, whether such funds were provided locally or took the form of Grants in Aid provided from the Imperial Exchequer.

Summarised, Mr. Haldane's scheme was to concentrate on two forces only—the Striking Force (Regulars) and the Territorial Army (non-Regulars).   At first he aimed at mobilising a Striking Force of four or five cavalry brigades, three army corps, with three regiments of Imperial Yeomanry, two brigades of Field Artillery, and sixteen battalions (Militia) for employment on lines of communication—some 150,000 to 160,000 troops in all.

To complete the organisation of the Striking Force and enable it to take the field, Mr. Haldane believed that he would have to draw on the Militia for such elements as railway, telegraph, artificers' duties, the manning of ammunition columns and parks, a good deal of the supply and transport work, and much of the medical assistance in the field.   With the exception of these earmarked units and specialists, he wanted the Militia, Yeomanry, and Volunteers to be welded into the Territorial Force. And it must be noted that the line of thought which led up to the formation of the Territorial Force held the possibility of that force being employed abroad, although men actually signed on for Home defence.

But—and this was the crucial question—Mr. Haldane was puzzled by the problem of reinforcements for the Striking Force, and exactly how he should treat the Militia.

For some time he played with the idea of the Militia as a sort of reservoir, into which the Regular Army should dip, and into which skimmings from the Territorial Army could be drafted in time of war ; but a midway force, retained as a separate entity, did not fit.

The Militia could not stand by itself : it was in an unsatisfactory condition, and the reason was that there was no definite function assigned to it—one might say that it had been robbed of the greater part by the creation of the Volunteers. The Militia was under no obligation to serve abroad; it did so of its own free will. It had been used to furnish drafts for the Regular Army, bled white, and then asked to go abroad in depleted battalions to fight ! The Militia never recovered. But the biggest blow of all was undoubtedly the creation of the Volunteers.

A tremendous lot of discussion went on amongst the Militia, the Yeomanry, and the Volunteers. All the Auxiliary Forces agreed that " things cannot go on as they are ! "—but when it came to radical changes they were conservative, with all the obstinate sentiment of antiquarians. An enormous Committee, dubbed the Duma, was appointed to inquire into the means of putting Mr. Haldane's ideas into practice, and accomplished little or nothing. It seemed as though the Secretary of State would fail over the Militia.

Apart from the not unnatural obstinacy of the Militia and Volunteers, there were strong objections to the scheme from military quarters, as may be gathered from this short expression of opinion from Lord Kitchener ; but it must be remembered that he was preoccupied with Indian requirements—while in England that soldier of vision, Lord Roberts, was thinking of Germany.

" We have all, of course, read Mr. Haldane's able statement of his confession of faith on military matters, and realise the fact that the present policy at the War Office has tended towards destruction of the substance while relying on the shadow of a patriotic and territorial levee *en masse*, conceived in the womb of time and which its progenitor describes as the gradual growth of years, while its success or otherwise can only be gauged by actual experience.

" We realise that for the present the Expeditionary Force when mobilised will include practically all England's fighting men of any value whatever. As, however, the Home Government have given neither hint nor suggestion that the pledge given to India last year by Mr. Balfour's

Government, which was heartily concurred in by the then Opposition, is to be ignored, we can but infer that the Expeditionary Force, which is roughly of a strength of eight divisions, is earmarked as the promised Indian reinforcements *en bloc* in time of war.

"Moreover, if we were to seriously follow the shuttlecock of the War Office changes of policy in its almost annual reversal of direction, I cannot help thinking we should never be able to enjoy any finality of policy in India. It seems to me, therefore, preferable to treat the recent departure as merely one of the passing clouds with which the military outlook at Home is so frequently overcast, and wait patiently for a brighter day."[1]

Feeling ran high, and when Mr. Haldane issued his Sixth Memorandum, crystallising the somewhat dispersed thoughts of previous memoranda, and making it clear that the Militia must go, that conditions of service must be altered, and that means must be found to maintain the Striking Force for six months in the field, it was all so startling that yet another Committee was appointed to inquire and consider the scheme of the Secretary of State.

The Committee consisted of Lord Esher, General Sir Neville Lyttelton, General Sir John French, Major-General Ewart, and Sir George Clarke. It was definitely laid down and accepted, as a basis for their inquiry, that the Expeditionary Force required was six infantry divisions, of three brigades each, and four cavalry brigades.

Their conclusions were that, under the existing organisation, we could not, even approximately, mobilise and maintain in the field the six divisions and four cavalry brigades ; that we had not sufficient reserves available to meet the wastage of war and to maintain in the field the forces demanded ; that the Auxiliary Forces, though available for Home defence,[2] could not be reckoned in the troops required to meet the external needs of the Empire.

The Committee reported that though the changes proposed were drastic, they might be justified by the actual unsatisfactory state of affairs, and that if Mr. Haldane's expectations were realised it was evident that the military strength of the country would be increased by the measures contemplated.

They had cleared the way for the Territorial and Reserve Forces Act, 1907.

The Militia became the Special Reserve, with the concession that units should retain their entity and connection with their Regular battalions,

---

[1] K. to E.   [2] The Militia was 40,000 below strength.

to which they would be the reserve. Thus the Regular battalion had its Reserve, and its Special Reserve battalion, or 3rd Battalion.

The following entry was made in the Records of the 3rd (Militia) Battalion Royal Welch Fusiliers, under date 21st July 1908 :

" In accordance with the terms of the Order in Council dated 9th April 1908, the 3rd Battalion, having completed the prescribed period of annual training on the 27th June 1908, has been transferred to the Army Reserve, as a unit of Special Reserve, with effect from the 28th June."

Under the Act there came into being the 4th (Wrexham), 5th (Flint), 6th (Carnarvon), and 7th (Newtown) Battalions Royal Welch Fusiliers, Territorial Force.

THE DECLARATION OF WAR.

One must not fall into the error of measuring the success of Mr. Haldane's Act by a counting of Regular and Territorial heads. Numerically the fourteen Territorial divisions were below strength in 1914 ; but the organisation was there, in working order.[1] And the interest aroused by all this discussion and wordy warfare did not die down : there followed, to keep the nation awake, the growing menace of Germany [2] and the Entente with France—like a volcano before eruption, Germany was always making rumbling noises.

That the Striking Force was ready in 1914 no one can deny ; that the use and requirements of the artillery should reach such phenomenal proportions in modern warfare is beside the point—within the limits laid down the small British war machine was prepared.[3] Over the intervening years the Expeditionary Force was perfected, the Special Reserve formed, the Territorial Army had been through five annual trainings, and the War Book was written.

The murder of the Austrian Archduke, at Sarajevo, was the spark that fired the magazine. Peace strategy had formed on one side the Triple Alliance of Germany, Austria, and Italy (also a secret understanding with Turkey) ; on the other, treaties between France and Russia, and what

[1] Total establishment of the Territorial Force was : 12,700 officers, 303,394 other ranks ; strength on 1st August 1914 was : 10,684 officers and 258,093 other ranks.

[2] The Algeciras affair, 1906 ; the annexation, by her ally, Austria, of Bosnia and Herzegovina, 1908 ; the Agadir crisis, 1911, etc. etc.

[3] How closely the German danger had been studied by the keenest military minds may be judged from the fact that in 1911 Sir Henry Wilson, then Director of Military Operations, gave to the Committee of Imperial Defence a forecast of the probable German plan of attack on France—under the existing treaties of alliance. He predicted that the German Armies would draw up on a line from the Swiss frontier to Aix-la-Chapelle ; they would then swing their right wing through Belgium, thus turning the line of fortresses by which the eastern frontier of France was protected.—*The World Crisis* (Churchill).

was called the Entente Cordiale with Great Britain. The latter was a limited promise of support to France in the event of unprovoked and concerted attack ; scarcely a pledge—a diplomatic handshake and expression of sympathy, in the nature of " I'll help you, if I can ! "

Events moved with dramatic and tragic speed ; in the attitude of Germany there was theatrical and criminal bombast, a determination to force war at any cost. The whole nation had been trained to " *Der Tag !* " —and when the crash was evident, Socialists, Communists, Reds of all shades, forgot their international fraternity and rallied round the Kaiser— their *Kriegsherr* !

It was dramatic and criminal in its day, and the lapse of time has not made those events seem less astounding. Still, it is probable that Great Britain would have stood aloof for a time—one can hardly imagine a victorious Germany allowing us to remain out of the war—had the German leaders not elected to attack France through Belgium.

Sir Edward Grey, Secretary of State for Foreign Affairs, did his best to avert war, but this last move of the Germans, against a small, defenceless State, in no way involved in the quarrel, and, moreover, a State whose neutrality the Powers of Europe were pledged to protect, was actually a declaration of war against Great Britain ! Technically we declared war against Germany.

Serving Officers, Royal Welch Fusiliers (1st August 1914).

c.o. = Colonial Office.
t. = Serving with the Territorial Force.
s. = Staff.
f.o. = Foreign Office.
e.a. = Egyptian Army.
r. = Serving with Special Reserve.
i.v. = Serving with Indian Volunteers.
r.e. = Regular Establishment.

Lieutenant-Colonels.

2 Delmé-Radcliffe, H.
1 Cadogan, H. O. S.

Majors.

f.o. Doughty-Wylie, C. H. M., C.B., C.M.G.
s. Berners, R.A.
c.o. Braithwaite, W. G., D.S.O.
1 Gabbett, R. E. P.

(3) 2 Hay, A. (Commanding Depôt).
c.o. Cockburn, J. B.
2 Williams, O. de L.
s. Hill, H.

Captains.

2 Walwyn, F. J., D.S.O.
2 Geiger, G. J. P.
2 Powell, D.
Kington, W. M., D.S.O.

1 Harris-St. John, W.
t. Norman, C. C.
2 Owen, C. S., Adjutant.
(3) 1 Stockwell, C.
e.a. Bayly, E. A. T.
t. de Pentheny O'Kelly, E. J.
1 Vyvyan, W. G.
e.a. Kyrke, H. V. V.
2 Phillips, R. N.
(3) 2 Gwyther, G. H.
t. Garnett, W. B.
(3) 1 Lloyd, M. E.
t. Minshull Ford, J. R. M.
e.a. Webb-Bowen, H. I.
1 Jones, S.
t. Lloyd, R. L.
1 Barker, R. V.
i.v. Venables, J. D.
r. Crawshay, C. H. R.
c.o. Fox, L. d'A.
2 Pery-Knox-Gore, W. H. C.
s. Hutton, G. F.
e.a. Kearsley, E. R.
1 Skaife, E. O.
2 Samson, A. L.
t. Wood, C. E.
2 Jones-Vaughan, E. N.
1 Edwards, C. H.
1 Smyth-Osbourne, J. G.
2 Lloyd-Mostyn, M. L.

Lieutenants.

2 Thomas, G. O.
(3) 2 Stable, L. L.
c.o. de Miremont, G. E. R.
2 Ormrod, L. M.
1 Anwyl, M. I. H.
c.o. Brunor-Randall, J. G.
2 Childe-Freeman, J. A. C.
(3) 1 Parry, M. D. G.

c.o. Davis, H. H.
2 Wynne-Edwards, J. C.
1 Dooner, A. E. C. T., Adjutant.
2 Maltby, P. C.
1 Hindson, R. E.
2 Fitzroy, C. A. E.
1 Hoskyns, E. C. L.
1 Chance, G. O. de P.
2 Holmes, W. G.
1 Barchard, D. M.
1 Courage, J. H.
1 Poole, B. C. H.
1 Alston, L. A. A.
2 Mostyn, P. G. J.

2nd Lieutenants.

1 Hardie, H. R.
1 Evans, J. M. J.
1 Peppe, C. G. H.
1 Ackland-Allen, H. T.
1 Snead-Cox, G. P. J.
1 Wodehouse, E.

Quartermasters.

1 Parker, E. A.
r. Hickman, E.
2 Yates, H.

SPECIAL RESERVE.
Captain.

Clarke, H. H.

3RD BATTALION.
Lieutenant-Colonel.
Jones-Williams, H. R.

Majors.

t. Philips, B. E.
r.e. Hay, A.

Captains.

Macartney-Filgate, A. R. P.
Lane, A. P.
Jones, E. B.
France-Hayhurst, F. C. (seconded).
Brennan, J. H.
Fairclough, R. (seconded).
r.e. Stockwell, C. I.
Tringham, L. W. H.
Jones, M. G.
r.e. Gwyther, G. H.
r.e. Lloyd, M. E.

Lieutenants.

Prichard, T. L.
Ormrod, J.
Lloyd, L. S.
Hadley, F. C.
Blosse, R. C. L.
Jones, E. T.
r.e. Stable, L. L.
r.e. Parry, M. D. G.
Cuthbert, J.
Raffles, R. L. S.
Richardson, A. K.
Stamper, E. P. F.
French, R. M. J.

2nd Lieutenants.

Thompson, E. J. V. C.
Gore, G. R.

Quartermaster.

Hickman, E. A.

4TH (DENBIGHSHIRE) BATTALION.
Lieutenant-Colonel.

France-Hayhurst, F. C.

Majors.

Johnson, A. E.
Wilson, W. R.

Captains.

Davies, J. C.
Mayes, G. R.
Bury, T. O.
Withers, W. N.
Roberts, R.
Davies, A. S.
Williams, W. C. B.

Lieutenants.

Evans, J. E.
Griffith, J. V.
Davies, A. L.
Foulkes-Roberts, P. R.
Rouffignac, F. D.
Davies, C. O.
Griffith, G. R.
Hugh-Jones, N.

2nd Lieutenants.

Bury, C. L.
Croom-Johnson, B.
Harrop, N. M.
Owen, R.
Minshall, T. C. W.

Adjutant.

Minshull-Ford, J. R. M.

Quartermaster.

Manfield, T.

5TH (FLINTSHIRE) BATTALION.
Lieutenant-Colonel.

Philips, B. E.

Majors.

Keene, T. M. (seconded).
Head, B.
Williams, E. J. H.

Captains.

Williams, J. L.
Borthwick, F. H.
Beswick, W.
Trickett, W. E.

Lieutenants.

Parry, T. H.
Marston, J. B.
Kingsbury, A. (seconded).
Jefferson, H. A.

2nd Lieutenants.

Roberts, E. H.
Parry, J. E.
Taylor, K. B.
Armstrong, T. H.
Hughes, J.
Owens, R. J.
Astbury, A. N.
King, F. J.
Alexander, G. A.
Horner, G. A.
Williams, H. O.
Davies, H. M.
Corbett, F.
Bate, T.
Mocatta, R. M.
Roberts, D. R. K.

Adjutant.

Wood, C. E.

Quartermaster.

Claridge, G.

III—2

6TH (CARNARVONSHIRE AND ANGLESEY) BATTALION.

Lieutenant-Colonel.

Roberts, H. J.

Majors.

Roberts, R. H. M.
Tuxford, W. A.

Captains.

Wheeler, A. H.
Jenkins, H. T.
Evans, J.
Griffith, R.
Battersby, G. L.
Hughes-Hunter, Sir W. B. H.

Lieutenants.

Darbishire, C. W. (seconded).
Cemlyn-Jones, J.
Roberts, J. H. S.
Miller, J.
Evans, E. H.
Jones, J. R. M.
Bracken, R. J.
Anthony, J. R.

2nd Lieutenants.

Stonor, C. H. J.
Russell, J. F.
Evans, J. H.

Adjutant.

Lloyd, R. L.

Quartermaster.

Armstrong, T.

7TH (MERIONETHSHIRE AND MONTGOMERY) BATTALION.

Lieutenant-Colonel.

Jelf-Reveley, A. E. R.

Captains.

Davies, D.
Corbett-Winder, W. J.
Arbuthnot-Briscoe, R. J. W.
Pryce-Jones, P. V.
Owen, O.
Lloyd-Jones, E. W.

Lieutenants.

Davies, D. O.
Williams, I. O. W.
Davies, J. A.

Jones, O. C.
Jones, A. M.
Beadon, B. H. E.
Johnston, T. C. S.
Hampson, W. (seconded).

2nd Lieutenants.

Price, E. P.
Harries, E. G.
Parkes, G. K.
Swift, C. B.

Adjutant.

Garnett, W. B.

Quartermaster.

Richards, W. F.

THE EXPANSION OF THE ROYAL WELCH FUSILIERS.

THE actual hour of Great Britain's declaration of war was 11 p.m. on the 4th August; but the situation in July was tense, and on the 27th July the precaution was taken of cancelling the order to the Fleet to disperse after manœuvres.

On the 29th July the Austrians commenced to bombard Belgrade; and the German Imperial Chancellor had a significant interview with the British Ambassador on the subject of neutrality. On the same day further precautionary measures, arranged by our General Staff, were put into force.

The 1st Battalion Royal Welch Fusiliers was at Malta, so we have to deal with the 2nd Battalion, which had just returned from India and was at Wool, for company training;[1] with the 3rd Battalion (Special Reserve), which left Wrexham on the 7th July to undergo twenty-seven days' annual training at Porthcawl; and with the 4th, 5th, 6th, and 7th Battalions (Territorial Force), also in annual camp for training at Aberystwyth.

On the 30th July the 2nd Battalion received orders to proceed forthwith to their peace stations at Portland and Dorchester (one company). On the 31st July the 3rd Battalion were ordered to move to Pembroke

---

[1] Bovington Camp.

Dock, where they took over the East and West Blockhouses, Milton Waterworks, the Wireless Station, and Pembroke Dockyard. On the 1st August both France and Germany ordered general mobilisation, and in England the orders for Army manœuvres and Territorial training were cancelled ; the 4th, 5th, 6th, and 7th Battalions returned to their respective headquarters on the 3rd.

Throughout England soldiers and civilians waited anxiously, eagerly buying the special editions of newspapers—one came out with the headline " To Hell with Servia ! " which probably represented the feelings of the great majority of the people.   But, having declared war on France on the 3rd, Germany extended it to Belgium on the 4th, and public opinion in England, from a state of shocked bewilderment, became firm and clear.

The 2nd Battalion was ready.   Captain Geiger, writing of those momentous days, says : " Williams and I had gone into Bournemouth for dinner on Thursday, 30th July.   On our return to Wool . . . we noticed flames, and my first idea was that the canteen was on fire !   However, on pulling up, Knox-Gore rushed up and, in a voice quivering with emotion, informed us that we were ordered back to our peace stations and were starting in ten minutes.   My company's peace station was Dorchester, the other three being in the Verne Fort at Portland.   I had my own car in a shed close by, and was wondering what I could do about it, when the C.O. came up and told me I could drive myself home and leave the company to be brought along by Samson (2nd Captain) and the two subalterns, Wynne-Edwards and Fitzroy.   I got back to Dorchester about midnight, and then waited weary hours for the company to arrive, which it eventually did in great spirits at about 3 a.m.

' The next few days were a period of anxious waiting. . . .   We had made all transport arrangements, etc., to set out at once for Portland as soon as the mobilisation signal came through, so when it finally did arrive at about 2.30 a.m. on the 4th August, we were under way by 3.15.   We started in the pouring rain, the men in the best of spirits, singing at the top of their voices.   I have forgotten what they sang, but it certainly was not ' Tipperary,' which was already out of date in Quetta the previous year. . . . We climbed the hill to the Verne at about 8 a.m.   I noticed a Red Cross flag flying from the Naval Hospital flagstaff at Portland, and so knew that war had been declared.

" The next hours were passed in a whirl of mobilisation, and at least two parties of reservists came in, the first one under the command of Clegg-Hill (R. of O.).   Our mobilisation equipment was not of the best, since, having only just arrived from India, we did not belong to any division or brigade, and did not, on paper, belong to the Expeditionary Force of six divisions."

A. M. Boreham, who became Sergeant-Major of the 2nd Battalion later in the war, and was then Company Sergeant-Major of B Company,[1] gives an account of the memorable march from Wool to Portland.

" At the outbreak of the Great War I was Company Sergeant-Major of B Company, 2nd Battalion Royal Welch Fusiliers. I have often thought since how in the April and May of 1914, when we were engaged in platoon and company training, Captain Douglas Powell would, in his lectures, picture us with Germans as our opponents. Few of us dreamt at the time that in a few short months we should have them as such in reality. I do not think that even when things were reaching a climax on the continent we discussed our chances of having to take any part in it. To me personally it came with the suddenness of a thunderbolt, and it was in this way. The battalion was in camp at Wool, in Dorsetshire, engaged in training and musketry. We were to return to Portland, our station, towards the end of July, stay there about a week, and then go to Salisbury Plain for manœuvres. We Company Sergeant-Majors had just received the detail for the moves from the Adjutant, Captain C. S. Owen, and I had not got back to my tent when the bugler sounded, ' Company Sergeant-Majors at the double.' Back we went to the orderly-room ; this time the orders were very brief : ' Strike camp and pack up. We march back to Portland to-night.' Then it flashed through my mind—' WAR.' The men were jubilant, as is usual in such circumstances. I'm not afraid to place it on record that I was not ; the South African War had taught me that there was nothing at all to get jubilant about. It is strange what thoughts pass through one's mind in times of crisis. The very first thing that came to my mind was the recollection of being verminous in South Africa, and of the intense horror of being so again. Then I began to think of other things.

" It was about seven in the evening when the order was issued, and we got to work at once and were on our way to Portland before midnight. Pickets had been sent out to round up the men who were out of camp, but of course there were the usual few absentees at tattoo ; these must have had a shock when they returned and found that the camp had disappeared. The goat, which had been unwell, died that night ; he must have known something. Fortunately the night was fine, but the march

---

[1] The 1914 Infantry Training Manual had just come into force, with the reorganisation of battalions in four companies, instead of eight. It made many drastic changes. The title of colour-sergeant was done away with and company sergeant-majors and company quartermaster-sergeants were created.

was long and dreary. Day was breaking as we came down the hills to Weymouth, and when we sighted the harbour we had our next forecast of the war : when we had last seen it the harbour was full of warships, now none could be seen. As the daylight increased, the awful sleepiness always associated with night-marching wore off and the march became less irksome. The band and drums started to play, and the good folks of Weymouth were roused about six a.m. by the ' drums ' playing ' I do like to be beside the sea-side.'

" The next sign of ' war ' was at the bridge half-way between Weymouth and Portland, over an arm of the sea, where a guard was mounted. It was strange how these various signs impressed one with the sense that things were very unusual.

" Portland rises abruptly from sea-level, and the final climb of nearly 600 feet was not a very nice finish to a march of about twenty-two miles in marching order ; needless to say that we were all very pleased when we reached the top. Here those of us who possessed wives found them waiting wide-eyed and apprehensive of the reason of our returning so suddenly.

" Then followed a week of preparation for the expected mobilisation. Though the order had not been received, our regimental authorities very wisely anticipated it, so that when it did come there was less to be done than would otherwise have been the case. The battalion had been fitted out with home-service clothing and equipment after our return from India in the previous March, the whole of the band and drums completed with their respective types of tunics, but everything had to be packed away or handed in to stores ; paybooks and identity discs checked up to date, nominal rolls for everything prepared. Fortunately for me, I had finished my tour of duty as Sergeants' Mess president the previous quarter. Bill Barling had the job of packing up the Mess in addition to all the other work.

" I've often reflected since on how many things ' came true.' When we first got the paybooks and identity discs about two years before the war, we smiled at the idea of ever having occasion to use such things. Behind the commanding officer's table in the orderly-room was a mobilisation chart—another smile. What an awful bore it was to have to listen to the ' King's Rules and Regulations ' relating to active service read out each quarter !—and when we had to make out family allotment forms the smile developed into a broad grin. As the days passed the situation became more critical and the work of preparation more strenuous. I had just time to rush home, snatch a bit of food, and then back to business. It was usual to be roused by a knock in the middle of the night and told by an orderly that I was wanted at the orderly-room. I don't think Jimmy Caldwell, the Orderly-room Sergeant, got much sleep at all at this time. When the day of departure arrived, there were not many of the administrative staff who were at all sorry."

. . . .

The first act of the Government had been to embody the Territorial Force and call out the Naval Reserves ; the order to mobilise the Army was not issued until 4 p.m. on the 4th August—but the Army sometimes moves slightly before time.

Meanwhile, from the 3rd Battalion, Major Hay, Captains Stockwell, Crawshay, Tringham, and Lieutenant Stable had, on the 1st August, returned to the Regimental Depôt at Wrexham to prepare for the expected mobilisation (the Quartermaster, Hickman, and eight drummer-boys had preceded them). The mobilisation order was received at Wrexham at 5 p.m., and within thirty-six hours 1,300 reservists had reported. Three hundred and fifty-nine were clothed and equipped and sent to the 2nd Battalion on the first day of mobilisation.[1]

The four Territorial battalions mobilised at their respective head-quarters, and were quickly made up to strength. They went into camp at Conway on the 22nd August, but they, too, were ready within twenty-four hours.

Departure of the 2nd Battalion.

The excitement was intense, but no one knew what was to happen —when they would leave, or what would be their destination ! There was plenty of news to discuss : two German cavalry divisions, followed by infantry, had entered Belgium on the 4th ; on the 5th they were engaged before Liège ; on the 6th, with the consent of King Albert, a French cavalry corps (Sordet) crossed the Belgian frontier. While, at Home, Lord Kitchener, who had been on the point of leaving England, was recalled and made Secretary of State for War ; and there was a great scene in the Commons when Mr. Will Crooks, member for Woolwich, gave the House a lead in the singing of the National Anthem !

The Cabinet decision was to send four infantry divisions and the cavalry division from the Expeditionary Force ; embarkation was to commence on the 9th August. The reason for cutting down the number of divisions was that Lord Kitchener still had in mind the possibility of a raid in force by the enemy and retained, for the time being, the 4th and

---

[1] 2nd Battalion was under strength.

6th Divisions. It is also curious that, although there had been many meetings between the French and British Staff, the area of concentration in France for the British Army had never been discussed : the Le Cateau—Avesnes area was now selected.

The 2nd Battalion was ordered from Portland to Dorchester on the 6th, the order causing considerable excitement, which fizzled out when they discovered their destination *was* Dorchester. [" First billet, Infants' School—block floor with pack for a pillow." (R.Q.M.S. Powell.)] The boys under age were replaced from the Reserve, the battalion was equipped and brought up to strength. The power of the trumpet-call was extraordinary.

" I remember two absentees returning, one a man who had deserted from our 1st Battalion (our predecessors at Portland) two years before to the Channel Islands, and who immediately returned at his own expense ; and the other one of the bad hats of my own company, who had cleared off nine days previously, and who was making his way to the South Wales coal-fields—this man, on reading the mobilisation posters, turned round and walked back again, a good example of proper spirit." (Geiger.)

Early in the morning of the 10th the battalion left Dorchester, still ignorant of their destination, in two trains—A and B Companies, under Major Williams, in the first, and Headquarters, C and D Companies in the second.

Major Williams prophesied " a sumptuous Cunarder, with unlimited champagne at the Government's expense," but was only right in so far as embarkation was concerned : on arrival at Southampton, A and B Companies marched to a wretched Irish pig-boat, the *Glengariffe*, in which they sailed ; C and D Companies—under Major Williams !—remained at Southampton until the 13th.

The Expeditionary Force crossed the Channel without a hitch ; both train and shipping arrangements were superb. Sir John French was given command, and crossed on the 14th. Lieutenant-General Sir Douglas Haig was appointed to command the I Corps ; Lieutenant-General Sir James Grierson the II Corps (he died suddenly on the 17th, and was succeeded by Sir Horace Smith-Dorrien) ; Lieutenant-General W. P. Pulteney the III Corps ; and Major-General E. Allenby the Cavalry Division.

THE 1ST BATTALION.

The Government started arrangements for the relief of battalions abroad, but the 1st Battalion did not return from Malta [1] until 16th September,

---

[1] Left Malta 3rd September on the s.s. *Ultonia*, a Cunard emigrant ship taken off the Trieste—New York service. Two days were spent at Gibraltar, while a convoy of troopships was assembled and escorted to Southampton.

when they went to Lyndhurst, near Southampton. They sailed from Southampton on the 4th October, amidst great excitement, for the whole town was up all night to give the 7th Division a " send-off." The orders were quite unexpected and caught many officers on leave visiting friends in the neighbourhood—servants were dispatched in motor-cars in all directions. A good number of men were also in Southampton on pass, but the number that did not reach the ship was insignificant.

The Territorial Battalions.

The four Territorial battalions of the regiment formed one brigade, the North Wales Brigade of the Welsh (Territorial) Division. The divisional war station was at Shrewsbury, but the North Wales Brigade remained at Conway until the division was ordered to Northampton, on the 29th August.

At the end of October the need for troops was urgent, and the 4th and 5th Battalions were earmarked for immediate service overseas. On the 5th November the 4th Battalion left the division, and embarked at Southampton for France.

The 5th, 6th, and 7th Battalions remained, being employed at intervals in the digging of trenches on the east coast. The division was again moved to Cambridge on the 21st December, and then to Bedford on the 5th May 1915. On the 13th May the designation of the division was altered to the 53rd (Welsh) Division, and the North Wales Brigade became the 158th Infantry Brigade, with the 1st Battalion Herefordshire Regiment (Territorial Force) in place of the 4th Battalion Royal Welch Fusiliers.

The 158th Brigade continued training until July 1915, when, on the 14th, the 5th and 6th Battalions entrained for Devonport and embarked on the s.s. *Caledonian*, to be followed on the 17th by the 7th Battalion, which embarked on the s.s. *City of Edinburgh*. The whole of the 53rd Division set sail for Gallipoli.

.   .   .   .

The 3rd Battalion and Expansion.

The 3rd Battalion left the Defensible Barracks at Pembroke on the 9th August 1914, and returned to their headquarters at Wrexham.

At Wrexham their strength varied between 1,500 and 2,000, and the troops were encamped in the football field at the back of the barracks.

The battalion was called upon to furnish detachments for certain war stations—Conway, Holyhead, Menai, Warrington, Lancaster, Queensferry, and Denbigh—and was drawn upon for reinforcements of various natures. Major Hay was promoted Lieutenant-Colonel on the 21st August, and appointed to command the 8th Battalion, the first *Service* battalion to be raised. With him went Captain G. H. Gwyther and Lieutenant M. D. G. Gambier-Parry.

On the 19th September Captains M. E. Lloyd, J. H. Brennan, 2nd Lieutenants C. R. Egerton, Hon. C. R. B. Bingham, A. Walmsley, T. Taylor, and a draft of 342 other ranks left Wrexham to join the 1st Battalion, which had arrived at Lyndhurst.

Orders were then received that the 3rd Battalion (all Regiments) was to be raised to a strength of 2,600 ; but at the end of October it was reduced to 1,500, and recruits in excess of that number were formed into the 12th Battalion, commanded by Major Glynn. By the end of December 1914, 35 officers and 2,429 other ranks had been sent as reinforcements from the 3rd Battalion to the 1st and 2nd Battalions.

But the whole idea of expansion and reinforcement, foreshadowed in Mr. Haldane's scheme, was swept aside by Lord Kitchener. He never extended his sympathy to the Territorial Force, or showed any enthusiasm for the possibilities of the Territorial County Associations. Although he allowed the Associations to raise 2nd, 3rd, and Reserve Battalions, he started Service Battalions, or Kitchener's Army, as it was called, at once. It is contended that the popularity of the Territorials had suffered from a cheap sneer, and that he was right to exploit the popularity of his own name ; and also that Mr. Haldane's scheme for expansion had not yet received statutory sanction [1]—which, considering Lord Kitchener's powers, means nothing. However that may be, the matter was trivial at the time ; men were wanted, schemes and names of the past were of no importance— men, and more men ! The 8th and 9th Service Battalions of the regiment were up to strength by the end of August 1914, and recruits continued to line up for enlistment.

On the 19th September 1914, at the Queen's Hall, London, the Earl of Plymouth, as Lord-Lieutenant of Glamorgan, presided over a meeting that was addressed by Mr. Lloyd George (Chancellor of the Exchequer) upon the cause of the Great War, and a proposal to recruit a Welsh army corps was put forward and adopted. This was followed, on the 29th, by a National Conference at the Park Hall, Cardiff, where Mr. Lloyd George announced official sanction for the raising of a Welsh corps, on condition that it would be independent of, and in addition to, the Regular battalions of the Royal Welch Fusiliers, the Welch Regiment, and the South Wales Borderers, and the existing Welsh Division (Territorial).

A Welsh Army Corps Committee was appointed, consisting of the

---

[1] *Military Operations,* 1914.

Earl of Plymouth, Mr. D. Lloyd George, Lord Kenyon, Lord Dynevor, Lord Treowen, Lord Rhondda, Mr. David Brynmor Jones, Mr. William Brace, General Sir Henry Mackinnon, Sir Watkin Williams Wynn, General Sir Owen Thomas, Lieutenant-Colonel David Davies, Lieutenant-Colonel Ivor Bowen, Lieutenant-Colonel Sir John Lynn Thomas, Sir Leonard Llewelyn, Mr. William George, the Rev. Colonel John Williams, Sir Frederick Mills, Mr. Edward Hughes, Mr. Henry Clement, Mr. Ivor Gwynne, Mr. R. T. Jones, Mr. David Davies, Sir William Davies, Major-General Sir Owen Philipps, and Mr. Owen W. Owen (Secretary).

The Army Council issued its formal authority to General Sir Henry Mackinnon, G.O.C. Western Command, on the 10th October, the new units to be raised as Service battalions of the existing Welsh Regular regiments, and the corps to consist of two divisions.

Until the financial and military organisation passed into the hands of the Army Council,[1] when voluntary recruiting ceased, the Welsh Army Corps Committee had raised the 13th, 14th, 15th (London), 16th, 17th (London), 18th, 19th, 20th, 21st, and 22nd Battalions Royal Welch Fusiliers, and had expended £1,750,000 of public money on their work. The 38th (Welsh) Division was formed, but no second division. A 68th (Welsh) Division was afterwards raised, but it was purely a Home-defence division.

Following on the numbers of the Territorial Force battalions of the regiment came the 8th, 9th, 10th, and 11th Service Battalions—these may be called the Kitchener battalions. The 12th was, as has already been stated, an offshoot of the 3rd, and was a reserve and draft-finding battalion.

Of the numbers 13 to 22, which were raised by the Welsh Corps Committee, the 13th, 14th, 15th, 16th, 17th, and 19th served abroad, but the 18th, 20th, 21st, and 22nd became Reserve training battalions, at one time finding drafts, as did the 23rd.

The 24th and 25th Battalions were the dismounted Denbighshire Yeomanry and Welsh Horse—in no sense were they raised as Royal Welch Fusiliers ; still, they bore the badges and name, and upheld the honour of the regiment.

Following the 25th came seven garrison battalions, of which the 2nd, 4th, and 6th served abroad (the 2nd became the 26th Reserve).

The numbering of the Territorial battalions was peculiar and sometimes leads to confusion. An oblique stroke was used, thus : the 1/4th was the original battalion, and was followed by the 2/4th and 3/4th; and then the

---

[1] The Derby Scheme of National Registration took effect on the 15th August 1915 ; Conscription, 9th April 1918.

Reserve battalion was numbered simply, 4th. Each Territorial battalion of the regiment raised three other battalions during the war.

Altogether forty-four battalions bore the badges of the regiment, and twenty-one served abroad.

To return to the 3rd Battalion.

On the 12th May 1915 Lieutenant-Colonel H. R. Jones-Williams was ordered to move his battalion to Litherland, near Liverpool, where they went into hutments.

By an Army Council Instruction, issued in August 1916, all Reserve battalions, other than Special Reserve and one Territorial Reserve battalion per regiment, ceased to have a regimental name or wear badges : they were designated Training Reserve Battalions, and were numbered. The 12th then became the 62nd T.R. Battalion ; the 18th became the 63rd T.R. Battalion, and the 20th, 21st, and 22nd became the 64th T.R. Battalion, sending at the same time 1,300 men from their camp at Kinmel Park to the 3rd Battalion at Litherland. In accordance with the order, three Territorial Reserve battalions disappeared, and were merged into one, the 4th.

In January 1917 the establishment of the 3rd Battalion, which had been raised to 2,000 in August 1916, was reduced to 1,586. Up to the 1st May Lieutenant-Colonel Jones-Williams had sent to the battalions serving on all fronts 423 officers and 10,722 other ranks.

At the end of October the numbers had increased to :

Officers :

To France	.	.	481	To Egypt	.	.	.	12
„ Mesopotamia	.		2	„ India	.	.	.	1
„ Salonika	.	.	10	„ Mediterranean	.		.	22
„ E. Africa	.		4	„ Other battalions	.		.	30

Other ranks :

To France	.	.	9,108	To Egypt	.	.	.	1,126
„ Mesopotamia	.		560	„ India	.	.	.	511
„ Mediterranean	.		1,128	„ Salonika	.	.	.	710
„ E. Africa	.	.	24	„ Garrison battalions	.		.	1,328

On the evening of the 2nd November 1917 a telegram was received ordering the recall of all officers on leave, and the mobilisation of a fighting battalion, in accordance with a standing secret scheme. This force was to hold itself in readiness to proceed to Ireland at short notice.[1]

1 The Irish Rebellion broke out 24th April 1916.

The battalion entrained at Seaforth on the 5th, and proceeded to Holyhead. No preparations had been made for them, and camp was pitched in a sodden field, in the teeth of a howling gale. The battalion passed through Dublin for Limerick on the 7th.

Major G. W. H. Wakefield had been left with a party at Litherland, but on the 12th December all ranks posted to the battalion were ordered to proceed to Limerick, and the rear party left Litherland on the 27th January 1918.

There was, however, little of an exciting nature. A mobile column, 150 strong, was dispatched under Captain R. A. Rigby to assist the Royal Irish Constabulary in dealing with cattle-driving about Ennis and Tulla. St. David's Day was observed in Limerick in the customary manner : the Colour was trooped in the morning, and after the parade the battalion marched through the town, all ranks wearing the leek ; and on the 3rd and 4th single soldiers walking out were attacked with stones and sticks, and a few strong pickets had to be sent to restore order—but whether this was cause and effect is hard to determine.

On the 14th March 1918 Colonel Jones-Williams, who had been on leave since the 14th December, published his farewell order, and one might well apply some of his remarks to his own work:

" On the 15th March my command of the 3rd Battalion Royal Welch Fusiliers comes to an end. I take this opportunity to thank all officers, N.C.O.s and men for their loyal support given me during my five and a half years in command. For the last three and a half years the greatest crisis in our Empire's history has taken place, and all have given ungrudgingly of the best that is in them for their King and country. Hundreds of men have undergone war training in the battalion since 1914 ; and I take pride to place on record the lasting honours the regiment has gained on the many fronts occupied by British troops, ever upholding the great traditions of the regiment to which I have had the honour of belonging for thirty-six and a half years, and leave with many regrets. I am proud to look back on the good feeling that has always existed in the regiment, but the one regret I shall always have is that I have not been privileged to go to the front with the men I have helped to train. My thoughts will always be with you. To soldiers of all ranks of the 3rd Battalion R.W.F., I wish you good-bye !

H. R. JONES-WILLIAMS,
Colonel, 3rd Battalion, R.W.F."

Major A. R. P. Macartney-Filgate succeeded Colonel Jones-Williams in command and was promoted on the 1st June.

In July the battalion was well over 4,000 strong, and was closed to recruits; but owing to the 4th Battalion (Reserve) being turned into a young soldiers' battalion, the 3rd acted as a Reserve for the Territorial as well as the Regular and New Army, or Service Battalions.

The drafts sent out by the battalion from the 1st December 1917 to 15th August 1918 were:

Officers:

To France	.	.	.	.	.	143
,, Egypt	.	.	.	.	.	14
,, Italy	.	.	.	.	.	2

Other ranks:

To France	.	.	.	.	.	2,290
,, Salonika	.	.	.	.	.	42
,, Italy	.	.	.	.	.	52

making a grand total, up to that date, of 19,265 other ranks.

On the 10th October Lieutenants J. E. McIntosh and W. J. Singleton lost their lives while proceeding on leave in the mail-steamer *Leinster*, which was torpedoed by a German submarine. The latter had served in France with the 17th Battalion. Orders were then given that drafts for the Expeditionary Force should proceed to a dispatching battalion in England, from which final leave would be granted and a double journey avoided.

On the 11th November 1918 the massed buglers of the 3rd Battalion sounded the "Cease fire" in the centre of the Square at Limerick.

.   .   .   .

For the sake of convenience in following with many divisions and on many fronts the fortunes of the regiment, we give here a list of all battalions, and the postings.

1st Battalion.—Went to Flanders with the 22nd Brigade, 7th Division, October 1914. The division moved to Italy November 1917.

2nd Battalion.—To France as line-of-communication troops, 11th and 13th August 1914. Posted to 19th Brigade, 21st August 1914. The brigade was under III Corps until the end of September 1914, then joined 6th Division until 28th May 1915. Brigade was transferred to 27th Division. On the 19th July 1915 the Brigade was moved to the 2nd Division, replacing the 4th Guards Brigade. On the 25th November 1915 it was transferred to the 33rd Division. The 2nd

Battalion was then moved to the 115th Brigade, 38th Division, on the 5th February 1918.

3rd Battalion.—The Special Reserve Battalion.

4th Battalion (Territorial Force).—To France, December 1914, and was posted to the 3rd Brigade, 1st Division, on the 7th December 1914. The battalion was transferred to the 47th Division (London) as Pioneers on the 1st September 1915.

5th Battalion (Territorial Force).—Sailed for the Dardanelles, 14th July 1915, with the 158th Brigade, 53rd Division. The division moved to Egypt, December 1915.

6th Battalion (Territorial Force).—As for 5th Battalion.

7th Battalion (Territorial Force).—As for the 5th Battalion. But this battalion was transferred to the 160th Brigade, 53rd Division, on 24th June 1918, when a number of battalions were sent to France.

8th Battalion (Service).—To the Dardanelles with the 40th Brigade, 13th Division, in June 1915. The division moved to Egypt in January 1916 ; and to Mesopotamia in February 1916.

9th Battalion (Service).—To France with the 58th Brigade, 19th Division, July 1915.

10th Battalion (Service).—To France with the 76th Brigade, 25th Division, September 1915. The brigade was transferred to the 3rd Division, the 14th October 1915. The battalion was amalgamated with the 19th Battalion, and designated the 8th Entrenching Battalion, on the 5th February 1918.

11th Battalion (Service).—To France with the 67th Brigade, 22nd Division, September 1915. On October 30th the division was sent to Salonika.

12th Battalion (Reserve).—Became the 62nd Training Reserve Battalion.

13th Battalion (Service).—To France with the 113th Brigade, 38th Division, December 1915.

14th Battalion (Service).—As for 13th Battalion.

15th Battalion (Service).—As for 13th Battalion. Was disbanded the 6th February 1918.

16th Battalion (Service).—As for 13th Battalion.

17th Battalion (Service).—To France with the 115th Brigade, 38th Division.

18th Battalion (Reserve).—Became the 63rd Training Reserve Battalion.

19th Battalion (Service).—To France with the 119th Brigade, 40th Division, June 1916. Amalgamated with the 10th Battalion, the 15th February 1918.

20th, 21st, 22nd Battalions (Reserve).—Became 64th Training Reserve Battalion.

23rd Battalion (Reserve).

24th Battalion (Territorial Force).—Was formed in Egypt by the Denbigh-shire Yeomanry (Dismounted), March 1917, and was posted to the 231st Brigade, 74th Division. Went to France with the division, April 1918. Was transferred to the 94th Brigade, 31st Division, the 21st June 1918.

25th Battalion (Territorial Force).—Formed in Egypt by the Montgomery-shire Yeomanry (Welsh Horse). Was posted to the 231st Brigade, 74th Division. Went to France with the division, April 1918.

26th Battalion (Service).—Went to France as the 4th Garrison Battalion, February 1917, and was posted to the 176th Brigade, 59th Division, on the 15th May 1918, and designated 26th Battalion.

1st Garrison Battalion.

2nd Garrison Battalion.—Formed 24th October 1915. Went to Egypt 6th March 1916. Was disbanded 22nd August 1919.

3rd Garrison Battalion.

4th Garrison Battalion.—Became 26th. See above.

5th Garrison Battalion.

6th Garrison Battalion.—Went to Egypt 23rd January 1917, and was on lines of communication until September 1918.

7th Garrison Battalion.

2/4th Battalion (Territorial Force).

3/4th Battalion (Territorial Force).   .

4th Battalion (Territorial Force Reserve).

2/5th Battalion (Territorial Force).

3/5th Battalion (Territorial Force).

5th Battalion (Territorial Force Reserve).

2/6th Battalion (Territorial Force).

3/6th Battalion (Territorial Force).

6th Battalion (Territorial Force Reserve).

2/7th Battalion (Territorial Force).

3/7th Battalion (Territorial Force).

7th Battalion (Territorial Force Reserve).

II

THE SHOCK

THE SHOCK

THE RETREAT FROM MONS.

THE SITUATION IN FRANCE AND FLANDERS.

THE Belgian Army stood like a courageous pigmy before the Teutonic giant. Realising that their 3rd Division, which had already repulsed the German attack before the frontier town of Liège, might be surrounded, the Belgian Staff withdrew it to Gette. The town itself then fell into German hands, but the gallant General Leman defended the fortress in such fashion that the last of the forts did not fall until the 16th August. It was a valuable gain of four days for the French and British Armies.

German troops then appeared to the north of that other frontier town, Namur, on the 19th, and drove in the Belgian outposts on the 20th; but they were again held up by the forts until the garrison withdrew on the 23rd August.

The effort of the Belgian Army during the eighteen days they fought the German invasion was not wasted. But the situation there, the strong German advance, had an effect on General Joffre's preliminary plan.

On the 2nd August, when he heard of the German Ultimatum to Belgium, he put into execution a plan which moved the French Fifth Army to the north, while General Sordet's Cavalry Corps made a reconnaissance to within nine miles of Liège. It appeared, from captured Germans, that five different German army corps were passing through Belgium, but it was thought by the French General Staff that the main German armies were round Metz, and General Joffre decided to throw the weight of his troops in that direction. The offensive had started in Alsace, when, on the 15th August, the Belgians reported 200,000 Germans crossing the Meuse below Visé.

Then commenced an extension of the French line to the north : the Third Army took over the objectives of the Fourth ; the Fourth occupied the ground vacated by the Fifth, as it, in turn, moved out on the left flank.

South of Metz the Germans appeared to be making no move.

General Joffre then decided to strike with his Third and Fourth Armies at the flank of those German forces across the Meuse, and make a secondary attack only between Metz and the Vosges.   The Fifth Army, the British Expeditionary Force (when it arrived), and the Belgian Army would oppose any German advance from the Meuse and gain time for the attack of the Third and Fourth Armies to develop.   The General Advance was ordered on the 21st.

Sir John French left London on the 14th.   During the 15th, 16th, and 17th he made himself acquainted with the situation.

Meanwhile the British Expeditionary Force was moving to its concentration areas :

Cavalry, east of Maubeuge, Jeumont, Domousies, Cousolre, with Divisional Headquarters at Aibes.

II Corps, east of Landrecies, with Headquarters at Landrecies.   3rd Division at Marbaix, Taisnières, and Noyelles.   5th Division at Maroilles, Landrecies, and Ors.

I Corps, east of Bohain, with Headquarters at Wassigny.   1st Division at Boué, Esqueheries, and Leschelles.   2nd Division at Grougis, Mennevret, and Hannappes.

The Royal Flying Corps had 63 aeroplanes at Maubeuge, and formed an aircraft park at Amiens.

Sir John French was also informed by the War Office that the 4th Division would be dispatched immediately (19th).

.   .   .   .

Headquarters, A and B Companies of the 2nd Battalion Royal Welch Fusiliers, on the Irish pig-boat *Glengariffe*, arrived at Rouen at 2 a.m. on the 11th.

" We sailed in the early hours of the 11th, and my next recollection is about 10 a.m., with no land in sight, falling in with a French tug-boat carrying our pilot.   They hailed us and asked our port of destination, to which our captain, who had now opened his sealed orders, replied ' Rouen '!   Whereupon the Frenchmen started cheering, to which our men, who were swarming over the rigging, replied with enthusiasm."

But Serjeant-Major Boreham, with the men, records :

" I'm afraid that had our French friends understood they would have been very disgusted, for our fellows, in the way peculiar to English soldiers, shouted most uncomplimentary remarks in answer ; anyhow the Frenchmen continued to cheer all the way into the harbour, so I suppose they thought we were saying nice things.   The trip up the Seine was very fine, the only drawback being that a couple of our subaltern officers found out how to work the ship's siren, and did not give it a rest the whole of the way. All the way up the inhabitants of the various towns and villages turned out and yelled greetings. We got to Rouen in the afternoon, and the first man of the regiment to land in France was Regimental Sergeant-Major M. Murphy. I am quite certain of this, for I was standing by the gangway trying to be first myself, but of course I had to give way to my superior officer. After disembarking, Headquarters and B Company crossed the river by means of the transport bridge and marched to our billet in the Ecole Pape Carpentier."

Arriving at Rouen, " it became very evident that we were in for a reception of some sort, as a French battalion was drawn up on the quay, and a lot of French ' Brass Hats ' were to be seen as well. As soon as we tied up, a French General came aboard, and I, as a reputed French scholar, was pushed forward to welcome him. I conducted him to the C.O., whereupon he at once launched into one of those graceful and charming little speeches which the French are so good at. I made a few halting remarks and then, there being nothing to offer him in the drink line, we conducted the General over the side again." (Geiger.)

The French nation were never under any illusion as to the might of Germany—some 1870 veterans were still alive, and, in any case, the memory of a nation is beyond that of man. They knew they must have help, and their joy at seeing a handful of British troops was hysterical.

The next day A Company was sent to Amiens.

" As our journey progressed it became more and more hilarious. Crowds seemed to be waiting for us at every station—and we stopped at all—and a good deal of osculation went on. The subalterns next door seemed more lucky than I, as far as I could see out of the corner of my eye. The climax of the ludicrous was reached at some station or other, where the town band met us and played the Marseillaise ; to which A Company responded with much solemnity by intoning ' God save the King ' ! We also received bouquet after bouquet at every station, and by the time we reached Amiens, about 10.30 p.m., there was barely room to sit down." (Geiger.)

Amiens was the Headquarters of the Lines of Communications, and the duties of A Company were to furnish orderlies where required, and to be ready at the station with rations and water for the troop trains carrying the Expeditionary Force to their concentration areas.

The company was billeted in some schools, and the officers found quarters outside. The latter took their meals at various restaurants, but the luxurious establishments that were so well known to the British

Army later on were not in existence—except the fish shop in the Rue des Corps Nus sans Têtes. " We used to wind up the evenings by attending a café in the Place Gambetta, where an orchestra played. The performance always concluded with all the National Anthems, when everyone stood up and solemnly saluted during the ten minutes it took to play them."

The flash was a thing of interest to the Frenchmen ; one ventured to verify a solution that occurred to him by asking an officer if he was a chaplain !

All officers wore the flash,[1] and some consternation was caused by the arrival of Sir John French at Amiens, he having ordered the flash off the 1st Battalion, when in service dress, during his command at Aldershot. The 2nd Battalion was in India at the time, and naturally took no notice of the order. However, although A Company mounted a guard over the Hôtel-du-Rhin, the Commander-in-Chief made no comment; he doubtless had other things to think about.

All four battalions that landed on the 11th—Royal Welch Fusiliers, Cameronians, 1st Middlesex, and 2nd Argyll and Sutherland Highlanders —were employed on the lines of communication[2] ; but when, on the 19th, G.H.Q. was informed [that the 4th Division was to be sent over from England, it was decided that these troops should form the 19th Brigade.

.   .   .   .

It was on the 19th that the British Flying Corps carried out their first reconnaissance from Maubeuge. The next day the British cavalry moved out as far as Binche without seeing any enemy ; but the airmen discovered a body of troops " stretching through Louvain as far as the eye could reach " ! This was part of the German First Army, which, under von Kluck, was pressing forward, to enter Brussels.

On the 20th the Belgian Army retired on Antwerp ; it was the day the Germans came within range of Namur, and the day given by General Joffre for a general advance.

The French Third and Fourth Armies prepared to attack the German centre. In the French Fifth Army, on the left flank, two reserve divisions occupied the place on the left of the XVIII Corps, north-east of Maubeuge, which General Joffre desired the British Expeditionary Force to occupy ; farther to the west there were three French Territorial divisions, under General d'Amade.

---

[1] Permission was given to wear the flash, in service dress, on the 13th May 1915 ; the size was limited to five inches in length.

[2] Among other duties the battalion found a guard—from A Company—for the body of General Grierson when taken from the train. They also buried two airmen who had crashed.

The French offensive, however, failed. The French Third and Fourth Armies met unexpected forces and could make no headway.

Meanwhile the British Expeditionary Force was moving up on the left. Sir Horace Smith-Dorrien arrived at Bavai, to take command of the II Corps, at 4 p.m. on the 21st August, the I Corps then being about ten miles to his right rear.

The I Corps moved up on the right of the Forêt de Mormal, while the II Corps, on the left of the forest, moved to Mons, to the line of the canal. The two corps were then in their proper positions according to the G.H.Q. time-table.

But on the afternoon of the 22nd, G.H.Q. learned that the French Fifth Army had been driven in about its centre, and that the right of the I Corps was some nine miles from the left of the French XVIII Corps.

Sir John then decided that the British advance should not proceed, but he agreed to help the French, who were falling back on his left, to the extent of holding his ground for twenty-four hours. The movement of the British Army, which was in progress, had not been completed : the two corps were in the midst of a wheel to the right, and in the ordinary course of events the I Corps would have stood its ground and allowed the II Corps to come up on its left. With the wheel incomplete, the two halves of the Army stood like the hands of a clock at twenty minutes to four.

MONS, LE CATEAU, AND THE RETREAT FROM MONS.

Having been formed, the 19th Brigade were ordered to move up on the left of the II Corps, and so, on the 22nd, our 2nd Battalion left Rouen, and passed through Amiens on their way to Valenciennes.[1] A Company followed later in the day with Brigade Headquarters.[2]

After breakfast on the 23rd, the whole brigade fell in on the Place de la Gare, and then proceeded along a pavé road in a north-easterly direction. The 2nd Battalion did not, however, go far ; they halted near the village of Vicq, where they took up a position on the Escaut, and scraped out " one-hour shelter trenches " with their small entrenching tools. The 1st Middlesex and the Cameronians were at the head of the brigade, but they did not move up into the line until 3 p.m.

" At Valenciennes some boxes which had been the objects of some speculation as to their contents were opened ; they were found to contain ordnance maps of sections of Northern France and Belgium. My share of

---

[1] See page 286, vol. I.
[2] Twenty-three officers, 2 interpreters, 752 other ranks, entrained at Rouen at 10.25 a.m. 5 officers, 221 other ranks, entrained at Amiens at 11 p.m.

these was eight, which was not a welcome addition to the already weighty
contents of my pack.   After some time we got off and marched out of the
town by the road leading to the Belgian frontier.   A number of lorries
passed us returning to the town, and although we had been away from
home for but a few days the familiar names on these lorries—one I remember
was a Maple's—made me feel quite homesick.   After a couple of miles my
company left the main road and went to a village named Rombies ; here
we put out one or two posts and then proceeded to get some breakfast.
The villagers were very interested in the operations of the cooks in making
the tea and expressed what amounted to horror when, after obtaining some
milk from a farm, the cooks put it in the tea.   As I have previously
mentioned, the battalion was engaged in training when the war broke out,
and as we had not yet become acquainted with real shells, etc., it seemed
that we were still going on with the training ; for when Captain Powell
read out the situation and said that the enemy's cyclists had been seen at
So-and-so, there was nothing strange about it.   In the afternoon we marched
to a place called Vicq, where we found the rest of the battalion.   It was
difficult still to realise that there was a war on, for we bivouacked in a
field where the corn had been recently cut ; it was a lovely Sunday afternoon, and the lads and girls of the village strolled around dressed in their
Sunday clothes." (Boreham.)

On that memorable Sunday morning (23rd August) the clash came
between troops of the German First Army and the British II Corps.   Von
Kluck was also attempting a wheel, to his left.   The left half of his army,
that is, the standing half, was opposite the Mons Salient ; the right half
was swinging round on the British II Corps.

It is of great interest to note that von Kluck did not know the position
or strength of the British Expeditionary Force, as landed, even on the
morning of the 23rd.   That a part of it had landed in France was established
by an encounter with a squadron of the 4th Dragoons at Casteau, north-
east of Mons, and by the shooting down of a British aeroplane ; but the
German Staff expected it to be in the neighbourhood of Lille.

It is said that about noon on the 23rd the German cavalry reported
to their III Corps—elements of which were two miles from Mons—that
there was no enemy within fifty miles, but shortly afterwards two Hussars,
covered with blood, galloped past, shouting that the enemy had occupied
the canal in front.[1]

Very early in the morning British cavalry had come into contact with
the enemy, and German cavalry exchanged shots with the 4th Battalion

[1] This incident is quoted in *Military Operations*, 1914.

Middlesex Regiment about 6 a.m. Before 9 a.m. German guns were in position and shells were falling on the 4th Middlesex and Royal Fusiliers, who held the apex of the Mons Salient. It was the right of the German IX Corps that advanced on the 4th Middlesex at Obourg, and as von Kluck continued his wheel, so the German III Corps came into action at 11 a.m. and the IV Corps during the afternoon.

Between 2 and 3 p.m. the 1st Middlesex and the Cameronians relieved the Cavalry Division on the extreme left of the British line, and extended it on to Condé, where they came into touch with General d'Amade's Territorial divisions. Soon after 5 p.m. the 1st Middlesex were attacked, but held their own with trifling loss.

Our 2nd Battalion remained on their position about Vicq. " While we were sitting peacefully round, at about 8 p.m., we began to hear gun fire—field guns ! This was, as far as we were concerned, the first sounds of war, and denoted the opening of the Battle of Mons—Charleroi in our part of the field. An hour or so later we heard that the Middlesex outposts had been engaged with the enemy across the canal, and that they had, at least, one officer wounded. We got a little sleep in the intervals of visiting our sentries, and at about 2.30 a.m. (24th) suddenly got orders to fall in." (Geiger.)

The news that reached the 2nd Battalion was exceedingly meagre. Of the great fight that had been going on all through the day they knew nothing. Stated briefly, it was that two British divisions, the 3rd and 5th, had met the attack of six German divisions. The left of the II Corps stood fast ; the right had evacuated certain positions which were bad, but had been forced on them, for better ones, some two miles in rear. In fact the situation was such that Sir John French had ordered the II Corps to stand the attack " on the ground now occupied by the troops. You will, therefore, strengthen your position by every possible means during the night."

All the fighting had been done by Sir Horace Smith-Dorrien's corps, whose total casualties were 1,600.

Later messages caused the Commander-in-Chief to cancel his order. As a result of operations by the French Third and Fourth Armies on the 23rd, a retirement had been ordered which would take with it the French Fifth Army. The gap between the latter and the Expeditionary Force was already considerable, and any widening of it would jeopardise the safety of the British Army.

Sir John French ordered a retirement.

The order to retire was given by Sir Archibald Murray, Chief of the

General Staff, at 1 a.m. on the 24th to the senior Staff officers who had assembled at Le Cateau (G.H.Q.).   The I Corps was in telephonic communication with Le Cateau, over a French wire ; the II Corps was not.   Consequently Colonel Forestier-Walker had to motor thirty-five miles before he could acquaint Sir Horace Smith-Dorrien with the decision.   Meanwhile Sir Horace had made his dispositions to carry out the original order, which was to stand fast.   The actual sequence in which the two corps would retire was to be settled between the two commanders, but they did not meet until midday, and by that time Sir Douglas Haig's I Corps had slipped away unmolested, the main bodies of the 1st and 2nd Divisions marching off without reference to the II Corps between 4 and 4.45 a.m.

On the II Corps front, before dawn, the Germans opened heavy artillery fire, and by 5 a.m. were developing an attack along the whole length of the line.

The 19th Infantry Brigade, who were under G.H.Q., received their orders to retire on Élouges about midnight.   It was pitch dark, and the company commanders of our 2nd Battalion, with their haversacks loaded with maps covering the whole of Belgium, led their companies along the road without the slightest idea of their destination.

" The first event of interest was our arrival at the small town of Quiévrain, just over the Belgian frontier.   Here the inhabitants were in an agitated state of mind ; firing could be heard again, and all arms were *en évidence*.   We marched straight on, the noise of gun fire getting nearer ; indeed, on our left, you could see the puffs of exploding shells falling on the other side of the nearest crest-line, about half a mile off.   Just as we were getting up to the village of Elouges we got the order to about-turn, and thus, unknowingly, began our long trek south."   (Geiger.)

The 19th Brigade had, as a matter of fact, passed under the command of General Allenby, and had, on his order, been directed on Baisieux, slightly south-west of Elouges.   The withdrawal of the II Corps had become complicated by a general engagement, and the 5th Division (Fergusson), on the left, was to hold its ground ; General Allenby, therefore, covered the left flank of the 5th Division with his cavalry in position on a line drawn through Elouges.   The 19th Brigade was then ordered to retire on Rombies, to be followed by the cavalry in successive brigades.

Our 2nd Battalion arrived at Rombies soon after midday.   They made scoops with their entrenching tools in obedience to what seemed a mechanical order.   Beyond the obvious fact that they were retiring, no one knew what was happening, or what rôle the 2nd Battalion was supposed to perform. They ate bully-beef and biscuits and were off again.

The next halt was at Jenlain, at about 6 p.m., but before they could settle down to rest the entrenching tools were again brought into play—excepting A Company, who managed to get hold of some picks and shovels from a small party of French Territorials.

It had been a hot day, but the men had marched well ; the reservists' boots, however, issued to the size which corresponded with the first number the man thought of, were beginning to give trouble—there had been a little straggling. But " on this, the first, and on all subsequent days, the march discipline was excellent, markedly better than in any other unit of the Brigade (this may have been due to our having fewer reservists)."

The 2nd Battalion had narrowly missed an engagement this day, as the withdrawal from the flank of the 5th Division was premature, and General Allenby had to send some of his cavalry back to fight in the neighbourhood of Elouges and Quiévrain. Indeed, the fighting of the II Corps, while extricating itself in the face of the enemy, was severe on the 24th : in the 5th Division alone, casualties amounted to 1,650 ; the return of the 19th Brigade was 40, and of the 2nd Battalion 1—Captain F. J. Walwyn, D.S.O., in the foot.

An interesting point to note is that at the end of the day Sir Horace Smith-Dorrien had so directed the movements of his corps that the divisions had changed places : the 3rd Division was now on the left, having crossed the rear of the 5th and passed to the west of Bavai.

The intention of von Kluck was now apparent, and was correctly gauged by G.H.Q. His order for the 24th August had been to throw the British back on Maubeuge and cut off their retreat to the west. To escape from this trap, and in view of further retreat by the French on the right, the orders for the Expeditionary Force were *to fall back on a position in the neighbourhood of Le Cateau.*

This movement, with the great Forêt de Mormal extended in length along the line of march, presented difficulties and risk. The I Corps moved on the east of the forest to Landrecies ; the II Corps had to move on the west of it. The I Corps marched at 2 a.m. on the 25th ; the task of the II Corps was further complicated by the passage of General Sordet's Cavalry Corps across their line of march.

It was a very trying day for our 2nd Battalion. They marched from Jenlain just before 4 a.m., and at 11 a.m. arrived at the village of Haussy. They were now close to the 4th Division,[1] which had crossed the Channel on the 24th, and was immediately ordered to occupy a position about Solesmes and assist the retirement of the II Corps. The situation on the left flank was becoming serious.

[1] There were eleven battalions of infantry and one brigade of artillery at this date.

General d'Amade's Territorial troops were falling back rapidly on the left of the British Army, and the pressure of the German pursuit was being felt ; added to which the roads were choked with refugees. The cavalry was becoming somewhat dispersed.

General Allenby, therefore, ordered the 19th Infantry Brigade to stand. The brigade was then at Haussy, and drew up, in mass formation, near the railway station.

" If we had been spotted by an enemy aeroplane or cavalry patrol, we could have been made very uncomfortable by an enterprising German horse battery. . . . Nothing untoward happened, however, and at about 1.30 p.m. we were off again. As we were marching through St. Python, word was passed that the enemy were near, and shortly after emerging a few shells fell in it. We thereupon extended, and lay down in a field of roots, facing north. I could see a troop of our cavalry, about 400 yards to my right front, when suddenly a shell burst in their vicinity, and they moved out of sight. The next moment there was a bang and a noise like tearing calico, as a couple of shells, in close succession, burst over the roots immediately on our right. This was the first time we had ourselves been under fire, and as no one was hit, the men began to make merry with one another on the subject. . . . After about a quarter of an hour we got the order to retire again, and proceeded to do so, this time alternately, by half-companies and in extended order. We eventually got to the road and resumed column of fours. Soon, at a cross-road, we began to get mixed up with other troops, mainly artillery, and there was considerable congestion for some time. We were marching along a shallow valley (the Selle). Looking through my glasses while the jumble was sorting itself, I suddenly saw a German patrol of four or five Uhlans on the western side of the valley, not more than a mile off. They seemed blissfully unconscious of our presence, and continued to advance in the same direction as ourselves, and were soon lost to view." (Geiger.)

The 2nd Battalion, with the 19th Brigade, passed up the valley of the Selle, by Briastre and Neuvilly, towards Le Cateau. The 4th Division remained on the position they had taken up, south of Solesmes, and covered the retirement of the 3rd Division, the Cavalry Division, and the 19th Infantry Brigade.

Darkness fell. " At last, about 8 p.m., we tumbled into the market square of Le Cateau, pretty well done in."

Already the men were beginning to show fatigue. Transport drivers were seen to be asleep on their wagons and artillerymen on their horses.

The position in which the corps commander now found himself is one of absorbing interest. From the first the brunt of the fighting had fallen on his corps, and the last stage of the retirement, along the west of the Forêt de Mormal, had been an anxious one. The German masses moved forward by sheer weight, but they were not anxious to meet the rapid fire of the highly trained British Regular (one has only to read their own accounts of the " pursuit " from Mons). Still, they had squeezed the corps against the Forêt de Mormal, and the increasing pressure of their enveloping movement had thrown a number of French troops, together with innumerable refugees, on to the roads the II Corps were bound to use. The corps commander's orders from G.H.Q. were to fall back on a position, with the idea of making a stand.

At 7.30 p.m. on the 25th Sir John French issued orders for the retreat to be resumed on the 26th.

At 11 o'clock that night General Allenby reported to the II Corps that his cavalry had retired from the high ground overlooking Solesmes (where the 4th Division had been), and that it had been occupied by the enemy. He also stated that the cavalry was much scattered, was very exhausted, and that he could not collect a sufficient force to recapture the Solesmes positions, which was necessary to cover further retreat.

The Germans then had their II Cavalry Corps, IV and III Corps ready to strike at the British II Corps in the early morning ; and their IV (Reserve), II, X (Reserve), and parts of the IX and VIII within a march and available if necessary.

The question Sir Horace Smith-Dorrien had before him was, could his corps slip away before daylight ? At that hour, 11 p.m., the units of his corps were not yet assembled on the positions he had indicated—indeed the rearguard of the 3rd Division was struggling along the congested road, and was seen by him at 4 o'clock in the morning !

He came to the conclusion that he must fight.

To guard his left flank he had only the Cavalry Division, which had been fighting rearguard actions all the way from Mons. There was a gap between his right flank and the left of the I Corps which he had intended to fill, in part, with troops from the 5th Division ; and there did not seem to be much hope of help coming from that direction, for the I Corps had a small affair during the evening at Landrecies—in which a few battalions were involved—and were extremely nervous. They appealed to Sir Horace for help about 3.30 a.m.

G.H.Q. was a long way off, at St. Quentin, and a message dispatched by motor-car at 3 a.m. and received there at 5 a.m. drew from Sir John French the reply : " If you can hold your ground, the situation appears likely to improve. 4th Division must co-operate. French troops are taking offensive on right of I Corps. Although you are given a free hand as to method, this telegram is not intended to convey the impression that I am not as anxious to carry out the retirement and you must make every endeavour to do so."

So far the last orders issued had been for the resumption of the retreat, and the corps commander's difficulty was to acquaint divisional commanders of his resolution to fight. General Hamilton, commanding the 3rd Division, was present at Sir Horace's Headquarters, but the 4th Division only reached its destination at Haucourt about 5 a.m., when a staff officer brought the new orders. Sir Horace took the orders himself to the 5th Division.

Weary with long marches and sleepless nights, units arrived on their positions, which had been selected under the first orders from G.H.Q. to stand. These orders had then been cancelled, and had it been possible to correct the positions taken up the necessity was not apparent. Troops stood to arms at 4 a.m. under the impression that the retreat was to be resumed, and then, at the last moment, the order came to fight. In most cases there was no time to occupy the most favourable positions.

Fate now played a curious game with our 2nd Battalion. They had slept in the market square of Le Cateau. While they were having hot tea and something to eat at 4.30 in the morning, the town was still blocked by British transport, which had been held up overnight by General Sordet's Cavalry. The Headquarters of the 19th Infantry Brigade could not be found by the messengers, sent round in frantic haste with the final orders. The Brigade Staff was working on the order to retreat, and marched off, in pursuance of that order, to Reumont.

The retreat had carried the 2nd Battalion off all the maps that had been issued to officers, and they had a very hazy idea of their whereabouts, and none at all of what was happening. " Nobody had been killed in the battalion, and everyone was getting fed. The worst events, so far, were the heat, two longish marches (about twenty miles each), and the fact that a lot of the reservists' boots did not fit.

" The men had finished their tea, and eaten some food, and were seated among the grounded arms of their respective companies. . . . Suddenly I heard a Frenchwoman calling out, ' Les Allemands arrivent ! ' —and getting up, saw a number of women pointing down a street on the opposite side of the square. They did not seem in the least alarmed, rather amused than otherwise, probably—poor creatures !—looking on the affair as one only affecting Germans and English, and with which they were not concerned." (Geiger.)

This was the appearance of the first German scouts—some cyclists—and the 19th Infantry Brigade were the last British troops to leave the town of Le Cateau. The moment the brigade had cleared the town it was quite apparent that a battle was expected, as the 5th Division could be seen hastily digging trenches. Orders eventually reached the brigade, while on the road, to halt at Reumont.

The right of the II Corps rested on Le Cateau, and two battalions of the 19th Brigade, the 1st Middlesex and the Argyll and Sutherland Highlanders, were sent forward during the morning to support the Suffolks against a desperate German onslaught. Later, about 10 a.m., the situation on the left of the corps, about Ligny, where the 4th Division was involved, called for support, and the 2nd Battalion Royal Welch Fusiliers and the Cameronians were ordered to move to Montigny.

" We swung off, left-handed, after a bit, and were soon passing II Corps Headquarters, which I think was the village of Bertry. . . . We cleared this village and then sat down by the roadside for a bit. A battery was firing close at hand, and there was quite a lot of noise all round. After about half an hour we went on again, and halted in a village which I believe to have been Montigny. Here we sat down in the midst of battle noises. A field hospital was established at the Mairie, but otherwise, except for the banging going on, all was peace. The inhabitants were strangely unmoved, like those at Le Cateau, probably for the same reason, and I remember buying chocolates and exchanging badinage with the old lady who sold it." (Geiger.)

For six hours the II Corps held and repulsed all efforts of the enemy, but in the afternoon the Germans made a gap immediately to the west of Le Cateau, where the Suffolks and a part of the Argyll and Sutherland Highlanders were overwhelmed after a terrible and gallant fight. The situation of the 5th Division seemed bad to Sir Charles Fergusson, and after consultation with Sir Horace Smith-Dorrien, the latter decided to withdraw.

Half of the 1st Middlesex and two half-companies of the Argyll and Sutherland Highlanders had been moved to the east of the town, and successfully held up the more feeble German attempts to pass that side. It is curious to note that the Germans fought the right flank of the II Corps, when, had they gone a short distance to the east, they would have passed through the gap between the two British corps. Von Kluck and his staff made many mistakes, as did other German commanders, and was completely mystified in the " fog of war." He thought, apparently, that the British were desirous of retreating on Boulogne, or one of the Channel ports, and his main effort seems to have been to interpose his troops between the British left and what he thought was their line of retreat.   Sir Horace was always keenly aware of the danger to himself and the I Corps if the Germans worked through the gap, but had to take the risk.

Our 2nd Battalion and the Cameronians were the only reserves held by corps, and had been nursed accordingly.   But now Sir Horace put them under the orders of Sir Charles Fergusson, and they were directed to move from Bertry and post themselves on the left of the Duke of Cornwall's at Maurois.   Their task might now well be of importance, as the retirement was to be carried out by divisions from the right.

" At about 3 o'clock we got orders to fall in again.   We all thought we were going to pass under General Hamilton's orders, but we were wrong again.   It began to appear that all was not as it should be.   Hostile shelling was appreciably closer, and as we emerged on to a road near a railway we could see shells falling in Bertry, where we had last seen Corps Headquarters, and where Charles Owen, the Adjutant, had just gone to collect some orders.   On his return he reported a certain liveliness along the road, and of having got his orders from a staff officer who had been left in a cellar, the rest of Headquarters having, very wisely, cleared off.

" It appeared that the line had given way somewhere on the right, and that we and the Cameronians were to form a rearguard—possibly only the infantry portion, but I never heard [1]—for the whole force.   There may have been other orders, but they never reached us.   We continued our march south along the railway, and finally extended in two lines facing north-east, in front of the road leading from Bertry to Busigny, and south of the Route Nationale. . . ."

These orders had been amplified by General Smith-Dorrien, who, meeting Major Williams, said, " Tell your Colonel to throw out a rearguard to cover the retirement."   Major Williams produced his map and the General marked the position he wished held.

" The afternoon was drawing on—firing seemed to have died down— but parties of stragglers could be seen coming along the Route Nationale. There was no sign of the enemy.   At last, just as it was getting twilight, I got my orders to retire ; so back we went and found the other two companies extended along the road."   (Geiger.)

It was about this time that a body of cavalry was seen, approaching at a gallop.   It was difficult to see who they were in the dusk.   " Solly Flood (afterwards Major-General), who was on the ground with a squadron

---

[1] A party of Argyll and Sutherland Highlanders and the 59th Field Company, R.E., held a spur ; behind them the Royal Welch Fusiliers, Cameronians, Norfolks, and one sixty-pounder gun of the 108th Heavy Battery.

of cavalry, was sure they were Germans "—and A Company opened fire. As the strange body of troops galloped past and out of sight, they were seen to be British.

Although the Germans had broken the line held by the Suffolks and part of the Argyll and Sutherland Highlanders, the remainder of the

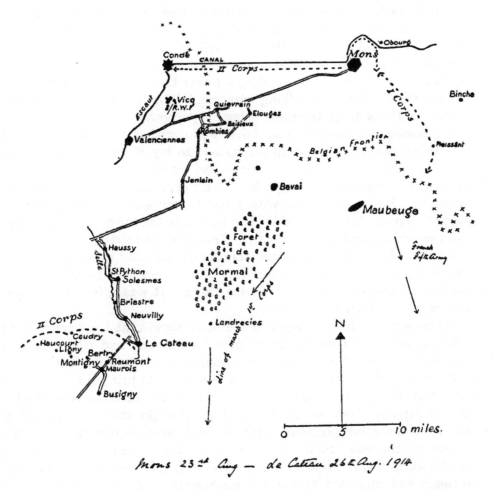

Mons 23rd Aug — Le Cateau 26th Aug. 1914

Highland Battalion, who were with the 1st Middlesex and the 1st Scots Fusiliers (two companies) east of the town, managed to hold them in check by long-range fire. At 3.47 p.m. the II Corps reported to G.H.Q. that the retirement had begun. The enemy showed no initiative on the right flank of the 5th Division.

By 5 o'clock the 5th and 3rd Divisions had commenced their retreat,

III—4

and the reappearance of General Sordet's Cavalry on the left of the 4th Division created a diversion during which that division extricated itself.

The Battle of Le Cateau put an end to the German pursuit—they merely followed the British Army.   But " the march on was now a painful business. Mercifully the night was cool, but we were all pretty dead-beat.   The marches had not been excessive—we had only done about twenty miles on each of the first two days, and we had already done but sixteen on this day—but no one had had more than a couple of hours' sleep a night since the previous Friday, and it was now Wednesday.   Consequently, after leaving Beaurevoir, people were reeling all over the road with fatigue, and I remember Owen, who was walking with me, falling into me several times, and I suppose I was doing the same thing." (Geiger.)

" We managed to keep the men fairly well together, though it was a bit of a job to prevent some of them falling out to lay down and sleep.   On one occasion I saw a man leave the ranks and wander towards the gates of a farm that we were passing.   I got hold of his arm and asked him where he was going to.   He looked at me with a fixed stare and mumbled that he was going to have a sleep.   I pushed him back into the ranks and the movement of the other men kept him going.   I'm quite sure that he had no idea of what he was doing, that his senses were simply numbed by being without sleep for so long.   This was the fourth night since we had left Rouen, and we had had no proper sleep since leaving there.   It was a few more days, too, before we got a fair night's rest.

" When it got light we began to see more signs that we were part of a retreating army ; for we began to pass lorries that had either broken down or had run out of petrol and were abandoned.   At one place rations were laid at the side of the road, so that the men could just help themselves as they went along.   Just after this we turned off the main road, and I thought to myself, ' Now we are for it,' for I thought that we were going to take up a defensive position.   But we had done so just to avoid the congestion on the main road.   During one halt the men were discussing the situation, and one of them said, ' Well, there's one thing.   We are advancing,' and appealed to me for confirmation of this.   ' Oh yes,' I said ; ' we shall be in Germany in a couple of weeks.'   I did not mean quite what the man thought I did.   Our men still kept very well together, but we began to pass stragglers of other units.   Our medical officer was marching at the head of my company and was telling Captain Powell how, when attending to a sick man during the night, he gave his horse to a man to hold, but both man and horse had disappeared when he had finished with his patient.   Almost as soon as he had finished his story, a man of the

Cameronians came past riding the very horse in question, and was very loath to give it up. We got to St. Quentin about breakfast time, but there was no breakfast. The officers went into shops and bought all the eatables they could, tinned fish, biscuits, chocolate, and anything that could be eaten. This was shared out to the men as far as it would go round." (R.S.M. Boreham.)

The 2nd Battalion reached Estrées about 2 a.m. on the 27th August, and literally dropped into a wayside field, where they had two hours' rest. On reaching another Route Nationale, they turned left-handed to St. Quentin, where Colonel Radcliffe " requisitioned " food from a grocer.

During the whole of the retreat food never became a matter for anxiety. Sir William Robertson's orders to dump supplies on the roadside had been carried out. " We received orders to go to different dumps to get rations. I never took any notice of the orders, but as soon as I had delivered one lot to the battalion I filled up from the first dump I came to. The officer would say, " Are you such-and-such a division ? "—answer was always, ' Yes '—and away I went loaded. I did hear that the C.O. in several places, at the request of a few officers, used to requisition various articles from the French—they used to like the French bread especially. Rations were taken up to them between Le Cateau and St. Quentin on the Wednesday evening, but I did not get to them again till the Thursday evening, General Smith-Dorrien having told me at the Mairie in St. Quentin to push on to Noyon as quick as possible, dump everything and pick up men that were not able to walk, leaving rations on the roadside for the troops to help themselves." (H. Yates, Quartermaster.)

Probably the British Army looked more ragged at St. Quentin than at any other period of the retreat. The close engagement had necessitated troops leaving the field in small bodies, and they marched along in the manner of a "football crowd." Staff officers sorted them out at St. Quentin, and they gradually got more or less together again.

Meanwhile Sir Horace Smith-Dorrien had chased G.H.Q. to Noyon, where he gave a personal account of the action and its breaking off to the Commander-in-Chief. Sir John French informed him that the orders issued on the 26th held good and that the retirement was to continue to the St. Quentin Canal—Somme Line (La Fère—Ham). The 19th Brigade orders, on this decision, were to march to Ollezy, four miles east of Ham, which gave them a marching distance of thirty-eight miles, with a two-hours' halt at Estrées.

The next day, the 28th, the 19th Brigade marched to Noyon, crossed to the left bank of the Oise, and reached Pontoise at 9 p.m., where it spent the following day.[1]

General Joffre was now forming a new Army, the Sixth, commanded by General Maunoury, between the British left and General d'Amade's Territorial divisions.

On the 30th August Sir John French decided on a further retirement (against General Joffre's wishes), and the 19th Brigade and 4th Division (which on this day became the III Corps, under General Pulteney) moved south and halted on the Aisne, near Attichy.

General Joffre concluded that he, too, must fall back before delivering a counter-stroke ; and so, on the 31st, after consultation with Sir John French, who agreed to retain his position in the Allied line of battle, the French and British continued to retire. The I Corps halted on the north side of the Forêt de Villers-Cotterets ; the II Corps south-west of Villers-Cotterets ; and the III Corps, after a flank march through the forest of Compiègne, at the south-west corner of the forest, about Verberie. Our battalion was at the railway station.

The last two days had been excessively hot and sultry. The " going " through the forest was very hilly and difficult, and " as the roads we used that day were unmetalled, it was trying work for the transport animals. The forest was full of other troops, and German cavalry was also reported to be about, so with everyone having flank guards out we should have looked rather a rabble from an aeroplane. As a matter of fact there was no confusion."

At Verberie A Company's sector was from the Compiègne—Senlis road to the railway bridge over the Oise, and Captain Geiger relates that " after posting my people, I took an hour off for some food and rest, and then set out along the railway line to look at my pickets. It was pitch-dark now. On approaching the bridge I was met by a very excited French officer, who explained rapidly that he was not a Regular ; that he had been ordered to prepare the bridge for demolition ; that the Germans were close up on the other side ; and that ' faut-il faire sauter le pont ? ' Only five weeks previously I had been peacefully engaged in company training, in the course of which had any of my men damaged so much as a cabbage I should have been held strictly to account. Consequently, with the fear of being held responsible for a sum of half a million francs or so, I sternly replied that if he blew up the bridge he did so on his own responsibility. At this moment an engine arrived from the direction of the station and

---

[1] The bridge was blown up, but the charge was badly laid and the bridge remained passable on foot, at least. The bridge guard was B Company and No. 3 Platoon of A Company.

the C.O. descended from it. I reported my conversation with the French-man, and he cordially approved my action. We then turned back down the line, after looking at the picket. We had not gone many yards when we heard a terrific explosion : my French friend's nerves had settled the matter, and the bridge had ' sauted ' ! I then set about seeing my remaining pickets. I was talking to a ' group ' at a small level crossing, when the sentry challenged. To our unspeakable astonishment, out of the night came the following words : ' For Gawd's sake don't shoot, gents ! I ain't no spy ! ' And from the darkness emerged a small fat man, in plain clothes, carrying a bundle, and so pale he positively illuminated the darkness. He added hastily, ' I'm a stable hand in these parts, gents. They told me the woods was full of Germans and that I'd better be off, so I 'opped it—but I ain't no spy, gents ! ' I sent him back to the reserve company under escort.

"The next incident was not entirely comedy. On my return journey there was suddenly an explosion of fire, beginning on my left—I was walking east—and continued almost in front of me. I hurried towards the level crossing and there found Williams. Apparently some cavalry had come dashing down the road, and had been fired on by the pickets, and had gone over the level crossing, which was stupidly open, and disappeared into the night. Williams and I went up the road to investigate, and soon came upon a dead horse with undoubted English saddlery and equipment. Going on for another 500 yards we came across the A Company picket watching the road. I was beginning a few honeyed words to the sergeant in charge when I suddenly saw another dead horse. Going up to this and putting my hand down, I picked up something furry, which, on inspec-tion, proved to be a Hussar's busby of unusual pattern, and very obviously not British. We then began to look carefully, and at once discovered a man lying full length by the horse. His hair was shaved close to his head and he looked, indeed, a typical Hun. He was also obviously shamming dead. Ordering a party to bring him along, we turned back towards Company Headquarters to interrogate him there. We had not gone far when groans made us turn round, and we found the wretched Boche being frog-marched along behind us. It was then discovered that, though far from dead, he had a bullet through his leg, so a stretcher was substituted for the previous mode of progression. At Company Head-quarters I started in on my prisoner and discovered he belonged to the 8th Hussars, and that patrolling along the road from Compiègne they had suddenly come upon a patrol of our cavalry just as these were dis-mounting. The Germans had gone for them, and the whole mob had come tearing down the road, fighting as they went, and with their horses by this time unmanageable. Arriving abreast of our outposts, they had, not unnaturally, been fired at, as the latter had taken the whole lot to be enemy troops. He did not know what had happened to his pals, except that they had careered down the road after he was hit. It was obvious that they were somewhere behind our lines.

" Looking round, I found that I was being watched by at least half the company, who, with eyes and mouths wide open, were contemplating their first prisoner with enormous curiosity. I sent him down to Battalion Headquarters and saw him no more."

The capture of this Hussar was important, as it confirmed the air report that von Kluck, who had been marching west, had now wheeled south-east. It appeared to Sir John French that the German First Army, which had left his troops alone (broadly speaking) since Le Cateau, was again closing in in great force ; and he ordered the retirement to continue : the I Corps to move to La Ferté-Milon—Betz ; the II Corps to Betz—Nanteuil ; the III Corps to Nanteuil—Baron, and the Cavalry Division to Baron—Mont-l'Evêque.

Our 2nd Battalion being relieved by the 2nd Royal Inniskilling Fusiliers, the march was resumed on the 1st September to Raray—after lying in a field of beet for a long time, watching the left flank of the retirement—and then on to Fresnoy. Again on this day the battalion narrowly missed an engagement near Néry, in which the 1st Middlesex were involved in the morning.

By this time the situation was viewed from London and Paris with the gravest concern. It seemed to both Governments that the retreat had been going on long enough, and that Sir John French was withdrawing the British Army too rapidly. At all events, Lord Kitchener went to Paris and there interviewed Sir John. An explosion between the Secretary of State and Commander-in-Chief was averted, but the meeting, apparently, had some effect in clearing up what might have been an estrangement between the Allied Commanders.

On his return to G.H.Q. Sir John found that his troops had been in close touch with the enemy, and ordered a night march to get them clear.

" We fell in about 4 a.m. on the 2nd September, and resumed our march south, moving for a long time in extended formation with scout parties in the woods. . . . After emerging from Montlongnon Wood, we passed through Montagny and found ourselves in the middle of our own cavalry. We therefore closed on the road again. . . .

" It was another scorching day, but proved entirely uneventful. As we were marching through Dammartin, quite a town, in the late afternoon, I pulled up at a shop to satisfy a perpetual craving for chocolate. . . . We halted on the main road, south-west of the town, and started cooking dinners, concluding that as we had done thirteen miles we should remain there for the night. This was, however, not to be, and soon after finishing our usual repast of bully, biscuit, and cheese, with this time the addition of tea, a rumour came through, which soon proved correct, that we were to continue our march, and accordingly somewhere about 1 a.m. (3rd) we ' hit the road ' again. The hours that followed were, I think, the most exhausting I ever experienced. Marching by night is always more tiring than by day, as there is no change in the landscape to keep one interested. Added to this, we had already had a fairly tiring day. All I can remember that night is a seemingly endless ribbon of straight white road, with an occasional village, and passing the usual crowd of fleeing villagers, who were always to be met with at any hour of the day or night. As the whistle blew for each halt, officers and men fell down in the road, and slept like logs until it sounded again. Whoever was carrying out that duty that night must have had an iron will to keep himself awake. . . . We finally struggled into Lagny at about 9 a.m."

The whole of the British Expeditionary Force crossed the Marne on the 3rd September, but still the order came for them to retire—only this time the right flank had to swing back before the whole force could get behind the Grand Morin, and our battalion, being on the left flank, did not move until 1 a.m. on the 5th.

" We arrived at the small village of Grisy at daylight and proceeded to bivouac in a rose-garden, although we were told that we might billet ; D. R. [Colonel Radcliffe], however, preferred to have us concentrated. As it was still warm and fine, and we were surrounded by rose trees, it was really more pleasant. We spent the night of the 5th at Grisy, and most of the 6th. It was our ' farthest south ' !" Also, as a date to note, the battalion received its first draft of reinforcements ; Lieutenant French turned up with 98 other ranks.

As the imperturbable General Joffre watched the movements of the German hosts, the spirits of some of his Generals rose to a point of elation. The German First Army, in spite of Le Cateau and a zigzag line of march, was a considerable distance ahead of the German Second Army, on its left, and was now marching from east to west across the front of the British Expeditionary Force, and against the left flank of the French Fifth Army and the gap which existed between the latter and the British Army. The discovery has been attributed to General Gallieni, Military Governor of Paris.

On the 4th September, General Gallieni, with General Maunoury, visited Sir John French, but found him absent. They waited for him three hours, and then left without seeing him ; but they pointed out to the Chief of Staff that the German First Army, by offering its right flank, had given them an opportunity which should be taken advantage of at once. General Gallieni stated that, with the concurrence of General Joffre, he wished to attack with the French Sixth Army and the garrison of Paris, and he suggested that the British Army should cease to retreat and take the offensive the next day, in co-operation with his forces ! [1] General Joffre, while agreeing, was not to be hustled, and he desired a little more room for the French Sixth Army.

The position of the British Army was then : I Corps in and to the west of Rosoy, the Cavalry Division on its right rear, about Mormont ; the II Corps, on the left of the I, was in and east of Tournan ; the III Corps, on the left of the II, from Ozoir-la-Ferrière to Brie-Comte-Robert, touching the defences of Paris. At the same time, on the order of General Gallieni, the French Sixth Army moved to the north of the Marne, and established contact with the enemy in the neighbourhood of Meaux, so that the British Army stood on its right rear, between the Marne and the Seine. The gap of fourteen miles, between the right of the British and the left of the French Fifth Army, was filled by General Conneau's Cavalry Corps.

The Allied line was open here like a trap, and into its jaws came the right flank of von Kluck's Army.

.   .   .   .

So the 2nd Battalion Royal Welch Fusiliers came through the Retreat from Mons practically unscathed : such is the fortune of war. But, though they were lucky in not sharing the casualties with other battalions of the II Corps, they shared in full the hardships of the march. The sun, on those sultry August days, beat on them unmercifully ; and then came intervals of rain and cold. As a feat of marching there is, of course, nothing in it—about 200 miles : the Regiment could accomplish the distance any fortnight of the year ; but as a high example of courage and endurance it is without parallel. Major Geiger's account of the march, from which we have drawn freely, puts the hardy spirit of the battalion before us. Company officers and men never knew what was happening, never knew

---

[1] He estimated the eventual strength of the Army of Paris, as he called it—which included the Sixth—at 150,000.

the intention of any of their movements—beyond the evidence of disaster round them. They left the road and extended across the fields to watch the empty countryside ; they closed on the road again and resumed their march. They halted, no one could say why, or for how long ; in a moment they were ordered to fall in and were off again. The sounds and sights of battle were all round them, but they hardly saw an enemy. The one obvious fact before them was *retreat*, without rest, without sleep. Need one comment on the courage required to resist such conditions ?

THE BATTLE OF THE MARNE.

The blessed word " psychology " finds its way even into military history. There is no evidence of moral or spiritual depression in the 2nd Battalion Royal Welch Fusiliers. It is true that they had not been knocked about ; a few men were missing, a few had been overlooked and left asleep at Estrées, and a certain number had gone sick, but officers and men were quite cheerful. The strain, however, had begun to tell on the Higher Command. General Gallieni was enthusiastic, and General Joffre, we are told, was in high spirits ; but British G.H.Q. was gloomy : there is evidence of irritability ; they were impressed by the unity of purpose and mutual support of the Germans ; the II Corps was described as shattered ; and undoubtedly the offensive power of the Expeditionary Force was questioned. Indeed they were approaching the condition of mind which the Germans, in accordance with their war philosophy, desired to impose. The end of the Retreat from Mons marks a dangerous moment.

Fortunately the nervous system of the German commanders was not of superhuman quality. If the Allied troops were weary from sleepless nights and continual marching, so were the enemy. Men and animals were dog-tired. And their commanders realised a threat and were afraid.

Sir John French was, apparently, at a loss to understand why the Germans retired.

" The time has come," says General Joffre's instruction, " to profit by the adventurous position of the German First Army and concentrate against that Army all the efforts of the Allied Armies of the extreme left."

Sir John came to the conclusion that the enemy had commenced to retire before he attacked—before the French Sixth Army attacked. Indeed, the movements of troops seem to have followed the mental condition of the Higher Commands : there was not the crash of a sudden, determined, and powerful thrust, but a cautious advance, and a cautious retirement.

Sir John French's order, on the 5th September, states : " The enemy has apparently abandoned the idea of advancing on Paris, and is contracting his front and moving south-eastward," and he directed the army to move eastward with a view to attack ; the Sixth French Army, on its left, would also attack east, and the Fifth French Army, on its right, would advance northward.

The III Corps order was that the 4th Division would find the advance guard, and march on Serris ; the 19th Infantry Brigade would follow the 4th Division.

So the stay of the 2nd Battalion in their rose-garden was not a long one. " On the afternoon of the 6th we started off again in the dark, and it was not until we had marched for half an hour in a steady north-eastern direction that I dropped back to comment on this with Powell, at the head of B Company. We had, as usual, been given no inkling of any development, and at this time we had not been told a word of any change of direction on the part of the enemy. We finally arrived at Villeneuve-St. Denis." (Geiger.)

The II and III Corps had advanced without any trouble, but the I Corps came into close contact with the enemy; and the II Corps, being about five miles to the left rear of the I, was ordered to close in the next day (7th). This meant that the III Corps would also feel its right.

The 2nd Battalion halted for the night at the village of La Haute Maison, having crossed the Grand Morin. The Grand Morin figures largely in orders at that time, but no one in the battalion noticed it ; small streams and brooks were frequently vested with more importance than their size seemed to warrant. At La Haute Maison the battalion found there was no outpost duty, and bivouacked peacefully.

On the right and left of the British Army, the French had made good progress : it will be realised that they started a day's march ahead of the British. The Sixth French Army had its left on Betz and the enemy was beginning to retire in some haste. The bridges over the Marne at La Ferté-sous-Jouarre were reported by airmen to be congested. Indeed, the situation of the German Armies is full of interest, if one can dismiss all natural glee at the spectacle, and study the arguments that went on between the thrusting von Kluck, the careful von Bülow, the active Colonel Hentsch, and the preoccupied and distant Supreme Command. Mental depression had now descended on the Germans.

On the 8th September the whole of the British Army was engaged in forcing the line of the Petit Morin. This tributary stream joins the main river, the Marne, below La Ferté-sous-Jouarre. At 6 a.m. a mass of enemy troops were seen from the air, waiting their turn to cross the bridges at that town. The 12th Infantry Brigade, 4th Division, was directed to advance on La Ferté, and the 19th Infantry Brigade on Signy Signets, on the left.

Our 2nd Battalion stood to arms at 3 a.m. and moved off as a flank guard to the brigade ; the 1st Middlesex formed the advance guard.

They were moving in close country, but when the battalion arrived within a mile of Signy Signets the ground fell away, and a view was opened right across the Valley of the Marne, but the river itself was not visible. Ahead of them the Middlesex could be seen, feeling their way towards the river. Over the river a flash revealed a German battery moving into position.

" This promised to be very interesting, so we all lay down to watch the performance. The 57th were advancing in artillery formation, and it was not long before the Germans opened on them, whereupon they all lay down and where possible took cover, and the advance ceased."

Captain Geiger states that he imagines the 2nd Battalion had no orders of a definite kind, as they were " in the air " and crossed one of the 11th Brigade battalions. They advanced in a north-easterly direction, across country that was much wired, and dotted with many orchards. They arrived on the crest of the heights south of the river, " but no enemy were in sight, although we could now hear machine guns, which, owing to their slower rate of fire, were rightly surmised to be German. Here we halted to take stock of the situation ; it must not be forgotten that we were always without maps, and had not the faintest idea where we were, the only thing we could identify being the river. We had been here for a few minutes when a gorgeous general officer burst upon our vision. He asked who we were, and on my respectfully informing him, waved his stick and pointed downhill, exclaiming, in that theatrical manner which later made him celebrated, ' Follow me ! ' He then strode off rapidly, and before one platoon had fallen in had disappeared—for two years, so far as I was concerned.

" However, we had now got some sort of orders, and we continued to advance in the same direction as before, and were suddenly brought up by a precipice. As we could not get forward, we lay down in the vicinity of the skyline. As already stated, the view across the river was excellent, and a well-placed shell over a wood, about two miles off, drove a party of the enemy out, and they started running down a road. Encouraged by the distant view of the foe, Wynne Williams asked for permission to fire, and although nothing more could be seen, I acquiesced, as it seemed a good thing for *moral*. So the platoon on the left started firing bursts of independent fire, which had the effect of drawing the invisible enemy's attention to ourselves, and within a couple of minutes we came under traversing machine-gun fire. News was passed down of three or four casualties, which decided me that it would be foolish to stay where we were. We thereupon retired over the skyline and soon came on Powell, ensconced with B Company in a long, deep ditch. Powell told me that C and D Companies had gone down into the town of La Ferté-sous-Jouarre by the main road, which was somewhere on our right, and that A and B Companies were in reserve. We accordingly sat tight in our ditch, listening to occasional outbursts of musketry and occasional shells, firing having nearly ceased.

" When it was nearly dark, we got our orders to advance, which we did by the road, and soon reached the first house of La Ferté, and also some of the men of the companies that had got in first, and who told us they had had some casualties, presumably from parties of the enemy still in the houses. Williams, who was in command of C and D, was installed in the château, and thither we all proceeded.[1]

" Williams, Glegg-Hill, and Company had taken steps to have a comparatively sumptuous repast prepared, and the sole remaining occupant of the château, one of the servants, who proclaimed himself openly to be an Austrian, but who added he only desired to lead a quiet life and had no use for war, provided sundry bottles of quite respectable Burgundy from the wood-stack under which it had been hidden. The battalion was set down to boil its tea in the drive, while our dinner, under the influence of the Chambertin, Hermitage, or whatever it was, became decidedly animated. Someone asserted that the Rifle Brigade were going to clear the town in the middle of the night ; whereupon someone else got up and asked why the hell the Rifle Brigade should perform a task we were quite capable of carrying out ourselves. It was carried unanimously that as soon as we had finished our meal, we should proceed to anticipate the Rifle Brigade. . . .

" Before starting off, I ran to see Parker [*an officer of the King's Own, who was lying in the house wounded*], who told me that as far as he could make out he had been hit by a machine-gun bullet from the other bank. He told me there was open ground which ran down to the river, and it was hereabouts that he had been hit. On going back, I found the war party just starting off under Williams.

[1] This spirited account does not explain that Major Williams, having taken C and D Companies into the town, where he found details of other units, was met, about dusk, by Generals Wilson and Hunter-Weston, and was ordered by them to take charge of the town for the night.

" We advanced slowly down a broad street, breaking into each house on either side. We found no one—not even a peaceful inhabitant. We next came to the open space Parker had told me about. The first house on the left-hand side was a large one, and here we struck oil, for on running upstairs we came into a large room with about fifty wounded Germans, all in bed, being tenderly nursed by a party of French Red Cross Sisters. . . . Clegg-Hill was already on the premises and very indignant, as he was under

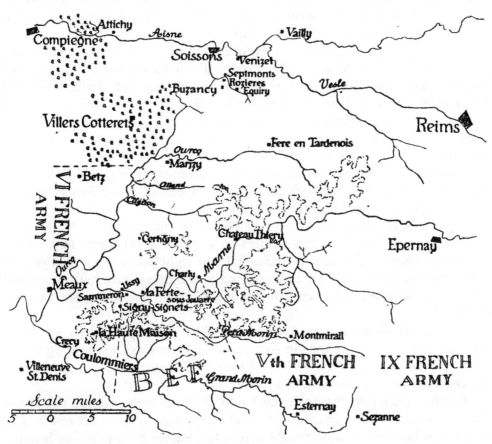

the impression these Germans were responsible for our casualties—which was afterwards found not to be the case.

" As soon as we got outside again I was told that half one platoon had been installed with Wynne Williams in another house at the extreme north-western corner of the open space, where they could get a view of the opposite bank, and where, very obviously, a German machine gun lay near at hand. Parties were also left out behind barricades to block the roads north, east, and west of the château ; after which we all went home, and I found a bed—the first for many days." (Geiger.)

The next day young Collingwood Thompson was killed, in the open space that led down to the river. He was the first officer of the regiment to be killed. A few minutes later the East Lancashire Regiment (11th Battalion) arrived to relieve the 2nd Battalion, and their Commanding Officer had his attention drawn to the spot where Collingwood Thompson had been hit, and to the German machine gun on the north bank of the river—for all that he, too, was killed by it before the day was out.

The situation reports on the evening of the 8th revealed the British Army over the Petit Morin ; the French Fifth Army, on the right, well forward ; but the Sixth, on the left, strongly opposed, indeed General Maunoury's centre had been forced back. But there was still a wide gap between the German First and Second Armies, and though von Kluck was putting up a stout fight against the French Sixth Army, the Supreme Command was getting more nervous than ever.

The British Army was ordered to force the passage of the Marne on the 9th, and move against the left flank of the German First Army, and so relieve the pressure on General Maunoury.

The I and II Corps were able to cross the Marne by bridges which they found intact and held by a few snipers only, but the III Corps had a hard task before them. The enemy defended the right bank with energy and determination, and when evening fell only six battalions had succeeded in crossing the river. Our 2nd Battalion, being in reserve, spent the day resting.

Military Operations, 1914, points out that although it does not seem a satisfactory day for the British Army, its advance was the deciding factor in the German decision to retire. There had been some stormy scenes between the German commanders.

By the evening of the 10th the I and II Corps were astride the River Alland, with the cavalry in front ; the III Corps was on their left rear. The latter corps had had to pass troops across the Marne by a pontoon bridge ; the whole of the 4th Division had preceded the 19th Brigade, so the 2nd Battalion was " very much in reserve."

The battalion moved to Certigny that night ; to Marizy St. Geneviève on the 11th, in pouring rain ; to Buzancy on the 12th, again in the rain ; Equiry on the 13th ; Venizel on the 14th ; and there remained till the 19th, when they went back to Septmonts to make up deficiencies.

Of this period a story is told by Sergeant-Major Boreham with an allusion to the " Angels of Mons." No doubt a yarn of the sort gave rise to that fable which, with the tale of Russian Armies passing through England, casts a curious light on the emotional state of the people in Great Britain. The Sergeant-Major's story provides a source for this particular supernatural adventure.

" Our billet in Buzancy was in a château that evidently dated from the Middle Ages. There were vast caverns in the hill immediately behind the house, which had been used as stables in the days gone by. I must confess that it was here that I did a mild bit of looting. We company sergeant-majors were accommodated in the hall of the château; the room in which the headquarter officers dined led off from this hall, and after dinner we went into the room to receive orders from the Adjutant. While we were in there I noticed some bottles of wine on a sideboard. When all was quiet, I went back in my stockinged feet with the idea of annexing one of the bottles. Just as I reached the door, someone approached the door on the far side of the room with a lighted candle. I hopped back, and when all was once again quiet I tried again. This time I got to the door, and as I stepped into the room a board creaked loudly enough to wake everybody in the house. Again I hopped back, and then started again, but this time on my hands and knees, and was at last successful. One bottle was not much between four or five, but still it was a case of ' stolen fruit being the sweetest.'

" The next day Sergeant Dealing told me a queer story. He and his platoon were billeted in an outhouse. While he lay awake before going to sleep, he heard in the distance the sound of mounted men approaching. He could distinctly hear the trampling of hoofs and the rattle as of armour and weapons. The cavalcade came nearer and passed right over where he and his men were lying, and the sounds died away in the distance. He maintained that he was wide awake the whole time. We had not heard of them at the time, or I should have suggested that it was a mounted section of the ' Angels of Mons.'

" In the afternoon of Sunday, the 13th September, we moved off again, through Rozières to Septmonts. Here we halted, and were told that we were to wait while the engineers put bridges over the Aisne, when we would continue our pursuit of the enemy. At night the battalion moved down to Venizel and came in for a bit of shelling, but without any casualties occurring. I should say that this shelling happened the following morning. We then went into the woods just above Venizel, where the battalion remained until the 19th. During this time the enemy shelled the ground in rear of the woods continuously, but no shells fell where we were. We must have kept very well concealed. Also rain fell pretty well all the time.

" About one in the afternoon of the 19th September the battalion moved out of the wood and returned to Septmonts. One hundred paces was kept between platoons on leaving the woods. This was the first time we had done this, and it was a good thing that we did it, for when about three platoons got on the road, which ran parallel to the enemy's position for some half-mile before turning into a gap in the hills, a half-dozen shells came over pretty smartly, one or two of which fell in the intervals, and would undoubtedly have caused casualties had the usual formation on the march been observed. Septmonts was reached without any further incident, and the night was spent in the open. My diary records that it was a ' beastly cold night.' "

THE BATTLE OF THE AISNE.

The German retreat took them behind the Aisne. The battle opened on the 13th September. By noon the I Corps on the right, and the III on the left, of the British Army had forced the passage of the river, although all the bridges were either down or much damaged, and the enemy's opposition in some places was strong. The II Corps managed, in the afternoon, by means of a single plank, to pass troops over to the north bank.

The prospects of the Allies then seemed good, as the gap between the German First and Second Armies was still open. Sir John French directed the Army to advance north on the 14th. In the III Corps it was the 4th Division that was ordered to resume the offensive ; the Divisional Artillery and the 19th Infantry Brigade remained on the south of the river.

But the German VII Reserve Corps, by the surrender of Maubeuge, was released from its investment and arrived on the scene to fill the gap between their First and Second Armies. When the British Divisions advanced on the Chemin des Dames Ridge, they found, instead of the scattered German cavalry that had been expected, a full entrenched defence of all arms.

The Battle of the Aisne was a confusing engagement for the British Army, with a patchy entrance into battle, hard fighting, gaps in the line, and so forth. It marks the end of the first German retreat.

On the 15th Sir John French issued a simple, innocent-looking order :

" On the right of the British Army the French have made some progress.

" The 18th Corps has occupied Craonne and the high ground on the left, and is in touch with the right of our I Corps.

" On the left the French have reached the general line Soissons—Noyon, and are making good progress on their left.

" Our Army has successfully maintained its position, and has repulsed numerous counter-attacks, inflicting heavy losses on the enemy.

" The 6th Division has to-day reached Rocourt and is marching early to-morrow morning to join the III Corps.

" The Commander-in-Chief wishes the line now held by the Army to be strongly entrenched, and it is his intention to resume a general offensive at the first opportunity."

The line to be strongly entrenched!

The important moves that followed the battle were made by the French. On the 17th September General Maunoury commenced an attempt to outflank von Kluck, but the Germans had brought their IX Corps from Antwerp, and the French attempt failed. The French Second Army was then moved up to the left on the 22nd, but fresh reinforcements, in the shape of the German II Corps, arrived to prolong the enemy flank, and at a critical moment the XVIII Corps.

The German line was then extended by their XXI Corps, I Bavarian Corps, II Bavarian Corps, and XIV Reserve Corps. By this time the battle-line had reached the Somme area.

The French put in their Tenth Army over the Arras region ; the Germans their Guard Corps, IV Corps, and I Bavarian Reserve Corps. The French replied with their XXI Corps ; the Germans with their XIV Corps. By the 9th October German Cavalry Corps were thirty miles from Dunkirk.

" But," says Sir John French, " all ended in the same trench ! trench ! trench ! I finished my part in the Battle of the Aisne, however, unconverted, and it required the further and more bitter lesson of my own failure in the north to pass the Lys River, during the last days of October, to bring home to my mind a principle in warfare of to-day which I have held ever since, namely, that given forces fairly equally matched, you can bend but you cannot break your enemy's trench line."

The trenches dug on the Aisne were short, narrow slits, to hold a section, and not connected.

Our 2nd Battalion was held in reserve throughout the Battle of the Aisne. " The part we are playing in the great battle is an absurdly tranquil one. Yesterday (26th September) the Royal Welch Fusiliers drove the woods here with beaters for straggling Germans, of which a few are often reported. They stood along the drives and round the edges of the woods like men waiting for pheasants. The wood contained exactly three rabbits." (2nd Lieutenant W. G. Fletcher.) The battalion remained at Septmonts till the 5th October, when it moved to Estrées-St. Denis, and entrained at 6 a.m. on the 10th, arriving at St. Omer at 10 p.m.

III—5

OPERATIONS IN FLANDERS.   (OCTOBER—NOVEMBER 1914.)

Shortly before the outbreak of war, Sir John French had pointed out to the Committee of Imperial Defence that the submarines and aircraft of a continental Power which might be in possession of the coast-line between Dunkirk and Boulogne would deny the passage of the Straits of Dover to any vessel not submersible.   " In fact the command of the sea, in so far as this part of the Channel is concerned, would not depend on the relative strength of the opposing navies, but would remain in dispute until one side or the other effected practical destruction of its adversary's aircraft and submarines."   (1914, Field-Marshal Viscount French of Ypres.)

He went on, with sound prophetic insight, to contend that the Straits of Dover would soon lose their maritime character, and, as a military obstacle, become no more than a river.

The " race for the sea," as it has been called, which followed the Battle of the Aisne is a misleading description : the danger foreseen by Sir John French was not the primary reason for extending the flank of the Allied Armies, although the menace to the Channel ports was always present in the mind of the General Staff ; those flank movements were started by General Joffre on one side and von Moltke on the other attempting an enveloping movement, the obvious move against an open flank.   Naturally a success by the enemy would have given them the coast-line, and so that a point might be held the General Staff requested the Admiralty to send a brigade of marines to Dunkirk ; it was landed on the night 19th/20th September.

The situation contained a further possibility, though slender and overweighted by what was becoming day by day a grave problem—a junction with the Belgian Field Army in Antwerp.   But the geographical position of Antwerp, buried in Holland, was unfortunate : an extension of the German line would complete the investment, which was then only partial, and the Belgian Army would be trapped.

An immediate reinforcement seemed necessary, and troops were scarce.   The suggestion of the First Lord of the Admiralty (Mr. Churchill) to send two Naval brigades, which, with the one Marine brigade at Dunkirk, would form a Naval division, was agreed to.[1]   The War Office also agreed to send the newly formed 7th Division and the 3rd Cavalry Division, the whole force under General Sir Henry Rawlinson.   The French Government

---

[1] The composition and equipment of these two Naval brigades have been much criticised.   The immediate problem which confronted British Ministers has, however, been ably dealt with by Mr. Churchill—never an advocate for " doing nothing "—in vol. i of *The World Crisis*.

was to co-operate by sending a Territorial division and some 8,000 Fusiliers Marins.

But the situation was grave. The Germans had decided to capture Antwerp, with the help of their heavy howitzers, and the Belgian Field Army was withdrawn to the west bank of the Scheldt on the night 6th/7th October.

The 7th Division and 3rd Cavalry Division were landed at Zeebrugge on the 6th and 7th, and were ordered by General Rawlinson to Bruges.[1]

The 1st Battalion Royal Welch Fusiliers was posted to the 22nd Infantry Brigade, 7th Division, and reached Zeebrugge at 9 a.m. on the 7th October. They proceeded by rail to Oostcamp, four miles south of Bruges, and marched on the 8th to Oudenburg, south-east of Ostend. This was their first experience of the continental *pavé* roads, which, until the men became accustomed to them, were very tiring. The traffic they had to march through was eloquent of the state of affairs, and at times the road was completely blocked.

The first news to greet them, that Antwerp had not fallen, was a satisfaction of short duration. A decision to evacuate the town was arrived at on the 8th, and Lord Kitchener wired the information to General Rawlinson, and instructed him to protect the withdrawal.

The position until the 9th was that two Expeditionary Forces were operating, the one under Sir John French, the other directed by Lord Kitchener from the War Office.

The evacuation of Antwerp came as a surprise to Sir John, who had not realised any immediate danger. He was never fully informed of what was going on, and the infantry and cavalry divisions were dispatched without reference to him.[2] His comment is that " as things actually turned out, the troops which were landed at Zeebrugge and Ostend had (to quote from General Joffre's wire to Huguet [3] on 8th October) no influence on the fate of the fortress, and what help they were in protecting the retreat of the Belgians and saving the Army from destruction might have been equally well rendered from a safer and more effective direction."

---

[1] The division was made up of the 1st Grenadier Guards, 2nd Yorkshire Regiment, and 2nd Border Regiment, who were in the United Kingdom when war broke out ; the 2nd Scots Fusiliers and 2nd Wiltshire, who came from Gibraltar ; the 1st Royal Welch Fusiliers and 2nd Warwickshire, from Malta ; the 2nd Queens, 2nd Bedfordshire, and 1st South Staffordshire, from the Cape ; and the 2nd Gordon Highlanders, from Egypt. They were deficient in artillery and some essential services, and did not constitute a formed division.

[2] This statement of Sir John's is curious, as General Rawlinson was in close touch with him— see the latter's Diary.

[3] Military Attaché in London, who played an important part in pre-war arrangements for military support under the Entente Cordiale.

At this moment Sir John was secretly withdrawing his army from the Aisne. The rapid passing of French troops to the left to outflank the Germans was placing his line of communication across an ever-growing French Army line of supply, and, from all points of view, it seemed more fitting that the British Army should be near the coast. To this General Joffre had agreed, and the first moves had taken place.

Lord Kitchener's instructions to General Rawlinson on the 8th were to cover the retirement from the line Ghent—Selzaete to the area Ostend—Thourout—Dixmude, and, when Sir John's Army moved out on the left flank of the Allied line and marched eastwards, to form the left column of the combined forces.

So, on the 9th, this disposition of troops being carried out, the 22nd Infantry Brigade marched to Ostend, where " we halted for several hours on a piece of waste land near a canal : this proved very unpleasant on account of smells. Many refugees passed us here, on carts, bicycles, and on foot, carrying as much as they could. A few of the Royal Naval Division wounded also passed us from Antwerp. Both refugees and wounded were very pessimistic and said Antwerp was bound to fall." (Hindson.) The brigade entrained for Ghent, arriving there at 6.30 p.m.—incidentally they passed the Naval Division *en route*, training back from Antwerp. They bivouacked a mile south-west of the town : the enemy was then reported to be about ten miles south of them. No fires were allowed, and there was a steady downpour of rain.

On this day General Rawlinson was placed under the orders of Sir John French, who gave to this force the name of IV Corps.

Sir Horace Smith-Dorrien's II Corps was then detraining at Abbeville. We have seen that the French XXI Corps was the last to be moved out on the left flank. On the 8th they had extended the line to Vermelles ; and to the north of them came two corps of French cavalry and a brigade of French Territorials extending the line to St. Omer ; and a second brigade of Territorials was dotted about connecting up with Dunkirk.

The Germans, with two cavalry corps, had attempted to break through between La Bassée and Armentières on the 9th, but were checked ; another cavalry corps, coming through Ypres, was turned back by the French Territorials on Bailleul. From Bailleul to the sea is thirty miles. Sir John French's orders to General Rawlinson were to retain his position as long as he could without becoming involved, and then to retire slowly on the line St. Omer—Dunkirk.

On the 10th October at 2 a.m. our 1st Battalion was moved a short distance from their bivouac area to a ridge about a mile south-east of the village of Melle, where they entrenched with the Royal Warwickshire on their left, in support of Belgian and French troops, who were in contact with the enemy south and south-east of Ghent. " French and Belgian troops were going to attack a small German force, and we were to co-operate by striking the German rear and left flank. The Germans, however, attacked first, and were surprised by the French and Belgians as they were coming over a railway embankment. The Germans left about 200 dead behind." (Hindson.) At 10 o'clock that night our 2nd Battalion detrained at St. Omer.

It looked as though the regiment might have a battalion on either side of the German line !

The 2nd Battalion moves North.

The arrangement arrived at between General Joffre and Sir John French was slightly modified, and the British Army was to concentrate about Doullens, Arras, and St. Pol, and then move as rapidly as possible to the left of the main French Armies and, it was hoped, turn the right flank of the German Armies.

On the 11th the II Corps had arrived in the neighbourhood of Bethune.

Our 2nd Battalion move from the Aisne was made with the utmost precaution, marching at night, bivouacking in woods, and remaining concealed all day. " We had to get off by night, march till morning, and then get into the wet and frosty woods before daybreak, and sleep in the woods till about 8 a.m.—hang about all day and go on the next night. Secrecy, of course—aeroplanes ! The men carry rolled great-coats, waterproof sheets, spare boots, socks, towel and washing things, three days' emergency rations, rifle, 150 rounds of ammunition." (Lieutenant W. G. Fletcher.) But they entrained at Estrées St. Denis. The train passed through Amiens, Etaples, and Boulogne. The latter completely mystified the men. " All sorts of conjectures were made—the best one being that as we were the first troops out we were going home."

The 19th Brigade was now attached to the 6th Division (6th October) in place of the 16th Brigade.

Although the III Corps had not completed its concentration, General Pulteney was ordered to advance on Hazebrouck, thirteen miles east ; and on the 11th, the 19th Brigade, being present, was sent forward as advanced guard to a line half-way between St. Omer and Hazebrouck. Our 2nd Battalion moved on this day to Renescure. " Billeted in a château—very nice it was," commented Captain M. S. Richardson.

The order was then issued for the corps to advance on Bailleul through Hazebrouck in five columns—6th Division on the right, three columns ; 4th Division on the left, two columns.

THE BATTLE OF ARMENTIÈRES OPENS.

On the morning of the 12th our 2nd Battalion marched to St. Sylvestre, south-east of Cassel ; and on the 13th to Strazeele, in reserve to the 6th Division. A stiff little engagement was fought at Meteren, in very close country, which was the first formal attack of the British in the war, the whole corps being halted to prepare for it. The battalion, however, was not required.

On the advance being resumed, the 19th Brigade was still the advanced guard to the division. Although it was not then known, the Germans were preparing a new plan. They had formed a new Army, the Fourth, which was to move forward between Menin and the sea while the Sixth Army stood fast on the line La Bassée—Armentières—Menin. The 19th Infantry Brigade found Bailleul evacuated, though small bodies of the enemy remained in the vicinity. " Marched off about midday through Bailleul. I was sent along the railway as flank guard—ran into the enemy and had two men wounded." (M. S. Richardson.) Our 2nd Battalion was put on outpost across the Bailleul—Nieppe road, south-east of the town. During the night they sent forward a reconnaissance party to Steenwerck, which was also found unoccupied. The next day the whole battalion moved to Steenwerck.

The road was " strewn with dead horses." They found the state of the town indescribable. Before leaving, the enemy had thrown furniture, clothing, half the contents of the houses, into the street, and only one remained untouched—owing, presumably, to the fact that it had been occupied by the German Staff. But the inhabitants were convinced that the woman occupier was a spy, and a riot was going on outside the house. To prevent violence, it was found necessary to put a guard over it. Two years later this same woman was running the officers' club at Steenwerck.

On the 16th October the 16th Brigade rejoined the III Corps, and the 19th Brigade passed into G.H.Q. Reserve. The battalion was immediately ordered to Vlamertinghe, and had to abandon two wagon-loads of letters and parcels, ten days' accumulation—a bitter sacrifice.

" We got to Vlamertinghe late at night and my company was billeted in a school. Sentries were posted on the doors of the estaminets (inns), which doubtless saved a few men making asses of themselves. A baker worked all night making bread, which was eagerly bought by the troops. The following day some of the officers went into Ypres to see the 1st Battalion, which was in that place, having marched there from Zeebrugge, where it landed a couple of weeks before. I may as well relate another pre-war experience which has some connection here. On our way home from India in the previous March, the 2nd Battalion called at Malta to hand over a draft to the 1st Battalion ; all the members of the Sergeants' Mess who could be spared went ashore and were entertained by the members of the 1st Battalion Sergeants' Mess. During the evening Sergeant-Major 'Shem' Williams, in the course of a speech, said that the two battalions had not met since 1881, and he did not think that it would happen again in our time. Here is another case of the war bringing about the unexpected, for here were the two battalions, if not actually meeting, within a few miles of each other. A few months later they were side by side in the trenches." (Sergeant-Major Boreham.)

The situation then was that the II Corps had become involved about La Bassée, and the battle was still raging ; and though it had been the intention to relieve Sir Horace Smith-Dorrien with French troops, none were available, and so he had to remain with his corps on the left of the French XXI Corps, and the gap between the II and III Corps was filled by Conneau's Cavalry Corps. On the left of the III Corps between Romarin and Ypres was Allenby's Cavalry Corps and the III Cavalry Division. In front of Ypres, from Voormezeele to Wieltje, was the 7th Division. The French Naval Brigade was at Dixmude, and the Belgian Army was on the Yser. Sir Douglas Haig's I Corps was detraining in the Hazebrouck area.

Sir John French's orders for the 16th include, for the first time, the Second Expeditionary Force, which had been sent to relieve Antwerp.

The 1st Battalion moves South.

We left the 1st Battalion south-west of Ghent listening to heavy firing. On the 11th October they were ordered forward to cover the retirement of Belgian and French troops ; and themselves retired, about 4 p.m., without being engaged, and marched to Hansbeke, via Ghent and Tronchiennes. It was again a retreat, similar in scene to that from Mons, but without the bitter fighting. Civilians, transport, other troops, were streaming along the roads. " A battalion of Marine Fusiliers marched parallel to us through the broad boulevards of the town (Ghent). We were impressed by their rapid and easy marching. We saw them several times during the march back to Ypres. Belgian cavalry were in the picture." (Alston.)

Arriving at Hansbeke at 7 p.m., the place was crowded with troops and billets were hard to find. The battalion moved off again at 2 a.m. On the line Hanime—Neyeze three companies held the crossings of the canal while Belgian engineers laid charges and blew up the bridges. That night (13th) they arrived at Thielt, having handed over the outpost line to the Northumberland Hussars and Belgian Cyclists. Then followed a tiring day as rearguard to the division marching on Roulers ; but here 150 men per company entrained for Ypres, leaving the transport and details to march by road with the division.

At Ypres they were billeted in the Kaserne, and spent the 15th out in the orchards round Zillebeke, returning in the evening to other billets in the east of the town.

The Intelligence before G.H.Q. gave three German divisions moving from Antwerp on Ypres ; and as the Germans were falling back on the III Corps front, Sir John French, in consultation with General Joffre, ordered his army to move eastwards. In detail, the III Corps was to move at first to the north-east and get into touch with the IV Corps, which would be marching east between Courtrai and Roulers. The II Corps was to try to move north, and draw towards the III Corps, but, as it turned out, could not do so.

In the early morning of the 16th the 7th Division marched from Ypres, passed through an outpost line about two miles out, held by the Royal Scots Fusiliers, who reported the presence of enemy patrols, and commenced to entrench on a six-mile position between Zandvoorde and Zonnebeke. On the left, our 1st Battalion, as advanced guard to the 22nd Brigade, arrived at Zonnebeke at 6.30 a.m. to see a Uhlan patrol gallop out of the far side of the village. They took up and entrenched an outpost position on the Wervicq—Passchendaele road.

The position was on a forward slope, with the Broodseinde cross-roads about the centre. It was close country. There were a lot of houses and gardens on the left, and a wood to the front. The reserve company was placed in a sandpit, about 400 yards in rear on the reverse slope. Rifle pits were dug and connected up as far as time permitted, but from all accounts there was not much done in this respect.

The IV Corps was now waiting for the advance of the III Corps, which had occupied Armentières. The II Corps was acting under the original order to capture La Bassée, and made a small advance towards that place.

It was still thought possible to turn the enemy's flank, and on the 17th Sir John French issued orders for attack in conjunction with the French. The II Corps was to capture La Bassée, the III Corps was to move down the Lys, the IV Corps was to attack and capture Menin ; but the word

" move " was used for the latter operation, whereas in the instructions to the II Corps " attack " had been employed, consequently General Rawlinson's orders were based on the assumption that the 7th Division might attack the next day, which would be the 19th.

On the 18th the 7th Division made a right wheel to face south-east, instead of east. The 22nd Brigade went into reserve and marched to the area round Hooge.

We arrive now at the situation of a thin line of alternate infantry and cavalry between the main French Armies and the sea, with our 1st Battalion in the forefront and our 2nd Battalion in G.H.Q. Reserve close up behind them.

The broad details of the picture, as the student knows it to-day, are that General Foch had elaborated a combined move of British and French to the east, seeing a chance of separating the German III Reserve Corps, which was advancing from Antwerp, from the main German Armies ; and while a portion of the Allied forces drove this corps on to the coast, the bulk would force the passage of the Lys, north of Menin, and attack the German Armies in flank and reverse. Sir John French was manœuvring his army in accordance with this plan. But neither he nor Foch nor Joffre knew of the approach of the German Fourth Army, between Menin and the coast.

General Rawlinson, therefore, was about to attack Menin across the front of a hidden army. He had been informed of his mistake on the 18th and had arranged to attack on the 19th.

It was a tense and dramatic situation. The advance of the German Fourth Army was one of the enemy's great moves in the war, and " on paper " the Allied flank was turned, the Channel ports were open to the Germans, with Paris, perhaps, to follow—a masterly move, as great, in its way, as General Gallieni's swoop with his hidden Paris Army on the flank of von Kluck.

THE BATTLES OF YPRES—THE BATTLE OF MESSINES.[1]

The ancient town of Ypres had a military history but little attraction. It was quaint enough lying by the side of a tree-shaded canal, with its

[1] The dates of all these battles overlap. The Battle of Messines dates officially from the 12th October to the 2nd November, and the area was along the Douve from Warneton to Dranoutre—Reninghelst—Dickebusch—Voormezeele, thence along the canal. This places the 1st Battalion out of the Battle of Messines on the 19th. On the other hand, the official date for the commencement of the Battles of Ypres, 1914, to which the action fought by the 1st Battalion might be a prelude, is the 19th, although the first of the series of battles commenced officially on the 21st. Inasmuch as the 1st Battalion was conforming to an Allied plan, the first moves of which commenced on the 12th October and were conceived in ignorance of the German Fourth Army, undoubtedly they took part in the Battle of Messines. Officially the honour seems to have been awarded to the 2nd Battalion, who marched through a part of the area.

cathedral and Cloth Hall, its old brick-faced fortifications, its moat, and its gates to the country beyond ; but apart from age, the architectural qualities of the two principal buildings had not sufficient appeal to draw many visitors. It was a town of narrow streets, with, of course, a square opposite the cathedral. Commercially it had reached its zenith and local industries showed no sign or promise of noteworthy expansion.

The surrounding country is flat—the military value attached to ridges during the war has given them a prominence which is not apparent to the ordinary traveller—and is highly cultivated. It was, in fact, uninteresting before the war, and is now, but for the association.

When our 1st Battalion arrived at Ypres, although there had been a little looting by the enemy, all the houses were intact and, in spite of the flight of many citizens, the business of the town was being carried on, the Mayor and Corporation were functioning and were filled with more than ordinary importance. There was the stirring and bewildering bustle of military movement—British troops, French troops, and Belgian troops passing through the streets, billeted in the houses and public buildings, buying souvenirs in the shops, drinking beer at the open cafés that invaded the footway with their tables and chairs.

A century lay between the Battle of Waterloo and the First Battles of Ypres, but the scene in this town was as extraordinary a prelude to the drama that was to follow as was the Duchess of Richmond's ball on the eve of Napoleon's eclipse.

Even the battlefield had not been, like the decks of a ship, cleared for action ; tenacious peasants continued their autumn work, cattle grazed in the fields, women and children appeared in the cottage doorway with the wondering air of possessors disturbed in their peaceful rights, but otherwise as unmoved by the marching of troops as by the flight of civilian refugees along the Route Nationale.

Houses, farms, labourers' cottages, here clearly defined, there half-hidden by the autumn foliage, dotted the countryside and clustered now and again into small villages.

But military transport rattled and crashed along the roads, and high up in the sky a puff of black smoke, thick and woolly, appeared in a silent burst, followed by a hollow explosion ; and a less echoing crash drew the eyes to another cloud of smoke rising from the centre of a distant wood, or perhaps to a house where the falling debris and dust gave movement to the cloud.

To the private soldier, cheerful and, apparently, indifferent, it was not quite the same as Army manœuvres. A march from Ypres, at first bold, would be broken by frequent halts as a vaguely defined danger-zone was approached. The company would draw up under a leafy hedge, or a bank by the side of a wood with the earthy smell of autumn in the air and the murmuring sound of conversation accentuating a strange silence through which, paradoxically, the expectant ear was assailed by a multitude of noises. For a moment the mind may have been attracted and absorbed in the movements of a bird.

Armentières had been occupied by the III Corps on the 17th. On the 18th the corps had been engaged in hard fighting about Frelinghien as it moved up the Valley of the Lys towards Menin ; on its left the Cavalry Corps had been pressing forward on the line Deulemont—Tenbrielan, being in touch with the 7th Division. From Armentières the British line ran in a general north-easterly direction, with the 7th Division on the line Kruiseecke—Terhand—Waterdamhoek, facing south-east.

The German main line was the Lys, with a line of posts, America—Koelberg—Kezelberg, covering Menin.

On the 18th October the 22nd Brigade was in reserve amongst the woods round the château of Hooge : the 1st Battalion was at Veldhoek, a little way off along the Menin road. The men received their first pay since landing, at the château. There were few sounds of battle. It was known that the division was going to attack, but there was not enough information to inspire speculation on how they themselves would be used, and where.

French cavalry were out in the direction of Roulers and Houthulst Forest ; the Belgian Army was on the Yser.

Late that evening the battalion marched to Becelaere and billeted there for the night. The Battle Orders arrived about 2 a.m.

The III Corps was to continue its advance on Menin down the Valley of the Lys ; Allenby's Cavalry Corps would keep in touch with the infantry of the III and IV Corps ; but stress was laid on the attack of the 7th Division on Menin from the north and north-west.

The 22nd Brigade, opposite Dadizeele, was the left of the division ; on its left were the 6th and 7th Cavalry Brigades of the 3rd Cavalry Division, with special orders with regard to Ledeghem ; there were also some armoured cars on this flank. The 7th Division was to advance from the left, and when the 22nd Brigade had cleared the enemy from the trenches in front of them, the capture of Gheluve was to follow, and then the whole division would advance on Menin.

The battalion was afoot in the darkness of the early morning, ghostly companies parading outside their billets ; they commenced to pass through the outpost lines, as advanced guard, at 6.30 a.m., heading for Dadizeele. (See Map, page 81.)

They reached Dadizeele without adventure—the villagers were still there.   Kezelberg and Klaythoek, occupied by the enemy, lay on the main Roulers road between them and Menin.   The order was given to attack Klaythoek.

The battalion deployed on the left of the road, with the Royal Warwickshire on the right, and the South Staffordshire in support ; the Queens were on the left rear, watching Ledeghem.

It was then about 11.30 a.m., and as the battalion advanced, with front and support companies extended, across the fields and up a gentle, almost imperceptible slope, the enemy artillery opened fire, and in a moment the whole area seemed covered by the overhead crash of shrapnel. Casualties, however, were slight.   They passed through Kezelberg, and pressed on to Klaythoek, the enemy retiring before them.   The advance was now against rifle fire, and was made in short rushes.   Casualties commenced to mount up, and the South Staffordshire reinforced the front line. They were now within a short distance from the second mile-stone out of Menin, on the forward slope of the swell in the ground, overlooking the town, and within assaulting distance of the German trenches defending Menin.

But alarming news had reached General Rawlinson.   The 6th Cavalry Brigade had taken Ledeghem, after considerable opposition ; the 7th Cavalry Brigade, on their left, was engaged with a strong enemy column advancing from Iseghem and, with the French Cavalry on their left, were falling back.   And before 11 o'clock airmen reported considerable enemy forces approaching the left flank of the IV Corps.

The perilous nature of the situation thus revealed forced General Rawlinson to order the attack to be abandoned.   General Capper, commanding the 7th Division, then ordered the 22nd Brigade to break off the engagement and fall back on the left of the 21st Brigade, but facing north, and in touch with the right of the 3rd Cavalry Division at Moorslede.

Brigadier-General Lawford had then to extricate his brigade, already within assaulting distance of the enemy covering-posts.   Runners left Brigade Headquarters and somehow reached the firing-line : the order was delivered to an officer—it does not seem to have been Colonel Cadogan or any of his staff.   But the surprise it occasioned may be imagined : the battalion was making good progress and felt its ascendancy over the enemy.   They were ordered to cover the retirement, and, where they could, commenced to scratch protecting holes.

There was a certain amount of mixing of units, which was, under the circumstances, a natural sequence, and the withdrawal was a piecemeal affair. The enemy made no attempt at pursuit, but the battalion casualties under this difficult manœuvre mounted up : Captain Brennan (3rd Battalion) and Lieutenant Chance were killed, and a number of men were picked off by emboldened snipers.

When the rest of the brigade was clear, the battalion withdrew through Kezelberg and Dadizeele—where the villagers still remained, though now thoroughly alarmed as the enemy had commenced to shell the village— and so, through Becelaere, to the rifle-slits they had already made at Broodseinde, near Zonnebeke. The scene on this last stage was one of the greatest confusion, for the road was blocked with fugitives before the advancing host, and the battalion transport had, eventually, to turn off the road and make its way across the fields. All through the night, when the battalion was disposed in its rifle-slits, a great stream of civilians flowed down the road from Roulers.

Company commanders spent part of the night re-sorting their men. But Captain J. H. Brennan, Lieutenant G. O. de P. Chance, and 15 other ranks had been killed ; Major R. E. P. Gabbett, Captains E. O. Skaife, W. H. St. John, S. Jones, 2nd Lieutenant R. E. Naylor, and 84 other ranks had been wounded ; 11 other ranks were reported missing.

The left of the brigade should have been on Moorslede, but the 3rd Cavalry Division had been forced back from that village ; indeed, pressure was being exerted everywhere. But in spite of the evident presence of strong enemy forces, the situation was not fully appreciated on the evening of the 19th October. The Intelligence placed three and a half enemy corps advancing, whereas there were actually five and a half ; and Sir John French, " still, apparently, mistrusting the intelligence received," informed General Haig, whom he had ordered forward, that " the enemy's strength on the front Menin—Ostend is estimated at about a corps, and no more." The II and III Corps were ordered to continue their operations, and the IV Corps (7th Division) was to entrench while the 3rd Cavalry Division covered the advance of the I Corps. The capture of Menin was also part of the 3rd Cavalry Division's task.

But on the 20th October the whole British Army was on the defensive.

In compliance with G.H.Q. orders, the 3rd Cavalry Division moved out early in the morning of the 20th to Passchendaele, where it was in touch with the French Cavalry Corps ; and on the right, the 7th Division sent two battalions of the 20th Brigade forward to Gheluwe, which was found occupied by the enemy, and two battalions of the 21st Brigade to Terhand, but they, after passing through Becelaere, could make no further headway. The enemy was closing in.

On the right of the 7th Division, General Allenby soon discovered that he must defend his own line, and not attempt to advance. His Cavalry Corps made a great fight during the day, and, though they had to retire, kept in touch with the right of the 7th Division.

On the III Corps' front General Pulteney's orders were not quite in accordance with the spirit of G.H.Q. orders : he did not like the reports of the 19th. He, therefore, ordered his divisions to maintain their positions, and attempted to get some depth in his dispositions. He had not, however, the time to carry out his ideas, as the enemy was on him early in the morning, and his right was bent back under the weight of the attack.

The II Corps was wheeling to the right, and still attempting to envelop La Bassée, according to the order. There was severe fighting on this corps' front, in which our 2nd Battalion became involved.

THE BATTLE OF LANGEMARCK.[1]

The 1st Battalion, however, remained in its rifle-slits and all the confusion arising from the previous day's withdrawal was smoothed out.

Soon after 11 a.m., enemy columns were seen approaching, and artillery fire was opened on the battalion line. Unknown to them, the 3rd Cavalry Division and the French Cavalry Corps on their left had been driven back ; and the reconnaissance companies from the 20th and 21st Brigades had been called in from their positions on the " high ground," where they had been in touch with the enemy. There was a drizzle of rain since the early morning.

Crouching in their rifle-slits, under the bombardment, the battalion waited. At last the guns ceased, and the enemy infantry advanced.[2]

Every man knew that the weight of artillery was against us, but his musketry training had given him confidence in his rifle. The German advance was thick—they always favoured superior weight in men and metal—and the excitement in the rifle-slits, from which a roar of fire, indistinguishable from machine-gun fire, arose, was intense as the waves of the enemy drew nearer—then seemed to hesitate as figures darted about unsteadily—and then receded.

After a pause there followed more artillery fire ; and then, at 4 p.m.,

---

[1] Official date: 21st–24th October. Area : Comines Canal to Ypres ; thence the Yser Canal to Steenstraat ; thence road to Bixschoote and along the southern edge of Houthulst Forest.

[2] The barrage, which moved slowly in front of assaulting troops, was a British artillery invention, and was not then used by the Germans or the French.

another attack. But the depleted ranks of the battalion maintained the accuracy and devastating rapidity of fire to which they had been trained, and this attack, too, withered away.

Several other attempts, perhaps less strong in numbers but equally determined, were made before darkness, but were repulsed.

" Owing to dead ground, the enemy were able to get up to within a hundred yards of our trench, but we kept them from leaving the shelter of the wood to our front.

" Our chief danger lay in enfilade fire, as our trench turned abruptly across the Broodseinde—Passchendaele road and our left was exposed.

" On our left were numerous cottages, which the Huns occupied and were thus able to fire down into the trench from the roofs and upper windows ; to our front and within 120 yards was a thick wood in which the Germans were able to concentrate, especially as part of it was dead ground. This wood was occasionally ' searched ' by machine-gun fire which covered some of the dead ground invisible from the trench, but with what result it is hard to say. One machine gun was in the main trench on the extreme left, and had an all-round traverse, so as to be able to fire to our front or to our left flank and half-right ; the other was in a well-concealed pit some thirty yards to our left front, in a cottage garden, and, in addition to lessening the amount of dead ground to our front, was able to bring enfilade and oblique fire on any party of the enemy attempting to rush the trench from the woods ; it covered some 400–500 yards of the trench front, as far as I remember.

" I had no good machine-gun targets, the best being a group of thirty to forty of the enemy, invisible from our trench, who were fully exposed behind some cottages about 150 yards away ; only a few escaped, although some were only wounded. About 120 yards to our left front were three haystacks, which the enemy used as cover and so worked round to our flank.

" We had no wire in front of our trench. About 7 p.m. the Colonel and Adjutant came up to the trenches from their headquarters in a small quarry north-west of the Broodseinde cross-roads. Shortly afterwards there was a sudden and evidently preconcerted outburst of shrapnel, machine-gun and rifle fire, which lasted for some time and then gradually died away. Most of the cottages round the trench and cross-roads were burning by now. We carried on digging a communication trench back to the road ; this was never finished.

" A listening-post of an officer and a private, sent out on our left flank, reported digging some 150–200 yards away ; on investigation they were found to be Germans. Captain Smyth-Osbourne, who was the senior officer in that part of the line, reported this to Headquarters and asked if he should charge, but the Brigadier considered such a step too hazardous with the small number of men at his disposal.

" During the night there were several violent outbursts of fire, lasting some time, but nothing followed. The enemy were blowing bugles and whistles most of the night, but with what object I am unable to say." (Hindson.)

Colonel Cadogan had placed his headquarters in the sandpit with his reserve company, and this spot received a lot of attention from the enemy artillery—a hole definitely marked on the map ! The Commanding Officer was knocked over once by the burst of a shell, but suffered no injury.

When night fell, the 3rd Cavalry Division was back on the line Poelcappelle—Zonnebeke, and the French Cavalry (de Mitry) had yielded Passchendaele and Houthulst Forest to the enemy.

The situation was not in accordance with Sir John French's early-morning hopes. The II Corps on the right was on the line Givenchy—Herlies—Aubers, with a weakly covered left flank. Conneau's Cavalry Corps stood between the II and III Corps, but the 19th Brigade had been moved from Vlamertinghe to Laventie, behind the French cavalry ; the right flank of the III Corps in front of Armentières and Ploegsteert Wood had been forced back ; Allenby's Cavalry Corps was on the line St. Ives—Messines—the Canal in front of Hollebeke ; the 7th Division held its position, Zandvoorde—Kruiseecke—Zonnebeke ; the 3rd Cavalry Division carried on through St. Julien to Langemarck ; thence, behind Houthulst Forest, came de Mitry's Cavalry Corps to join with the 87th and 89th French Territorial Divisions, the Belgian Army, and the French 42nd Division.

Still, the order for the next day, the 21st, presumed that the enemy would retire. The principle laid down by General Foch earlier in the war—" My centre cedes ; my right recoils ; situation excellent : I attack "—prevailed. The head of General Haig's Corps was now behind the 3rd Cavalry Division, and was to advance on Thourout, with the 3rd Cavalry Division on its right and the French Cavalry Corps on its left, and was to roll up the enemy to the right or left as seemed most advantageous : the remainder of the British Army was to stand fast.

So far as the 7th Division and the 3rd Cavalry Division were concerned, they stood fast before the attack of two German army corps.

The artillery of the German XXVI and XXVII Reserve Corps moved forward during the night, and early in the morning of the 21st October opened on the 22nd Brigade—especially from Passchendaele, whence they

enfiladed the whole line.   It was a day of furious bombardment and many casualties, with frequent assaults, which, however, were always repulsed by the 1st Battalion.

"About 10 a.m. the enemy began to bombard us with 'coal-boxes,' having previously sent an aeroplane over.   They soon found the exact range and began to flatten our trench very systematically.   The brunt of the fire fell on the trenches on either side of the Broodseinde—Moorslede road, held by A Company, who lost heavily, the occupants being killed or buried in the trench.

"This bombardment went on until about 2.30 p.m., and machine guns occasionally traversed our parapet.   The enemy also fired shrapnel.

"My machine guns had both been put out of action, and Lieutenant Duke, of the Royal Warwicks, brought his two guns to replace mine; he only got one good target—a group of the enemy retiring from some cottages to our right front.

"We lost a good many men from snipers, some being in the cottages and roots to our immediate rear, men being shot from behind." (Hindson.)

The Germans were able to concentrate for their assaults in the wood to the battalion front; and they worked round on the left into the houses and gardens on the road.   At one moment it looked as though the left of the brigade would be enveloped, and the 7th Cavalry Brigade was moved up into the line.   But by midday the arrival of the I Corps eased the situation, and General Rawlinson withdrew the Cavalry Brigade to his right flank, which was being badly hammered, and their place was afterwards taken by the Irish Guards of the 4th (Guards) Brigade.   Before the latter arrived, however, Germans had spotted the weakness in the line, and had advanced to within 200 yards of the 22nd Brigade.

Lieutenant Wodehouse, supported by the fire of a party placed in a barn, tried to clear the left flank, but his casualties were so heavy he had to give up the attempt.   Several efforts were made to occupy the edge of the wood to the battalion front, and, apparently, some fifty to sixty men succeeded in passing through a raking flank fire and attained the wood, but were held there and lost.   About half a dozen won their way back again.

"We got several messages telling us to 'hold on at all costs,' and saying the 3rd Army was coming up.

"We also had several messages passed down the trench telling us to retire.

"As the day went on, it became more and more difficult to get messages to and from Battalion Headquarters, and for two hours before we were taken we had lost touch; our only means of communication was by runner. . . .

" I do not know the losses of the rank and file.

" After the bombardment we found it impossible to use many of the rifles and we had to hammer our bolts open with entrenching tools ; our maximum rate of fire was about three rounds per minute.

" In the afternoon we were being shelled from our left rear with shrapnel—at the time we thought our own guns were bursting short, but apparently they were German guns.

" Parts of our line had been reinforced by platoons of the Royal Warwicks (three, I think), who came up in our centre. About 4.30 p.m. I was captured with two other officers and 42 men ; we had been holding about a hundred yards of trench." (Hindson.)

It was evident that the position occupied by the 22nd Brigade was bad : it was a nasty salient, and the enemy artillery had found the range accurately. Brigadier-General Lawford asked for General Rawlinson's permission to draw back his left in line with the Irish Guards on the right of the I Corps, and this was given. So, at midnight, the Queen's took up a position about Zonnebeke station, and our 1st Battalion was moved into reserve at Eksternest. The brigade connected with the 21st Brigade at Reutel.

But it was a sadly depleted battalion. There remained the Commanding Officer, the Adjutant (Lieutenant C. T. Dooner), Lieutenant B. C. H. Poole, 2nd Lieutenants E. Wodehouse, R. de B. Egerton, and Captain E. A. Parker (Quartermaster), with 206 other ranks.

Captains Kington, D.S.O., M. E. Lloyd, Lieutenant E. C. L. Hoskyns, 2nd Lieutenants H. T. Ackland-Allen and G. P. J. Snead-Cox, with, as far as could be ascertained, 37 other ranks, had been killed ; Lieutenants L. A. A. Alston, J. M. J. Evans, J. H. Courage, 2nd Lieutenant A. Walmsley, with some 80 other ranks, had been wounded ; while amongst the missing, whose fate was uncertain, were Captains J. G. Smyth-Osbourne, W. G. Vyvyan (died of wounds as a prisoner), Lieutenants R. E. Hindson, D. M. Barchard, C. G. H. Peppe, 2nd Lieutenant the Hon. G. Bingham, with 213 other ranks. A certain number of the latter rejoined, a certain number became prisoners of war. The withdrawal in the night from a line smashed by bombardment, so that troops had become scattered, had undoubtedly meant that small parties were overlooked and left to their fate : it was an inevitable loss.

An effort was made by parties from all battalions of the brigade, under Lieutenant-Colonel Cadogan, to collect the wounded in the early morning, but was met with opposition and had to be abandoned.

The position of the battalion was now behind Polygon Wood, and beyond shelling the 22nd October passed without incident for them.   But the enemy continued his attacks against the I Corps on their left, and the 21st Brigade on their right (the South Staffordshire came in for these attacks at their junction with the 21st Brigade).   As on the previous day, losses were occasioned by shell fire, which ceased when the German infantry advanced in closer formation than any practised by the British Army ; their dead on this day have been described as lying in heaps.

Although there was but insignificant loss of terrain, the situation was none the less serious for the Allies ; the enemy had already two divisions to our one, and more troops were reported moving up through Belgium.

The French IX Corps was arriving behind Ypres, and General Foch, true to his principles, suggested that counter-attack would ease the situation, that the French 17th Division would attack, and that under the impetus given by these fresh troops the British Army should advance. Sir John French was also optimistic, and considered the German attack as their last effort.   General Haig, however, took a graver view and sent a Staff officer to explain the situation to the Commander-in-Chief.

The French 17th Division came up on the 23rd, caused much confusion, did not attack, but relieved the 2nd Division.

For our 1st Battalion the 23rd was much the same as the previous day.   The 7th Division was heavily shelled, and on the right, in the neighbourhood of Kruiseecke, the enemy advanced to the assault, but was again defeated by rifle fire.

The complications of the great battle were increased enormously on the 24th October.   The French 17th Division attacked on the left of the 7th Division and the right of the 1st Division and made slight progress. This enabled General Haig to assist General Capper with troops of the 2nd Division, in reserve, against furious enemy attacks on Polygon Wood and the right of his line.   It also enabled the 22nd Brigade to move to the right in support of the 21st Brigade, although they were not used.

Our 1st Battalion was now at Veldhoek.   Every reinforcement had been eagerly seized, stragglers and lost men had trickled in, and there had been a rigorous combing out of employed men, so that services behind the battle-line were short-handed : the strength of the battalion had been raised to a little over 400.

The 24th October marks the end of the first of the series of Ypres battles.   The defence of Ypres was now in the form of a semicircle, with the British holding the southern half and the French the northern.   From now on, it must be remembered, it was an Allied defence, French and British troops fighting shoulder to shoulder, as was the case, indeed, farther south, on the II Corps front. So far as the battalion was concerned, no change was noticed in the condition of affairs. They were unaware that Polygon Wood, which had been before them as a friendly but not very effective screen for the last two days, had been lost and recaptured. They had, during the morning of the 24th, before they moved to Veldhoek, been subjected to a furious shelling which they attributed to the work of a spy ; it was but the prelude to the German attack.

THE BATTLES OF LA BASSÉE (2ND BATTALION) [1] AND ARMENTIÈRES. [2]

General Smith-Dorrien had been ordered by Sir John French to capture La Bassée, and he had commenced a wheel to the right by his whole corps to do so.

On the 19th October the intelligence before G.H.Q. seemed to point to more reinforcements being brought up by the enemy in front of La Bassée, and that our efforts to outflank the enemy about La Bassée should be transferred north, to the neighbourhood of Ypres, where General Haig's I Corps was already detraining. There was a big gap between the II and III Corps, which had been filled by Conneau's Cavalry Corps, but the situation on the left of the II Corps was not considered satisfactory. The 19th Brigade was, as we know, in G.H.Q. Reserve, and had been waiting at Vlamertinghe. They were dispatched to the II Corps by bus (our 2nd Battalion marched), and ordered to entrench a position between Fauquissart and Fleurbaix, behind the junction of the French Cavalry and the II Corps.

This while our 1st Battalion was on its way to capture Menin.

The 2nd Battalion arrived at Laventie, and went into some trenches which " were very comfortable, with plenty of straw." The River Lys, some distance in rear of them, meanders through this flat country, which is one of those plains intersected by a complicated system of dyke drainage. It was possible, in dry weather, to dig trenches of a workable depth, and it was done in 1914 ; but when the rains came, and the line settled down, the absurdity of digging *into water* was obvious, and breastwork defences were made. It remained, however, a hopelessly wet sector, in winter.

The great " feature " in this part of the country was the Aubers Ridge, a mere swell in the ground but of inestimable military value. The

---

[1] Official date : 10th October—2nd November. Area : road Noyelles-les-Vermelles—Beuvry— Bethune (exc.)—Estaires (exc.) ; thence a line to Fournes. The battalion, in trenches near Laventie, would appear to be within this area.

[2] 13th October—2nd November. Area : Fournes—Estaires—Hazebrouck Station—Caestre Station—Dranoutre (exc.) ; thence the River Douve.

eye became trained to appreciate these slight rises, and magnify them—under the influence of bullets.

The attack of the German Fourth Army, which developed at Ypres on the 20th, was accompanied by an attack of the German Sixth Army directed chiefly on the right of the III Corps, but embracing the II Corps front as well. We know that the 6th Division, on the right of the III Corps, had given way under the weight of artillery and infantry assault, to the extent of some two miles. The line held by these troops on the night of the 20th October was Touquet—Bois Blancs—Le Quesne—La Houssoie—Château d'Hancardy, three-quarters of a mile west of Epinette. On their right was Conneau's Cavalry with the 19th Brigade.

This was the day when Sir John French issued the order for the II and III Corps to stand fast while the I Corps attacked at Ypres.

The 19th Brigade moved forward to a position in front of Fromelles, where they had French cavalry on their right and left. They were still attached to the II Corps.

("Moved out this morning. A big battle on—we ordered to fill a hole between Second and Third Armies. Dug trenches. Ordered forward to Fromelles, which we occupied. Germans in strength at Fournes, 3 K.s in front. Occupy outposts round village. In a stinking house. Wonder if they will attack.")

But this position, in the middle of French troops, was not too satisfactory, and Brigadier-General Gordon arranged that the 19th Brigade should take over the left, or northern, side of the gap they were filling, next to the 6th Division. The battalion took over from some French Dragoons, who wore their brass helmets, with horsehair tails and cuirasses, and were armed with carbine, lance (in lieu of bayonet), and sword. The brigade was transferred to the 6th Division on the 21st, but, apparently, the arrangement had not been completed on that date, as there were French cyclists on the left of the 19th Brigade.

The German attack was continued, from the sea to La Bassée. At 6 a.m. on the 21st they advanced against the 3rd Division, on the right of Conneau's Cavalry, and against the III Corps, who were heavily engaged; but, nevertheless, General Pulteney had to send assistance to the cavalry on his left, who were in difficulties about Messines.

There is some meaning in the phrase " the far-flung battle-line " ! Our 1st Battalion was at Zonnebeke, being heavily shelled and repelling infantry assaults; our 2nd Battalion was before Fromelles, on the right of the Argyll and Sutherland Highlanders, who held Maisnil; and at 11 o'clock in the morning the German artillery opened on the 19th Brigade.

The shelling continued until the afternoon—as the Germans gained respect for our musketry skill, so the artillery preparation was increased—when they launched a strong infantry attack. The French cyclists, it is stated, gave way ; the Argyll and Sutherland Highlanders held on till 6 p.m. and then fell back on the reserve line at Bas-Maisnil, with the exception of one company, which remained on the left of our battalion.

Our 2nd Battalion was isolated before Fromelles,[1] with a two-mile gap on its left. But the Germans, fortunately, did not discover the evacuation of Maisnil, and about midnight the battalion was withdrawn to the new line, Rouges Bancs—La Boutellerie, and entrenched at La Cordonerie Farm, which was still inhabited.

("We occupy the French trenches. Rotten bad ones. Cleaned up one of the rooms in the château. Caught hens and made a stew. Chased by big shells about a field. Ordered to dig fresh trenches that night. Cancelled. Move in ten minutes to La Boutellerie, where the rest of the brigade is. Our position was too forward.") (Stockwell.)

The French Cavalry, on the right of the 2nd Battalion, was also driven back during the day, and the 3rd Division of the II Corps had to conform.

At the close of the day's fighting we find both the 19th and 22nd Infantry Brigades had been engaged at points of weighty enemy thrust, and had been obliged to give ground.

The next day, when visiting General Moreland, commanding the 5th Division, Sir Horace Smith-Dorrien received a shock. He says in his diary that " the incidents of the last few days disclosed a worse state of affairs than I had thought. The men appear to be quite worn out with the incessant digging and fighting of the last ten days. The Germans in front of them are increasing in strength, and it seems doubtful whether the men in their present state, with their heavy losses (for in the last ten days the corps has lost about 5,000 men), would be able to maintain their position against another determined attack."

All this fighting from La Bassée up to and around Armentières was no less severe than at Ypres, but it has not attracted attention like the defence of one town which tickles the imagination. General Smith-Dorrien decided that " there was nothing left " but to retire his whole line to a prepared position a mile to two miles in rear.

---

[1] " Here we were, in a ' deserted village.' In the houses it looked as though the inhabitants had just gone out for a few minutes, and though plenty of the houses had been damaged by shell fire somehow or another, it did not seem at all—how shall I say—unusual. Captain Powell told Miners and myself to make ourselves comfortable in one of the cottages. As we were going to lay down fully dressed and equipped, we took the sheets off the bed, so as not to dirty them. As if it mattered ! " (Boreham.)

It was reported that men had actually been observed falling asleep over their rifles in the midst of an action.

Sir John French has commented on what he calls the " needlessly pessimistic " point of view of the II Corps Commander, a pessimism which is not revealed in Sir Horace Smith-Dorrien's diary, but there can be no doubt that the situation was grave and appreciated by the Corps Commander. His troops were physically worn out, and there is ignorance of fact in the Commander-in-Chief's statement that " the 4th Division and 19th Brigade were all just as heavily engaged at Le Cateau as the II Corps, but that their spirit and condition, as I had seen for myself the day before, were excellent."

Sir John French gave what help he could and dispatched the remains of the Lahore Division from Estaires. There were only two brigades of this Indian division in France, and the Ferozepore Brigade was with Allenby's Cavalry Corps, so the one brigade (Jullundur) was given to the II Corps and employed to relieve Conneau's Cavalry, which then formed a reserve.

On the night 23rd/24th October the Jullundur Brigade came into line between Fauquissart and the right of the 19th Brigade. This reinforcement was no sooner in place than the enemy launched an attack on the II and III Corps fronts from La Bassée to the Lys. He was repulsed everywhere.

The assault on the 2nd Battalion, now in the line, was delivered at 6.30 p.m. and easily stopped by rifle fire.

The enemy effort was then directed to the capture of Neuve Chapelle, which they effected, the Jullundur Brigade being heavily engaged and our 2nd Battalion again coming within the limits of the attack. " Attacked in force in pouring rain," says Captain Richardson of the 25th October, and the attacks were continued into the night and during the following afternoon, when Captain E. N. Jones Vaughan, Lieutenant Stable, and 2nd Lieutenant Stone were killed.

The 28th was a quiet day, devoted by the enemy to shelling and sniping ; but the 29th was again a day of assault. At 2 a.m. a heavy attack developed against the 19th Brigade, and the 1st Middlesex trenches, on the right of our 2nd Battalion, were entered. The situation was restored by the Argyll and Sutherland Highlanders, from Brigade Reserve, and a portion of the 2nd Battalion " charged, got six German dead and at least two wounded." (Richardson.) This was the last concentrated attack on the 19th Brigade, although general attacks on the II and III Corps continued.

The sort of position held can be gathered from Stockwell's diary :

" *22nd October.*—Marched off at 6.30 and entrenched in front of Cordonerie Farm. Clay and sand in a ploughed field. D Company on our right, then C Company; B in reserve. Dug on, unhindered, a good position, but a lot of houses in front at Ver Touquet, 450 to 700 yards away.

" *23rd.*—Started communication trenches, deep and narrow, to join up the whole place. Got milk from a farm, for which I paid—also a shave. Fine but cold. Got some straw to sleep on. Shell fire at guns over us.

" *24th.*—They attacked on the right, but did not bother us. Still fine and pushing communication trenches. Changed socks—very glad— feet were sore. Quail did a shave—I didn't. Night attack—not much as far as we were concerned.

" *25th.*—They started shelling us early, burst four on the parapet of one section in which I was. Infantry advanced but swung. Shelling at intervals. We downed two or three of their infantry; no casualties. Heard that Stone had been killed and Buffalo (Tudor-Jones) wounded in the arm. At 6.30 they began night attacking. Kept it up till 11.30— then from 2.30 till dawn. An awful night—pouring rain—so muddy could hardly move.

" *26th.*—Snipers everywhere in the houses. Hear Stable has been killed bringing in a wounded man. Another night attack.

" *27th.*—Same old game, shelling and sniping all day, but they do no damage. Night attack—up most of the night. Sloper's (Clegg Hill) lot got the worst of it.

" *28th.*—Wet and beastly. Night attack. Sloper most of it.

" *29th.*—Sent a patrol out in front in the morning. Found German trenches about 600 yards in front, and two dead.

" *30th.*—Night attack all night. Left platoon, Richardson's; got into mess a bit. Sloper has 150 dead in front of him. A quiet day. Wet in evening, but a quiet night. Got some sleep."

The 2nd Battalion remained in the line, and the period can be visualised by extracts from Captain Richardson's diary and letters.

" It has been most awfully cold in these clay soil trenches, as I have nothing but my burberry and waterproof sheet with me, all the kits being three miles off. I was taken unprepared. I am in the most awful state of filth, not having been able to get a wash for ten days. It poured the other night when we were attacked, and everybody and everything became covered with slimy mud, which is just beginning to rub off. All the officers and men are in the same box, and have long beards, looking awful ruffians. I have to sleep in a trench with all my men and no officer within 250 yards. I shall be very grateful for an air pillow when it arrives.

" *2nd November.*—I have had eight men wounded in my trench, seven from shrapnel and one from a bullet. Shells are going over our heads all day ; one has to keep one's head pretty low in the trench or one gets picked off by one of those beastly snipers who are all over the place. I have got some sacks which I get into at night, and keep me fairly warm, the nights being awfully cold.

" *5th.*—I wish to goodness they would send out the Canadian people, let us get a move on these Germans, and have done with it, as it has got to come in the end ; personally I think the war will last another two or three months at least. The Russians seem to be making mincemeat of them. It is pitiful to see houses and villages all destroyed by shell fire, and to see poor people trudging along the roads, dozens of fine cattle lying in the fields round, killed by the bullets and shrapnel. I am getting awfully bored by the trenches and am feeling fearfully tired. I hope we won't be in them much longer. I wish they would order the advance.

" *12th.*—Last night I was on the watch from 9 p.m. till midnight. At about 11.30 an awful hail-storm came on, with stones nearly as large as marbles, and fairly stung our faces. After that the wet had loosened the parapet, and it fell on top of two men who were sleeping, and buried them from their waists down, and I had to dig them out, which took about half an hour ; luckily they weren't hurt. The Germans are scared stiff to attack us with any vigour, and we are just waiting for the order to advance and give them a hiding such as they have never had yet, to pay them out for their underhand sniping way of fighting, and their shells, to which infantry cannot reply. Twelve hundred Germans were found in front of the brigade trenches after a scrap the other night ; they won't face us by day. We are being quite well fed and are in good condition, considering the wet and other troubles."

On the night of the 14th/15th November the IV Corps, now composed of the 7th and 8th Divisions, relieved the inner flank brigades of the Indian and III Corps. On the left the 20th and 22nd Brigades of the 7th Division took over from the 19th Brigade.

Our 2nd Battalion was relieved by the 2nd Battalion Scots Guards, and marched back to Sailly to billets.

THE BATTLES OF YPRES CONTINUE.

On the 24th October Sir John French warned the Home Government that the supply of artillery ammunition must be maintained, or the infantry would have to fight without support. The consumption of ammunition, the continuous firing, was beyond anything anticipated, and soon the gunners were to be strictly limited to a daily number of rounds.

There was a pause of several days in the major attack on Ypres, but locally the pressure was maintained. To the Allied Command the prospect seemed brighter and the order for the offensive held good. But the form of advance, which may be described as successive bounds from the left, yielded poor results.

A local enemy effort on the 26th drew our 1st Battalion into the fight. The loaning of troops to the 7th Division had resulted in a great mixing of units, so that later on it was customary to speak of " groups " rather than brigades.

Units of the 2nd Division had been ordered to attack from the Kruiseecke—Reutel line to ease the situation for the 7th Division on their right. General Haig's objective was Becelaere, but the enemy, although he had failed in his previous efforts, determined to try again to capture Kruiseecke salient, as it was called, held by the 20th Brigade : he fore-stalled the British attack, and succeeded about midday in breaking through the southern side of the salient, and getting behind the 1st South Stafford-shire, some companies of Grenadier and Scots Guards, and the 20th Brigade. Brigadier-General Lawford was ordered to counter-attack.

Our 1st Battalion and the 2nd Royal Warwickshire advanced from Veldhoek into the gap on the left of the 20th Brigade and forward in the direction of Tenbrielen. They came under heavy shell fire, but before they closed with the enemy they were ordered to stand fast.

There was, naturally, much confusion in this part of the line, many contradictory reports, and no facilities, in that flat and close country, for observing the battlefield. The Brigadier had been informed that the 20th Brigade was falling back, which was not the case, and had counter-manded his previous instruction. The result of it all was that instead of holding a salient, the 20th Brigade was on the right and the 22nd on the left of a re-entrant. The enemy, however, made no effort to follow up this success.

THE BATTLE OF GHELUVELT.[1]

During the pause in the German major attack from the 24th to the 30th October, they put in operation yet another well-conceived plan.

The German Supreme Command had recognised, on the evening of the 24th, that their Fourth Army would never get through the British line

[1] Date: 29th–31st October. Area : as Langemarck.

at Ypres, and that the Sixth Army had equally failed to pierce the II and III Corps front. They decided, then, to form another Army under General Fabeck, which would attack the line Messines—Hollebeke—Zandvoorde on the 30th October. And further, that they would mass, in support of this onslaught, no fewer than 250 heavy guns—an unheard-of number in those days.

Now that the line was held by both sides from Switzerland to the sea, it was not easy for agents to get information through to the Allied commanders. All the same, one must admire the second secret assembly of an Army Group—the Allies had no warning : French and British General Staffs were serenely optimistic, and continued punching the German line with divisions, winning here and there a few hundred yards on the northern side of the Ypres salient. The French IX Corps was half-way between Zonnebeke and Passchendaele ; the British 2nd Division, on their right, joined up about Reutel with the 1st Division ; the 7th Division, much battered, was opposite Gheluvelt, with the Cavalry Corps on their right.

The 29th October was a typical day : the French IX Corps attacked and gained some slight successes ; and the enemy attacked the junction of the I and IV Corps. A hammer-and-tongs battle took place about the cross-roads on the Menin road a mile south of Gheluvelt. Trenches were taken and retaken, troops driven back were reinforced and advanced again. It was a misty day, bullets were flying in all directions, and the battlefield was a mass of small fields, hedges, and houses. The continual shifting and reinforcement of the front line had resulted in a tangle of units. Finally, the Germans retained the cross-roads.

Our 1st Battalion was in reserve, and was moved during the day into line on the extreme right of the division, in touch with the cavalry ; and there they remained—the German assault did not reach them. The 2nd Royal Scots Fusiliers were on their left, then came the 2nd Green Howards and the 2nd Queen's ; the Warwickshire and South Staffordshire Battalions were in reserve.

The night passed quietly—although the noise of an unusual amount of transport was reported—and the order stood for the resumption of the " offensive." No sight or sound of the five new divisions of Fabeck's Army Group, with its 250 heavy guns, reached the eyes or ears of the Intelligence Corps ; but the guns were in position and had registered on the 29th, and the reliefs took place during the night 29th/30th October, in preparation for the great effort to break through.

The German Fourth Army opened the battle at 6 a.m. on the left of the I Corps, about Zonnebeke, but the infantry advance was repulsed.

Fabeck's heavy guns opened on the 7th Division and Allenby's Cavalry Corps at 6.45 a.m., and at 8 o'clock the infantry advanced.

Our 1st Battalion, little over 400 strong, was scattered about in short slits of trench, without inter-communication, on the forward slope of a roll in the plain ; their field of vision was short in the midst of the hedge-enclosed fields, and it was impossible to know what was happening to the

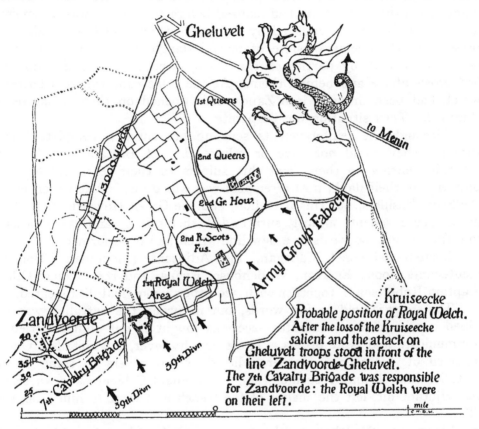

right or left. But the advancing lines of German infantry were mowed down by their rifle fire.

On their right a disastrous situation arose.

The Cavalry Corps held a wide front. Immediately on the right of our 1st Battalion were the 1st and 2nd Life Guards, in alternate squadrons. The greater part of Fabeck's artillery bombardment was concentrated on them and the 1st Battalion. The cavalry suffered heavily, and when, at 8 o'clock, the German masses advanced in overwhelming numbers, the order was given them to retire on the support line. No news of this reached

Brigadier-General Lawford, or anyone else. The right of the 7th Division was made aware of the presence of the enemy by enfilade fire from his field guns brought into Zandvoorde village.

Various bodies of troops were put in motion to restore the situation— the 6th Cavalry Brigade, the 2nd Gordon Highlanders, and the 1st Staffordshire; later on the 1st Northamptonshire, the 2nd Sussex, and a detachment of cavalry; but time had elapsed before the enemy was discovered, and our 1st Battalion, engaged by a frontal attack which was still being pressed by the enemy in spite of fearful slaughter in their ranks, were taken in reverse by parties of the enemy who had worked round the hedgerows above and behind them. At the same time the field batteries which had been brought into Zandvoorde opened on them a shower of shrapnel. Their situation was desperate.

Although the reinforcements sent up prevented a complete breakthrough, they could not save or relieve the 1st Battalion. With the attacking enemy on their front, his snipers to their rear, and his field batteries on their flank, post after post was wiped out. A few men joined the Scots Fusiliers, but this battalion, and the Green Howards, now stood in an acute salient, almost surrounded themselves, and were ordered to retire some 1,200 yards to a new line which had been formed.

Lieutenant-Colonel Cadogan, his Adjutant (Lieutenant Dooner), Lieutenants Poole, Egerton, Wodehouse, Evans, and the Medical Officer (Captain Robertson [1]), together with 320 other ranks, had disappeared.

The story is told in few words, but naturally the battalion was not wiped out in so many minutes—sections fought it out—officers tried to communicate and issue orders. There are, however, few details. One is reported of Lieutenant Dooner, who delivered orders to some of the battalion himself and, returning, fell. Lieutenant-Colonel Cadogan, seeing his Adjutant hit, left the shelter of the trench and went to him; he, too, fell.

Lieutenant Wodehouse, who was wounded and captured, can only give a short account :

" 30*th October*.—We were holding a line about three-quarters of a mile long, A Company on the right, then B, D, and C on the left. Battalion H.Q. was in a dugout about 600 yards to the rear. The trenches were not well sighted for field of fire. So far as I know, no one was on our right; some ' Blues ' were supposed to be there, but I did not see them. It was foggy in the early morning, so that the Germans could not shell us much, which was lucky, as they had two batteries on Zandvoorde Ridge. About

---

[1] This gallant officer refused to leave the wounded and was taken prisoner.

8 a.m. the shelling increased, and we saw large numbers of Germans advancing down a slope about 1,500 yards to our front. Also I believe large numbers were seen coming round our exposed right flank. The batteries on the ridge were now firing point-blank into our trenches, so that it was difficult to see what was happening, and the rifle fire also increased from our right rear. No orders were received, so it was thought best to stay where we were, and about midday the whole battalion was either killed, wounded, or taken prisoners.

" Casualties : Colonel Cadogan, Dooner, Egerton, and an officer of the Cornwalls killed, self wounded and prisoner, Poole, Evans, and Barrow (Cornwalls) prisoners. During that day or the next Barker, who was doing Staff-Captain, was killed. I was taken to a dressing-station in Zandvoorde and patched up.

" The Germans were suffering heavily from our shell fire and were unable to use the road. I saw some of their guns get stuck in the mud behind the village. I do not know what the strength of the Germans was, but I believe it was at least a regiment (Hanoverians). I was struck with the fact that they had ' Gibraltar ' on their shoulders."

Recapitulating what was known of the various actions fought by the battalion, General Capper said, in an order of the day :

" On the 19th October the battalion attacked Kleythoek with much gallantry and dash, and later on the same day acted with coolness and discipline under trying conditions. On the 20th and 21st October, at Zonnebeke, the battalion held the left of the line under very heavy enfilade fire and enveloping attack of the enemy's infantry, until withdrawn by orders of the Brigadier. During these two days' fighting the battalion lost three-quarters of its strength in officers and men.

" On the 30th October the battalion occupied the right of the division line. Owing to troops on their right being driven back, the battalion became very exposed, and was subjected to an enveloping attack by the enemy. The battalion, however, held on and lost nearly all its effectives, including the Colonel and all other officers, only 90 men rejoining the brigade. This battalion has fought nobly and has carried on its best traditions by fighting until completely overwhelmed. As a battalion it had for the time ceased to exist."

In forwarding the General's communication to units, Brigadier-General Lawford said : " I wish to add my sincere appreciation of the splendid behaviour of the 1st Battalion of the Royal Welch Fusiliers on all occasions. The battalion has nobly maintained the glorious traditions of the regiment, and has again added to the honours gained in former campaigns. All ranks have always responded to calls made on them under severe conditions. I am very proud to have had the honour of having the battalion in the brigade under my command. The heavy losses, both in officers and men, witness to the efforts made by this battalion to uphold the honour of the Army and the Empire."

The result of the Battle of Gheluvelt was that the enemy succeeded in bending the line to the extent of a mile and a half.

As though to complete the tragic number of casualties, Captain R. V. Barker of the Regiment, Staff-Captain to the brigade, was killed the next day, when the brigade, little more than a battalion in strength, was being led in person by the Brigadier and his staff. Before the end of the battle Brigadier-General Lawford was left with four combatant regimental officers and some 700 men.

And so, for a time, the battalion practically ceased to exist. Less than 90 men were attached to the Queen's. It is not quite clear whether they remained in the line or not.

·   ·   ·   ·   ·   ·   ·

Meanwhile, Messines was lost, Wytschaete was lost—the odds in favour of the Germans were six battalions to 415 men in this part of the field—and the wide circle defending Ypres was narrowed down to the well-known Ypres salient. Ammunition was running short ; a third of the artillery was withdrawn by Sir Douglas Haig's order, and the remainder limited to 20 rounds per day for each 18-pounder and 10 rounds for each 4·5 howitzer.

During the night of the 5th November the 7th Division was relieved by troops of the II Corps, which had come out of the line near La Bassée on the 30th/31st October. The 7th Division had been under intense artillery fire since the 19th October, and though their original front of seven miles had been reduced, the number of yards held per man had increased.

Back in the town of Ypres, where the Queen's with a handful of Royal Welch Fusiliers were billeted, reinforcements arrived, 109 other ranks under 2nd Lieutenant F. R. Orme. They were thrust into the firing-line at once.

On the 6th the enemy attacked down the Menin road, and on either side of the Comines Canal. It was a foggy morning, and the French, holding the line near the Comines Canal, were driven back, losing the tunnel under the canal, about a mile west of the bend. Other French troops were, for some unaccountable reason, seized with panic and abandoned their line. All this happened south of the canal.

North of the canal (following events from right to left) were other French troops, in touch with the right of Lord Cavan's force. A heavy

LIEUTENANT-COLONEL H. O. S. CADOGAN.

attack was made on these troops and their front was pierced. The enemy pursued his advantage, and reached Zwarteleen, only 3,000 yards from Ypres. He then started to roll up the British line, pressing back the Irish Guards. Two companies of a French battalion, and the Household Cavalry, attacked and checked the enemy advance. The 3rd Brigade and 2nd Munsters were hurried to the threatened zone, and the 22nd Brigade was ordered forward from Ypres.

It was, however, too dark to do anything that day—the 22nd Brigade did not arrive at Zillebeke until 10 p.m.—and the situation remained with the enemy in possession of Zwarteleen, making a deep dent in the Allied line.

Although the French had promised to re-establish the original line held by them, Lord Cavan decided that he could not afford to wait, so he ordered the 22nd Brigade to a point in his line about 500 yards north-east of Zwarteleen, just above the bite in the line. The intrepid Brigadier-General Lawford, leading his brigade (now consisting of 14 officers and 1,100 men), drew up for the attack in front of the 3rd Brigade, under cover of a slight rise. He put the Queen's and attached Royal Welch Fusiliers to lead the attack in two lines, supported by the South Staffordshire, and he held the 2nd Warwickshire in reserve.

At 6.15 a.m., as the darkness of the night was giving way to the thick, enveloping gloom of a morning fog, he gave the order to charge—the enemy was only about 150 yards away. The composite battalion swept over the first enemy trenches, capturing three machine guns, but all efforts to press further forward were held in check by enfilade fire. The battalion held on till dusk—the French did not appear—when, having both flanks in the air, they were withdrawn.

The brigade lost ten of its fourteen officers, and amongst them was 2nd Lieutenant Orme ; of the 1,100 other ranks, 304 were casualties.

On the 8th November the brigade was withdrawn to Locre, and marched to Bailleul on the 9th. Here Major R. E. P. Gabbett and Captain Minshull Ford arrived with a draft of 99 other ranks.

The next day, under Major Gabbett, the battalion marched to Merris, and on the 11th was joined by Captain W. G. Garnett and 2nd Lieutenant G. R. Gore with 303 other ranks ; and on the 12th by a further draft of 151.

The battalion was now strong enough to be organised into four companies—A Company was given to Captain Minshull Ford, who doubled the duties of Company Commander with those of Adjutant ; B Company to Captain Garnett ; C Company to 2nd Lieutenant Gore ; D Company to 2nd Lieutenant S. B. Jones, who had joined with the last draft.

On the 14th November the battalion took over three-quarters of a mile of the line in the neighbourhood of Touquet, within a few hundred yards of the line which had been held by the 2nd Battalion.

With the second meeting of the two battalions, in the Armentières sector, the first period of the war ends.   The British Army had hovered on the brink of disaster and had been saved by the steadiness of the men. In the movements of our two battalions, the one in the Mons retreat, the other in the retreat from Antwerp, we have in brief the history of the opening phase, the struggle to arrest the advance of overwhelming numbers.

The multiplicity and rapidity of movements are bewildering, but a record of them does not convey the confusion through which everyone, down to the latest-joined second lieutenant, had to battle his way.   In the story of the first draft, H. G. Picton-Davies gives a good idea of the fog of war behind the fighting line during this period.   He was the " latest joined."

" After leaving Sandhurst in July 1914, I joined my father's old regiment at their depôt at Wrexham in North Wales, where soon the order for mobilisation was to change the ordered quiet into crowded turmoil. Reservists were joining daily.   The accommodation at the barracks proving inadequate, billets for officers and men were speedily requisitioned in and around the town.   The aim and occupation of the staff was to clothe and arm the arrivals.   Ere long a unit was formed of reservists, consisting of 1 officer, 1 sergeant, and 98 men.   This was to be the first draft, and its command was entrusted to me.

" After receiving orders and counter-orders, on a date I cannot remember, accompanied by the Commanding Officer and the Mayor of Wrexham, escorted by the band and amid the cheers of the populace, we marched off to the station with orders to proceed to the 2nd Battalion in the 19th Brigade with the Expeditionary Force in France—or Belgium.

" We soon found ourselves at Southampton, where we were joined by a unit of the Argyll and Sutherland Highlanders, under an officer whose name, I think, was Campbell.   We journeyed to Le Havre in a South American meat-boat of 15,000 tons.   At Le Havre we disembarked and, marching through the town, proceeded to the high ground to the east, where a camp was being formed.   All was confusion, and rumours were perpetually arriving.   Nobody seemed to have the slightest idea of exactly where the Army was, but we seemed quite sure that it was advancing on Brussels.   We were expecting to get orders from someone to proceed hourly and were simply standing by.   Rumours suddenly became alive !   It was reported that Uhlan patrols had been seen ten or fifteen miles to the west.   We were hurriedly commanded to dig trenches on the edge of the heights with a view to placing Le Havre in a state of defence.

"For two days we dug steadily, along with all sorts of units. We were beginning to feel satisfied that we would occupy and hold our trenches against overwhelming swarms of Huns when we heard definitely that the Army was in action at Mons on the 23rd August, and that orders were given to it to fall back to other positions ! We heard this news at the railway station, whither we had marched to entrain, consequently we were held up. Then suddenly we were ordered to proceed to the docks instead of returning to the camp. When at the docks we were ordered on board a ship and at once put to sea. (Later we heard that some days afterwards the base at Le Havre was moved, but when we left everything was carrying on as arranged.) We proceeded at once to St. Nazaire (the port for Nantes), at the mouth of the River Loire, where we disembarked and marched through the town amid scenes of great enthusiasm, as, I believe, we were the first troops to arrive there as a unit.

"At the railway station we were met with rumours and the news that a train would be almost impossible ! However, after a delay of several hours, a train was accumulated ; the Argylls and 2/Royal Welch Fusiliers units with some artillery and oddments were bundled in, and off we went.

"The train went straight to Paris and continued on round the suburbs. All along the line was great excitement and everywhere we were treated to all the people could give—apples, cigarettes, cigars, and always with great glee by the French population. At Paris we tried to obtain news, but not arriving at a central station could find no one from whom information could be obtained. Our only source became the engine-driver, who knew very little—he was practically driving from signal to signal. We did not wait at Paris, but continued on, and we were under the impression that we were making for Lille or some place in that direction. We had passed through Noyon and had come to, apparently, nowhere in particular, when the train stopped. After a while, and wondering why the stop arose, we journeyed along the train to our source of information, who could only tell us that, the signal being against him, he could not continue on. After a longer delay we decided to send someone to investigate ; on his return we learnt that a bridge about a mile on was down, evidently blown up, but by whom or why was unknown.

"It sufficed, however, for both us and the driver. He was for getting his train back to somewhere where orders could be received ; and we for getting on and finding someone with even a hazy notion of the whereabouts of our respective units. We therefore detrained and held a council of war.   I am unable to give the date of this, but as far as I can recollect it was early in September.   We decided that we would strike east and try to pick up communication with some official in the rear of where we fondly imagined our Army's position to be—somewhere near Maubeuge ! Hence our object was to make for Laon and see what happened.   While in a big wood on the way we met some units of the Army, who told us that they were in retreat and that Uhlan patrols were about, that the Army was somewhere north and ' coming down this way.'

"Another council of war : at which we decided to put out outposts and keep clear of towns at night.   And we decided to strike south until we met a biggish place where we could get into touch.   We were afraid that the Army might retire past us farther east or between us and the sea ; and, again, visions crossed our minds of a sanguinary ' break through ' the Hun and a happy meeting with our own forces.

"We lived by giving ' chits ' for bread and meat in the villages through which we passed, and for which I am always wondering why no appeal has been made on me for payment, for I signed my name as O.C. 2/R.W.F. Detachment.   Perhaps the villages were all smashed up and the ' chits ' lost.

"In striking south we came eventually to Méaux, where we found English officers in possession of information !   They told us that ' the French had made a mistake, that we were nearly surrounded, and that our Army had been falling back on Paris ; that we were in front of them, but that no one could tell what was going to happen ; that we had better continue south, but do our best to find out all information we could ; that Staff officers were in all the towns and, as the situation progressed, we could no doubt— later on—hear more explicit news.   This seemed the best thing we could do ; and so more marching and more ' chits.'   At one place we came across a field cashier anxious to get rid of some money, so we promptly drew some pay for ourselves and our men, who by this time had increased in numbers, for oddments had joined us from time to time.   All the men signed for pay in their army books, and so we realised we were somewhere in front of or behind our own forces.

"Somewhere near Paris we met the Army or bits of it, but never the 19th Brigade, and we commenced a weary round looking for it.   If the brigade had been heard of somewhere, it was never there when we got there. After about the first week in September we trekked after an obviously advancing Army, up through La Fère-en-Tardenoise, where again we heard news of the brigade.   It was at Soissons, so said the report : so on we went, bivouacking at night and rather wondering where we were.   We had no official maps, and I was working from a very poor cyclist's map purchased in some village now away back !

" As we went on we felt we were nearing our goal, and on the night of the 13th September (it may have been the night of 14th/15th September) we were marching till dusk and, as was usual, decided to bivouac in a field by the side of the road and put out sentries. It was very misty, and my Argyll friend had left me in the morning as he thought he had definite news of his unit—so had many of the various units who had joined me from time to time. At dawn I was wakened by my sentries saying they could hear the movement of troops quite close. We stood to arms very quietly. With the sergeant I pushed on to reconnoitre; as visibility was very poor, only a few yards could be seen. About fifty yards down the road we saw a sentry and were challenged—in English. To our relief and astonishment we discovered that he was R.W.F. We got our men and were escorted to H.Q. by the side of the road and reported to Lieutenant-Colonel Delmé Radcliffe, in command, Major O. de L. Williams, and Captain C. S. Owen, the Adjutant. We were given a breakfast at the mess-cart by Sergeant Mallory. The mess-cart had been appropriated, I believe, at Le Cateau or somewhere on the retreat; it was a travelling draper's cart. I was detailed to Captain Clegg-Hill's company; to him I reported and became his ' wart.' I commanded No. 2 Platoon, A Company.

" Years afterwards I had an official letter from the Army Paymaster stating that for several years he had been chasing the wrong officer, but had now definitely settled that I was the officer to whom (I think) 780 francs for payment to men had been made in September 1914, and as no record could be proved that this had been paid over, would I send a cheque for its equivalent? I replied that ' the Army books of any of the men would show the payment.' After ceaseless correspondence, it was discovered eventually that one man could be found somewhere who had an entry on that date; the remainder were not to be found, but the Paymaster's Office accepted the situation that as one payment was found, no doubt the others were O.K. The matter was only definitely cleared up about 1925, when the balance of the 780 francs was charged to ' Public Services.' "

The same officer adds, what was often said :

" I look back on that time spent with the battalion with a sense of acute pleasure and pain—pleasure to remember the wonderful men there, for they were wonderful ; pain for the loss of splendid men and pals very dear to me. I can recall Lieutenant-Colonel Delmé Radcliffe and Major O. de L. Williams walking along on top of a scratchy trench and telling me that my men should remember always the value of cover, that they should always improve any position they were in to ensure as much protection as possible. (They, in the open!) Captain C. S. Owen with his wonderful flow of language—efficient, capable, kindly, yet covering it always with the most wonderful language. . . . " Tiger " Phillips, for whom I have the very greatest admiration. I was with him only a short time ; it was a bad time and we were up against it. He was magnificent, and he was kindness personified to me. Stockwell, the efficient, keen soldier ; a hard worker who expected hard work and implicit obedience. Brusque in speech, he knew well what he wanted and saw he got it. Holmes the whimsical, the wit of the unit. I was young and green, and Phillips and Holmes did everything they could to help at a time when I wanted help ; I had left a bit of the line I knew to come to a bit of unknown line, for A and C were quite a bit away from each other. There were nasty little gulleys running up to C Company's trenches where many dead Germans lay and where they always crowded in times of ' war.' . . .

" And what of the men ? They were fine ! They possessed discipline, good physique, and more—they could shoot. Their rifle was not a thing to carry or something to stick a bayonet on. It was their soul. The Hun could never break through a line of resolute men who could use their rifles. Later on in the war one was to come across the disciples of the bomb— men who said the day of the rifle had gone ; that bombs were the only offensive and defensive weapon. If they had ever seen the rifle at work, had seen a line held over and over again by a few rifles, but well worked, the energies of all would have been concentrated on the ' shooting ' of the Army.

" The N.C.O.s were magnificent. There was R.S.M. Murphy, as stout an effort as ever wore uniform ; Stanway, the marvel of the war, afterwards to be a Brigadier-General."

III

OFFENSIVE OPERATIONS: FIRST PERIOD

OFFENSIVE OPERATIONS: FIRST PERIOD

WINTER, 1914—1915.

Stockwell's diary. (2nd Batalion.)

" 15*th November.*—Got the Company reclothed and straightened up. Went to 7th Division H.Q. Saw Parker, who told us the news of the 1st Battalion being wiped out, and about T. C. Capper. Quail goes to command C Company—Cuthbert comes as sub.

" 16*th.*—We move to-morrow. 4.30—ordered to go at once with Brigade Staff to take over trenches from Royal Irish Fusiliers east of Houplines.

" 17*th.*—Went with R.I.F. Colonel to trenches. Rotten trenches. R.I.F. found the Moated Farm the best. Dublin Fusiliers' trenches very bad. Returned to Houplines. A Company to go to Farm. Got some wine out of château, also bought some food.

" 18*th.*—Trenches very comfortable for men, but dangerous. Cameronians on our left up to the edge of Frelinghein. We live in a room in farmhouse. Sleep in dog-hole in moat.

" 19*th.*—Wet and muddy.

" 20*th.*—Very cold. Snow.

" 21*st.*—Freezing all day. Very cold, though fine.

" 22*nd.*—Still freezing. W. Edwards went into Armentières.

" 23*rd.*—Went in myself. Had a bath. The people are coming back.

" 24*th.*—Heard we are to be relieved to-morrow by Middlesex. Heavy firing towards Ploegsteert.

" 25*th.*—Went with Guillaume (O. de L. Williams) and Joe (Powell) and had a damned good lunch in the Café Comte-d'Egmont, Armentières.

" 26*th.*—Got a jolly good billet. Very nice to have a bed and a bath, and clothes off—especially boots.

" 27*th.*—Went into Armentières and found the pâtisserie a good egg.

" 30*th.*—Rode over to see Scatters (Minshull Ford) and 1st Battalion. Saw Wood, Killaloe (Gabbett), and Gore. Scatters has done awfully well— blew up a farm and will get a D.S.O.

"1st *December*.—King here. 1st Battalion find guard—Scatters commanding. Congratulated by King on gallant conduct.

"2nd.—Went with 200 men, Quail, Maltby, Freeman, Richardson, to find guard of honour for King. P. of W. there. King shook hands with us all, and looked at guard. Sergeant Taylor presented with D.C.M. for bringing in Stable. Company Sergeant-Major Fox (mine) commanded guard. Officers were formed up in front—rather a unique occasion—guns firing half a mile away.

"3rd.—We go into Cameronians' trenches. A bright moon—very dangerous—no casualties.

"4th.—Their trenches beastly and dirty—150 yards from enemy—they in a brewery. We are right up against the houses of Frelinghein and on the Lys.

"5th.—Rain, rain, rain. Trenches under water—parapet falling in right and left. At work all night shoring up. Beastly cold and a frost."

The 4th Battalion.

The 4th Battalion sailed from Southampton and arrived at Le Havre on the 6th November.[1]

After a few days at St. Omer, the battalion, under Lieutenant-Colonel France-Hayhurst, moved to Heuringhem for training in trench digging and attack.

Training, to meet the actual conditions they were faced with, was exercising the mind of the Higher Command. The new *Infantry Training Manual* had been issued in August 1914, and it was an excellent little book. It had not, however, been thoroughly assimilated, even in organisation— the 4th Battalion, for instance, arrived in France with the old eight-company organisation.

The Manual provided, as such books do, principles for guidance in war rather than definite and detailed action, but the heavy casualties that had been incurred suggested to the General Staff that it might be amplified, although the instructions they issued do not seem to have expanded the provisions of the various handbooks already published by the War Office.

The whole question could, probably, have been covered by the one word " quantity." Artillery, machine guns, tools, were insufficient for static warfare.

It would not be right to say no one had foreseen the stalemate that prevailed after the First Battles of Ypres, with all possibility of manœuvre

---

[1] Changes had already been made in the posting of officers, but no useful purpose would be served in trying to follow them.

in the open field at an end, with the armies facing each other in a double line of trenches from Switzerland to the sea ; but the training of the British Army had been for open warfare, and siege conditions had not been much studied ; also, at that time, it was still hoped that the slough of despair, which they seemed to be rapidly approaching, might be avoided. The instructions issued must not be read as a forecast of the future ; they were based entirely on the experiences of officers up to the end of the Battles of Ypres.   But their recommendations had to be studied by new formations.

In the first " Notes " issued it is stated :

" One of the principal lessons of the war, hitherto, from a tactical point of view, is the necessity of screening positions for the defence from the enemy's artillery fire. The enemy's artillery is numerous, powerful, and efficient, and our infantry has suffered much from its fire. The German infantry, on the other hand, is inferior to our own in developing fire effect. A short field of fire (500 yards, or even less) has been found sufficient to check a German infantry attack. Tactically, therefore, in occupying ground for defence, every effort should be made to combine the fire of our own guns and rifles against the enemy's infantry, while denying to the enemy the use of his artillery by the siting of trenches, in positions which it is intended to hold on to, behind rather than on the crest line or forward slopes."

It would seem that the Hythe School of Musketry, which had given officers and men such confidence in the power of rifle fire, had a tendency to deliver them, by their selection of fire positions, into the hands of the enemy artillery.

The " Notes " continue, on the subject of trenches, to lay down that " trenches should be commenced at once with the light entrenching tool and improved later on as opportunity occurs. They should be deep and narrow, and should show above the ground level as little as possible, and all trenches should be traversed at intervals of five to ten rifles."   To obtain head-cover from shrapnel, troops were recommended to undercut the trench on the enemy's side.

But there is a hint of the real difficulties with which troops had had to contend in " Notes from a Conversation with a Battalion Commander who has recently been Wounded and Invalided Home " :

" It has been found that the best form of entrenchment is a deep, narrow trench without parapet or head-cover. Parapet and head-cover form too much of a mark for the German artillery. Trenches two feet wide for ' fire standing ' with the earth thrown in rear are recommended. The difficulty of draining trenches has not been overcome. If possible, trenches should be dug to communicate with hollow lanes. . . . Shallow trenches dug with the portable tools are worse than no trenches at all against artillery fire, as they give the German artillery a better target. . . . Infantry battalions have often been handicapped because the battalion picks and shovels were a long way in rear in a wagon, which has been unable to reach the battalion."

There is enough here to indicate that the thought of all commanders was, that units were stuck up as a line of " cock-shies " for the enemy artillery to bombard, and they were finding it extremely unpleasant. They were modifying their ideas on " field of fire " and " observation." They were ready to sacrifice the long-range power of the rifle, and cut it down to 300 yards and less. Dead ground was not anathema ; the false crest and reverse slope were welcome.

The " Notes " always came back to the same thing—the effect of the enemy artillery fire. " The error of the gun appears to be almost non-existent, and it is quite common to see four high-explosive heavy shells dropped within two or three yards of each other. It is difficult to find any explanation for this, possibly the design of the shell has much to do with it. The enemy's time-fuses are also astonishingly accurate, particularly those of the field howitzers. . . . The shooting of the German artillery can only be described as uncanny," [1] and so on.

But the battalion commander quoted touched on the two points that really mattered : the portable tool, a diminutive combination of pick and hoe, was useless, and drainage had not been solved.

The battalion establishment of tools provided 222 shovels and 148 picks, which seems a goodly number ; but the problem of swift digging-in, as it appeared in 1914, could not be solved unless the shovel and pick were in the hands of the men—and that problem exists now. Quantity was wanted—large margins for waste—for this was a war of shovel and shell.

All further recommendations as to construction of trenches may be swept on one side—they were already in the Manuals—before the insuperable difficulty of drainage.

It is in the nature of man to adopt a makeshift and murmur "sufficient unto the day is the evil thereof." So the astounding truth that if a hole is dug in the ground and sufficient rain falls, the hole will fill with water, and can only drain to a lower level, was realised after many attempts to reverse the order of things. In the Valley of the Lys, with which our battalions were for the moment concerned, there was no lower level, for the

---

[1] Exaggerated.

sluggish stream has practically no banks and the country is little above the level of the sea, thirty-five miles away.

The left of the line held by the 2nd Battalion had, for example, been sited in dry weather in the bed of a tributary brook to the Lys, just below the Frelinghein brewery. When the river rose with the winter rains, the company holding it was, very naturally, flooded out. The Royal Engineers boxed it in with thick planks and raised a breastwork ; even so the water rose at times above the floor-planks.

The condition of trenches during the first winter was terrible. " Duck-boards " made their appearance, and were placed at the bottom of the trenches in the hope that they would provide a solid foothold : as they sank in the mud, others were placed on top !

Undoubtedly every claim made for British rifle fire was justified ; but there had been cases when the mud of the trench had had a disastrous effect on this weapon. " Rifles must be kept clean and well oiled, and it has been found necessary to make an inspection daily, or even oftener. . . . When in trenches in wet weather, every precaution must be taken to prevent the bolt of the rifle from becoming clogged with mud." (Official Notes.)

In this respect the experience of the 1st Battalion at Broodseinde, as related by Lieutenant Hindson, was shared by the 2nd Battalion near Fromelles. Picton Davies's diary, 27th October : " It poured with rain all last night. Difficulty in using rifles, as clogged with mud. Many bayonets are broken."

Company Sergeant-Major Boreham paints a more lurid picture : " A great many rifles were rendered useless owing to plugs of mud getting into the muzzles and so causing the barrels to bulge or burst when the weapon was fired. This meant that the serviceable rifles in possession of the men of the reserve company had to be sent up to the front line. On one occasion when things were rather threatening the C.O. ordered those who had no rifles to arm themselves with picks and shovels—a few lucky ones had German rifles and bayonets that had been brought in."

The recommendations for training were put in the following order :

(1) Entrenching, especially in the dark.

(2) Rapid fire.

(3) Cover from view of artillery for the trenches.

(4) Bringing enfilade fire to bear on the enemy trenches whenever possible.

(5) Skilful use of machine guns.

Finally, general training in the organisation of entrenched positions in " defended localities." Eight hundred yards between two " localities " was regarded as the maximum.

The number of machine guns employed by the enemy and the effect of machine-gun fire was also being closely observed. It was claimed, in these Notes, that machine guns were easily knocked out by artillery fire and rifle fire, but it was admitted that they caused many casualties against advancing troops. During the winter the establishment was increased from two to four guns.

A new weapon, or rather an old weapon reintroduced, made its appearance during the first winter—the bomb. But those first bombs were clumsy things, made out of jam tins, scrap iron, some high explosive, and a length of indifferent fuse. Rifle grenades were of better construction, but very scarce. And some awkward trench mortars were constructed out of iron piping.

During the winter the line settled down to what has been called the " routine of trench life," with dumps for picks and shovels, and sandbags, which, however, were not plentiful during the first winter ; with sentry reliefs day and night, and " stand to arms " an hour before dawn, and an hour before dusk ; with fatigue parties for rations, trench " stores," and ammunition ; with " braziers," cook-houses, and a " tot " of rum at daybreak.

There remained, and one finds it in the Staff " Notes," a hope that a move forward might soon take place, but it was not very strong.

" History teaches us that the course of campaigns in Europe, which have been actively prosecuted during the months of December and January, have been largely influenced by weather conditions. It should, however, be thoroughly understood throughout the country that the most recent developments of armaments and the latest method of conducting warfare have added greatly to the difficulties and drawbacks of a vigorous winter campaign," said the Commander-in-Chief in his dispatch covering the period.

Only one attack of any importance was made during the winter, and that by the Indian Corps.

The Raid at Touquet.

Small enterprises were, however, undertaken, and one of the first raids into the enemy lines was made by the 1st Battalion.

This little affair is a fine example of the fighting qualities and spirit of the battalion. There were only from eighty to ninety of the original ranks left, the companies being filled up by newly arrived drafts, but they were as grimly determined or as indifferent to blows—whichever way one cares to look at it—as the first highly trained men from Malta.

German snipers had caused a good deal of trouble, especially from some farm buildings situated just in front of their own line. The scarcity of ammunition prevented the artillery from dealing with these buildings, so Captain Minshull Ford, lately Adjutant to the 4th Battalion, and Lieutenant E. L. Morris, of the Royal Engineers, raided the place with fifteen men and blew it up with gun-cotton.

The incident is mentioned in Sir John French's dispatch. The battalion went into the line on the 14th November, and the raid took place on the night of the 24th/25th November, over snow-covered ground. The party was half-frozen while crawling to rushing distance. The enemy was alert, and the party was seen. Captain Ford led the charge, which was met by wild fire—a bullet cut the peak from his cap—and the enemy fled. The explosive was successfully laid and fired.

Later in the war the regiment earned an enviable and well-merited reputation for raiding the enemy lines, the foundation of which was laid at this time. The aggressive spirit required for this form of enterprise was fostered in these early days by patrols of four to six men led by an officer. Lieutenants P. Mostyn and Fletcher distinguished themselves in patrol work. Mostyn was indefatigable, and on one occasion shot Maltby in the foot while he, too, was on patrol! Fletcher, who knew German, spent many hours curled up under the enemy parapet—neither rain, snow, mud, nor standing water deterred him. On one occasion he entered the German trench by the aid of a tree, and brought away a flag which the enemy had stuck up to the annoyance of the 2nd Battalion. After his death from a sniper's bullet in March 1915, this flag was presented to Eton College, where he was, before the war, a master : it was hung in the Great Hall.

The Defence of Givenchy.

The attack of the Indian Corps, mentioned above, took place on the 19th December, on the Givenchy front, and was not a success, inasmuch as the ground gained had to be abandoned, being considered untenable. But on the 20th the enemy, after a bombardment by artillery and trench mortars, launched an infantry attack on the village and drove the Sirhind Brigade—recently from Egypt—out of their trenches.

For a while the situation was uncertain, and Sir Douglas Haig's I Corps, then in reserve, was ordered to send first a brigade and then a division in support of the Indian Corps.

The 4th Battalion of the regiment had been posted, on the 3rd

December, to the 3rd Brigade, 1st Division, and had moved from Heuringhem through Hazebrouck to Bailleul. They were immediately ordered to conform to the 1914 organisation of four companies.

At that time the Territorial battalions were temporarily posted as fifth battalions to brigades, and, as a rule, were entrusted with a shorter length of line.

The 1st Division being ordered to move down to Givenchy, our 4th Battalion marched from Bailleul at 7 a.m. on the 20th, while it was still dark. Their first lesson was to be a hard one. They had no field kitchens, and no provision had been made for feeding the troops. Their road lay through Merville, Bethune, and Gorre, a distance of 26 miles. They had a few hours' rest at Bethune, and completed the march during the afternoon of the 21st. But no rations were issued until 7 a.m. on the 22nd.

Meanwhile the 1st Division had steadied the line at Givenchy and the 4th Battalion took over some trenches near Festubert. They remained in the line for three weeks, and the men suffered a good deal from trench feet, or frost-bitten feet.

CHRISTMAS DAY, 1914.

In some parts of the line the first Christmas Day of the war witnessed extraordinary scenes.

" I think I and my company have just spent one of the most curious Christmas Days we are ever likely to. It froze hard on Christmas Eve, and in the morning there was a thick ground fog. I believe I wrote and told you the Saxons opposite had been shouting across to us in English. Strict orders had been issued that there was to be no fraternisation on Christmas Day. About 1 p.m., having seen our men get their Christmas dinners, we went into our shelter, which is about five yards behind the trench, to get a meal. The sergeant on duty suddenly ran in and said that the fog had lifted and that half a dozen Saxons were standing on their parapet without arms, and shouting that they did not want to fight. I ran out into the trench and found that all the men were holding their rifles at the ready on the parapet, and that about half a dozen Saxons were standing on their parapet and shouting, ' Don't shoot! We don't want to fight to-day. We will send you some beer ! ' A cask was hoisted on to the parapet and three men started to roll it into the middle of No Man's Land, which is the name for the strip of mud between the opposing trenches. A lot more Saxons then appeared without arms.

" Things were getting a bit thick. My men were getting excited and the Saxons kept shouting to them to come out. We did not like to fire as they were all unarmed, but we had strict orders, and someone might have fired, so I climbed over the parapet and shouted, in my best German, for the opposing captain to appear.

" Our men were all chattering and saying, ' The Captain's going to speak to them.' A German officer appeared and walked out into the middle of No Man's Land, so I moved out to meet him amidst the cheers of both sides. The Germans were all out in No Man's Land by this time, but made no attempt to approach our lines, as our men were all in the trench. We met in the middle of No Man's Land and formally saluted. He introduced himself as Count something or other, and seemed a very decent fellow. He could not talk a word of English. He then called out to his five subalterns, and formally introduced them, with much clicking of heels and saluting. They were all very well turned out, while I was in a goatskin coat. One of the subalterns could talk a few words of English, but not enough to carry on a conversation.

" I said to the German Captain, ' My orders are to keep my men in the trench and allow no armistice. Don't you think it is dangerous, all your men running about in the open like this ? Someone may open fire.' He called out an order, and all his men went back to their parapet, leaving me and the five German officers and a barrel of beer in the middle of No Man's Land. He then said, ' My orders are the same as yours, but could we not have a truce from shooting to-day ? We don't want to shoot, do you ? ' I said, ' No, we certainly don't want to shoot, but I have my orders to obey '—to which he agreed. I then suggested that we should return to our trenches and that no one should come out of the trench. We agreed not to shoot until the following morning, when I was to signal that we were going to begin. He said, ' You had better take the beer ; we have lots.' So I called up two men to bring the barrel to our side. I did not like to take the beer without giving something in exchange, and I suddenly had a brain-wave. We had lots of plum-puddings, so I sent for one and formally presented it to him in exchange for the beer. He then called out ' Waiter,' and a German private whipped out six glasses and two bottles of beer, and with much bowing and saluting we solemnly drank it, amid cheers from both sides. We then all formally saluted and returned to our lines.

" *Later.*—A hard frost last night. Not a shot all night ; our men had sing-songs—ditto the enemy. He played the game and never tried to touch his wire or anything. At 8.30 a.m. I fired three shots in the air and put up a flag with ' Merry Christmas ' on it, and I climbed on the parapet. He put up a sheet with ' Thank you ' on it, and the German captain appeared on the parapet. We both bowed and saluted and got down into our

III—8

respective trenches, and he fired two shots in the air and the war was on again.   I wish my German had been more fluent."   (Stockwell.)

The 1st Battalion was out of the line on Christmas Day, the Brigadier having allowed the routine of reliefs to be changed by arrangement with the 8th Royal Scots [1] (who wished for New Year's Day), and so ate their dinners in billets at Rue Bataille.

The 4th Battalion was in the line at Festubert, but their puddings had, apparently, not arrived.   There was no special incident to record.

On the 8th January the 2nd Battalion moved to Bois Grenier, and held the line on the immediate left of the 1st Battalion.

The conditions here [2] were exactly the same as farther south, in the Laventie, Neuve Chapelle, and Festubert sectors—that is to say, marsh land, where it was impossible to dig trenches, and defences consisted of breastworks.   By late spring it was described as " a pleasure to be in the line," so much work had been done.   A great deal of this was due to what was called the " Sapping Platoon," then a domestic institution, but later to be enlarged to Pioneer Battalions.   Their *chef d'œuvre* was the communication trench.   It was about 500 yards in length and was wide enough for troops to move along in column of route ; at its entrance were orange trees in green-painted tubs.   It was plainly visible to the enemy, but three years later, when the 2nd Battalion returned to this front, it was untouched, with the orange trees still there in green tubs, but dead.

The Sapping Platoon worked continuously in the line, as a separate unit, the men rejoining their companies when the battalion was out of the line in rest-billets.   The grasping hands of brigade were soon laid on them to form the Brigade Working Company—this about a year later.

One company—Captain Samson's, of the 2nd Battalion—solved the ration fatigue, through the acquisition of a draught dog and cart, such as the Belgians used ; and down the communication trench trotted " Fouche " with the rations.

During that first winter people in England were generous to " our boys in the trenches " and sent such quantities of socks, mufflers, and

[1] The 8th Royal Scots (T.F.) became the 5th Battalion in the 22nd Brigade on the 12th November.

[2] Lieutenant A. K. Richardson says : " During December 1914 the 1st Battalion was holding the line between Touquet and La Boutellerie, and owing to the very wet state of the trenches an order was issued that one platoon from each company was to go out of the line into a ruined farm about 150 yards to our rear, and there the men were to be given a chance of cleaning themselves and resting.   One platoon went out each day at ' stand-to ' in the morning and returned at ' stand-to ' at night.   An old woman arrived at the farm one day, dug a safe out of a manure-heap, placed it in a wheel-barrow, and departed with her rescued savings in broad daylight and in view of the enemy."

shirts that many men, rather than wash what they had, threw them away and applied for new. But in time the lavishness died down, and a battalion laundry was set up, each company detailing a man to wash ; later still this important duty was undertaken by Divisional Headquarters Laundry Company.

When the 2nd Battalion went out of the line to rest, every alternate five days, the billets were round " Streaky Bacon Farm," where all officers slept and had a battalion mess. Expenditure on extras in the mess was limited to 1½ francs per day, and all gifts from home were supposed to be turned in for general consumption ; the most popular of the latter were the fresh Irish salmon, butter, and honey which arrived for Captain Knox-Gore.

Sport, of a kind, existed when the battalions were out of the line, although both polo and football were apt to be interrupted by enemy shrapnel.

Armentières was accessible with its shops, restaurants, estaminets, and tea-rooms. Also the 4th Division had taken and staffed a theatre for their own " Follies." This original company of entertainers was the only one—and that not for many months—allowed to have real " girls," or rather, feminine assistants, in the person of two French *ingénues* to whom the British Expeditionary Force gave the names of Vaseline and Glycerine. Armentières, although occasionally shelled, was a centre of life and entertainment at that time. The first rest-house for officers was established there.

St. David's Day was celebrated in Streaky Bacon Farm, when many uninitiated ate the leek—only the goat was missing from the ceremony in this part of the line ; but farther south, at Essars, the 4th Battalion borrowed a white goat from a farmer, gilded its horns, and paraded it round the table to the tap of a—biscuit tin.

The most interesting event was the inevitable decision to grant temporary commissions to N.C.O.s and men of the Regular and Territorial Forces. Within the regiment the first of such promotions were :

Regimental Sergeant-Major Murphy.

Company Sergeant-Major Stanway, a noted sniper and the first commander of the Sapping Platoon.

Regimental Quartermaster-Sergeant Welton.

Murphy became the first bombing officer, and gave terrifying instruction in the use of the early " jam-tin " bombs.

Early in January Corporal Moody and Privates Higginson, Barlow, and Owen, of the Artists' Rifles (Territorial Force), reported, having been given temporary commissions. They arrived in their ranker uniforms and were given leave at once to buy kit. They were posted to the 2nd Battalion.

THE SPRING OFFENSIVE, 1915.

During the winter months much correspondence and discussion went on between the Commander-in-Chief and the Cabinet in London. Sir John French was of the opinion that an attack along the coast, supported by the Fleet, would produce good results. In consultation with the First Lord of the Admiralty (Mr. Churchill) he had been promised 200 heavy guns on the sea.

" For four or five miles inshore we could make you perfectly safe and superior," said Mr. Churchill. " We could bring men in at Ostend or Zeebrugge, to reinforce you in a hard south-easterly push. There is no limit to what could be done by the extreme left-handed push and swoop along the Dutch frontier."

In support of this plan the British Government communicated with the French Government, asking that the British Army might be moved to the extreme left of the Allied line. General Joffre, however, rejected the scheme, and the Cabinet weakened in their support, finally refusing to entertain the idea at all, on the grounds that it was found difficult to supply drafts for the twenty-four Territorial battalions already in France, and would be impossible if that number was increased to the fifty demanded by Sir John French for his scheme ; also that it was impossible to supply the ammunition considered indispensable for such an operation.

" You have pointed out that offensive operations, under the new conditions created by this war, require a vast expenditure of artillery ammunition," Lord Kitchener wrote, " which may, for even ten or twenty days, necessitate the supply of fifty or a hundred rounds per gun per day being available, and that unless the reserve can be accumulated to meet expenditure of this sort, it is unwise to embark on extensive offensive operations against the enemy in trenches." And he pointed out that it was impossible to say how long an offensive, once begun, would last, and that to break it off for want of ammunition might well lead to disaster.

Sir John considered the reasons given for the refusal illogical, especially as the Cabinet was considering an offensive in a new theatre. The gloomy prospect of a stalemate on the Western Front loomed with the appearance of conviction through the uncertain mist of the future, and the War Council considered that " projects for pressing the war in other theatres should be carefully studied."

Sir John, perhaps prejudiced by the work he had in hand, ventured the opinion that the impossibility of breaking through the enemy lines in Flanders had not been proved, and that there were no theatres, other than France and Flanders, where decisive results could be obtained.

General Joffre, when opposing Sir John, had in his mind the probability of an enemy offensive in the near future, and the massing of reserves to meet it and regain the initiative. His offensive plan was to break through the enemy line at Reims and Arras, and Sir John French says, " it brought about for the British Army the Battles of Neuve Chapelle, Ypres, Festubert, and Loos ; and for the French other important actions which . . . did not result in achieving any appreciable advance towards the objectives which the plans sought to attain "—which is true.

THE BATTLE OF NEUVE CHAPELLE.[1]
(1ST AND 4TH BATTALIONS.)

It would, however, be unwise to state that an offensive along the coast, at that period of the war, would have been crowned with any greater success than the battles mentioned.

According to Sir John French's despatch, the considerations which led him to attack at Neuve Chapelle were : " The general aspect of the Allied situation through Europe, and particularly the marked success of the Russian Army in repelling the violent onslaughts of Marshal von Hindenburg ; the apparent weakening of the enemy on my front, and the necessity of assisting our Russian Allies to the utmost by holding as many hostile troops as possible in the Western Theatre ; the efforts to this end which were being made by the French forces at Arras and Champagne ; and, perhaps the most weighty consideration of all, the need for fostering the offensive spirit in the troops under my command after the trying and possibly enervating experiences which they had gone through of a severe winter in the trenches."

The second consideration would, however, seem to have been the most vital, as the Intelligence at General Headquarters, commendably accurate, suggested that a great opportunity presented itself in March 1915. It was known that, owing to the situation on the Russian Front, the Germans had thinned their line, and between La Bassée and Bois Grenier the German VII Corps had been reduced to two weak divisions, the 13th and 14th. Opposed to them, between these boundaries, was General Haig's First Army, consisting of seven divisions.

This country had been the scene of all the heavy fighting in 1914,

---

[1] Date: 10th–13th March 1915. Area : road Richebourg-l'Avoué—Croix Barbée—Pont du Hem—Fauquissart—Aubers.

when the II Corps attempted to envelop La Bassée, and the line held in March 1915 was the prepared position to which Sir Horace Smith-Dorrien had decided to withdraw in October 1914. But the village of Neuve Chapelle had been lost to the enemy, and the German line formed, here, a salient offering special facilities for effective artillery bombardment.

The decision to attack on the Neuve Chapelle front, and to capture that village as a preliminary to a general advance over the Aubers Ridge, was arrived at in February. The first phase was to be an assault on 2,000 yards of the enemy trench system, to be followed by an advance on a five-mile front.

In the first phase of the attack three British brigades (fifteen battalions) would meet one and a half German battalions with two companies in reserve, and in a Special Order of the day issued on the 9th March, General Haig, referring to the main attack, states, " We are now about to attack with forty-eight battalions a locality held by three German battalions," which was true.

The opportunity was, therefore, favourable, with the weight of numbers on our side.

On St. David's Day the 7th Division slipped south, and our 1st Battalion took over the line south of Fauquissart village.

The battle that followed was a failure, and costly—there were 12,500 casualties. The first phase, the capture of Neuve Chapelle, was accomplished, but the main attack was arrested by the determined and gallant defence put up by a handful of Germans armed with machine guns which our artillery failed to destroy.

At that stage of the war the massing of artillery gave to the First Army —beyond the fixed establishment—no more than :

> 38 4·7-inch and 60-pdr. guns ;
> 24 6-inch howitzers ;
> 5 6-inch guns ;
> 4 9·2-inch howitzers ;
> 1 12-inch howitzer ;
> 1 15-inch howitzer.

One result of the battle was to raise in England a tremendous outcry against the meagre strength of the artillery and the inadequate number of shells, especially high-explosive shells. Great play was made with the cutting of wire entanglements by means of shrapnel, but the considered opinion of artillery officers, at that time, was that shrapnel was preferable to high explosive, and that 35 minutes was sufficient to cut the wire and destroy the enemy breastworks.

The regiment was not deeply involved in the Battle of Neuve Chapelle. Situated on the extreme left of the main attack, the 22nd Brigade was not to move until the Du Pietre Mill, slightly north of that hamlet, had been captured by the 21st Brigade. At first encouraging reports were received, and our 1st Battalion, with gaps cut in their breastworks, expected to move forward at once, but it was soon evident that all was not going according to plan. Time passed, and no orders arrived—nothing happened, beyond a good deal of enemy shelling and a lot of machine-gun fire. 2nd Lieutenant H. E. Parkes, who was liaison officer with the 21st Brigade, was killed early in the day, and 2nd Lieutenant J. C. Poole took his place, but was soon wounded. The battalion did not move. Occasionally targets presented themselves and were immediately engaged from the breastworks.

On the extreme right of the main attack our 4th Battalion held the original line on the flank of the advance. They were able, from time to time, to assist with rifle and machine-gun fire whenever any Germans showed themselves.

The high ground about Haut Pommereau and Illies remained with the enemy. Being the first prepared attempt by the British Army to break through the German trench system, protected by wire entanglements and defended by carefully sited machine guns, it is an interesting study. At First Army Headquarters the greatest optimism reigned, and twice the Cavalry Corps and Indian Cavalry Corps received orders to move, with the immediate prospect of an advance through the enemy lines and a swing round in rear of La Bassée. The possibility was always there, the probability trembled in the balance, but one of the outstanding features of the battle was the breakdown of control. Again and again orders for attack either did not get through to battalion commanders, or were issued without sufficient regard for the time necessary to reach the units concerned, with the result that it was impossible to co-ordinate the movements of the infantry with the action of the artillery. In some cases the infantry did not advance, having missed the covering bombardment; in others, gallant attempts were made, only to meet with inevitable failure.

THE BATTLE OF AUBERS RIDGE.[1]
(1ST AND 4TH BATTALIONS.)

In spite of the disappointing result of Neuve Chapelle, it was thought that the experience gained promised well for future success. Correspond-

---

[1] The battle includes two attacks, one at Fromelles, the other at Rue du Bois, both on the 9th May. The area for the first was: road Aubers—Fauquissart—Laventie—Rouge de Bout—Fleurbaix (exclusive)—La Boutillerie—Bas-Maisnil. For the second: road La Quinque Rue (exclusive)—Le Touret—Lacouture—Croix-Barbée; thence a line to the Bois du Beiz.

ence passed between Sir John French and General Joffre on the subject of a combined Allied attack between Armentières and Arras, which was finally decided upon.   Sir John released a certain number of French troops in the north by extending his line to the Ypres—Poelcapelle road, and preparation commenced for a second attempt on the Aubers Ridge.

Strictly speaking, the Battle of Aubers Ridge was the opening of the Battle of Festubert—that is to say, the two battles were one, as will be seen.

The enemy opened his spring offensive at Ypres on the 22nd April with " a cynical and barbarous disregard of the well-known usages of civilised war, and a flagrant defiance of the Hague Convention. . . . The enemy has invariably preceded, prepared, and supported his attacks by a discharge in stupendous volume of these poisoned-gas fumes." (Despatches.)   This was the commencement of the Second Battles of Ypres, which continued until 25th May.

While this was going on in the north, the French attacked between Arras and the right of the British line, and Sir Douglas Haig was ordered to attack with his First Army.[1]   Between Neuve Chapelle and Givenchy the attack was to be delivered by the I and Indian Corps ; and in the neighbourhood of Rouge Bancs by the 8th Division of the IV Corps.

Our 4th Battalion took part in the right attack.   They were in billets at Hinges, and marched on the 8th May to a position in rear of the Rue du Bois.   The task allotted to them was to follow the assaulting waves of the 3rd Brigade, and deal with any small groups of the enemy overlooked by the leading battalions.

The bombardment commenced at 5 a.m., and after forty minutes lifted.   It was insufficient.   The assaulting infantry were simply driven back to their breastworks the moment they attempted to cross No Man's Land.   Wire and Germans had, apparently, been untouched by the bombardment, and very few of the 3rd Brigade succeeded in advancing beyond their own line of wire.

The 4th Battalion, waiting behind the support line of breastworks for their first plunge into battle, started, at the hour of assault, to cross to the first line over the open.   But the volume of fire directed on the assaulting troops, and sweeping across the flat country, was such that they never succeeded in reaching the front line.   Lieutenant-Colonel France-Hayhurst, Captain Eric Evans, Lieutenant B. Croom-Johnson, 2nd Lieutenant J. T. C.

---

[1] Sir Douglas Haig and Sir Horace Smith-Dorrien took over new " Army Headquarters " of the First and Second Armies, respectively, on the new year.   Sir Horace was, soon after, succeeded by General Plumer.

MAJOR (BATTALION LIEUTENANT-COLONEL) R. E. GABBETT.

Hazeldine, and Lieutenant M. Pern of the R.A.M.C. were killed; the casualties in the ranks amounted to 65.

A second assault was ordered at 4 p.m., Major Meares being in command. Two companies of the battalion were then attached to the Royal Engineers, to follow when the enemy line had been won and consolidate the position; the rôle of the remaining two companies was the same as in the morning.

Major Meares led his troops forward under the shelter of a communication earthwork, only to find that the assaulting battalions had again not been able to leave their line.

The attack was abandoned, and the 4th Battalion was withdrawn that night to Harisoirs.

The same story was repeated on the IV Corps front. Here the 8th Division was to attack, and break the first trench system; the 7th Division would then follow, take up the advance and capture Aubers village, La Pouich, and Le Cliqueterie farms.

The 8th Division took the first line of breastworks, but " the position was much stronger than had been anticipated," and they could get no further into the system of first-line defences. Our 1st Battalion did not leave their line.

Stockwell's diary is eloquent:

" 25*th March* 1915.—A memo to say I'm transferred to the 1st Battalion. Went to Laventie—Scatters in a stew. Dickson commanding, Berners coming out, no place for me—I shall only get a company.

" 30*th.*—Said good-bye to Guillaume and the others and rode over to Laventie. Great preparations for an attack in which we are to take part—but which I think are a mere bluff. . . .

" 9*th May* 1915.—At 7 p.m. last night the show put off till Sunday. I gather the French started a day late. We are due to deliver the attack to-morrow morning—it is a portion of a very large operation. We are to have the whole of the First Army in—120,000, and two cavalry divisions, backed by the Canadians and two or more Territorial divisions. The idea is to attack the Aubers Ridge from the north-east and south-east simultaneously, the north-east attack to be made by the 4th Corps (ours), the south-east by the Indian Corps, there to join hands. The French are pushing at north-east of Arras and hope to be in Douai on Sunday. If both are successful, the German line in between will be pushed out and scuppered. Everyone seems to know about it, which is bad.

" 9*th May.*—At 5 punctually the guns opened—a terrific din—the line a mass of flame and then shell smoke. No reply from Germans. The VIII Division moved forward, the guns firing on distant targets. The

Queen's and Warwicks moved up nearer—very little news. We have taken the first-line trenches and parts of the second line ; then the telephone reports only holding first line, and only that in parts. The show has gone wrong—wounded cursing the gunners. Reports have it that the artillery bombardment was a failure, and divisional artillery knocked our own people about very much.

" 12.30 p.m.—Another terrific bombardment by our guns. Germans have brought up guns and are beginning to reply. The 8th Division are going to assault again. At about 2.30 they assaulted. It is reported that the assault has failed. We hold portions of their front line—a heavy casualty list. The German shelling is increasing, and as it is now getting dark they are counter-attacking. We still hold a footing, R. Brigade, the others have been driven out. The Indian Corps has failed also. 11.30 p.m.—We are to move forward at once. I suppose the 7th Division is to try now. 12.—Our move cancelled.

" 2.30 a.m. (10th).—Very heavy firing and shelling ; spent ones are whistling by and over us. We are to move at once. Spent a very chilly night, no food, no smoking, no lights, but managed two and a half hours' sleep and feel frozen now. Lots of bullets passing between us. I had three men wounded yesterday, B had none, but C three. Curious, as they were whispering round everywhere. Shelling coming nearer. We moved back half a mile into a field and then dug in. Men very cheery."

THE BATTLE OF FESTUBERT.[1]

In the evening General Haig reviewed the situation, and proposed to abandon all further attempts at Rouge Bancs and concentrate his attack on the Festubert system. The Commander-in-Chief agreed, and preparations were put in hand at once for the 7th Division to move from the IV Corps area into that of the I Corps. The Battle of Aubers Ridge was, of course, broken off.

This decision caused great inconvenience to the French, who, according to plan, had launched their offensive on the Vimy Ridge and Arras sector, and, to placate General Joffre, orders were drawn up for the 2nd and 7th Divisions to move south of the La Bassée Canal and attack on the left of General Foch's Tenth Army. At the last moment the orders were cancelled, and it was decided to go on with General Haig's plan.

The breaking off of the Aubers Ridge Battle had caused the Germans to move their two reserve divisions, the 58th and 115th, on the British

---

[1] Date: 15th–25th May. Area: La Bassée Canal to Gorre ; thence road to Le Touret ; Lacouture—Croix-Barbée ; thence a line to the Bois du Biez (south-west corner).

front, to the south against the French, leaving two divisions of the German VII Corps, each made up to nine battalions with practically no reserves at all, opposed to General Haig's First Army.

The plan, similar to that of the 9th May, was to consist of two separate attacks, though the distance between them was only 600 yards as compared to 6,000 yards, and the first objective was La Quinque Rue. The 2nd Division, between Chocolat Menier Corner and Richebourg l'Avoué, a frontage of about 1,600 yards, was to assault and capture the first two lines of German breastworks at night; at dawn the 7th Division was to attack immediately north of Festubert, on a 750-yards front.

After a pause at La Quinque Rue, the two divisions were to advance on the second objective, Rue d'Ouvert—Rue du Marais.

But the Battle of Festubert marks a change in the use of artillery: it was no longer deemed sufficient to bombard the enemy lines for thirty-five minutes; a slow bombardment over several days was ordered. It commenced on the morning of the 13th May and, originally intended to be for twenty-six hours, was extended to sixty hours. The wire was cut in lanes.

.   .   .   .

The 7th Division was then moved from the IV Corps area to take part in this attack.

The 1st Battalion was in billets at Essars when Lieutenant-Colonel Gabbett received a warning order for the attack. All officers immediately visited the line and the observation posts to study the lie of the land. Captain Stockwell, commanding A Company, felt uneasy about the River des Layes. The course of this stream is confusing, as it is joined by drainage ditches, and itself controlled and straightened by the peasants; but it seemed to Captain Stockwell that it might well run, according to his map, down the centre of No Man's Land. So he obtained permission from the Commanding Officer to carry out a night reconnaissance, as no information was available from the battalion holding the line. He went out, accompanied by Lieutenant Woodward and 2nd Lieutenant Walmsley of B Company, on the night of the 12th, and found a " considerable obstacle from 5 to 10 feet broad and everywhere a depth of 5 to 6 feet of water."

The nature of the river, or ditch, was reported to Brigade, and it was agreed, there being no time to bridge it, that A Company, leading the attack, should carry trench-boards and put them out about every ten yards.

The reconnaissance was, therefore, of the greatest value, and enabled the 22nd Brigade to avoid the fate of troops farther to the north who were unable to cross the river. The stream had played a great part in the Battle of Neuve Chapelle, opposite that village, and it is curious that its presence, or that of a tributary, was unreported to the south.   Indeed, Stockwell was not too pleased by what he saw : " Took platoon commanders down to trenches.   Very unpleasant.   Our guns are dangerous and the Huns are firing high-explosive at the parapet.   No provision for massing troops has been made.   No sniping, no loopholes, nothing."

The German line extended from Richebourg l'Avoué in a south-westerly direction.   The enemy had been stirred up by the attack on the 9th, and the unusual artillery activity made it evident to them that we were about to repeat the effort.

The 22nd Brigade on the extreme right was attacking with the Queen's and our 1st Battalion.   The German line here formed a salient, to be taken by the Queen's, and a re-entrant, which fell to our battalion.

The idea was to penetrate some 450 yards into the enemy lines, and change direction half-right, to take and hold, as a flank to the general advance, a long communication trench.   A Company was to lead the attack, followed by B, C, and D, all in lines of half-companies.   A company would have the most distant point of the oblique-lying objective, an orchard known as Canadian Orchard, about 1,200 yards from their jumping-off line.   The other companies would come up in echelon to the right rear.

Zero hour was 3.15 a.m., when the artillery would lift from the German front line ; but " as far as the assaulting infantry were concerned, they had no knowledge of what the further action of the artillery would be, but we were told that if we got into the fire of our own guns we were to indicate the fact by firing Verey pistol flares.   The arrangements, in fact, were extremely sketchy."   (Stockwell.)

On the left of our 1st Battalion was the 2nd Battalion Scots Guards. What was known as Indian Village was reached through a communication trench running from the corner of the Rue du Bois and the Rue d'Epinette. The Indian Corps and 2nd Division attacked on the left four hours before the 7th Division, so the enemy was again on the alert.   Their attack had been successful.

Captain Stockwell describes the entry into battle :

" The battalion moved into the line on the night 15th/16th, through Indian Village, and assembled in lines immediately behind the front parapet, and proceeded to dig themselves such cover as they could from the enemy's counter-bombardment.   I sent out patrols to cover the putting out of the trench-boards, and to report on the wire and enemy parapet. The patrols reported that the wire was well cut, but, as far as they could see, the front trench was not much damaged.   As a matter of fact, practically no damage was done by our guns to the front system : the high-explosive fire was so limited by shortage of shell that even if accurate it would not have accomplished a great deal, and it mostly went over the enemy line.

" At 2.45 a.m. our intense bombardment began. We suffered a fair amount of loss through our own shorts, which kept catching the top of the high breastwork. The enemy's guns opened at 3.5 a.m.

" At 3.15 I gave the word to ' Go ! ' and the first line went over, followed by the second line twenty seconds later.[1] It was extremely dark and the enemy were shelling No Man's Land heavily.

" We got across the Rivière des Layes all right, but then came under intense machine-gun fire from our right, and were opposed by rifle fire from the trenches we were assaulting. The men of my company whom I could see seemed to thin out rapidly, but the remainder went straight on to the enemy trenches, where half an hour's strenuous hand-to-hand fighting took place in a frightful tangled system of trenches."

The deep formation of the assaulting troops, in lines of half-companies, meant that the whole of No Man's Land, some 120 yards at this point, was soon filled by a stream of passing troops : enemy fire, directed against A Company—which they escaped the moment they entered the enemy line—caught succeeding companies as they left their lines to cross the fatal 120 yards. Only three officers of the last two companies succeeded in getting over. Lieutenant-Colonel Gabbett was killed while climbing over the breastworks, as was Captain Jones, commanding B Company ; the second-in-command, Major Dickson, and Lieutenant Chapman, commanding C Company, were severely wounded.

The crossing of the battalion took some time, and to add to their troubles the Queen's, on the right, were held up for a while, which gave the enemy opportunities for cross-fire. The formation lost its symmetry, and became a headlong rush for the German line.

The success really depended on the action of a few during the " half-

---

[1] In his diary, written in terse, telegraphic style, Captain Stockwell said :

" 2.45 a.m.—Our guns have begun and one can hear nothing but shells screaming over and exploding. The shelling is pretty intense—it is an awful dark morning.

" 3.5 a.m.—The enemy's guns are beginning to reply—several of my men already wounded. It is getting pretty close and exciting. It is still beastly dark.

" 3.15 a.m.—It is time to go. I've been standing gazing at my watch, but times are apparently not exactly the same as the artillery—one of our shells has just cut the top of the parapet above me. I wish to God our artillery would lift.

" 3.16 a.m.—I've shouted ' Go ! ' and the front line are scrambling over the parapet. I counted sixty and then yelled ' Go ! ' and climbed the parapet with my second line. An awful crashing and banging going on, and a sort of steady hissing. Got through our wire all right, and then over a bridge."

hour's strenuous hand-to-hand fighting " in the " tangled system of trenches," and those few were to hand.   When Company Sergeant-Major Barter jumped into the German first line he called on the nearest men to join him, and collected eight, one of whom was a Queen's man.   Barter acted with the utmost speed and with confident leadership, the men following him, catching some of his reckless enthusiasm as he bombed his way along the trench to the right.   He forced 3 officers and 102 men to surrender to his swift and fearless attack, and also found and cut no less than eleven mine leads.   Altogether he made 500 yards of trench secure, and materially helped the Queen's in their advance as well as his own battalion.   He was awarded the Victoria Cross.

The rush across No Man's Land to that maze of defences resulted in much confusion.   Captain Coles, with men from A and B Companies, joined a company of the Scots Guards, which was probably F Company. Their adventures are not known, beyond the fact that Captain Coles was mortally wounded.   The Scots Guards Company was annihilated.

Captain Stockwell says : " I could find few men after we had cleared up the enemy in the trenches, and no officers of my company—as a matter of fact, all four of my subs were killed, and the second in command of the company died of wounds somewhere in the enemy line.   I endeavoured to collect what men I could, but they were all excited and ' blood mad,' and had got all over the place.   I finally succeeded in collecting some fifty men of the regiment and about thirty Scots Guards,[1] and I had also with me Company Sergeant-Major Warner of A Company, and Company Sergeant-Major Harrison of B Company, who were invaluable.   I got this small force clear of the trenches and deployed them and moved due east. It was still extremely dark and we could see no signs of simultaneous advance on our left.   [*The bulk of the Scots Guards had, apparently, edged to their*

---

[1] *Stockwell's diary :*

" We are nearing the smoke.   Can't say I feel excited.   There is a breach in the parapet in front of me.   I decide to go through there.   No Germans were apparent.   Got through breach. Just as I got through a German comes round the corner of a traverse at me with a bayonet.   I lift my pistol quickly and let drive—three times, quickly (one awful moment—will it work ?).   The Hun crumples up, and can see two more farther on being bayoneted by our men.   Went on through the German trench and met a crowd of Scots Guards coming from the left, yelling.   Am now in the German second line.   One can hardly see from smoke of our lyddite shells, which is hanging all round the place.   A Hun comes out of a dugout and holds up his hands—a Scots Guard sticks him— pretty beastly.   Then they all go mad, and all stick him, and stand round in a bunch yelling.   I walk up to a man and say, ' What in the name of Hell are you doing ? '   He answers, ' Who the devil are you ? and what's it got to do with you ? '—so I hit him as hard as I can in the face and knock him down.   I've cut my knuckle and jarred my wrist.   I yell out, ' Come on, boys,' and they all come along, about thirty of our men, the Company Sergeant-Major, Warner, Bridgeman, my servant and about thirty Scots Guards."

left.]   As we advanced we came under more and more enfilade fire from our left, men kept getting hit, and our numbers gradually dropped to about fifty.   I kept halting at intervals to try to get the men in line again, and see if any reinforcements came up.   I managed to collect two officers of

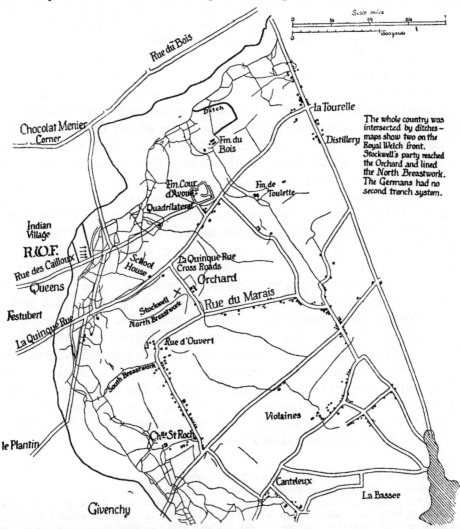

the regiment—2nd Lieutenant Walmsley, who was with me throughout the day, and 2nd Lieutenant Garnons Williams, who was later wounded but got back all right—also eight men of the Border Regiment [*they attacked on the left of the Scots Guards*] and a platoon of the Warwicks, who were supporting us and had got lost."

Captain Stockwell was then obliged to halt owing to the fire of our own artillery, and his force was again diminished by a German machine gun firing at their backs. This lasted for about twenty minutes. He had no idea of his exact position, but moved right-handed to try to find the communication trench—the battalion's final objective—and was rewarded by recognising a house, which had been pointed out as a machine-gun post, about 200 yards east of that communication trench.

As he moved forward, now sure of his bearings, an enemy machine-gun team appeared in a trench which ran towards the house, and tried to get their gun in position. Captain Stockwell's party opened fire and killed every man of the team.[1] " We then worked up the trench towards the house supposed to hold a machine gun, at the corner of the Canadian Orchard, but came only under rifle fire from that and other houses in the vicinity. The machine gun for this back position was probably the one we had just put out of action. I organised an assault, under Lieutenant Walmsley, on the nearest house to the end of the communication trench, and under the covering fire of the rest this was successfully carried, the Boche garrison being killed. We reached this position about 6 a.m. Any further advance was useless, as we were entirely in the air and could find no one on our left or 500 yards behind us. I then proceeded to consolidate the position and get the German machine gun working from the house. We found we were in line with and about 400 yards from a German battery which was not firing. We succeeded twice that day in shooting down his teams coming up to take off the guns. Six runners sent back failed to get through. At about 10.30 an officer of the Queen's with a forward observation officer came up the communication trench and telephoned back our position. Reinforcements began to come up at 1 p.m. In the meantime the enemy from Canadian Orchard attempted to attack us twice, but were driven off: We held the position till 7.30 p.m., when we were withdrawn to our original line, but south of the Rue Cailloux." [2]

---

[1] This was the first machine gun captured by the regiment.

[2] Stockwell's diary gives more detail than his considered report :

" Walmsley comes pushing along, and not seeing us goes prancing on. I manage to call him back and collect E. Williams, a sub, and also a few more Scots Guards. We now number about sixty. My Company Sergeant-Major, Warner, is with me and also Company Sergeant-Major Harrison, of B Company. Nobody knows where anyone is. I decide to make half-right for where I think the objective is. We move off. It is getting lighter. Our own shrapnel then open on us, bursting behind us. Several men are wounded, and I order a halt just beyond a deep broad ditch. The men try to dig in and get some cover. I have already sent back two men to bring supports up to me. A machine gun is raking us in the back—the same one that had been enfilading us. The Queen's ought to be in trench on our right, and the Scots Guards on my left—there is nobody. Walmsley gets a piece of shrapnel on the side of the head, without much damage—in fact except to raise a

COMPANY SERGEANT-MAJOR (NOW CAPTAIN) BARTER, V.C.

Lieutenant A. K. Richardson, who was in command of the 22nd Brigade Trench Mortars, supplements the end of the story :

" My orders were to support the advance of the 2nd Battalion Queen's. As their first line went over, a very hot enfilade fire caught them from the right. We succeeded in detecting some German machine guns, who caused the first line of the Queen's very heavy casualties, and immediately opened fire on them, as fast as the guns could be loaded,[1] and eventually succeeded in silencing them. The Queen's continued their advance, although greatly depleted in numbers. When we arrived at the Queen's objective we found only two officers left, Captain Furze and Major Kirkpatrick. The latter, although wounded in the head, was in command of the new line.

" Captain Stockwell made his way over to get into touch with Major Kirkpatrick, and on his arrival he heard I was there with the trench mortars, and asked for me to be sent up to bomb the orchard. On arrival I proceeded to bomb the orchard, which was a nest of German snipers. My ammunition was not powerful enough to dislodge them ; they were hidden in several ruined buildings and behind haystacks. I thereupon sent a message for the 60-pounders to come up, but they, too, were unable to silence them. Captain Stockwell then endeavoured to get our artillery to shell the orchard ; but it was not until very much later in the day,

bump it did nothing. I get one on the side of the boot and bruises me badly. Walmsley and I get in the ditch.

" It's getting lighter. I see a German High Command trench in front of us and an orchard and a road—this looks like our objective. My haversack falls—the strap has been cut through, and there are five bullet-holes through it. Walmsley says he is facing wrong, and some argument, which was almost cut short by a high-explosive shell—one of ours—which exploded about twenty yards in front of us. We have not enough men to carry the orchard in front of us. I order everyone to crawl to the right, and we presently see some of our men in a ditch. They turn out to be a lost platoon of the Warwicks. I take charge of them. Germans are seen running up the trench in front of us carrying a machine gun, which they try to put up. We open rapid fire and rush them. Our fire must have been accurate, as the officer is dead and a couple of his train wounded. I order the men to move up the trench to the left and seize the orchard and houses—Walmsley in charge. He pushes on. Shortly afterwards some Queen's, under Kirkpatrick, come along. He has been wounded but has his telephone with him, and reports to B.G.C. that I have reached machine gun and orchard. He tells me Gabbett and Jones are both killed, and Dickson wounded, so I am in command.

" Walmsley could not get the orchard—it was strongly held and we had only about fifty men. The Huns have a machine gun or sniper in all the houses. My bombers get them out of one, which we seize and fortify and dig a trench to join in up with our trench. Can't do any more. Reinforcements are coming up, but we are in the air and the enemy are working round behind us. The attack of the brigade on our left which should join up with us seems to have failed.

" 12 noon.—The mortar battery arrives and mortars the place ; not much effect. The long trench is fully manned now—Queens, Warwicks, and S. Staffords. It is a rotten trench and neither shell- nor bullet-proof."

[1] These were Vickers guns, and did not have a rapid rate of fire. The Stokes mortar was not yet in use.

III—9

and after we had suffered many casualties, that the artillery succeeded in driving out the Germans.

" Captain Stockwell went off again to the telephone at the Queen's objective, and asked for reinforcements. On his return a message came for him that Major Kirkpatrick had again been wounded, and that he, Captain Stockwell, must go at once and take over command of the new line. He left me in charge. Shortly afterwards a party of the 19th London Regiment arrived, having received orders from Captain Stockwell to take the orchard at the point of the bayonet.

" Later our artillery commenced to shell the orchard, and the German snipers bolted up the communication trenches leading to the road, Rue d'Ouvert, where the main German line had fallen back to—a distance of some 400 yards.

" The communication trench we were holding was composed of wire netting with posts at intervals and earth thrown up thinly against the wire. Our position was getting more and more untenable—no reinforcements coming—our ammunition expended—when, late in the evening, about 7 p.m., the German artillery began to bombard our position, causing heavy casualties.

" The Queen's and the Warwicks had been withdrawn when I received urgent messages from Captain Stockwell to retire. We eventually arrived back at our original line."

Here the battalion remained until the night of the 17th/18th, and during that time the bodies of 4 officers and over 100 men of the regiment were recovered from No Man's Land.

The orchard was retaken by the Canadian Division some days later.

There remained a gap between the 7th and 2nd Divisions, held by the enemy, which was not cleared until the next day, when both divisions made a further slight advance. The task allotted to the 7th Division was to push in the direction of Rue d'Ouvert, Château St. Roch, and Canteleux ; and the 2nd Division towards Rue du Marais and Violaines. By the 18th the 7th Division were on the La Quinque Rue—Bethune road. They were relieved by the Canadian Division, which had been in France for some weeks.

The battle resulted in an average advance on a four-mile front of 600 yards, but Captain Stockwell's party had gone 1,200 yards forward.

The Divisional Artillery, which consisted of the 22nd and 35th Brigades, 18-pdr., and the 37th Brigade, 4·5-inch howitzer (less one battery), were supported at Festubert by the

7th Siege Brigade, R.G.A., of 6-inch howitzers ;
8th London Brigade, R.F.A., of 5-inch howitzers ;

47th London Battery of 4·5-inch howitzers ;

36th Brigade, R.F.A. (less one battery), of 18-pdrs. ;

12th London Battery, R.F.A., of 15-pdrs. ;

14th Brigade, R.H.A., two batteries of 13-pdrs. ;

1st Indian Brigade, R.H.A., three batteries of 13-pdrs. ;

and one section of No. 7 Mountain Battery.

Some idea of the strength of the enemy opposing the 7th Division may be gained from the fact that the front attacked by the division was a part (less than half) of the 2,000 yards held by the German 57th Infantry Regiment ; the front and support lines were held by two battalions of this regiment ; while the third, at the opening of the battle, was in rest-billets at Violaines and La Bassée.

The strength of our 1st Battalion on the 16th May was 25 officers and 806 other ranks ; only 6 officers and 247 other ranks came out of the battle.

Amongst the killed were Lieutenant-Colonel Gabbett, Captain S. Jones, Lieutenants R. E. Naylor, R. H. Ackerley, 2nd Lieutenants Morris, H. F. Lynch, and 118 other ranks ; 2nd Lieutenants J. B. Savage (Adjutant) and H. L. G. Edwards died of wounds.

The wounded included Major G. F. H. Dickson, Captain M. L. Lloyd-Mostyn, Lieutenants H. Chapman, F. G. Williams, C. E. Woodward, 2nd Lieutenants W. G. Farren, R. C. D. Owen, R. Gambier-Parry, the Medical Officer Lieutenant W. Kelsey Fry, and 271 other ranks.

Captain H. S. Coles, Lieutenant L. Jones, and 170 other ranks were missing.

Soon after the Battle of Festubert, Sir John French, breaking away from Army tradition, gave interviews to the Press on the subject of ammunition. He had never been able to get what he asked for, and was informed privately that members of the Government accused him of wasting ammunition. Mr. Lloyd George was made Minister of Munitions as a result of the scandal that ensued, and a new order of output was established.

THE INTRODUCTION OF GAS.

The attempt of the Commander-in-Chief, and the British Government, to make an ethical question of the use of gas met with poor success.

We know that treaties and undertakings between individuals are broken every day of the week, neither party incurring ostracism ; between nations we know that they never stand. The German idea of war departed in every respect from the jousts and kingly contests of the Middle Ages, which were tournaments that could be watched in comparative safety by a civilian, or at least, being restricted in area and scope, avoided. The German view—and a clear-sighted one—of war was an affair between nations. Every soul comes into it. Thus one finds the catch-phrase " the will to fight " applied to the whole nation, and, indeed, it is logical and sound. Old conventions based on the discrimination between combatant and non-combatant, soldier and civilian, fell automatically into abeyance. And so the Germans exercised the greatest severity against the civil population of Belgium—a deliberate war policy ! And aeroplanes, which provided a new and formidable branch of artillery, carried the shell far back into industrial centres—the country as a whole being, in fact, a fortified area. " It is clear," said Marshal Foch, at a later period, " that aircraft attack on a large scale, owing to its crushing moral effect upon a nation, may impress public opinion to the point of disarming the Government and thus become decisive." Moral effect—the will to fight ! Is it a new conception of war ?

We should try to think clearly about the use of gas, which, after all, must be classed with high-explosive, both being chemical compounds.

The first gas attack at Ypres, in April 1915, consisted of a discharge of chlorine gas from cylinders ; some lachrymatory gas was also apparently used. Its use, in this case, was a military one only, but terror, the breaking of the will to fight, applies as much to the Army as the civil population, although to the latter—as Marshal Foch points out, and the Germans were soon to discover—terror would have a more far-reaching effect ; for gas, as a weapon against the soldier, was not very effective. In the whole war there were slightly under 181,000 casualties in all from gas, and only 3·3 per cent. were fatal ; it was, therefore, a more merciful weapon than shell fire. The difficulty in every form of " cloud " gas was to concentrate it in sufficient volume, whether discharged from cylinders or liberated from a bursting shell : the concentration automatically decreased ; the air, in continual eddies, wafted it up, loosened it, diluted it. The most effective used in the war was " mustard " gas, which was in the form of a liquid of a very volatile description which would continue to give off fumes for a long time ; the liquid itself had a burning or corrosive effect, and was very deadly, but the mask was a safeguard against the fumes.

The use of gas was foreseen, but all nations, except the Germans, ran away from it by signing The Hague Convention and, like Mr. Macawber, gave their attention to something else. The Germans signed, but went on thinking. The enemy had, then, the advantage of surprise and preparation, but did not profit by it. It is true that for a time they created a state of deep anxiety in the British Army. All sorts of weird respirators were used and recommended—men were even advised to dip a rag or handkerchief in urine as an efficacious and quickly made respirator. Apparently it is not difficult to improvise a filter for chlorine gas. The Canadians, who stood well against the first discharges of gas, had the wit to cram something in their mouths, and, above all, remained calm and did not run ; their breathing remained normal. But very soon a bag with goggles sewn in it was provided by the authorities ; it was saturated with a glycerine mixture which was found effective. Before other and more penetrating gases were used by the enemy, the British box respirator, with a charcoal filter, was introduced with satisfactory results.

Professor Haldane points out that the first discharges of gas were well carried out by the Germans, but that their respirators were bad, and they were unable to follow the cloud. " This was, apparently, because the most competent physiologist in Germany with any knowledge of breathing was a Jew ! " Thence he argues that the anti-Semitism of Germany lost them the war, for they could have got through the biggest gap they ever created in the Allied line, and so marched on the Channel Ports and, perhaps, Paris.

The important question raised by the introduction of gas is its use against the civil population. The Army is controlled and disciplined, and defensive measures can be applied easily ; but in future wars the problem that seems to loom before us is civil panic.

THE BATTLE OF LOOS.[1]
(1ST, 2ND, 4TH, AND 9TH BATTALIONS.)

After Festubert the 1st Battalion remained in the Richebourg—Givenchy sector through June, July, and part of August. Lieutenant-Colonel R. A. Berners assumed command at St. Hilaire on the 24th May.

The 2nd Battalion, which had been transferred with the 19th Brigade from the 6th Division and attached to the 27th Division (Major-General Milne) on the 28th May, remained in the Bois Grenier sector until the 23rd July, when they were again transferred to the 8th Division (Major-General Davies) and moved to the Laventie sector, slightly south.

The 9th Battalion [2] arrived in France on the 19th July with the 58th

[1] Date: 25th September—8th October. Area: road Aix-Noulette—Nœux-les-Mines—Bethune (exclusive)—Gorre—Festubert (exclusive).

[2] Lieutenant-Colonel H. J. Madocks ; Major C. Burrard ; Captains C. A. Acton, K. I. Nicholl, E. G. Payne, B. W. E. Hoyle, F. M. Jones, L. S. Hogg (Adjutant) ; Lieutenants M. M. Lewis, M. H. Davies, H. J. Williams, C. Heald, C. F. J. Symons, A. T. Orr, G. H. Charlton, L. G. Meade, W. G. Thomas, Stephens ; 2nd Lieutenants R. J. Williams, C. Y. Fawcett, R. H. Higham, C. G. Roberts, V. E. Owen, R. E. Ruck-Keene, R. N. Thomas, T. W. Karran, H. C. Wancke ; Lieutenant and Quartermaster Lawry ; Lieutenant A. G. Gilchrist (Medical Officer).

Brigade, 19th Division. Crossing from Folkestone to Boulogne, they waited at the latter place for a couple of days, until they were joined by an advance party which had sailed one day earlier from Southampton to Le Havre ; they then proceeded to Merville and underwent a course of training.

This battalion had been taken over at the last moment by Lieutenant-Colonel Madocks from Sir Horace McMahon, who had failed to pass the medical test for active service owing to defective eyesight. The battalion, however, owes him a deep debt of gratitude for the soundness of its training and the spirit he implanted.

The sector allotted to the 2nd Battalion was between Fauquissart and, on the left, a small salient known as " Red Lamp Salient." The Lahore Division was on their right. Just behind them was Laventie. At this period, with the exception of the church and buildings round it, Laventie was little damaged. Many of the inhabitants were there, a fair restaurant hotel was open, and the reserve battalion found comfortable billets in undamaged houses. Five miles behind the line was the town of Estaires, where battalions went for their periodical rest.

The line was held by four companies, each with a platoon in support. On the right, where the trenches were 400 yards apart, there was comparative quiet, but at Red Lamp Corner the trenches were only 60 to 100 yards apart, the ground was higher and drier than at Bois Grenier, and mining and countermining were being actively carried on ; until the men got used to it, the tread of an unseen sentry, or some other repeated sound, was apt to be mistaken for underground work by the enemy. And the nearness of the trenches led to a great deal of bombing. We had a battery of catapults, and abusive messages, as well as bombs, were hurled across to Fritz !

From the very commencement of the war, stories of espionage had been rife ; in time they died a natural death, for few of them were true, but in the early part of 1915 units arriving from England were very suspicious. The 5th Scottish Rifles joined the brigade at the end of 1914[1]; they were filled with Scotch suspicion and determined vigilance. Major Williams, accompanied by the Medical Officer, Captain Harbison, passing through their area on his way to Armentières, was stopped, and had to be very persuasive before he was allowed to proceed. Before leaving them, he warned the guard that he might be followed by some suspicious persons who might call themselves officers of the Royal Welch ! The desired result was achieved—Captain Owen, the Adjutant, and the company commanders,

[1] This Territorial unit was always referred to as the Scottish Rifles and the 1st Battalion under their title of Cameronians.

who were following, were clapped into the guard-room until someone could be found to identify them. Captain Owen, however, was prompt in asserting that " Guillaume was at the bottom of this ! "

Several arrests among civilians were made while the battalion was in the area, which added strength to less well founded rumours.

There was also a rumour during the summer that the war would soon be over. " The mere infantry officer is cynically incredulous, unless some improbable political deal is being negotiated. A more likely rumour is that the 19th Infantry Brigade will soon cease to be Army troops on absorption into a new division." (Dunn.) The latter proved to be true. On the 17th August the brigade marched out of the Fauquissart—Picartin line, shed the supply train, ammunition column,etc., it had possessed as Army troops, and on the 19th marched to Bethune to take the place of the 4th (Guards) Brigade in the 2nd Division. On the road the battalion marched past Lord Kitchener, whose remarks were unusually complimentary ; but he did not know that the surplus baggage and other items that would have detracted from the " turn-out " were sent by another route.

The 2nd Battalion, being in shorts, created a mild sensation among the inhabitants of Bethune. The town was of moderate size, but it had good shops and offered a variety of amusements not obtainable in Laventie and Estaires. As September advanced it became more and more thronged. Men who had not seen or heard of each other for ten or twenty years, living oceans apart, met in its squares, in the barber's, in the Café du Globe, in the Hôtel de France !

On the 1st September our 4th Battalion was posted to the 47th (2nd London) Division, and moved to Les Brebis. They then became a Pioneer Battalion, working under the Royal Engineers.

The 9th Battalion had moved to Neuve Eglise on the 20th August, and companies had been instructed by Suffolk and Manchester battalions in trench warfare : they took over a length of the line south of Festubert on the 30th August.

.   .   .   .

The Battle of Loos was preceded by heated argument. The French reached the high-water mark of man-power in 1915, the British would not develop their full power until 1916. In 1915 the Germans were hotly engaged on their Eastern Front, and had an effective strength of 800,000 rifles on their Western Front, opposing 1,185,000 of the Allied Forces.

The policy of the British Government had been to remain on the defensive on the Western Front until the New Armies were ready in the spring of 1916 ; meanwhile they desired that all men and material that could be spared should be sent to Gallipoli. This policy had practically been accepted by the French Government in June, but they then gave way before the arguments of General Joffre, who had always been opposed to the Gallipoli adventure, and declined to send any more troops to the Mediterranean.

General Joffre had conceived an attack on a grandiose scale. The line between Reims and Arras formed a great salient which was held by the German Seventh, First, and Second Armies ; north of Arras were the Sixth and Fourth Armies ; south of Reims the Third and Fifth Armies. The French and British were to attack the German Sixth Army, and advance in an easterly direction, across the Plain of Douai ; while from the Champagne the French would attack the German Third Army and move in a northerly direction. Both attacks were to strike into the plain behind Douai, the natural converging point of all the main roads and railways which fed the three German Armies in the salient.

For this attack other parts of the line were to be thinned out, men and guns would be massed. After a bombardment lasting four days, which would effectively destroy all wire and trenches, the assaulting divisions would advance, each on a 1,500 yards front, disposed in depth from 3,000 to 4,000 yards. All formations would move forwards simultaneously, the picture presented being a steady stream of men, several miles long, advancing irresistibly, the leading divisions being followed by the reserve divisions and cavalry. All divisions not participating in the attack (that is, on other sectors) were to be ready for a general advance should a break-through be successful.

The argument that had arisen—whether the attack should take place in 1915 or 1916—now shifted its ground. Sir John French had at first agreed that the British Army would attack on the left of the French Tenth Army and south of La Bassée Canal ; but General Haig, having considered the proposal, reported strongly against it—he was definitely of the opinion that the ground selected was unfavourable, and that the chances of success were beyond reasonable hope. He proposed, as an alternative, an attack astride the canal, fixing the defences round the village of Auchy as the key of the strong position held by the enemy

General Joffre, however, maintained that the ground between Loos and La Bassée Canal would be found favourable, and gradually, as the series of disasters to the Allied cause accumulated in other theatres of war, the British Military Authorities abandoned their objections.

Meanwhile, through the latter part of June and July the Germans, apprehensive of the state of their defences on the Western Front, had constructed a strong second line, sited on reverse slopes, strongly wired, and beyond the effective range of field guns.

. . . .

The general orders to the British Armies were that the First Army, under General Haig, should conduct the battle ; the Second Army was to hold the enemy between Armentières and Ypres, and attack the enemy line north and south of Bellewaarde Lake [1] with the 3rd and 14th Divisions under General Allenby ; the Third Army, of nine divisions, which had taken over the line in the Somme area, south of the French Tenth Army, was to support the French attack with its artillery and be prepared to advance should the attack be successful.

In his own hand, disposed behind the First Army, Sir John French held the Cavalry Corps and the XI Corps, consisting of the Guards Division and two New Army divisions, the 21st and 24th.

At the commencement of the battle the German forces opposing General Haig's First Army were, south of La Bassée Canal, the 117th Division (22nd Reserve, 157th, and 11th Reserve Regiments), and the 16th Regiment and 11th Jäger Battalion of the 14th Division ; the other two regiments of the 14th Division, the 56th and 57th, were north of the canal, with the 2nd Guard Reserve Division on their right.   The organisation of the regimental area placed one battalion in the front line, one in support, and one in reserve, about five miles behind the line.

The general reserves of the German Sixth Army, three divisions, were at Lille and Valenciennes ; but there were at hand, as immediate reserves, part of the 2nd Guard Reserve Division and the 8th Division on the flanks of the British attack.

The total strength of the British Expeditionary Force on the 24th August 1915 is given as slightly over 850,000, but these figures are always misleading : an estimate of " effectives " gives 250,000, or slightly more than two-thirds, employed on services out of the fighting line.

Sir John French had received the last possible Regular division on the 15th January,[2] but created the Guards Division in August, which gave him eleven Regular divisions.   Territorial battalions commenced to arrive in France in 1914, and were still, for the most part, posted as 5th battalions to Regular brigades.   Territorial divisions commenced to arrive in February,

---

[1] There were other minor diversions along the Second Army front.

[2] The first eight divisions were Regular divisions, the 8th arriving in France on the 5th November 1914 ; then followed the 27th on the 13th December 1914, and the 28th on the 15th January 1915 ; the remaining Regular division, the 29th, was at this date in Gallipoli, and did not arrive in France until the 20th March 1916.

the first being the 46th ; followed by the 47th, 48th, 49th, 50th, and, on the 30th April, the 51st. The New Army divisions commenced to arrive in May, and on the 25th September there were fifteen in France.

The growth in number of divisions meant growth in artillery strength, and the shell question was now well on the road to settlement. In the Loos despatch the Commander-in-Chief says : " Our enemy may have hoped, not perhaps without reason, that it would be impossible for us, starting from such small beginnings, to build up an efficient artillery to provide for the very large expansion of the Army. If he entertained such hopes, he has now good reason to know that they have not been justified by the result. The efficiency of the artillery of the New Armies has exceeded all expectations, and during the period under review excellent services have been rendered by the Territorial Army." Associated with this excellence was an encouraging increase in the number of heavy guns.

Briefly, although he had taken over a new sector with his Third Army in the Somme area, Sir John was able to assemble 70,000 men to attack some 10,000 Germans ; also 35 siege and heavy artillery pieces, 36 long-range guns, and massed divisional artillery amounting to 498 pieces. This on the I and IV Corps front, which was about double the amount possessed by the Germans on their corresponding front.

ʹ The field of the main attack was a coal-mining district, dotted with slag-heaps and the gigantic machinery of the industry. The main features of the battlefield were Hill 70 on the right, behind the village of Loos ; on the left Fosse 8, a coal-pit, on which was based the Hohenzollern Redoubt, a strong enemy system, jutting out from their main line and having, slightly south of it, the Quarries, behind which lay the mining village of Cité St. Elie—all strongly entrenched and wired.

The distance across No Man's Land varied between 100 and 500 yards.

It was a bare and open country that created an unfavourable impression, but at General Headquarters a change of view seems to have occurred with the decision to use gas. It is lightly touched upon by the Commander-in-Chief in his despatch : " Owing to the repeated use by the enemy of asphyxiating gases in their attacks on our positions, I have been compelled to resort to similar methods ; and a detachment was organised for this purpose, which took part in the operations commencing on the 25th September for the first time. Although the enemy was known to have been prepared for such reprisals, our gas attack met with marked success, and produced a demoralising effect on some of the opposing units, of which ample evidence was forthcoming in the captured trenches."

Many thousands of cylinders were despatched to France—on the I Corps front 2,500 were used alone—and after a demonstration in a back area the possibility of breaking through the two enemy systems of defence was firmly believed in : the first despondency had completely evaporated.

So we get, then, in the First Army area, a picture of industry and much movement stretching back miles behind the line. The storing of ammunition and the work it entailed may be gathered from the allotment, for the last hour before the assault, of 100 rounds per field gun and 60 rounds per howitzer (4·5-inch, 5-inch, and 6-inch) ; the gas required 8,000 men to carry it to the trenches ; on one corps front it was estimated that over 600 miles of telephone wire had been laid ; and then there were small-arm ammunition, hand-grenades, smoke-candles, ladders for climbing out of trenches, bridges for placing across trenches, wire, shovels and picks, a whole list of articles described as battle stores ; and finally the assembly of units, in billets, ready to move forward in the successive lines which were to break a road through the German defence and end the war.

These " set-piece " battles were progressive in size, and each time they occurred they created, naturally enough, a lot of preliminary excitement behind our lines. Troops of the six attacking divisions were informed that their objective was Douai. It was known that the XI Corps, consisting of the Guards Division and the 21st and 24th Divisions of the New Army, was held in reserve to give the final " push " which would allow the British Cavalry Corps (assembled round St. Pol) and the Indian Cavalry Corps (assembled at Doullens) and a large force of French cavalry to ride through and behind the enemy lines. It was spoken of as the greatest battle in history.

On the 5th August the 1st Battalion went into the line in front of Vermelles ; and on the 24th the 2nd Battalion to Givenchy and alternately to Cambrin. South of the canal the trenches had been made by the French, and were deep and narrow ; the communication trenches still retained the French name *boyeaux*, and were mostly wired, fire-stepped, and traversed to form in need a defensive flank.

The Cambrin, Cuinchy, and Givenchy sectors were interesting parts of the line, on either side of the canal—the latter on the north bank.

The brickstacks on the Railway Triangle and Canal Embankment of the Cuinchy sector were celebrated for unpleasantness. The company commander holding the line lived in a sandbagged culvert in the embankment, and learned to be vigilant. His right platoon occupied the Bluff, from which the ground fell to a small marshy area, impassable in wet weather—defended by an earthwork keep, the Cabbage Patch—and rose again to the brickstacks. The latter were mostly in the enemy's hands and were adapted for observation posts, machine-gun, or snipers' posts ; the stacks were perfect cover, but flying fragments of brick frequently wounded men in the open.

The Givenchy sector had a dry trench system running northwards to the Warren, which ended in the Duck's Bill, when the ground fell sharply and a breastwork re-entrant ran westwards in a sweep in front of La Plante and then north to Festubert.

The line, having been pushed on to the ridge, gave opportunities for underground warfare, and mining was actively carried on ; the ridge was pitted with craters. Frequent minor changes took place in the front line as new-blown craters were connected up by saps. At one point the British and German lines were only 25 yards apart.

Some 1,100 yards behind the front line was Harley Street, running north from the Bethune Road ; it crossed the canal at Pont Fixe and continued to Windy Corner, the northern limit of the divisional area. In the ruins of this one-time single-street village the two support battalions were housed with the R.E. workshops and the Advance Dressing Station. One familiar ruin was the Bath House : in 1915 the number of tubs became too small, but some coffins were found in an abandoned workshop and these, when puttied, made excellent baths. Each night the street was thronged with working parties, reliefs, runners, vehicles ; and the nearest guns were in the orchards bordering it. Until mid-September a few civilians remained, who lived by ministering to the creature comforts of the troops.

From Cuinchy the rattle and clatter of the enemy limbers on the *pavé* road, bringing up rations at dusk, was plainly audible. The artillery on both sides respected the enemy's ration limbers.

Our 4th Battalion, in their new rôle of pioneers, did not have too easy a time in all the battle preparation. Lieutenant Picton Davies, recovered from the wound he had received early in the year, returned to France and was posted to the 4th. " I travelled up with Lieutenant-Colonel Pereira, of the Grenadiers, who had been appointed commanding officer. When we arrived, the battalion was doing ordinary trench duty at Vermelles —four days in and four days out. The battalion had been badly cut up at Festubert and never made up to strength since. The N.C.O.s were good fellows but inexperienced. Once the C.O. had sized up his command, he obtained a Guardsman as Regimental Sergeant-Major, whose arrival was resented at first by the men, but whose tact and the efficiency he introduced were soon recognised and appreciated.

" On 25th August we moved to the Cambrin area.

" On 2nd September I was posted to B Company as company commander, and as such I remained during the sixteen months of my service with the battalion.   This same day the battalion was warned that it would be transferred to the 47th Division.   It had been found that the Londoners could not dig, and to a few of us it was confided that gas was to be installed in their front line, which would entail much preparatory trench digging, etc.   At night we were told that we were to become a Pioneer Battalion, whereupon the C.O. exclaimed, ' Good God !   We shall have to dig latrines for the rest of the war ! '

" From the 3rd to the 9th September we dug nightly, making assembly trenches behind the front line.   On the night of the 16th three new trenches were begun in front of the front line—to be called W1, W2, and W3.

" W2 and W1 were to accommodate the first and second waves respectively in the coming attack.

" W3 was the trench to contain the gas cylinders.

" All these three trenches were begun simultaneously and they were got down two feet the first night, in spite of discovery and interruption by the enemy.   I thought my company lucky to have only twelve casualties. Three nights' work sufficed to complete the system of trenches.   The   work   was done behind infantry covering parties, who lay out in shell-holes some way in front of the work.

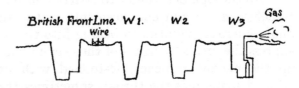

" W1 was a mere shelter trench, but W2 was fire-stepped.

" W3 had to be of special construction to shelter the cylinders of gas from shell splinters, and to conceal them from air observation.   The method used was an overhanging parapet supported by special revetment.   A fire-step was made on the rear wall of the trench for the use of the garrison who were to protect and release the gas.

" Duck-boards were laid along each of the trenches, which were to be available and in position as bridges over which the assaulting troops would cross the trenches at zero.   All these trenches had to be connected up by communication trenches, and furnished with the usual annexes of a trench.

" In order to assist the assault, once it was launched, advanced machine-gun and trench-mortar emplacements were made, and shell-holes close to the German wire were adapted, and to conceal the existence of new work all the soil excavated had to be taken back in sandbags for disposal.

" All this preparatory work was practically completed by the 18th September.

" On the 19th the gas cylinders were brought up. So far only the officers were supposed to know of the intended use of gas ; men remarking on the unusual form of W3 were told that it was to provide additional shelter from shell fire. This night an enemy patrol came right over, but it was believed that every man was scuppered.

" The men were then instructed in the method of working the gas cylinders, in what to do in case they became casualties, or in the case of a direct hit on one of the cylinders both prior to and during that attack.

" By the 20th everything was ready. The cylinders were all in position. The long, double, rectangular nozzles that were to discharge the gas clear of the parapet were ready to be joined up. W3 was manned by us, and the front was strongly patrolled by night. For nearly three weeks prior to this all our work had been done at night ; by day we slept and rested in the cellars of Les Brebis."

All through September the battalions not in the front line dug assembly trenches, made gun emplacements in the support line, carried up stores, and numerous cylinders to be dug into the front line—no vocabulary could express the men's thoughts of those cylinders as they struggled and sweated up the narrow trenches, festooned with detached telephone wires that gripped sometimes the throat, sometimes the feet.

Patrols were active, too. Lieutenant H. M. Blair, of the 2nd Battalion, went out a few days before the battle, on the Cambrin front. " Samson, who was always relieved to know that anyone in his command these days was not married, sent me with a corporal and a bomber to examine the German wire. We started at 9.30 p.m. We were in shorts, so I soon felt I was well over the age limit for patrolling by night in bare knees. I was a subaltern, but the C.O. was the only officer older than I.

" We had been out a long time and I was straddling a disused German trench when a flare fell close to us ; in that posture—even to holding my breath—I stood fast till the flare burned itself out. Beyond the trench were patches of standing corn, which made progress easier. Suddenly we came out of the corn, with the moon at its brightest shining on us and on a party of Germans working on their parapet, and there were only thirty unpleasant yards of burned grass between ! Unseen by the Germans we lay low, hoping they would go to bed and let us get on. We had been out for 2½ hours already. Next day I discovered that we had strayed from our course and were well inside the re-entrant in the German line. As the Germans did not go we started a snail crawl—myself, then the bomber, then the corporal—at a yard a minute. Arriving at their wire, I signed to the bomber to stop while I crawled in and tested it. The Germans were busy and not throwing flares ; the officer or N.C.O. in charge was quite near me, standing in a gap smoking.

" Rejoining my men, we crawled back at the same breakneck speed to the friendly cover of the corn—it was an hour since we left it, an hour of strain, so we sat down for a breather before making for home. Nearing our wire, I changed places with the corporal—he was leading and I was in rear—for I wanted to warn the listening post, who might not be expecting us after nearly six hours' absence. Not a minute after our change of places two shots were fired from the post. The corporal was hit in the chest and stomach and died, poor fellow, soon after being carried into the trench.

" The sentry told me he had been warned that two only had gone on patrol ; spotting a third man, he inferred that we were being stalked and fired. It was a tragic mischance that the two snap shots at 40 yards, fired by moonlight at a crawling figure, took effect."

New batteries kept coming in and " registering." There was little secrecy in the arrival of guns and no concealment of their emplacements. Observation balloons were up through the day, and there was more aerial activity than had yet been seen. Day after day of fine weather passed with accompanying wonder at the delay in attacking.

Early in the morning of the 21st the artillery opened fire in a way there was no mistaking. At the time the bombardment was impressive. The enemy made little reply, and that on back areas ; our casualties were scarcely more than normal. While the British artillery was active, the men could lean their arms on the parapet and watch the shoot ; but during pauses in the fire a few enemy machine guns would sometimes traverse the parapets.

On the 23rd there was rain after 7 a.m., and thunder, and more rain later ; the roads and trenches that had been clean so long became muddy and slippery.

On the 24th September our 1st Battalion was at La Bourse, in billets ; the 4th was looking after smoke-candles and gas, three parties of 80, 54, and 59 men, under Lieutenants P. R. Foulkes-Roberts, H. G. Picton Davies, and C. O. Davies, having been detailed for this duty with the 47th Division on the extreme right of the attacking line ; the 9th Battalion was at Festubert, between what was known as Barton Road and Fife Road ; the 2nd Battalion was in billets at Bethune.

Between dusk and dawn important decisions had to be taken. All faith in success had been placed on the gas attack, but the gas attack depended on the wind. The bombardment of the enemy positions had been going on for four days, and it would have been easy to continue it and wait, if necessary, for a favourable breeze ; but such a decision would have had a disastrous effect on the French double attack—that of the Tenth Army on the right, and the greater attack in the Champagne. Without gas the artillery was thought insufficient to support the attack of six divisions, and an alternative plan had been prepared : only two divisions would attack, the 9th assaulting the Hohenzollern Redoubt, and the 15th a limited objective about Loos no deeper than the first-line system of defence.

At 9.45 p.m. on the 24th the weather forecast was considered favourable, and a message to the effect that the gas discharge would take place was sent out. By that time a great movement had started : the assaulting brigades of the six divisions were marching up to relieve the front-line troops, and the movement stretched away back into the distant assembly areas of the XI Corps, the three divisions of which spent the night marching forward to within six miles of the front line.

About 5 o'clock in the morning the breeze veered to the south—it was a faint, puffy, baffling breath of air—and at 5.25 a.m. General Haig attempted to stop the discharge of gas : it was then too late to get the order to the front line. At 5.50 the intense, last-hour bombardment was opened on the German trenches and the gas liberated.

" With the approach of zero hour on the 25th September we were ready. The nozzles had been screwed on to the cylinders, and we were standing by in our gas-masks. At 5.30 a.m. the gas was released. It was the first time gas had been used by the British. On the front of our division the wind was in the right direction and the right strength—the gas went over well. When the cylinders were exhausted, a smoke screen was put down, the trenches were bridged over with duck-boards, and the infantry, wearing their gas-masks, went over at 6.30 a.m.

" The 4th Battalion had played its part, and we moved back to the railway cutting. My company had thirty casualties, for as soon as the gas began to drift over, the German guns opened on the trench. We collected and sent back the casualties. We all felt sick as a result of the fumes, and nearly all of us were sick." (Picton Davies.)

Following events from the right, the 47th Division, advancing forty minutes after the gas discharge, found the wire well cut ; they formed a flank to the south of Loos. Next to them the gallant 15th Division of the New Army (Second Hundred Thousand) went over Hill 70 as far as Cité St. Auguste, but they swerved off their line of advance to the right. On their left the battle began to go wrong with the right brigade of the 1st

Division, which was checked by wire and a stout defence ; the left Brigade of the 1st Division pushed through the village of Hulluch with its right flank in the air.   Everywhere, excepting the right of the line, the gas went wrong, hindering the advance of the troops and causing no damage to the enemy.   Casualties were extremely heavy, and opportunities which were undoubtedly opened up by the rush of the gallant Scots (15th Division) drifted away—the picture of a stream of men, always advancing in successive lines, remained a dream.

In the I Corps area, the 7th Division were on the right and were to capture the Quarries ; while the 9th Division (First Hundred Thousand) were responsible for Fosse 8 and the Hohenzollern Redoubt.

The I Corps had to attack over a hard, featureless country.   There was Fosse 8, with its slag-heap, and to the left of it many cottages and buildings which practically joined on to the village of Auchy.   The corps was to press on to the Haute-Deule Canal, with the 2nd Division forming a defensive flank on its left.   But it had always been recognised that Auchy would be a hard nut to crack, and that above all other places its capture was dependent on the successful discharge of gas.   Should the 2nd Division fail to capture Auchy, the 9th Division was to form a protecting flank and the 7th Division advance on the canal.

The attack of the 7th Division on a frontage of 1,400 yards was made by the 20th Brigade on the right and the 22nd Brigade on the left.   The general scheme was a simultaneous advance from five successive lines of assembly trenches, some eighty yards apart ; and the artillery, in two groups—the 22nd Field Artillery Brigade supporting the 20th Infantry Brigade, and the 35th Field Artillery and 14th Horse Artillery Brigades, with two batteries of the 56th Field Artillery Brigade, supporting the 22nd Infantry Brigade—were to follow the advance of the attacking battalions.[1]

The German defences were unusually strong, with strong-points at intervals in the front line.   They were, however, lightly held by two companies of the 11th Reserve Infantry Regiment in the front line, a company in the Quarries and another at Cité St. Elie.   Only two German regiments (the 11th Reserve Infantry Regiment and the 16th Infantry Regiment) and the 11th Jäger Battalion opposed the advance of the I Corps.

The 22nd Brigade attacked with the 1st South Staffordshire and 2nd Royal Warwickshire leading, our 1st Battalion in support, and the 2nd Queen's in reserve.

.   .   .   .

---

[1] The 37th Brigade (Howitzers), less one battery, and the 57th Field Artillery Brigade were in Divisional Reserve.

On the 22nd September our 1st Battalion had marched from Gonnehem to La Bourse. The next day Lieutenant-Colonel Berners was ordered to Corps Headquarters as Reserve Brigadier, and Captain E. R. Kearsley took command of the battalion. On the 24th the battalion paraded at 10.45 p.m., and to the tune of the terrific bombardment, as they then thought, marched through the night to Vermelles, and so to their battle position at Clerk's Post, arriving at 2.30 a.m.

The instructions issued were that the attack was not planned to capture any particular locality, but to break down the enemy's defensive system and " shake free from the present indecisive trench warfare." Four objectives were given : the enemy's first-line trenches ; the Quarries ; Cité St. Elie ; the Haute-Deule Canal crossings at Wingles and Meurchin with the high ground east of it.

The South Staffordshire would attack on the right, the Royal Warwickshire on the left. Our 1st Battalion was drawn up in rear and would move forward to the trenches occupied by the Warwickshire as soon as they were vacated by the assaulting troops.

When the leading troops reached the German first-line trenches, the battalion would advance in support and also cover the left flank of the brigade. On gaining the enemy's first line, the battalion was to swing half right.

It was raining hard when the artillery commenced rapid fire and the selected parties in the front trench opened the gas cylinders, alternating gas with smoke from Roman candles.

At 6.30 a.m. the leading brigades of the division advanced, climbing up their ladders over the parapet. The 20th Brigade, on the right, were in the middle of the gas cloud with their flannel-bag masks adjusted. These masks, or smoke-helmets, kept out the gas and also the air. Suffocated, the men had to remove them to breathe, and although they advanced rapidly, many were gassed. They had 350 yards to cross before reaching the German line, and the German artillery, having had plenty of time to note the gas and smoke cloud, was bursting shrapnel in the midst of it. Casualties were heavy. The wire had been cut in gaps and men had to crowd to the gaps to get through, which gave the enemy further opportunities of inflicting heavy loss. But as soon as the trench was entered, the enemy surrendered. The remnants of the attacking battalions, reinforced by their supports, then moved forward, captured a German battery, and reached the Lens road, about the Vermelles—Hulluch cross-roads. They were unable to go any farther.

The 22nd Brigade had 500 yards of No Man's Land to cross. The gas cloud hung thick round their trenches, and their experience was similar to that of the 20th Brigade.   However, the Staffordshire and Warwickshire rushed through the smoke and gas and found themselves in the middle of No Man's Land, in full view of the German position.   They also found that the wire had hardly been damaged, and had actually to scramble over and through it.   The trenches also were in excellent condition after the four days' bombardment, and although the enemy were numerically weak the losses they were able to inflict while the attackers were entangled in the wire may be imagined.

While this was going on, the 26th Brigade of the 9th Division was attacking the Hohenzollern Redoubt on the left.   This was a mighty work to which the Germans attached much importance.   The slag-heap of Fosse 8 was behind it, tunnelled for observation and machine guns, and the Redoubt, well dug and strongly wired, had been made on a sort of " hump " in the ground in front of the Fosse, and connected up with the main line by the Big Willie Trench and Little Willie Trench.   This work was to be assaulted whether the plan of attack with gas or the alternative of two separate attacks by the 9th and 15th Divisions was executed ; consequently there had been special artillery preparation, and the assault of the 26th Brigade was quite successful, but it took time, and the assaulting troops had not worked their way down the north and south faces to the main line.

Our 1st Battalion had moved at 6.30 into the trenches vacated by the Warwickshire, and a quarter of an hour later went " over the top."   The leading battalions were not yet through the wire.   Our battalion, with A and B Companies leading, D and C in support 100 yards in rear, advanced over the 500 yards of No Man's Land and were met by terrific machine-gun fire, from the direction of the Hohenzollern Redoubt, from Big Willie and the slag-heap.   The Commanding Officer, Captain Kearsley, seeing what was happening, ran forward from the supporting line, and managed to swing some of the troops round to deal with this fire ; advancing then with the leading companies, he was badly wounded as they entered the German front line.

What happened is not clear.   Officer casualties were heavy, and the three battalions, Warwickshire, South Staffordshire, and Royal Welch Fusiliers, were intermingled.   No one knew who had been hit and who survived.   The advance was delayed by fire from a strong-point on the right, dealt with eventually by the 20th Brigade.   But at 8.30 a.m. the Queen's arrived from reserve, and the advance then swept forward over the Quarries to the defences of Cité St. Elie.   Here the brigade was held by machine-gun fire, and found that the trenches before the village, and a wide belt of strong wire, had been untouched by the bombardment.   What remained of the brigade fell back to the Quarries and consolidated that position.

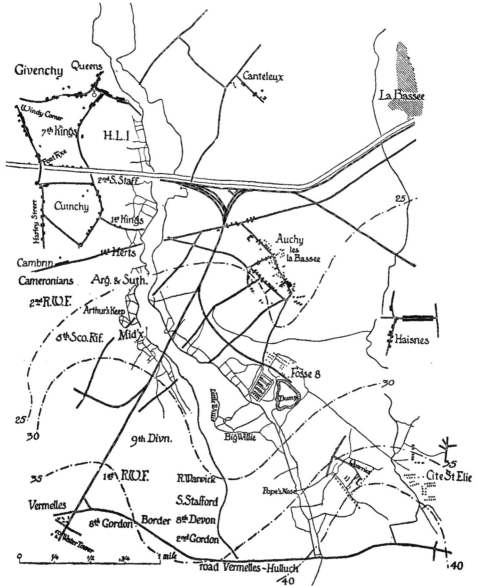

Lieutenant W. B. Reeves found himself in command of the battalion. Meanwhile the 21st Brigade had been sent forward (five battalions) to support the 20th and 22nd and carry on the advance.   The left half-brigade, 2nd Green Howards and 1/4th Camerons, arrived at the Quarries, and an officer patrol confirmed the report on the defences of Cité St. Elie. A further bombardment was ordered but did no harm to these defences, and at 7.30 p.m. orders were received to consolidate the positions won.

The situation of the 7th Division then was that the 20th Brigade held the Vermelles—Hulluch and Lens—La Bassée cross-roads ; the 21st Brigade from the Vermelles—Hulluch road to the southern edge of the Quarries ; the 22nd Brigade the east and north edges of the Quarries. Two brigades of artillery had moved up to within 1,500 yards of the captured positions.

.   .   .   .

Auchy was on the front of the 2nd Division. " The attacks," says Sir John French, " . . . were successful all along the line, except just south of La Bassée Canal." The 2nd Division attacked, on the immediate left of the 9th Division, with all three brigades, two south of the canal, on the Cambrin and Cuinchy sectors, one north, on the Festubert sector.

Only two German battalions held the front opposite the 2nd Division, the width of No Man's Land between them and the 2nd Division being on an average 100 yards. But they, no doubt realising that there were still mines below them (two were to be sprung in preparation for the attack), abandoned their front line, after levelling the parapet, and manned their support trench, which was only 100 yards behind.

The attack of the 19th Brigade, on the right, was led by the 1st Middlesex and the 2nd Argyll and Sutherland Highlanders ; our 2nd Battalion were in support. The picture presented to them by the plan of battle was a short intensive artillery bombardment during which the gas was to be released, making all the Germans casualties. The leading battalions would then stroll across to the enemy lines and proceed to occupy an orchard about 1,000 yards distant. The final objective was, however, the other side of Auchy.

Of the preliminary bombardment Captain Owen (Adjutant) says : " Our artillery fire was at the time considered to be heavy, but was nothing in comparison to what we became accustomed to later. The enemy's retaliation was slight, and it was quite easy to observe the effect of our fire without much risk. On the night of the 23rd the 1st Battalion Middlesex Regiment took over our trenches, and we moved back to Bethune, where we remained until the next night, when we moved to the assembly trenches in front of Cambrin."

Disaster on this front was easy to predict. The wind, though but a faint breeze, was distinctly against the assaulting troops, and one engineer officer refused to take the responsibility of turning on the gas ; he received, however, a direct order to carry out the programme, which seems an unnecessarily stringent devotion to discipline.[1] The gas left the parapet to the extent of its compressed force in the cylinders, and then blew gently back into the faces of the assaulting troops. In some places it was turned off, in others the cylinders were apparently allowed to empty themselves. Many were gassed.

The Middlesex and the Highlanders climbed over the parapet and stepped out of the cloud of gas and smoke.

Every German, warned by the gas cloud, was standing in his place—there had even been time to light straw fires to disseminate the cloud should it, by chance, blow towards them—and was ready to fire. Undeterred, the troops advanced, but had to bunch to get round the craters. Then the storm broke loose. The assaulting troops fell in heaps. Still, a few managed to reach the wire, which was uncut, of the original German front line.

While the leading battalions were being shattered, the supporting companies knew nothing of what was going on as they moved forward in the deep, narrow trenches to occupy the vacated front line.

Captain Freeman led B Company, and with him were Moody, his only subaltern, and Company Sergeant-Major Pattison, and a few bombers. They had gone only a little distance when the trenches were found blocked with debris, wounded, runners, and stretcher bearers. Arriving at what was thought to be the front line, and was found to be the support, Freeman discovered that only twenty of his men had got through the jamb and kept up with him. As he was due in the front line in twenty minutes, he sent Moody and Company Sergeant-Major Pattison over the top to find and bring up the rest of the company. Just as these two returned to report their failure, Lieutenant-Colonel Williams ran forward with a wound over his eye, from which the blood streamed down his face ; he was very concerned, as he had seen that the attack was failing, so he ordered the troops in the vicinity to advance over the top at once.

At that moment Freeman collapsed—it was found later that he died of heart failure—and Moody led the party forward. Six had become casualties by the time the front line was reached, most of the party thinking, in the confusion and excitement, that it was the German line.

The scene in front was indescribable. The ground was strewn with dead and wounded, thick near the parapet, thinning beyond. Many of the wounded were crawling back through the grass. The gas was still drifting

[1] The Brigadier asked to have the gas order cancelled on the 19th Brigade front, but was informed he was " too late."

up from the right and rising from the cylinders in our trenches to come back over our line.

Moody again made search for the main body of his company, and having found it, reported to Headquarters for orders. Lieutenant-Colonel Williams and Major Clegg-Hill had both been hit, and the Adjutant, Captain Owen, was in command. In lurid and characteristic fashion he told Moody to advance.

Moody got his company into line and went forward. Half the company fell in the first thirty yards. As there was no prospect of the remaining 200 yards being covered by any but those born to be hanged, the remainder dropped in their tracks and stayed where they were.

At 9 a.m. a runner was given a message requesting orders from Headquarters, and failing to return, another was dispatched at 10.30 a.m. B Company then received orders to stand fast and take part in a renewed attack which would be launched at 11 a.m.—the appearance above the parapet of the bayonets of the attacking troops would inform them when to move !

At 4 p.m. Moody, tired of watching for bayonets, crawled back to the trench " like an earthworm," and sought fresh orders. He was greeted at Headquarters by Captain C. S. Owen with, " Hullo ! I thought you were dead ! "—and told to bring his company back.

B Company crawled back to the trench in ones and twos, under cover of the long grass.

The experience of C Company was similar. Captain Samson was mortally wounded just outside the front-line wire.

" I saw no shells bursting over the German trenches, so, the morning being bright and sunny, the German riflemen and machine gunners took their toll of us undisturbed. We may have gone 40 yards, and then the line just fell down. Samson was killed ; Goldsmith and I were badly wounded ; the casualties among the men were heavy. I was out of the picture with a fractured pelvis. A less wounded man near me wanted to carry me in, but I told him we would both be shot ; however, he started to get up and was wounded again immediately. I crawled back slowly, and was laid in the bottom of the trench, where I was nearly suffocated with gas before the Doctor came and had me moved to a narrow communication trench. I lay there for five hours. No stretcher could be used, even if one had been available. Eventually I was carried down slung on my putties between two rifles. It was an exceedingly painful journey. Once clear of the trench the medical arrangements were very good." (Blair.)

In both companies casualties were increased by men attempting to get their wounded comrades back to the trench.

" It was considered hopeless to send any more troops forward. The attack, as far as it concerned our front, was stopped. Many of our own men were gassed. I was in the front line and got a really good stomachful, and my head was splitting for forty-eight hours after it." (C. S. Owen.)

" Some 600 wounded of the 19th Brigade passed through my hands in an improvised dressing-station 1,000 to 1,100 yards behind the front, also about 300 gas and ' wind-up ' cases, during the thirty-six hours after zero." (J. C. Dunn, Medical Officer.)

The 9th Battalion fared no better in the attack about Festubert. They advanced in line with the 9th Welch, but again the gas blew back and the wire was uncut. Lieutenant-Colonel Madocks, watching the advance of his battalion from the parapet, was killed at once. The men could do nothing.

So far as the regiment was concerned, the attack of the 1st Battalion only was successful, they having reached the outskirts of Cité St. Elie. After-comments state : " With both flanks in the air, as usual, and a strongly entrenched and wired enemy in front of us, what could we do but fall back ? There were no reinforcements ! "

Errors of judgment abound in military history, and sometimes appear incredible : one cannot assume the mentality and enter the atmosphere of the moment. The first conception of this battle seems clear, the picture of successive lines of troops advancing, a simultaneous advance of front and rear units ; but there was a misunderstanding between Sir John French and General Haig. General Haig understood that he was to have the XI Corps, and only discovered shortly before the battle that Sir John intended to keep the corps under his own hand. Different ideas prevailed in the minds of the Commander-in-Chief and the First Army Commander as to the nature of the battle. Sir John, apparently, never believed a break-through possible. General Haig had based his plans on that possibility, and expected the XI Corps to be close up in rear of the attacking divisions and advance with them. With difficulty he persuaded Sir John to move the corps within six miles of the battle-front, and divisions marched all night (24th/25th) through pouring rain to get there ; but they were not handed over to him until late in the morning of the 25th, and the difficulties of getting into position were such that they could not be used that day.[1]

[1] The question of wisdom in using inexperienced divisions can never be argued satisfactorily, as the 9th and 15th fought with the greatest gallantry and determination, and there is no reason why the 21st and 24th should not have done likewise. The Commander-in-Chief was in favour of using these new formations by brigades, even by battalions.

LIEUTENANT-COLONEL H. J. MADOCKS.

So the 24th Division, which might have supported the assault of the I Corps, and given the necessary impetus to secure Haisnes and Cité St. Elie, was not available.

The confusion behind the battle-front was indescribable. The question of the reserve had been settled about midday, and First Army Orders had been issued to drive the attack through the German second line (which was believed to have been pierced), but the 73rd Brigade, the leading brigade of the 24th Division, did not reach its allotted place in Fosse Trench till past midnight.

The enemy had tottered, but the moment was lost. The German 117th Division, reinforced by the 26th Reserve Infantry Brigade of the 2nd Guard Reserve Division, was ordered to attack in the north on a front Fosse 8—the Quarries—Gun Trench. They delivered this attack about midnight, with the guns at Auchy taking the 9th Division in flank.

The remnants of the 22nd Brigade—one cannot now distinguish battalions—held the greater part of the Quarries, but touch had never been gained with the troops of the 9th Division on the left. The latter were about 500 yards to the left front of the 22nd Brigade, and the German attack found this gap, and turned the flanks of the 22nd and 27th Brigades. It was impossible to retrieve such a situation, in the middle of the night, with shattered battalions and few officers. The whole of the 22nd Brigade fell back and rallied in the original German front-line trench, 1,000 yards in rear. The Brigade Commander of the 27th Brigade, who had moved his headquarters into the Quarries, was captured. It was, there is no doubt, a scramble.

Our 1st Battalion remained in the German first line through the 26th, and moved into the old British first line on the 27th ; the next day they went back to Sailly la Bourse, and on the 1st October into the line again at Cambrin.

.   .   .   .

The casualties [1] of the 1st Battalion were : killed, Lieutenant G. W. S. Morgan and 43 other ranks ; wounded, Captains E. R. Kearsley, R. M. J. French, Lieutenants J. M. J. Evans, A. Walmsley, S. Williams, E. I. Jones, F. Jones-Bateman, W. I. James, H. J. F. Brunt, 2nd Lieutenants H. E. Farmer, H. J. Brett, and 264 other ranks ; missing, 135 other ranks.

Of the 2nd Battalion : Captains A. L. Samson, J. A. C. Childe-Freeman,

---

[1] Three divisional commanders were killed at Loos. With deep regret the 1st Battalion heard that Major-General Sir Thompson Capper died on the 27th from wounds received the previous day. Major-General Thessiger (9th Division) and Major-General Wing (12th Division) shared his fate.

G. O. Thomas, and 34 other ranks killed ; Lieutenant-Colonel O. de L. Williams, Captains C. R. Clegg-Hill, P. B. Welton, Lieutenant H. M. Blair, 2nd Lieutenant H. E. G. Goldsmith, and 71 other ranks wounded.

Of the 9th Battalion : Lieutenant-Colonel H. J. Madocks, Captains C. A. Acton, E. G. Payne, L. S. Hogg (Adjutant), B. W. E. Hoyle, Lieutenant C. F. J. Symons, 2nd Lieutenants R. J. Williams, and 24 other ranks killed ; Lieutenants H. J. Williams, G. H. Charlton, 2nd Lieutenants R. H. Higham, C. Y. Fawcett, and 129 other ranks wounded ; 85 other ranks missing.

.   .   .   .

All efforts to improve on the situation created by the first assault failed. The 21st Division on the right (IV Corps) and the 24th on the left (I Corps), having gone into battle without food or rest during the previous thirty-six hours, were called upon to attack, sustained heavy casualties, and eventually broke, retiring from the right and centre of the battlefield. The Guards Division was then sent forward but did no good, for the redoubt over the crest of Hill 70 was not taken, and Hugo Wood remained in the hands of the enemy. The enemy also retook Fosse 8 and practically the whole of the Hohenzollern Redoubt ; at the latter the fighting developed into bombing attacks.

Gas was tried a second time, at the Hohenzollern Redoubt, where, although the wind was in the right quarter, it was a failure ; and on the 2nd Division front. " On the 26th and 27th," says Captain Owen, " a continual bombardment was kept up on both sides, and at 5 p.m. on the 27th the 2nd Battalion was ordered to attack the enemy's position. Gas was to be again released prior to the attack. Brigade Headquarters rang up and ordered very careful observation to be made of the effect of our gas on the enemy. It was found that the enemy was very little affected and were holding their line in strength as if expecting an attack. On Brigade Headquarters being informed of this, the attack was stopped just in time to save many casualties."

There remained then nothing—the village and valley of Loos, the reverse slopes of Hill 70.

In the 19th Infantry Brigade the feeling was that the High Command had made a mess of things, and denunciation of " the cavalry Generals " who monopolised these commands was bitter.

The Battles of 1915.

The battles in which the regiment took part in 1915 were a failure. On each occasion, at Neuve Chapelle, Aubers Ridge, Festubert, and Loos, the enemy had been greatly inferior in numbers, and the promise of success seemed assured ; but the experience of the regiment in 1914, when, greatly outnumbered, battalions had repulsed or arrested advancing hordes of Germans, was repeated in 1915, when they, in turn, attacked a numerically weak but brave and determined foe.   Obviously attack demanded a greater sacrifice than defence, and good German troops on the defensive might be expected to do as well as British, but, apart from quantities, there was a great contrast in the idea of armaments : at the time of Neuve Chapelle and Festubert shrapnel was still considered by the Army authorities to be effective for wire-cutting and general use against trenches ; it seems that the importance of flattening trenches as well as wire had not been sufficiently considered.   On the other hand, the Germans had been, from the first, strong advocates of high-explosive shells which would actually destroy trenches and the infantry in them—as the regiment knew from 1914 experience.   The conditions of attack were, therefore, not equal on both sides.   Although gaps may have been cut by British shrapnel in the enemy wire, the German machine gunner remained in the shelter of his trench with his fire power unimpaired ; whereas the British, always, by unaccountable short-sightedness, inferior in machine guns, had to resist attack by rifle power alone and in vulnerable trenches.

In spite of the poor artillery support, there had been a great opportunity at Neuve Chapelle.   Opinion, within the regiment, was freely expressed at the time that it had been thrown away by faulty command : it was justified.

Festubert was the sudden change in plan of Aubers Ridge, and does not appear to have offered the same promise of success as Neuve Chapelle. But these two battles impressed on the enemy the immediate necessity for a strong second line ; and so at Loos, although some cause of our earlier failure had been met by increased artillery and high-explosive ammunition, the task of our infantry was infinitely greater, as was that of the artillery.

One can say that the front line was completely smashed at Loos.   For a couple of hours, perhaps a little more, there was, owing to the weakness in German numbers, an opportunity, which had to be snatched, to get through the second line, but one wonders, if the XI Corps had been at hand, whether they could have been in time to grasp it : the congestion and confusion behind the British front before the first assault were hopeless.

Lessons were learnt on both sides.   See the preparations in 1916 for the Somme, the roads and railways that were constructed to deal with the traffic to and from the battlefield ; see, too, the German lines of defence, becoming infinite.   The regiment grew, battalions continued to arrive in France ; the Army passed the million figure ; guns could be counted by thousands : and the task became increasingly difficult.

THE WINTER 1915—1916. WAITING FOR THE SUMMER OFFENSIVE.

The major operation was over, but the Loos front was still in a state of unrest, which continued for some time. The regiment, however, was not involved.

Bethune remained a " social " centre. When battalions, on relief, went to the back areas and were billeted in rather dull little mining villages, everyone who could borrow a horse or a bicycle—or " jump " a lorry—went into Bethune, which was never so thronged or so gay. Peasants, workpeople, and townspeople of all sorts crowded the streets, together with hundreds of officers and men representing every arm of the Service. Milk-carts, drawn by dogs, moved along the streets by the side of heavy guns, lorries, mess-carts, limbers, despatch riders, all the " wheels " of an army. Nurses had come up to the hospitals, and those in hospital barges on the canal offered cress sandwiches and tea to their acquaintances. " Brass hats and red tabs were as the sand on the sea-shore." In a side-street a house numbered 3, and otherwise distinguished by a red lamp, was the origin of that curious alteration in the popular game of " house " when Number Three became, reminiscently, Red Lamp. A more select rendezvous was the Point-du-Jour, an estaminet presided over by Camille and her frail but amiable sisters. But all friendly and social gatherings in Bethune were liable to be broken up by the sudden arrival of a Staff officer with the order, shouted out, that all officers of a certain division were to return forthwith to their headquarters.

In the line the artillery on both sides was active. On the Cambrin—Givenchy front mining operations were resumed, and crater after crater was " blown." A great deal of repairing work had to be done, and new trenches, breastworks, and keeps constructed.

The word " camouflage " came into use. With both sides tied down during the winter to what has been fitly described as " nagging tactics," the old idea of concealing guns in cottages and snipers in the foliage of trees was improved upon. Aeroplane observation, combined with photography, had shown the importance of shadow in the art of concealment, and the French had experimented with paint, applying to objects a confusion of colour which deceived the eye. Scientists, Royal Academicians, and theatrical scene painters were employed to invent means of concealment for anything from a 15-inch gun to a Stokes mortar. A shattered tree-trunk in the front line was replaced in a night by a steel facsimile to conceal a sniper or observer ; a dead cow in No Man's Land was similarly replaced by a work of art, armour-plated. All kinds of ingenious devices were thought out for concealment and protection.

The Stokes mortar, which was first used for propelling smoke bombs at Loos, was now issued to some divisions. It was to become a favourite amongst all those contrivances ; the idea of dropping the shell and pro- pelling charge with a percussion cap straight down the muzzle on to a striker enabled a trained team to open rapid fire which was most effective, though it could not last long. The alternative weapon was generally the Vickers trench mortar, a much smaller affair on the principle of rifle and rifle grenade, the bomb being fitted with a rod which was inserted in the muzzle of the gun. Both were a vast improvement on the old " drain- pipe " trench mortar, improvised at an earlier period, and extremely dangerous to those who fired it.

A rearrangement took place with the brigading of machine guns—a step towards the construction of machine-gun corps—and the introduction in battalions of the Lewis gun. There was also introduced an improved hand grenade, the Mills bomb, and new rifle grenades ; later the Mills bomb was made to serve both purposes.

The introduction of these new arms necessitated training, and con- sideration " of the tactics to be employed in their use in co-operation with our own principal weapon the rifle. Previous experience had shown that, owing to faulty tactics and indifferent training, we had always come off second best in bombing and rifle-grenade encounters with the enemy.[1] Moreover, the training of the drafts arriving from England pointed to the fact that unsound tactics in bombing were being instilled into them, and that the rifle was being neglected to a large extent. The number of efficient instructors in rifle grenade, bomb, and Lewis gun in the battalion was limited, and it appeared impossible to train the battalion in the use of these arms in co-operation with rifle fire before the great summer offensive unless drastic reorganisation was made in the battalion. Lieutenant Colonel Minshull Ford therefore decided to reorganise the 1st Battalion into five companies, the fifth company to be known as the Grenadier Company, and consisting of four platoons, A, B, C, and D, each platoon being recruited from A, B, C, or D Company, who supplied it with its best all-round men-at-arms. When in the line the Grenadier Platoon was attached to its own original company, if required. Each platoon in the Grenadier Company had one of the Lewis guns then issued to the battalion

---

[1] During Sir Horace Smith-Dorrien's command at Aldershot, before the war, an attempt had been made to practise troops in bomb-throwing, but the cost of the bomb (6*d.*) was considered too great, and the training was limited to one demonstration by Royal Engineers—an empty affair.

(four).   In the line these platoons, under their respective commanders, not only assisted in the defence of the line, but carried out intensive training in the new weapons among the rank and file of the companies to which they were attached.   Out of the line, tactical training in the co-operation of all infantry arms was carried out in attack on trench systems.   As a result of this reorganisation, about 150 men were instructed in the Lewis gun, of whom 50 were fit to act as Number 1, and the fact that co-operation between the Lewis gun, rifle grenade, bomb, and rifle was essential, if good results were to be obtained, was firmly fixed in the minds of all ranks.'' (Stockwell.)

Various suggestions for the organisation of bombers were adopted by other battalions, but that of our 1st Battalion was pre-eminently successful.

The new weapons called for " specialists " which battalions had to find, and, although in the case of machine guns and trench mortars the teams supplied by battalions were still fighting forces, they were gradually removed from the control of battalion commanders.   Concurrently with the new fighting formations, administrative formations drew from battalions : baths, gas, entertainments, canteen, laundry, were some of the necessary services, but each officer taken required a servant, each mounted officer a groom as well ; small parties of men were called for by Brigade for some special but temporary service and became absorbed in the ever-growing permanent personnel of Brigade or Divisional Headquarters ; commanding officers saw their battalions dwindling ; the system of requisitioning men from fighting battalions for back-area jobs became a scandal and continued till the end of the war.   The " effective " figure was ludicrous.

The winter 1915–16 was open ; only at the end of February and beginning of March was the weather really trying, and then, for about two weeks, frost, thaw, and snow alternated rapidly ; there were, too, some very cold wind and rain in April.   But provision was made for the men.   Cardigan jackets and flannel-lined leather jerkins were issued ; and long thigh-boots of rubber were given out as trench stores to be taken over by relieving battalions.   The boots were not much good for keeping the feet dry, for although they kept the water out they kept perspiration in, and could never be dried inside.   As a preventive of " trench feet," whale oil and camphor powder, rubbed on daily, was more efficacious.   (Our 2nd Battalion had only one hospital case during the winter.)

After the New Year hot broth, for consumption during the night, was sent up in double-lined (thermos) containers ; the ration tea came up

in petrol tins packed in hay.   The old Regular soldier did not view these
innovations with favour ; he resented the diversion of his rations to a
communal pot, and preferred to cook and eat them in his own way and time ;
also he feared that the broth was a substitute for rum—which was attempted,
in some corps areas.

The winter landscape was intensely depressing.   The outlook in this
part of the line—and it did not differ much from others—was over fields
that had not been cultivated for two years.   The greyness of last year's
dead and tangled vegetation, the deeper grey lines of the thick belts of wire,
the reddish earth, or the chalk where the surface was scarred with trenches,
chilled the heart.   Amidst this desolation and beyond it were the empty
doorways and windows, the broken walls and tumbled masonry of villages
all silent, in which it was rare indeed to see a creature stir.   The occasional
curl of smoke where a soldier cooked under cover, even the sinister report
of a sniper's rifle, eased the sadness of the scene.

It was in February that a party of sailors from the Grand Fleet visited
the lines—they left expressing an emphatic preference for the North Sea.

By the second week in March, while snow still lay on the ground,
there were many signs that winter was passing.   Little frogs appeared
in the trenches ; owls flew about the ruined cottages, though there were
no other birds to be seen then—the Cambrin kestrels of the previous summer
were gone, and they did not return ; in the garden of an isolated villa,
that had a battalion headquarters in its basement and a gunners' observa-
tion-post built into its upper floor, there were snowdrops, primroses,
primulas, and violets.

．　　　．　　　．　　　．　　　．　　　．

After Loos the 1st Battalion did a tour of duty in the Cuinchy sector,
under Lieutenant-Colonel Minshull Ford, until the 23rd November.   They
then passed through Bethune to Gonnehem, and on the 5th December
entrained at Lillers for Saleux, south-west of Amiens, and marched eighteen
miles to Montagne.   Here they remained training until the end of January,
when they moved up into the line in the Somme area, east of Meault.

The 2nd Battalion, who were relieved on the 19th November, were
also at Gonnehem on the 21st, and on the 25th were transferred, with the
whole of the 19th Brigade, to the 33rd Division, passing under that command
while at Gonnehem.   But the 19th Brigade lost two of the old battalions,
the 1st Middlesex and the 2nd Argyll and Sutherland Highlanders.   The
two new battalions were the 18th Royal Fusiliers, recruited from the
Universities and " old Public School Boys," and the 20th Royal Fusiliers,
consisting mainly of Manchester Grammar School " old boys."

Of the winter 1915–16 the Medical Officer of the 2nd Battalion (Major J. C. Dunn) notes :

" For four months there were not even minor operations on the Bethune front, but the guns on both sides were at times only less active than at the height of the Loos engagement. Mining activity, too, continued, and with the formation of crater after crater, especially to the north of the main road, the opposing front lines with their saps underwent constant change. New trenches and keeps were made ; much labour was expended in repairing and remaking parapets, wire, and communication trenches, for the trenches were a year old and they were cut so perpendicularly that their sides crumbled and sagged, apart from damage done by shelling. There was an almost unlimited supply of sandbags for reveting ; hundreds of miles of trench-boards (duck-boards) were laid on the B.E.F. front to mitigate the mud. The Cambrin—Cuinchy—Givenchy front was by no means a wet part. The consistence of the mud where there were no duck-boards varied with the weather from that of pea-soup to that of dough, and it might be a foot deep. Only in the hollow of the Cabbage Patch— Grouse Butts area did the water lie, and there it was upwards of two feet at times ; so for several weeks there was an unoccupiable gap of 150 yards in that part of the Cuinchy sector. An active and destructive mortar, well covered by a brickstack, added much to the labour of repair in this sector ; it was superior to any British mortar of the period ; it threw a projectile with a thin metal casing 2½ to 3 feet long. Sentries indicated by whistle-blast the line of leisurely flight of this demoralising charge of high explosive.

" The routine of trench life was never so systematic as in the winter of 1916. The line was stable. The antagonists had brought into the field a large, partially trained civil population which had to be inured to campaigning ; both sides were marking time ; they had the experience and the material that were lacking in 1914–15.

" While the four months between Loos and February 1916 were devoid of incident in the battalion, there were circumstances that affected it, some temporarily, some permanently. Excepting the Commanding Officer, Adjutant, and Captain Stanway, the Regular officers remaining were too junior to be regarded as being of the Old Army ; temporary officers from the civil population predominated, and by the middle of November one of these became Adjutant, when Major C. S. Owen was promoted to the command of a battalion of the Queen's West Kents.

" On 7th November Captain Harbison, Royal Army Medical Corps, left after a year's service with the battalion ; a sociable Irishman with sporting tastes, he was a general favourite.[1]

" By 12th December the battalion was at rest at Le Cornet-Boordois, between Lillers and St. Venant. St. Venant, the refilling point, is a drab seventeenth-eighteenth-century town, containing a red-brick fortification of the same date. The regiment took part in its siege by Marlborough in 1710, when it resisted capture by more months than Bethune had resisted days. The district was in great part under water, and so waterlogged that a bombing range was the greatest area of reasonably dry ground off parts of the roads on which parades had to take place. There was neither professional nor recreational training, nor a sing-song. Even estaminets were far to seek. Officers who could get into Lillers, another very dull little town, found there a remarkably good oyster-bar in a wine-shop.

" Preparations for the celebrating of Christmas went forward. To the distress of some of the messes, not a turkey was to be had within twenty miles, but there was no lack of other fare. To exchange greetings with the battalion the acting Commanding Officer and Adjutant had to visit eighteen detachments, for the billets were small and scattered. So great was the variety of spirits, wine, and ale taken, that lunch was an impossibility.

" On 27th December the fatiguing rest came to an end. After a night in the tobacco factory at Bethune, the battalion moved to Beuvry. On 29th December two companies went into the Cambrin trenches ; the others remained at Beuvry to provide working parties. At 11 p.m. on 31st December, and at midnight, the enemy put down a five-minutes' and a two-minutes' strafe as a New Year greeting : the latter was preceded in the Givenchy sector by a shout from the Germans—' Keep down, you bastards ; we're going to strafe you.'

" At this period the enemy was particularly active underground. He had blown two small mines a few days previously, to the customary accompaniment of a short, intense bombardment. On the 2nd January he blew, just north of La Bassée road, what was, at that time, his largest mine.

" Hitherto reliefs on the Bethune front had taken place by day, though the roads by which detachments and even battalions marched were under observation, and regimental bands must have been audible sometimes from the point to which some of them accompanied their battalions. Even during the action in September the main road through Cambrin was little shelled, but of late it and lesser roads leading to the communication trenches

---

[1] J. C. Dunn, who became Medical Officer, was with the 19th Field Ambulance, which he had joined on 23rd July 1915.

III—II

had been receiving an increasing amount of attention from the enemy's guns. From now movement by daylight was reduced to a minimum, and individuals were forbidden to take short cuts over open ground leading to tender spots."

Lieutenant-Colonel O. de L. Williams (known to his friends as Guillaume) had to go to hospital in December, and for a short time the battalion was commanded by Captain Dennison, K.R.R., but towards the end of February Lieutenant-Colonel Williams returned. The battalion was then on the point of leaving the line. Lieutenant C. R. J. R. Dollings, " a level-headed and keen officer," noted for his eager pursuit of German patrols in No Man's Land, had just bombed a German working party with great success, having crawled up to them with three men. Unfortunately the Adjutant, Lieutenant H. Robertson, was, during the same tour of trench duty, killed ; but the tour covered the Kaiser's birthday, and the battalion was " on its toes," ready for trouble. Nothing further happened, however, and the relief took place ; the battalion marched back behind Bethune.

Lieutenant-Colonel Williams was then placed temporarily in command of the 100th Brigade in the Auchy left sector, immediately south of the Bethune—La Bassée road. In this area the trenches converged, and mining operations had been active. As craters were " blown " they were occupied by one side or the other and linked up with the trench system. Such a crater had recently been made by the Germans at the end of a British listening-sap, and was, together with two others of earlier formation, occupied by the enemy.

" I was sent for," says Colonel Williams, " by the General Officer Commanding 33rd Division, who told me that the enemy had blown three craters close to our front line and were occupying them. Several unsuccessful attempts had been made by the 100th Brigade to dislodge them. The corps and Army were very anxious that the Germans should be ejected, as our mining galleries were in serious danger as long as they held the craters. I was told to take command of the 100th Brigade and capture the craters that night. I asked if I might use my own battalion, and was told I might do anything I liked so long as the craters were taken.

" Plans were at once made for the attack, which was entrusted to Captain Stanway. The attack was carried out that night with great dash and determination ; the craters were captured, and strong counter-attacks repulsed."

They were taken by a swift charge of bombers, under cover of a slight artillery bombardment. But, as was often the case in similar raids, the most trying part of the affair was that of the trench-digging parties, who had to connect the craters with the main system : this was done before dawn. " A good trench was dug, linking up the craters with our front line, and by daylight the position was thoroughly consolidated. These craters were named by the corps, R, W, and F craters, and remained a permanent part of the line."

Casualties were : 8 other ranks killed ; Lieutenants J. M. Owen and C. R. J. R. Dollings and 28 other ranks wounded.

In the early part of 1916 the Staff, unmindful of the work of the 1st Battalion and such officers as Lieutenant Fletcher, became greatly excited over a Canadian raid into the enemy lines. It was an exceedingly well-planned raid—the Canadian Corps possessed that genius which is the aptitude for taking infinite pains—and thenceforth raids by order of the Higher Command became part of the ordinary duty of fighting battalions.

On the 8th April Lieutenant-Colonel Williams planned such a raid for the 2nd Battalion, with the assistance of Lieutenant-Colonel Rochford Boyd, commanding a group of the 33rd Divisional Artillery. The idea was to close on an enemy sap in the Cambrin sector and scupper or capture the garrison. The raid was carried out by volunteers from A, B, and D Companies, but failed in its object. It was the first time the battalion had used the Bangalore torpedo, a contraption for blowing up the enemy's wire, and the laying of it was entrusted to D Company party. The torpedo failed to explode, and was left under the German wire. As it was a new invention, the relieving battalion was ordered to get it in again, but this did not suit D Company. Lieutenant Coster, recently joined from the Honourable Artillery Company, went out with a small party to recover it. Unfortunately it was in two pieces, and the butt of it came away, leaving the front piece firmly fixed under the wire. All efforts to explode it by rifle fire failed—it had to be abandoned.

Disappointed with the result of the first, a second raid was planned and carried out on the 25th April on the road at Cuinchy right sector. Captain Stanway was put in command of the operation, which was entrusted this time to sixty men from B and C Companies. Both parties got into the enemy trench, but both the officers of C Company—Dollings and T. R. Conning—and of B Company—Hopkin, R. H. Morris and D. B. Morgan—were wounded, and the raiders came back without a prisoner.

These raids, miniature battles, soon became most unpleasant : if the enemy had any inkling of what was afoot, the concentration of artillery on the few yards selected was infinitely worse than in a big set battle.

An interesting note by the Doctor covers the period up to June :

" At Hohenzollern, and other parts of the Loos Salient, the Germans sought to improve their position by a gas attack on several occasions. One of these was about 7.30 a.m. on the 27th April. The battalion was then in support at Annequin North, and the wind brought the gas on to the billets, but it travelled at a fair speed and was so diluted that it did not inconvenience anyone. Animals felt the gas. Horses and cows were agitated ; chained dogs ran round in fright ; fowls flew up on to out-houses and little chickens strained on tip-toe to get their gaping mouths above the vapours that crept along the ground ; mice came out of their holes and climbed walls to reach fresh air ; seedling vegetables turned yellow and wilted. There was a great hullo-balloo in Bethune, where all the bells clanged out a tocsin.

" Another release of gas was made on the 17th June, when the battalion was in billets at the extreme west of the town ; it drifted slowly, but fairly well diluted, through the streets nearly to the level of the first-floor windows. Masks had to be worn for a time, but there were no casualties. The one good effect it had was to reduce temporarily the number of rats, dirty pests which swarmed in the trenches. One of Stanway's amusements was to keep a revolver by him and shoot rats as he played cards in dugouts.

" By the 30th April the weather was so genial that bathing in the canal near Pont Fixe was largely indulged in. On the 1st May the battalion returned to the Brickstacks. Soon after dark a piece of paper, weighted with a piece of chalk, giving the news of General Townshend's surrender at Kut was thrown into a sap-head.

" In the first week in May a likely-looking draft arrived, but the battalion remained below strength. German measles came with the draft, and for a couple of weeks men were going to hospital with the disease.

" On the 17th May the battalion went into the Cambrin sector, left front, after an absence of five weeks, to find that a very aggressive regiment had come in opposite. It was reported to have got the upper hand completely, so that the observation of No Man's Land and of the enemy parapet was denied, every periscope being shot down as soon as it was put up. The first morning experience confirmed the report. The enemy's use of rifle grenades and trench mortars made this the hottest tour in the line the battalion had experienced since the end of January. Rifle-grenade retaliation was organised at once. So effectual was it that soon the close array of enemy periscopes had been greatly thinned and observation of his parapet obtained. For four days the grenade and periscope-shooting contest continued, and though it was necessary sometimes to evacuate a stretch of trench, casualties were remarkably few. Counting periscopes as points, the battalion was easily the winner.   The experience was a severe test for the new draft, but it came through it well.

" Throughout the turmoil a lark sat on her eggs just outside the wire, and a pair of martins made persistent attempts to build under an overhead traverse."

On the 7th June Lieutenant-Colonel O. de L. Williams was appointed to command the 92nd Brigade, 31st Division, and was succeeded by Lieutenant-Colonel Crawshay.   On the 17th the battalion was at Gorre, in the château which was large enough to billet the whole battalion, and was due to take over the Givenchy sector on the 20th.   The day before they moved, the officer commanding the Mining Company dined with Lieutenant-Colonel Crawshay, and after dinner, over a glass of port, demonstrated that a recent camouflet and two small mines had so damaged the German underground works that six or eight weeks must elapse before the front line could be again menaced.

The battalion went into the line—B, C, D, and A Companies in line. Being midsummer, reliefs were late, and this one had not long been completed when, at 2 a.m. on the 21st, the enemy exploded a mine under B Company, completely wrecking about eighty yards of the front line and doing considerable damage to the support line ;   at the same time the enemy put down an intense bombardment on the front and support lines and Battalion Headquarters which lasted about an hour and a half.   They then attacked with 150 men and entered the front trench, but were promptly evicted by C Company and the remnant of B.

It was a big mine, and the experience is interesting.   B Company was most involved, and Captain H. M. Blair's narrative commences in the billets at Gorre :

" We were billeted in a farmhouse with big outbuildings, surrounded by a large fruit and vegetable garden ;   several well-built army huts had been put up in the orchard—there were beds for all and to spare.

" We took over from Heaven knows who—a corporal and one weary sentry were all I and my company sergeant-major ever saw.   The taking-over was noteworthy for two things, the filthy state of the latrines and the casual way in which a dump of Royal Engineer stores and clothing was handed over.   Of the stores the corporal said he had never been given an inventory, nor had he made one.   Nobody seemed to know anything about the stores, or to take the slightest interest in them.   Excellent news for B Company !

" All dirt and rubbish were quickly cleaned up, new duck-boards were laid in front of every hut, inside the huts was almost everything the heart of man-at-the-front could desire.   Our billets were a model.   The company was a delight to the eye—new uniforms and equipment.   Indeed Gorre was a nice place.

" Two days before taking over the trenches at Givenchy, the Commanding Officer and Company Commanders had a look round.   My opposite number was quite reassuring regarding the underground position.

" At night we had a dinner party in our billets.   Besides my company officers—Pryce Edwards, Barrett, Banks, and Crosland—there were Moody, Higginson, and Heasty : a very cheery crew.   Full of good food and bonhomie, we afterwards played follow-my-leader across country, with me as leader.   It was practically dark when we started, but we got along safely till I tried to jump a brook too wide for my powers—I landed on the far side in the mud, my cap fell off and I sat on it.   I am glad to say there were at least two other casualties.   Obstacle number two was a haystack which the farmer was cutting up into trusses ; the steps were high, but we all got to the top safely.   It was quite dark now.   We lined up on the ridge of the haystack, and on the word ' go ' we all tobogganed down the side, and off into space !   This part of the show was repeated three times. Then someone suggested that we raid D Company's mess, which we promptly did.   They were playing cards, so we were vastly unpopular.   We withdrew. Thereupon some lunatic suggested climbing through the barbed wire where it was high and thick and many yards in depth—this in pitch darkness. We got through, but in spite of the aid of two of my subalterns the seat of my trousers was torn right out.   And so to bed.

" Late in the evening of 20th June we moved up to Givenchy.   It was a lovely midsummer evening.   The march to the trenches was all too short. I marched with young Crosland and his platoon most of the way.   He was thrilled.   It was the first time he had been in the trenches.   Poor boy ! three hours later he was dead.

" We took over from the 4th Suffolks shortly before midnight.   The Company Commander I relieved assured me that the German mines had been ' knocked into bits ' since we blew camouflets the previous day, and not a sound had been heard.   This was comforting, but—— !

" About half an hour after midnight I began a round with my sergeant-major, Pattison.   The trenches had been knocked about in places by shelling during the day.   A perfect network of saps ran out for a considerable distance between mine-craters.   In one of the saps I met Conning, the bombing officer.   He told me he could not spare more than two-thirds the complement of bombers, but I insisted on having the full number.   I had an uncomfortable foreboding of impending trouble—I cannot say why.

I was neither worried nor depressed, but the feeling grew as time went on. It was a lovely, peaceful night. Perhaps it was the almost uncanny stillness—too quiet to be natural in that unpleasant part of the line. Anyhow, I was filled with a haunting unrest. I sent my sergeant-major to have boxes of bombs placed on the fire-steps, and the pins pinched ready for use ; boxes of reserve S.A.A., too, were to be ready to hand.

" It was nearly 1.30 a.m. on the 21st when my sergeant-major reported again. Conning had made up the complement of bombers ; we all went for a last look round ; everything was quite in order. So we strolled towards the company dugout to have a last drink before turning in. A few yards from the dugout somebody—Conning, I think—looked at his watch : it was twenty minutes to two. He said he was dead-beat, and if I didn't mind he would prefer to turn in at once. So we postponed the drink. He and another, whose name I forget, went off in the direction of C Company. Conning's change of mind saved his life at the time, and mine.

" After they left us I went back with Pattison to the far end of one of the saps, and spoke to the sentry and Lance-Corporal Morris. There was stillness everywhere. I had just stepped off the fire-step into the sap— Pattison was about five yards from me—when I felt my feet lifted up beneath me and the trench walls seemed to move upwards. There was a terrific blast of air, which blew my steel helmet Heaven knows where. I think that something must have struck me on the head (it was said in hospital that my skull was fractured) ; anyhow, I remember nothing more, until I woke to find myself buried up to the neck, and quite unable to move hand or foot. I do not know how long I had been unconscious. I was told afterwards that there was a heavy bombardment of our trenches lasting nearly an hour after the explosion of the mine, but I was unaware of all that.

" I awoke to an appalling ' shindy ' going on, and gradually realised that heavy rifle and machine-gun fire was taking place, and that bullets were whistling all round. Several men passed within a few feet of me—I saw them distinctly by the light of flares, and I remember hoping they would not trip over my head. The men were shouting to each other, but I was too dazed to appreciate that the language was German. When I heard a hunting-horn I was certain I was having the nightmare of my life—pegged down and unable to move, with a hailstorm of bullets all round, and men rushing about perilously near kicking my head ! The firing died down, and I realised that it was no nightmare but that I was very much awake."

The explosion which had buried Blair had been felt at Divisional

Headquarters in Bethune, whence a telegram was sent for information. In the line itself the two centre platoons of B Company and Headquarters were buried, out of sight, in the ruins of their trenches. The remainder of the company had barely collected their senses when an intense bombardment burst out on B, C, and D Companies' fronts—all companies were in line.

C Company had merely received showers of earth, but the occupants of Company Headquarters dugout were imprisoned.

After fifteen minutes the German gun fire lifted, and the reserve line and communication trenches were shelled. Battalion Headquarters, in front of what was known as Windy Corner, and Brigade Headquarters, on the canal bank two miles in rear, were both heavily shelled. With the lifting of the guns the German infantry assaulted. The new crater gave them cover to enter and get behind B Company's lines.

C Company's officers were released from their dugout with outside help when the guns lifted. Stanway, expecting a raid, was getting his men on the parapet when the enemy came over; they did not get through C Company front, but came round behind through the gap in B Company. A regular dog-fight took place near C Company's Headquarters. All the officers were in it. Craig was disarmed, and was being dragged away when he was rescued. Conning, who had been in the support line, collected and brought forward a few of the 18th Middlesex Battalion (Pioneers). Sergeant Roderick and Private Lane, of B Company, earned the D.C.M. for their action here : Lane used his fists when his bayonet was stuck fast in a German. Here, too, Banks, just out from Sandhurst, fought and died like a hero.

Moody had just returned to D Company's Headquarters when he felt the shock of the explosion, and the bombardment commenced. His front was not attacked—on his left A Company was not even shelled.

Back at Battalion Headquarters the Doctor—

" Wakened at 2 a.m. by heavy gun fire which suggested a raid. Went up to Headquarters. The ' strafe ' lasted about an hour and a half, and after it was over a runner from Stanway brought a report of a mine on his right and heavy casualties to B Company ; then Moody, on Stanway's left, reported a mine on his right and five casualties to his company, D. At length Stanway came down and told that B's centre had been engulfed, including Company Headquarters. A bombardment on our front and support had followed, flattening out our trenches : he anticipated a raid and got ready ; with the lifting of the bombardment to the rear the Hun attacked as his company was getting on the parapet. The attack was on both sides of the crater. Hand-to-hand fighting occurred. Banks was dead ; and there were six dead Huns in C Company's trench. The mine was under the front and extended back to our support line. Conning had found the right platoon of B Company on the other side of the crater.

" The Commanding Officer returned with Stanway.

" Later in the morning a Lewis gun of B Company was found between the parapet and the wire, and one of the gun team and a Boche beside it—dead. All B Company's officers were missing—Blair, Price Edwards, Crosland, Company Sergeant-Major Pattison—but all four platoon sergeants had escaped.

" The Boche got round behind C Company's front, which held, Stanway lining his parapet and firing from there. Everyone spoke well of Banks, C Company, who had shot two, if not three of the raiders before being stabbed in the neck and killed (the dagger used by his assailant was found).

" The Commanding Officer made a thorough survey of the line, and cleaning up was put in hand at once. In the edge of the crater three partially buried men were found, one of whom died at the aid-post.

" After daylight, Blair (Company Commander) and two men were seen half-way up the side of the crater, apparently buried to the waist. Throughout the day Blair exchanged signals with those below, but rescue was impossible till after dark.

" One wounded Boche stated that the raiding party was 150 strong.

" It is remarkable that though the shock of the mine going up was felt in Bethune, no one at Battalion Headquarters felt it, nor in the regimental aid-post above Windy Corner.

" Our casualties in the mine and raid were about 100. The remains of B Company, about 40, were relieved by a company of the Cameronians.

" The crater is huge to look at—approximately 75 by 150 yards at the base ; the lips are 40 feet high."

Blair and the corporal remained out, buried in the debris of the explosion. Blair says :

" Soon day began to dawn. I was extremely uncomfortable with violent cramp in my left leg ; also I was in a very exposed position. It was then for the first time I noticed Corporal Morris ; he was wedged up against me and was evidently in great pain (both his legs were broken). The dead body of Private Baylis was lying close to us, partly under my left side. After some struggling I got my right arm loose, pulled out my big pocket-knife and started busily to make a dugout as far as my cramped quarters would allow. I managed during the next two hours to excavate a good-sized hole, and carefully piled the earth, handful by handful, between us and the Germans. Thanks partly to this parapet and partly to the unevenness of the ground, Morris and I were able to hide from the German snipers. Later in the morning we must have been seen by some of our men. A rescue party of Cameronians tried very gallantly to come to us, but it was shelled immediately by the Germans, and any attempt to rescue us had to be abandoned during daylight. Foolishly I waved my arm to them. Whether the Germans saw the movement or not I cannot say, but they had discovered or suspected my whereabouts and turned a machine gun on to the spot. The bullets kept hitting the top of the parapet, or passing some inches above us, but we were able to crouch down in the hole I had dug.

" The weary hours dragged on. I continued to dig ; it was something to do. Every handful of earth was disposed of carefully, lest the Germans detect the movement and intensify their fire, or bomb us. After several hours I freed my right leg, but my left leg was fixed down firmly under me and felt quite dead. The sun was very hot and beat upon my bare head, which ached badly ; but my eyes were very much worse—they were full of grit and dirt, and were running in streams, and were excessively painful.

" By the early afternoon we were in rather a bad way. Morris was in great pain and was becoming light-headed. He begged for water. He said he would put his head over the top of our little parapet and finish things off. For a time I was able to persuade him to carry on. At length the poor fellow, who was half-crazy with pain and thirst, raised himself right up. There seemed only one thing to do—I hit him with my fist in his wind, and he collapsed. Personally I felt less discomfort as the sun declined ; though my eyes and head throbbed, there was no pain in my leg or body, and I did not feel so thirsty. So I tried to take an intelligent interest in our surroundings and prospects. My appreciation of the position was that if we kept quiet, the Huns would not trouble us—they probably thought we were dead by now. As soon after dark as possible the rescue party would come for us, therefore all was well—provided the party found us, and the Germans did not send a party to investigate. For I felt qualms : our rescuers might fail, and the Huns might gather us. Morris was quiet during the later afternoon, partly numbed, I think, by the pain in his legs, about which he was extremely plucky. We talked in whispers of the certainty of rescue at dark. Again and again, too, he could not help asking me to give him a few drops of water.

" Very slowly the long summer evening closed in. It seemed ages before the darkness of the night began to fall. Our one topic, our one thought, was how soon the rescue party would come for us. The last two hours of our imprisonment were far the worst of that long day.   9.30—no, too light.   10 o'clock—still too light.   10.30—they ought to come now ; if they let it get too dark they may not be able to find us.   11 o'clock—the worst time of all !   Had the rescue party been unable to find us and given up in the dark ?   We were parched with thirst, and had visions of lying out another twenty-four hours without water.   We were getting depressed and losing hope when—it must have been nearly 11.30—I heard footsteps and a muttered whisper—English, thank heaven !   I called softly, and the rescue party came up to us—our Doctor (Dunn) and a covering party of the Cameronians. We were given water. It took about three-quarters of an hour to release me, and it was two hours before Morris was carried back to our lines."

The Doctor himself writes in his diary :

" *June 22nd.*—The Cameronians provided a covering party—I had a digging party, and a bearer squad was at hand. We left the trench at nightfall and got to work. One of the men, Baylis, was dead ; the other, Morris, was exhausted and moaning ; Blair was irritable and impatient, but quite rational—they both craved a long drink.

" Blair had scraped one of his legs free, but the other was held fast to above the knee. The Boche started firing, but a slight elevation protected us. The work was delicate and arduous, for the soil was dense and moist, and sandbags, pickets, barbed wire, and legs were intermixed. It took three-quarters of an hour to free Blair, who assisted in the work ; he was considerably bruised about the face and head, but otherwise uninjured. Morris was a case ; and the early discovery that he had a fractured thigh increased the difficulty of freeing him ; much of the work had to be done with bare hands. Daylight had almost come before he was freed.

" At Headquarters Blair described how he had gone to the head of the sap to inspect the bombing-post ; whilst he was talking to the men the soil began to fly up before him, and he was lifted off his feet. He and the men clutched each other for support ; they went up in darkness together, and fell in darkness together ; and soil, stones, sticks, etc., fell on them and about them, supporting them upright but holding them fast by the legs. But he could see, by what light there was. He saw the enemy shell bursting below him ; then the shell burst farther off ; and then the raiders passed by and below them in a mass, but returned singly or in small groups. Eventually all was silence.

" With the coming of daylight he could recognise objects and individuals. His left leg, being bent at the hip and knee, was much less buried than the right, and by scraping throughout the day he got the left free and the upper part of the right thigh.   His companions seemed unable to help themselves at all : Baylis was calling out, and had to be kept quiet while the raiders were passing.   Thirst was their chief distress throughout the day." (Diary of J. C. Dunn, Medical Officer.)

This crater was named Red Dragon Crater.

Shortly after the enemy raid, Captain Stanway was appointed to command a New Army battalion of the Cheshires in the 39th Division. He had risen in the ranks to Company Sergeant-Major, and during the winter 1914–15 had been given a commission.

On the 27th June the battalion was relieved in the line by the 5th Scottish Rifles and went back to Préol.   The Germans fired three more small mines on the Scottish Rifles' front.

The disaster to B Company roused a general desire for retaliation. The German salient, on the left of the sector the battalion had just handed over, and known as the Warren, was a likely spot.   The idea was approved by the division, and during the rest at Préol, Higginson and Moody, commanding A and D Companies, were busy planning and arranging the operation, with the help and advice of Lieutenant-Colonel Rochford-Boyd, R.H.A.

On the 3rd July the battalion returned to the line, taking over from Red Dragon Crater to La Plante.   The night of the raid was fixed for the 5th/6th July—after the opening of the Somme offensive.

The question, How are the men ? was frequently asked both before and after an engagement, but beyond a general statement that they were all right nothing could be said—it could not be developed.   At this time, however, one can grasp some of the excitement that was seething through the battalion.   The summer offensive had long been a topic of conversation, the Somme Valley was known to be the selected spot—even German prisoners, captured in raids, named the Albert front—only the date had been vague.   But now the din of battle was in every ear.

At 9.45 a.m. on the 24th June the British artillery opened fire all along the line.   On the Bethune front it was intermittent—it was governed largely by plans for a succession of raids, which battalions of the division carried out.   But for two weeks the rumble of guns to the south was continuous, and that noise has a peculiar stirring quality.   There was, too, evidence of anxiety on the German side when, at night, brilliant star shells rose and fell against the dark sky that shimmered with the flashes of guns like summer lightning ; but that ominous rumble—drum fire, distant, deep, bubbling up and down, relentless and amazing in its ceaseless roll— that sound brought with it a sort of fever.

All this, and their own raid !

When the battalion returned to the line on the 3rd July they stepped, metaphorically, into the ring.

The salient in the German line, which was to be the objective of the raid, had at its apex three mine-craters. D Company was to cross via the craters, while A Company, on the left, attacked the side of the salient.

A Company's rôle was to push through this northern side to the reserve line, which they would hold while D Company, coming in at the apex, mopped up and destroyed the trenches, saps, and mine-shafts ; in the latter task they were to be helped by a detachment of the 222nd Company, R.E. Captain J. V. Higginson commanded A Company, Captain P. Moody commanded D. B Company was to carry extra bombs across from La Plante. All ranks wore a white band on each arm.

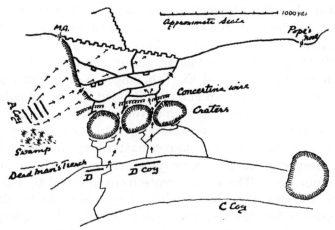

It was arranged that a " jumping " bombardment of three-quarters of an hour should start at 10.30 p.m., after which a " box " barrage would be put round the salient and the raid would take place. The jumping bombardment consisted of a continual change of target, a skipping to and fro from front to support, to reserve trenches.

Also, to distract the enemy's attention, the 5th Scottish Rifles made a bombing attack at the Duck's Bill, a number of mines were blown under the enemy lines along the sector, and gas was discharged from the Brickstacks.

At 11.15 p.m. the assaulting companies left our front line. The Commanding Officer watched his men start. " They went away," he said, " like a pack of hounds ! " D Company took advantage of the cover afforded by the craters ; A Company, in single file, moved across No Man's Land to the left. The ground scout who preceded Captain Higginson was shot through the head when he had gone only ten yards, but the company reached a selected " jumping-off " point without further casualties and lay down in close column of platoons facing the steep bank of the northern re-entrant of the small salient.

" The men were very happy and soon had their cigarettes going ; they were cracking jokes and calling Fritz a few choice names whilst the guns carried on the good work.   Then the box barrage was formed and the companies rushed into the enemy's position, each platoon in its allotted place.

" A Company's sergeant-major began badly, when, standing on the parapet, it gave way and he fell in a heap at the entrance to a dugout, unable to help himself, having a Verey pistol in one hand and a rifle and fixed bayonet in the other.   ' Are you hit, Sergeant-Major ? ' his Company Commander asked.   But the next moment he was calling the Boche from the dugout—the reply was a bullet, so a Mills bomb was thrown in.   When the dugout was searched, four dead men were found in it ; later a land mine was placed in the mouth of it, and so they were buried.

" The next dugout also contained four men : they came out with their hands up—' Kamarad ! '   Their belts and bayonets having been taken off them, they were told to get on the top and sit in a shell-hole.   One of them, speaking good English, said, ' Not for you or your officer '—he got a wallop on the chin and was hoisted up by his pals.   Soon after a man of the company came up with a wound in his arm, and he was given a revolver and told to take the prisoners back to the company's trench and hand them over to the company quartermaster-sergeant (Powell), who was waiting in a deep dugout to receive prisoners.   But those four prisoners never got to our line.   The escort wrote from hospital to a pal in the company that he thought they were going to slip him, so he shot them ; but he was sorry he lost the sergeant-major's revolver ! " (Sergeant Fox.)

A dozen half-stupefied occupants of the front line surrendered to D Company ; but in the support and reserve lines a stout resistance was met with—the conduct of one German officer was referred to with special admiration.

When resistance was overcome, looting and destruction followed. Everyone had personal souvenirs.   The deep and solidly built German dugouts were admired and envied, but as many as could be found were destroyed with explosive, as were the mine-shafts, and a trench mortar, too large to carry away.

Most of B Company, after carrying up the extra bombs, joined in the hunt and destruction ; also D Company's quartermaster-sergeant, who, having brought up his company rations to our own lines, strolled over himself to see how they were getting on.

Forty-three prisoners were taken, some of them wounded.   " The first batch of twenty-five came down under the sole escort of Moody's servant. They were Saxons of the 241st Regiment—all well-looking men with English speakers amongst them. A trench mortar and a machine gun, of British make, were brought away—these were eventually sent to Wrexham. The machine gun was carried by Private Buckley, whose selected weapon was a bill-hook—one of the wounded appeared to have been pursued by him ! Buckley's affable handshake with the Chaplain reflected not only his own supreme satisfaction, but that of all the raiders." (Dunn.)

The two companies remained in the German lines for two and a half hours.

Company Sergeant-Major Fox states : " When I got back to our trench I went to the dugout to see how Powell was getting on. He was in a fine stew. A German shell had hit the parados opposite and nearly filled the entrance. I think he had had a worse time than we had in the raid. Now comes the most awful part of the show. A man of A Company had a brother in C Company ; when he got back after the raid he said, ' Pass the word to my brother I am all right.' A few minutes later he was sitting with two others in the trench when a shell landed plum among them, killing them all. Shortly after daybreak I met his brother coming to see him—he asked me if I knew where his brother was. His brother's body had been taken back to Cambrin for burial, but I couldn't tell him. When he did find out, he nearly went out of his mind."

The German retaliation was, of course, very severe, and a number of our casualties were caused by shell fire, and inflicted on the men holding our own line.

Our field batteries were stated to have fired 6,000 rounds, the 4·5-inch howitzers 150, and the 6-inch howitzers 30 rounds. The trench mortars fired 3,500 rounds, and nearly 5,000 rifle grenades were discharged.

The next day the Germans shouted across that they had captured a corporal of A Company (Roberts).

Casualties were : 2nd Lieutenant R. A. R. Hollingberg and 10 other ranks killed ; 47 other ranks wounded.

The importance of this raid drew the congratulations of Sir Douglas Haig, who remarked that " raids of this sort are of great material assistance to the main operation "—which had opened on the 1st July.

During the first six months of the year many smaller raids were carried out, Lieutenant D. B. Morgan, 2nd Lieutenants Dollings, T. R. Conning, R. H. Morris, E. Coster, and R. O. Barrett being some of the leaders.

.   .   .   .

The 4th Battalion remained on the Loos—Hulluch front till the 8th

March, when they moved, with the 47th Division, to the Vimy Ridge sector. At Loos they had tunnelled the slag-heap known as the Double Crassier at the rate of 14 feet 2 inches per day, a feat of which they were justly proud.

. . . .

The 9th Battalion remained throughout the winter in the Festubert—Neuve-Chapelle—Laventie area. Major C. Burrard, who had reorganised the battalion after Loos, was invalided home at Christmas, and was relieved by Lieutenant-Colonel R. A. Berners. On the 7th May the battalion moved, with the 19th Division, to Montonvillers, and commenced intensive training for the summer offensive.

New Arrivals.

On the 27th September 1915 the 10th Battalion embarked at Dover on the s.s. *Onward*, and sailed for Boulogne, landing with a strength of 29 officers and 996 other ranks.[1] After a stay at Caestre they moved to Bailleul on the 5th October, and into the Ploegsteert area on the 7th. Thence to the Ypres Salient, two companies at a time, for instruction from the 2nd Royal Scots, eventually relieving that battalion in the line near Hooge on the 15th October.

The battalion went out to France with the 76th Brigade, 25th Division, but on the 14th October the whole brigade was transferred to the 3rd Division.

From Hooge they moved to St. Eloi at the end of November, where, on the 27th December, Lieutenant-Colonel Beresford Ash was wounded. Major F. L. Macgill-Crichton-Maitland (Gordons) assumed command, to be succeeded in a few weeks by Major S. Binny.

The salient took its toll of casualties.

On the 2nd March the 76th Brigade attacked in the neighbourhood of the Bluff, the battalion being in support to the 2nd Suffolk. The attack was successful in its object of retaking a stretch of lost line, but the battalion losses were 11 other ranks killed ; Captain W. P. Griffiths, Lieutenants Maynard, H. J. M. Lewis, 2nd Lieutenants J. L. T. Davies, and 67 other ranks wounded.

The next day a chance shell fell on the Headquarters dugout, and killed

---

[1] Lieutenant-Colonel W. R. H. Beresford Ash, Major F. N. Burton, Captain W. T. Lyons (Adjutant), Quartermaster-Lieutenant E. H. Chapman, Captain B. Grellier (Medical Officer), Major E. Freeman, Captains R. A. Adamson, G. P. Blake, F. A. Samuel, E. W. Bell, W. P. Griffiths, B. D. Jones, J. A. Walker, Lieutenants W. B. Morgan, A. J. S. James, M. Murray, H. A. V. Maynard, 2nd Lieutenants W. Hughes, H. J. M. Lewis, A. W. Fish, H. E. Wynne Williams, A. V. Cree, F. C. G. Larkworthy, C. A. R. Follitt, A. G. Buchanan, A. Nevitt, J. L. T. Davies, C. L. Locke, O. S. Hughes.

TRENCH, FESTUBERT SECTOR.

Imperial War Museum photograph, Crown copyright.

176]

Major S. Binny, Major Freeman, Captain Lyons (Adjutant), 2nd Lieutenant W. Hughes, and 9 other ranks.   After this tragic event Major G. R. Crosfield (South Lancashire Regiment) assumed command, but was wounded on the 20th March during a bombing raid carried out by 2nd Lieutenant Nevitt. The casualties during the raid, mostly from shell fire, were Captain Griffiths, 2nd Lieutenant H. E. Wynne Williams, and 8 other ranks killed ; Captain C. P. C. Daniell, 2nd Lieutenant Nevitt, and 30 other ranks wounded.

Ill-luck dogged their footsteps, for the following day, 3rd March, Captain Jackson, who had assumed command on arrival from the 1st Battalion, was wounded, and he was succeeded by Captain F. A. Samuel.

The next minor affray to be briefly recorded was on the 30th April. The battalion was given warning by two deserters of an impending attack and successfully repulsed an assault delivered after a gas discharge.   It was a stout bit of work, as the trenches were only thirty-five yards apart, which favoured the gas attack, a fact which was appreciated by the Army Commander.   The battalion had 25 casualties and about 50 gas cases.

In the middle of June the battalion went out of the line and started a circuitous march to the Somme.

.   .   .   .

The 11th Battalion did no more than pass through France, arriving in September with the 22nd Division and embarking in October for Salonika.

.   .   .   .

The 13th, 14th, 15th, 16th, and 17th Battalions were all posted to the 38th (Welsh) Division, which arrived in France during the first week of December 1915.   The first four battalions formed the 113th Brigade, the 17th Battalion was posted to the 115th Brigade.   The division was sent to the Laventie sector and received instruction in trench duties from the Guards Division.   There is no special activity to record during the winter.

The 14th Battalion, on the 4th June, sent a party of 60 men, under Captain H. Williams, to raid the Moated Grange.   After an artillery bombardment the party penetrated the wire and entered the trench, only to find that the enemy had retired to the support line.   With only ten minutes to inflict such damage as they could, they bombed some dugouts and engaged the support trench.   The return journey was not so easy, and Captain Williams and 2 other ranks were killed ; Lieutenants A. Lloyd Jones, J. Glynn Jones, and 24 other ranks were wounded ;   5 men were missing.

The 15th Battalion was the first battalion of the 38th Division to raid the enemy line : this was on the night of the 7th May.   Captain Gorony Owen, 2nd Lieutenants N. Osborne-Jones and H. Taggart, with a party of

50 men, left the Laventie line and approached the enemy trenches with the object of inflicting loss and securing identification. Advancing silently across No Man's Land, the party discovered an enemy wiring party just finishing their work. Captain Owen immediately altered his plan, and followed the enemy party into their line. Taken completely by surprise, the Germans were thrown into confusion, and some 60 were killed and wounded as they vainly attempted to get bombs from a trench store. Captain Owen then gave the signal for retirement, but the two young officers, Osborne-Jones and Taggart, who had dashed forward eagerly to attack, were killed, with 4 other ranks ; 10 other ranks were wounded. The battalion was mentioned in Sir Douglas Haig's next despatch for this raid.

. . . . . .

The battalions of the Welsh Division soon became accustomed to the fixed trench routine, which varied very little : at night ration parties went up to Battalion Headquarters, or near by, and other parties were detailed to repair damage to breastworks, renew the wire, or attempt to make a dry and clean pathway behind the breastworks—they were on the low-lying plain below the Aubers Ridge. The breastworks were between six and seven feet high with fire-steps in the bays, which sometimes had a parados ; built up with loose earth and earth-filled sandbags, they were always giving way in the wet weather. Close up against them trench-boards, or duck-boards, were laid as a path, and these were continually sinking in the sodden clay. All along the line, behind the breastworks, were excavations, varying in depth and width, where troops had dug, either to fill sandbags or for some other purpose, and these excavations, filled with water, presented to the eye a series of ponds, at places of considerable length. To add to the flood troubles, which were the principal ones in this sector, the military works had interfered with the carefully planned dykes and natural watercourses of the district, so that even a moderate rainfall put large tracts of country under water.

Under the shelter of the breastworks so-called dugouts had been constructed—funk-holes is a more descriptive name : the framework was generally made by the engineers, and the men built up walls with earth-filled sandbags ; the roof, of corrugated iron, was also covered with a layer of sandbags. They were in no sense shell-proof.

Sanitation had improved. Latrines were carefully inspected, and buckets had been provided.

Cook-houses were built in the line, and at night the glow of the fire could be seen by the enemy, who would amuse himself sniping at it for hours. There were, too, stores for ammunition, sandbags, spades and picks, and the stocks had to be renewed from time to time by fatigue parties. All this necessitated a trench store list, which was checked by relieving battalions or companies.

The quartermaster brought up all stores and rations at night, generally to a point near Battalion Headquarters, which presented an animated scene—no lights, but the glow of cigarettes, the flash of a match, restive horses, impatient drivers, men calling for a comrade, laughter, chat. And with it the distant pop of a rifle, or regular popping of a machine gun ; the whine of a shell overhead ; the sharp crack, swish, or whisper of near-by bullets, according to the distance they had travelled. Along the road, approaching or leaving the meeting-place, parties of men in file, shadowy in the gloom.

These points were well known to the enemy, who would occasionally shell them ; and we, knowing his ration points, would retaliate. The Germans had also a number of fixed rifles, trained on such points, which a sentry could fire when he felt so inclined by merely pulling the trigger ; the rifles were fixed in pairs, threes, and at one place five, and were often at a considerable distance, so that one could hear the pop of the rifles—on a fine night—followed by the whisper of the bullets a few yards off. The ear became trained to the different sounds of a bullet.

Inter-battalion reliefs in the front line took place at intervals of two or three days, when companies would change over to the support line, sleeping in barns, ruins, strong-points with slightly better dugouts than in the front line ; and then the whole battalion would march back five, six, or seven miles to some small village or township, for a week, to rest, clean up, and drill. A football match, a boxing match ; with the approach of summer a cricket match ; a race meeting, a horse show ; St. David's Day ! Then back to the line.

Farms some two miles behind the front line were still occupied. Laventie had a thinning population, but a few shops were still trading ; La Gorgue flourished on the troops. So it was everywhere behind the line—a zone of devastation, ruin of a milder kind, a few inhabitants, a packed town.

The spring passed—the Summer Offensive approached.

IV

OFFENSIVE OPERATIONS: SECOND PERIOD

OFFENSIVE OPERATIONS: SECOND PERIOD

THE BATTERING-RAM

ON the 17th December 1915 Sir John French handed over command of the British Armies in France to Sir Douglas Haig; at the same time Sir William Robertson was moved to London and became Chief of the Imperial Staff.

The change of command opened a new phase in the war, not due to any individual, for had Sir John remained it is probable that the same policy would, in the main, have been pursued; it was inevitable, because it was obvious to British, French, and Germans.

Nobody had any suggestion to offer, after the last chance of a swift break-through disappeared at Loos, except to use the great British Army that had now been assembled and the mass of artillery and abundance of ammunition as a battering-ram to punch its way slowly through the enemy defences. Sir Douglas Haig, Sir William Robertson, and General Falkenhayn certainly had the same idea; Falkenhayn was the first to commence at Verdun.

The Germans, however, quickly condemned the method, but Haig and Robertson (and Joffre) could see no alternative, and having started, continued through the winter of 1916–17, and moreover, when the series of battles between the Somme and the Scarpe died down, in the spring of 1917, recommenced with no modification the battering-ram policy at Ypres.

The attempt to avoid the static warfare in France and Flanders by the ill-fated Gallipoli expedition had failed, and those soldiers who maintained that the Western was the decisive front considered that their argument had been demonstrated. The French adventure under Nivelle, early in 1917, was additional confirmation that their theory was correct.

The Germans and their Allies, attacked on all fronts, had imposed if not the fear of invincibility at least the dullness of perplexity on their opponents. There was an impasse, and in searching for the solution the

British Imperial Staff created a hell on the Western Front which had its effect in breaking down German *moral*.

Henceforth battles on the grand scale continued for months. Units of the Army fought in relays, the battle being carried on by others while each rested, reorganised, and refitted. And the objectives they were called upon to win were limited and strictly defined.

The after-effect of the Battle of Neuve Chapelle was that the single-fire trench became a fortified zone, or a network of trenches to a depth of some two hundred yards. The French met a defence of this kind on the Vimy Ridge, in May and June 1915, with such weight of artillery that the Germans, if they had not come to the conclusion before, were convinced that a second line, well sited, solidly built, and strongly wired, planned at such a distance from the first line as would necessitate moving the attacking artillery forward in order to reach it, was essential. The first line could not withstand the artillery bombardment, but a second line, out of effective range, would bar the progress of the assaulting infantry when the first fell, and force a pause in the attack : this is what occurred at Loos. But although the method of defence had succeeded at Loos, the German Command thought it advisable to supplement it by a third line. It was a mechanical progress.

Starting with a conception of war which, in the continental view of strong artillery support, gave prominence to heavy guns, the Germans led the way to a general military vision of artillery " assault " to gain ground which the infantry would occupy and hold. Infantry movement and the initiative of lower unit commanders were restricted. The General Staffs saw a methodical advance, with limited objectives, won primarily by the artillery. The German methods at Verdun and the British methods on the Somme are similar. A battering-ram to break the wall.

The Allied scheme for the 1916 offensive was first outlined in December 1915 : the decision was the mutual responsibility of the Allied General Staffs. It was a part of a co-ordinating endeavour by all the Allies. The Russians were to make an onslaught with their reorganised and enlarged armies on the Austrians ; and while the Germanic Powers were deeply involved on the Eastern Front, two British Armies and three French Armies were to attack astride the Somme.

The ultimate objective is somewhat vague : the plains behind Douai are indicated, and a general rolling-up of the German line, to the north by the British, to the south by the French. Equally vague is the vision of time in this " break-through," which combined limited objectives for the infantry with movements of cavalry in the back areas to positions of immediate readiness.   The problem of attack was baffling.   The solution was sought in " straight-forward action."

Whatever the merits of the original scheme, the German offensive at Verdun forced a modification.   The French, instead of being the senior partners in the combined attack, became the juniors, and the military objects of the battle are confused by such statements as that it was undertaken to relieve the pressure on Verdun, to assist our Allies in the other theatres of war by stopping any further transfer of German troops from the Western Front, and to wear down the strength of the forces opposed to us—all of which is only moderately true, the situation being forced by the enemy in face of preparations made with quite a different object.

The last of the " objects " given by Sir Douglas Haig, the wearing down of the enemy strength, was a polite variation of Falkenhayn's declared object at Verdun, to bleed France white.   By the middle of June the French were unable to undertake an offensive on the Somme with a greater frontage than nine miles ;   the British frontage remained about 18,000 yards, from Maricourt to Serre.   The plan was therefore modified because of Verdun, and was never made to relieve Verdun.

Our 1st Battalion went into this area on the 2nd February.   Colonel Minshull Ford was soon promoted to command the 91st Brigade, 7th Division, and Major Stockwell was ordered to leave his appointment of Brigade Major to the 59th Brigade and take command of the 1st Battalion. He handed over to his successor on the 19th February.   " We had a special dinner and drank my health in bubbly.   Very sorry to go, as I have learnt a lot.   The General [Shute] has been awfully good to me in all ways."

The 59th Brigade was then in the line at Ypres, and the new commanding officer describes his journey to the 1st Battalion.   He left at 5 a.m. on the 20th.   " Damned cold.   Got to Pop [Poperinghe], and just as we were starting they started bombing and shelling the station.   Glad to get off.   One plane chased me, but was drawn off by one of ours.   Changed at Hazebrouck and had breakfast—then to Boulogne ;   then caught the express to Abbeville about 4.30 p.m.   I got a billet in a hat-shop.   Went out to buy some papers.   Dinner at the Tête de Bœuf, a mixed assembly —French and British officers, wives of the former and mistresses of both. Found I had dropped my *porte monnaie* in the street—result only five francs.   Went round to the paper-shop and the police.   As I talked French the man in the paper-shop lent me 25 francs.   To bed.

" *21st.*—9.30 a.m. left Abbeville.   Reached railhead at Méricourt 1 p.m.   Got my horse about 3 p.m. and rode to Merlancourt, where I met

Cottrell (Transport Officer). Battalion in the trenches. Saw the General (Brigadier) Steele. Everybody glad to see me. Dined with Brigadier.

"*22nd.*—Went out to trenches—bare, rolling down of chalk. We have got the upper ground, delighted to find. Fry, our doctor; young Richardson, my sub. in the 2nd Battalion, a company commander; Anderson, another; Reeves, Adjutant; Compton Smith, second in command, a junior captain from the Suffolks. We are in second line. Went round the companies and saw all officers. On my way back the devil of a bombardment opened on our front and the battalion on our left. Communication broken down with the front line—sent off orderlies and officer to maintain it. At 5.30 p.m. a gas alarm—all bunkum. We stood to arms. Sent up to the 20th Manchesters, the front-line battalion, to find out what was happening. Nothing happened, except shell, but are attacked on our left. Informed brigade and stood down."

Stockwell then went round the section of line on this bare, rolling down. "A curious place. About 500 yards of front consists of a continuous row of craters—the whole place white chalk. The Huns seem to have it mostly their own way, though I gather our miners are holding their own now. Huns have pushed bombing posts within 40 yards of our front line. Wire rotten; parapet everywhere bad and nowhere bullet-proof. Went back to Headquarters and wrote a memo to company commanders that we must drive in those posts as soon as we come into the line. Cold; snowing and freezing hard."

From one place in the line Fricourt could be seen—in enemy hands—on the left, and the two lines of white chalk trench stretching away north.

The battalion was in the line six days, and out three at Merlancourt. The work of improving the line went on steadily—the wire was strengthened and a new front-line trench made. The enemy was "up-ish" and used trench mortars freely. "Our guns rotten—can't hit anything, and are very slow. They have rotten, cold-footed ideas, too, about shooting for fear the Huns may shoot back!"

Captain Jackson left the 1st Battalion to join the 10th Battalion, after the death of Majors Binney and Freeman. Captain Richardson was wounded on the 18th March, and died the next day. Casualties continued.

On the 25th May Lieutenant N. Stansfield raided the enemy with 25 men. The party ran into "masses of wire and got hung up." Stansfield was wounded; 1 man was killed and 11 wounded. All the wounded were brought back, "largely owing to Sassoon's bravery."

.   .   .   .

Meanwhile preparations were going on for the summer offensive. The

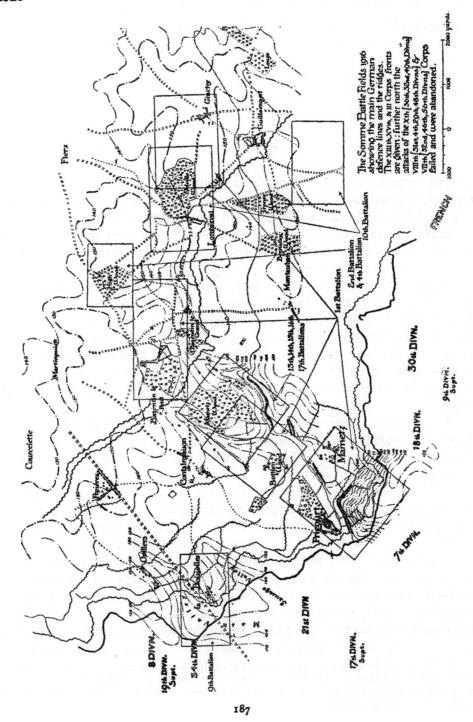

The *Somme Battle Fields* 1916 showing the main German defence lines and the ridges. The XIIIth, XVth, & III Corps fronts are given; further north the attacks of the Xth [36th, 32nd, 49th Divns] VIIIth [31st, 4th, 29th, 48th Divns] & VIIth [32nd, 46th, 50th Divns] Corps failed and were abandoned.

magnitude of Loos shrank before the vastness of the Somme.   The front
to be attacked, from Méricourt to Serre, formed a great salient with Fricourt
at the apex.   Between the Somme and the Ancre observation on the enemy
front-line trenches, which generally lay above ours, was good, but practically
nothing could be seen of his rear systems, the second of which was between
3,000 and 5,000 yards away on the summit of the high ground in front of the
Fourth Army.

As far as was possible the German Higher Command tried to keep
their units in the same part of the line, and there was a competitive spirit
between companies, battalions, and regiments in the construction of
trenches, dugouts, and wire entanglements.   The result was an impregnable
position against attacks not supported by massed artillery and prepared
by lengthy bombardment.   Each separate trench system was strongly
wired in, and contained deep dugouts at regular intervals.   But the great
feature of the defence was the linking up of the first- and second-line systems
by a series of fortified positions : each wood and village had been prepared
for defence, every advantageous piece of ground had been entrenched,
often provided with dugouts, and wired ; not a single provision for an
obstinate and determined defence had been neglected.   All that vast area
between the first and second lines had been made, to all intents and purposes,
into one wide, defended zone ; and farther back the construction of a third
line was in progress, being linked up in a similar manner with the
second.

The summer offensive was a formidable undertaking and Sir Douglas
Haig's preparations were methodical.   There was no secrecy.   It was a
straightforward fight—the obvious trial of strength with faith in massed
artillery and unlimited shells.[1]

" Vast stocks of ammunition and stores of all kinds had to be accumulated beforehand within a convenient distance of our front.   To deal with
these, many miles of new railways—both standard and narrow gauge—and
trench tramways were laid.   All available roads were improved, many
others were made, and long causeways were built over marshy valleys.
Many additional dugouts had to be provided as shelters for the troops, for
use as dressing-stations for the wounded, and as magazines for storing
ammunition, food, water, and engineering material.   Scores of miles of
deep communication trenches had to be dug, as well as trenches for telephone
wires, assembly and assault trenches, and numerous gun emplacements and

---

[1] Up to the 3rd April 1915 the total number of shells sent to France from the outbreak of war
(eight months) was 2,133,942.   The next figure that strikes the eye is that in thirteen weeks, ending
31st December 1915, 2,500,000 shells were sent to France.   In the four weeks of July 1916 the
number of shells rose to 3,500,000.

observation posts. Important mining operations were undertaken, and charges were laid at various points beneath the enemy's lines.

" Except in the river valleys, the existing supplies of water were hopelessly insufficient to meet the requirements of the numbers of men and horses to be concentrated in this area as the preparations for our offensive proceeded. To meet this difficulty many wells and borings were sunk, and over 100 pumping stations were installed. More than 120 miles of water-mains were laid, and everything was got ready to ensure an adequate water-supply as the troops advanced."

All through the spring and early summer this work went on, unceasing and obvious. Traffic on the roads increased, working parties bent to their task, fatigue parties carried stores. Behind the front line, parallel with it, motionless, sausage-shaped observation balloons stood in mid-air.

. . . .

The mass of artillery and ammunition we had assembled was sufficient to destroy all trenches and wire; in time we could batter through. The effective defence was dugouts.

The enemy would be driven into his dugouts, and the problem then facing our Staff was that the assaulting troops would have to be assembled in positions above ground, vulnerable to enemy artillery; that although the enemy trenches had been smashed by artillery fire, the ground itself would be so cut up as to present a serious obstacle to swift movement and assaulting troops must take some time reaching the enemy dugouts, during which time they would have to pass through an enemy barrage; that our artillery, although firing on the line of enemy trench to the last moment, would have to lift and so permit the enemy to come out of his dugouts; and that success or failure must rest on the time required by the already battered assaulting troops to reach the enemy dugouts after the artillery lift. But the strength of the German dugouts and their number were under-estimated, and too much faith was placed in the power of the artillery to destroy or block them.

For covering the attack, 1,513 guns and howitzers had been placed in position, averaging a field gun [1] to every twenty yards, and a heavy gun to every sixty yards of front, and during the preliminary bombardment and the first day of assault they fired 1,628,000 rounds of ammunition.

Thirteen British and five French divisions were assembled for the assault.

---

[1] On the 1st April 1915 there were 1,153 guns and howitzers, of all calibres, in France; on the 1st October 1915, 2,529; on the 1st July 1916, 4,037; on the 30th December 1916, 5,000. These figures do not include trench mortars.

Facing the thirteen British divisions was the German XIV Reserve Corps, with the 26th Reserve Division holding the front Serre—Thiepval—Ovillers, and the 28th Reserve Division holding Ovillers—Fricourt—Maricourt. The Guard Corps, of three divisions, was on the German right, holding as far as Arras ; the XVIII Corps, of three divisions, on the left as far as Roye. Behind these three corps were two divisions in reserve.

In artillery the Germans had less than a sixth of the quantity opposing them.

.   .   .   .

" All the arrangements are now made (27th)—our action is subsidiary. Scatter's [Minshull Ford] Brigade bears the brunt, and we support the 20th Manchesters. Scatter is very optimistic—too much so, I think. The enemy have pretty well destroyed our front line, and we theirs. I don't think our gas has had much effect. German prisoners captured say, ' Yes, we thought it might be gas and put on our masks, but were not sure.' Foch and the French seem very confident. This will be the biggest battle and the hardest yet fought by us on the Western Front. Reports seem to show that the Boches are getting alarmed. Will they get Verdun before we get them ?—that is the question. We go up to-morrow night.

" 28th June.—A filthy wet morning. Saw General Watts, also Steele. Everyone full of beans.

" 11.30 a.m.—A last conference of officers. 1 p.m.—Order for the brigade to stand fast. 2 p.m.—Ordered up to the trenches to relieve the Manchesters and Borderers. Everyone very bored—show off for forty-eight hours—no one quite knows why. Relief completed at 1 a.m. Devil's own bombardment going on.

" 29th June.—Bombardment on all night. German lines very knocked about. Gas and smoke daily. Nothing but the roll of guns and the crash of shells can be heard. Hun retaliation is feeble. Prisoners seem fed up. 5.30 p.m.—We let off a smoke cloud in the middle of an intense bombardment. Got off with three casualties, which is lucky, as they shelled like the deuce. 2 a.m.—An S.O.S. from a division south of us. Our men out all night trying to clear our wire—difficult work, as one is in danger from our own short shells and also the Huns shelling heavily.

" 30th June.—We move to our battle assembly positions this morning, everyone in his proper place by about 3 p.m. All the officers in reserve under Holmes have gone back. The following go into battle :

C.O. (self).
Adjutant—Reeves.

A Company—Morgan, Dobell.
B Company—Williams, Alexander, Smith.
C Company—Greaves, Sassoon, Garnons-Williams.
D Company—Davies, E. I. Jones, Baines.
Bombing Company—Stevens and Newton.
Lewis Guns—Anscombe.
Medical Officer—Kelsey Fry.

" Our battle headquarters are good and safe.

" The 20th Manchesters, who are to assault, are in front of us ; we are to support them.

" In addition, Brunicardi is Brigade Observation Officer, and young Dadd commands the Brigade Mobile Reserve.

" The bombardment has been terrific—a huge expenditure of ammunition.   If all goes well we ought to break the Hun line to a depth of a mile or more the first day, taking the first two lines of defence.   We assault on a 30- or 40-mile front at 7.30 a.m."

.   .   .   .   .   .

Other battalions of the regiment were on the move.   As at Loos, the area behind the battle-front held immediate reserves, while farther afield divisions were on the march towards the Somme district—although not on the scale of a few weeks later, when there was a continual in-and-out flow from the battlefield.

The 19th Division had been training since the middle of April about Aire, Abbeville, and Amiens.   Commencing on the 10th June, the march of our 9th Battalion led through Bruchamps, La Chaussée, St. Gratien, Bresle, and they arrived on the 30th June at Albert.   Their position that night was in the railway cutting running south from the Amiens—Albert road.

At 10 a.m. on the 1st July the whole division moved forward into trenches in rear of the front line.

The terrific bombardment, the quivering air, the spouts of earth and chalky dust, the thunder of explosion, the drone of aeroplanes and the motionless balloons, the waiting thirteen divisions.

The XV Corps orders state that the Fourth Army " has been ordered to take part in a general offensive with a view to breaking up the enemy's defensive system, and of exploiting to the full all opportunities opened for defeating his forces within reach."

Three successive tasks were allotted to the XV Corps : (a) To capture the German defences as far as Mametz Wood, level with the XIII Corps, on the right at Montauban, and the III Corps, on the left at Contalmaison.

(*b*) To pivot on the XIII Corps and take Bazentin-le-Grand, with the III Corps up to Bazentin-le-Petit. (*c*) To capture Guinchy, Longueval, and Delville Wood, with the XIII Corps taking Guillemont, and the III Corps High Wood.

It was calculated that (*a*) would conclude the first day's operations, " when preparations will immediately be undertaken to commence the second phase " (*b*). No time seems to have been allotted to (*b*) and (*c*), but, presumably, when " preparations " were complete, one day was deemed sufficient for each bound forward.

" The Corps Commander wishes to impress on all commanders that the success of the operations as a whole largely depends on the consolidation of the definite objectives which have been allotted to the 7th and 21st Divisions. Beyond these objectives no serious advance is to be made until preparations have been completed for entering on the next phase of the operations." In this manner firm control of the battle was to be kept in the hands of the Higher Command—whatever befell, all troops halted on a line. If the line was not completely won, still those who had reached it must halt, and wait while the lagging battalions battered their way to it. It is the keynote of the Somme adventure : centralisation of control ; the artillery as the battering-ram ; a straightforward attack.

In addition to a prelude of intense artillery fire, hurricane Stokes-mortar fire, smoke discharged in some parts of the line, " whiffs " of gas in others, there was to be a " Flammenwerfer attack, commencing ten minutes before zero, ' provided the apparatus is received in time ' " ! A curious after-thought in this carefully prepared battle !

So far as the XV Corps front is concerned the attack was to be " developed to the north and south of Fricourt village and Fricourt Wood by the 21st and 7th Divisions respectively, with the object of isolating the triangle formed by these localities, and which will be afterwards dealt with in a subsidiary operation." The two divisions would join hands at Willow Avenue, prolonging the line northwards through the Quadrangle towards Contalmaison.

The 91st Brigade (Minshull Ford) was on the right ; in the centre the 20th Brigade ; on the left the 22nd Brigade.

The brunt of the fight fell on the 91st Brigade, who were to advance in three phases through the village of Mametz, while the 20th Brigade formed a defensive flank from the north-eastern outskirts of Mametz, down Orchard Alley to its junction with Apple Alley, and so to our front trenches.

" The 22nd Brigade will clear the German trenches north of the Bois Français at an hour to be decided later, when the main attack has reached

ROYAL WELCH FUSILIERS IN BIVOUAC DURING SOMME BATTLE.

Imperial War Museum photograph, Crown copyright.

192]

its final objective. This operation will take place in conjunction with two battalions of the 50th Infantry Brigade, who will clear Fricourt village and Wood."

Finally, each man was to carry " (1) rifle and equipment, less pack, (2) two bandoliers of small-arm ammunition, (3) haversack on back, containing two tins of meat, eight hard biscuits, and canteen packed with grocery ration, (4) waterproof sheet, with jersey rolled inside, fixed on back of waist-belt by the supporting straps of the pack, (5) sandbags to be carried as directed by brigade, (6) two Mills grenades, one in each lower jacket pocket, (7) two smoke helmets, (8) a square patch of pink flannel will be sewn on the flap of the haversack, the top edge level with the seam marking the turnover of the flap—this will allow the patch to hang loose over the haversack, with the bottom level with the bottom of the haversack when filled."

THE BATTLE OF ALBERT.[1]

(1ST AND 9TH BATTALIONS.)

" 1st July.—Up at 5 a.m., the morning of the greatest battle the world has ever seen. We assault on a 30- to 40-mile front at 7.30 a.m., and the Russians at the same time and moment with 40 corps, or something near 2,000,000 men [2] ; we, the French and British, with about a million men.

" A heavenly morning. At 6.45 the most colossal intense bombardment started—the air does nothing but quiver and shake. The noise is terrific, a continuous soughing of shells passing overhead. We have 580 guns on this corps front of about two miles, and some hundreds of huge trench mortars, and they are all firing as hard as they can go."

The impression of rocking and quaking in the atmosphere was no exaggeration. It was a stupendous noise. From a distance the German word " drumfire " was appropriate, but standing in the midst of the pandemonium the sensation was of a seismic nature.

Looking out from his headquarters, a deep dugout in the chalky soil, Stockwell notes in his diary that at 7 a.m. there was " a damned machine gun traversing just over the door of our dugout." At 7.25 a.m. the British mines were fired, and then Stockwell could see " our men going over the top for a mile on each side."

---

[1] Date: 1st–13th July. Area: the Combles Valley to Hardecourt, thence road to Maricourt—Suzanne—Bray—Albert—Bouzincourt—Hedauville—Forceville—Bertrancourt—Sailly-au-Bois (exclusive)—Hebuterne—Puisieux.

[2] The Battle of the Strypa ended on the 30th June. The Battle of Baranovichi commenced on the 2nd July. Stockwell's diary records what was said on the Western Front.

The assault had commenced. The guns had lifted, but did not cease firing. News came in slowly. At 9 a.m. Stockwell ordered A and B Companies to their positions of assembly—he had heard that all was going well on the flanks. But an hour later he received orders to postpone all action.

The nature of the enemy's resistance may be gauged from the fact that the 20th Brigade had been obliged to shift their assembly positions an hour before the assault, as their front line had been blown flat by the enemy artillery ; troops had then to advance from the support line two minutes before zero.

At zero hour the 22nd Manchester and 1st Staffordshire, of the 91st Brigade, had little difficulty in passing over the German first line ; but the 2nd Gordon Highlanders (20th Brigade), who came next in line, had no sooner crossed No Man's Land than they were met by machine-gun and rifle fire—the Germans had had time to get out of their dugouts ! And the 9th Devon, starting from the support line, suffered from machine-gun fire before reaching their own flattened front line, near Mansel Copse. But they all got across.

In spite of the bombardment, the enemy was very much alive, and throughout this main attack troops suffered severely from the machine guns in Mametz on the right and Fricourt on the left.

Soon after midday Stockwell received orders to the effect that the postponed attack of the 22nd Brigade would take place at 2.30 p.m. The 91st Brigade were then fighting at close grips with the enemy on the outskirts of Mametz and Dantzig Alley, and by 4 p.m. had cleared Mametz and were established in Fritz Alley ; the 20th Brigade were striving to attain their final objective.

Thus, when the time came for the 22nd Brigade and the 50th Brigade (17th Division) to attack the nose of the salient, both the other brigades of the 7th Division and the whole of the 21st Division were engaged in hand-to-hand fighting on the flanks.

The subsidiary attack, to which our 1st Battalion was in support, started badly. Owing to an error, the 50th Brigade had advanced earlier in the day without artillery support, and had been badly cut up, so when the real attack was ordered at 2.30 p.m. the life had been taken out of them, and they failed to advance.

But on the 22nd Brigade front the 20th Manchester went forward covered by a rolling barrage. The leading line crossed to the German trench without opposition, but lost direction and swung to the right. They found the enemy in Bois Français, and bombing commenced. The second line were not, however, so fortunate in crossing No Man's Land. The failure of the 50th Brigade, on the left, enabled the German machine gunners at Wing Corner and Fricourt to devote their attention to the 20th Manchester, and the bombing detachments crossing with this second wave were annihilated. The attack lost half its strength, for the bombers of the second line were to have cleared Sunken Road Trench, Kitchen Trench, and Copper Trench, and worked their way towards Fricourt.

The enemy was holding Sunken Road Trench, Rectangle Support, Zinc Trench, and Orchard Alley in strength, and the attacking battalion found itself confined to the Bois Français Trench and Support.

. . . . .

At 3.45 p.m. Lieutenant-Colonel Stockwell, anxiously watching events, was informed that the 50th Brigade had only succeeded in getting to the German front line between Tambour and Wicked Corner, and that the 20th Manchester and troops crossing No Man's Land were badly enfiladed from Wing Corner. The situation at 4 p.m. " was not quite nice." The hill, which had to be cleared, was defended by a regular system of trenches, with the Rectangle, a " keep," on top of it. At 4 p.m. Stockwell notes : " Lewis (commanding the 20th Manchester) has gone over himself ; his right has apparently been bombed in by Papen Trench, and his left is in the air. His reserves and the Mobile Reserve (Dadd) have been sent over to Bois Français to clear up the situation and connect with the 20th Brigade in Apple Alley." Shortly after this Stockwell received the order to support the 20th Manchester and carry the hill.

To cross No Man's Land on his immediate front would be to offer a target to the German machine gunners at Wing Corner and Wicked Corner, and was out of the question. R. M. Stevens (Bombing Company) and C. D. Morgan (A Company) were, therefore, ordered to cross under shelter of the craters, behind the defensive flank already formed by the 91st Brigade. This occasioned a little delay.

The special training and organisation of the battalion under Minshull Ford were now to be put to the test. Stevens was ordered to bomb westwards, from the captured portion of the enemy trenches, along the parallel lines of Sunken Road and Rectangle Trenches. He was to be supported by Morgan's Company, and Williams was ordered to move up with B Company and be ready to meet any enemy counter-attack.

" 5 p.m.—The 20th Manchesters are in a bad state bunched up in Bois Français Support. Lewis killed. Morgan and A Company are over, but he will not get a move on.

" 7 p.m.—Masses of prisoners coming through.

" 10 p.m.—Enemy counter-attack developing through Fricourt. Morgan not yet at Rectangle. Reeves (Adjutant) has done splendidly—he has been over twice to ginger Morgan up.

" 10.30 p.m.—Stevens and Morgan have got the Rectangle and are consolidating. About 100 prisoners have been taken in Sunken Road by our men, who have done well. Morgan and Stevens did A1. They consolidated the Rectangle, and Stevens pushed on and seized Sunken Road Trench as far as Wing Corner—this was found to be strongly held. Lewis's body recovered."

The 20th Brigade, on the right, was now firmly established on the final

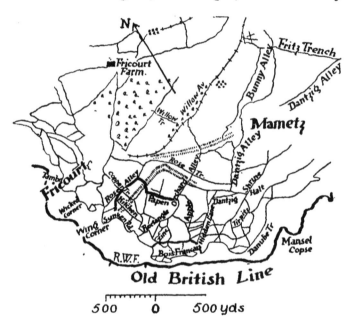

objective, and the 22nd Brigade orders were that they should not push on into Fricourt, which would be bombarded and taken by assault the next morning. But the enemy seemed to be shaken, and Stockwell sent parties of bombers to see if they could get into the village. These parties found little resistance, and in the morning the capture of Fricourt was reported just in time to prevent an unnecessary bombardment. In fact Stockwell was admonished " for exceeding orders and upsetting the programme—an example of the rigidity of our operations."

Bombing continued till 11 a.m., when the line quietened down and the commanding officer was able to ramble over the captured position. It was of great strength. Each line of trenches was supplied with a double tier of dugouts, connected to each other by tunnels. Canteens and a quartermaster's store were discovered.

" The principal feature of the operations had been the success of the Grenadier Company and the tactics they employed. The dreaded German bomber proved entirely futile when opposed to them, and thanks to them the battalion was able to capture five lines of strong trenches on a front of 800 yards, also Fricourt itself, with exceedingly small casualties (4 other ranks killed and 35 wounded). We are to be relieved to-morrow. Everyone very pleased with the battalion, as they saved the situation on this front. A quiet night, and a good sleep for three hours or so."

The whole of the 22nd Brigade concentrated on the 3rd July in a valley close to Mametz.

.   .   .   .   .   .

Meanwhile, on the left of the XV Corps, the III Corps attack did not go well. The 34th and 8th Divisions had been given the task of breaking through the enemy front-line system and capturing the line Acid Drop Copse—Cutting—Pozières, when the 19th Division would pass through them and advance on Bapaume.[1]

On the 1st July the 58th Brigade, with our 9th Battalion, was in trenches " about 1,000 yards east of Albert," opposite La Boisselles. Their rôle was, at the commencement of the battle, a waiting one, and the news that reached 19th Divisional Headquarters was grave : the 8th Division had secured no more than patches of the German front line, and was held. Finally, the 19th Division was ordered to advance and complete the task of the 8th Division.

" The 58th Brigade will capture La Boisselles this afternoon without fail, and regardless of losses, as the success of the whole operations there depends on its capture."

It was late in the afternoon when this decision was arrived at. The Divisional Commander called a conference of brigadiers at his advanced headquarters and explained the situation : the check was definite. He ordered the 57th and 58th Brigades to attack at 10.30 that night. Troops commenced to move at once—it was then about 6 p.m. Shortly before the attack was timed to commence the Officer Commanding 9th Cheshire Regiment arrived at Brigade Headquarters (58th) and reported that the congestion in communication trenches was so great that his battalion, which was to lead the assault, had become hopelessly scattered and he could only find a portion of it. Our 9th Battalion, moving up to support the Cheshire Battalion, was wedged in the long communication trenches, and could not move. The Officer Commanding the Cheshire Battalion was ordered to carry out the attack as soon as possible.

By 3 a.m. (2nd July) three companies of the 9th Cheshire had managed to cross No Man's Land to some craters already held by troops of the 34th Division.

---

[1] On the left of the III Corps was the 32nd Division, X Corps.

At 5 a.m. there was no sign of an attack being carried out. About that time a message was received at 58th Brigade Headquarters that the 9th Royal Welch Fusiliers were not yet in position, and that the 57th Brigade would not be able to carry out their attack. The Brigade Major was then sent down to the front line to report.

He found the communication trenches and front line, which had been much knocked about, were filled with wounded (and dead) men. Most of the 9th Cheshire were in the craters in the German line, but the Royal Welch Fusiliers were still, for the most part, blocked in communication trenches, though some had reached the old British front line. He consulted with the Commanding Officer, Lieutenant-Colonel Berners, and they arrived at the conclusion that an attack could be launched in the afternoon, after the trenches had been cleared. It was also decided that there should be no bombardment of La Boisselles, but of Ovillers, with a view to deceiving the enemy.

At 4 p.m. the advance commenced, our 9th Battalion and the 6th Wiltshire crossing No Man's Land with comparatively small loss. But the account of what followed is confused and leads to no clear statement. It was a hard fight with bombs, " all ranks behaving with the utmost gallantry." Captain E. K. Jones and 2nd Lieutenant C. D. McCannon were killed ; Lieutenant W. J. Jones and 2nd Lieutenant L. A. Nea were wounded. But the southern end of La Boisselles was secured by nightfall.

At 2.45 a.m. on the 3rd July, B and C Companies once more started to bomb their way forward, with A and D Companies in support. They were in the midst of the ruined village, bombing from one tumbled house to another, with trenches and shell-holes intervening. No one could tell exactly where he was, but pushed forward. So it went on till midday, when the enemy launched a strong bombing counter-attack and forced the battalion back to the edge of the village.

The Adjutant, Lieutenant C. G. Roberts, and 32 other ranks were killed ; 2nd Lieutenants H. C. Wancke, H. T. Jones, and J. L. Hughes and 128 other ranks were wounded.

The position remained the same until the battalion was relieved that night and bivouacked in the Tara-Usna line. They returned to hold the line between La Boisselles and Contalmaison on the 7th and 8th.

·　　·　　·　　·　　·　　·　　·

The first day's fighting is disposed of in a short paragraph in Sir Douglas Haig's despatch :

" On our right our troops met with immediate success, and rapid progress was made. Before midday Montauban had been carried, and shortly afterwards the Briqueterie to the east and the whole of the ridge to the west of the village were in our hands. Opposite Mametz part of the assembly trenches had been practically levelled by the enemy artillery, making it necessary for our infantry to advance to the attack across 400 yards of open ground. Nonetheless they forced their way into Mametz, and reached their objective in the valley beyond, first throwing out a defensive flank towards Fricourt on their left. At the same time the enemy's trenches were entered north of Fricourt, so that the enemy garrison in that village were pressed on three sides. Farther north, though the villages of La Boisselles and Ovillers for the time being resisted our attack, our troops drove deeply into the German lines on the flanks of these strongholds, and so paved the way for their capture later. On the spur running south from Thiepval the work known as the Leipzig Salient was stormed, and severe fighting took place for the possession of the village and its defences. Here, and north of the Valley of the Ancre as far as Serre on the left flank of our attack, our initial successes were not sustained. Striking progress was made at many points, and parties of troops penetrated the enemy's positions to the outer defences of Grandcourt, and also to Pendant Copse and Serre ; but the enemy's continued resistance at Thiepval and Beaumont Hamel made it impossible to forward reinforcements and ammunition, and, in spite of their gallant efforts, our troops were forced to withdraw during the night to their own lines."

Farther north still, at Gommecourt, the attack was a complete failure.

The first onslaught had not, then, justified the optimistic faith in massed artillery : the zone of artillery fire, this first day, extended in depth beyond the German second line. Opinions and orders were modified. Although certain notes of encouragement were circulated here and there, to the effect that " the enemy seemed demoralised," General Headquarters realised the full stubbornness of the defence. Sir Douglas Haig decided that he would not press the attack on the left, where it had been repulsed, and restricted the activities of the Fourth Army. The two left corps were placed under the command of Sir Hubert Gough, with instructions to act as a pivot on the front La Boisselles—Serre Road to the attacks, as they made progress, on his right. " During the succeeding days the attack was continued on these lines. During the 3rd and 4th July, Bernafay and Caterpillar Woods were also captured, and our troops pushed forward to the railway north of Mametz."

QUADRANGLE TRENCH.

Our 1st Battalion rested, sleeping mostly, all through the 3rd July in their valley near Mametz village. At 10 o'clock that night they were called out.

" I got some mysterious orders to go and dig a trench. Apparently the edge of Mametz Wood is not occupied, and we and the Royal Irish have to go and make a position there, but I can't make out on what authority. They say these places are unoccupied—it is pretty sketchy. Orders say, if opposed we are to come back. A guide is coming from the 91st Brigade."

The guide arrived about midnight, and seemed to have a hazy idea of direction—at 1 a.m. he was still trying to find the road. In front of him was a labyrinth of trenches and shell-holes.

" I refused to move the battalion till the guide had found the way. At 2 a.m. he decided to take us through the communication trenches. Got to destination about 3—men dead-beat. Went out to see where I was to dig—an impossible place, on a bluff (see map), within fifty yards of the forest. A bombing fight broke out at the end of the wood and we had to do a guy ! " (Stockwell.)

The intention of the orders which had so puzzled Stockwell was that the 2nd Royal Irish and the Royal Welch Fusiliers should consolidate a line from the south of Mametz Wood to Strip Trench, Wood Trench, and the Quadrangle as far as its junction with Bottom Alley. A rumour had been started, and was apparently believed by the Staff, that the wood was unoccupied.

The 2nd Royal Irish sent out covering parties to the edge of the wood, and ran into a strong force of the enemy. In the murky light of dawn they claim to have killed some fifty Germans, and undoubtedly inflicted loss and drove the enemy back, as they returned with the breach blocks of two field guns they had found.

It was obvious that the enemy was within a few yards of the line on which the two battalions were supposed to dig, and it was getting light (some parties of the Royal Irish had to be extricated from the wood with the aid of the artillery), so Stockwell decided to withdraw his battalion and return to the bivouac camp near Mametz village.

But the situation seemed slightly clearer to the Higher Command, and during the forenoon on the 4th July orders were issued that the line which the two battalions had been ordered to consolidate the previous night should be attacked during the night 4th/5th. Stockwell sent his company commanders to see the ground. They saw little, as it was raining hard,

LIEUTENANT-COLONEL RONALD JAMES WALTER CARDEN, COMMANDING 16TH
BATTALION, 1916. KILLED IN ACTION, 10TH JULY, 1916.

and although the British line ran along the edge of Bottom Wood, the enemy line could only be seen from some high ground about 2,000 yards in rear.

The attack was in conjunction with the 17th Division, on the left. At 12.30 a.m. our battalion was in position on the line of Bottom Wood, with the Royal Irish on the right and the 7th Northumberland Fusiliers on the left.

The night was very dark ; the ground heavy after the rain.   The attack had been mounted in a most casual way.   The wire in front of the German trenches was to have been cut during the afternoon, but the light was not good and the artillery did not fire.   The uncut state of the wire was not reported to Divisional Headquarters (7th) until 8 p.m. and " the 35th Artillery Brigade were hurriedly turned on to this work."

It was then reported that the wire in front of Quadrangle Trench was well gapped, but in that in front of Wood Trench there was only one gap.

Under these unfavourable conditions the attack was launched at 12.45 a.m., on a two-company front ; the assaulting troops disappeared in the darkness and there followed some hours of uncertainty at Battalion Headquarters.   Stockwell was in a communication trench in rear.

The artillery was firing now ; the German, too ; soon machine guns added their rattle to the noise that filled the night, but nothing could be seen.

" Wire won't work.   No news.

" 1.15.—News that the right company has lost its way ; then news that the battalion has been cut up—that the Royal Irish got in but have been driven out. Finally Williams (right company) turns up wounded. No news of the left company. Sent up the support company, A.

" 2.10.—Hear A and D are in, but hard pressed—sent up Stevens, C Company, and bombers. Dadd came back to explain the situation—bombs and bombers required, but no more men. Stevens and Dadd clear the trench and we gain our full objective."

The right company and the Royal Irish had been held up by wire. The latter made several attempts to enter Wood Trench, where one gap had been reported, but without success.

For our 1st Battalion it was once more a bombers' fight. " No doubt they have paid us hand over fist," Stockwell declared. " Stevens and Dadd did splendidly, as did Sassoon also." The moment the assaulting troops gained a footing in the line, the bombers cleared the trench right and left. On the right, where the trench ended near the railway, there was a gap of some 200 yards swept by a machine gun, which effectively prevented any help being given to the Royal Irish ; but a block was made in Quadrangle Alley. On the left considerable help was given to the Northumberland Fusiliers.

The 2nd Royal Irish were withdrawn and the trench garrisoned by our 1st Battalion ; the bombers and surplus men were sent to Bottom Trench.

About 6 a.m. the Germans launched a counter-attack. The German support line was not visible from the captured trench, but was connected to it by a long communication trench—Quadrangle Alley—and down this the Germans came. It was rather a shallow trench, and the heads of the enemy bombers could be seen : they were allowed to approach the block and were then bombed and enfiladed by Lewis guns. One of our bombing platoons immediately took the offensive and drove the Germans back to their support line. A new block was made some 300 yards farther along the trench, and close to the German support line. From this vantage-point two other attacks were repulsed during the day.

That night our 1st Battalion was relieved by our 14th Battalion, under Major Gwyther. The 1st Battalion was about 400 strong, the 14th near 800 ; the trenches were overcrowded.

The whole of the 7th Division marched back to rest ; our 1st Battalion at Heilly. Casualties in the last attack had been 8 other ranks killed ; Lieutenant H. B. Williams, 2nd Lieutenant C. D. Morgan, and 55 other ranks wounded.

MAMETZ WOOD.

The 38th Division had moved from the Givenchy—Laventie area on the 10th June, and had marched to the neighbourhood of St. Pol, where battalions underwent a short course of training. They arrived in the battle-area on the 4th July.

The 113th Brigade took over the line between Marlborough Wood and Cliff Trench, with the 18th Division on the right and the 17th on the left. Information on what was in front of them was circulated ; it was taken from the report of the Royal Irish.

Mametz Wood " is very dense, with thick undergrowth in that portion which was entered, and movement for infantry is not easy. There is a trip wire at the edge of the wood which would not form a serious obstacle by day. About 100 yards inside the southern face of the wood is a small shallow trench, or dip. Strip Trench is strongly wired and well traversed ; trees from the wood have fallen across the trench and make movement difficult."

Battalions realised, of course, that they were for an early attack. There had been conferences, at which verbal instructions had been given. There was a rearrangement of the line, a side-slipping to the right by the 17th Division, who took over an extra length of trench ; and the 113th Brigade was relieved by the 115th.

Operation orders were issued late on the 6th July. The objective of the XV Corps was Acid Drop Copse and Mametz Wood, and the operation was to be carried out in two stages. At 2 a.m. on the 7th the 17th Division was to attack Quadrangle Support and Pearl Alley, and if successful a combined attack would be launched by the 17th Division and the 38th Division on Mametz Wood at 8 a.m. But if unsuccessful, the second stage would take place at 8.30 a.m.

The first stage failed, and so the hour of assault for the 115th Brigade was 8.30 a.m. The 16th Welch Regiment and the 11th South Wales Borderers were met by machine-gun fire, which stopped them before they reached the edge of the wood. A second attempt was made at 11 a.m. with a similar result. A third was ordered for 4.30 p.m. It had been pouring with rain the whole day, the ground was sodden, the trenches were half-filled with mud and water, and the approach to the wood, down a slope and, on the greater part of the front, a cliff, was difficult. Communication was bad ; all the telephone wires had been cut and the linesmen were slow, under the conditions, in repairing them ; also the artillery was inaccurate and ineffective. So the 4.30 attack was cancelled.

The wood seems to have been a puzzle. There was still, for some reason, a belief that the enemy would relinquish it, though why he should do so with such easy access to it is not clear. The 115th Brigade and a battalion of the 17th Division having failed to secure even the edge of the wood, our 14th Battalion received orders to attack early in the morning of the 9th with parties of bombers and capture from Wood Trench to point G.

After an artillery bombardment " at 2 a.m., bombing parties will go down the cliff against the southern end of Strip Trench and will move up it, keeping a party above ground as long as possible," and " another attack of 50 men, and 4 Lewis guns, will leave the road below the cliff, with their left near the junction with the railway, and will attack point G." With the darkness, the fearful condition and congested state of the trenches, the 14th Battalion did not reach their assembly position in time, and the attack was cancelled.

At this moment the division was in some difficulty. During the morning Major-General Ivor Phillips vacated command, and Major-General Watts, commanding the 7th Division, was given temporary command. Reliefs took place, and the line was held by the 114th and 113th Brigades. In the evening orders were issued to attack next day at 4.15 a.m.

Mametz Wood was to be captured by the 114th and 113th Brigades, with some help from the 17th Division, who were to bomb up Quadrangle Support and Wood Support. It was to be a slow and deliberate attack, with three separate artillery lifts within the wood.

For three-quarters of an hour the artillery was to bombard the southern portion of the wood, and during the last half-hour form a smoke screen. The guns would then lift, and the infantry were required to gain the edge of the wood and push through the tangle to the first ride. They were given two hours to gain this objective. Meanwhile the artillery would be firing between the first and second rides ; but their subsequent action and that of the infantry are not clearly expressed :

" At 6.15 a.m. the artillery barrage will lift to the line W, V, Y, O, and K, and the infantry will capture and consolidate the line, making strong-points at V, Y, O, and K."

At 7.15 a.m. the artillery would again lift to the north edge of the wood ; and at 8.15 a.m. to the German second line.

Throughout the operation machine-gun fire was to be directed from Marlborough Wood and Caterpillar Wood on to the long communication trench between Mametz Wood and Bazentin le Petit Wood ; while three heavy trench mortars and the medium trench mortars were to assist against Cliff Trench.

The dividing line between brigades was the centre drive, the 113th Brigade having that part of the front marked GI.

Our 16th Battalion was to deliver the assault in eight lines, or waves, from behind White Trench. Immediately behind them was the 14th Battalion, drawn up in four lines; the 15th and 13th Battalions were back in the neighbourhood of Bunny Trench, Fritz Trench, and Mametz village.

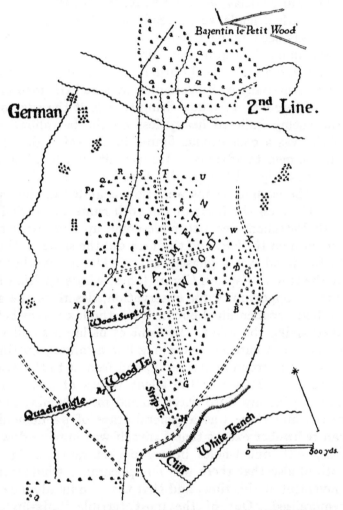

Brigadier-General Price Davies met the officers of the 14th and 16th Battalions in Queen's Nullah and went through the orders with them, explaining any doubtful points. Colonel Carden, commanding the 16th Battalion, was told that although the time for starting was fixed for 4.15 a.m., he must not start before the 114th Brigade, as he was nearest to the edge of the wood.

Lieutenant-Colonel Carden was a gifted leader with a touch of fanaticism. He addressed his battalion before going into action: "Make your peace with God. You are going to take that position, and some of us won't come back—but we are going to take it." And tying a coloured handkerchief to his walking-stick he said, "This will show you where I am."

The Attack.

As the action progressed, all became confusion. The instructions to the 16th Battalion to wait till the 114th Brigade had started seem to have caused delay, as Major F. R. H. McLellan stated that when he started, the 114th Brigade were already well down the slope to the wood, and their left was seen to be retiring, which caused the 16th Battalion to waver. German machine guns were already at work, and there was some hesitation, but Lieutenant-Colonel Carden, supported by Captain G. C. W. Westbroke and Lieutenant A. V. Venables, steadied the men and led them forward.

There was a shallow firing trench at the edge of the wood from which the enemy inflicted heavy loss on the battalion. Carden, with his stick aloft, was a conspicuous figure, in the soft light of early morning, calling on the men to advance. He was hit, and fell, but rose again. He led to the very edge of the wood, where he was killed.

The leading troops were now engulfed in the thick undergrowth.

Close on the heels of the 16th came the 14th Battalion. In fact the 14th Battalion seems to have come up level with the 16th, but the 16th bunched on the left, and the 14th did the same on the right. The approach to the wood was a ghastly affair. Major Gwyther was severely wounded at the start. Captain Glynn Jones, whose position in the rear waves gave him an opportunity for observation, describes the scene. " Before dawn we had our men lined out in the orthodox waves behind the rising ground overlooking the wood. In front of us lay a small valley, in the centre of which was a cutting, something like a railway cutting (the Cliff). To that cutting the ground fell steeply, and from it to the wood was a more gradual slope. . . . Presently the silent waves of men started moving forward, and I, with my third wave, joined in. Machine guns and rifles began to rattle, and there was a general state of pandemonium, little of which I can remember except that I myself was moving down the slope at a rapid rate, with bullet-holes in my pocket and yelling a certain amount. I noticed also that there was no appearance whatsoever of waves about the movement at this time, and that the men in advance of us were thoroughly demoralised. Out of the most terrible ' mix-up ' I have ever seen I collected all the men I could see and ordered them into the cutting. There appeared to be no one ahead of us, no one following us, and by this time it was broad daylight and the ridge behind us was being subjected to a terrible artillery and machine-gun fire.

" I well remember thinking, ' Here comes the last stand of the old Carnarvon and Angleseys ' as I ordered the men to get ready, and posted a

Lewis gun on each of my flanks. At this stage, too, I remember seeing wounded Major Gwyther, our commanding officer, and giving him certain attention. Meanwhile, men were crawling in from shell-holes to our front, with reports of nothing less than a terrible massacre, and the names of most of our officers and N.C.O.s lying dead in front were mentioned. Shortly after there was a lull, and from the wood in front a number of Germans— about forty—came out, with hands up. Suspecting a trick, I ordered my men to cover them, but allowed them to approach us. When they got about half-way I went out to meet them, accompanied by a sergeant, and sent them back to our headquarters.

"As this appeared to point to the wood being unoccupied, I sent a small patrol to examine it ; and then we all moved forward. Crossing the trench on the fringe of it, we entered the wood at the entrance of the main ride, and with two patrols in front advanced up the ride in file, as the under-growth was very thick. Presently on our left we met men of another battalion (the 16th), who reported the wood taken as far as the first objective. Later I found this to be the case."

Meanwhile the Brigadier had ordered up the 15th Battalion and two companies of the 13th, in response to appeals for reinforcements. All went into the wood, and naturally enough, once the troops reached the thick tangle, control became extremely difficult, if not impossible. Many officers of all battalions had fallen while crossing the open space on the hill-side ; leaders were few and the thick underwood, fallen trees, and shell-holes made for confusion. Reports sent back to the brigade and division were wild and contradictory—no one could say with certainty where he was. One fact stood out, that Wood Support was still held by the enemy and was causing a lot of trouble. The 16th Battalion and part of the 15th were in Wood Trench; both claimed to have bombed the enemy from Strip Trench : elsewhere all was uncertain, but a strong impression was created at Divisional Headquarters that troops had passed through our own barrage. The artillery was therefore ordered to lift on to the German second line, between Mametz Wood and Bazentin le Petit Wood.

To clear up the situation the Brigadier ordered Lieutenant-Colonel Flower to take the two remaining companies of his battalion forward (13th) and reorganise the 113th Brigade. About the same time he went forward himself, accompanied by Colonel Gosset, attached from the Fourth Army. In Strip Trench "a party of men were found running back in panic." Flower and his two companies had arrived at the edge of the wood, and he was ordered to take them in two lines through the wood, the leading line to carry the troops in front forward, the second line to dig in. Actually these companies joined the mass of troops assembled south of the first ride.

The situation at 9 a.m., as appreciated by Brigadier-General Price Davies, was that the 113th and 114th Brigades were in touch at the central ride on the first objective ; that units were mixed in a most hopeless way ; that the Pioneer Battalion (19th Welch Regiment) and the detachment of Royal Engineers, sent forward about 7 a.m., were trying to consolidate a line but were much hampered by fire from Wood Support ; and that the brigade generally were being *bombarded by our own artillery*. It was, however, clear that no troops were beyond the first objective. On the extreme right the 114th Brigade were in difficulties and uncertain about point X.

Orders were now issued to the heavy artillery to bombard the northern part of the wood, and arrangements were made for the infantry to advance on the next objective—the second ride. Our 17th Battalion was sent from the 115th Brigade to support the 113th Brigade, and the 10th South Wales Borderers to support the 114th Brigade. Unfortunately the 17th Battalion lost Lieutenant-Colonel J. A. Ballard, who became a casualty on the way up, and the attack was delayed.

The situation was somewhat eased by the 13th Battalion bombing the enemy from Wood Support, where a number of prisoners were taken. But on the right, the 114th Brigade was counter-attacked, and the unit on the eastern edge of the wood was having a rough time.

At this stage of the proceedings there were no less than eleven battalions in the wood. The Brigadier withdrew our 15th and 16th Battalions—at least some of them.

At 2 p.m. Lieutenant-Colonel Pryce (G.S.O.1) arrived from Divisional Headquarters and found the troops " in a somewhat confused state, except for three companies of the 17th Royal Welch Fusiliers." As there was no rifle or machine-gun fire from the north, he ordered these three companies to advance " as a covering party " to the second ride, which they did without trouble. An attempt was then made to sort out the troops on the first ride.

By 4 p.m. the 10th South Wales Borderers and the 15th Welch Regiment were ready, and moved forward east of the central ride till they came abreast of the 17th Royal Welch Fusiliers ; our 13th Battalion moved up on the extreme left, between the edge of the wood and the railway ; and the whole line advanced to within 40 yards of the northern edge. Here they were met by fire from the German second line, and though our artillery was firing on that second line, it is only fair to state that it was unobserved fire.

LIEUTENANT-COLONEL O. S. FLOWER.

Once more our 15th Battalion was brought up to reinforce the 13th, and after further bombardment an attempt was made to get through the remaining portion of the wood, but was unsuccessful.

The line held that night was said to be about 100 yards from the northern end of the wood.

But night fell on the most bewildering state of affairs. No one could either see or move. Messages commenced to arrive at Brigade and Divisional Headquarters that the enemy was attacking. Lieutenant-Colonel Pryce, who had remained in the wood, could only report that the situation was not clear, but that the line was, apparently, not broken. Still the firing and confusion were such that the 22nd Brigade, resting behind Mametz village, was turned out—this was about 10 p.m.—but the order was shortly afterwards cancelled, and the Brigade returned to its bivouacs.

There was, however, a great deal of wild firing through the night, and the relief of troops by the 115th Brigade was not possible until the morning.

" There was a good deal of confusion in the wood, particularly during the night time. Groups fired on one another, mistaking one another for the enemy. It was impossible to see on account of the darkness, and most difficult to hear or give orders on account of the weird din. A machine gun gave the impression it was a few yards in front on account of the strange reverberation through the wood. Many of our shells fell short—or perhaps it was that they struck the tops of the trees and burst prematurely." (John Edwards, O.C. C Company, 15th Battalion.)

Brigadier-General Evans, commanding the 115th Brigade, was now responsible for the wood, and he made a personal reconnaissance. He found the line not so advanced as he had been led to believe. It ran in an irregular way from a point about 300 yards below the north-eastern corner to the point K, near Wood Support. The enemy was holding the northern part. The men were tired, and " the *moral* of some units was shaken." He proposed to straighten out the line from the north.

It was then arranged that the infantry should advance at 3 p.m. without artillery support and drive the enemy out at the point of the bayonet. But at 2.45 p.m. " our artillery opened a heavy barrage on the northern end of the wood, making it impossible for our infantry to advance. Many casualties were caused by shells falling short ; the telephone wires being cut made communication to our rear an extremely difficult matter." Orders were given to the infantry to advance as soon as the unwelcome barrage ceased—which was about 3.30 p.m. It was then found that although the artillery had effectively stopped our advance, it had failed

III—14

to drive the enemy out of the wood.   Still, progress was made on the western side, and the whole line drew up level, about 300 yards from the northern edge.   And so it remained.

The secret of this unhappy state of affairs is probably to be found in the German second line.   It was easy for parties of the enemy to get into, or retire from, the wood ; and simple enough to keep the northern part of it under machine-gun fire.   Our gunners could not see this portion of the German second line, and failed to get the range from the map.

.   .   .   .

One cannot ignore the reports of eye-witnesses.

" The impression gained of the fight is that the initial advance from the cliff to the wood was carried out with great gallantry in the face of heavy fire from the enemy's artillery and small arms.   Subsequently there appeared to be no sting in the attack, and *moral* gradually became reduced until the smallest incident caused a panic."   (Brigadier-General Price Davies.)

" That evening there developed a terrible enemy shelling of the wood, and this resulted in perfect pandemonium.   Out of the wood emerged scores of men, from every battalion in the division, all making headlong for the rear.   Being more collected ourselves, and supported with a sheltered home and a steep hill behind, Sergeant Thompson and I, sometimes with the aid of revolver threats, very soon increased our force in the cutting to about 250 men."   (Captain Glynn Jones.)

Brigadier-General Evans confirms the disorganised state of the troops.

On the other hand, there is much to be said in mitigation.   " Our own guns were firing short, and in spite of our attempts to communicate with the rear this continued.   The numerous casualties we sustained because of this had the effect of making the men very panicky.   Further, the difficulty of seeing more than a few yards in front caused ignorance amongst the men as to where the front lay and whether any of our fellows were there : any noise in the bush in front meant a hail of bullets into it.   I, myself, saw an officer of the 15th Royal Welch Fusiliers killed in this way." (Captain Glynn Jones.)

The artillery programme had not been an easy one to carry out, and the wood was thickly packed with troops.   Something like misgiving occurred to Brigadier-General Price Davies.

" This account (to Division) was made up after the receipt of the accounts furnished by battalion commanders and from my own personal experience.   Since then I have had accounts of certain gallant actions performed by officers and other ranks, and I feel that possibly I may not have given my brigade full credit for what they did in Mametz Wood. This is probably in great part due to the painful impression left on Lieutenant-Colonel Bell, 15th R.W.F., and myself (the only two senior officers and the only Regular officers of the brigade who witnessed the fight and did not become casualties) by the discreditable behaviour of the men of the division who fled in a panic, about 8.45 p.m. on July 10th. The result has been that the initial success in entering the wood in the face of heavy artillery and small-arms fire has not been brought to notice sufficiently.

" I feel that some brigadiers would have made a most readable story with the material available. They would no doubt have dwelt upon the capture of guns in the wood, and on the number of machine guns to our credit, as well as upon the difficulties of attacking through a thick wood in the face of the fire of snipers and machine guns. Though I deprecate all forms of bragging and consider that when failure is disclosed it should be faced, I think it possible that a certain amount of praise, in fact making the most of such successes as we obtain, is good for *moral* and improves the confidence and self-respect of the men.

" Further, from rumours which reach me, I believe *other troops operating in High Wood and Bois des Trones found it extremely difficult to organise an advance under such conditions.*[1]

" I realise it is now too late to add to any account which has been sent forward, but as I feel I had, in conversation, painted rather a gloomy picture to the Divisional Commander of the conduct of the troops I saw in Mametz Wood, I thought I might be permitted to represent the above facts.

" PRICE DAVIES."

.   .   .   .

During the night the 38th Division was relieved by the 21st Division. Our 14th Battalion had moved into the wood again. " About midnight a message was passed down that I was wanted on the left. Proceeding there, I found an officer of the Warwicks, who stated that he had come to relieve us. Words cannot express the meaning of that word ' relief ' as it applied to us at that moment. To a war chronicler it cannot mean more than a trifling operation, but its effect in our case was that after handing over our little line to the new-comers, we were making our way back down the main ride at a pace that I never would have dreamed us capable of. I remember very little about that long journey back, except that as a parting gift we had a direct hit on our tail, which killed a number of men as we were nearing Mametz village. But I well remember my Quarter-

[1] Our italics.

master-Sergeant meeting me somewhere with the words ' Thank God you're all right, sir,' having a dixie of hot soup, and falling off into a deep sleep." (Glynn Jones.)

The division was billeted round Treux.

Casualties had been particularly severe. The 13th Battalion lost their gallant Lieutenant-Colonel Flower (died of wounds), Captain E. W. Lawrence (Medical Officer), Lieutenants Vivian Jones, 2nd Lieutenant A. S. H. Barrett, killed ; Major O. J. Bell, Captains L. S. Ayer, F. R. Graesser-Thomas, 2nd Lieutenant J. Pritchard, wounded.

The 14th Battalion : Major R. H. Mills, Lieutenant J. F. Venmore, 2nd Lieutenants A. S. Roberts, B. Harrison, A. C. Stagg, and 67 other ranks killed ; Major G. H. Gwyther (Commanding Officer), Captains H. C. Gorton, J. Williams, Lieutenants B. B. Cotterill, J. B. Martin, 2nd Lieutenants C. H. Stork, J. Jack, W. J. Williams, N. L. Harris, and 233 other ranks wounded.

The 15th Battalion (unrecorded) : 12 officers, 250 other ranks from 5th to 11th July.

The 16th Battalion : Lieutenant-Colonel Carden, 2nd Lieutenant H. H. T. Rees, and 43 other ranks killed ; Lieutenants J. S. Humphries, R. J. Atkinson, 2nd Lieutenants G. A. Black, Hepworth, J. Fairclough, and 186 other ranks wounded ; 64 other ranks missing.

The 17th Battalion : Captain H. Williams, 2nd Lieutenants J. V. Sinnett Jones, W. C. Wright, L. Lewis, T. O. Thomas, and 30 other ranks killed; Lieutenant-Colonel J. A. Ballard, Captain and Adjutant P. B. Welton, Lieutenants A. S. Edwards, A. H. Styles, 2nd Lieutenants J. R. Jones, L. R. Jones, P. F. Kunkler, H. E. Van Derplank, F. W. Walsh, C. Gates, E. Thomas, Captain P. Walsh (Medical Officer), and 197 other ranks wounded ; 37 other ranks missing.

" In particular the names of Lieutenant-Colonel Flower, Lieutenant-Colonel Carden, and Major R. H. Mills should ever be remembered by us as officers who have set a glorious example, an example we should all endeavour to copy. Such officers can never be replaced, but it is hoped that their courage and self-sacrifice may long act as an inspiration to those who witnessed their gallant conduct." (Brigadier-General commanding 113th Brigade.)

.   .   .   .

Meanwhile, on the left of the Fourth Army, at the junction with Sir Hubert Gough's two corps, the position had been strengthened. After the capture of La Boisselles, the 19th Division had made a further advance, and on the 7th July our 9th Battalion had left their Albert billets and moved up to the front line. They were to take over from assaulting troops, who were forming a flank. The line was still in a loose state, and a party of Germans held up the leading company with machine-gun fire which enfiladed the communication trench. There was some considerable delay, but when darkness fell the enemy party was driven from its position, and the battalion took over from the 12th Durham Light Infantry. On the 10th July they returned once more to Albert, to move later to Mametz Wood.

THE RIDGE.

When the 2nd Battalion was relieved in the Givenchy sector and commenced to move south, Bethune had a depressing and tawdry appearance. The glamour of battle had departed and left a small, drab, provincial town, surrounded on three sides by coalfields.

The battalion entrained at Fouguereuil and arrived at Longueau at 7 a.m. on the 10th July—20 officers and 686 other ranks. Then commenced the march to the Somme.

The route lay through Amiens, with its cathedral partly sandbagged, and through the pleasant rolling country to Cardonette. On the 11th the British and Indian cavalry lines were passed on the road to Daours, where the Ancre and the Somme meet and a road was named Rue Na Poo (the soldier's catchword from the French shopkeeper's " Il n'y en a plus ").

The 38th Division transport was met on the 12th, moving north after the Mametz slaughter.

The camp at Buire, where tents were pitched in an orchard, was in " a pocket of silence," only $7\frac{1}{2}$ miles from the battle-front, and the guns could not be heard, though the flashes could be seen : here the battalion remained for some days. They had had a pleasant march, in easy stages, and through country resembling parts of southern England ; also the weather had been fine.

The 33rd Division was now in the XV Corps, under General Horne.

Seven and a half miles away preparations were complete for a second great effort to break through the German lines before dawn on the 14th July. While the battalion was breakfasting on the 13th, a cavalry division rode by : all arms were to be represented in this battle. " Apparently the High Command was hopeful of making a sufficient gap in the third line to let the cavalry through—to the regimental officer it seemed a futile hope." During the afternoon Lieutenant-Colonel Crawshay and the company commanders rode forward to Mametz, where the artillery in ranks was pounding the second German line, preparing the way for an infantry attack in the early morning. Back in camp the " pocket of silence " was silent no longer ; that night the guns were heard, and in the morning the sound increased.

A break in the weather had been threatening, and on the 14th the camp woke in a drizzle of rain. The great battle was raging. " The situation is satisfactory " was the official news, which the cynical regimental officer interpreted as meaning that the cavalry would not be required. At 11 a.m. the battalion moved out of camp at the tail of the brigade, and while halting at Meaulte for a haversack ration saw for the first time a big batch of prisoners—some 900—being marched back.

The first site selected for the brigade to bivouac was on the forward slope of a hill, opposite some German observation balloons ; the brigade was promptly shelled, and the Brigadier ordered a move to the reverse slope. From here, just above the Fricourt Road, the steady grind of traffic was heard all night.

Brigade réveillé was at 2.30 a.m. on the 15th. The battalion moved off at 4 a.m. in a thick mist. Soon after the road was reached they entered the uncleared battlefield. Broken wagons, dead horses and drivers, casualties of the midnight shelling, were passed. The soil " exhaled tear gas " ; eyes and noses ran, and the taste of tobacco was spoiled. Ambulances, stragglers, detachments, messengers, broken guns, a dead German lying on a stretcher, equipment, clothing, rifles, all the litter of battle was strewn over the shell-pitted ground. Bécordel—except the church tower—and Fricourt were flattened out.

The march had been interrupted several times by shell fire, but at midday a halt was ordered, and, the mist dispersing suddenly, the battalion found itself among the dead of the Welsh Division in front of Mametz Wood. The bodies of several friends were recognised and buried.

. . . . . .

Despatches, published in the midst of a war, are treacherous foundations for history : they so often cover disappointment by accepting a situation as a natural incident, foreseen and provided for in the original plan, and the hope that was cherished is suppressed. Thus the somewhat empty results of the first five days' fighting drew the explanation from Sir Douglas Haig :

" In normal conditions of enemy resistance the amount of progress that can be made at any time without a pause in the general advance is necessarily limited. Apart from the physical exhaustion of the attacking troops and the considerable distance separating the enemy's main systems of defence, special artillery preparation was required before a successful assault could be delivered. Meanwhile, however, local operations were continued in spite of much unfavourable weather.

" An attack on Contalmaison and Mametz Wood was undertaken on the 7th July, and after three days' obstinate fighting, in the course of which the enemy delivered several powerful counter-attacks, the village and the whole of the wood, except its northern border, were finally secured. On the 7th July also a footing was gained in the outer defences of Ovillers ; while on the 9th July, on our extreme right, Maltz Horn Farm—an important point on the spur north of Hardecourt—was secured.

" A thousand yards north of this farm our troops had succeeded at the second attempt in establishing themselves on the 8th July in the southern end of Trones Wood. The enemy's positions in the northern and eastern parts of the wood were strong, and no less than eight powerful German counter-attacks were made here during the next five days. In the course of this struggle portions of the wood changed hands several times ; but we were left, eventually, on the 13th July, in possession of the southern part of it.

" Meanwhile Mametz Wood had been entirely cleared of the enemy, and with Trones Wood practically in our possession we were in a position to undertake an assault upon the enemy's second system of defences. Arrangements were accordingly made for an attack to be delivered at daybreak on the morning of the 14th July against a front extending from Longueval to Bazentin le Petit Wood, both inclusive. Contalmaison Villa, on a spur 1,000 yards west of Bazentin le Petit Wood, had already been captured to secure the left flank of the attack, and advantage had been taken of the progress made by our infantry to move our artillery forward into new positions. The preliminary bombardment opened on the 11th July. The opportunities offered by the ground for enfilading the enemy's lines were fully utilised and did much to ensure the success of our attack."

THE BATTLE OF BAZENTIN RIDGE.[1]

We must take stock of our position.

On the 13th July our 10th Battalion, 3rd Division, was at Carnoy, having entrained at St. Omer on the 1st July for Doullens and marched through Gézaincourt, Naours, Rainneville, and Franvillers ; the 1st Battalion was at the Citadel, a camp in rear of the original British line ; the 2nd Battalion was at Buire-sur-Ancre, and moved the next day to Meaulte ; the 9th Battalion was back in Albert. The bombardment in preparation for the attack on the German second line was in progress.

[1] Date: 14th-17th July.   Area: road Hardecourt—Maricourt—Fricourt—Bécourt—Albert (exclusive), thence the Ancre.

THE 1ST BATTALION.

Part of the 7th Division was already in the line. The XV Corps had taken over a portion of the Montauban Valley from the XIII Corps, which was held by the 2nd Gordon Highlanders, and the 7th Division had also taken over, from the 38th Division, from Marlborough Wood—Caterpillar Wood—east of Mametz Wood.

A great attack this of the 14th July. Hope soared high at General Headquarters. The XV Corps issued instructions on the 13th:

" In the event of the attack to-morrow being successful, the first task of the XV Corps will be to consolidate Bazentin le Grand Wood and Bazentin le Petit village and Wood. Later on to secure High Wood and Martinpuich, and ultimately to secure the enemy's third line between Flers and Eaucourt l'Abbaye, both inclusive. XIII Corps are to secure Ginchy and Guillemont, and part of the enemy's third line, towards Flers. III Corps are to secure the enemy's second line, between Bazentin le Petit Wood and Albert—Bapaume Road, Pozières, and later Le Mouquet Farm. Ultimately to secure Courcelette and Le Sars.

" Should the enemy's line be broken and Delville Wood and Bazentin le Petit be secured, the 2nd Indian Cavalry Division will be sent on by order of the XIII Corps to seize High Wood and the enemy's switch line immediately to the east and west of the wood. XV Corps will then take over High Wood from the 2nd Indian Cavalry Division, who will then come under the orders of the XV Corps, and will push forward to Flers and Eaucourt l'Abbaye to cover the deployment of the XIII and XV Corps and the advance of the 1st Cavalry Division."

The French on the right and Gough's Reserve Army on the left were attacking with the Fourth Army. With the knowledge of after-events the optimism of Sir Douglas Haig is a difficult mood to capture—the second line pierced, the cavalry good enough to take the third line !

" In the early hours of the 14th July the attacking troops moved out over the open for a distance of from about 1,000 to 1,400 yards, and lined up in the darkness just below the crest and some 300 to 500 yards from the enemy's trenches. Their advance was covered by strong patrols, and the correct deployment had been ensured by careful previous preparations. The whole movement was carried out unobserved and without touch being lost in any case. The decision to attempt a night operation of this magnitude with an Army the bulk of which had been raised since the beginning of the war was perhaps the highest tribute that could be paid to the quality of our troops. It would not have been possible but for the most careful preparation and forethought, as well as thorough reconnaissance of the ground, which was in many cases made personally by divisional, brigade, and battalion commanders and their staffs before framing their detailed orders for the advance.

"The actual assault was delivered at 3.25 a.m. on the 14th July, when there was just sufficient light to be able to distinguish friend from foe at short ranges, and along the whole front attacked our troops, preceded by a very effective artillery barrage, swept over the enemy's first trenches and on to the defences beyond."

The XV Corps attacked with the 7th Division on the right and the 21st on the left. The XIII Corps placed the 3rd Division on their left, but our 10th Battalion was in reserve with the 76th Brigade, and was not called upon to attack until later.

In the 7th Division the 20th Brigade led the assault on the German second line, and the 22nd Brigade, at first in support, went through the 20th Brigade to take Bazentin le Petit village.

"We attack to-morrow at dawn. Men very keen. To bed early, and move off at 2 a.m.

"14th.—We moved off from the Citadel to White Trench. The 20th Brigade are assaulting the trenches in front of Bazentin le Petit Wood. The Warwicks and Royal Irish are to go through and consolidate the village as far north as the Cemetery; we are in support; the 20th Manchesters in reserve. We had some difficulty in getting into White Trench as the intense bombardment was on, and we had to dodge the guns. The assault was for 3.45 a.m." (Stockwell.)

The assaulting companies of the 20th Brigade entered the German line with ease, and the 22nd Brigade was ordered to advance. The 2nd Warwickshire, passing through Bazentin le Grand Wood, attacked Circus Trench, which they took. The 2nd Royal Irish then passed through them, and attacked Bazentin le Petit and the Cemetery, which they secured about 8.15 a.m. Meanwhile our 1st Battalion was waiting in White Trench.

"About 4.15 a.m. we learned that the Warwicks and Royal Irish were going forward, and pushed forwards by companies across the valley to occupy their positions in the hammer-head of Mametz Wood. No trenches, but lots of shell-holes—and lots of shells falling. Did the best we could to dig in, but it was a death-trap if the Huns had shortened 100 yards.

"About 11 a.m. we got orders to advance after the cavalry, and take and hold High Wood about 1½ miles farther on. Made all arrangements. Smith wounded."

The antics of the cavalry always created the greatest amusement, mortifying though it probably was for them. While Stockwell was making arrangements, the situation in Bazentin le Petit was not comfortable. The Royal Irish, in the village, were under fire from the wood on their left ; troops of the 21st Division were repeatedly shelled out of the wood as soon as they entered it. At 11.30 a.m. the enemy launched a strong counter-attack : the situation then became critical.

The Royal Irish were driven out of the northern end of the village, and the line Windmill—Cemetery, which had been occupied, was lost. A company of the Warwickshire had moved out to the right, and with Northumberland Fusiliers of the 3rd Division were hotly engaged before Longueval, where the German counter-attack was to some extent stopped. But at Bazentin le Petit parties of Germans were getting through between the Windmill and the Cemetery, and from the north as well.

South of the village, Captain Lowe, of the Royal Irish, collected " a crowd of men of several regiments, including the Royal Irish, who had retired through the village " of Bazentin le Petit, and leading them to the lower end of the wood, beat up through it and emerged to the north. At the same time a company of the Warwickshire moved up from Circus Trench into the village, and became engaged in severe house-to-house fighting.

At 12.30 p.m. the 2nd Gordon Highlanders, 20th Brigade, were ordered to clear up the position in Bazentin le Petit Wood, and the 1st Royal Welch Fusiliers were ordered to attack the Windmill and Cemetery.

" About 12.30 was ordered to counter-attack the Boches, who were counter-attacking the Royal Irish near the Cemetery. It took some time to get the battalion out of the wood, what with shells, other units, and pioneers at work, and other battalions advancing. Rallied the battalion on the road to put them on the right direction ; while doing so Reeves and I were knocked flying by a big shell which landed about 20 feet from us—one man killed and five wounded alongside me. Pushed the battalion up the hill, under a pretty hot high-explosive and shrapnel fire. On arriving at the top had some difficulty in finding out the situation. Sent patrols out, and ordered A and C Companies to attack and hold the line Cemetery to Windmill ; B and D in support.

" Established headquarters in a shell-hole on the hill-top, close to the wood—a pretty rotten place, but shells were everywhere. A and B carried out the attack and forestalled the Boche ; we then held the line Windmill—Cemetery, with a flank thrown back along the sunken road, in touch with the Royal Irish on our left and the Northumberland Fusiliers (3rd Division) on our right. Casualties : Baines killed, Morgan mortally wounded,

Greaves, Brunicardi, and Smith wounded, as well as 50 men killed and wounded."

The move of our battalion, with the Gordon Highlanders going through the wood on their left, was most opportune. The Windmill—Cemetery line was a commanding position : in the hands of the enemy he could see down into the valley as far as Mametz Wood ; in our hands it gave us observation as far as a slight ridge just north of the Bazentin le Petit—High Wood Road, masking High Wood. The two attacking companies advanced from Circus Trench, with their right on the Windmill. The

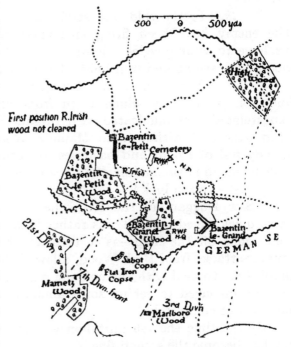

left company became engaged at the Cemetery, which lies in a hollow, and drove the enemy out of it ; but the right company was unopposed, and suddenly topping the rise saw lines of the enemy advancing over the rise from High Wood. Presumably the enemy was reinforcing his troops in Bazentin le Petit, and imagined that the Windmill—Cemetery line was still in his possession. But fire was opened on him at once at from 300 to 400 yards range, and his troops were scattered, bolting back in the direction of High Wood.

A Lewis gun was then mounted on the top of the Windmill, and the companies were posted from about 200 yards west of the Cemetery, above the Cemetery, past the Windmill, and then south-east, along a banked road, and obtained touch with the 3rd Division facing Longueval ; touch was obtained with the Royal Irish on the left as they and the Gordon Highlanders cleared the wood and village.

There were no trenches, at that time, between the position taken up and the Switch Line, hastily constructed by the Germans prior to the attack.

" Spent a most uncomfortable afternoon, being shrapnelled and shelled in this shell-hole. The, or some of the, cavalry passed through on their way to tackle High Wood." [*A squadron " came into action," according to*

*Despatches, " killing several of the enemy and capturing some prisoners."
This on a report to Army Headquarters that it was possible, early in the
afternoon, to advance to High Wood.*] " At 7 p.m. the South Staffordshire
and Queen's attacked High Wood, assisted by the cavalry—a badly run
show, but lucky, as the gunners botched it and gave no artillery support.
We helped with our Lewis guns from the Windmill against the German
Maxims, which were enfilading the Staffordshire.   However, they managed
to get hold of the wood, except one corner.   The 33rd Division came up
on our left."   [*Our 2nd Battalion came up as far as Mametz Wood the next
day,* 15*th.*]

" 15*th.*—Pretty cold and stiff.   Everything seems to be going well.
The enemy have been firing lachrymatory shells—most unpleasant, as
we have to wear goggles.   Found a lot of Hun artillery dugouts in the
wood, very strong and well built—better than a shell-hole.

" 16*th.*—A man of the 1st Glasgow Highlanders arrived in my front
line from their own, which is in front of mine.   Refused to budge—
expostulated—communicated with Brigade, who, after a time, told me to
hand over and withdraw to Mametz Wood.   Did so—a rotten place,
already full of troops and batteries in position.   Got the men to dig in.
A shell landed in the middle of an open space and killed Sergeant Clay, one
of my best—rotten luck !

" Saw Duggan, of the Irish—he full of thanks.   Said our coming
up so quick saved him.   I was rather lucky to strike off the exact line to
hold—done off the map—as it turned out most important, checked all
counter-attacks from High Wood, allowed the assault to be launched, and
enabled me to deal with the enfilade machine-gun fire from the Windmill.
We also managed to get up some ammunition for the Royal Irish—they
had run out completely."

By the time the 1st Battalion was relieved the Windmill—Cemetery
line had become the second line.

The two Regular battalions met in Mametz Wood.   That night flights
of small shells twittered over and fell with a quiet plop ; they emitted
bromine fumes, which were choking to anyone near a burst.   The enemy
had not used lethal shells against the regiment before, but from the date
of the Somme they superseded the gas cloud from cylinders.   A few
casualties occurred, and the 2nd Battalion moved their bivouac a hundred
yards, near the road and behind the artillery positions : not a good position
for sleep, as a French ·75 battery was close by and kept everyone awake
through the night with its high-pitched bark.   And the air was heavy with
the reek of dead in the wood.

There was nothing to be done there but watch the guns moving forward to Happy Valley, in rear of the Bazentins, where batteries were aligned one behind the other, and discuss the rumours that were brought back from the front line. The 33rd Division " had been biffed, owing to the Queen's saying they held the whole of High Wood when, as a matter of fact, the Huns held a strong-point in the north-west corner, from where they enfiladed the advance of the 33rd Division. Had a buck with Tibs [Lieutenant-Colonel Crawshay], and saw Higginson and Moody, who used to be my subs.—they have both done splendidly and are recommended for D.S.O." (Stockwell.)

Far from being captured, High Wood, with Longueval and Delville Wood, was the scene of heavy fighting, of attack and counter-attack, for days to come. At midnight, 17th/18th, the 2nd Battalion were roused and marched to Bazentin le Petit, where they relieved the 4th King's, with their right on the Cemetery and their left on the Martinpuich Road. As the morning mist cleared they could see the Middlesex dead lying on the glacis before them ; and an artillery team galloped up, hitched on to an abandoned German gun, and galloped away with it.

The morning was quiet, but in the afternoon the enemy shelled heavily, and the battalion lost 5 killed and 32 wounded.

After attempting to establish Battalion Headquarters (unconsciously) in a cess-pool, some good and substantial German dugouts were discovered ; they were ornamented with brocade hangings, taken no doubt from some neighbouring house. Apparently they were the headquarters of an engineer unit, for the workshops above-ground, and now wrecked, were remarkable, with the solidity of permanent wood buildings, and with reinforced glass windows. There was also a small kitchen garden with a hothouse and frames for which the reinforced glass had also been used. There was no fault to be found with these quarters.

The 33rd Division was engaged in High Wood, and the 2nd Battalion was soon to be called up, but before they went into action our 10th Battalion moved to Delville Wood.

THE BATTLE OF DELVILLE WOOD.[1]

(1st and 10th Battalions.)

The situation about Delville Wood and Longueval was recognised as critical.

As we know, the 3rd Division had fought on the great day, the 14th

[1] Date: 15th July—3rd September. The area was Delville Wood. The 1st Battalion came into the battle later on.

July, on the right of the 7th Division, and had been in and out of Longueval, but had never secured it firmly.   On the early morning of the 18th the 1st Gordon Highlanders assaulted and took a line running along the north-west edge of Delville Wood, through the north of the village and along the avenue to the west.   During the afternoon, 4.30 p.m., the enemy launched a counter-attack, which had been prepared by an artillery bombardment since midday, and drove the Highlanders out to the west of the village.

The 3rd Division was ordered to recapture Longueval and Delville Wood,[1] the southern portion only of the latter being in our hands.   The 2nd Suffolk were ordered to attack the village from the west, and the 10th Royal Welch Fusiliers were to " push through " to the north of the wood from a line about Princes Street—a ride in the wood.   Owing to the intricate position held at that moment, all troops taking part in the attack or holding the line were warned that no firing was to take place.

The deployment of the Suffolk Regiment was carried out about 3 a.m. on the 20th.   There is no definite information as to what happened.   " Two companies undoubtedly passed through the village from the west, and as none of them have since returned it is feared that they have been annihilated, as it is highly doubtful that any of the unit would surrender."

Our 10th Battalion, however, got into trouble at the start with bad guides and incorrect information as to the line held by the 53rd Brigade of the 9th Division.

The battalion had been ordered to parade at 10 p.m. and arrived at the first rendezvous, a sunken road behind the line, without casualties from shell fire.   From this point their road lay across country, and they proceeded by compass bearing.   Before topping the last rise between them and the front line, heavy machine-gun fire opened to their front and they halted under protection of the rise.

The firing died down.   It was very dark, and the commanding officer, Lieutenant-Colonel A. M. L. Long,[2] feared that platoons might lose direction and risked closing up the battalion.   The guides were met at the south-west corner of the wood, and they led the battalion up the side of Buchanan Street, held by the South Africans.   " At this point our troubles began. Although, apparently, we were nowhere near Princes Street, we were met by a considerable amount of machine-gun fire : Verey lights went up a short distance to our front, and the Germans were heard shouting all over the wood.   It was maintained by the guide that we were close to Princes Street, but this could not be the case as we had advanced only 150 yards

---

[1] See Sketch 15, p. 241.
[2] Long took over on the 6th April from F. A. Samuel.

from the south edge of the wood. The only possible course seemed to be to deploy, so a compass bearing was taken and a star selected due east for the leader of the deployment to march on."

The original intention was that three companies should deploy behind the line Princes Street, each on a 200-yards frontage ; Captain G. P. Blake (B) on the right, Lieutenant V. H. Piercy (D) centre, Captain G. D. Scale (C) on the left. Captain C. P. C. Daniell (A) was to be in reserve with his company and the bombers, under Lieutenant D. T. Williams.

" Captains Blake and Follit and 2nd Lieutenant Godfrey advanced on this point [the star], the intention being that Godfrey should halt after 200 yards to mark the right flank of C Company ; Follit to march 400 yards to mark the right flank of D ; Blake to advance to the edge of the wood. Companies would then halt, turn left, and extend back to officers marking their flanks.

" B Company had moved out along the line of deployment about 100 yards, when the Germans appeared advancing, sending up Verey lights, and shouting. B Company, firing steadily, repulsed them.

" After this incident, a further deployment of 200 yards was made, and another attack was made by Germans and was beaten off." (Long.)

Wood fighting in the middle of the night is, necessarily, an impossible action to follow, unless special details are recorded at the time. The story of Corporal Davies is in the *Gazette*.

Between these two German attacks, Corporal Joseph Davies, with eight men, became separated from his company (D). Before he could rejoin them the second German attack was made, and he, with his eight men, was surrounded. He took cover in a shell-hole, and by throwing bombs and opening rapid fire routed them. " Not content with this, he followed them up in their retreat, and bayoneted several of them. Corporal Davies set a magnificent example of pluck and determination. He has done very gallant work and was badly wounded in the Second Battle of Ypres." The credit of repulsing the second German attack was, therefore, entirely Corporal Davies's.[1]

And then occurred an unfortunate accident : the battalion was fired on by the 11th Essex Regiment. The line was admittedly intricate, hence the strict orders against firing, but the officer commanding the Essex stated that he had not been informed that the attack would take place

---

[1] He was born at Tipton, Staffordshire, on the 28th April 1889. He entered the Army on the 19th August, 1909, joining the 1st Battalion Welch Regiment. He returned with his battalion from India, and was wounded at Ypres in 1915. He was transferred to the 10th Battalion Royal Welch Fusiliers.

at dawn. However that may be, the battalion suffered severe casualties from this fire, but behaved with the greatest coolness. The mistake was discovered, and the battalion eventually aligned, but on a restricted front.

The advance commenced at 3.45 a.m., but naturally the wood was, by this time, in a turmoil, and C Company, on the left, was met by machine-gun fire and bombs, and checked. Scale, however, rallied his men and led them forward level with the other companies. But the line was broken up—officer casualties, and men, were severe, and " with the resultant lack of co-operation it became impossible for the advance to continue. The line had to be withdrawn." Many parties, however, could not get back, or never received the order, and lay out all day, engaged in sniping duels with the enemy.

Private Albert Hill had " dashed forward, when the order to charge was given, and meeting two of the enemy suddenly, bayoneted them both. He was sent later by his platoon sergeant to get into touch with his company, and, finding himself cut off and almost surrounded by the enemy, attacked them with bombs, killing and wounding many, and scattering the remainder. He then joined a sergeant of his company and helped him to fight the way back to the lines. When he got back, hearing that his company officer and a scout were lying out wounded, he went out and assisted to bring in the wounded officer, two other men bringing in the scout. Finally, he himself captured and brought in as prisoners two of the enemy. His conduct throughout was magnificent." [1] Corporal Davies and Private Hill were each awarded the Victoria Cross.

With darkness several of the lying-out parties got back, and at 3.30 a.m. on the 21st the battalion was relieved.

Captains G. B. Blake and G. D. Scale, 2nd Lieutenants L. G. Godfrey, H. Page, and 33 other ranks were killed ; Captain Daniell, Lieutenants D. T. Williams, A. W. Fish, V. H. Piercy, 2nd Lieutenants W. A. Bouette, W. Macaulay, W. G. Daniel, O. L. Jones, J. F. Dale, W. A. Cowie, W. C. Wells, and 130 other ranks were wounded ; 50 other ranks were missing. It was a gallant effort by the 10th Battalion.

The shattered remnants remained in Breslau Trench until the 25th, when they marched back to camp at Bois des Tailles.

THE ACTION AT HIGH WOOD.

With equal tenacity the enemy clung to High Wood on the left. On the 19th High Wood was once more in German hands. The 19th Brigade

---

[1] He was born 24th May 1895, at Manchester. He joined the Army 3rd September 1914.

PRIVATE A. HILL, V.C., 10TH BATTALION.

CORPORAL J. DAVIES, V.C., 10TH BATTALION.

224]

attacked at 2 a.m. on the 20th, together with the 2nd Worcestershire. The 1/5th Scottish Rifles and the 1st Cameronians were employed for the assault ; but when they entered the Wood, " owing to the casualties amongst senior officers and the confusion and intermingling of units inevitable in wood fighting, it now becomes rather difficult to make out exactly what happened, but at 9 a.m. a report was received from the officer commanding 1st Cameronians to the effect that we were holding the southern half of the wood, meeting with strong resistance from the enemy in the northern half, that casualties amongst officers had been heavy, and that hostile reinforcements were being brought up." (Division Diary.)

Our 2nd Battalion had been sitting on the left of the Cemetery, continually shelled, when at 8 a.m. they were ordered to go to High Wood and clear the enemy out of the northern half. Two Stokes trench mortars and four machine guns were also sent up.

The road to High Wood was visible from some part of the Switch Line, and the enemy on the alert, after several hours' fighting. He put down a heavy barrage on the 2nd Battalion as they advanced across the open country, but although they suffered many casualties they " pushed through the barrage with great steadiness and courage." Lieutenant-Colonel Crawshay had his attack organised by 2 p.m. The summons to the wood had arrived when B Company and detachments of the other companies were away on a carrying fatigue, so that D, C, and A were weak when they formed up on the eastern edge of the wood, with their backs to Delville Wood. The plan was to go straight through, although there were still elements of the Cameronians, 5th Scottish Rifles, and 20th Royal Fusiliers in the wood—these were complications, being met with unexpectedly. But on the right D Company, under Moody, had nothing but the enemy in front of them and suffered casualties from the start.

The advance was slow, as the fallen trees, in foliage, not only blocked the rides but made it difficult to see more than a few yards. About the centre of the wood the companies came up against rifle fire, and it seemed to them that the artillery of both sides were concentrating on that point. Still they pressed forward, from tree to tree and shell-hole to shell-hole : they cleared the enemy from some shallow trenches, " there was the hopeless mix-up of bush fighting. Some Cameronians joined in. There were small opposing parties, scrapping and bombing, pursuing and pursued all over the north-west of the wood." Finally Lieutenant-Colonel Crawshay was able to report the whole wood and the sunken road at the far end clear. " This was only achieved by the gallantry and tenacity of all units engaged. The Royal Welch Fusiliers were determined to get the northern half, and stuck

III—15

to it until they eventually succeeded, displaying fine fighting qualities and spirit." (Brigadier's Report.)

Casualties had been heavy. Heasty, who had joined from Sandhurst in June with Banks and Cruikshanks, was killed—the last of that gallant trio ; Bowles, who had travelled from the Argentine to join, was carried out dying ; and the rank and file were sadly reduced. The return of B Company and other details on fatigue duty made the situation slightly more comfortable.

Nevertheless the situation on the Brigade front can only be described as one of confusion. The early morning attack of the 19th Brigade had left those units in a fluid and disorganised state : the Cameronians had lost 13 officers, including all their Company Commanders ; the 5th Scottish Rifles had only one officer left ; only a few Royal Engineers were left and they were short of stores ; no strong points or defence work had been started anywhere. This was the

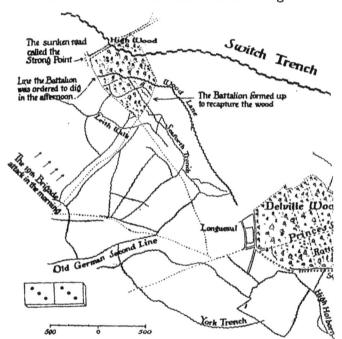

state of affairs when Lieutenant-Colonel Crawshay was appointed " O.C. High Wood " early in the afternoon.

Suddenly an order came from the Division (confirmed later by a Staff Officer) to dig and wire a diagonal line well inside the edge of the wood, which gave to the enemy the northern triangle and the sunken road leading into the Switch Strong-point. This order was, apparently, due to the fact that the Switch Line was outside the scheme of the day's attack.

The work of constructing the new trench was given to the Royal Fusiliers on the left and B and D Companies (now under Coster and Conning) of our battalion on the right. By nightfall B and D had dug a good trench, but the Royal Fusiliers, still consisting of men unused to manual labour, had not made much progress.   There was no wire for any of the working parties to put out.

After the capture of the Wood the artillery on both sides was silent for about two hours ; then the enemy commenced to shell intermittently. The dispositions of our troops at that time were : a covering party (under Sergeant " 10 Jones ") to B and D Companies, who were digging the trench ; A and C Companies, with Headquarters, in support in a shallow trench along the south-western edge of the Wood, in touch, on the right, with the 2nd Gordon Highlanders ; the Cameronians and 5th Scottish Rifles still lay along the south-western edge of the Wood.   The eastern side of the Wood was an uncomfortable place, being under long-range fire from machine guns, apparently in Delville Wood.

Late in the afternoon enemy movement was seen beyond the Flers road, and reported.   It soon became apparent that the enemy were trickling back into the Switch Line : the covering party were " glued to the ground " ; what was thought to be a ration party came up after sunset and entered the Switch ; soon afterwards a solitary German strolled across the open towards D Company's right flank, and was shot by a man who did not realise the importance of capture ; finally Sergeant 10 Jones found his advanced position too hot to hold and withdrew his men.

Without warning, at nightfall, the enemy broke through the Royal Fusiliers, and our B Company's left flank was enveloped before a German appeared on the Company front.   The left half of the Company, under Company Sergeant-Major Miners, became casualties, while the remainder commenced to fall back.   On the right Conning maintained a little order and tried to withdraw to the south-west edge of the Wood.   But in the bewilderment of surprise and bush fighting nothing clear can be ascertained. Regimental Quartermaster Sergeant Powell (then Company Sergeant-Major of D Company) relates that while he was unaware of what was happening on the other side of the Wood, " a strong body of Germans appeared on D Company's front, advancing without formation or apparent leadership.   It looked as if they were going to give themselves up, when they started firing, and we replied.   Sergeant Hinder, of the Machine Gun Company, who was on our right flank, ran forward, clear of the Wood, with his two guns to try to bring flank fire to bear on them.   Feeling we were outnumbered, I ordered the men to retire to the edge of the Wood.   When we had moved back there was such a jumble of units that it was not easy to sort out the Company again."

When Sergeant Hinders, and sundry others, came into view, as they fell back to a position behind the eastern corner of the Wood, their shadowy forms and uncertain movements excited suspicion, but A Company was steady enough to refrain from firing. The enemy was satisfied to remain in occupation of the trench he had captured.

Later in the night a fresh Royal Engineer Company arrived with the wire and stores that had been lacking all day, and the 18th Battalion Middlesex (Pioneers) reported to dig a communication trench, but left when they heard of the situation.

All through the battle communication with Brigade Headquarters was practically impossible.

Only the southern half of the wood was retained. After seven days under heavy shelling it was a bitter conclusion. The battalion was relieved and marched back to Buire.

Besides Heasty and Bowles, 29 other ranks were known to have been killed ; Captains R. R. Graves, P. Moody, Lieutenants G. E. B. Barkworth, N. O. Parry, R. Gambier-Parry, 2nd Lieutenants A. G. Lord, O. M. Roberts, G. W. Lowe, H. L. Crocket, and 180 others ranks were wounded ; 29 other ranks were missing.

.   .   .   .

Sir Douglas Haig divided the operations on the Somme into three phases. " The first phase opened with the attack on the 1st July, the success of which evidently came as a surprise to the enemy and caused considerable confusion and disorganisation in his ranks. The advantages gained on that date and developed during the first half of July may be regarded as having been rounded off by the operations of the 14th July and the three following days, which gave us possession of the southern crest of the main plateau between Delville Wood and Bazentin le Petit.

" We then entered upon a contest lasting for many weeks, during which the enemy, having found his strongest defences unavailing, and now fully alive to his danger, put forth his utmost efforts to keep his hold on the main ridge. This stage of the battle constituted a prolonged and severe struggle for mastery between the contending armies, in which, although progress was slow and difficult, the confidence of our troops in their ability to win was never shaken. Their tenacity and determination proved more than equal to their task, and by the first week in September they had established a fighting superiority that has left its mark on the enemy, of which possession of the ridge was merely the visible proof.

" The way was then open for the third phase. . . ."

Obviously, too, the policy and aim of the Higher Command had been modified beyond recognition. Nearly three weeks had been required to reach a position which, it had been hoped, would be secured on the first day.   In spite of the prolonged and tenacious resistance met with, reports of enemy disorganisation were continual : we were pounding our way forward, like a battering-ram, and the enemy might crack—the possibility was a legitimate consideration.   Also, although it was not the object of the original attack, the relief of pressure on Verdun now came to the front as a battle aim.

Both Hindenburg and Ludendorff have written of the Somme in dismay.   The question " Can the enemy stand more of this ? " had to be answered.   The battering-ram was a definite idea.

The end of Sir Douglas Haig's first phase marks a period of rest for the regiment.   The 1st Battalion, relieved on the 21st July, went right back to La Chaussée ; forward to Dernancourt on the 12th August ; into the line again on the 26th August.

The 2nd Battalion, also relieved on the 21st July, marched back to Buire ; to Fricourt Wood on the 13th August ; front line on the 18th.

The 9th Battalion, employed first on various digging fatigues about Mametz, held the line 300 yards north-east of the Five Ways at Bazentin le Petit from 23rd July, were relieved on the 29th July,[1] and went, by easy stages, out of the Somme Battle area to Bailleul, and were employed about Wytschaete and Ploegsteert.

The 10th Battalion, relieved from Breslau Trench on the 25th July, marched back to Bois des Tailles ; into the line once more on the 17th August.

THE SECOND PHASE.

" There was strong evidence that the enemy forces engaged on the battle-front had been severely shaken by the repeated successes gained by ourselves and our Allies ; but the great strength and depth of his defences had secured for him sufficient time to bring up fresh troops, and he had still many powerful fortifications, both trenches, villages, and woods, to which he could cling in our front and on our flanks.

" We had indeed secured a footing on the main ridge, but only on a front of 6,000 yards ; and desirous as I was to follow up quickly the successes we had won, it was necessary first to widen this front."   (Despatch.)

An advance by the Fourth Army and Reserve Army on the 23rd July gave nothing of importance to the Fourth Army, but General Gough captured Pozières.   The attention of the Higher Command was, however, more deeply concerned with the situation on the right.   The salient which had been formed was becoming a danger, inviting counter-attack, and placing our troops under a concentration of artillery fire from a semicircle

---

[1] This brings them into the Battle of Pozières Ridge.

of German guns. The boundary between the Fourth Army and the French ran from Maltzhorn Farm up the Combles Valley ; and General Headquarters was anxious to push forward between Delville Wood and the Somme. A series of attacks were launched against Guillemont, a dominating position on Sir Henry Rawlinson's right flank, but without success. Convinced that Guillemont could not be taken as " an isolated enterprise," an advance, in conjunction with the French, on limited objectives, to include Maurepas, Falfemont Farm, Guillemont, Leuze Wood, and Ginchy, was arranged.

The first attempt on the 16th August was admittedly a failure.

Throughout the entire period of rest which the battalions of the regiment enjoyed the guns never ceased firing—there was either slow, deliberate fire from a few batteries or rapid from many. There was really no pause between " Army " attacks. There were always points which had to be taken or retaken, and the fighting was a daily affair. A main attack which met with some success sometimes brought the attacking troops over a slight ridge, and fighting would take place in fields—cut up, but recognisable as fields, with crops. But soon the landscape would change to uniform mud, for the weather was not kind, and the rainfall was above the average through July and August. The incessant pounding of the artillery destroyed everything. Engineers and pioneer battalions were indefatigable in maintaining the roads behind the battle-front, and constructing ways for troops and supplies to reach the front line. The rain continued ; the artillery pounded ; the feet of men and the " wheels " of the Army churned up the soft country roads, and the tracks leading to battalion or brigade headquarters ; the engineers and pioneer battalions carted stones, tree trunks for corduroy tracks, duck-boards. Night and day the work went on amidst shelling—always shelling.

The rain, the haze, and the low clouds interfered greatly with the shooting of the artillery. The line of observation balloons would rise the moment visibility improved, and aeroplanes would come droning over, but on some days there was scarcely a balloon to be seen, and few aeroplanes. Still the shelling went on.

The 10th Battalion was the first to move along the congested roads and the deep mud-covered tracks. The 55th Division had attempted to improve the line by the capture of Cochrane Trench prior to the abortive attack of the 16th August, and their failure to pass beyond it was partly due to a newly constructed German trench, named Lonely Trench, which was mistaken by the gunners for our front line. The 3rd Division was now ordered to take over the line and clear the enemy out of Lonely Trench, as a preliminary to further operations. It was one of those minor enterprises which passed unnoticed, but were frequently more costly to the units engaged than a major operation.

The 3rd Division, on taking over, was on the extreme right of the Fourth Army, in touch with the French ; on their left was the 24th Division. The attack was to be made on 17th August by two companies of our 10th Battalion and two companies from the 9th Brigade.

It was clear that Lonely Trench was a much more formidable obstacle than had been anticipated. It was strongly held and wired ; it had a low command, and was irregularly sited. Lying in some places close to our own front line, at others it was concealed from artillery observation. It was decided to vacate our front line to allow the heavy batteries to bombard what could be seen. The bombardment was to continue throughout the day and the attack to be launched at 10 p.m., at which time the full moon would be rising. But there was to be an element of surprise in the assault.

The very nature of the fighting which took place on the Somme gave to the line most peculiar shapes : it zigzagged about to such an extent that a battalion might find itself facing opposite ways at its flanks. The most complicated wheels were demanded of troops after leaving their trenches in order to present a united front in attacking the enemy. To obviate this difficulty it was arranged that the attacking companies on this occasion should form up on a tape line, previously laid out across the front to be attacked, and that the artillery should cease fire at 8 p.m. to allow this manœuvre to take place. A sudden burst of artillery fire at 10 p.m. and a quick leap forward by the assaulting troops would, it was hoped, take the enemy by surprise.

" At 8 p.m. the companies moved off [*from trenches some way in rear*], led by specially detailed guides. After proceeding some distance up a French trench, a heavy barrage was put on and the order came down that the column must move back. This was countermanded, and my Adjutant was sent up to ensure that it was carried out. There was a delay of half an hour.

" The two companies got into line and were in position by 9.30 p.m.

" At 9.30 I moved along the companies, telling them it was time to go forward to the tape. On my left flank I found the Officer Commanding 12th West Yorks and the Brigade Major, and was told that the attack was postponed until 10.30 p.m. [*The reason was, apparently, that our 10th Battalion was expected sooner, and was believed to be late.*] I immediately said that this was impossible, as my men were all over the parapet and could not be withdrawn, that it was impossible to communicate with the artillery in time, and that the surprise effect we were relying on would be lost. I advised the O.C. West Yorks to get his men over at once, which he proceeded to do.'' (Lieutenant-Colonel Long.)

But the delay was fatal. The advance did not take place, as a whole, from the taped line ; some of the troops were still in the irregular trench line it was intended to avoid, as much as 100 yards behind the tape : the attack did not take the enemy by surprise and was not the quick bayonet charge contemplated. The assaulting troops were driven back.

A second attempt was made at 4 a.m., but failed.

Nothing more could be done, for this was the 18th August, the day for the bigger attack in conjunction with the French, whose 153rd Division were to advance with the 3rd and 24th Divisions. Lonely Trench would have to be taken with the other objectives.

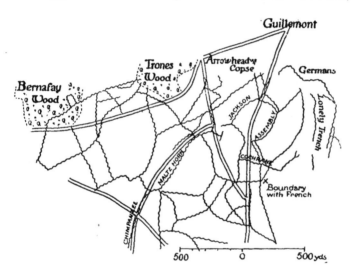

The two unused companies of our 10th Battalion were brought up by Major Samuel. The 1st Battalion Gordon Highlanders were on their right, and, after a heavy bombardment, the assault was delivered at 2.45 p.m. With the additional weight in this attack, our companies entered the southern part of Lonely Trench, and went on to the further objective, the road. But the attack of the 9th Brigade, on the left, did not go so well ; and on the right the French were counter-attacked and gave ground, taking with them some of the Gordon Highlanders. This led to a report that all the captured positions had been lost, which caused a certain amount of confusion ; the artillery barrage was brought back, and the orders for a renewed attack by the 9th Brigade were cancelled. The mistake was, however, discovered, which was fortunate for our two companies, and during the night and early morning the whole of Lonely Trench was occupied and consolidated.

Our battalion was withdrawn on the 19th and marched back to Morlancourt. The casualties were : 2nd Lieutenants J. E. Hughes, L.

DELVILLE WOOD.

Imperial War Museum photograph, Crown copyright.

232]

Williams, E. Dixon, A. O. Williams, and 32 other ranks killed ; Captain C. A. R. Follitt (died subsequently), Lieutenants W. J. D. Hale, S. F. Bancroft, 2nd Lieutenants G. H. Jennings, W. D. Evans, S. J. Thomas, A. B. Brotherton, F. A. Lawson, and 180 other ranks wounded.

From Morlancourt the battalion moved to the Loos sector.

The 2nd Battalion at High Wood.

The fighting for High Wood and Delville Wood was interminable. The northern half of the former, where the Switch Trench ran through the wood, was still held by the enemy.   On the 18th August the 98th Brigade attempted to capture it, after treatment with Flammenwerfer (which did not work), and failed.   During the night the Argyll and Sutherland Highlanders were relieved by our 2nd Battalion.[1]

It was a most unpleasant tour of duty.   The wood and its approaches had changed greatly, and from open warfare had become the scene of trench warfare, reeking of the dead.   It was continually shelled.   The battalion bombed the enemy line, but failed to move him ; he, in his turn, crawled forward on two occasions and bombed ours, but equally failed to make any impression—he was jumpy and nervous.   The battalion was relieved by the 1st Cameronians on the 22nd ; went back into the line again on the 26th, and was relieved next day, when the 1st Brigade, 1st Division, took over the line.

The German gunners had taken their toll.   2nd Lieutenants C. R. Dollings and P. S. Wilson, with 6 other ranks, had been killed ; 9 other ranks wounded.

THE BATTLE OF GUILLEMONT.

It is of interest to take note of the extracts from a General Headquarters Memorandum circulated about this time (26th August) to divisional commanders :

" In confirmation of verbal instructions already given, the C.-in-C. directs me to say that he wishes you to impress on all concerned under your command the urgent importance of capturing Ginchy, Guillemont, and Falfemont Farm as a necessary step towards further operations.   The capture of these places is well within the power of troops who have shown themselves capable of overcoming such difficulties as the Fourth Army has mastered since 1st July.

" The attack must be thoroughly prepared for in accordance with the principles which have been successful in previous attacks, and which are, or should be, well known to all commanders of all ranks.

[1] This places them in the Battle of Pozières Ridge area.

" It must be made known to all arms and all ranks taking part in the operations that a great effort is called for, and that a well-combined attack driven home with energy will certainly succeed. A few more successes now, such as the capture of Guillemont, Ginchy, and Falfemont Farm, will undoubtedly have great effect on an enemy whose defensive power is known to be strained to the utmost ; whereas any relaxation of effort at this juncture would mean failure to reap all the advantages which have been brought within reach by the splendid energy and gallantry already displayed.

" Without desiring to hamper the proper initiative of subordinates, the C.-in-C. desires that you will impress on the higher commanders under you their responsibilities for assuring themselves that plans and preparations are complete and thorough, that no detail is overlooked, and no possible aid to success is unemployed, and that every individual understands clearly what is required of him before the attack is launched.

" In actual *execution* of plans, when control of higher commander is impossible, subordinates on the spot must act on their own initiative, and they must be trained to do so. But in *preparation*, close supervision by higher commanders is not only possible but is their duty, to such extent as they find necessary to ensure that everything is done that can be done to ensure success. This close supervision is especially necessary in the case of a comparatively new army. It is not ' interference,' but a legitimate and necessary exercise of the functions of a commander on whom the ultimate responsibility for success or failure lies. It appears to the C.-in-C. that some misconception exists in the Army as to the object and limitation of the principle of the initiative of subordinates, and it is essential that this misconception should be corrected at once, when it does exist.'

It suggests a tightening of the already rigid control, or that it had been unduly relaxed in some quarters.

.   .   .   .

The 1st Battalion, rested and strengthened by a draft, were at Derlancourt. Orders for the forthcoming big attack on Ginchy and Guillemont were issued on the 23rd August. " They seem fairly simple, as far as we are concerned, so long as our left is covered." The Commanding Officer had a field day on the 24th—" rather good "—and went to Amiens the next day.

Nothing to worry about ! But his attention was suddenly called to that left flank.

On the 26th Lieutenant-Colonel Stockwell was ordered to go at once to Montauban, and arrange to take over the line preparatory to one of those troublesome preliminary attacks for the purpose of making a front square with the advance planned for the major operation. The battalion was to follow the Commanding Officer.[1]

The enemy was still clinging to the eastern side of Delville Wood, and it had been decided that the wood and the trenches east of it must be cleared before the attack on Ginchy took place, and fresh assembly trenches dug to the west of Ginchy.

" Rode off to Montauban and got guides. I was first taken to the Quarry—enemy shelling like the deuce. Got in and saw the O.C. 7th R.B.s. : pretty rotten and shelling damnably. Then pushed on to the Battalion Headquarters of the 7th K.R.R., from whom I take over this Delville Wood part of the line. Got there dodging shells more or less the whole way. Saw the Commanding Officer. The situation is as bad as can be. The corner of the wood, from which my left company should attack, is in the hands of the Boche. A gap of 300 yards exists between the left of the line and the right of the next division, which gap the Boche holds strongly, including portions of the wood. His battalion is badly shaken, has suffered severely, and the shelling is very bad. No one will do much to clear the wood—about six attempts have been made, and failed.

" Went round most of the line, being shelled the whole time ; practically no trenches, so went over the top—probably safest.

" Delville Wood is indescribable. Dead and bits of people everywhere. Our trenches choked with dead, and the stench something awful. We shall have to try to clear the wood as soon as we get in—it is the only thing.

" Got in touch with the Battalion Commander on the left, Durham Light Infantry—turned out to be Morant. Arranged a combined push. Got back to the deep dugout, which is most unhealthy, being in the barrage, and wrote orders for the battalion, who were then on the march, and sent them off by Conninghame, my orderly. Lucky I did, as I learned afterwards that the Manchesters had no idea of the situation and were in an awful state of confusion. The battalion finally got into the line, and the relief was completed by 3 a.m.—a few casualties." (Stockwell.)

Rain was falling heavily, which interfered with the relief, and no work on the trenches could be carried out that night.

The rôle of the battalion in the main operation was to attack eastward, with its left on the east corner of Delville Wood, and capture Pint Trench and the north of Ginchy. The principal objection to the scheme was that a flank had to be secured and formed along Ale Alley simultaneously with the attack on Pint and Ginchy. Stockwell had been informed that the whole of Delville Wood was in our hands as well as Hop and Beer, and

---

[1] Brings the 1st Battalion into the Battle of Delville Wood.

portions of Ale. He now learned that we held Hop and Beer but none of Ale, and the gap of 300 yards between the battalion left and the right of the next brigade ran along the north-east corner of Delville Wood, and was always strongly held by the Germans, who could reinforce up Ale if attacked. Ale Trench ran along the crest of the ridge, and commanded the gentle slope to the south as far as Guillemont, and could not be touched by the artillery where it passed close to the wood owing to the height of the trees.

Stockwell reported the situation to the Brigadier (Steele), and a plan was formed to clear the wood with the grenadier company and B Company. The arrangement was that at 5 a.m. on the 27th, B Company and a portion of the grenadier company, starting from the west end of Hop Alley, were to attack north, along and in the edge of Delville Wood, clearing the wood as they advanced. They were to be supported by an intense long-range bombardment of rifle grenades (about 3,000 were brought up). A similar attack was to be made from the north end of Beer Trench, along Beer Sap, with a view to cutting into Ale farther east. At the same time the 10th Durham Light Infantry, posted along the north edge of the wood, were to try to clear Ale, with the assistance of trench mortars, and join hands with our battalion at the corner of the wood.

" Stevens arranged it. We started to bomb at 5 a.m. At 6.15 a.m. the attack was held up owing to a lack of rifle grenades. More grenades sent up, and orders to push the attack north. This was done. The bombers pushed forward under a heavy fire from their artillery (rifle grenades) and drove the enemy back. They finally established a block within 30 yards of the west end of Ale Alley, thus practically clearing the enemy out of the wood. In the meantime we pushed 100 yards along Beer Trench, towards Ale Alley farther east. Casualties heavy."

The enemy had put down a heavy barrage on the wood, and the attack of the Durhams had apparently been checked at its commencement. So a platoon of grenadiers, under Stevens, was sent round, through Delville Wood, into the lines of the Durhams, and a simultaneous attack by that battalion and the grenadier company cleared the trench as far as the corner of the wood, and they joined hands. " The wood is now clear, though there is still a gap of 30 yards in the line. B and D Companies have suffered heavily—the former having 35 per cent. knocked out. Every attack leads to intense shelling."

Stockwell now ordered the attacks to cease and the position to be consolidated. The battalion had a fairly good jumping-off ground for the big operation. About 60 prisoners had been taken.

" All due to Stevens, Black, and Newton, and to the general steadiness of the men. I am now happier in my mind as to this attack—I can take Ale longitudinally with my left as I advance, and have a proper front from which to attack. Sergeant Whitbread did well.

" *29th.*—At about 4 p.m. I heard a shout that the dressing-station had been blown up. Kelsey Fry was over there at the time. The servants and orderlies rushed over despite 5·9 shells, which were dropping all round Headquarters dugout and the dressing-station. Everyone had been blown to bits except Fry, who was sitting in a corner of the dugout. Pearce and Sheasby, his pet stretcher-bearers, and both D.C.M.s, also Gorst and Kelly, all obliterated round him in a second. He was absolutely untouched, but suffering from shell-shock. I gave him an injection of morphine, which quietened him down. Poor little man ! Sent him off to the ambulance. Turnbull, the Medical Officer of the Manchesters, did his best for us.

" The shelling has been, and is, very heavy. We are to be relieved by the South Staffordshire. Peter and Moody very shaken—the latter has been buried twice and the former once. One poor devil got buried three times in twenty minutes, and was sent down almost mad ; he was so bad he was sent off on a stretcher, but near the dump a 5·9 killed three of his bearers and wounded him, and he went clean off his head. My dugout has been rocking all day, and the lights have been blown out fifty times."

The battalion was relieved and marched wearily back to a camp at Bonté redoubt.[1] General Watts was " awfully pleased " and the men seemed " as cheery as can be."

During this time the battalion had also dug the first assembly trench, Stout Trench, and the communication trench, Ginchy Avenue, leading to it. The weather was still bad, and on the 29th, the day they were relieved, the main attack was postponed for forty-eight hours.

The 91st Brigade then started to dig a second assembly trench, Porter Trench, in front of Stout. Operations were further postponed by the XV Corps, and Brigadier-General Minshull Ford took over command of the wood from Brigadier-General Steele—this at 3.30 p.m. on the 31st August, while fighting of great importance was taking place in the wood.

At 10 o'clock that morning the enemy opened an intense bombardment with heavy guns and lachrymatory shells, and attacked the north and north-east corner of Delville Wood at 1.30 p.m. The attack, delivered by bombers, was repulsed, whereupon the bombardment was started again, continuing from 4.15 to 7 p.m., with occasional pauses for an infantry assault. The third attempt, made about 7 p.m., succeeded in driving the

---

[1] One thousand yards east of Becordel, behind 1st Battalion line, 1st July.

South Staffordshire out of the north-east corner of the wood and retaking Hop Alley.

Meanwhile our 1st Battalion, in camp, was being made exceedingly uncomfortable by the shelling from a German long-range gun, and at 10 p.m. on the 31st decided to shift camp. With Brunicardi as guide they started off, " but he lost his way in the dark, and we did not reach our new ground, which was about 1,500 yards away, till midnight."

Within half an hour of arriving at the new ground Stockwell received orders to go to Montauban at once and see the 91st Brigade ; the battalion was to follow as soon as possible. It was reported then that the enemy might have captured the whole of the eastern side of Delville Wood.

Everything in camp was, naturally enough, in the utmost confusion : it was pouring with rain, and the men were pitching tents, their rifles and kits stacked anywhere in the dark.

Stockwell gave his orders and left with four orderlies. It was an eight-mile walk and the roads were fearfully bad.

" Finally found some empty R.E. carts and got a lift in them for three miles. Reached Montauban about 3 a.m.—choked with guns and limbers, an awful smell of lachrymatory gas, and very dark. Pushed on through the village. Just outside about forty tear shells fell on both sides of the road. Put on goggles and found it impossible to see with them in the dark. A few minutes later the orderlies began to be sick—felt rather queer myself. We hurriedly put on gas helmets and tried to move on. Gas very bad and movement most exhausting—tumbled all over the place. Could not find the entrance of Brigade Headquarters, which is in a trench, and had to go round Bernafay Wood, which was being heavily shelled. Finally reached Scatter's headquarters about 3.30 a.m."

The battalion arrived an hour later, which was an excellent piece of work, and went into the Montauban defences. Meanwhile the 91st Brigade made several attempts to recover the lost trenches, or at any rate improve their position, without success. The evening of the 1st September fell on an unaltered situation.

" *2nd September.*—A quiet night, except for gas and lachrymatory shells, which bothered the men a good deal and spoilt their rest. In the afternoon I saw Steele (Brigadier) : he thinks the situation bad. The 91st Brigade are attacking Hop under cover of smoke as we push out of the wood—it is a mad scheme, but has to be, as there is a big attack. I hope the people on our left play up ; it may save us. We attack to-morrow— zero hour noon—from Delville Wood. We have to get our left on Ale, and finally take Pint and the north end of Ginchy. Warwicks support us. Manchesters to take Ginchy and hold it. Rather a big job as the brigade is weak—we and the Manchesters muster about 400 men. Went down to the dugout headquarters, our old ones in York Alley."

The 22nd Brigade took over command of the line at 8.30 p.m. on the 2nd. The gravity of the situation lay in the east corner of the wood being the highest point of a small ridge, along which Ale Alley had been dug, and from it the enemy was able to bring fire to bear on a wide stretch of ground to the south and south-east. In view of the big operation the next day, which meant much movement that night, with battalions taking up their assembly positions, it was decided not to make any further attempt to retake the fatal wood corner, but it was arranged that the 91st Brigade bombers should attack three minutes before zero on the 3rd.

Our battalion formed up for attack on the south of the Longueval— Ginchy Road : " Davies and Peter on the right ; J. Dadd[1] on the left." There was a heavy bombardment all through the night.

THE ATTACK.

" 3rd September.—A fine morning. Got J. Dadd on the 'phone, and told him that I feared for his left, but that he must try to engage the enemy in Ale and Hop while the other two companies pushed on. Told Peter the same. Newton and one platoon of bombers with the left attack to clear up Ginchy.

" 9 a.m.—Carrying party of Staffs arrived—sent them to the dump with sergeant-major.

" 10 a.m.—91st bombers turned up, very late. Cursed them and pushed them off.

" 11 a.m.—Carrying party returned. Sergeant-major knocked out, and they went astray. Sent them off again with a guide.

" 12 noon.—We must be moving forward ! "

Zero hour ! A dramatic moment. The direction of the whole of this operation had been left to Stockwell, and though the hands of his watch pointed at 12 he knew he would receive no news for some time. The vibrating thunder of " drum fire " throbbed in the air. The French, on the right, and the two British Armies were attacking, as far as the Ancre. How was Dadd progressing on the left—and those bombers ? And Davies and F. H. Peter ? He made notes on a sheet of paper.

" 12.10 p.m.—Warwicks move forward in open order over our head-

---

There were two—J. Dadd and E. H. Dadd. Many references are made to " Lieutenant Dadd " without initials !

quarters. [*In support ; they were to move forward and dig in on a line west of Pint.*]

" 12.45 *p.m.*—Observers report our infantry in Ginchy—left hung up. Enemy shelling headquarters like the deuce. Gregory and Smalley both came into my headquarters—if they hit us they will get a bag !

" 2 *p.m.*—Dobell arrived back wounded. Ed. Dadd is killed—J. Dadd wounded—Jones killed. The 91st bombers played the fool and did not attack, having given the show away by firing their smoke. Our men came under heavy fire at once from Hop and Ale, and Dadd was at once killed. They tried to reach Hop and failed, but got Beer. Dobell knows nothing further. I hope B and D Companies have pressed on."

At first the attack of the Manchesters progressed favourably. They entered Ginchy with little opposition, went through the village, and began to consolidate the eastern edge. The northern end of the village, on the left of the Manchesters, was, it will be remembered, the objective of our battalion, but they were not up, and the Manchesters do not appear to have realised it at first : when they did, the left company turned its left flank to face the enemy, but the enemy suddenly appeared in rear. The Manchesters were eventually forced to retire, but the first reports sent back gave them the village.

The news that reached Stockwell of his own battalion was scrappy, and not good.

" 4.30 *p.m.*—Message from Findlay to say he is dug in with about thirty men opposite Hop, and about forty yards from it. Enemy pressing.

" Later message from Cartwright that he is in a trench with Warwicks, but does not know its name. Closely engaged. Very few of our men.

" Observer reports our troops retiring out of Ginchy.

" 91st bombing officer came in and said his men would not stand, and enemy were pressing into Delville Wood. Pushed up Warwicks and reserve bombers to take over.

" Brigade ordered one company of Royal Irish and Irish bombers to attack and gain Hop—bombers to attack from west. Wrote out orders and carefully explained them to officer commanding company : he was to deploy by ones and twos along Pilsen, and then try a surprise rush. We would cover him with fire (Findlay). Zero 5 p.m. The rest of the Irish ordered to attack Ginchy.

" 6 *p.m.*—The attack on Hop failed. The situation in Delville Wood is serious, as there is no one to keep the Boche out—the brigade on our left did nothing and are very shaken. Seized all available men of all battalions

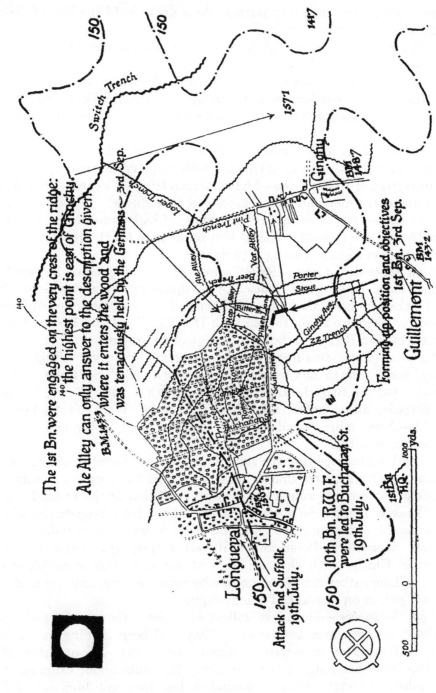

150.

150

1457

Switch Trench

1571

Loger Trench — 3rd Sep.

Ginchy.

BM. 1467

The 1st Bn. were engaged on the very crest of the ridge: the highest point is east of Ginchy.

Ale Alley can only answer to the description given, where it enters the wood and was tenaciously held by the Germans.

B.M.143.3

140

140

Pint Trench

Var Alley

Ale Alley

Beer Trench

Porter

Stout

Forming up position and objectives
1st Bn. 3rd Sep.

Guillemont

BM 143·2.

Hop Alley

Bitter Trench

Pilsener Trench

Ginchy Ave.

ZZ Trench

South Street

Princes St.

Rotten Row

Buchanan St.

Buchanans

Longueval

143·2

150

Attack 2nd Suffolk
19th July.

150

10th Bn. R.(O.F.
were led to Buchanan St.
19th July.

1st Bn.
H.Q.

1000 yds.

500 0

III—16

and on my own responsibility pushed them up to hold the line of Delville Wood and prevent penetration.

" Message from Peter that he is with Warwicks just by the north of Ginchy—very few men."

Meanwhile contact aeroplanes reported to Division that troops of the 22nd Manchester Battalion were still in Ginchy, and the Divisional General urged Brigadier-General Steele to push forward more troops and secure the village.

" 9 *p.m.*—Divisional General orders us to be relieved and to move with all men we have and take Ginchy, which he says is unoccupied. 20th Brigade is coming up in lorries—I have no men left. We can, when relieved, muster about 120 men and four colonels—it is madness.

" 10 *p.m.*—21st Manchesters arriving. Chad came down and fixed up the line we are to hold. Asked him to arrange for the relief of Findlay and Peter—don't know where Cartwright is.

" *4th September*, 3 *a.m.*—Relief complete. Findlay came in with forty men and three Lewis guns under Povey—quite steady and self-confident. Said Manchesters had taken over and then fallen back. Woodward furious, and ordered them up again to join with Delville Wood and Beer. Findlay saw some men in Beer—he thought it might be Cartwright.

" 4 *a.m.*—Forty-two men, and headquarters ! Reeves cracked about midday, and Freeman has been doing his work well. Sent the battalion on, and went to Brigade Headquarters, where I saw Green, Brigadier 20th Brigade, and Steele. Explained situation. Went on to Pommier Redoubt—three miles—dead to the world. Slept. Marched back to camp at 9 a.m. (4th)."

It had been realised that the 22nd Brigade had suffered severe casualties, was much scattered, and that it was impossible to reorganise units with the lack of officers, the rough and broken condition of the ground, and in the darkness of night. So it was decided that the 20th Brigade should take over command of the line, and the 22nd Brigade would be withdrawn.

" *4th September*.—Peter and Williams turned up. Peter had been in front of Ginchy with the remnants of our men and some Warwicks. He was talking rather rot about no one being in Ginchy, and yet said they could not get on on account of machine guns !

" *5th September*.—Moved to billets at Buire. Cartwright and Johns and about eighteen men turned up. They had been holding out in Beer Trench, without food or water—damned good work. About three others turned up from shell-holes close to Ginchy. No doubt about Edmund Dadd being killed. Newton seriously wounded, but they got him out of Beer and back. Jones killed. Pountney, Evans, Dobell, J. Dadd wounded. No news of Davies or Tudor Jones, but I believe they are dead."

Efforts to take Ginchy continued till the 7th, when, during the night 7th/8th, the 7th Division was relieved by the 16th and 55th Divisions.

Commenting on the battle, General Watts wrote:

" The task allotted to the division was a difficult one, as it involved an advance from a salient with the left flank exposed, and the magnitude of the task was much increased by bad weather, which rendered the ground very difficult to move over, especially during the dark nights. The tactical situation became more unfavourable after the enemy had regained possession of the eastern corner of Delville Wood on the 31st August. . . . When the corner of the wood was captured by the combined operations of the 43rd and 22nd Brigades on the 27th August, steps should have been taken without delay to dig a fresh trench clear of the wood, joining up with the posts already established by the 14th Division in front of the north-east of the wood. Such good progress was, however, made by the 1st Battalion Royal Welch Fusiliers in bombing down Hop Alley, Ale Alley, and Beer Trench, that I felt confident of being able to consolidate Beer Trench, which would have been the better line."

The casualties were: Captain E. H. Dadd, 2nd Lieutenants H. Jones, J. I. L. Davies, and 22 other ranks killed; 2nd Lieutenants J. Dadd, C. M. Dobell, H. Llewellyn-Jones, V. F. Newton, F. Fisher, P. Pountney, W. E. Evans, and 129 other ranks wounded; Captain E. T. Jones and 87 other ranks missing.

The battalion was given eleven Military Medals for this battle.

They left Buire on the 8th September, and entrained at Albert for Ypres area.

THE THIRD PHASE.

Ginchy was not captured till the 9th September.

" The way was then opened for the third phase, in which our advance was pushed down the forward slopes of the ridge and further extended on both flanks until, from Morval to Thiepval, the whole plateau and a good deal of ground beyond were in our possession. Meanwhile our gallant Allies, in addition to great successes south of the Somme, had pushed their advance, against equally determined opposition and under most difficult tactical conditions, up the long slopes on our immediate right, and were now preparing to drive the enemy from the summit of the narrow and difficult portion of the main ridge which lies between the Combles Valley and the River Tortille, a stream flowing from the north into the Somme just below Peronne.'' (Despatch.)

The commencement of the third phase, which dates from the 15th September, is noteworthy for the first use of tanks. Mr. Winston Churchill, who fathered these machines with such enthusiasm, never ceased to regret their hasty and unconsidered use in the Battle of the Somme. His enthusiasm was not contagious ; there was much scepticism ; and to ask that they should be held back, accumulated, and launched in a major operation which would depend entirely on their success required an equal flame of faith in the unemotional bosom of General Headquarters. One cannot deny, however, that they were put to a terrible test in their infancy.

The tanks were landed in France on the 25th August, and on the 26th the 7th Middlesex were put through a practice attack with five tanks. They were to work in combination with the recognised form of infantry attack in '' waves.'' The tanks were to cross our front line at zero hour ; one minute later the first infantry wave would advance, three minutes after zero the second wave, five minutes after zero the third wave. The infantry advance was to be in '' short rushes '' up to the tanks. If a tank broke down, they were to proceed as if it was not there.

The practice was continued for several days, and was viewed by Sir Douglas Haig, General Joffre, and H.R.H. the Prince of Wales. Two tanks broke down in the course of the exercise, which was not to be wondered at, but had an effect, no doubt, on the minds of the spectators.

The first tanks had a tail, an arrangement like a bogy carriage. There was a '' male '' and a '' female,'' the difference being one of armament, the '' male '' having machine guns and two small 3-pdr. guns mounted in side turrets, the '' female '' Vickers and Hotchkiss machine guns only.

The opinions expressed by brigade and battalion commanders after the battle were very contradictory. Sir Douglas Haig mentions the successful advance of tanks at Flers, but on other parts of the front they broke down, or were disabled by enemy artillery—at least one caught fire. The derelict tanks became firing-points for the German gunners and machine guns, and the opinion was freely expressed, wherever the tanks failed, that they drew the enemy fire and caused heavy casualties.

So far as the regiment was concerned, tanks scarcely came within their view, as they were now represented on the battlefield by the 4th Battalion only.

The 4th Battalion left the Vimy Ridge sector (Villers au Bois) on the 26th July, and marched for days, round by St. Pol, pausing in villages sometimes for a week, and arriving finally at Bresle, behind Albert, on the

20th August. " Bresle was a filthy little village, abounding in German prisoners, refuse dumps, manure heaps, and bluebottles."

The roads were now in a terrible condition. The congestion at Loos had been bad, it was infinitely worse on the Somme ; added to the wear of a mass of traffic, which sometimes remained locked for hours, there was the pitiless weather, the rain flooding everything.

On the 27th August the battalion was put on the " German Road " running from Fricourt through the " Valley of Death " south of Mametz to the two Bazentins, where they worked without ceasing, constructing and maintaining it.

The 47th Division was moved up into the line at High Wood on the 11th September, and our 4th Battalion was then employed in digging assembly trenches for the big attack on the 15th. It was a combined Allied attack, with Morval as the objective of the Fourth Army. The New Zealand Division was on the right of the 47th, the 50th Division on the left.

At 6.30 a.m. on the 15th the advance commenced. There were, of course, no tanks in High Wood. The attack progressed fairly well on the right, but the 47th Division had some hard fighting in High Wood before they finally drove the enemy out of it. Our 4th Battalion then commenced their arduous and most unpleasant task of digging communication trenches in the midst of heavy shell fire ; they had also to construct artillery tracks.[1]

BATTLE OF MORVAL.[2]

But the line of Morval had not been attained, and a further Allied attack was launched on the 25th which secured this objective. The 47th Division was not actively engaged, but our 4th Battalion was still employed on making artillery tracks.

THE BATTLE OF LE TRANSLOY RIDGE.[3]

Eaucourt l'Abbaye was secured by the 47th Division, the assembly trenches for the attack having been dug by the 4th Battalion. On the evening of the 2nd, companies went up to consolidate the line won.

All the work of the 4th Battalion was carried out under the most appalling conditions. The rain had turned the battlefield into a morass— they dug into mud, they lived in mud, with the bodies of the festering

[1] This gives the 4th Battalion the Battle of Flers-Courcelette.
[2] Date : 25th–28th September. Area : the Combles Valley to Hardecourt ; thence road to Maricourt—Fricourt—Becourt—La Boisselles—Bapaume.
[3] Date : 1st–18th October. Area : the valley from Sailly Saillisel to Combles ; thence road to Ginchy—Longueval—Martinpuich—Courcelette ; thence the valley to Warlencourt.

dead around them. But their valuable work was carried on. Still, one cannot wonder that relief on the 9th October was welcomed. They left Albert on the 13th for the Pioneer Camp between Vlamertinghe and Dickebusche, in the Ypres sector.

.   .   .   .

About this time the 2nd Battalion also returned to the Somme area. The Doctor's notes cover the period :

" The battalion proceeded by route march on 31st August via Ribemont, Rainville, Bernaville, Beauvoir, and Bonnières to Blangermont, where it arrived on 5th September. March discipline was satisfactory the first day, but upwards of twenty fell out the second day, mostly with sore feet. The fifteen-mile march in packs to Bernaville on a sultry day caused large numbers to fall out ; only a day's rest and cool weather on the 4th September enabled many to reach Beauvoir and Bonnières with their companies after a ten-mile march through the pleasant Valley of the Authie. There was a halt for two days at Blangermont ; on these the G.O.C. expected the battalions to go for a route march, as if the previous day's moves had not sent plenty of the new men to hospital. Nearly all the foot-soreness was the result of neglect of individual habits of cleanliness. Cleanly habits kept the old Army men remarkably free from minor ailments. Neglect also caused the vast amount of itch, lousiness, and consequent debilitating maladies that ravaged the Territorial and New Army troops, and taxed the capacity of hospitals. The march was resumed on the 8th ; it was via Moncheaux, Ivergny, and Humbercamps. Unlike the rest of Flanders (Artois and Picardy that had been seen), the country about Moncheaux and Ivergny was enclosed ; its well-trimmed hedges and the window-boxes of Ivergny were like England.

" On the 11th the battalion went into trenches at Fonquevillers (Funkeyvillas), which were reported to average one casualty per week, and remained there until the 21st. The enemy trenches ranged from 300 down to 140 yards distant. Trenches and billets in the neighbourhood were overrun with rats. The tour was without incident.

" After six days in billets at Bienvillers the battalion went into trenches in front of Hannescamps, with Pigeon Wood and Gommecourt on the right front.

" On the 29th, to avoid night relief, the line was left in small parties by day. After a night at Souastre, Loucheux was reached by route march on the 30th. On the way there was evidence everywhere of preparations for wintering troops."

Loucheux was in a pleasant vale adjoining Ivergny ; its cottages and flower gardens made it even more reminiscent of home. Eighteen days were spent at Loucheux. The billets were good. Unfortunately troops from Gallipoli had been on the ground and infected it with dysentery, of which a few cases occurred in the battalion. Every morning, some afternoons, and one night were given to strenuous training, which was the Commanding Officer's hobby. After the night operation the men swung in to breakfast in a way that was heartening—they were not recognisable as the timid drafts of six weeks earlier. None the less it was observable that with the practical disappearance of the old Army men from the ranks the snatches of song that had stimulated the weary disappeared too : " Tipperary " with variations, " Keep the Home Fires Burning," " Pack up your Troubles," or the challenging call " Are we downhearted ? " and its defiant response, were no longer heard towards the end of the stages of a route march. Henceforward the Army kept its breath to cool its ardour, not to fan it. But the old ardour still burned in one junior N.C.O. of the old Army stock—he expressed it on the door of his billet in these lines :

> Bravo ! Brave Fusiliers,
> You're soldiers tried and true ;
> Neither Kaiser's Huns nor giant guns
> Can daunt such men as you.
> And yet again in the dear homeland
> The plain will ring with cheers,
> For the men who claim Givenchy fame,
> The Second R. Welch Fusiliers.

At Loucheux the Headquarters details were organised as a fifth company —it was a battalion arrangement only, and was allowed to lapse.

" On 14th October the transport proceeded by road to the XIV Corps area (Lord Cavan). On the late afternoon of the 19th the company officers stood aside while the Brigadier managed the detail of embussing the battalion in French vehicles with Megalassy conductors. Méricourt was reached soon after midnight.

" On 21st October the battalion marched to the Citadel—a tented camp on the hillside, beyond Méaulte, on the left of the Bray Road. The weather had become very cold—the ground, greasy by day, was frozen firm during the night. German bombing planes were unwelcome visitors : a milk goat which Headquarters had acquired always gave warning of the approach of aeroplanes by her bleating. The march was continued across country ; the going was heavy for the men, but the transport skidded or stuck on the muddy slopes before getting into its allotted area of the vast expanse of mud at Carnoy, whence the companies continued by road to Trones Wood.

" Trones Wood consisted of branchless, shattered trunks standing amidst shell-holes and crumbling trenches. Only a few hours were spent choking and blinking round green-wood fires, for in the dark of the morning of the 23rd a further move was made.

" The battalion was lent to the 4th Division, which was in action on the Les Bœufs—Morval front. The first part of the march was on narrow congested parish roads, that had to carry an immensity of French as well as British traffic. The roads were lined by men of labour units, who made shift to maintain them amidst the constant stream of men, animals, vehicles, tripping, stumbling, lurching on the untrimmed branches and other timber thrown into shell-holes to overcome a momentary difficulty. The macadam surface had got beyond repair, even by the Germans, whose substantial corduroy was the only stretch on which the going was good.

" The route was by Guillemont and Ginchy, which were passed unnoticed, so complete was their destruction. Beyond these sites vehicles did not go. Artillery ammunition, as well as small arm, and rations were taken on tracks marked by the foundered and killed pack animals. Short as was the distance to Serpentine Trench—a portion of the German Delville Switch—it was daylight when the battalion got there. The morning was misty and chilly, the ground was soggy, and any tolerable shelter was already occupied by the artillery, whose guns were in line only fifty to sixty yards in rear.

" The attack, in which the 4th Division had a part, took place at 2.30 p.m. The ground shook as the sweating gunners fired shot upon shot from the leaping guns, and ear-drums were jangled by the clangour. The first accounts of the attack were good—the early walking wounded are always optimists. Later accounts were not so good ; then there was word of that awesome situation which is ' obscure ' : in short, the attack, like others on the same ground, had failed, and rain had come on.

" It rained all night, and the only relief anyone had was to vary the posture of discomfort. It rained most of the day on the 29th, which the men spent in making themselves ' comfortable.' The gunners objected to any fires but their own ; there had been little sleep for four nights, so nerves were frayed.

" As night fell, the battalion went forward again. The 33rd Division was relieving the 4th. Difficulty began when a cross-country track had to be found a mile behind Morval. Goldsmith, who had the only guide, raced on with his company ; touch was lost and no one else knew the way —but we got in somehow. The men, wet, weary, and mud-caked, were overladen for such going—they sank over their boots. Our youths of

A BARRAGE, SOMME BATTLE.
Imperial War Museum photograph, Crown copyright.

248]

poor stamina were coming in, tired out, up to noon on the 25th, and not a few had sought rest at the Ambulance Relay Posts and been sent to hospital. In a sunken road several exhausted men of the out-going units were stuck fast, and had to be dug out of the tenacious clay soil.

" The battalion was disposed on a two-company front, in touch with the French extended from Sailly-Saillisel. The dead and wounded of the 11th Brigade, whom we had relieved, were everywhere. For the three days the battalion was in the position the stretcher-bearers worked tirelessly, but the absence of communication trenches restricted the work to the dark hours, and many died.

" Daylight on the 25th showed the position to be a hollow, overlooked by the enemy, to whom situation maps allotted ' Hazy Trench,' ' Misty Trench,' etc. There was aptness in such names for trenches that were figments of the Staff imagination—the enemy was dispersed in shell-holes which served him admirably.

" On the 27th the battalion had orders to be relieved at night. It was cheering news, for the physical conditions were most trying, and spirits were flagging. Food could neither be cooked nor sent up hot : even Head-quarters lived on sandwiches prepared at the Transport, and its personnel shivered with cold when not blinded and choked with smoke in a hazardous, extemporised German dugout. The weather was misty and dull until the afternoon of the 27th, when rain fell.

" Getting out was less tedious than getting in, but it was 6 a.m. on the 28th before the last of the companies got back to Guillemont, a distance of less than three miles as the crow flies. By evening the men had made themselves shacks, and some were singing. There was a rum issue, a very rare event now, for it had to be wrung out of the new G.O.C.

" The 29th was a day of rain and bitter cold, and yet more mud; and some used-up men had to go to hospital. On the 30th a short move was made to ' Reserve,' among old gun emplacements in Trones Wood. On the 31st a further move was made to La Briqueterie, beyond Bernafay Wood, into tents in a sea of mud. Here the battalion remained for three days, finding fatigue parties. The days were sunny with occasional heavy showers, and the clear nights brought German aeroplanes with machine guns over the camp.

" At 2 p.m. on the 3rd November the battalion went forward again to relieve the 1st Middlesex in front of Les Bœufs. The route was through the site of Ginchy, and was by road until Les Bœufs was approached. Progress was very slow, and the platoons moved in single file amidst the congested up-and-down traffic. With the mass of movement on these

Picardy roads the silence was awesome. There was the monotonous grind of feet and wheels on the crumbling macadam, or the swish-swish where the water lay deep, and the occasional burst of a shell ; but of talk there was none. Mechanically a subaltern or sergeant ordered his men to ' close up,' or ' lead on ' ; wearily a driver muttered a curse when his horse stumbled or his wagon skidded ; stolidly thousands of men plodded forward or rearward. The last mile of the route, round the left of Les Bœufs, was by a heavily shelled track, in which the feet sank and slithered and slid. The rear of the column had hardly entered on it when Regimental Sergeant-Major Boreham was wounded.

" While the 19th Brigade was in reserve, the 98th Brigade had gained a little ground at the shambles that was called Dewdrop Trench—nowhere were our dead so numerous, nor did they comprise so many units as on the ground crossed to reach it. The battalion was disposed with B Company (2nd Lieutenant W. H. Fox) in front with its left on the Le Transloy Road, and a gap on its right, on the far side of which was the 100th Brigade at Morval ; D Company (Lieutenant Coster) in Dewdrop, in close support of B's right ; A Company (Lieutenant R. Greaves) in support on the left ; and C Company (Lieutenant W. H. Radford) in reserve.

" A patrol of thirty, under Lieutenant A. W. Loverseed, was sent out to explore the gap—lost itself, and stayed out all night and the next day, returning on the 4th November, after dark.

" The 4th was a grey day, with glints of sunshine and no rain. The day was spent studying the ground in anticipation of an Anglo-French attack in the morning. Three schemes, with a diminishing objective, came in quick succession. To those on the spot only the last seemed practical. The battalion was to go forward to a line roughly 250 yards in advance of B Company's position, to the forward slope of the last undulation before the ground dipped to the glacis crowned by Le Transloy village, with the cemetery as an outpost—the sort of ground which delighted the German machine gunners.

" In the early morning of the 5th C Company was ordered forward into Dewdrop Trench, on D Company's right. Such were the conditions that they only settled in just before dawn—fortunately it was a grey, damp morning with a mist, and visibility was bad. The Commanders of C and D Companies foregathered in a German dugout later in the morning for a cup of tea, when D Company's operation order arrived. Coster read it and passed it to Radford. The attack was to be carried out by strong patrols pushed up over the crest to seize and hold the ground, the remainder of the companies to advance later and consolidate the ground thus gained.

Zero had not been fixed, but would be notified later if possible : in the event of time not permitting notification to the attacking companies, the opening of the French ·75 bombardment would be taken as zero.   Such was the order when read subsequently at leisure.

" Radford was half-way through with the first reading when the French barrage fire commenced—it was then 11.10 a.m.   The two company commanders looked at each other, roared with laughter, shouted, ' The show's begun ! ' and, neither having had time to grasp the orders, ran out and tumbled their men from the trench—the companies advanced *en masse* and surged up the slope.

" There was luck in this pell-mell evacuation of Dewdrop, for the companies had barely got out when the German counter-barrage fell on it, and on A Company, whose orders were to occupy it when vacated.   In spite of their casualties, it was a less unhealthy spot for A than that which they quitted.

" In the meantime B Company had also got on the move, but were held up by an unharried machine gun on their right ; so a Lewis gun was played on it, which helped C and D Companies to get into line.

" The attack of the 33rd Division and the French happened on an enemy disposed to shorten his line.   From the salient of the shell-hole area of Hazy, etc., some 200 Germans emerged, and made for the cover of the reverse slope.   The three companies carried on the advance, until the ground sloped towards the main German position, and they came under direct machine-gun fire.   A line of shell-holes was occupied temporarily, and digging started to connect them up, while patrols worked their way forward on to the objective.   The decision to consolidate behind an outpost line was taken by Fox, Radford, and Coster in consultation—it had regard for the exposed position.

" C Company overran the machine gun that had enfiladed B, and secured four prisoners of the 81st (Frankfurt a/M) and 24th Regiments. They were 19, 19, 22, and 26 years old, one of them a pleasant, talkative youth.

" The weather became increasingly depressing as the day wore on. After dark C Company sent out a small patrol, under Lieutenant Mair, to seek touch with the 100th Brigade.   The patrol had gone about fifty yards when a shot was fired under the leader's nose, which caused them to scuttle back.   Quartermaster-Sergeant Deeling suggested that anyone on the flank should be mopped up, so the patrol was reinforced and he went out with it, enveloped in the flowing mackintosh cape affected by Quartermaster-Sergeants.

" The night was fine and the atmosphere clear under a star-lit sky ;

for the first time in two weeks not a gun disturbed the silence, in which sounds carried far. In the fresh breeze that blew from the right Deeling's cloak flapped like the sides of a tent in a gale. Every note of his deep bass voice was audible in the trench as he asked or gave directions. ' Where are they, sir ? ' . . . ' Form a horse-shoe round them.' . . . ' Heave one amongst them, sir.' There was the crash of a Mills bomb—' Come out, Allemands '—and in no time four scared Germans were flung into the Company Headquarters shell-hole.

" The four Germans, extracted from their lair so summarily, were provided with five days' rations. Among them, wounded, was one of the missing from Loverseed's patrol : he said he had been treated properly— had his wounds dressed and had been given food and drink.

" By daylight on the 6th the front companies were linked up by a trench of sorts.

" The 7th was a quiet day of rain, which filled much of the new trench. The 1st Devons, of the 8th Division, came up after dark. The relief was long, in spite of a clear sky and moonlight, for movement was slow on the greasy, soggy ground, and so tiring that there was even reluctance to bring out the wounded ; each stretcher required triple squads carrying on short relays. It was well on in the morning of the 8th before anyone reached the clay field, intersected by shallow, fallen-in trenches at Briqueterie, in which the battalion bivouacked." (J. C. Dunn.)

. . . .

About the middle of September, when the French had captured Sailly-Saillisel, Sir Douglas Haig, according to the despatch, realised that " the moment for decisive action was rapidly passing away," and that the weather was a serious obstacle to further progress. But, he says, " while continuing to do all that was possible to improve my position on my right flank, I determined to press on with preparations for the exploitation of the favourable local situation on my left flank." Our 9th and 10th Battalions, having been " rested," came back to the Somme on this left flank.

THE BATTLE OF THE ANCRE HEIGHTS.[1]
(9TH BATTALION.)

The main assault of this battle was delivered on the 21st October, in the neighbourhood of Courcelette-Pys, and resulted in the capture of Regina and Stuff Trenches and the Schwaben Redoubt.

[1] Date : 1st October–11th November. Area : road Pys—Le Sars—Martinpuich—Contalmaison—La Boisselles—Aveluy—Martinsart—Mesnil—Hamel.

Under the battering-ram system of limited objectives divisions were continually on the move. They were sent in to battle, " used," and taken out to recuperate, absorb drafts (which were very mixed), hold a quiet sector of the line, and then, frequently, moved again into the battle area for further operations. So our 9th Battalion, in the Ploegsteert area, marched with the 19th Division on the 5th October to Bailleul and entrained for Doullens. They passed through Sailly-au-Bois, Vauchelles, Toutencourt, and arrived on the 11th at Ovillers.

On the 26th, after the main attack, the battalion relieved the 10th Warwickshire in Regina and Hessian Trenches, still under heavy shell fire. They lost Lieutenant C. G. Lawes and 11 other ranks killed ; Captain H. L. Williams, Lieutenant J. L. Hughes, 2nd Lieutenants F. E. Wormesley, F. G. Davies, and 29 other ranks wounded.

THE BATTLE OF THE ANCRE.[1]

(9TH AND 10TH BATTALIONS.)

The 9th Battalion continued to hold Regina and Hessian Trenches, going back to Ovillers for rest. The journey, on each relief, was some three miles. The ground was in a fearful state, the shell craters being filled with liquid mud, and balanced on the edge of the craters was a duck-board track : it eased the journey, but even so troops arrived in the line or camp in an exhausted condition.

Meanwhile our 10th Battalion, who had been holding the line in the Loos sector since the 8th September, moved south and came into the V Corps area at the beginning of October. Preparations for the attack were commenced at once under the belief that it would be launched in a few days. But postponement followed postponement as the weather steadily grew worse. The troops in the front line, soaked to the skin, wading in mud, were bombarded daily, and the assembly trenches which they dug with so much labour were knocked to pieces—an easy operation when they would scarcely stand up by themselves. To add to the general discomfort, the billets in the back areas, which should have afforded them shelter and rest, were limited and bad.

The attack planned had for its objectives Miraumont, Beauregard, Dovecot, Serre, also Pys, Irles, and Achiet le Petit, to be attained in three bounds. The 19th Division were to pass over Grandcourt Trench to a final line on the Miraumont—Beaucourt road ; the 3rd Division were to capture

[1] Date: 13th–18th November. Area: the Bapaume Road to La Boisselles ; thence road to Aveluy—Martinsart—Englebelmer—Mailly-Maillet—Colincamps—Hebuterne—Puisieux.

Serre and form a defensive flank from John Copse across Pendant Trench to Puisieux Trench. But all plans had to be altered ; while the ultimate scope remained the same, the opening attack became with each postponement less ambitious.

On the 9th November a spell of frosty weather set in, and on the 11th the bombardment opened and was continued till the 13th, when at 5.45 a.m. the assaulting troops advanced from Schwaben Redoubt to the north of Serre. The 10th Battalion attacked on that day.

The village of Serre stands on a small hill, the slope rising gently from our lines. The soil, in this part of the country, is soft clay, which had been pounded by the intense bombardment of the 1st July and, less intensely

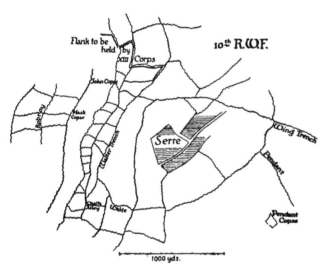

but continuously, since the commencement of October. The enemy's lines defending Serre looked like a tumbled mass of shell craters. From the air the lines of trenches could be distinguished, on the map they were definitely marked, but on the ground their position and formation were extremely vague.

The weather had again changed. The night of the 12th/13th November was very thick, a dripping fog making the ground wet and greasy. The peculiar silence of such wet foggy nights brooded over the battlefield, broken now and again by an occasional shell from an enemy field gun or a burst of machine-gun fire, and punctuated by slow, regular fire from some of our own batteries.

Troops filed into their places.

The 76th Brigade were on the left of the V Corps, and 3rd Division front ; on their left troops of the XIII Corps were to make a short advance to complete the defensive flank. The attack was on a two-battalion front, each battalion on a front of two companies, each of the leading companies on a front of two platoons.

Our 10th Battalion was on the right, the 2nd Suffolk on the left ; the 1st Gordon Highlanders and the 8th King's Own Royal Lancaster were in support.   Before taking up their final positions, all men were given hot tea, rum, and a cheese sandwich.   Then the assaulting battalions pushed forward four Lewis guns into No Man's Land, to keep down any enemy machine-gun fire, and the leading assaulting waves formed up just behind them ; the remaining waves remained in the front line and Copse Trench.

The preliminary arrangements, the forming up, the artillery barrage (100 yards in 5 minutes) were satisfactory.   South of the river, on the II Corps front, the operation was a great success.   St. Pierre Divion and on the north bank Beaumont Hamel passed into our hands with many prisoners ; only about Serre did the attack go wrong.

The movements of troops could not be seen in the fog—they simply disappeared.   The ground, a mass of shell-holes, was so heavy that men sank up to the middle of the calf, in some places to above the knee, and had continually to pull each other out of the mud.   The mist and mud combined to destroy the cohesion of the attack ; men were inclined to bunch ; parties lost touch, and arriving in the German trenches found themselves isolated.

Our 10th Battalion, except for the heavy going, met with practically no opposition, but the 2nd Suffolk on the left got hung up before some new concertina wire and the barrage went on.   The ground on the left of our battalion then appeared " alive with Germans," who, when the barrage had passed over them, came out of their dugouts.   As our waves advanced, they were forced to form a defensive flank to their left, draining the forward thrust.

But the conditions were in any case bad.   Cohesion seems to have been lost the moment the advance commenced ; direction was lost ; leading troops could not see where the barrage was ; and there were gaps everywhere in the assaulting line.   The second line was reached—the third line—and about two platoons entered the fourth line.   In the fourth line the enemy was strong, and came streaming out of dugouts on the left to counter-attack : knowing the ground, they worked swiftly round our leading troops, most of whom, with their brave and capable commander, Captain Rudd, disappeared.

All the officers of the two leading waves were killed.   The next two waves reached the German third line and, with some thirty Gordon Highlanders, held it for an hour ; but neither party was in touch with the other, and the Germans, working round, drove them back.

The next two waves were badly cut up by machine-gun fire between the German first and second lines.   They lost all their officers but one. The last two waves had fewer casualties, but did not pass the German first line.

It was a most confusing operation.   The Gordon Highlanders, leaving their trenches to advance in support, had no idea of the progress made by our battalion.   They reached the German third line in about an hour's time, having seen only one Royal Welch Fusilier.   The trench was knee-deep in mud ; the number of Highlanders remaining was small—they could not maintain their position.

By 8.30 a.m. it was clear that the attack had failed, but the last of our troops did not return from the German lines until 7 p.m.

Efforts were made to renew the attack, but the disorganisation was so great it was abandoned.   It was learned from prisoners that an attack had been expected, and the bells, which had been heard ringing in Serre about 3 a.m., were a warning to stand to arms.

The remnants of our battalion gathered together in Rob Roy Trench, and at dusk the following day moved back to Courcelles.

Captains W. F. Rudd, E. W. Bishop, and 156 other ranks were missing ; 2nd Lieutenants A. E. Capell, H. G. Thomas, P. Williams, H. M. Jones, G. Thomas, D. Davies, R. H. Williams, H. L. Harries, and 17 other ranks were known to have been killed ; Captain W. N. Davies, 2nd Lieutenants E. Vaughan-Jones, I. H. Hughes, and 102 other ranks were wounded.

.   .   .   .

South of the river the 19th Division did not attack.   They had been ordered to attack Grandcourt on the 14th, but the order was cancelled, and our 9th Battalion, and the 58th Brigade, who had been for the attack, came, in the new order, in reserve.   The whole of Beaucourt fell to the II Corps on the 14th.

The battle then eased down ; but on the 18th, the 19th Division attacked with the 26th and 27th Brigades and occupied a portion of Grandcourt.   During this operation our battalion was in billets at Aveluy.

The whole of these operations, which were in the main successful, yielded 7,500 prisoners.

The 9th Battalion moved back through Warley to Doullens and Le Meillard, where they arrived on the 25th November.

Meanwhile, on the 20th, Colonel Berners had been appointed to command the 11th Infantry Brigade, and on the 4th December Lieutenant-Colonel L. F. Smeathman assumed command, with Major Lord Howard de Walden as his second-in-command.

.   .   .   .

" The three main objects with which we had commenced our offensive in July had already been achieved at the date when this account closes ;

in spite of the fact that the heavy autumn rains had prevented full advantage being taken of the favourable situation created by our advance, at a time when we had good grounds for hoping to achieve yet more important successes.

" Verdun had been relieved ; the main German forces had been held on the western front ; and the enemy's strength had been very considerably worn down.

" Any one of these three results is in itself sufficient to justify the Somme battle. The attainment of all three of them affords ample compensation for the splendid efforts of our troops and for the sacrifice made by ourselves and our Allies." (Despatch.)

One cannot judge the 1916 Offensive by looking only between the Somme and the Ancre : co-operation between the Allies had been agreed, and the Somme, though an operation in itself, was part of a far bigger scheme which must be taken into account.

Brusilov commenced his successful and spectacular advance against the Austrians on the 4th June, whereupon the Austrians broke off their attack on the Italians. The Italian Army then started a counter-offensive, and Rumania declared war on the Central Powers.

The Battle of the Somme opened ; further Russian attacks were launched in the east ; and there is no occasion for surprise at Ludendorff's admission that " We went through a terrible time," and " Our nerves were strung to the highest pitch." But everything does not, in war, always go " according to plan." The western part of the Allied Offensive was complicated by the Battle of Verdun, which, under the circumstances, was no less a complication for the German Headquarters Staff.

One can assert that the true battle-aim of the Somme operations was not attained ; but that is not to say they had no effect.

The system of limited objectives had taken us from Fricourt to Le Transloy, a distance of nine miles, in five months—and the enemy line was unbroken. We had pinned our faith on an artillery assault—the massing of guns on a restricted front with a limited depth of fire—and the principle, at first sight, seemed sound enough ; but we never succeeded in so smashing and demoralising the enemy that he was unable to launch a counter-attack at will, counter-attacks which frequently succeeded in throwing us back to our original positions ; and he remained always a fighting Army before us. The advance of nine miles meant nothing—there was no vital objective in front of us on which the enemy's organisation and security were centred.

The Germans, however, recognised that their system of defence was endangered by this form of attack. Ludendorff's comments are interesting, the more so when referring to the infantry, for there is a familiar ring about them, almost as though they had been spoken by one of our own Generals.

The course of the battle, he says, had supplied important lessons on the construction and plan of the German lines. The deep dugouts and cellars often became " fatal man-traps," and what he calls underground forts in the front trenches must in future be replaced by shallower constructions. Lines of trenches, wherever sited, could be photographed, and observed by the artillery from aeroplanes; and "large thick barriers of wire, pleasant as they were when there was little doing, were no longer a protection. They withered under the enemy barrage." He, too, is forced to the conclusion we had arrived at in 1914, that " forward infantry positions with a wide field of fire were easily seen by the enemy " and provided too good a mark for the artillery. The whole system of defence had to be made " broader and looser and better adapted to the ground." And he realised the value of concrete pill-boxes.

When Falkenhayn was dismissed and Hindenburg with Ludendorff became the chiefs of the German Army, they attended a conference at Cambrai, and heard, for the first time, the true conditions on the western front and the effect of the artillery battle on the infantry. " The barrage had come to be regarded as a universal panacea. The infantry insisted on it, but unfortunately it had come to confuse many sound theories. A barrage is all very well in theory, but in practice only too often it collapses under the storm of the enemy's destruction fire. Our infantry, which had come to rely on the barrage alone for protection, were far too inclined to forget that they had to defend themselves by their personal efforts. . . . The use of the rifle was being forgotten, hand-grenades had become the chief weapon. . . . The excessive use of hand-grenades had come about because these could be usefully and safely employed from behind shelter, whereas a man using a rifle must leave his cover. In the close fighting of some of our own raids, and also in the large-scale attacks by the enemy, where the fighting at any moment came to be man to man, hand-grenades were readier weapons for the unpractised men and easier to use than rifles, the latter having also the disadvantage of getting dirty easily. One could understand that ; but infantry must keep able to hold the enemy off and fight from a distance." (*My War Memories*, 1914–1918.)

THE BATTLES OF ARRAS, 1917.

The region of the Somme remained the centre of military attention. The Allied Commanders considered that a favourable situation had been created there for a further effort early in 1917.

They met at Chantilly in November and decided that the attack should be renewed with the British Fourth and Fifth Armies (Gough's Reserve Army was now the Fifth), and to add to it an attack of the Third Army (Allenby) and the First Army (Horne) at Arras and Vimy. The French would attack south of the Somme.

The offensive was to be resumed by the British in February ; three weeks later the French would launch their main attack, which would be south of Reims. Orders were issued for the preparation of a scheme which was to be ready on the 1st February.

The fact that the Allied Nations had a common enemy was not lost sight of—the Russians and Italians were included in the schemes for 1917 ; it was to be " an all-front offensive." But the Russian Revolution, as we know, soon took them out of the picture.

Man proposes—but in war there is also the enemy. Ludendorff makes his position abundantly clear. He claims that 1916 closed with success for the Germanic Powers, and when one considers the great weight of the Allied assault in that year, the claim must be admitted—with qualifications. On the Western Front the Allies had nothing much to show : Nivelle's spectacular recovery of ground at Verdun, which placed him in the position of popular hero, was of no consequence. But Ludendorff does not conceal the gravity of future threat : he sees coloured troops filling the gaps in the French Army—England brought up to strength—Russia calling again on her enormous man-power—the defeated Rumanian Army reorganised under French officers—and any falling off in quality of troops compensated for by an improved and enlarged technical equipment of all Allied Armies. " They [German General Headquarters] had to face the danger that ' Somme fighting ' would soon break out at various points on our fronts, and that even our troops would not be able to withstand such attacks indefinitely, especially if the enemy gave us no time for rest and the accumulation of material." He thought that if the war lasted, defeat would be inevitable.[1]

It was a depressing outlook. But no one knew better than Ludendorff how the pendulum of war may suddenly swing in the opposite direction : the Germanic Powers were not defeated, were still dangerous and capable of exchanging fierce blows. His aim was to economise men, keep large reserves in hand, and wait for opportunity. He did not propose to undertake any great offensive in 1917.

The remedy for the malaise was to shorten his line, and at the same time strengthen it.

This conclusion was arrived at long before the Allied Commanders

[1] Ludendorff, *My War Memories*, 1914-1918.

met at Chantilly—it was in September, while bitter and costly battles were still being fought on the Somme. A new line was sited, running from Arras to Cambrai—St. Quentin—La Fère—Vailly-sur-Aisne, and construction was commenced. When we knew of its existence, we called it the Hindenburg Line—the Germans, with their love for the myths and sagas of legendary days, called it Siegfried!

The date of the retirement was not settled immediately, but that such a retirement must affect the plans of Joffre and Haig is obvious. Ludendorff's object was, first, " to avoid a battle, our second to effect the salvage of our raw material of war and technical and other equipment that was not actually built into the position, and finally the destruction of all high-roads, villages, towns, and wells, so as to prevent the enemy establishing himself in force in the near future in front of our new position."

And a further complication arose to upset the Allied plan—the French Government decided to dismiss General Joffre, and place General Nivelle at the head of their Armies.

Our 4th, 13th, 14th, 15th, 16th, 17th Battalions had already left the southern field—that is to say, the Somme area—and were at Ypres. After the attack on Serre, the 10th Battalion remained but a short time in the sector, moving north on the 6th January to Arras, where they were to take part in the spring offensive.

We have to deal first with the 1st, 2nd, 9th, and 19th Battalions.

THE 19TH BATTALION.

The 19th Battalion was raised under what was known as the " bantam " standard of height, and was posted in February 1915 to the 119th Brigade —with the 12th South Wales Borderers and the 17th and 18th Welch Regiment—of the 40th Division, a " bantam " division. The division trained at Whitchurch (Salop) until September 1915, when they moved to Aldershot. On the 1st June 1916 the division sailed for France.

Our 19th Battalion received instruction in trench warfare from the 1st Gloucestershire and 2nd Munster in the Calonne sector, where they remained until the end of August. They then did a tour of duty in the right sub-sector at Loos, till the end of October, when they moved by easy stages south, arriving at Suzanne on 26th December. They went into the line at Rancourt, taking over from the 17th Welch. They were in touch with the French.

Casualties were light, but on the night of the 22nd January Lieutenant-Colonel B. J. Jones was wounded, " having encountered an enemy patrol while visiting some isolated posts." Major J. H. R. Downes-Powell took command.

.   .   .   .

On the 16th September Lieutenant-Colonel Stockwell left our 1st Battalion, who were in billets at Merelessart, to take command of the 164th Brigade, 55th Division. Major W. G. Holmes assumed command. The next day the battalion proceeded to Ploegsteert Wood. This was a quiet part of the line, but the advent of the 7th Division meant that in a short time it was exceedingly lively. Many raids were carried out, one of the most successful being that by our battalion on the last night of September. Casualties, however, were not heavy.

The battalion was in fair strength, two drafts of 160 and 350 having arrived since the Ginchy battle; of the latter Stockwell had time to note in his diary, " A draft of 350 second-line Terriers—good, I think," before he left.

In November they were ordered back to the Somme area.

The 7th Division took over the line in front of Beaumont Hamel on the 25th November; the 22nd Brigade did not go in till the 29th, our battalion being then in reserve.

The first news that greeted them was that the division had been ordered to capture Munich Trench in front of the village—these were V Corps instructions, but the division came under XIII Corps almost immediately. Also brigades were informed that a reward of £5 a head would be paid for the first twenty prisoners taken.

It was part of Sir Douglas Haig's scheme that the enemy should be allowed no rest on this front. A major operation was out of the question, but a series of minor attacks would, it was hoped, place our troops in possession of the Beaumont Hamel spur with its facilities for observation. There was then, about Beaumont Hamel, the indication of an active winter—and it was, indeed, a memorable one.

The situation since the capture of Beaumont Hamel village had been obscure, and when our battalion took over the front line from the 2nd H.A.C.[1] on the 2nd December, their position was not too happy. That it should be so must not cause surprise, as the conditions were abnormal and horrible. The area was a quagmire. Trenches, when it was possible to dig them, soon became a series of holes in which a sentry-post existed and which slowly filled with mud and water: the digging of a new hole would improve the situation for a while, and so it went on. They had

[1] The 2nd H.A.C. took the place of the Royal Irish, who were transferred to the 16th Division on the 14th October.

scarcely oriented themselves when they were relieved by the H.A.C. When they returned again to the line they were puzzled : " The advanced posts, when taken over, though relatively the same, were found to be farther to the right than had at first been thought. There was still doubt as to their exact position. A reconnaissance was made by 2nd Lieutenant Garnon-Williams with a view to establishing their position."

If possible, the ground had become worse since our 10th Battalion had attacked at Serre. The long winter nights, when all movement took place, were an improvement in misery on the popular idea of Hades. The glow from the rising Verey lights, fired in the front line, was dimmed by a driving veil of rain or wet mist, but was reflected in pools of water and humps of slimy mud ; and through the drizzle or sweep of rain, mud-plastered figures would stagger along uneven trench-boards, laid on the insecure crests between shell-holes, and stretching for miles across the desolate pulpy country. Someone would slip, fall with a splash, and flounder in filth while he cursed France and Germany ; but the next man would dump his load and laugh as he helped his fallen comrade to rise, only to curse in his turn when he found his rifle, and anything else he happened to be carrying, had become embedded in the mud. Even the exploding shell was so clogged with mud that its effect was reduced.

In contrast to the memorable Christmas Day scene recorded by the 2nd Battalion in 1914, the 7th Division diary notes : " To celebrate the occasion of Christmas Day there was no offensive artillery fire from our side between the hours of 6 a.m. and 8 a.m., 11.30 a.m. and noon, and 4.45 p.m. and 5 p.m. ; but at 8 a.m., noon, 5 p.m., and 5.5 p.m. every gun and howitzer in the Fifth Army fired one round." No expression of German gratitude, or even acknowledgment, is recorded. Perhaps their perception was dulled by the monotony of mud. At least one of their ration parties blundered into one of our posts during the morning : three were shot and the remainder—six—captured. And a little later in the day an Intelligence Officer, Captain Blennerhasset, accompanied by 2nd Lieutenant Freeman, approached their line and attempted to pursuade them to surrender—but the replies he received showed a lack of initiative. Hostilities were then resumed, nothing having been gained but a certain amount of information about the German line.

Prisoners came in freely during the winter.

On the 10th January the 2nd Border Regiment commenced to nibble at the enemy and captured some advanced posts, A and C Companies of our battalion holding the line during the attack and helping to consolidate the gains. The next morning Munich Trench was taken, 2nd Lieutenant T. D. Jones and 10 bombers co-operating.

On the 21st January the division went out of the line for six weeks' training about Rubempré.

It was during this rest that Ludendorff gave the signal for retreat. The first " Alberich " day, as he called it, was 9th February, and the general retreat to the Hindenburg Line was to commence on the 16th March.

. . . .

Our 2nd Battalion was, during this time, on the right sector of the British line, opposite St. Pierre Vaast Wood. They had taken over the line on the 18th December, after a month of rest at Forceville. Conditions were no better here than in the Beaumont Hamel sector. There were days of frost, when it was possible to walk with some comfort over the frozen surface of the ground, but the mud was appalling.

" The battalion went into line at Bouchavesnes, near the southern edge of St. Pierre Vaast Wood, where the Division had relieved the 30th French Division two weeks earlier. Headquarters was in a louse-infested dugout, excavated in the chalk at the side of the Peronne—Bapaume road. The companies were in rudely constructed trenches, the front so exposed that no movement was possible by day. Save for occasional coils of French wire, there was only a single strand of wire in front : but the sector was quiet ; there seemed to be a tacit armistice, though Rancourt, on the immediate left, was shelled ceaselessly.

" The weather had been bad for two weeks, snow and rain alternated, and there was always mud. Enforced inactivity chilled the two front companies ; fatigues on the steep gradients and heavy going exhausted the support companies. Just behind men struggled under loads, and pack-horses foundered in the mud, taking up ammunition of which the guns could not get enough." (Dunn.)

They spent Christmas Day out of the line [1] near Bray and returned to the Clery sector, where they relieved the French 90th Regiment.

The picture here is the same as in the other parts of the Somme battlefield : the exhausting physical effort required to get in and out of the front line ; the soaked and mud-caked equipment, clothing, and greatcoats ; the wobbly duck-boards ; and the congested roads. The last were terrible. All movement up to the line took place at the same time— rations, engineers' stores, artillery ammunition, etc.—and the heavy and

---

[1] The men's dinners consisted of soup, roast meat, potatoes, carrots, turnips, plum-pudding, apples or oranges, and sweets. At 6.30 p.m. tea was given them, with cake, candied fruits, sweets, and beer for an improvised sing-song afterwards.

dilapidated condition of the roads meant that loads had to be lightened, with the result that the volume of traffic increased. The hour of dusk was amazing.

The division remained in the Clery sector until the middle of March. The final word on that exhausting winter, shared by all battalions of the regiment, excepting those in the northern and, in a military sense, quieter sectors who were spared the artillery activity, must be left with Major Dunn.

" The outstanding circumstance was the weather conditions and their resulting casualties, for the winter 1916–17 was the most severe the Expeditionary Force had experienced. With the arrival of the division in the area, keen frost set in and did not relax until the middle of February. The ground was ice-bound and the Somme was mostly frozen over ; the starving waterfowl were game to the poachers among the troops. Many nights there were 15 to 20 degrees of frost, and there were frequent snow-showers. The beauty of the scene was striking, but it did not warm chilled bodies. There were no braziers in the trenches ; fuel near the trenches was so scarce that the rude crosses were taken from the casual graves. Except for a tepid tea that came up in tins wrapped in hay, food was mostly cold, for solidified alcohol was a rare issue. The G.O.C. was obdurate in his opposition to a rum issue. The trenches were never so vocal, all the occupants coughed—a circumstance which, added to the whiteness of the ground, suspended patrolling. Owing to the reduced and rationed output of coal at home the issue of coal to the Army was limited, so the fortunate occupants of dugouts had coke issued. In these ill-ventilated tenements, and with men sleeping on the floor, cases of coke-fume poisoning were common.

" Home leave for troops on the Somme began and ended with a severe test of endurance. The direct route, by Boulogne, was reserved for senior and privileged officers, all others had to make the long round by Havre. Three to five days might be spent on the journey. The trains were unheated ; the windows, even the doors, of most compartments were broken. The tented rest-camps were apparently sited for fresh air. An officer who had spent a night in the camp at Havre could not sleep for cold ; he was roused from one of his fitful dozes to find three rats snuggling in next his shirt for warmth. Trying as was the cold, it was nothing to the week of thaw when sick-parades exceeded a hundred a day.

" During the two months the division was at Clery, operations were of a minor kind—two or three raids, or attempted raids by both sides. But the artillery had bursts of destructive activity. On the night of the

25th January Lieutenant-Colonel Crawshay was severely wounded in the arm and back by an enemy rifleman while inspecting the wire. Until Lieutenant-Colonel W. B. Garnett was transferred from the 20th Royal Fusiliers, Captains Cuthbert and J. M. Owen were alternately in hospital and acting Commanding Officer.''

A raid, ordered by the Higher Command, but looked on by all officers as the utmost folly, was averted by the sudden thaw, which filled the lines with ice-cold liquid mud, and caused the trenches to fall in. It was attempted, later, by the Argyll and Sutherland, who were shot down as they left their assembly lines.

Lieutenant-Colonel Garnett assumed command on the 19th February, and that night the battalion was withdrawn to support, near Marrières Wood. Over eighty men were sent to hospital the next day, the majority with trench feet.

From the 23rd February to the 3rd March the battalion was resting, on an hour's notice to move, at Suzanne.

On the 25th February the Fourth (and Fifth) Army sent out a wire: '' Reliable information received enemy contemplating retirement to line north and south through Cambrai. Infantry brigades must take immediate steps to ascertain if hostile trenches are empty or only thinly held. If hostile retirement is in progress infantry brigades in the line will keep touch pushing forward detachments.'' But on this front the enemy was found in normal strength, although before our battalion left the line a road crossing No Man's Land had been blown up by a mine.

But St. David's Day was celebrated at Suzanne in a broken shrine. Parry, chef at one of the large London restaurants, prepared an excellent dinner. Major Roger Poore, recently transferred from the Hants Yeomanry, and now second-in-command, presided. A German shell-case served as loving-cup. And neither leek nor goat was absent—a fine Welsh goat from the Wynnstay Hills, the gift of officers at the depôt, had joined the battalion.

'' On the 3rd March the battalion marched via Eclusier to the lower-lying, right sub-sector at Clery. The frost had returned and the ground was firm. On the 5th more than an inch of snow fell, but did not lie. A trench strength of 450 was got by taking into the line the drums and some of the details usually left out. The enemy was more active than he had been hitherto. A raid he attempted on a sap-head was checked. He was covering his withdrawal by artillery activity, which caused an unusual number of casualties. Numerous fires could be seen in his rear positions, where houses and stores were being destroyed. The last relief on the Somme front was on the 9th March—the night was spent at Frise Bend, where a ration of sardines was issued in place of meat.   The battalion remained, after a night at Suzanne, at Camp 13."   (Dunn.)

.   .   .   .

But on the left of this area, about Beaumont Hamel, the Fifth Army message on enemy retirement was found to be correct.   Patrols from the 21st Manchester found the front line evacuated (Ten Tree Alley), and it was thought that Serre was also unoccupied.   Our 1st Battalion moved up from Rubempré, and was attached to the 91st Brigade, in support to the 21st Manchester.   Our 9th Battalion, with the 58th Brigade, was in reserve to the 19th Division, and remained during the whole of this period training at Louvencourt.

The retirement was discovered on the 25th February, but it was confined to this northern side of the Somme battlefield.   Our 1st Battalion was ordered to concentrate above the Serre road and to the west of that ruin, and prepare to attack Puisieux ; then the order for attack was postponed till the next day, but they lost 10 killed and 30 wounded from shell fire.

The advance of the battalion commenced at 4.45 p.m. and was largely an affair of patrols : the enemy was there, fighting a delaying action, but would not stand up to anything like a fully mounted attack.   The village of Puisieux was entered, and the patrols, passing through to the northern edge of it, were held up.   2nd Lieutenant Montgomery was sent with twenty-four men to clear the church : he lost most of his force, and failed, the church being strongly held.   Casualties were heavy, Captain A. W. Anscombe, Lieutenant J. R. P. Adams, 2nd Lieutenants C. H. Owen, C. E. Montgomery, and A. M. Syrett were wounded ; 11 other ranks were killed, 22 wounded, and 5 missing.

The situation bristled with difficulties and everyone passed through a most trying time.   This sudden order to advance over a maze of shell-hole positions, against an enemy who had sited machine guns with great skill, with a prearranged line of retreat to another site, was unexpected. The ground was favourable for such enemy tactics, and the state of it clogged our advance.   It was difficult to keep in touch with neighbouring units, and much time was expended in sending patrols to a flank while the forward movement was delayed.

The 1st Battalion was relieved on the 28th February and went back to Bertrancourt.   When they went forward again on the 16th March—the date of the general retirement of the enemy—they relieved the 2nd H.A.C. at Puisieux.   The whole of the 17th was spent in feeling their way through Bucquoy (which they had been ordered to attack) to Ablainzeville, which was burning.   The next day they moved on to Courcelles, which had been occupied by the Royal Warwickshire and two squadrons of the Lucknow Cavalry Brigade.

Progress was slow.   The nature of the operation led to the cancellation of many orders.   On the 19th the battalion was to attack St. Leger, but it was found evacuated and they remained at Courcelles.   They moved back to Puisieux on the 21st, and forward once more to Courcelles on the 27th.

The Fourth and Fifth Armies had been forced to conform to Ludendorff's plan.   " The country we had traversed was devastated, and before military operations could be made possible upon it a certain amount of restoration was essential . . . an infinite amount of road and bridge building would have to be done.   The enemy, therefore, established himself in relatively low strength in front of our new line."   (Ludendorff.)

Meanwhile, the change in the French command had made itself felt. General Nivelle, while not actually discarding the plan which his predecessor and Sir Douglas Haig had decided upon, modified it to some extent.   The British were asked to take over more line, which reduced the weight of the contemplated attack ; on the other hand, the French undertook an even greater part—they were to deliver surprise attacks on either side of Reims.   Unfortunately, French orders revealing the most essential details of their scheme were taken into the front line, and captured by the Germans in a local raid.   Warned of the " surprise," the Germans could, if the plan was persisted in, turn it to their advantage.   The French did persist.   They were full of confidence.   Nothing mattered—the cry was " à Berlin ! " The German retreat to the Hindenburg Line was of no consequence—the British attack could proceed, with certain modifications to meet the situation !   Friction arose.   Nivelle tactlessly revealed his opinion of the British Army, which was in all respects opposed to that held by British Headquarters.   Meanwhile, the salient which Sir Douglas Haig hoped to attack, between the Ancre and Arras, had disappeared.

The German retreat was not completed for some time.   Starting on our left, it ended on our right.   Our 19th Battalion, working during the first weeks of April on roads about Bouchavesnes, moved up to Gouzeaucourt, and attacked near Gonnelieu on the 21st.   It was a small affair, the Germans holding a rearguard position.   Troops of the 8th Division were on the right of our 19th Battalion, opposite Gonnelieu ; the 12th South Wales Borderers were on the left.   Captain J. Williams and Lieutenant V. H. Piercy led their companies with success.

But while the Fourth and Fifth Armies were floundering in the morass of the Somme battlefields, and the enemy, with a short step back, set his feet on dry ground and marched airily to the Hindenburg Line, the preparations of the Third Army were complete. This front was hardly affected : the Hindenburg Line came sliding into it obliquely and the Germans only relinquished the forward elements of their trench system, lessening in depth towards the left of the Third Army. The prospect of turning the whole of the newly constructed defence system was, then, offered if a break-through was attained. But the Germans had foreseen this possibility and were busily engaged in building a switch line, covering the rear of the old system : it ran from Quéant to Drocourt, and was unfinished in April. Ludendorff foresaw an attack on this front.

The immediate objective of the Third Army was Cambrai, with the plains behind Douai as the ultimate goal. The French attacks, planned by Nivelle, were in the direction of Mezières—converging railway lines, unlimited objectives !—and would also turn the southern extremity of the Hindenburg Line. (See Map, page 306.)

The record of General Allenby, who then commanded the Third Army, is clear. Military text-books and the military experience of ages lay stress on the value of surprise, and this was his conception of battle and the trend of his thought. Complete surprise was not possible, but to a limited extent it might be obtained. He wished to discard the lengthy artillery preparation which had heralded the Somme attacks and trust to a twenty-four-hour preliminary bombardment. His attacking brigades were to be concealed to a great extent in the underground quarries and sewers of Arras, St. Sauveur, and Ronville—remarkable excavations which were improved, joined up, lit by electricity, and carefully organised by the Royal Engineers.

In the discussion of these plans Allenby found himself opposed by General Headquarters, and in the end had to give way to the fatal battering-ram policy, tried and found wanting on the Somme.

Under the revised plan the front to be attacked contained some five miles of the Hindenburg Line and, in some parts, the original three-line trench system. Sir Douglas Haig contended that " the great strength of these defences demanded a very thorough artillery preparation. . . . Three weeks prior to the attack the systematic cutting of the enemy's wire was commenced, while our heavy artillery searched the enemy's back areas and communications. Night-firing, wire-cutting, and the bombardment of hostile trenches, strong-points, and billets continued steadily and with increasing intensity on the whole battle-front, till the days immediately preceding the attack, when the general bombardment was opened."

And so, on the 6th April, Ludendorff had no doubt that a great British offensive was imminent at Arras. " I begged the Group Headquarters to bring up their reserves nearer to the line in the area of the 6th Army."

The system of infantry attack used in the battles of Arras was known as " leapfrogging," and was a succession of short advances, " the separate stages of which were arranged to correspond approximately with the enemy's successive systems of defence. As each stage was reached, a short pause was to take place to enable the troops detailed for the attack on the next objective to form up for the assault."

Although the reports on tanks in 1916 were not encouraging, they were to be used again, and one might have expected a variation in tactics as the result of study and experience, but they were again dealt out to corps with the impartiality generally associated with useless trench stores : there were but sixty, and each corps was fairly treated.

.   .   .   .

The situation arrived at is that the Fourth Army was still following retreating Germans ; the Fifth Army was facing the Hindenburg Line, scrapping fiercely with the enemy ; and the VII Corps, on the right of the Third Army, had also moved forward to occupy the vacated enemy trenches.

The plan of the Arras battle was that the 21st Division on the right should be the pivot on which the 14th, 30th, and 56th Divisions were to wheel (VII Corps). On the left the VI Corps were to attack with the 3rd, 12th, and 15th Divisions—the 37th Division waiting to " leapfrog " through. While north of the Scarpe the XVII Corps had the 9th, 34th, and 51st Divisions in line—with the 4th ready to go through the 9th. Still north of them the Canadian Corps were to attack the ill-famed Vimy Ridge.

The 3rd Division front lay south of the Cambrai road and included the village of Tilloy.

.   .   .   .

THE FIRST BATTLE OF THE SCARPE, 1917.[1]

(10TH BATTALION.)

The opening battle is a story of hard fighting, but the " leapfrog " gave short objectives. Regimentally we must look at it from the Hindenburg Line angle, for battalions were concerned principally along that line.

Our 10th Battalion left Wanquetin at 7 p.m. on the 6th April, and

[1] Date : 9th–14th April.   Area : Cherisy—Hamelincourt—Marœuil (exclusive)—Willerval (exclusive).

marched to Arras. They went into billets in the cellars of the Rue Ronville close to the station.

For the next two days officers reconnoitred their assembly positions, and watched the progress of " wire-cutting " about Tilloy. The battalion was to follow the Gordon Highlanders, go through them at the fourth German line and capture Devil Wood, or what was called the Black Line, drawn through the far end of the wood to the divisional boundary, on the

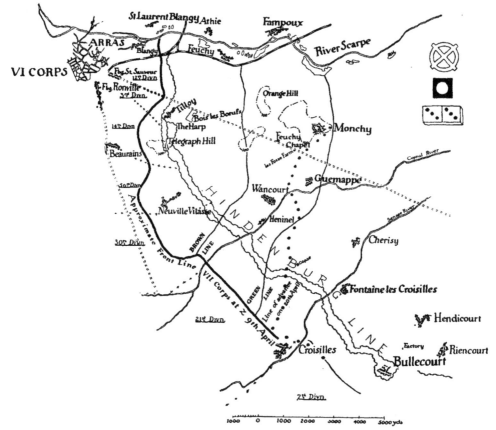

right, and the Cambrai road on the left. The enemy had, however, evacuated their front line, which we had occupied, so the Gordon High-landers had only three lines to capture. The position was quite familiar to officers and men, as the division had held the line since the 12th February.

The wire-cutting programme was completed, strong-points, back areas, trenches, and billets had received special attention—the intense bombardment commenced.

Our 10th Battalion moved into position after dark on the 8th, and were drawn up on their allotted front by 11 p.m. Lieutenant-Colonel Compton Smith held a last conference at midnight.

The general attack opened at 5.30 a.m. on the 9th April, " under cover of a most effective barrage. Closely following the tornado of shell fire, our gallant infantry poured like a flood across the German lines, over-whelming the enemy's garrison." (Despatch.) The debouching of brigades from the caves and sewers of Arras was a triumph of organisation.

At first everything went " according to plan." The Gordon High-landers moved to the assault close behind a " magnificent barrage," with the 10th Royal Welch Fusiliers at their heels. These two battalions started so well that the enemy's counter-barrage, which opened at 5.38 a.m., and was laid on our front line, fell on empty trenches.

The Gordon Highlanders captured their objective with little trouble—opposition was slight ; so also our 10th Battalion.

" A and C Companies followed closely on the barrage. The instruc-tions to keep up close to the barrage were at last being appreciated, the men realising that the bursts of our ' shorts ' were far less to be feared than machine-gun fire. The advance companies were into and through the wood before the enemy realised our approach, and his surprise at the speed of our advance was ludicrous. From a cellar under a destroyed house in the wood, eighty-three prisoners poured (this included some from dugouts), and two machine guns were captured." (Captain Watcyn Williams.)

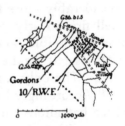

The 9th Brigade passed on to Neuilly Trench ; the 8th Brigade went through the 9th, and made for the Feuchy—Wancourt line. The latter movement was about noon. All had then been up to time, but now the leading battalions were checked at Chapel Road.

Meanwhile our 10th Battalion took over the defence of the whole captured position, and were told to rest as much as possible ; while the 1st Gordon Highlanders and 8th King's Own were moved forward to attack. The attack failed, and a fresh attack was ordered for the next morning.

The Hindenburg Line—at least the end of it—had been smashed through the first day ; it was a promising opening. But, as was often the case on both sides, certain points held out and influenced the result. At first Telegraph Hill and the Railway Triangle defied the stormers—the advance in these two areas was behind the scheduled time—and then the Feuchy—Wancourt line held up the whole attack. On the VI Corps front the 37th

Division did not go through the attacking divisions, as it should have done.

The attack was renewed at noon on the 10th and cleared the ground as far as Wancourt and Guémappe. Our battalion remained in the old German front line throughout the day, but moved up to the Feuchy—Wancourt line in support to the 76th Brigade attacking Guémappe at 7 a.m. on the 11th.

It had been raining, and there had been a fall of snow—the ground was in a terrible state.

" The battalion advanced in artillery formation in support of the King's Own. Extended order was adopted after we had advanced 500 yards. The promised barrage on the village (Guémappe) was not forthcoming, and our artillery was negligible. The attacking battalions in front were driven to ground very soon, and suffered heavy casualties. The machine-gun fire from the high ground to the left of Guémappe, and from our immediate front, was the hottest I have ever encountered. For considerably more than 1,000 yards the battalion advanced through heavy shell fire, mostly 5·9. By 8.10 a.m. it was evident that further advance was impossible, and the men had been driven into a line of shell-holes, with its left on Le Fosse Farm and its right curving back to a sunken road. The only thing left to do was to reorganise.

" Accordingly I reconnoitred the whole of the line, and found men of all three battalions mixed up in shell-holes. At the extreme right I got into touch with a Suffolk officer, and after agreeing on the line to be held, handed over the right to him. Reorganisation was not completely possible, owing to the fact that it would have to be done over the top.

" At 2.30 p.m. the Gordons attempted to advance, and we prepared to assist them, but they never reached our line. By this time the enemy had brought field guns up to the high point to the left of Guémappe and was shelling us point-blank. We received a little help from our artillery, who were undoubtedly hampered by the terrible state of the ground.

" All day, anyone moving from shell-hole to shell-hole was sniped and machine-gunned, and movement, except singly, was folly. A few German snipers and a machine gun were silenced by a party of Royal Welch Fusiliers with a Lewis gun, who spotted them and advanced to a small cut trench, just ahead of Le Fosse Farm.

" The conduct of the men, who early on must have realised the hopelessness of their task, was beyond praise." (Captain Watcyn Williams.)

For our battalion it was a wretched time. The weather had been fine up to dawn on the 9th, when rain commenced. This was followed by snow.   The rest which they had been recommended to get was impossible, as the battalion, although in support, was continually on the move, generally starting in the middle of the night.

On the night of the 11th the whole brigade moved back into divisional reserve about Tilloy and the Harp.   The men of the battalion were bitterly cold and had been " practically without sleep for three days."

Lieutenant E. Evans (R.A.M.C.), 2nd Lieutenants E. Williams, J. C. Davies, and 32 other ranks were killed ; Lieutenant-Colonel Compton Smith, Captain W. S. Brocklehurst, 2nd Lieutenants T. Rea, J. Thomson, J. M. Wardlaw, H. D. Taylor, J. A. James, J. W. Broxup, T. E. Williams, C. W. Jones, and 165 other ranks were wounded.

The next morning Wancourt fell to the 56th Division, but the Germans were counter-attacking strongly, and the battle, as an effort with a definite objective, petered out by the 16th April.   We were held—we had failed to break through.   As Ludendorff puts it, " A further withdrawal to the Wotan (Drocourt—Quéant) position . . . was not found to be necessary, though contemplated for a time by the 6th Army."   We had, however, captured 13,000 prisoners and 200 guns, and when the battalion returned to the line on the 24th they took over trenches at Monchy—the farthest point of our advance south of the Scarpe, and an impressive position. They remained in and out of this part of the line till the 15th May.[1]

Amongst the casualties during this period were Captain W. J. D. Hale, 2nd Lieutenants H. Curran, E. G. Williams, killed ; Captain H. Pritchard, 2nd Lieutenants A. P. Comyns, F. A. Lawson, A. G. Williams were wounded.   A return gives 146 other ranks killed and wounded.

Our chief success in this battle was north of the Scarpe, where the Canadian Corps advanced beyond the Vimy Ridge.   South of the river our swift piercing of the main line of defence had startled the Germans, and, according to Hindenburg and Ludendorff, had given them a bad twenty-four hours facing disaster—they both declare that our success was complete, but that we did not know how to exploit it.   There would appear to be some truth in this criticism.   Lieutenant-Colonel Compton Smith notes that the troops of the 76th Brigade were held up at Feuchy Chapel and on the Wancourt line by uncut wire, and this line marks the limit of the artillery attack—troops had overrun the effective range of field artillery.   Batteries commenced to move forward on the 9th, but this phase of the battle suggests the moment for the use of tanks.   A fatal

---

[1] The area places this Battalion in the Battle of Arleux, 28th–29th April.   Bourg Notre Dame —Monchy-le-Preux—Beaurains—Rolincourt—Vimy—Acheville.

pause took place which enabled the Germans to organise resistance on the last line between us and the unfinished Drocourt—Quéant line.

Our own eagerness to take advantage of the preliminary success is once more pathetic. With the tactical handling of tanks reduced to an equitable distribution between four corps, and with the last completely organised enemy line beyond the effective range of our field guns, the congestion behind the battle front was made infernal by the prancing about of cavalry, " in readiness to be sent forward should our infantry succeed in widening this breach. . . . South of Feuchy, however, the unbroken wire of the German third line constituted a complete barrier to a cavalry attack, while the commanding positions held by the enemy on Monchy-le-Preux hill blocked the way for an advance along the Scarpe." (Despatch.)

Fighting, however, did not cease. The situation became complicated by the action of our Allies. Haig declares he never saw that any great strategical results were likely to be gained by following up a success on the front about Arras, and he had determined to transfer his main offensive for the year to the north. It is quite evident that he had gathered in all that was likely to accrue from the Battles of Arras. But the French launched their main offensive on the 16th April. It was disastrous.

Sir Douglas Haig says " it would have been possible to have stopped the Arras offensive at this point, and . . . to have diverted forthwith to the northern theatre of operations the troops, labour, and material required to complete my preparations there." He decided, however, to continue to press forward at Arras, although it was clear that " except at excessive cost our success could not be developed further without a return to more deliberate methods." He was not ready for another week, and by that time there was no French advance to support. At a conference on the 30th April he was still determined to continue his attacks, although he showed little faith in any renewed French offensive.

THE SECOND BATTLE OF THE SCARPE.[1]
(2ND AND 10TH BATTALIONS.)

Our 2nd Battalion now comes into the picture. At the opening of the Battle of Arras they were at Bailleulmont, having arrived there through Corbie, Villers Bocage, Beauval, Loucheux, and Saulty. This was in the XVIII Corps area, in reserve to the Third Army. Late on the 11th they marched to the Boisleux-au-Mont—Mercatel area in a heavy snow-storm. Here they found that the German devastation had been most carefully

[1] Official date : 23rd–24th April. Area : the River Sensée from Vis-en-Artois to Ervillers (exclusive) ; thence a line to Dainville (exclusive)—Bailleul-Oppy.

carried out ; all buildings had been destroyed, and they had to make shift to build up shelters with such material as was found lying about.

With the battalion was Lieutenant S. L. Sassoon, who had rejoined the regiment while the 2nd Battalion was in Camp 13, in the Clery sector, on the 12th March.   He says : " Posted to B Company, I found myself in command of No. 8 Platoon (which contained eight Joneses).   Its total strength was 34 (including 2 sergeants, 1 corporal, and 6 lance-corporals) ; 8 of the 34 were Lewis gunners, and these being deducted my compact little command was unimpressive on parade, and seldom mustered 20 strong.   We were in corps reserve, and Battalion Headquarters had issued its order : ' Carry out platoon training.'

" A recent draft had added a collection of undersized half-wits to the depleted battalion.   Several men in my platoon seemed barely capable of carrying the weight of their equipment.   In my case platoon training commenced with the platoon commander teaching a man how to load his rifle.   Afterwards I felt that the poor devil would have been a less perilous ingredient of my command had he been left in his first ignorance.

" Of Camp 13 the less said the better ; I cannot believe that anyone has ever said a good word of it—mud and smoke were its chief characteristics.   The long, gloomy, draughty chamber where company officers took their ease was seldom free from the smoke that drifted in from the braziers of the adjoining kitchen.   Of an evening we sat and shivered in our British-warms, reading, playing cards, writing letters by the feeble glimmer of guttering candles.   Orderlies would bring in a clutter of tin plates and mugs ; machonachie stew was consumed in morose discomfort.   How peculiar was the taste of tea during the Great War !   One sip of that nasty concoction would bring the whole thing back to me more than a hundred war histories by Field-Marshals and Cabinet Ministers ! [1]

" I could scarcely have begun my acquaintance with the battalion under worse conditions.   Naturally no one was feeling over-bright.   As for myself, I endured my first week minus my valise, which had gone astray on the way up from Rouen ; my new trench-coat had been pinched off me on the boat ; I was inclined to grumble because I had been posted elsewhere than to the 1st Battalion, which I regarded as my spiritual home in France ; and the M.O. greeted me with a double anti-typhoid injection.   The O.C. B Company began by regarding my presence with hauteur and aversion.

" One expedition to Amiens (with Greaves, Conning, and ' Binge ' Owen) for a bath and a good dinner at the Godobert Restaurant—this was a cheer-

---

[1] Apart from the chlorinated water, tea was generally made by flinging a handful, more or less dry and more or less free from mildew, into warm water and letting it boil.

ful experience, anyhow! We were photographed the next morning, I remember, but otherwise I have no record of what occurred, except a note of beverages consumed :

> 2 John Collins,
> 1 Japanese ditto,
> 1 oyster cocktail,
> 1 sherry and bitters,
> Pommard Eclatante, trois verres,
> 1 Benedictine.

" Then back to Camp 13, per feet, and a lucky lift on a hospital ambulance going to Corbie.

" Aerodromes loom in the dusk as we approach the Camp, and a brazier glows redly at the cross-roads, where the sentry stands. Down in the hollow our brigade has got through another day of corps reserve. News of the fall of Peronne, and other places, falls flat. The Boches are withdrawing to the Hindenburg Line, and we are told that we shall probably go to St. Pol before proceeding to the battle. What a hope !—as the troops used to say.

" In spite of hankering for the good old 1st Battalion, I was now beginning to identify myself with the equally good old 2nd Battalion, but it was not until we quitted Camp 13 that I became aware of the identity of the battalion as a whole. Hitherto my brain had not gone beyond B Company ; now, while the column was trudging and swaying along the main road to Corbie, on that cold, grey Monday morning (2nd April), the four companies knit themselves into a unit, and I was glad to be going with them on their journey into a somewhat hazardous future.

" As we went up the hill to the Bray—Corbie road, the smoke from the incinerators gave the impression that we had fired the camp on leaving it. As second-in-command of B Company I toddled along behind it, while Kirkley ambled in front, in full possession of some patient quadruped whose face I cannot recall.

" To Corbie was a seven-mile march, and the battalion was settled in its billets by 1.30. I can remember my own billet—an airless cupboard in a greengrocer's shop. Also I can remember that several of us spent a convivial evening drinking bad champagne in a small room in a wine merchant's house, while Ralph Greaves drew pleasant sounds from a piano. He played as though he was saying good-bye to all music for ever—three weeks later he had lost one of his arms.

" We left Corbie at 9 a.m. on the 3rd April in brilliant sunshine, and went 21 kilometres, reaching the village of Villers Bocage at 2.   I had some difficulty in keeping the company up to strength ; several undersized men were beat to the world at the end of the march, and I covered the last lap trundling two of them in front of me while another struggled along behind, hanging on to my belt.   Not one of the three stood more than five foot high.

" The woman of our billet told us that troops had been passing through for fifteen days, never staying more than one night, and always going toward Doullens and Arras.

" Next day (4th April) we marched 12 kilometres to Beauval. Wet snow was falling all the way. Our Corps Commander (Maxse) was waiting to welcome us on a long straight stretch of the Amiens—Doullens road. We ' eyes lefted ' him without enthusiasm. Colonel Garnett rode up to him and received a volley of abuse in response to his salute. Apparently the Corps Commander resented the fact that brooms and other utilitarian objects were being carried on the cookers ; or it may have been some minor detail of march discipline.[1]

" We left Beauval at 4 p.m. the next day and covered another 12 kilometres to Loucheux, where we billeted by 8 p.m. in some huts amongst wooded hills. We passed through Doullens on our way—Arras, 32 kilometres, said a signpost. The wind was from the east—it was only a slight breeze, but it brought us heavy murmurs of the huge firing at Arras. I can remember going down the hill to Doullens in the pleasant evening sunshine ; I was walking with Major Poore, and we were talking about cricket and fox-hunting. It was a calm night, and we dined in the moonlight, sitting round a brazier with plates on our knees. Next day was Good Friday, and I awoke with sunshine streaming in at the door and broad Scots being shouted by some Scottish Rifles in the next huts. Someone was practising the bagpipes on the edge of the wood, and a mule contributed a short solo.

" We remained at Loucheux that night and went to Saulty (15 kilometres) in cold wind and sunshine on the 7th April. When the company had been safely bestowed and I had stuffed myself with coffee and eggs, I sat on a tree-stump in the peaceful park of a big white château, with the sun just looking over the tree-tops, a few small deer grazing amongst the purple undergrowth, and some blackbirds and thrushes singing. Nothing was there to remind me of the war except the enormous thudding of the guns twelve miles away, and an aeroplane humming in the clear sky over-

---

[1] The Corps Commander's remarks concerned the intervals between companies, which were greater than those laid down in the drill book. Also he desired all rifle muzzles to be covered. (Lieutenant-Colonel Garnett's diary.)

head. Sitting alone I felt happy and contented, and confident—and the men had seemed cheery and almost elated the last day or two, but they were always their best when they knew they were 'for it': there was a chance of a 'blighty one,' anyhow. The air turned chilly, and the sun was a glint of scarlet beyond the strip of woodland—and away on the horizon that infernal banging continued. 'The sausage machine,' we called it.

"*8th April* (*Easter Day*).—Left Saulty 9 a.m.; reached Basseux, about 11 kilometres south of Arras, 11.15 a.m. Until recently the place was only a mile or two from the front-line trenches, but doesn't appear to have been heavily shelled. Walking out to inspect the old trench line, I was struck by the appalling inferiority of our position to that of the Germans.

"We are living in a derelict château which must have been very pleasant in peace time. Some officers are playing cricket with a stump and a wooden ball and an old brazier for a wicket. Our conscientious and efficient little Adjutant, J. C. Mann, bustles across the foreground, with papers in his hand—no time for cricket among the orderly-room staff.

"*9th April.*—Still at Basseux, but under orders to move at the shortest possible notice. Everyone talking very loud about success reported from the line—'our objectives gained'—'5,000 prisoners'—and so on. I am chiefly interested in my own physical condition, which is beastly—sore throat, gastritis, festering scratches on my hands, and no clean pocket-handkerchief or socks.

"We were having a single-brazier (!) cricket match on the Wednesday afternoon (11th April), in the sunshine, when someone blew a whistle, and the match came to an abrupt end. An hour later (5 p.m.) the battalion left Basseux. We'd been on the march about half an hour when heavy snow began falling. We passed through villages that were less than heaps of brick; a couple of inches of snow covered them altogether. The most demolished village was Ficheux—Fish Hooks, the troops called it. The snow had stopped when at the end of eight miles we bivouacked in the dregs of daylight in a sunken road near Mercatel. Casson and I spent the night in a very small dugout—how we got there I can't remember, but we considered ourselves lucky to be sitting huddled over a small brazier in that coke-fumed den.

"Daylight of the 12th April found us bleary-eyed and somewhat dejected. By 4 p.m. we had moved on about 6 kilometres, relieving the 17th Manchester (21st Division) in reserve at St. Martin Cojeul. The afternoon was wet and the snow had left its legacy of bad mud. B Company occupied an old German third-line trench. The village was a heap of brick. A few 5·9s arrived while I went to the underground dressing-station to get my festering fingers dressed—small discomforts of that kind did much to dissipate heroic attitudes of mind. Company Headquarters were the nearest thing to a rabbit-hole I have ever experienced ; there was just space for K. and myself. The dugout contained a small stove. Rations were short—K. and I had one small bit of bacon between us. I was frizzling my fragment when it fell off the fork into the stove, where my unfortunate fingers recovered it—I don't think it tasted bad, even then.

" The night was bitterly cold ; sleep was unprocurable, since there was nowhere to lie down, though K. showed a capacity for sleeping soundly in any position and under the most inappropriate conditions. E., the only other officer with B Company, supplied a continuous obbligato of Welsh garrulity.

" B Company contained a typical contrast in C. and E. C., aged 23, had been to Winchester and Christchurch ; he was a sensitive and refined youth and an amusing gossip. E. was about the same age, but had not ' enjoyed the same social advantages ' ; he was very noisy and garrulous, always licked his thumb when dealing cards, and invariably answered ' Pardon ! ' when any remark was made to him. That ' Pardon ' became a little trying at times. Equally good when tested, these two merged their social incompatibilities in the end—both were killed on 26th September.

" There was nothing to do but to wait where we were for further orders. So there we sat, on Friday the 13th, while the 62nd Division attacked unsuccessfully from a hill about three-quarters of a mile away. There was a serene sunset, with huge peaceful clouds. C. and I walked up the hill ; I wanted to get him accustomed to the unpleasant sights—there were a lot of our yesterday's dead on the slope."

The 33rd Division was then in the VII Corps, and the 19th Brigade was placed under the orders of the 21st Division as a reserve for the attack north of Fontaine-les-Croisilles on the 13th. This attempt failed, and the 19th Brigade repeated it on the 14th, making a little ground along the Hindenburg Line by bombing. Our battalion did not take part.

The 33rd Division took over from the 21st on the 15th—the 21st Division, it will be remembered, was the pivot of attack at the opening of the battle. They were, therefore, still engaged with the Hindenburg Line, although to the left the British line ran through Wancourt, not, as yet, through Guémappe, and so to Monchy—well behind the Hindenburg work.

The 33rd Division was ordered to advance to the line of the Sensée River at 3 a.m. on the 16th.

Our 2nd Battalion took over from the 13th Northumberland Fusiliers, in the Hindenburg Line itself. Relief was not completed till 4.30 a.m. on the 15th. Their rôle was limited to the supplying of 100 bombers in support of the Cameronians, who were to work their way up the Hindenburg Line. In the attack of the 16th April 75 of these bombers became engaged. The attack was not a success. At one time some 300 yards had been won, when 2nd Lieutenant Sassoon and Sergeant Baldwin distinguished themselves.

The whole of this adventure is described by Sassoon :

" At 9 p.m. the relief of the 21st Division began. The companies at Henin moved forward with guides who knew little of the ground, to a rendezvous for which wrong map references had been issued by Brigade. The leading company was 3½ hours in covering 4 kilometres and the night was bitterly cold. On the left B Company fell in at the top of the ruined street called St. Martin Cojeul. When we left the road and were going uphill over the open ground, the two cheerful 13th Northumberland Fusilier guides were making the pace too hot for the rear platoon. Like nearly all guides, they were inconveniently nimble, owing to their freedom from heavy equipment, and they were insecurely confident that they knew the way in the dark. The muttered message, ' Pass it along—steady in front,' was accompanied by the usual muffled clinkings and rattlings of arms and equipment. Unwillingly retarded, the guides led us on—we had less than two miles to go. Gradually the guides became less confident, and the Company Commander's demeanour did not reassure them. At a midnight halt they admitted they had lost their way completely. Kirkley decided to sit down and wait for daylight ; I went blundering off into the gloom, expecting to lose myself independently. By a lucky accident I stumbled into a sunken road and found myself among a little party of sappers who could tell me where I was. With one of them I returned to the company and we were led to the Hindenburg trench.

" There must have been some hazy moonlight, for I can remember the figures of men propping themselves against the walls of the communication trench ; seeing them in some sort of ghastly half-light I wondered whether they were dead or asleep, for the attitudes of some were like death, uncouth and distorted.

" When we arrived in the Hindenburg support trench my Company Commander told me to post the sentries. He then vanished to Company Headquarters, which were situated somewhere down a shaft with fifty steps. The company we were relieving had departed, so there was no one to give me any information. I didn't even know for certain that we were in the front line.

" The trench was deep, roomy, and unfinished-looking. I had never occupied such a trench before. The sentries had to clamber up a bank of loose earth in order to see over the top. The length of the intervals between our sentry posts made me conscious of our inadequacy in that wilderness of destructive activity. When I had posted the sentries, I went along the trench to look for the company on the left.

" Poor devils, they belonged to an amateur battalion, which suffered badly in the dud attack thirty-six hours later. I came round a corner and found a sort of panic party going on at a point where the trench was like a wide nullah. A platoon had taken alarm, N.C.O.s and men jostling one another in their haste to vanish through a narrow doorway, which led down to the bowels of the earth. As I stood there in astonishment, one of them, panting excitedly, told me that ' the Germans were coming over.' Two officers who were with this rabble seemed to have no idea except to get everyone downstairs as soon as possible. Unlikely as it may sound, they all disappeared, and I was left alone. But in No Man's Land there wasn't the slightest indication of an attack. As there seemed nothing to be done, I returned to my own sector."

The situation was not of the best. There was a bomb-carrying fatigue for B Company the next day.

" We were out in the rain till 4.30 p.m. (15th). As soon as I got home to my mug of tea, I was told I had been detailed to take command of 100 bombers to act as reserve for the 1st Cameronians next morning. When it was dark I went with a cheery little guide to discuss the operation orders with the Cameronian Company Commander in his front-line dugout. (Was it the front line ? I don't know. I only know that I felt very incompetent and misinformed, and that the officer I talked to seemed full of knowledge and trench topography which meant nothing to my newly arrived mind.) It was regarded as possible that the bombing attack would function along the underground tunnel as well as above ground. There was a barrier in the tunnel.[1] The Germans were on the other side. We should climb over it—could anything, I thought, be less pleasant ! and I tried to adapt myself to the self-protective cheerfulness of the Captain and his colleagues.

" I returned with the feeling that I hadn't the faintest idea what it was all about or what I should do in the way of organising my command. Something had to be put on paper and sent to Battalion Headquarters.

---

[1] In this part of the Hindenburg Line there was a long gallery beneath the main trench, fitted with bunks and other conveniences. There were entrances, alternate wide stairs and inclined planes for stores, every forty to fifty yards. Within the part of the tunnel occupied by the battalion were units and detachments of two brigades, jostling amidst new mud and old refuse, improvised and intended latrines, British and German dead. A dreadful place.

By the mercy of God I got hold of Ralph Greaves ; I found him sitting in a little chamber off the underground trench ; to him I confided my incompetence, and while I sat and ruminated on my chances of extinction the next morning, he drew up some scheme for me and wrote it down.   His little room contained a mirror and a clock ; the clock's dumb face stared at me—an idiot reminder of real rooms and real domesticity.   Greaves, with his eyeglass, and his whimsical, debonair looks, and his gentle, stammering voice, was a consoling link with real life, for I had known him before the war.   When he had fixed up my immediate future we shared our common knowledge of a certain part of the county of Kent.

" At zero hour (3 a.m.) I was sitting self-consciously in the Cameronians' Headquarters, with a rumbling din going on overhead, and my 100 men sitting on the stairs—there were 50 steps up to the outer world.   A bone-chilling draught came down the stairway, and our men must have regretted our 33rd Division General's edict against the rum ration.

" The Cameronians' Colonel and his Adjutant conversed in the constrained tone of men who expect nothing but ill news.   There was a large cake on the table.   I was offered a slice, which I ate with embarrassment.   I wasn't feeling at all at home.   I couldn't make myself believe that the Cameronian officers expected me to do them any good when I was called upon to take part in the proceedings upstairs.   (The underground attack had been cancelled.)   The tapping telephone orderly in the corner very soon announced that communication with the attacking company had broken down.

" After, I think, nearly three hours of suspense, it became obvious that someone was coming downstairs in a hurry.   This messenger finally arrived outside the doorway in a clattering cascade of tin utensils.   He entered and proved to be a dishevelled sergeant, who blurted out an incoherent statement about ' their having been driven back after advancing a little way.'

" I got up, stiffly, aware that my moment had arrived.   Probably I mumbled something to the Colonel, but I can't remember his giving me any instructions.   I was, however, sensitive to the fact that both Colonel and Adjutant were alive to the delicacy of my situation.   Their muttered message was, ' Well, old chap, I suppose you're for it ! '   Helmet on my head, I went up, and told my two under-officers that I was going to take 25 men up to the show.   I can easily remember how I hustled upstairs and emerged into a sunlit but noisy morning.   The section of 25 men who were sitting at the top of the stairs bestirred themselves at the instigation of Sergeant Baldwin, and at once I was hurrying up a trench with my chilled and flustered little contingent at my heels. ' 15 bombers (each carrying 10 Mills bombs), 4 rifle grenadiers (each carrying 5 grenades), 5 carriers (also act as bayonet men), 1 full rank (Sergeant Baldwin).'

" I hadn't the slightest idea what I was going to do, and my destination was in the brain of the stooping Cameronian guide, who trotted in front of me. After dodging and stumbling up a narrow communication trench, we arrived at the wide main trench. And there we met the Cameronians.

" I must have picked up a Mills bomb on my way, for I had one in my hand when I began my conversation with their leader. I had the advantage of him, since I was advancing, and he and his men were out of breath and coming away from the objective. I was told that the Germans were all round them, and that they were out of bombs. Feeling myself to be for the moment an epitome of R.W.F. prestige, I became unnaturally jaunty and unconcerned. ' But where are the Germans ? ' I asked carelessly, tossing my bomb from left hand to right. ' I can't see any Germans ! '

" My effrontery had its effect—he looked a little embarrassed. My behaviour became more and more patronising and complacent. ' All right,' I remarked. ' You needn't bother—we'll see to all this ! '—Or words to that effect.

" I led my party past the Cameronians ; told them to wait a bit ; went up the trench with Sergeant Baldwin—an admirably impassive little man—about 100 yards without meeting anyone. I think we climbed over some sort of barrier at the beginning. Noticing that there were a good many Mills bombs lying in little heaps, I told Baldwin to go back and arrange for them to be collected and brought up the trench. Then, with a slightly accelerated heart-beat I went round the corner alone. A small man was standing there, watchful and resolute, with a bag of bombs slung over his left shoulder. He was a Cameronian corporal whose name was, I afterwards learned, Smart. Neither of us spoke. I also was carrying a bag of bombs. We advanced and went round the next bay. I experienced a sobering shock then, for a young, fair-haired Cameronian private was lying propped against the wall, in a pool of his own blood. His open eyes were staring vacantly at the sky. His face was grey and serene. A few yards up the trench was the body of a German officer, crumpled up and still. The wounded Cameronian made me feel angry with our invisible enemies, and I slung a couple of bombs in their direction, and received a reply in the form of an egg-bomb which exploded harmlessly behind me. I went on throwing bombs and advancing, while the corporal, who was obviously much more artful and efficient than I, dodged up the saps at the side—a precaution which I should have forgotten. Between us we created a considerable demonstration of offensiveness. In this manner we reached our objective. I had no idea where our objective was, but the corporal told me we had reached it, and he seemed to know what he was about. This, curiously enough, was the first time he spoke to me.

" I had caught an occasional glimpse of a retreating German, but the whole thing had been so absurdly easy I felt like going on still farther. There was a narrow sap running out of the place where we halted. ' You stay where you are,' I remarked to Smart, and then I started to explore the sap. What I expected to find there I can't say. Finding nothing, I paused for a minute to listen—there seemed to be a lull in the proceedings of the attack ; spasmodic machine guns rattled ; high over head there was an aeroplane. I thought what a queer business it all was, and then decided to take a peep at the surrounding country. No sooner had I popped my head out of the sap than I received what seemed like a tremendous blow in the back, between the shoulders. My first notion was that I had been hit by a bomb from behind. What had really happened was that I had been sniped from in front. Anyhow, my attitude towards life and the war had been instantaneously and completely altered for the worse. I leaned against the wall and shut my eyes. When I opened them again, Sergeant Baldwin was beside me, discreet and sympathetic. To my great surprise, I discovered I was not dead. Baldwin assisted me back to the main trench, investigated my wound, and left me sitting there while he went back to bring up some more men.

" After about a quarter of an hour I began to feel active and heroic again, but in a different way—I was now not only a hero but a wounded hero ! I can remember talking excitedly to a laconic Stokes mortar officer, who had arrived from nowhere with his weapon. My seventy-five men were no longer on the scene. My only idea was to collect all our available ammunition and renew the attack while the Stokes mortar officer put up an enthusiastic barrage. It did not occur to me that there was anything else going on on the Western Front excepting my own little show. My overstrained nerves had stirred me up to such a pitch of febrile excitement that I felt capable of the most suicidal exploits. This convulsive energy might have been of some value had there been any rational outlet for it, but there was none. Before I had time to do anything rash and irrelevant to the military situation, Conning arrived on the scene to relieve me. Conning's unruffled behaviour sobered me a bit : he seemed to have the situation sized up. Nevertheless I was still boiling over with the offensive spirit, and my activity was only quelled by a written order from the Cameronian Colonel, who told me that we must not advance owing to the attack having failed elsewhere. This caused an anticlimax to my ardours, and I returned to the 2nd R.W.F. Headquarters. On the way I met Dr. Dunn, strolling along the trench with the detached air of an amateur botanist. I was back in the tunnel within four hours of leaving it."

. . . . .

On the 17th the 19th Brigade was relieved by the 98th, and marched to Mercatel in a storm of hail and snow, to bivouac. The confusion in the celebrated tunnel when they left it was beyond description : one battalion started to leave at 7 p.m. on the 16th, and Headquarters, the last to go, did not move until 8.30 a.m. on the 17th.

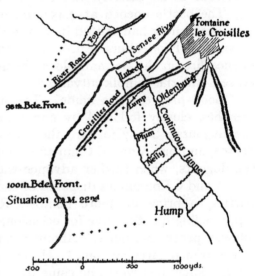

The old trenches at Mercatel, in which the battalion bivouacked, were not provided with tunnels, and were not comfortable. But Major Poore and company commanders left early on the 18th to look at another bit of line, in front of Croisilles, which was taken over on the 19th. Back again on the 21st to Mercatel, having been relieved by the 2nd Worcestershire.

The battalion was warned that on the 23rd they would be lent to the 98th Brigade, who were to attack. A and C Companies, under Captains Owen and Radford, were in the line by 9 p.m. on the 22nd, with a special task ; B and D followed early in the morning of the 23rd.

The Second Battle of the Scarpe ran from Croisilles, across the River Scarpe to Gavrelle—a front of about nine miles. While the attack on this front was to sweep forward, the 98th Brigade were given the task of pushing along the Hindenburg Line on the extreme right. The 62nd Division, now holding the left of the neighbouring V Corps, was to take no part beyond artillery assistance.

The 33rd Division was to attack on both sides of the Sensée River. The front held, astride the Hindenburg Line and astride the Sensée River, was somewhat peculiar. On the right of the divisional front, east of the Sensée, the 100th Brigade, holding a main line 1,500 yards from the

Hindenburg Line, were to make a frontal attack ; on the left of the divisional front the 98th Brigade were to attack down the length of the Hindenburg Line, and behind it, from high ground falling to the Sensée River. Two companies (A and C) of our 2nd Battalion were lent to the 98th Brigade to work exclusively along the Hindenburg Line.

The 4th Suffolk were to lead the attack on the right, that is along the Hindenburg Line ; our two companies were to mop up, and picket the entrances to the tunnel. In the centre of the brigade front were the 2nd Argyll and Sutherland Highlanders ; on the left the 1st Middlesex, in touch with the 30th Division. The advance of the centre and left battalions would therefore be behind the Hindenburg Line, over the shoulder of a spur that runs in an easterly direction to the Sensée. (See Map, page 288.)

The battle opened at 4.45 a.m. on the 23rd April.

The Suffolk had waited in vain for two tanks which were to help them down the Hindenburg Line. A detachment of Stokes 4-inch mortars opened fire on the German blocks in the line, using thermite ; at zero they ceased and the Suffolk advanced.

Good progress was made. The men swept along the double line of trenches, closely followed by our A and C Companies, the latter picketing the dugouts. At 7.30 a.m. the Suffolk were about 200 yards from the Sensée, and our A and C Companies had extracted over 200 prisoners from the dugouts, when further advance was held up by lack of bombs.

A and C Companies disposed of their prisoners, and organised carrying parties to bring up more bombs. Radford states that this work was " proceeding quietly, save for occasional shots from the left. By 7.30 a.m. all was peace and quiet. About 8 a.m. a German made his appearance in the trench carrying soup ! He was seized and the soup was consumed. No one knew just where he came from—apparently from a communication trench on the left, behind where the Argyll were to have attacked at zero. His arrival was, then, somewhat ominous, especially as a good deal of movement was observed in that direction shortly afterwards." Owen and Radford tried, without success, to find the Stokes mortars, so they treated the area with rifle grenades. At 8.30 urgent messages came from the Suffolk that they had run out of bombs. Soon after 9 a.m. a mixed lot of Suffolk, machine gunners, and others started to swarm back—they had been counter-attacked. Soon they had all passed through the companies.

A company was, at the time, strung out over the trench carrying bombs. The Germans descended on them, and a bombing contest commenced. Behind A Company, C Company was making haste to rebuild the barricade, and just before 10 a.m. A Company had fallen back behind it.

For two hours there was a bad time at the barricade. We had a good supply of rifle grenades and bombs, and parties were organised to use them, but, says Radford, " it was the turn of the Germans to be in the ascendant. They manned their trench mortars (which the Suffolk had captured and they had now recovered, together with our four Stokes mortars) and sent over a colossal collection of every kind of aerial torpedo, ' pineapple,' bomb, and rifle grenade."

Casualties increased every moment. Owen called for volunteers to go over the top. He and Ralph Greaves took out parties who bombed the enemy back some distance. " But by that time the enemy had rifle-men posted in one of the cross-trenches, so the volunteers were driven off with a good few casualties, including Llewellyn Jones and Brooks, both of A Company—all of these, however, were got back to the barricade.

" Next a Lewis gun was mounted in a trench flanking the barricade ; it kept down the riflemen effectively. The rifle grenadiers were making good practice and the enemy did not seem inclined to press the matter. A stray N.C.O. of the Middlesex turned up and did good work. C Company men were in the trench behind A, and we felt fairly happy. We tried to get in touch with our artillery, but they were completely at sea as to the situation. I was attending to a man's rifle that had jammed with a grenade, when he called to me to ' look out ' and ducked into a trench. I looked up and saw one of ' Jerry's ' grenades in the air right above me. It hit the barricade level with my chest and I got the issue in my arm, and was carried down the trench." (Greaves.)

Soon after Owen, who was preparing to take another party over the top, was killed by a trench-mortar bomb. Rhys Jones, of C Company, was wounded about the same time. A Company had no officers left at the barricade, so Radford brought up his own company from support and relieved A. He remained in command at the barricade for the rest of the day.

At noon all was quiet. Radford had lost his three subalterns, all wounded, and Sergeant Hughes, a fine N.C.O., who was killed. Shelter was at hand, for all but a guard, in the tunnel below.

While the bombing attack was going on in the Hindenburg Line, the Argyll and Sutherland Highlanders and the 1st Middlesex had attacked on the left, that is to say behind the Hindenburg Line.

No doubt if the Argyll and Sutherland had succeeded in the centre, their advance would have had some effect on the Germans in the trench ;

but they were held in front of the copse on the hill, and only two companies of the Middlesex, and a few Argyll and Sutherland on the left, passed over the shoulder of the spur to their objective. This little force got into a trench and remained there, but they were completely cut off from their Headquarters, and it was supposed, in view of the failure of the whole attack, that they had been killed or captured. The situation seemed very definite.

Meanwhile B and D Companies and Headquarters had breakfasted at Henin, and then reported to the 98th Brigade, and moved on to the Hindenburg Line at about 11 a.m.

Late in the day the attack was ordered again, down the Hindenburg Line and to the east of it. B and D Companies were to advance towards the copse, with the remnants of Argyll and Sutherland ; the 5th Scottish

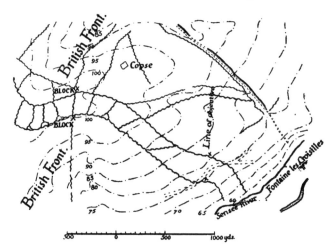

Rifles were to repeat the bombing attack, supported by our A and C Companies.

Lieutenant-Colonel Garnett has a note in his diary that the order to attack at 6.24 p.m. was placed in his hands at 6 p.m. He hastened off, with Captain Mann (Adjutant) to see the Commanding Officer of the Argyll and Sutherland, only to find that the latter and his Adjutant had just become casualties. He had, therefore, to forgo the co-operation of what Highlanders were left.

Events moved quickly. " The last platoon of B Company was barely on the ground when, at 6.24 p.m., there were some splutters of 18-pounder shells in front of the German line. A fresh breeze from the left swirled the smoke away at once. A hen pheasant with a broken wing ran clucking between the lines, and divided attention with another splutter of shells in rear of the German line. Officers and N.C.O.s looked at each other, doubting ; looked over at Headquarters officers, who were standing by a German gun emplacement in dead ground, just a few yards behind the shallow trench ! Mann waved and shouted, ' Get on ! ' Hanmer, commanding D Company, had just been wounded by a shell splinter, so Jackson jumped out and waved to the company, as Company Sergeant-

Major Gitters blew his whistle.   Owing to a misunderstanding, two platoons of B Company did not follow Phillips.   Among shell-holes and the dead of ten days' failure all ranks dashed for the German position on the reverse slope of the spur, 150 to 200 yards distant.

" But the Germans were quick—they had rehearsed the situation already during the day.   Our men dropped fast—killed, wounded, or to escape the spray of bullets.   The two platoons of B Company, on the flank, scarcely got going at all—Phillips was one of the first to be killed—some were hit on the parapet and fell back in the trench.   D Company was mostly in dead ground for half the distance.   Where the ground rose to the general level of the spur there was a nearly solid obstacle, about 30 yards long, of Scottish Rifles, Royal Fusiliers, and Middlesex dead, lying where they fell as the German machine guns swept the crest.   Jackson, Company Sergeant-Major Gitters, and Platoon Sergeant ' Ten ' Jones were among the few who passed it.   They were close to the German wire when Jackson was wounded—he was killed by a shell soon afterwards.   Gitters and Jones had the luck to survive unhurt.   All was over in a little more than a minute. But in the stillness that fell on the battalion front the whistling shells of the creeping barrage crashed in successive lines that were traced by the quickly lifting wreaths of smoke.

" The empty trench was manned by the two remaining platoons of B Company, Headquarters signallers, servants, and any others.   On the left were two weak companies of the Middlesex.

" While the daylight lasted there was nothing to do but watch Monchy-le-Preux being reduced to dust ; or follow a to-and-fro movement of khaki figures where Guémappe had been, and bombs were being hurled."   (J. C. Dunn.)

On the right, that is in the Hindenburg Line, the renewed bombing attack failed.   Radford says : " The 5th Scottish Rifles were splendidly led by their late Sergeant-Major, now an officer.   They had no previous knowledge of the ground—very few got beyond the barricade.   The only result was that the Boche once more plastered the barricade and its neighbourhood with shells and trench-mortar bombs, and the brunt of the defence fell on C Company.   The bomb-throwing competition started all over again.   A bomb thrown by one of the company hit the top of the trench and blew into fragments the feet of a young private of the company who had been sitting there for hours, imperturbably straightening out the pins of the Mills bombs.   The officer of the 5th Scottish Rifles, who endeavoured to get the men remaining with him to attack, was mortally wounded, and then Company Sergeant-Major Marks (C Company) was

III—19

hit, and died in the tunnel.   Casualties became heavier every minute, and the number of men to call on was fading away.   By 8 p.m. the garrison at the barricade consisted of myself, Sergeant Jack Williams, Lance-Corporal James, and Private Bennett, all of C Company, and one man of the Scottish Rifles.   By then the place was a shambles.   At 98th Brigade Head-quarters it was reported that the barricade had given way—documents were burned and all else done appropriate to a disaster.   Two weeks after I overheard a Staff Captain at a divisional meeting giving a graphic and detailed account of the forcing of the barricade—I told him fairly and forcibly that he was recounting a pack of lies.

"I demanded of the O.C. Scottish Rifles to be relieved, as we were worn out.   At midnight we were relieved by a company of the Cameronians.   We spent the night in the tunnel.   Next morning we were astounded and annoyed by the news that the Germans abandoned their barricade and hundreds of yards of the trench during the night.   When we came out, the tunnel gave up a larger number of men than I knew were left—some of them must have hidden themselves damned well the previous day."

The Germans had also retired on the east side of the trench during the night.   "Before dark two Germans appeared and gave themselves up —more would have come, but they were fired on from the left.   None could have been so scared as they when a bombardment of our trenches was started by the enemy, which suggested that a counter-attack might follow.   As they shivered with cold and fear, Mann stamped and swore at them, then gave them some whisky : to abject expressions of thanks he retorted that he hated them—his only brother was killed during the spring.   No counter-attack developed.   On relief we learned that so hope-less was 19th Brigade Headquarters of our position and the retention of the Hindenburg Line under the reported assaults that the transport was ordered farther back.   Yates 'misunderstood' the order and stayed—but no rations were sent up.   My servant, who relieved the famine at Head-quarters, was four and a half hours making his way through the jam of many mixed-up units and detachments sheltering in the short stretch of tunnel through which he was directed.

"The night was fine and cold.   The immediate front was lighted by frequent enemy star shells—more frequent were the bursts of fire from a machine gun that ceased before dawn.

"As it got less dark on the 24th some wounded were seen looking out of shell-holes.   While individuals who crawled out were bringing them in, a wounded Argyll mounted the German slope of the spur and came through the wire ; he was looked at with much surprise and some suspicion, but he came on confidently and shouted something. Someone ran out from B Company and called back, ' They've gone ! ' The companies were ordered forward at once with patrols in advance. The isolated Middlesex and Argyll came in, bringing some prisoners with them. The Adjutant, Mann, ran on, searching the ground from side to side in advance of the patrols, who got close to where the Hindenburg Line was crossed by the Fontaine—St. Martin Cojeul road before exchanging shots at short range with the enemy. By direction of the G.S.O.2 a line of outposts was established here.

" The ground from which the enemy had withdrawn was honeycombed with shell-holes, and dispersed about it were concrete strong-points—the pill-boxes of Passchendaele. A few wounded, and unwounded, Germans were found." (J. C. Dunn.)

The doctor had more to do with this than is apparent in his account, as he and Mann were out in front of the line early in the morning.

Our casualties in this hard and unprofitable fighting were Captain J. M. Owen, 2nd Lieutenants A. Phillips, S. L. Blaxley, J. B. Jackson, and 30 other ranks killed ; Lieutenant R. Greaves, 2nd Lieutenants Llewellyn-Jones, Brooks, J. Farrand, R. H. Hanmer, R. Jones, G. W. Lowe, W. G. Lloyd, R. Nield-Siddell, and 70 other ranks wounded ; 5 other ranks were missing.

On the right of the divisional front, east of the Sensée River, the attack of the 100th Brigade, after a preliminary success, also failed.

The battalion was relieved by the 20th Royal Fusiliers, and went back to Boiry Becquerelle. On the 26th, when the 21st Division relieved the 33rd, the battalion moved to Blairville, where, as one cynical writer records, " bouquets from G.H.Q. and downwards were being handed out."

.   .   .   .

From the 27th April to the 2nd May the 2nd Battalion was at Basseux. The billets were good.

During the war, men, who in peace time would scorn to notice such things, not only perceived that the sky was blue and the apple trees in blossom, but actually wrote of them. The doctor, in this case, observes that " to lie down again warm and soft, to sit about in the sunshine among flowers and trees in leaf and in blossom, to hear the birds sing and twitter, and the church bells in the neighbouring village of Beauval—even with the drone of an aeroplane overhead—was paradise after such a life as that of the past eight months." He gives, too, a picture of Major Poore, brother of a noted cricketer, himself a keen player, and a swordsman of repute in the fencing schools of England (he won the championship with the sabre on one occasion), going on leave. Poore was a solicitor, a charming man with a slight stutter. It was his first leave. He was restless, anxious, and questioning, wondering if he was going the right way, how much money he would need, and so on. He got up in the middle of the night to make sure he would catch the staff car four hours later ; he packed and repacked his travelling kit ; he tramped about the uncarpeted room ; thrice in forty-five seconds he would say " You see " and twice " What ! " At last he went away and the other occupants of his billet went to sleep.

On the 2nd May the battalion moved to Monchy-au-Bois, near Adinfer Wood, to bivouacs. The wood had been in German occupation. On its front, but concealed in a hedge, were machine-gun emplacements of concrete, like large letter-boxes ; inside the wood were gun emplacements and shelters built of the trunks of large trees and planted over with ferns : they were unobtrusive and did not detract from the charm of the wood. Its trees were erect and unbroken ; it was carpeted with moss and ivy, violets and anemones, bluebells and jonquils, and wild strawberry. For the most part of the two weeks spent at Adinfer Wood the weather was very fine.

THE BATTLE OF BULLECOURT.[1]

(1ST BATTALION.)

The 62nd Division, which had supported the 33rd Division attack with artillery fire, was then launched against the village of Bullecourt, while Australians attacked on their right. The 7th Division had been resting close behind them since the beginning of April, and the 22nd Brigade moved from Courcelles to Mory in support of the attack.

The battle commenced on the 3rd May at 3.45 a.m., but after entering Bullecourt troops were driven back to their original line.

Our 1st Battalion had marched across what was called the " devastated area," from Courcelles at 1.30 a.m., and Lieutenant-Colonel Holmes had gone on to Brigade Headquarters. He rejoined the battalion south of Mory at 3 p.m. with orders to relieve the 185th Brigade and attack Bullecourt afresh. Company commanders went forward to reconnoitre ; the battalion was to be in position and commence to advance at 10.30 p.m. The arrangement was that the H.A.C. should attack on the right, the objective being a trench running through the centre of the village. If all went well, the 20th Manchester and

---

[1] Date : 3rd–17th May. Area : road Quéant (exclusive)—Noreuil—Vaulx Vraucourt—l'Homme Mort—Ecoust—St. Mein—Hendecourt.

2nd Warwickshire would pass through and carry on the advance to the Hindenburg Line in rear of the village.

The Royal Warwickshire and Manchester Battalions had already taken over the railway embankment from the 185th Brigade, and at 7.45 p.m. our 1st Battalion moved forward to take up their position in the cutting on the left of the Longatte road.

A few minutes before zero Captain R. M. Stevens reported that the H.A.C. were not yet in position, but as they were known to be on the way and at no great distance, he was ordered to advance slowly. This was done, in the face of machine-gun fire which, in the darkness, was for the most part high.

On the right of the battalion front, 2nd Lieutenant Soames, of C Company, entered the trench with slight opposition, but on the left of him A Company was held up by strong wire. Soames was not in touch with the H.A.C. on his right (who were, neverthe-less, in the village), and was driven out of the trench by a counter-attack ; he established him-self in a post near the German wire.

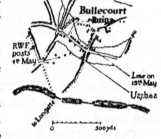

The gap on the right of the battalion was repeated on the right of the H.A.C., where Australians should have operated but did not advance. At 2.30 a.m. the H.A.C. were driven out of the trenches they had taken, and retired. (A small party held out in the centre of the village till the 7th, when they were relieved in the course of a subsequent attack.)

Our battalion, however, clung on to posts in front of the German wire, and to the sunken road on the left of the village, and at 3.10 a.m. the Manchester and Warwickshire Battalions passed through. They, too, failed to make the objective, but some of the Warwickshire established further posts on the right of our battalion.

It was extremely dark and disorganisation was complete. Small parties of men without officers were dotted about and no one could state the situation. About midday 2nd Lieutenant H. A. Freeman was ordered to locate the posts, with the result that they were placed as shown on the map, though a few small parties were nearer the Crucifix. This was con-sidered a hopeful spot, and during the night, 4th/5th, D Company, on the right of a company of the Royal Warwickshire, started from the sunken road to make a bombing attack on the Crucifix. This junction of sunken roads and trench proved to be a strong and well-organised post, and they failed.   D Company was ordered back to the starting-point and was relieved by the 9th Devon.

2nd Lieutenants A. S. Lewis, D. A. Thomas, A. M. Syrett, D. T. Jones, and 20 other ranks had been killed ; 2nd Lieutenants H. L. M. Ellis (subsequently died of his wounds), J. A. Soames, and 65 other ranks were wounded ; 22 other ranks were missing.

The battalion returned to Courcelles till the 10th, and then to Sapignies till the 13th.

The 20th Brigade were called upon to make another attempt to capture the village, and the attack was pressed for three days.   It was costly, and showed small gains.

On the 11th May the 91st Brigade was ordered to continue the attack. The Queens and South Staffordshire Battalions advanced behind a creeping barrage of 100 yards in six minutes, and the infantry formation is interesting. They advanced at 3.40 a.m. on the 12th on a two-company front, each with a " frontage of one platoon, waves to follow each other closely and to be in close order, or very slightly extended."   The " mass attack " did no good.   It was followed by an attack of the 2nd Royal Warwickshire with two companies of the 22nd Manchester at 3.40 a.m. on the 13th, and again at 7 p.m. by a company of the South Staffordshire, but neither made any headway against the severe German fire.   The feature of the defence was intense artillery fire ; any small advance was immediately wiped out.   The place was a shambles.

Our 1st Battalion was training at Sapignies.   That night (13th) they were ordered forward to Bullecourt, with orders to clear the south-western part of the village on the morning of the 14th.   B and D Companies were led to their forming-up point by guides of the 22nd Manchester ; A and C Companies went to the sunken road south-east of the village.

They found as the only result of all the fighting that we held the southeast corner of the village, our line running up the Longatte road, but not to the west of it, and turning sharp to the right in the village, about a third of the way to the church.   B and D Companies formed up between the old German front line and the cross-roads in the village.

The attack of these two companies was launched at 2.10 a.m., but broke against the strong-points in this patch of village which had resisted so many onslaughts.

A and C Companies were promptly brought up from the sunken road, and while B and D barraged the Crucifix and Point U27.b.6.2 with rifle grenades aided by Stokes mortars, attacked at 4.10 a.m.   The struggle continued for several hours, but at 10 a.m. a message from C Company informed Lieutenant-Colonel Holmes that the attack had once more failed. Posts had, however, been established in close touch with the enemy at the two points of stubborn resistance, U27.b.6.2 and the Crucifix. C Company was ordered to renew the attack at 2.30 p.m., when other posts were formed close to the enemy.

Later in the afternoon the battalion was yet again ordered to attack, but Lieutenant-Colonel Holmes informed a Staff officer, who had gone to him from the brigade, that he considered a further effort with tired troops was not possible until the Crucifix was taken : the attack was, therefore, cancelled.

The Chaplain, Captain the Hon. M. Peel, had been killed, as had 2nd Lieutenants L. G. Madley and R. P. Evans ; amongst the wounded were 2nd Lieutenants R. R. Brocklebank (died of wounds), C. H. Lloyd Jones, H. Allison, and J. F. Jones ; 14 other ranks were killed and 45 wounded ; 9 other ranks missing.

During the whole of the day the Germans had kept up a steady bombardment of our forward posts and the village, and, to add to the troubles of the battalion, the main dump for bombs had been blown up, so that the supply was inadequate.

Orders for relief were issued during the afternoon of the 14th May, and B and D Companies had actually been relieved when the battalion was once more ordered to renew the attempt. A and C Companies were, therefore, left behind.

The 91st Brigade Headquarters had received, during the afternoon, several reports from the 173rd Brigade, that the Germans were massing near the Factory. Our heavy artillery fired on them. Battalions were not, apparently, informed, and the incident passed. Later, when darkness fell, the steady enemy bombardment increased in volume, spreading to our battery positions, and included gas shells for special points such as Ecoust, the railway embankment, and communication trenches.

After dawn the enemy was seen advancing from the Factory, but was scattered by our artillery. But about 5 a.m. he again advanced from the Factory at the double and at the same time launched bombing parties from the dugouts he still held in the village. He emerged from U27.b.6.2 and drove in posts from A Company ; he also advanced from the Crucifix against posts established on the west of the village, drove them in, and advanced along the valley to within 300 yards of Battalion Headquarters by the railway embankment.

Captain T. Black, 2nd Lieutenants Freeman and J. M. Davies were sent forward with any men they could collect to hold the Germans by the cross-roads until a counter-attack could be organised. Lieutenant-Colonel Holmes took command of the " garrison," and gathering troops from where he could, H.A.C. and 21st Manchester, he launched them against the Germans, held in check by Captain Black, and re-established the line. A Company, in the village, also reported having retaken all lost ground and were in touch with 2nd Lieutenant Davies.

The enemy advance from the Factory had been broken up by our barrage, while in the village our line was, at a few points, slightly improved. The remainder of the day was spent in consolidating, digging supports, making dumps for bombs and ammunition, and general organisation.

2nd Lieutenant Freeman had been wounded ; 5 other ranks killed and 25 wounded ; 15 were missing.

The battalion was relieved during the night, 15th/16th, by the 8th London Regiment (174th Brigade, 58th Division) and marched back to Achiet-le-Grand, where it remained for the rest of the month.

The final capture of Bullecourt was completed the next day by London Territorial troops.

The obstinate defence of this place was no less remarkable than the determined and unceasing attack. On the 3rd May the Australians, on the right, had secured a length of the Hindenburg Line, and on the west bank of the Sensée our troops were also astride of that line : the defending troops were exposed to attack on three sides. Sir Douglas Haig gave the Germans a " mention " in his despatch, and rightly says that the defence of this 1,000 yards of double trench, " through two weeks of almost incessant fighting, deserves to be remembered as a most gallant feat of arms."

.   .   .   .

The Battle of Arras had now been maintained for six weeks. General Nivelle's reputation had foundered in a sea of blood. Every effort had been made to hold and to draw further German reserves into the Arras battle : after the first opening days the enemy counter-attacks had been swift and strong. " The strengthening of the enemy's forces opposite my front necessarily brought about for the time being the characteristics of a wearing-out battle " (despatch)—in other words, an exchange of heavy casualties ; but the object in continuing the battle had undoubtedly been achieved. There was, however, no excuse for prolongation after the French attack on the Chemin des Dames on the 5th May.

Sir Douglas Haig felt what Freudian theorists would call an " urge " towards Ypres. He determined not to spend any more of his strength at Arras, but transfer it to the flats of Belgium. Sir Herbert Plumer was ordered to be prepared to deliver an attack on the 7th June against the

Messines Ridge. In order to assist in these northern operations the French agreed to take over a portion of the front which we had accepted from them early in the year. This was done on the 20th May, the boundary between us and our Allies then being the River Omignon.

But sufficient activity was to be maintained on the Arras front to keep the enemy in doubt as to whether the offensive would be proceeded with. On the 20th May that portion of the Hindenburg Line which was still uncaptured between Bullecourt and our front line west of Fontaine-les-Croisilles received attention.

.　　　.　　　.　　　.　　　.　　　.　　　.

Our 2nd Battalion had had a much-needed rest at Adinfer Wood, with little to do, although the use of the rifle left much to be desired, and some sport.

Yates, the Quartermaster, had a wonderful horse—at least it was the apple of his eye—called Girlie. Yates himself might sleep in inclement weather on the ground, but Girlie was invariably sheltered under a tarpaulin, or her head would appear over a sheet enclosing a corner of the Quartermaster's store tent. On the 2nd May, Girlie, ridden by Yates, who was giving away two stone, ran a race against François, a horse owned and ridden by Captain Montgomery, the G.S.O.2. The battalion lost a few hundred francs. But at the divisional race meeting at Ayette, on the 7th, Yates and Girlie defeated all comers, and the battalion was in funds.

At this time an order from the Higher Command trickled down to the ranks that the German line known as Drocourt-Quéant was to be referred to in future as Quéant-Drocourt, Quéant being on the right. " Now," said the troops, " we ought to be able to get on with the war ! "

On the 12th May the battalion moved forward to Moyenville, and into support, west of St. Leger, on the 15th. The 16th and 17th were cold and wet days of waiting and preparation. On the 18th another move was made into German dugouts west of Croisilles—they were the only completed part of an outpost work to cover the Sensée valley. Some excitement was caused by the statement of a prisoner taken by the V Corps, that the enemy intended to retire to the Drocourt-Quéant line on this day. Patrols discovered there was no such intention. Late on the 19th, yet another move was made to the south of Croisilles. The 20th and 21st were days of morning mist and battle in which the whole of the 33rd Division, excepting the battalion, was engaged.

The 33rd Division attacked the " island " in the Hindenburg Line, between Bullecourt and the Sensée, on the 20th May, our 2nd Battalion, Cameronians, and 18th Middlesex (Pioneers) being in reserve. Our A and

C Companies did excellent work carrying for the 100th Brigade throughout the day. The fighting was severe, the enemy stubborn, and the front line only was captured. The next day [1] our battalion took over from the 6th Northumberland Fusiliers, A and C Companies between Plum Lane and the left communication trench, D in Plum Lane, B in shell-holes behind A and C Companies. D Company of the 5th Scottish Rifles was attached and occupied shell-holes in rear of B Company.

The attack was renewed on the 27th. The 2nd Battalion objective was that portion of the Hindenburg Support Line between Plum Lane and Oldenburg Lane. A and C Companies, on a two-platoon front, formed the first two waves. Their orders were to push across the support line and establish a line of posts about 100 yards beyond it. A Company was to establish a bombing block in Oldenburg Lane on the flank of these posts. [2]

The entrances to the tunnel, which ran below the support line, were to be dealt with by " moppers-up " from B Company.

D Company was to bomb up Plum Lane and, after clearing it, turn their attention to the support line, clearing it to the south for 80 yards or so ; one platoon would attack the support line across the open as the bombing was in progress.

The remains of B Company would form the third wave behind A and C ; and D Company, of the Scottish Rifles, would form a fourth wave. Zero was 1.55 p.m. The Cameronians attacked on the left.

Captain Mann, the Adjutant, had gone to hospital, " so Conning was entrusted to adapt the battalion dispositions to the brigade order. Moody, just returned after a few weeks with the 1st Battalion, shared Conning's misgivings. During fifteen months with the battalion Conning had been a happy-go-lucky fellow ; this time he arranged his private affairs as if, for him, the end of everything had come. After a large sick-parade had been disposed of, the battalion moved into positions already marked off." (Dunn.)

This was on the night 26th/27th. Companies were over-strength, as a large draft had been received which went in with the battalion. Headquarters was situated in the Quarry, " where the bull-frogs croaked all night," about a mile from Croisilles.

The doctor, who watched the fight, continues his account, to which Moody and Picton Davies (lately with the 4th Battalion) contribute. It

---

[1] The 1st Battalion were holding their sports and had challenged the 2nd Battalion to pull a tug-of-war. A few officers and a team were allowed to take up the challenge and attend. The 2nd Battalion won. This was at Achiet-le-Grand.

[2] See Sketch, page 285.

cannot be improved upon and squares with the official diaries in essential facts—the official diaries are curt and free from detail.

" On the battalion right was Plum Lane, a communication trench shared with the enemy. Tunnel Trench, 300 yards distant, was on a reverse slope, and screened by the crest even from a man standing on the parapet (parados as constructed originally), though he might be seen from the left, from the Cameronian area, where the ridge flattened as it fell to the Sensée. Between Tunnel Trench and the crest the enemy had connected up shell-holes as an intermediate line, with some light wire in front ; at one spot the tops of the pickets could be seen from our fire-step.

" The 27th was a fine May day. Our guns were unusually quiet in the morning, but the enemy scattered shell all round. Minutes are never so long as when waiting for zero, and this day hours had to pass in stillness, for German air observers were hovering about.

" After lunch Division and 19th Brigade Staffs assembled on the slope of a commanding spur about 3,000 yards in rear, to see the show. The spectators had not long to wait—or stay.

" The opening of the bombardment at 1.55 p.m. brought Conning and Picton Davies on to the parapet, followed by C and A Companies. Conning chaffed the stiff-limbed, and gave some a hand to climb out ; again he told those about him not to hurry—' Just stroll over behind our shells as if you were out for a quiet Sunday afternoon walk ' ; and at that pace he led on, in line with Picton Davies. To Moody, waiting on the parapet to go over with D Company, he called ' Cheerio ! ' B Company, led by Lawrence Ormrod, formed a third wave, supporting the two waves of C and A ; it was to ' mop up.' The Cameronians, already lying out fifty yards in front of their trench, got going at once, so there was a gap between the two battalions—slight, but it tended to widen. Four hundred yards to the right the 9th Highland Light Infantry were demonstrating on Nellie Trench with rifle grenades and Lewis guns." (Dunn.)

" Five minutes after zero the rear of the companies was on the crest. Already the second wave and B Company were closing up. The first wave had reached the wire of the intermediate line when the German shells began to burst behind the companies in No Man's Land and in the trench ; then the guns lifted to the back area." (Picton Davies.)

" For two hours the enemy shelled his barrage lines. The rôle of D Company, on the right, was to attack up Plum Lane and astride it. Bombs were flying about there as the last wave receded over the crest." (Dunn.)

Assured of his right, Picton Davies crossed to his left, where Company Sergeant-Major Prime was charged to keep touch with the

Cameronians. But the Cameronians had sidled off, and were advancing more than half left. Picton Davies sent a runner asking that the 5th Scottish Rifles fill the gap. C Company's first wave was checked momentarily by shorts from our artillery, that caused some casualties. Though the wire of the enemy's intermediate line of shell-holes was not considerable, it caused delay enough to allow the succeeding waves to come up, and the men closed in to the places where passages were being made.

" The leading troops were on to and over the active enemy in the intermediate line when, with the lifting of our artillery from Tunnel Trench, the enemy there manned his parapet and opened fire. The left of my company (A) had occupied the intermediate trench, but to my right they had not. The Germans in Tunnel Trench were now firing. Their fire seemed concentrated on my right centre and my men were having difficulty in getting through the wire. My left was dealing with the enemy in the trench. It was so important to get the centre of my line up that, leaving Prime in charge on the left, I ran along the Tunnel Trench side of the shell-hole line shouting to the men to come on. Some of the Germans in the shell-hole line were leaving it and making for Tunnel Trench, but others were remaining and firing. Some of my company, on the right, had passed through the wire and were fighting at close quarters with the enemy in the shell-hole line. Farther to the right I could not see.

" I was about the centre of my company, urging the men on ; the bulk came up and were approximately in line, advancing on Tunnel Trench, when I was hit by a machine gun right opposite me in Tunnel Trench, but as yet out of bombing range. I dropped, and I remember no more for an unknown period. I recall dimly that I was conscious my left was in danger—I think I made off in that direction, and I could not make out where my men had gone. I did not get far before I fell again. The next thing I recall is that two slightly wounded Scotsmen had picked me up, and I was being half dragged, half supported along. I do not know how long after zero that was, but I remember shells falling to right and left. The machine gun had registered five ' bulls ' on my person in various places." (Picton Davies.)

" As seen from behind, the advance had been made in good order over the crest ; then there was swaying and bunching, but progress was not quite arrested. A brisk rifle fire was opened and machine guns rattled. A moment later a few men ran back—then most of the men ran back. The collapse was stupefying in its suddenness and the manner of it. The Cameronians on the immediate left had come back, too. The men said they were stopped by wire ; that they had orders to ' retire.' There were no officers with them.   Individuals and little groups kept coming back ; there was Talkington, wounded in the arm, and Storey Cooper with a wound in the foot ; then Ormrod, and later Picton Davies—both badly hit—were carried in ; last of all a couple of senior N.C.O.s sprinted back singly. In one of the last little groups was Moody, who hurried into Plum Lane. A man struggled for a time, trying to free himself from the wire.   That was all until after dark." (J. C. Dunn.)

" The leading troops were in a hopeless position.   They were ringed in by good Germans who were well led—an officer stood on his parados, a revolver in each hand, choosing his targets.   From shell-holes and over the top, round A Company's open flank, the enemy came and fought at close quarters.   Enemy in the shell-hole line turned and fired to their rear when the menace on their front dissolved.   Conning had been killed at the first wire.   Three other officers were killed.   Richards fell wounded in front of Tunnel Trench (his leg was amputated in a German hospital) ; Sergeant Parry and a few others reached Tunnel Trench." (Shelley.)

" In Plum Lane, D Company had bombed their way until they faced a machine gun in Tunnel Trench firing down the Lane.   While they were trying to bomb the gun, the Germans came at them over the top on the right ; some of these Germans jumped into the trench, where they were dispatched, but some of D Company were cut off.   When I saw that the attack in the open had failed, I went up Plum Lane to secure the block, and took part in the bombing that covered the reconstitution of the defence. A Royal Fusilier Lewis gun on the right fired on the enemy who appeared in the open.   Until the defence was made secure, the bombing was fiercer than it had been at zero." (Moody.)

" Moody was the only officer in action not a casualty.   In reorganising the companies he was assisted by Captain McChlery, the only 5th Scottish Rifles officer on the ground.   While this was being done, a German concentration in Fontaine was seen from another part of the line and broken up by machine-gun fire.   Its suggestion of a counter-attack was sent as a warning to companies, so Moody asked the trench-mortar officer to open fire.   The wounded still lying out, who could see Tunnel Trench, described how all the trench-mortar bombs were overs ; none the less they ' put the wind up ' the Germans, producing the same apprehensive restlessness that a trench-mortar bombardment caused in the British Expeditionary Force, for these large visible bombs have a peculiarly demoralising effect as they come lurching through the air.

" Late in the afternoon de Miremont, who had been at Headquarters, was sent up and took command of the two left companies.   The C.O.

paid a visit and was satisfied that Moody had the situation in hand. All was quiet by then, and continued quiet throughout the night, save that at 9 p.m. our guns bombarded Tunnel Trench and killed some of our wounded still lying out. The wounded who came in, or could be got in after dark, numbered little more than a dozen, including Shelley, Sergeants Onions and Ibbotson. The enemy behaved well to our wounded near his trench ; in the heat of the afternoon a N.C.O. came out and gave them water.

" The Corps called for a report on the failure of the operation, whereupon Lieutenant-Colonel Chaplin, of the Cameronians, with the generosity which distinguished his relations with other units, took blame for his Battalion." (J. C. Dunn.)

The actual reason for this retirement was never discovered, but it is supposed that the left company of the Cameronians walked into our own barrage, and was ordered by the company commander to draw back a short distance ; this was taken as an order for retirement. The Company Commander was seen trying to rally his men and lead them forward when he was killed—the only other officer with the company had been wounded—and the retirement continued. Unfortunately the word was passed along the line, and came right down to the flank of the attack.

The whole of our battalion was back in the Hindenburg front line by 2.45 p.m. Heavy machine-gun fire caused many casualties, and only two officers returned unwounded.

Captains L. M. Ormrod and Picton Davies, 2nd Lieutenants Shelley, T. Torkington, and 76 other ranks wounded ; missing, 2nd Lieutenants T. E. G. Davies, W. O. Lewis, T. B. Williams, J. D. M. Richards, Lieutenants E. L. Orme and T. R. Conning ; 19 other ranks were killed, and 59 missing.

The battalion was relieved by the 1st Queens on the 28th, and marched back to Moyenville, thence to Basseux and Bailleulval. They remained training at Bailleulval till the 18th June, when they relieved the 9th Leicestershire in Moyenville trenches.

The division was relieved on the 30th, and moved on the 2nd July to take part in the Flanders operations.

.   .   .   .

The next engagement in this Arras area was fought by the 10th Battalion on the 14th June. Tool and Hook trenches, in front of Monchy, had been stoutly defended by the Germans : Tool had, after several efforts, been taken by troops of the 56th Division. The 76th Brigade attacked at 7.20 a.m. and captured Hook, one company of our battalion attacking with the 2nd Suffolk on the right, one with the 1st Gordon Highlanders on the left. The assault was punctual, the first wave arriving in Hook Trench, as intended, before the barrage opened. The enemy was completely surprised.

The enemy counter-attacked in the evening, but, thanks to a timely warning from the 56th Division, a warm reception was waiting for him.

" The right of the 56th Division was held by the Queen's Westminster Rifles, and a few minutes after five o'clock in the evening sentries noticed enemy movement behind a wood (Bois du Vert) which was opposite the 3rd Division and on the left flank of the 56th. Careful watching revealed the massing of troops. A warning was sent over the telephone. The 76th Brigade, immediately on the left of the division, was informed, as was the artillery. . . . At 5.30 p.m. the grey waves left the enemy trenches, and at once a storm of artillery, machine-gun, and rifle fire met them." (*The 56th Division.*)

In the assault our battalion lost 10 other ranks killed ; Captain H. H. Morgan and 40 other ranks wounded. But after the abortive counter-attack the enemy shelled our trenches unmercifully, and Lieutenants L. P. Vernon and D. E. Davies were killed ; Captain O. S. Hughes, 2nd Lieutenants L. E. Roberts, Ll. Jones, F. A. Stringer, were wounded ; other ranks were returned as 96 killed and wounded.

A second counter-attack—estimated at 1,000 strong—was delivered by the Germans on the 16th, at 3 a.m., when they drove in several advanced posts and retained one : the next day an attempt was made by the 1st Gordon Highlanders to recapture the one lost, but without success —our two companies had remained in support to the Highlanders. Commenting on the affair, Brigadier-General Porter stated that " the disadvantage of the system of a forward line of posts was clearly shown. It was found that when the enemy counter-attacked it was not possible to get our front line to open fire, since those holding it had the knowledge that there were posts in front of them, and naturally refrained from firing for fear of causing casualties among our own men. . . . The post was quickly put out of action by the enemy, all its occupants becoming casualties."

At the end of June the 10th Battalion moved back to Halloy, and in July to Velu Wood, rather more to the right, with the Somme battlefield behind them. On the 11th July they took over the line about Louverval, with Fremicourt as a rest centre.

.   .   .   .

After a rest the 1st Battalion returned to hold the line at Bullecourt, now on the far side of the ruins. The enemy, however, still held posts about the Crucifix, while the Bovis Trench, or Hindenburg Support, was their main line.

The offensive spirit of the battalion was maintained at high level, in spite of the heavy losses around this battered village. By this time Sir Douglas Haig had already opened his northern offensive with the Battle of Messines, and no major operation was contemplated about Arras ; it seemed, then, that some small enterprise was necessary.

A double raid was arranged by the 19th Brigade for the night 22nd/23rd July. The H.A.C. were to raid on the right of Bullecourt and the Royal Welch Fusiliers on the left. The object of the H.A.C. raid was to kill Germans, take a prisoner, and distract the enemy's attention from our raid on the left. Both raids were to be carried out " by stealth," and the artillery were not to fire until our raiding party had entered the posts near the Crucifix, on the Hardecourt road.

The ruins of Bullecourt
1st Battalion raid 22/6/17.
——————— 1000yds
German Posts—objective found unoccupied.

Bovis

The task was entrusted to D Company of our battalion. One platoon was to capture the posts and block the trench leading to them ; the remaining platoons were to be used as carrying parties and be ready to dig a communication trench to the captured posts if it was decided to hold them.

The idea was to blow gaps in the enemy's wire in front of the posts, but when the raiders reached the wire they discovered that the posts were not manned. They found many bombs stored in them and two deep double-entrance dugouts. They, therefore, decided to push on and find the Germans.

The explosive they were using was contained in long, flat cases, which fitted into each other like the lengths of a fishing-rod, and were pushed under the wire and fired by electricity : the invention was called the " Bangalore torpedo." It was a cumbersome arrangement, and they left it behind with a guard over the empty posts.

The one platoon pushed on towards Bovis Trench—moving on either side of the road from the Crucifix to the Factory. Bovis Trench was found to be strongly wired and in good condition. Men were sent back to bring up the Bangalore torpedo.

But the raiding party was observed, and the scene soon became lively, as bombs were hurled from each side of the wire. A machine gun opened from the right, too. And then, before the torpedo carriers arrived, our own artillery started to fire, as arranged, on Bovis Trench, and drove our party back.

"BILLY," CAIRLLON, 18TH JULY, 1917.

Imperial War Museum photograph, Crown copyright.

As observation from the captured posts was not considered good enough to justify their retention, the dugouts were destroyed, and the raiders returned to their lines.

The H.A.C. had also found their objective empty.

On the 8th August the 7th Division was withdrawn and proceeded to train at Blairville until the end of the month. They then moved to Godewaersvelde.

The Somme-Scarpe battles were over. They constitute an amazing military adventure—an obstinate effort carried on for a year. One need not consider what had happened to our Allies: whether the battles were fought to help them or not, there was a plan, however fantastic it might have appeared to regimental officers at the time, and a great trial of strength based on massed artillery and limited objectives for the infantry. In that trial of strength and method our advance on those distant and vital goals was negligible. On the question of effect, however, something had been achieved, although it was not apparent to those who survived: the enemy thought of this series of battles with horror—he was shaken, though still strong. The cost of this achievement was fearful: all those allusions to enemy losses being greater than our own, which one finds in the Despatches, were what the Army called " Eye-wash," and were not believed by those who wrote them ; no one imagined the old military axiom that losses in attack are greater than in defence had been suddenly reversed by command of the Imperial General Staff and the Commander-in-Chief. Dust had to be thrown into the eyes of our own Army, the civilian population at home, the enemy, and all neutrals : the ignorant masses were to some extent blinded—figures, of course, were not published.

This great effort had also an effect on our own Army, which was serious. As the old trained soldiers gradually disappeared, the regiment must take note of a great change.

Of the 2nd Battalion, Major Dunn, writing with the expert knowledge of a doctor, notes after the attacks on High Wood that " from now on the battalion approximated more and more to the standard of a New Army Battalion : the officers were nearly all temporary ; with three or four exceptions the N.C.O.s, however, were nearly all the Old Army, though in dwindling numbers ; but there were very few of the Old Army left amongst the privates, with the exception of the transport, drums, and signallers. Hitherto bombing raids, trench raids, etc., had been made by volunteers, but from now onwards men were detailed for everything.

" The next few weeks were spent in reorganising, and the quiet, rest, sunshine, bathing in the stream, and peaceful nights restored the nerves of the men, and they ceased uttering cries of hate and fear in their sleep. Drafts were received, including many Welshmen ; it was said that only 10 per cent. were Welsh when the battalion left England, Birmingham being the best represented of the English localities, but by this time the battalion was nearly 50 per cent. Welsh, amongst them being clerks, schoolmasters, and small tradesmen whose physique was fairly good ; but they were not in condition and were only partly trained ; a few simple

The B.E.F. area showing the main railways, of two or more tracks, behind the enemy lines.

hurdles put up showed that very few, even the youngest, whether town-bred or country-bred, could clear them."

The exhaustion of the Old Army had an effect on the New Army. The doctor points out that on the 31st May 1917, when training commenced at Bailleulval, there were only six officers available for duty, and none was a specialist. The same applies to N.C.O.s. The intensive " training " at home was very little use ; men could neither shoot, throw bombs an effective distance, nor understand manœuvre. Again and again the ignorance of the rifle is emphasised. The state of affairs penetrated to G.H.Q., and in May 1917, in order to accentuate the seriousness of the untrained state of the Army, they burst into verse.

THE MAN OF MONS.

Alf is old, as a soldier goes,
　　With hair that is rapidly turning grey ;
Ever since Mons he had strafed our foes
　　In his cool, calm, methodical way.
He learned to shoot on a Surrey range,
　　His aim is steady, and quick, and true ;
" Bombs," says Alf, " are good for a change,
　　" But it's the rifle will pull you through ! "

Lads who have scarcely been out a year,
　　These are to Alf but as untrained boys.
The name of Mills to their heart is dear,
　　And they won't be happy without those toys.
" Not," says Alf, " that they're much to blame,
　　Bred in a trench, as one might say ;
But when it comes to the open game
　　It's the well-aimed bullet that wins the day."

With his cheek to the stock he will cuddle down
　　While the swathes of Huns as grass are mown
At a burst of rapid into the brown—
　　Alf is a Lewis gun on his own.
" Clean her, and oil her, and keep her neat,
　　She's a wonder," says Alf, " when she gets her chance.
She stood by our boys in the great Retreat,
　　She will do the same in the Great Advance ! "

The training in England gave men a knowledge of, but not an instinct for, discipline. In France there was no opportunity to train them behind the line, and in the line the system of attack did not provide lessons in fire and movement. Plans were drawn up, as one severe critic observes, " with no more knowledge of the ground than might be got from a map of moderate scale. Generally remote and ineffectual in a battle, brigades were not always open to receive battalion information regarding local detail, or willing to transmit it to the rear. So even brigade might have no substitute to recommend for high-explosive shell, which so often advertised an assault it could not assist. By the time high explosive came into general use, infantry manœuvre had come to an end, or passed into abeyance. High explosive was expected to blaze the trail the company or battalion would follow. If the partly trained infantry cast a look to right or left, it was in apprehension of cross-fire, not to help by cross-fire a flank unit in difficulty." [1]

The money saved by cutting down the Establishment during years of peace was quickly lost in the Great War, and there was nothing left but an Army of amateur soldiers.

If, then, the quality of our battalions deteriorated, it should occasion no surprise. The astounding marvel of the War was that they stood, unskilled, and with the spirit of our Old Battalions.

[1] Compare with Ludendorff's remarks on the Somme operations. The only difference is that the criticism comes from the junior ranks. Its justice was recognised in so far as the training of infantry was concerned ; but the barrage was so firmly believed in that it seemed to kill all enthusiasm for infantry training. To be absolutely fair, however, the latter was a colossal task.

V

OFFENSIVE OPERATIONS: THIRD PERIOD

V

OFFENSIVE OPERATIONS: THIRD PERIOD

YPRES

SINCE the first German gas attack in 1915 the defences of Ypres had stood firm. There had been local gains and losses on both sides, the storming and restorming of a few hundred yards of trench, affairs which did not alter the general trench defences of the town. The main line, a semicircle from Wytschaete on the south to the neighbourhood of Boesinghe on the north, remained intact.

Practically every unit in the British Expeditionary Force visited Ypres at some time or other (the exceptions are extremely rare), and all retain a memory of its peculiar spell. In detail individuals were not similarly affected, but in general it is a memory of terror, of sweating anxiety, of cold fear.

One speaks of Ypres being overlooked by the enemy, of high ground ; but the stranger, visiting the place for a glimpse of the celebrated battle-field, will be disappointed if he expects to see hills in the accepted form ; the gentle undulations of an extremely flat country stand before him— a careful study of the map shows him a rise of, say, thirty feet in a mile, or a mile and a half ! But, on a winter day, when the foliage does not offer concealment, let him stand on the Menin road, on the road to Potijze, or even on the west of the canal, and note the distance of his vision. In the war years an orderly, having to move about the salient in daylight, thought of the skyline as an overhanging eminence.

The flatness of the country, the position of Ypres with the enemy's horns on either side, thrust so far forward that their tips were behind the town, gave to the least imaginative the sense of walking into a trap : he could not face his enemy and meet eye to eye the threat of death—the enemy was on his flank, and behind him whichever way he turned ; the Germans were watchful, and did not disdain a " small target " ; the solitary orderly knew well what it meant to be sniped by a field gun.

No bombardment was square—every trench could be enfiladed. And in that waterlogged country the trenches gave little protection from shell fire ; there could be no dugouts for front-line troops. Nowhere on the whole front was inferiority of position so acutely felt as in the Ypres Salient.

By midsummer 1916, when our battalions in the 38th Division moved up from the Somme to Ypres, the town was just a mass of ruins. A jagged remnant of the cathedral tower brooded over a pile of stone ; the streets, cleared by fatigue parties, were outlined by heaps of broken brick between tottering walls, pierced and rent, retaining, as by a miracle, their balance for yet another hour, a day, a week, perhaps. The pounded prison walls stood defiantly ; the old brick battlements above the moat, to the east of the town, grimly resisted the German artillery ; but otherwise the habitable town was represented by its cellars. It remained always a target for the German gunners—it remained always a centre for British troops, an active centre, but, at times, singularly weird and ghostly. There were moments of great stillness in Ypres when the solitary figure of a soldier, wending his way down the ruin-lined road, gave an awesome sense of loneliness to the scene of destruction—and also of horror that the town should still be pounded, hammered, crushed, though it lay there dead and desolate.

The position of the town, encircled north, east, and south by trenches, with the main feeding road running due west to Poperinghe—presenting on the map, and in the mind's eye too, a curious regularity of design— may have had something to do with the sense of nerve tension the great majority experienced in the salient : the German gunners must have felt as familiar with the Poperinghe road as the multitude of transport and artillery drivers who used it nightly ! One felt as though the east and west line of it was of great assistance to the enemy artillery. But oddly enough, although Poperinghe was by no means beyond enemy reach, nerviness and anxiety evaporated somewhere between Vlamertinghe and Poperinghe.

Poperinghe possessed a few simple pleasures which cheered the soldiers' hearts. Talbot House (Toc H) has its place in history, but so, too, has Ginger's Restaurant. The latter drew its name from a girl of, perhaps, twelve or thirteen years old, a carroty-haired, sharp-tongued little wretch who delighted in chaff. There were other restaurants, but none so celebrated as Ginger's. There were shops, and in the evening concert parties—nothing of any real merit, but the Army, generally, had a great affection for " Pop."

Undoubtedly there were plenty of " horrors " in the sector held by the Second Army—horror was never entirely absent : maybe the Angel of Death hovered closer there than over any other sector of the front—but with it there was an affection, born of pride (for the British had made that portion of Belgium their own), and nurtured and fostered by a remarkable Army Staff.   The Second Army was the best Army to serve in ; the fore-sight and administrative ability of Sir Herbert Plumer were recognised by every private soldier through the sheer force of contrast.   It was a firm and determined Command, where loose ideas did not exist ; at the same time it was a sympathetic Command and receptive to ideas and suggestions. With the most awkward front to feed, the Second Army was always better supplied than any other.   The organisation had perfect elasticity which surmounted all difficulties and maintained a steady flow of material for the use and comfort of troops.

No doubt the contradictory sense of affection, for an Army front where horror stalked unwearied, was the direct result of Sir Herbert Plumer's peculiar genius.   He never forgot either the duties or the difficulties of the regimental officer, and he directed the efforts of an able Staff, headed by General Harington, to help the front-line soldier and provide for his fighting needs.

It was to this front that our battalions in the 38th Division came during the Battle of the Somme, and our 4th Battalion at its close.

The position in the salient taken over by the 38th Division, and held by them for the next year, was on the extreme left of the British line, where the salient joined the canal, north of Ypres, whence the line ran along its bank.

The reserve companies in this sector were accommodated in dugouts in the canal bank, and were quite happy, although the diminishing size of the bank did not give them such secure protection as was obtained nearer to Ypres ; but, if not shell-proof, the dugouts were extremely difficult to hit, especially those on the eastern bank.

The front line was peculiar.   Much of it was not held and was allowed to fall into disrepair on the extreme left, and the left battalion, facing east, disposed of its platoons and posts sharply echeloned to the left rear as far as the canal, leaving wide patches of No Man's Land.   At the end of the year the division became responsible for the canal bank up to Boesinghe.

On the 19th August, when the division took over the line, the salient was covered with long, rank grass and a mass of poppies.   After the thunder of Mametz Wood it was quiet ; but battalions were soon called upon to act.

An officer of the 14th Battalion describes the long tour of duty under the Second Army as " months of monotony and moments of hell " : Ypres was something more than that ; the aphorism might be applied to any sector—a bombardment is always hell for those against whom it is directed. A different kind of hell is the small fight, or raid, which our battalions were called upon to undertake at frequent intervals—what was called the " offensive spirit " was maintained at a high level.

They are very similar, these raids. A small party, or a large one, waiting ; the opening crash of a hurricane bombardment ; lights shooting up from the German lines, throwing a shimmering brilliance over the dark, broken, tumbled strip of No Man's Land, in which men suddenly appear as small black shadows moving swiftly in the mystery of the revealed night—revealed by tossed-up balls of dazzling white, mingled with red lights, green lights, strings of lights, showers of golden rain : on the horizon flickering flash of guns ; ear-splitting din ; whistles blown ; men returning, tumbling into the trench, panting, excited, crouching against the parapet for protection against retaliation.

The first raid was successfully accomplished by the 13th Battalion on the 12th October.

The raiding party consisted of 4 officers, 11 N.C.O.s, and 74 men. Their object was to secure identification and kill Germans. They were to penetrate to the support line under the protection of a box barrage.

On this occasion the party was split up into a larger number of sections than usual, each with a distinct task : both front and support lines of the German system had to be blocked on right and left, and each line had to be cleared, or " mopped up " ; parties were also detailed to protect each line against possible counter-attacks while the mopping-up was proceeding.

All details of the plan were worked out and practised in the back areas, and on the selected night the raiders left the Château des Trois Tours, near Brielen, at 6.15 p.m., halted for a few moments at the canal bank to hear a short oration from the Brigadier, and were formed up in readiness behind the parados of our front line at 8.45 p.m.

The most important point in all these raids was direction—to strike through the darkness the exact spot selected, where the enemy wire had been cut by previous bombardment ; an error of a few yards would cause delay which might prove fatal to the enterprise.

The sections detailed to block the right and left of the support trench went first, when, at 9 p.m., the artillery opened with a crash ; but the others followed closely, and all the raiders were soon across No Man's Land and on the German wire.

The right blocking section, under Sergeant E. J. Hughes, found the gap in the wire and crossed the front line. Sergeant Hughes outdistanced his men, but keeping good direction jumped into the support line at the right spot. He was promptly attacked by two Germans. Before his section arrived he had shot one German and knocked the other down with his fist. These men were found to be without tunics and no identification was secured—they were supposed to be part of a working party.

The front-line blocking section bore too much to the right, but were fortunate in finding another gap in the wire and also in jumping into the trench practically on top of a machine gun. No Germans were, for the moment, visible, and they started to make a block in the trench. But the German machine gunners came running up to man their gun : the first was killed, the second was seized by Privates P. B. Roberts and H. Hurrell, the third ran away. The prisoner seems to have been a stout-hearted fellow, for Roberts and Hurrell had a fearful struggle before they secured him. The trench was narrow and the two privates hindered each other as they tried to hold the German. Finally Roberts caught him by the throat and called, " 'It 'im, Bert," to his comrade, which the latter promptly did and the German was still.

The blocking sections on the left got into position without incident. But the clearing party, under 2nd Lieutenant G. R. Paton, had rushed forward rather too soon at the first crash of the artillery, which was directed on the actual trenches to be raided, and most of them were hit. However, three survivors got into the German lines, led by Paton, who was himself wounded, and made their way up a communication trench to the support line. They found nothing ; but on their way back to the front line, by a second communication trench, they encountered two Germans, one of whom was shot by Paton, the other bayoneted by Lance-Corporal Westwood. The bodies were searched and identification secured. Meanwhile Paton had sent Lance-Corporal Westwood forward to watch the junction of this communication trench with the front line, and Westwood was attacked by three Germans : he shot one, bayoneted a second, and the third escaped. These bodies were also searched and identification secured.

The only section of the raiders which did not carry out its task was the front-trench section, under 2nd Lieutenant Thomas, consisting of himself and 14 other ranks. Thomas was, unfortunately, wounded, as was the sergeant, and with the loss of their leaders the men became disorganised, and joined in with any section they happened to see.

Captain Lees, stationed at the entrance to the enemy line, gave the signal to retire, and the raiders, having killed 15 Germans, returned to their own lines with one prisoner and one machine gun.

On this same night, the 12th October, the 15th Battalion (Lieutenant-

Colonel R. C. Bell) carried out a successful raid which was led by 2nd Lieutenants W. M. Morgan, Wilson Jones, and R. Bowes. They returned with 4 prisoners, after inflicting many casualties.

The report of Lieutenant-Colonel A. G. Jones (16th Battalion) on a raid in which mats were used to cross the German wire gives an insight to the careful preparation carried out prior to these raids. He says :

" Three officers and sixty other ranks were withdrawn from the battalion on the night 15th/16th October and sent to D Camp to prepare for the raid. A scheme was made out and an exact replica of the German trenches was dug, wire being added. The men were given the usual forms of infantry training, also special instruction in bayonet fighting, bombing, and crawling. Much attention was paid to discipline.

" On seven successive nights officers' patrols were sent out to reconnoitre the point to be raided and the intervening ground between it and our trenches. Besides this, all men were sent out into No Man's Land in turn, in the form of fighting patrols, ten to fifteen strong, to accustom them to being in the open near the enemy.

" A reconnoitring party of one officer, one N.C.O., and four men left our trenches at 7.45 p.m. (29th October) and moved to ' jumping-off ' point. From there two men laid a tape back to ' point of exit ' from our trenches. The remainder marked the jumping-off point with two luminous discs, and then moved out to the German wire at the point to be raided. They stayed there for some time, and reconnoitred to the right and left to make sure they had selected the right spot. They then laid the tape back to the jumping-off point, and, in order to make certain the point of entry had been marked in the right place, they again went back to the German wire. Being satisfied, they returned to the jumping-off point about 10.30 p.m., meeting the raiders half-way across No Man's Land at 10.50 p.m. They then returned to the point of exit as arranged.

" The raiding party left the point of assembly at 9.30 p.m. and moved to the point of exit, reaching it at 10.25 p.m. The officer in charge waited in our trenches for ten minutes to see if the reconnoitring patrol was coming in, and then moved out into No Man's Land in three columns, the centre column following the tape.

" Having crossed our own wire, the columns were halted for ten minutes, to ensure that every man was in his place and out of the trenches ; after which the whole column moved forward. No difficulties were encountered as far as the jumping-off point, which was reached at 11.16 p.m.

" At 11.20½ p.m. (½ minute after zero) the party left the jumping-off point and moved along the tape towards the German trenches. Now the

ground became very difficult, and the men carrying the mats were continually falling into shell-holes. The columns moved to within thirty
yards of the wire, beyond which it was found unsafe to go on account
of our bombardment.

" At 11.24 p.m. the bombardment shifted to barrage, and the raiders,
quickening the pace, moved up to the German wire.

" The left column got into difficulties with their mat, owing to
irregularity of the wire ; they eventually crossed over by the same mat
as the centre column. Beyond the wire the ground was very cut up and
odd ends of the wire and knife-rests lay about ; there was a confusion of
shell-holes and the ground was soft and boggy, having been ploughed up
by the bombardment. This caused five minutes' delay in entering the
German trenches.

" The parties entered the trenches in the order arranged, and the
blockers proceeded to their appointed places. The trenches were so broken
in places as to delay progress."

The result of this raid was three prisoners and some half-dozen of the
enemy killed.

Sometimes the rôles were reversed, and it was the Germans who
raided, as on the night of the 23rd December, when the 17th Battalion
(Lieutenant-Colonel J. B. Cockburn) was raided just after taking over
the new stretch of line along the canal bank from the French—part of the
extra sector towards Boesinghe. The enemy was successfully driven off,
but the raid is of interest, as the Germans crossed the canal on rafts.

The 14th Battalion made their most ambitious raid on the 18th
February, 1917, the party consisting of 5 officers and 145 other ranks.
It was not an unqualified success, as the raiders came under heavy fire,
2nd Lieutenant James being killed, Lieutenant Ormsby mortally wounded
(he died the next day), and 2nd Lieutenant R. Williams wounded.

A few days later, at 2.45 a.m. on the 25th February, the Germans
returned the visit and secured one prisoner. Our artillery was caught
napping on this occasion, and was a quarter of an hour before replying
to the S.O.S. from the front line. The enemy raiders got away without
casualties. We, on the other hand, suffered severely from their bombardment, Captain P. F. Craddock, Lieutenant W. J. Williams, and 2nd
Lieutenant Stanley Jones being killed with 10 other ranks, and 9 other ranks
were wounded. It was the fortune of war.

At the southern end of the salient was the 47th Division, with our
4th Battalion encamped between Vlamertinghe and Dickebusch in " Pioneer
Camp." The 4th Battalion had interesting work the moment they arrived

(for the infantry who watched them) on the 20th October. Amongst the various jobs they undertook was the tunnelling of the Bluff, the spoil-heap from the Ypres—Comines Canal, and the construction of cupolas in the Ravine and Larch Wood : the cupolas were corrugated iron huts with a little cement plastered over them, and would resist a direct hit from field guns, but nothing heavier. Their programme of work also included trench tramways and a light railway, roads and tracks. " Dumps of trench stores, ammunition, and all the other beastly impedimenta that one associates with the term ' push ' were already beginning to show themselves. A big scheme for the construction of trench tramways, of which there already appeared more than enough, was evidently in operation. Altogether the future looked none too rosy." (*4th Royal Welch Fusiliers in the Great War*, by Captain C. Ellis.)

Anything in the nature of a bank was being bored into to provide shelters from at least splinters, but the deep dugout, peculiar to the Germans, was not attempted in that low-lying country. There had always been, however, in this part of the salient, a bitter underground war, mining and counter-mining having been carried on since the winter 1914–15. Hill 60 and the Bluff were notorious centres for this form of warfare. A number of mines were already completed when our 4th Battalion arrived ; others were being rapidly sunk.

Our battalions saw the wet summer pass into a wet autumn ; the rank grass and poppies died down ; the winter, with snow to relieve the monotony of rain, with the trenches knee-deep at times with liquid mud, slipped by ; but they were more comfortably situated for rest-billets than the battalions in the Somme area. In May the 38th Division received the first official intimation of the 1917 offensive in the form of an instruction to take advantage of the diversion caused by an attack, which was to be launched on the Messines—Wytschaete Ridge, to construct assembly trenches in preparation for the subsequent main offensive.

The battle planned by Sir Douglas Haig was the same, if not in detail, in its main features and in its aim as that conceived in 1915 by Sir John French. He would advance from Observation Ridge to Boesinghe, the right of the attack on a line through Becelaere to Roulers, the left on Houthulst Forest. In conjunction with this advance a landing would be made on the coast, between Ostend and Nieuport, while the XV Corps would attack along the coast from Nieuport on a two-division front. He hoped that the Belgians would participate in the latter advance.

He explained this general plan in a warning note to Sir Hubert Gough, to whom he had determined to entrust the main thrust of the movement.

Sir Herbert Plumer was to open the offensive by a preliminary assault on the Messines Ridge.   When this ridge was secured, Gough and the Fifth Army Staff would take command of all north of the Menin road, leaving Plumer to build up a flank on the right of the main advance.

The situation must be borne in mind : the Battle of Arras had opened with promise and had developed into the general blood-sink of a battle of attrition ; Nivelle had failed.   All the high hopes which had been centred for the past year between the Somme and the Scarpe were at an end.

Haig's confidence in the southern issue would seem to have weakened during the winter months, and evaporated after the first few days of the Battle of Arras.   On the 7th May he asked Plumer when the attack on the Messines Ridge could be delivered, and Plumer replied, " In a month from to-day ! "   This promise he kept to the hour.

THE BATTLE OF MESSINES.[1]

(4TH AND 9TH BATTALIONS.)

The operation had a precise end—the battle map was not scored by sweeping pencil strokes to mark the indefinite hope of a cavalry advance. The problem was envisaged from the siege-war point of view, and its solution entrusted to engineers and artillery.   On the front selected twenty mines were either completed or in course of construction ; guns were massed at the ratio of one to every seven yards ; and the somewhat complicated movements of the infantry were worked out in consultation with the lower commands, who had special knowledge of the sectors they were defending or holding.

The point of this southern horn of the Ypres encirclement was in the neighbourhood of Wytschaete, the horn in itself being a sharp salient, and the area to the chord across its base was treated as a fortified place it was desired to capture.   The advance of the infantry would, then, be a converging one, on a shrinking front.

Our 4th Battalion had been working through the winter on preparations for this battle ; and our 9th Battalion, leaving Serre on the 2nd March, arrived in the Second Army area and took over a length of line about Hooge.   The whole of the 19th Division spent the month of May training, and in June took over the line on the left of Wytschaete.

There was not, of course, anything in the nature of a surprise

---

[1] Date : 7th–14th June. Area : road Frelinghein—Le Bizet—Petit-Pont—Neuve Eglise—Dranoutre—Locre—La Clytte—Dickebusch—Kruisstraat ; thence a line to Zillebeke—Gheluvelt.

contemplated by the Second Army—every movement, every bit of work, was overlooked by the enemy.   The German Higher Command warned their front-line troops that the coming battle might well prove decisive, and that they were to resist to the last.   " They were assured that strong reserves were available to come to their assistance and to restore the battle should the British attack succeed in penetrating their lines." (Despatch.)   But, curiously enough, a surprise was effected.   Apparently the general opinion at German Headquarters was that mining operations had died down ; no report of underground working had been made—nothing had been heard.   " It was long since any sounds of underground burrowing had been heard."   (Hindenburg, *Out of My Life*.)   We, on our side, were unnecessarily anxious, and believed that the Germans knew of their danger. " After the 1st February, 1917, the enemy showed signs of great uneasiness, and blew several heavy mines and camouflets in the endeavour to interfere with our working.   One of these blows destroyed our gallery in the Spanbroekmolen mine.   For three months this mine was cut off, and was only recovered by strenuous efforts on the day preceding the Messines attack."   (Despatch.)

From St. Yves to Mount Sorrel our preparations were complete. The 19th Division was to attack from their position on the left of Wytschaete ; the 47th would advance astride the Ypres-Comines Canal, with D Company of our 4th Battalion allotted to the 140th Brigade on the south bank, and B Company to the 142nd Brigade on the north.   These two companies were to consolidate the positions gained and link them up with our old trenches ; while A Company was to rush through the repair of an old road as far as our old line, and C Company was to run a tram line from the canal bank to the old line.

On the 5th June the Second Army was anxious to obtain identification and a raid " to capture, not to kill," was suddenly ordered to be made by C Company of our 9th Battalion then at Weston Camp, near Locre, and by two companies from the 56th Brigade on their immediate left.   Our D Company took over the line from the 9th Welch Regiment while C Company went " over."

The raid, led by 2nd Lieutenants E. O. Roberts and D. W. Thomas, was a great success ; they penetrated to the German support line—Thomas shot two Germans and stunned a third with the butt of his revolver, while Sergeants Bannister and Evans attacked and destroyed a machine gun— and 37 prisoners were sent back to Battalion Headquarters, besides many through the 56th Brigade.   The raiders had two killed, 2nd Lieutenant Thomas and 9 other ranks wounded, and one man missing.   Major-General

RUINS OF CLOTH HALL AND CATHEDRAL, YPRES, 1916.

Imperial War Museum photograph, Crown copyright.

Shute, who was never extravagant in his praise, sent the battalion a hearty message of congratulation.

The attack was due less than thirty-six hours after the raid. The 19th Division was the left of the IX Corps, with the 16th Division on its right, and the 41st Division, X Corps, on its left. The final objectives were the Black and Mauve lines ; that is to say, when the Black line was taken, outposts were to be pushed out to Oosttaverne Wood. The total depth of the advance was 2,500 yards.

The first phase was the capture of the intermediate Green line by the

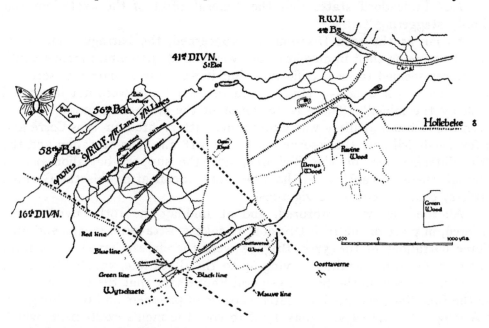

56th and 58th Brigades, after which the 57th Brigade would pass through to the Black and Mauve lines.

The first phase was subdivided by the Red line, which was to be taken by the 9th Royal Welch Fusiliers and the 6th Wiltshire Regiment, the other two battalions of the 58th Brigade being responsible for the Blue and Green lines.

The assembly was made without a hitch—there were but six casualties in the whole division. A desultory bombardment went on throughout the night, growing in intensity as zero hour approached. " At 3.10 a.m. hell itself burst forth along the whole of the Second Army front " as nineteen mines, containing 600 tons of explosives, were fired simultaneously.

The battle was so successful that there is very little to be said of it from the British side, but from the German side it affords, like all disasters, an opportunity for the story-teller. " The English prepared their attack in the usual way. The defenders suffered heavily, more heavily than ever before. Our anxious question . . . received the manly answer : ' We shall hold, so we shall stand fast.' But when the fearful 7th June dawned, the ground rose from beneath the feet of the defenders, their most vital points collapsed, and through the smoke and falling debris of the mines the English storm-troops passed forward over the last remnants of the German defence." [1]

And Ludendorff states that the " moral effect of the explosions was simply staggering."

So far as the 19th Division was concerned, the barrage came down and the mine on their immediate front went up at 3.10 a.m. ; farther south the mines seemed to be a trifle late, but it was only a matter of seconds. The infantry got over No Man's Land to time " and were not interfered with by the mine." There is no doubt of the staggering moral effect— even the German artillery was dumb ; one battery fired on Bois Carré and a few shells fell near the reserve line. By 4.18 a.m. our battalion and the 6th Wiltshire were on the Red line, and the support battalion passed through them, advancing on the Blue line. Soon after this the German artillery commenced to fire vigorously.

All the lines were captured, and at midday the 19th Division was ordered, in place of the 16th Division, to take Oosttaverne village and line. Three battalions of the 57th Brigade were therefore relieved to perform this task, our 9th Battalion moving up to the Black line, vacated by them.

Commenting on the battle, General Shute says that the two-hour halt on the Blue line prevented a greater capture of prisoners and possibly guns. " A long halt," he says, " may tend to cool the men's excitement, which has been worked up to the highest pitch and which, if once lost, is difficult to rekindle."

Most of the 9th Battalion casualties occurred in the Black line. Fifteen other ranks were killed ; 2nd Lieutenants J. B. Tippetts, V. Hazlewood, S. G. Manders, A. G. Brommage, and 99 other ranks were wounded ; 3 other ranks were missing.

Between 80 and 90 Germans were captured, together with 5 machine guns. The total captures in the battle by the Second Army were 7,200 prisoners, 67 guns, 94 trench mortars, and 294 machine guns.

Our 4th Battalion got to work quickly behind the assaulting troops of the 47th Division, and had soon connected our old front line with the

---

[1] Hindenburg, *Out of My Life*.

enemy support line.   There was, however, a big programme of work, and they were kept hard at it constructing tracks and tramways for the next eight days.

The 9th Battalion was relieved on the 9th June, was back in the line on the 14th for four days, when they marched out to Bailleul and remained in camp until the 10th July.

.   .   .   .

The success of the Battle of Messines raised the spirits of the whole Army ; everyone knew that a break-through had not been planned, and that there were no reservations in the official report.   It was a relief to know that some of the high ground was no longer in German hands, but troops in the northern half of the salient, and generally round the ruined town of Ypres, did not find that their condition was much improved.   The shelling, by both sides, was continuous.

Arrangements for the preliminary battle of Messines had been elaborate, but the preparation for the main offensive was the greatest of all ; and every movement was under the eyes of the enemy.   The details of this preparation are enumerated with cold precision by Sir Douglas Haig :

" The various problems inseparable from the mounting of a great offensive, the improvement and construction of roads and railways, the provision of an adequate water supply and of accommodation for troops, the formation of dumps, the digging of dugouts, subways, and trenches, and the assembling and registering of guns, had all to be met and overcome in the new theatre of battle, under conditions of more than ordinary disadvantage.

" On no previous occasion, not excepting the attack on the Messines—Wytschaete Ridge, had the whole of the ground from which we had to attack been so completely exposed to the enemy's observation.   Even after the enemy had been driven from the Messines—Wytschaete Ridge, he still possessed excellent direct observation over the salient from the east and south-east, as well as from the Pilckem Ridge to the north.   Nothing existed in Ypres to correspond to the vast caves and cellars which proved of such value in the days prior to the Arras battle, and the provision of shelter for the troops presented a very serious problem."

The sheltering of troops was a problem never solved.   Camps and hutments sprang up within view of the enemy, and within range of his guns. Every new track laid was seen ; only by chance did a few batteries escape detection—in the words of the showman at the country fair, quoted by a gunner, " Every shy a coco-nut ! "

On the left of the salient our battalions in the 38th Division had seized the opportunity afforded by the Messines diversion to dig assembly trenches, and to advance portions of their line some two hundred yards. The patrolling and raiding activities of the division were maintained.

The introduction of the Fifth Army Staff was made on the 10th June. Sir Hubert Gough took over from Observatory Ridge to Boesinghe, " owing to the great extent of front to be dealt with." Sir Herbert Plumer was then thrust away on the right flank with a secondary part in the operations.

Other changes were carried out : the Belgians, left of Boesinghe, were relieved by General Antoine commanding the First French Army, and British troops relieved French troops on the coastal sector. On the latter front the enemy caused some discomfort by wresting from our grasp a bridge-head on the Yser—an unfortunate incident.

.   .   .   .

THE BATTLE OF PILCKEM RIDGE.[1]

(13TH, 14TH, 15TH, 16TH, AND 17TH BATTALIONS.)

In the beginning of June the 38th Division was informed of the definite rôle it would have to play in the coming battle. There was a redistribution of corps areas, and the sector was now taken over by the Staff of the XIV Corps (Cavan). With Lord Cavan came the Guards Division, which now slipped into line on the left, next the French, the 38th Division giving up the Boesinghe sector.

In the elaborate preparations training occupied an important place. Aeroplanes photographed the enemy lines, prisoners were questioned, and maps of the complicated system of enemy defences were kept up-to-date. From the latter a replica of the 38th Division front was constructed in the back areas between Enquin and Delette, and the various phases of the attack, Blue, Black, Green lines, were marked.

The division left the line during the last days of June and marched to the St. Hilaire area to train. Here the Infantry Orders were carefully studied and troops " walked over the course in slow time " until all knew their positions ; the exercise was then carried out with a watch, timing the creeping barrage. Arrangements were also made to practise the machine-gun barrage, which was found to be of the greatest value, as none of the machine gunners had fired for long periods at a time.

On the 19th/20th July the division returned to the line, taking over its old front from the 29th Division.

[1] Date : 31st July–2nd August. The area defining all the 1917 Ypres Battles is the same : Comines—Ypres Canal to Voormezeele ; thence road to Vlamertinghe Château—Elverdinghe Château—Woesten—Bixschoote.

Conditions had changed : the situation was tense. In the forward zone, from the infantry in the front line to the heavy artillery in rear, there had been a thickening of troops which was increasing daily. Heavy guns poked their snouts from woods, spinneys, clumps of trees, and groups of houses ; they were covered with a queer sort of network interwoven with coloured strips of canvas to break their sharp outline which might be observed from the air.

In the line offensive activity had increased, and from the moment of taking over the trenches casualties were heavy from shell fire and gas. The Germans had once more flung a surprise at us in the form of mustard gas, which created a good deal of alarm.

On our side the artillery programme was continued with increased violence—it had already commenced when the 38th Division left for the training area. Aeroplanes were droning overhead, observing fire.

It was discovered that the enemy was withdrawing his guns to sites offering greater security, and zero day, which had been fixed for the 25th, was postponed, first for three days and then till the 31st July. Aeroplanes also reported that the enemy front line appeared unoccupied, and on the 27th July divisions on the left of the Fifth Army front were ordered to test it.

The 113th and 114th Brigades were ordered to send, each, a company to reconnoitre, and if the report was correct the remainder of the battalion would move forward. In the 113th Brigade, A Company of our 15th Battalion was selected for this duty.

At 5 p.m. the company advanced. They had almost reached Cactus Junction with no opposition, when the enemy opened a murderous fire on them. In a few minutes the company was cut to ribbons. Lieutenant-Colonel Norman, who was watching the reconnaissance, said that he thought the men did not use their rifles, and if they had done so they should have been able to withdraw ; as it was, the majority of the company were either killed or captured.

This air report was found to be true on the Guards Division front and in front of the French. The whole line was advanced and the passage of the canal secured, bridges being thrown across with all speed and in great numbers. All attacking divisions were now over the canal, and the fear that existed of the Guards and the French being delayed by having to fight their way over the canal was at an end.

Our bombardment went on steadily and without intermission.

Enemy shelling was continuous, though not heavy. On the 28th July he shelled the support line for a quarter of an hour, about eleven o'clock in the morning, and from midday onwards gave attention to Skipton, Essex, Yorkshire and Fargate Support Trenches ; this continued at a slow rate until 10.30 p.m., when the nature of his ammunition was changed and gas took the place of high explosive.   About 2 a.m. on the 29th he returned to high explosive and shrapnel and continued for an hour.   The next twenty-four hours were the same, continuous shelling, now on the front-line system, now on the support, now on the canal bridges.   He used up to 15 cm. shells.

Over the same period great activity was maintained in the air, especially in the evening.   Reports for the 28th show that at 7 p.m. several planes were patrolling the enemy lines.   " 7.13 p.m., Albatross Scouts, flying high.   7.18 p.m., one D.F.W. Aviatik flying low over our lines.   7.40 p.m., three Aviatiks flying low over our lines and firing on same—they dropped a string of white lights over Lancashire Farm.   8 p.m., engagement between our A.E.5's and nine Albatross Scouts over the enemy lines—no result, but the Aviatiks retired.   8.30 p.m., three Aviatiks again fly over our lines. 8.45 p.m., four Aviatiks low over our lines—one drops a white light."   And so on.   And the observation balloons, like motionless sausages suspended in the sky, gave a real feeling that the sky was peopled as the earth.   The drone of aeroplanes, the moan of shells, and the motionless balloons !

All this in the sky, and a great deal of movement and labour on the ground, even close up to our front line, as though, now that the hour was near, no one cared.   But on the German side the movement was only in the air—precious little to be seen on earth.   Observers, crouching over a telescope in a hollowed tree on canal bank, or at some point in the line which gave an elevation of a few feet, watched wearily.   On the 29th, " early in the morning, four Germans were seen going towards Cæsar's Avenue, carrying what looked like packs.   And at 8 a.m. a sniper in Harvey Trench reported that he had seen a party estimated at sixty strong, wearing full marching order, and visible from the waist upwards, enter dugouts about Kiel Cot and Caddie Trench.   They entered from the right, and what appeared a relief moved out from the left.   Rapid fire was opened on them."   Nothing else was seen that day.

At 2 a.m. on the 30th 2nd Lieutenant W. J. Williams, of our 16th Battalion, entered the German line with a patrol of ten men : he saw no enemy, but the enemy's front line was being shelled by his own artillery. He found the ground was very muddy.

The general plan of attack, revealed to our battalions with the 38th Division, was that the XIV Corps, with the XVII Corps on the right and the XXXVI French Corps on the left, would attack the German lines.

The 38th Division, with the 51st Division on the right and the Guards Division on the left, would attack the enemy's position on the Pilckem Ridge as far as Langemarck. The attack would be made in a series of bounds—first Blue line, second Black line, third Green line, fourth Green dotted line—and subsequent bounds would be made to the ground gained by our cavalry.

The 114th Brigade on the right and the 113th Brigade on the left would attack up to the Green line. The 115th Brigade, in Divisional Reserve, would, on the capture of the Green line, push through and secure the passage of the Steenbeek, eventually taking over the ground gained by the cavalry.

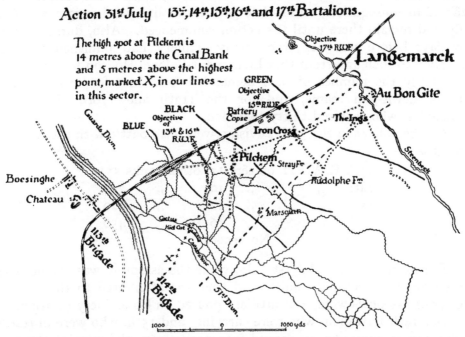

Action 31st July   13th, 14th, 15th, 16th and 17th Battalions.

The left battalion of the 114th Brigade to the Blue line would be the 13th Welch Regiment, and to the Green line the 14th Welch Regiment. The battalion on the right of the 2nd Guards Brigade would be the 1st Scots Guards up to the Black line, thence to the Green line the 3rd Grenadiers.

On the 30th July Major-General C. G. Blackader sent a message to his troops :

" To-morrow the 38th (Welsh) Division will have the honour of being in the front line of what will be the big battle of the war.

" On the deeds of each individual of the division depends whether it shall be said that the 38th (Welsh) Division took Pilckem and Langemarck and upheld gloriously the honour of Wales and the British Empire.

" The honour can be obtained by hard fighting and self-sacrifice on the part of each one of us.

" Gwell angau na chywilydd."

There had been some uncertainty as to the exact date of zero day, and it was difficult to arrange reliefs in a satisfactory order : the 16th Battalion suffered in consequence, and had to go into the line on the night 28th/29th July and remain there until the action commenced. Also, during the last few days before zero day, the enemy artillery had punished the 14th Battalion to such an extent that Lieutenant-Colonel Hodson found he could not supply the number of men demanded from him for carrying duty, for six Lewis-gun teams, and for the 113th and 176th Machine-gun Companies, who required thirty-two men.

Our battalions in the 38th Division went into battle with the following strengths :—

13th R.W.F. : officers 15, other ranks 551
14th   ,,   ,,   10,   ,,   294
15th   ,,   ,,   12   ,,   420
16th   ,,   ,,   16   ,,   456
17th   ,,   No record

During the night 30th/31st July, while the assembly was taking place, the enemy was unusually quiet, and this was attributed to the plentiful shower of gas shells which our artillery poured on his artillery positions.

Our 14th Battalion, who were carrying, and 15th, who were in reserve during the opening phases, moved into position on the west of the canal without any trouble. The 13th Battalion crossed the canal at 10.30 p.m. ; the 16th Battalion were already in place.

The 13th, on the right, and the 16th, on the left, were to capture the Blue and Black lines. Each of these battalions detailed two companies to take the enemy front-line system as far as the Blue line, and two companies to follow, go through the Blue line, and carry on to the Black line. The 15th Battalion would then take up the advance.

The whole of the 115th Brigade was in reserve, and our 17th Battalion would only operate later in the day.

Enveloped in the roar of cannon, with the whistling, soughing, moaning of the overhead stream of shells—the heaviest making a throbbing, grunting sound—the men of the Royal Welch Fusiliers waited in the darkness for zero. The artillery commenced to fire thermit shells and oil drums, which burst into flame—it was the hour. The field-gun barrage rolled out, and the long line of assaulting troops advanced—except on the left of the 38th Division, as the Guards Division were already ahead of them, and, with the French, were not to move until thirty-eight minutes after zero hour.

It was extremely dark at ten minutes to four, as the 13th and 16th Battalions advanced: it was impossible to pick up landmarks, the whole country presenting a dull brown aspect. The barrage was some guide, but could not correct swerves to the right or left; officers did their best to keep direction by an occasional glance at their compasses.

After stumbling over the German front lines, some rifle and machine-gun fire was encountered from the left—the German barrage was late in opening, and not very effective when it did fall. Our 16th Battalion cleared a few Germans from the railway cutting, but otherwise the advance to the Blue line caused little trouble. Between the Blue and Black lines opposition increased: Cancer Avenue and Telegraph House gave trouble to the 16th Battalion, while the 13th Battalion encountered the enemy at Pilckem village and had to fight.

This was the first encounter by the Royal Welch Fusiliers with pill-boxes (or concrete machine-gun shelters). On the 38th Division front it was estimated that there were 280 of these structures: they were generally individual little forts, made of concrete reinforced by iron bars, and able to withstand direct hits from all but the heavier guns; but where the site suited them, the Germans sometimes converted ruined houses into pill-boxes, building them inside the brick walls of the houses. Corner House had been treated in this fashion, and there was, near it, a pill-box of the more ordinary type.[1]

The 13th Battalion was definitely held up in front of the pill-box. Several attempts had been made to outflank it, but its flanks were protected and each effort resulted in the men being shot down. There was no long pause in front of the pill-box—these events happened quickly— but the assaulting line had dropped into the protecting cavities of shell-holes when Corporal James Llewellyn Davies advanced by himself, was hit, but rushed the pill-box, bayoneted one man, and the second threw up his hands. With this garrison disposed of, the battalion was able to move

---

[1] Generally speaking, all farms and houses mentioned were actually pill-boxes, on the sites of the original buildings.

forward, but not far, for Corner House was causing casualties. Corporal Davies took charge, gathered some bombers together and led them, though wounded, against Corner House. This garrison was also disposed of. Still the gallant Corporal found work to do. He had again been wounded, but crawled forward and succeeded in spotting and shooting a sniper on the left. He then died on the field of his wounds. A posthumous award of the Victoria Cross appeared in the *Gazette* of the 6th September.

The Black line was won. The 114th Brigade had found Marsouin Farm a centre of resistance, but this was overcome, and they also were on the Black line.

Our 15th Battalion now came up, accompanied by six Lewis-gun teams from the 14th Battalion, and carried the advance from the Black to the Green line.   The 114th Brigade, on their right, met with considerable opposition from Rudolphe Farm, in the 51st Division area ; a platoon had to be detached to attack the farm, which eventually surrendered, yielding fifteen prisoners. But the 15th Royal Welch Fusiliers found sterner resistance in Battery Copse, and from the houses and concrete structures about the railway crossing : the barrage ran away from them, and the smoke barrage, which, it had been arranged, should be put down at definite intervals, falling in the middle of the battalion, tended to confuse the men. Casualties amongst junior officers were heavy, and about this time Lieutenant-Colonel Norman was wounded. Seeing how things were going, he ordered the battalion to consolidate on Iron Cross Ridge, some way in rear of the Green line.

While the 114th and 113th Brigades were attacking up the Iron Cross Ridge, the 115th Brigade, with the 11th South Wales Borderers on the right and the 17th Royal Welch Fusiliers on the left, were gradually working their way forward.

The advance of our 17th Battalion from the positions held on Iron Cross Ridge to the Steenbeek was the hardest of the day. Most of the houses along the road on top of the ridge and beyond contained concrete machine-gun shelters, and casualties were heavy. But though these points held up the troops facing them, others on the flanks pushed forward, and one by one the houses were taken, and the Steenbeek was crossed. The battalion had to be reinforced by a company from the 10th South Wales Borderers.

It was now past midday, and from 2 p.m. onwards the enemy were seen to be massing for a counter-attack which developed at 3.10 p.m. The attack was repulsed everywhere, except at the Bon-Gîte, where a party of the 11th South Wales Borderers were driven across to the west bank of the Steenbeek. The enemy attempted to launch a second attack later in the afternoon, but it was broken up by our artillery.

All objectives had been won, but the mistake of trying to move cavalry was not committed.[1] During the afternoon the weather broke—it had been dull all morning—and rain fell heavily and continuously.

The heavy shelling which followed the action and the severe casualties in the 115th Brigade necessitated them being relieved, and on the night of the 1st/2nd August the 113th Brigade took over the line.

There is little else to record in this part of the line. The state of the weather put an end to all further operations, and the 38th Division was relieved on the 6th August.

.   .   .   .   .   .

On the extreme right of the salient we left our 9th Battalion (Lieutenant-Colonel L. F. Smeathman), after the Battle of Messines. They had been training at Bailleul for a month and returned to the salient on the 10th July. On the 31st July they were in reserve to the division, which was on the ground gained after Messines.

On this day the 56th Brigade only assaulted. But, owing to the scarcity of guns on that front, which was the pivoting end of the British line, the 63rd Brigade of the 37th Division was attached (less 2 battalions) to the 19th Division; and, for the same reason, the 37th Division advance was not to take place until four hours after zero. The junction of the right of the 19th Division with the 37th Division is the interesting spot for the regiment. At this point the objective marked a short advance of 500 yards; north of Green Wood it was 1,000 yards. The jumping-off line which ran west of Green Wood and Junction Buildings had been secured on the 9th July, posts having been gradually pushed forward after the Messines Battle.

The advance on a frontage of 2,400 yards was supported by 72 18-pounders, 27 4·5 howitzers, and 46 machine guns. Zero was 3.50 a.m.—forty minutes later than our battalions on the left of the salient—and all troops were to be in position by three o'clock.

The 56th Brigade attacked with three battalions in line, the 7th Royal Lancaster (King's Own) on the right, the 7th East Lancashire in the centre, and the 7th East Lancashire on the left; the 7th South Lancashire were held in Brigade reserve.

---

[1] The movement of cavalry through the infantry on the line of the Steenbeek had been abandoned before the battle opened. A note from G.H.Q. dated 22nd July lays down: " There is no intention of moving any cavalry divisions from their present areas prior to zero day, but as a first step towards meeting the possibilities stated above, an area for two divisions should be reconnoitred," etc. Only the 1st Cavalry Brigade was at Dickebusch on 31st July.

All went well, except that on the extreme left Forret Farm was not secured (so that the left of the North Lancashire was refused), and that on the right flank things went decidedly wrong.

Soon after four o'clock a message was received from the right company of the Royal Lancaster that they were on their objective and in touch with the 4th Middlesex on their right : this was the last that was heard from this company.

The message seems to have been true enough, but the company

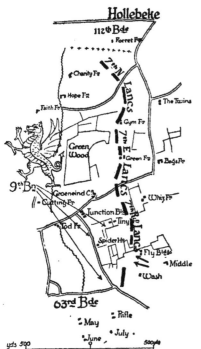

obviously thought itself in touch on both flanks, whereas the company on its left had split, and a gap of some 300 yards was created. About an hour after receiving the message, brigade observers saw small parties of the enemy approaching from the direction of Bab Farm and along the hedges north of Fly Buildings. Enemy machine-gun fire became more intense, and a considerable amount of smoke appeared between these points. Under cover of the smoke the Germans advanced, and at 6.45 a.m. a report was received that Rifle Farm had been lost.

The 37th Division attacked at 7.50 a.m., and at the same time the enemy launched a counter-attack from about Fly Buildings, which was repulsed by the two remaining companies of the Royal Lancaster, but succeeded in pushing back the left of the Middlesex : some of our men were seen to be in the hands of the enemy.

A company of the South Lancashire and of the Middlesex failed to drive the enemy back, and a second attempt, made by the South Lancashire about midday, also failed.

Meanwhile Captain Irwin and Lieutenant Philips from our C Company had been sent up at 9 a.m. to reconnoitre the ground and acquaint themselves with the situation. Rather late in the day C and D Companies were ordered to the front line. They arrived about 4 p.m. The news they received was that observers had seen the enemy dribbling in small parties along the hedges between Fly Buildings and Spider House.

Captain Irwin promptly occupied the hedges running east from Tiny Farm, the farm itself being held by some of the South Lancashire. D Company filled the gap from Tiny Farm to the divisional boundary, obtaining touch with troops of the 37th Division.

At 8 p.m. the 63rd Brigade tried to recapture Rifle Farm, and hurried orders were issued to D Company to co-operate by sending a platoon forward along the road, which was the divisional boundary. Time was, however, too short, and before the platoon could reach the objective, momentarily secured by the 63rd Brigade, the enemy counter-attacked and drove all the assaulting troops back to their original front line.

The battalion was relieved that night by the 9th Welch Regiment.

2nd Lieutenants H. Kilvert, A. G. Davies, S. G. Davies, and 20 other ranks were killed in this action ; 2nd Lieutenant N. A. Buck and 32 other ranks were wounded.

.   .   .   .

The opening of the Ypres offensive was, on the whole, quite satisfactory, the Second and Fifth Armies having gained the objectives given them ; but now the question so often put by the regimental officer as to the advisability of attacking at Ypres after the experience of the Somme arose with tragic fatality.   Haig's despatch admits it.

" The weather had been threatening throughout the day, and had rendered the work of the aeroplanes very difficult from the commencement of the battle.   During the afternoon, while fighting was still in progress, rain began and fell steadily all night.   Thereafter for four days the rain continued without cessation, and for several days afterwards the weather remained stormy and unsettled.   The low-lying, clayey soil, torn by shells and sodden with rain, turned to a succession of vast muddy pools.   The valleys of the choked and overflowing streams were speedily transformed into long stretches of bog, impassable except by a few well-defined tracks, which became marks for the enemy's artillery.   To leave these tracks was to risk death by drowning, and in the course of the subsequent fighting on several occasions both men and pack animals were lost in this way. In these conditions operations of any magnitude became impossible, and the resumption of our offensive was necessarily postponed until a period of fine weather should allow the ground to recover.

" As had been the case in the Arras battle, this unavoidable delay in the development of our offensive was of the greatest service to the enemy.   Valuable time was lost, the troops opposed to us were able to recover from the disorganisation produced by our first attack, and the enemy was given the opportunity to bring up reinforcements."

Indeed one might say that all chance of success vanished after the first day's fighting, for as the battle continued, so the stretch of bog was widened, creating in itself an obstacle harder to overcome than the determined resistance of the German troops.

The German resistance was carefully thought out. The ground had been plentifully sprinkled with pill-boxes, but was otherwise lightly held, with reserves in readiness to launch a counter-attack the moment our objective was known—not a difficult conjecture. And we, in these first battles, invariably advanced with divisions on a two-brigade front during the " first phase," when the reserve brigade would go through the other two to take and hold the final objective : this last brigade was then near the limit of effective barrage fire, and had to meet the strength of the enemy, launched in counter-attack.

It was not until the 16th August that the Fifth Army attacked again —none of our battalions was involved—and though slight success was attained on the left, on the right, and in the centre, counter-attacks generally resulted in our troops being forced back from the line won in the initial stages.

The 38th Division had moved back to Proven on the 6th August, but moved up to the battle-front again on the 19th and 20th, taking over from the 20th Division, who had captured Langemarck. The weather was still vile. An attempt was made by the 16th Royal Welch to make a slight advance on the 27th August, but " the men, lying in shell-holes that were gradually filling with water, found great difficulty in getting out and keeping up with the barrage, and were unable to reach their objective." Nothing further was attempted.

The division was relieved on the 11th September, moved back to Proven, thence on the 13th to Croix-du-Bac.

Our 4th Battalion went to Bouvelinghem on the 15th August, and for the first time in ten months had a week out of the battle area. They returned to Vlamertinghe and continued the struggle, which seemed so hopeless, of improving the communications to the front line : amongst other jobs was the construction of a tramway from Hellfire Corner, on the Menin road, to the advanced positions. This cheerful and hard-working battalion left the salient on the 18th September for a sector just north of Arras.

The 9th Battalion trained at Affringues.

There was now a long pause in the major operations at Ypres. Meanwhile, in the rearrangement of troops prior to the 31st July, British troops had taken over a strip of front next to the sea at Nieuport. It was a country of sand-dunes and marsh, where several canals met, running into the canalised Yser. North of Ypres a wide tract of the low-lying land, naturally marsh, had been flooded by the Belgians, and the Allied lines

SITUATION 19TH SEPTEMBER AFTER TWO MAJOR OPERATIONS.

lay to the west of the Yser. On the sand-dune strip of the coast, however, our Allies had succeeded in holding the east bank of the Yser, between Nieuport and the sea—all the various canals join the Yser at Nieuport. The foothold on the east bank was divided by a dyke, or creek, and on the

10th July the enemy, after a furious bombardment, which destroyed all the bridges across the Yser and the creek, attacked and captured the area between the creek and the coast up to the Yser.

Our 2nd Battalion was placed under the XV Corps, holding the coastal sector, and arrived at the Bray Dunes on the 31st July. They had moved on the 2nd July to Acheux, on the 3rd to Talmas ; on the 4th via Vignacourt to Belloy ; on the 5th, via Hangest to Airaines. On the march the usual daily crowd of men with sore feet presented themselves to the doctor.

Three and a half weeks were spent at Airaines, where everyone was in " holiday mood " and little training was done. Guard-mounting was the event of the day in Airaines.

No troops had been quartered in the town for some time and the inhabitants were well disposed. The weather was fine, and when once the billets had been cleaned up they were comfortable. Officers could get leave to visit Amiens, or the sea at Tréport. The notables of the town invited Major Poore to shoot wild boar, an adventure which filled him with delight : he returned with one rabbit done up in a brown-paper parcel—it was the day's bag. There was a divisional horse show on the 17th and 18th, in which the battalion secured 1st and 2nd prizes for officers' chargers, and 3rd and 4th for draught horses. This was followed on the 20th and 21st by a battalion athletic meeting, and later by a brigade boxing contest.

It is interesting to find that a mess meeting at Airaines decided against having a band again—there had been none since leaving Bethune.

On the 31st July the battalion left by route march for Pont Remi, and entrained for Dunkirk ; thence by barge to a tented camp at Bray Dunes.

" The population was Flemish-speaking. The cottages were gaily painted in vivid blues, greens, and yellows. It rained continuously for four days, and at frequent intervals for the next two weeks. After one exceptional period of downpour the entire battalion turned out bare-legged to drain the camp. The daily sea-bathing was much enjoyed ; but an attempt by officers to play polo on the sands proved their inability to do so : paper-chases, however, were good fun.

" A dash of sport attended visits to Dunkirk. At any moment the electric alarms might sound ; they were worked by spotters at Nieuport of a big gun at Ostend : two minutes elapsed between the flash and the arrival of the shell—two minutes in which to find a ' cave ' to plunge into !

" The sea and the White Ensign were a never-failing interest. Once in a while a monitor would slip its moorings, pass sedately along the coast, fire a few shots with provoking deliberation, and sedately return.

CORPORAL J. L. DAVIES, V.C., 13TH BATTALION.
POLYGON WOOD.

YPRES BATTLEFIELD, NEAR GLENCORSE WOOD.
Imperial War Museum photograph, Crown copyright.

" By now most of the remaining Old Army N.C.O.s had become applicants for commissions, not from choice but in self-defence, as many of their subordinates with short service of doubtful quality were making successful applications for a rank that could be counted in tens of thousands.

" On 15th August a move was made to billets at Oost Dunkerque, within the shelled area. As the Germans were making frequent use of a new shell-gas, the draught animals were provided with masks, worn at the ' alert ' position on the nose-bands of the head-stall. The use of this noxious gas (mustard) was compelling the evacuation of the civilian population which had remained to cultivate the land.

" On the evening of the 16th a move was made to Nieuport, a roofless shell of a town. A communication trench with a stout timbered roof led through the town, about which the faint nasturtium-like smell of the new mustard gas hung—and so to the crazy floating bridges across the Yser.

" Progress was slow when the bridges were being shelled. A permanent staff of engineers stood by to keep them in repair. These engineers amused themselves when it was quiet by putting up such notices as, ' You may loiter on the bridge—it inspires confidence,' ' Don't look for a handrail—all wood is required for repairs, and there's none for crosses,' etc.

" The battalion went into the Lombartzyde right sector. Headquarters was in the Redan, a small brick fort built originally by Vauban for Louis XIV, kept in repair and recently reinforced by concrete ; it was so impervious to shell fire that it was called the ' Rubber House.'

" On 28th August the division was relieved. The battalion marched in rain to La Panne. A short march was made on the 29th to Adinkerke, whence there was conveyance by barge to Condikerke. Condikerke was quitted on the 31st. By a strange bit of Staff work the battalion and the buses that were to carry them moved on the road side by side for two kilometres to the rendezvous. The buses had all plied formerly on the London streets, and they bore the device of the reverse of a penny and the motto ' All the way.' The route was via Bourbourg and Watten to the villages of Houle and Moule, not far from St. Omer. Again the buses dropped us about three kilometres short of our billets ; Staff work which excited the outspoken comments of the V Corps Commander, Lieutenant-General Fanshawe, into whose area we had come." (Dunn.)

On the 14th September the 33rd Division started to march towards Ypres. They passed through Lederzeele, Steenvoorde, and Thieushouk. " Two days of leisure were passed in this pleasant hop-growing district. Volunteers were offered three francs a day to get in the hops, and a kiln was given as a free billet in return for attention to the furnace. Not far

III—22

off was the Augustinian monastery on the Mont des Cats ; in a field a friar worked, wearing his brown gown over khaki. Through this charming hill-country the rumble of guns at Ypres echoed day and night. The gun-flashes flickered and blinked against the night sky. From the high ground star lights could be traced to Bethune, rising and bursting into brilliance, quivering, fading, and falling. It was an eerie spectacle and fascinating ; not least so to those familiar with it, and most aware of its significance.

" Before 4 a.m. on the 20th the battalion was preparing to move. The sky was clear and star-spangled after heavy rain. It was drizzling again when the move began in daylight. The officer commanding the company wearing their ground sheets was heavily dropped on by the Brigadier. Our crocks, those who had not been sent to hospital, were pushed off to find their way on by-roads, and in their own time, to Westoutre. This method of conserving man-power was a serious offence to the brigade ; it had to be resorted to by myself and the Adjutant conniving without the C.O.'s knowledge." (Dunn.)

And so after three days at Westoutre the 33rd Division relieved the 23rd Division in the line north of the Ypres—Menin road on the 24th September.

Our 10th Battalion, after a period of training at Barastre, entrained with the 76th Brigade at Bapaume on the 17th September, for Watou, where they remained until the 23rd.

THE BATTLE OF THE MENIN ROAD RIDGE.[1]

By this time the battle had boiled up again. The first weeks of September showed a slight improvement in the weather, and preparations for an advance by the Second and Fifth Armies were hurried on, as fast as the slush would permit. The left of the Second Army was extended to take in the whole of the high ground crossed by the Menin road, and the 20th September was selected as the day for an attack from the Ypres—Comines Canal to the Ypres—Staden railway north of Langemarck.

The 19th Division went into the line on the east of the Ypres—Comines Canal, and stood on the extreme right of the whole attack ; their task was to secure the right flank of the 39th Division and X Corps.

The advance here was not deep, but was fiercely contested by the enemy. Zero was at 5.40 a.m., and the first phase of the attack went well ; but the second phase found the Welch Regiment engaged in a desperate

[1] Date : 20th–25th September.

scrap at Hessian Wood. Their commanding officer was killed. Eventually they reached the north side of the wood, having suffered severe casualties. Our 9th Battalion (Lord Howard de Walden), in reserve, was hurried up to hold the line, and arrived in time to ward off the German counter-attack which followed. Shelling was heavy: 12 other ranks were killed; 2nd Lieutenants J. W. Phillips, H. R. Davies, N. A. Buck, and 73 other ranks wounded.

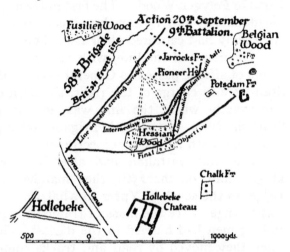

An advance was made all along the line; on the left of the Second Army Australian troops captured Nonne-Bosschen and were on the edge of Polygon Wood, while farther north, in the Fifth Army zone, the line ran before Zonnebeke, and approached Poelcappelle. The Germans carried out their plan, and counter-attacked all along the line, attaining minor successes here and there; actually it meant several days' fighting on the same ground. The enemy launched three strong attacks about Polygon Wood before the 26th, the date fixed for the next drive forward by the two Armies.

BATTLE OF POLYGON WOOD.[1]

(2ND AND 10TH BATTALIONS.)

Our 2nd Battalion was at Westoutre; the 33rd Division was waiting to relieve the 23rd Division on the north of the Menin road. They were now under the X Corps, which had attacked on the 20th with success, except for the left brigade of the 41st Division, in the centre of the corps front and on the right of the 23rd Division.

The 33rd Division relieved the 23rd during the night 24th/25th September. The orders for the forthcoming battle were that the 33rd Division, on the left of the X Corps, would cover the right flank of the Australian Corps (5th Australian Division) in their advance through the remainder of Polygon Wood; this task entailed the occupation of a line

---

[1] Date: 26th September–3rd October.

giving observation to the south and east, over the Reutelbeek Valley. The 19th Brigade were to be in Divisional Reserve.

The Divisional General[1] was to have assumed command of the line at 7 a.m. on the 25th, but the relief was not complete when, at 5.15 a.m., the enemy launched an attack along the whole division front, from Menin Road to Polygon Wood. The first authentic news was received at Divisional Headquarters at 7.15 a.m. by pigeon from the Queen's, who reported that the enemy had captured their front line.

Command of the line, with an obscure but obviously unpleasant condition of affairs, passed to General Wood about 10 a.m. The 100th Brigade Staff were in charge of the right, the 98th of the left of the division front, but exactly where the line was no one knew. The Cameronians and Scottish Rifles, of the 19th Brigade, were placed under the orders of the 100th and 98th Brigades respectively.

Our 2nd Battalion had already moved from Westoutre. Starting at 5.45 a.m. on the 25th, they marched via La Clyte, Dickebusch, Café Belge, to the south of Ypres to what was known as Shrapnel Corner. " It was strange to see the mass of traffic at high noon, on a road on which for so long men had hurried in the dark." They remained here until 8 p.m., when they moved by road and tracks round the south of Zillebeke Lake, Hell Blast Corner, the Dormy House, and so through Sanctuary Wood to Stirling Castle, where 98th Brigade Headquarters was situated, arriving there after midnight. The march in the dark was without disturbing incident, but some men were missing at the end of it. " Brigade advised us to dig in well, for the battle would be resumed in the morning ; but the men's reluctance to make cover for themselves and their ability to lie down and sleep on so cold a night, even if they were tired, were remarkable. I had to keep moving for warmth." (Dunn.)

Meanwhile several attempts had been made by the 98th Brigade to recover the lost line without success. It was said that the advanced troops were just east of Verbeek Farm. The plans for the attack on the 26th, with an advance from the Brown line to the Red line, had to be modified. Times, of course, could not be changed, and so zero hour remained at 5.50 a.m.

The 98th Brigade reported a thick mist before 5 a.m., and later a heavy barrage by the enemy which prevented the fresh assaulting troops getting into position. Lieutenant-Colonel Spence, commanding the 5th Scottish Rifles, says that the 98th Brigade guides wandered about Inverness

---

[1] Major-General Pinney went to hospital on the 2nd September, and Brigadier-General P. R. Wood was in command of the division.

Copse so effectively with the attacking battalions (his and the 4th Suffolk) that only two companies of his battalion got off the mark to time : a half-company was twenty minutes late, and the remainder with the Suffolk did not come into the picture. All suffered in the German barrage—an uncommonly good one. Orders were vague. The position of the front-line troops, Middlesex and Argyll and Sutherland, was unknown, and the 5th Scottish Rifles were to pass through it wherever found ! Under the circumstances there could be no creeping barrage.

The attacking companies found parties of the Middlesex and Argyll and Sutherland on the line of Lone Farm, and eventually dug in there. The 4th King's (Liverpool Regiment), on the far side of the Reutelbeek, were still on the Brown line, waiting for the attack to come up in line.

At this time (8 a.m.) our 2nd Battalion was placed under the orders of the 98th Brigade, who were told that the gap between the 15th Australian Brigade and the 100th Brigade must be filled at all costs.

Our battalion was still in the Stirling Castle area, and received instructions that it was to move north of Glencorse Wood, through the Australian area to Black Watch Corner, and launch an attack from this flank—an awkward task.

Time was passing. The Australians were on the Red line and hoping to gain touch with the 98th Brigade about Jerk House ; the 4th King's had not moved. At 9.30 a.m. three tanks left Glencorse Wood and were placed under the 98th Brigade.

Orders, issued at 8 a.m., arrived in due course, and our battalion moved at 10—zero was fixed for midday.

" Major Poore, who was in command of our battalion, called a conference of company commanders. The conference was somewhat protracted, an initial embarrassment being that there were no maps for the company officers. Eventually it was given out that B and D Companies would advance in line in the direction of Polderhoek Château, and that the support Company A or the reserve Company C would follow, advancing in the direction of Jut Farm, thus covering the left flank, and allowing the Australians to bring up their delayed right. The advice of the Officer Commanding 11th Field Company R.E. regarding the line of approach was invaluable ; while it entailed a time-consuming detour round Glencorse Wood, it avoided the barrage on Inverness Copse and the direct road to the north of it." (Radford.)

" With Headquarters leading, followed by D Company (Coster), B (Williams), A (Lloyd Evans), and C (Radford), the battalion moved off in single file. The Menin road was crossed east of Clapham Junction on the fringe of the barrage, one man being hit. Behind Inverness Copse half a dozen tanks lay foundered in a bog.[1] The bog, over which the battalion had to pass, extended a great part of the way behind Glencorse Wood. The spongy ground and soft places that had to be jumped caused delay. Soon the track was lined with Lewis-gun magazines and rifle grenades cast aside by their carriers. Between Glencorse Wood and Nonne Bosschen the barrage had to be gone through : less than a dozen casualties were sustained in it.

" At 11.45 a.m. D Company formed, under some machine-gun fire, on an east and west line, their left close to Blackwatch Corner ; B Company was coming up. The only covering fire given was a few smoke shells, so uncertain was everybody's position. Two platoons of B Company arrived in time to advance with D at zero. Mann saw them off, and had only just got the other platoons of B away also when he was shot through the throat and died almost immediately. Coster was killed about the same time, shot through the head as he was entering a scraggy orchard, north of Jerk Farm. B Company had got clear of a crescent-shaped line of pill-boxes centred about Blackwatch Corner that enclosed Carlisle and Jerk Farms in its horns, when Williams and Colquhoun, among others, were hit. At this early stage touch was lost between the two companies—they could not see each other.

" As A Company came up, Poore ordered first one platoon and then another into the gap he saw occur between B and D Companies. They remained on B's left, but never gained touch with D.

" D had closed to the left rapidly after getting through the Jerk Farm enclosure, changed front and advanced eastward. They found some of the 31st Australians in shell-holes ; with these the company arrived at a north and south trench, midway between Carlisle and Jerk Farms in rear, and Jut Farm and Cameron House in front. There the mixed force remained, firing to their front and right, into the wooded slope of Polderhoek Château, whence the enemy's fire came.

" Nothing of this was known at Headquarters for several hours. B Company was met, on coming into the open beyond the pill-boxes, by machine-gun and rifle fire from the same wooded slope, and soon came to a stop with their left on Jerk Farm and facing south-east. In shell-holes were some wounded Germans and some dead Australians.

" The remaining platoons of A Company were soon sent to support B, while the original two remained echeloned on B's left—these two (the

---

[1] This is the only allusion made by the battalion to tanks. They did not attack, and those ordered forward may have stuck in this or another bog.

former) platoons edged off to the right, merely extending the line south-westwards, and when Evans was wounded (he died a few hours later) they came to a standstill with their right on Lone Farm.

" When the medical officer got up, Williams, who had remained in command of his company, was sent to hospital. Colquhoun, whose wound was not severe, remained longer and directed an unskilled enthusiast how to handle an abandoned German machine gun, until it jammed ; he then went to Headquarters to report on his way to hospital.

" At 1.30 p.m. Radford had received no orders, so he reported personally at Headquarters, in a pill-box behind Blackwatch Corner.

" Seeing that no more ground was to be made, Poore sent C Company to a less exposed position in rear of the line of deployment (two platoons came up again at nightfall ; the other two were got up next morning).

" Headquarter details had been sent already to a shell-hole position 250 yards behind Polygon Wood ; Poore now went there to await events and instructions. It was an ill-chosen position, for 5·9 shells were plentiful behind the Wood. The Australian Headquarters (near by) was also their aid-post ; the ground round it was encumbered with their wounded, and it was the site of much movement of which the enemy gunners may have been aware. In the companies' area the enemy relied on machine guns and a few rifles, skilfully placed amongst the leafy trees between Polderhoek and Reutel. With the companies lying low, the German small-arms fire had subsided, though even individual movement was apt to draw fire." (From notes by Dunn.)

" About 2.30 p.m. I saw Radford over by A Company on the right, where he had gone to have a look at things. I had had no food since dinner last night, and was going to the Headquarter area, where there was a chance of finding my servant and getting some tea. There the sight of someone drinking stimulated the craving of a young Australian who had been laid down a little way off, and he called out. Because of the nature of his wound I had to refuse him the drink, and was trying to placate him when a signaller came and told me Poore was dead. While he and Casson (Assistant Adjutant) and Colquhoun, who had joined them, were sitting in a shell-hole talking, a shell fell on them, killing all three. So I went off to look for Radford to tell him he was in command.

" At one moment, about 150 yards off, two men suddenly rose into the air, fifteen feet, perhaps, amidst a spout of soil : they rose and fell with the constrained, graceful poise of acrobats ; a rifle, revolving slowly, rose high above them before it fell. I saw Radford at one of the pill-boxes behind B Company. It was then about 3.30 p.m. We went to the

Headquarter area and sat in a shell-hole, while a report to Brigade was written. The writing was interrupted several times by the quantity of soil that was being thrown about us. On completion of the report Radford moved Headquarters to a pill-box behind B Company, where it was pretty quiet.

" I was going to join Radford by way of the rifle-pit—it was hardly a trench—in which the aid-post sergeant had settled. The sergeant shouted to me to ' Look out ! ' and pointed to a German aeroplane that was only a hundred feet up, or thereby, and as many yards away. ' Get down,' he shouted ; ' the —— thing has hit me ! ' It went away, turned over Becelaere, and came over us again, amidst a fusillade. It turned again at Lone Farm and crashed on the north side of Polygon Wood. The pilot was found to have been shot. My sergeant showed me the nose of a bullet projecting between two of his ribs in front (I think it had been fired from Polderhoek). He did not realise that it had gone through from his back, and he did not feel ill, but it was to cause septic pneumonia : he died ten days later, close to Beachy Head, where he played as a boy. His condition in that rifle-pit recalls to me the last incident of the kind memory retains in which we had been concerned together. I had turned from examining a man who had been brought in dying. The sergeant remarked sardonically, as he ran the pages of a little book between his finger and thumb, ' They've all got these —— things on them now, them what's going to die ! ' ' What things ? ' I asked. ' Noo Testimint ! ' [1]

" The rest of the day passed in comparative quiet. Nothing had been seen of any of the 98th Brigade parties, but in a trench at Carlisle Farm there were a lot of Middlesex dead.

" As it was becoming dark, a sudden commotion arose as D Company fell back on their line of deployment. They reported that the enemy was massing in Polygon Wood, and that they had very little ammunition left. The decision to fall back was made in consultation with the officer in charge of the Australian detachment, who fell back with them, and remained interspersed with the companies during the night. D Company's movements induced A and B Companies to swing back also, except two sections of A on the extreme right. As no one knew what the supply arrangements were (all those who knew were casualties), the rations and ammunition Yates sent up to the rendezvous were not collected. Some ammunition was collected from the dead, and from equipment abandoned by the wounded.

---

[1] Observe there were sufficient New Testaments about to attract the man's attention. On the other hand, the essence of the man's bitter reflection was shared by many, who thought seriously, but not enough.

" Before urgent requests to the 5th Scottish Rifles could be complied with, the S.O.S. call went up on two occasions between dark and midnight in the Reutel direction, and was repeated by some other units.   It was a red over green over yellow at that time, a pretty combination of colours over the outline of the trees that was so dark against a midnight sky. Each time the gunners opened on their night lines in a frenzy of emulation, and every gun on both sides fired rapid.   The noise was as a rending of our portion of the firmament.   The staccato of the machine guns filled the intervals of the larger reports of the shell-bursts, and the rush of bullets through the nearly still air was like the whistling of a cutting wind.   A veil of smoke drifted over us, polluting the freshness of the autumn night.

Neither time was there any movement on the battalion front, and no one joined in the tumult.

" After the second spell of drum-fire ceased, Sergeant 'Ten' Jones arrived with others off leave.   They brought with them the company's mail (D) and one jar of rum.   One ! "   (Dunn.)

An official report gives the situation with our battalion about 100 yards to the west of Carlisle Farm, with posts about the same distance from Jerk Farm ; the 5th Scottish Rifles behind them from the junction of the Brown line with the Reutelbeek, to Lone Farm, to Black Watch Corner.

Our 2nd Battalion was ordered to attack the next morning and recover the position between the 100th Brigade and the Australian right.   The manner in which orders reached battalions is instructive.

" About 1 a.m. an Australian officer arrived at Headquarters with the news that the Australians had orders to attack in the morning ' in conjunction with the Imperial troops on the right.   Are you them ? ' he asked.   He could only be told we had no orders.

" Between 2 and 3 a.m. 2nd Lieutenant Liddall, who was patrolling the front, reported a small enemy patrol in front of Jerk Farm.   Otherwise there was no sign of the enemy during the night.   At dawn there was a preventive barrage, followed by comparative quiet.

" Being still without orders, Radford went to the 5th Scottish Rifles at Fitzclarence Farm to ascertain by telephone what Brigade intended. He was told that Major Kearsley, who had been in reserve, was already on the way up to take command with orders to advance in conformity with the Australians. In anticipation of such a move, and because the Australians were concentrating east of Blackwatch Corner, the battalion had been closed up on the corner.

" Kearsley arrived at Fitzclarence Farm while Radford was there. Together they came up, calling on the way at the Australians' Headquarters. There they met the Australian Brigadier, who had been up to Polygon Wood. He told them there were few, if any, Germans in front of the position ; he had ' been to look ' !

" Kearsley arrived and took command about 8 o'clock. After having the position explained to him, he moved the battalion yet further east, and sent to get the deficiencies in Lewis-gun magazines, rifle grenades, and small-arm ammunition made up.

" At 9 a.m. a patrol was sent to investigate the position east of Jerk Farm. It did not return until 11.30 a.m., when it reported that the Australians were in Cameron Covert, and that Polygon Wood was under enemy machine-gun fire. Without waiting for the return of the patrol, Kearsley had sent C and D Companies at 11 o'clock to occupy the trench D had occupied and withdrawn from the previous day. In the meantime the 5th Scottish Rifles had come up to the line Carlisle Farm, and lent us their D Company, under Captain McChlery.

" The Australians had got on the move early and were impatient of their right flank being still uncovered. At 11.30 a.m. a message was received from Brigade to push forward at once. Officers commanding companies were summoned to Headquarters in a pill-box north of Jerk Farm, and instructed as to their procedure ; they were told, too, to collect what loose ammunition could be found on the ground, for the supplies sent for had not arrived.

" The position of units was still considered by the Command too uncertain for the artillery or the machine gunners to give any covering fire. It would be about 12.30 p.m. when D Company, with the 5th Scottish Rifles, began to dribble forward, supported by B and C Companies. As the advance developed, men of both B and C Companies came in between the leading companies, and all the companies became somewhat mixed. Jut Farm was seen to be occupied as C Company's right approached it. Sergeant Moon was active in the small party that rushed it on the blind side ; the garrison of fourteen did not demur when called upon to surrender. The lower ground, in front of Jut Farm, in which the shallow Reutelbeek flowed sluggishly, was the battalion objective. Companies were on it an hour after beginning the advance, and settled in a shell-hole line. The 5th Scottish Rifles, their left south of Jut Farm, were on the stream facing southwards ; then C, B, and D Companies extended in a north-easterly direction, facing Polderhoek Château and the Reutelbeek Spur.   D Company was in touch with the Australians in Cameron Covert. On the right the 100th Brigade was understood to be not far off across the stream.

" The advance, during which no German was seen except in Jut Farm, was scarcely hampered by small-arm fire, and, as on the previous day, the German artillery respected the ground east of Lone Farm, between the Reutelbeek and Polygon Wood, as scrupulously as did our own artillery. So there were few casualties." [1]

During the day, while inspecting his line, Major Kearsley was wounded and had to be evacuated, so command once more devolved on Radford. " It was then 5 o'clock.   The quiet in which the companies had made their advance they continued to enjoy ; but all day long the Headquarter area was shelled persistently, with sustained bursts, and marksmen on the slopes of Polderhoek made good practice while daylight lasted on anyone moving about the area."

That night the 33rd Division was relieved by the 23rd. " In the absence of trenches the relief was a quick one.   A few casualties occurred. The fourteen German prisoners were employed in carrying as many of their wounded compatriots found in Carlisle Farm as they could take. Once clear of the barrage lines, officers were astonished at the strength of their companies. The shell-holes in rear had yielded their secrets. During the morning I had remarked to an officer that his company was on a very narrow front. He explained that his strength was only 25 : after relief furtive accretions raised the strength of that Company to 60." (Dunn.)

Casualties had been fairly heavy. Besides Major Poore and Captain Mann, Captain E. Coster, 2nd Lieutenants R. A. Casson, E. F. C. Colquhoun, H. Ll. Evans, I. Williams, and 31 other ranks had been killed ; Major Kearsley, Lieutenant M. Williams, 2nd Lieutenant E. H. Evans, and 122 other ranks were wounded ; 27 other ranks were missing.

Mann was one of the outstanding figures of the 2nd Battalion during the two years he served with it.   There was, the Doctor writes, much discrimination in Colonel Williams's early and, at the time, not very popular selection of him for the work at Headquarters. Of shortish, athletic build,

---

[1] With the death of Poore, and so many officer casualties, the Doctor, always keenly interested in the military situation, became Radford's "right hand man"! He provides this interesting account.

he was all activity in whatever he was doing, and when he joined the battalion was a careless chatterbox. But as time passed he was overtaken by increasing silence. Most capable and conscientious of Adjutants, he was devoted to his battalion and regiment. At any time in 1917 he might have gone to brigade or division, where he was wanted, but his loyalty to the battalion rose as its efficiency became less, and he would not be influenced to leave it.

While all this was going on in Polygon Wood, our 10th Battalion attacked at Zonnebeke.

This Battalion had been relieved in the Morchies—Louverval—Lagnicourt part of the line on the 7th September (by the 56th Division), and had spent ten days training in the back area. It was an open secret that they were destined for the Ypres battle. Time was short for preparation, but advantage was taken of the fact that the camps were in the old devastated area of the Somme battles, and suitable ground was selected for brigades to practise assembling at night on taped positions, and, by daylight, attacking strong-points with rifle and rifle grenade. The 3rd Division commenced to move on the 17th and was concentrated in the Watou area by the 19th.

The battalion was then in the V Corps, and orders had been issued for the corps to attack towards Zonnebeke on zero day. The Australians would be on the right and the 59th Division on the left of the 3rd Division, and the line of advance for the latter would be astride the railway, straight on Zonnebeke village. The actual zero date had not then been communicated.

The 9th Division was holding the line which the 3rd Division was to take over on the night 22nd/23rd September, and, when the 26th was announced as zero day, General Deverell (3rd Division) decided that the relief should be carried out by the 9th Brigade of his division, and that the 8th and 76th Brigades should be kept fresh for the attack, and brought up on the morning of the 26th.

This decision entailed a lot of careful preparation, for which great credit is due to Major A. J. S. James, of our 10th Battalion, who was detailed for the work.

From the 21st September onwards all officers and N.C.O.s of the two assaulting brigades were ordered to go up into the line, and make themselves acquainted with the conditions and features of the country ; but this was not possible, and only a few of the 10th Battalion ever saw the front they were to attack until the battle was in progress. Other measures and preparations were, however, more thorough. Definite lines of approach were allotted and marked by coloured lamps, shaded on the enemy side ;

the assembly lines were marked with ropes and discs for each platoon, and, at the last moment, the ropes were wound with white tap to make them more visible.

Major James was in charge of the tracks and track guides for the whole of the 76th Brigade. Each battalion had sent a party of 25 N.C.O.s and men, and they all lived with Major James in a mine-shaft at Railway Wood. Each batch of guides worked on its own track, and all were rehearsed several times before zero day.

The 10th Battalion had been one of the first of the division to arrive at Watou, on the 17th. They practised the attack at Brandhoek on the 23rd. That night German aeroplanes bombed the camp severely; fortunately casualties were limited to mules in the transport lines. The other battalions of the brigade had been moved forward to the east of Ypres to avoid congestion through the town on zero night, and the 10th Battalion entrained for Ypres on the night of the 25th. Again German aeroplanes attacked them, dropping bombs close to the train—" a nerve-racking experience," says Captain Watcyn Williams. The troops detrained at the Asylum Station, and, " meeting our guides, who under Lieutenant Owen had been over the ground several times, we moved up to our positions along duck-board tracks (after passing through Ypres). Most of the tapes had been blown to atoms by shell fire, but the guides led us to the line of shell-holes which we were to start from without a hitch. None of the officers or men had seen the position before."

The leading troops of the 76th Brigade were the 8th King's Own (R. Lanc. R.) on the right and the 1st Gordon Highlanders on the left, with their left on the railway. The brigade front was crossed by the Steenbeek and the Zonnebeke. The first-named stream, normally a narrow, insignificant rivulet, had been blocked by the destruction of culverts and the pounding of its banks by shell fire, with the result that it was now a morass, in some places 50 feet wide. But the left of the Gordon Highlanders took over a position on the east of the stream, where it runs under the railway, while the rest of the battalion and the King's Own assembled on the west. It was an awkward position from which to advance, but any attempt to divert the stream was out of the question—it would have been a considerable engineering work—and troops had to get through as best they could with the help of duck-boards, which had been laid, after careful reconnoitring, over the narrower parts of the morass.

The 2nd Suffolk, on the right, and our 10th Battalion on the left, were to go through the leading battalions at the first objective, or Green line, and capture the village of Zonnebeke. Their line of advance was crossed by the Zonnebeke, but this streamlet could not be reconnoitred.   It seemed reasonable to suppose, however, that it would not be any wider than down below, where it ran into our lines, and was easily negotiable.   As a matter of fact, on the 8th Brigade front this stream was a considerable obstacle.

Our battalion was in position by 12.30 a.m. (separated from our 2nd Battalion by the Australian Corps).

The divisional artillery opened a false or Chinese attack at 3.40 a.m. ; whatever the intention may have been, the only result was a considerable amount of retaliation from the enemy.   Otherwise the night was quiet and clear.   But by 5.50 a.m.—zero hour—there was a heavy ground mist.

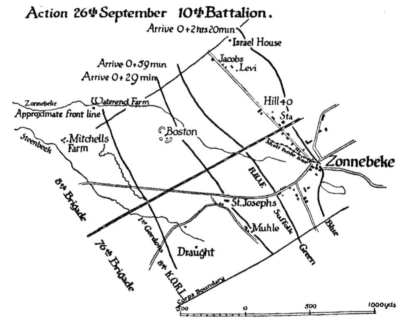

Action 26th September 10th Battalion.

The leading battalions, starting the advance behind a barrage, lost direction to a certain extent, partly through the mist, and partly through troops trying to find the crossings over the Steenbeek : but, once over the Steenbeek, the advance continued without undue loss and the Green line was occupied.

Then our battalion came up with the Suffolk and went through the Green line.   They soon found resistance.   After crossing the Zonnebeke with some difficulty, few men were to be seen, and heavy machine-gun fire was coming from the station.   Our right company, under Captain A. W. Fish, reached the centre of the village, and the church was entered by Fish, followed by fourteen men and a few of the Suffolk.   On the left the ruins of an old hut caused some trouble until it was outflanked and the garrison surrendered ; but it was found impossible to get nearer than 200 yards to the station.

Except for the extreme left, the battalion was on its objective. There was a gap of 200 yards between the right and left halves of the battalion where there was a swamp—indeed the troops had been much hindered by the state of the ground about the Zonnebeke, although on this front it was not so bad as the Steenbeek.

The advance had been up to time, and the Royal Welch Fusiliers were able to improve the shell-hole position they had occupied before the first German counter-attack was launched about 2.30 p.m. There was no weight in it and it was easily repulsed.

The main counter-attack was launched about 6.35 p.m. This was a determined onslaught, and a number of the enemy succeeded in getting through our artillery barrage and approached within 100 yards of our left company. The steady rifle and machine-gun fire from our battalion and the Suffolk either stopped them or drove them back ; the Germans were thrown into confusion, wandered off to our right, in the direction of the lake, and lost heavily. But on our immediate left, and beyond, the counter-attack met with better success : the battalion on the north side of the railway had been thrown into confusion by the swamp formed by the Zonnebeke and was driven back ; the situation on the 59th Division front was obscure.

Our battalion had lost its Commanding Officer, Lieutenant-Colonel Compton Smith, who had been shell-shocked, and Major A. J. S. James had been sent for to assume command. The situation in the front line was grave, as ammunition was giving out—some of the men were down to their last clip—and the left flank was entirely uncovered.

The enemy, however, did not exploit their success, and the night passed quietly until 3 a.m., when St. Joseph's and the area round it were subjected to a fierce bombardment. Nothing further happened. But during the afternoon of the 27th an attempt was made by a stout German party to capture the church : Corporal Thomas, of A Company, and his section, accounted for seven and one prisoner (wounded) ; the remainder ran.

On the left, the 8th Brigade was ordered to take the Blue line on the 28th, and Major James was instructed by the 76th Brigade to co-operate, although efforts to ascertain what the exact plans of the neighbouring brigade were failed to get any response. The new attack was, however, cancelled, but the verbal message only reached the 76th Brigade Head-quarters at dawn. Our battalion, being in an exposed shell-hole line, could not be reached in daylight by runners—the only means of communication—and it was necessary to inform companies of the altered plans. Four runners were dispatched ; two were seen to be hit, but two reached the left of the Royal Welch Fusiliers.

The situation in the front line was such that no communication was possible between right and left : the orders that had been received about the attack were vague enough, but they had been passed down the line. It is probable that no definite time had been mentioned for the 8th Brigade attack. The day passed quietly, but at 6.15 p.m. our artillery opened an intense bombardment on the enemy lines, for no known reason, and the men on the right of our battalion, who had no knowledge of the cancelling order, left their shell-holes and tried to advance : the barrage, however, did not lift—a few casualties occurred—and the men, puzzled, returned to their shell-holes.

The battalion was relieved that night and marched back to Ypres and Winnezeele.

The casualties were : Lieutenant D. L. Jenkins, 2nd Lieutenants C. W. Rowlands, T. S. Jones, and 39 other ranks, killed ; Captains M. Watcyn-Williams, F. H. Sewell, D. G. Isaacs, 2nd Lieutenants R. V. Jones, T. M. Davies, A. P. Comyns, E. G. Williams, D. C. Hunter, S. A. H. Granville, and 202 other ranks wounded ; 38 other ranks missing.

.   .   .   .

Sir Douglas Haig's despatch puts the position following the Battle of Polygon Wood :

" As had been the case on the 20th September, our advance was at once followed by a series of powerful counter-attacks.

" There was evidence that our operations had anticipated a counter-stroke which the enemy was preparing for the evening of the 26th September, and the German troops brought up for this purpose were now hurled in to recover the positions he had lost. In the course of the day at least seven attacks were delivered at points covering practically the whole front from Tower Hamlets to St. Julien. The fiercest fighting prevailed in the sector between the Reutelbeek and Polygon Wood, but here, as elsewhere, all the enemy's assaults were beaten off.

" On the 30th September, when the enemy had recovered from the disorganisation caused by his defeat, he recommenced his attacks. Two attempts to advance with Flammenwerfer north of the Menin road were followed on the 1st October by five other attacks in this area, and on the same day a sixth attack was made south of the Ypres—Roulers railway.

Except for the temporary loss of the two advanced posts south-east of Polygon Wood, all these attacks were repulsed with great loss."

The scene of action for the regiment remains about Polygon Wood.

On the 13th September our 1st Battalion was on the march from Godewaersvelde to Wardreques, when they received an order to proceed at once to Cassel. Here they entrained and were wafted off to Etaples to quell a mutiny that had broken out in the camp there. They arrived at midnight and found, as war reports read, " the situation well in hand." In the afternoon of the 14th, C Company mounted guard over the Field Prisoners' Compound, while the rest of the battalion " stood to." A display of discipline put an end to the disturbance, and on the 17th the battalion, having enjoyed a breath of sea-air and a swim in sea-water, entrained once more for the battle-front, arriving on the 18th at Leuline.

On the 30th September the 7th Division relieved the Australians east of Polygon Wood. The situation was much the same as when our 2nd Battalion had left, the line running north and south up the eastern side of the wood. The 22nd Brigade, with our 1st Battalion on the right and the 20th Manchester on the left, took over the line with their right rather south of Jetty Wood, next to the 6th Leicestershire, who were the left battalion of the 21st Division.

The German counter-attacks, referred to in the despatch, opened at 5.15 a.m. on the 1st October with a heavy barrage on front and support lines. No one had had time to get acquainted with the country, visibility at that hour of the morning was not good—company commanders spent an anxious hour waiting for the assault.

Our battalion was disposed with D and B Companies in the front line, A in support, and D in reserve. At 6.30 a.m. Lieutenant-Colonel Holmes received a message from D Company that the enemy was advancing on its front and on that of the Leicestershire. He sent two platoons of C Company to the right of D, to find out the situation and counter-attack if necessary. But at seven o'clock the reassuring news arrived that the enemy had been driven off.

The Germans had advanced in three waves, and had almost reached our trenches before the first wave was wiped out by our rifle and machine-gun fire ; the succeeding waves hesitated, and commenced to retire. D Company, reinforced by two platoons from A, immediately left their trench and advanced on the wavering Germans, drove them back into our artillery barrage, captured four, and also drove the garrison from a pill-box which they occupied, appropriating a machine gun the enemy had abandoned.

III—23

On receipt of this satisfactory news the question of taking the important ridge to his front presented itself to Lieutenant-Colonel Holmes. The opportunity seemed favourable, but the situation on the 21st Division front was not at all clear ; no one could give him any information, and he had to abandon the idea.

The estimated strength of the German attack on the junction of the two divisions was three battalions and three Sturm Truppen of 80 men each —they were of the 46th Reserve Division—and one prisoner stated that if the first attack failed, their orders were to attack again.

This information proved to be true. The artillery on both sides quietened down, but about 9 a.m. the German guns opened again, and at 9.50 a fresh attack was launched on the 21st Division front. D Company was able to give assistance, but the men only had the ammunition they carried, and this began to run short. Urgent calls resulted in a company of the Royal Warwickshire bringing up 50 boxes of ammunition, with orders to remain at Lieutenant-Colonel Holmes's disposal to stiffen the defence. This company had to go through the German barrage, and suffered heavily before reaching Battalion Headquarters.

The second attack failed, but the enemy continued to bombard our front and support trenches and back areas, making reorganisation and the despatch of messages difficult—the power buzzer was smashed by a direct hit.

No further assaults were delivered, but the artillery broke up a concentration of enemy troops in Cameron Covert and about Joist Farm, and to the north of it at 1 p.m. ; and at 2.50 p.m. and 7.20 p.m. were so prompt in opening fire in response to S.O.S. rockets that attacks were " nipped in the bud."

The situation was never in doubt. During the afternoon Brigadier-General J. Steele had ordered a second company of the Royal Warwickshire to carry up ammunition and place themselves under the orders of Lieutenant-Colonel Holmes, but soon after midnight they returned with the message that the commanding officer no longer required their support.

The battalion, with the rest of the 22nd Brigade, was relieved on the night of the 2nd October, and went back to the Dickebusch area, while the 7th Division made a further advance on the 4th October. This was part of a general attack from the Menin road to the Ypres–Staden railway— about seven miles—and was carried out under bad weather conditions. The coverts east of Polygon Wood were captured with the village of Reutel ; the latter was, however, lost in the subsequent counter-attack.

At this point in the great offensive, which had followed the same course as the Somme and Arras attempts and become a battle of attrition, Sir Douglas Haig considered the advisability of breaking off the battle. The condition of the field was infernal.   The despatch, like those on former battles, bristles with excuses—but they were not invented.   " The weather had been constantly unpropitious, and the state of the ground in consequence of the shelling and rain combined made movement inconceivably difficult.   The resultant delays had given the enemy time to bring up reinforcements and to organise his defence after each defeat.   Even so, it was still the difficulty of movement far more than hostile resistance which continued to limit our progress, and now made it doubtful whether the capture of the remainder of the ridge before winter finally set in was possible."

That vast quagmire had engulfed a holocaust of dead, and the devotion of labour corps, toiling with unceasing zeal, could do little more than maintain slender causeways to feed the armies.   And with each advance the difficulties increased, while those of the enemy remained the same.

The resultant decision on these reflections was to continue the battle with a combined British and French attack on the 9th October—there was, it was said, no reason to anticipate an abnormally wet October, and our Allies, who were to carry out operations in the neighbourhood of Malmaison, might be assisted thereby.

" Unfortunately, bad weather still persisted. . . . On the 8th October rain continued, and the slippery state of the ground, combined with an exceptionally dark night, made the assembling of our troops a matter of considerable difficulty."

The main attack was from a point east of Zonnebeke to Draaibank, on the French front.   The 7th Division launched a subsidiary attack east of Polygon Wood.

THE BATTLE OF POELCAPELLE.[1]

(1ST BATTALION.)

The battalion played but a minor part.   After the attack on the 4th October (the Battle of Broodseinde), the 7th Division had gained its final objectives ; but on their right the 21st Division had only succeeded in holding its first objective.   This left the right of the 7th Division in a sharp salient, and the enemy retained Judge Cottage, Judge Copse, and the village of Reutel, giving them observation over the valley of the Reutelbeek.   The

Date : 9th October.

7th Division was ordered to capture what had been on the 4th the final objective of the 21st Division.

The task was given to the 22nd Brigade, and Brigadier-General Steele detailed the H.A.C. and Warwickshire to carry out the attack.

Our battalion had been resting at Château Segard Camp, north of Dickebusch, since the 2nd October, and went back to Polygon Wood on the 7th, taking over from the 6th Leicestershire at Jetty Warren. The relief took some time, partly owing to the bad state of the ground, but chiefly to guides losing themselves. Relief was completed at 3.45 a.m. on the 8th.

Major-General Shoubridge was given, for the purpose of the attack, command over part of the 21st Division front. Our battalion had relieved the left battalion on that front ; the next two, 7th and 8/9th Leicestershire, remained in line under the 7th Division. Command of the front line was relegated to Lieutenant-Colonel Holmes, and Major Alston took charge of the battalion.

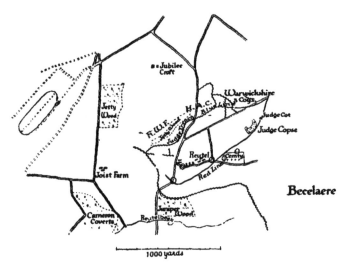

During the night of the 8/9th October a forming-up line was taped out in No Man's Land. While this was being done, our A and C Companies sent out patrols to report on the situation.

Lieutenant H. A. Freeman reported that Reutel was clear. 2nd Lieutenant I. Thomas found the Cemetery clear, but there was a trench in front of it occupied by the enemy with a machine gun, and they also held a mound to the east of it. 2nd Lieutenant D. M. John found that Judge Copse was held, but said he thought he could take it with two platoons. 2nd Lieutenant I. R. Cartwright, who was sent to Judge Cottage, did not return, and nothing more was heard of him. All this information was sent to the H.A.C. and Warwickshire Battalions.

The assaulting battalions took up their positions, and at 5.20 a.m. on the 9th our artillery opened. The enemy was prompt in replying with his protective barrage, which fell across our front and support lines within a few minutes, and caused a number of casualties. The H.A.C. and Warwickshire disappeared in the morning haze.

It had been arranged that the assaulting troops should fire green Verey lights when their objectives were attained, and half an hour after zero green lights began to rise; but they kept on rising—there was a profusion of green lights, and from many points. It began to dawn on the minds of observers that the enemy was using green lights—green was one of the normal colours by which he signalled to his artillery. For some time the situation was obscure. Lieutenant-Colonel Holmes sent out patrols and found that Reutel and the Cemetery were occupied by our troops. The objective was won all along the line.

Our casualties were 7 other ranks killed; Lieutenant W. T. C. Moody, 2nd Lieutenants W. E. Evans, W. J. Norris, and 36 other ranks wounded.

The battalion was relieved in the early morning of the 11th and went back to Zillebeke Lake.

THE SECOND BATTLE OF PASSCHENDAELE.[1]

(1ST BATTALION.)

The main attack in this battle was launched between the Ypres—Roulers railway and a point north of Poelcapelle; the 7th Division was concerned in a subsidiary attack south of the Menin road on Gheluvelt. Our battalion was only slightly involved. They moved, on the 25th, from Zillebeke to Bodmin Copse and Hedge Street, and were held in reserve. It rained heavily all night, and when the attack was launched the Queen's found a marsh between them and an enemy post, Lewis House, which barred their progress. Safe from a frontal attack, the German gunners turned their attention to the Gordon Highlanders, on the left of the Queen's, and stopped their advance. Our battalion was placed under orders from the division to capture Lewis House with two companies, but the order was, fortunately, countermanded, and all they had to do was to take over the line from the 20th Brigade, who were back in their original trenches.

There was a considerable amount of sniping the next day, and 2nd Lieutenant I. Rees was killed, and 2nd Lieutenants T. W. Lewis and J. Evans were wounded.

The battalion was relieved by the 1/1st Hertfordshire on the 28th.

The 7th Division generally seemed to feel the failure of this, their last attack on the Franco-Belgian front, deeply: there was no need. The mud was simply appalling. Even the optimism at General Headquarters

---

[1] Date: 26th October–10th November.

had been checked, for " the persistent continuation of wet weather had left no further room for hope that the condition of the ground would improve sufficiently to enable us to capture the remainder of the ridge this year." But the regiment, in spite of all difficulties, had come through gloriously.

The Second Battle of Passchendaele continued, however, into November. Sir Douglas Haig intended to press forward, when and where conditions of weather and ground permitted, and by a series of limited blows work his way to the crest of Passchendaele Ridge. But events in Italy had placed our Ally in a precarious position, and it really seemed that pressure must be maintained in Flanders for fear that even one division might be sent to exploit the Germanic success on that front.

Ludendorff calls these days " the culminating-point of the crisis." The 1917 Offensive at Ypres was a trial of strength, as the Somme had been— in the parlance of the prize-ring, a " mix-up," a desperate remedy, when strategy fails and tactical movement is limited to frontal attacks. One may deplore the welter of blood, and wonder, with after-knowledge, whether we were really pinned down to the Western Front for the decision. One must take note of the admissions of Ludendorff, who was the active agent of supreme power. His *War Memories* must not be relied upon to any greater extent than our War Despatches—there are sufficient good reasons in each case for ample discount. But if the object of our battles, the direction of our effort, the precise intention of the Higher Command, undergo a complete change between the writing of orders and the writing of the despatches, and become merely an unimaginative " mix-up," the final contention of our Headquarters that blows had been struck at the *moral* and strength of the enemy must not be dismissed when they are borne out by enemy admissions. " In the west we began to be short of troops," says Ludendorff. " The two divisions that had been held in readiness in the east, and were already on their way to Italy, were diverted to Flanders "—and this in October, on the eve of the Italian débâcle.

Concrete protection was not enough for the German troops—" At some points they no longer displayed the firmness which I, in common with the local commanders, had hoped for "—and anxious conferences were held on the further development of tactical defence. The local commanders, bereft of ideas before the stupendous artillery battle, desired, as our own invariably did, more men : their front line was to be thickened, and a reserve division was to be held behind every front-line division to launch counter-attacks. As a method of strengthening their defence it was, as Ludendorff observed, a simple sum of arithmetic, and—it could not be done.

On our side General Headquarters was also anxiously searching for improved methods of attack. Questionnaires were issued to Divisional Generals, and General Shoubridge's replies to some of them are interesting.

With regard to distances between assaulting waves of infantry, the normal distances in the 7th Division were 30 yards between lines and 100 yards between waves, mopping-up parties being placed about 30 yards in rear of each wave. " On each occasion that the division attacked, the enemy's barrage lines were carefully noted and arrangements were made to form up between these lines. In practically every case leading battalions formed up within a depth of about 150 yards. The distance in rear of battalions detailed to leap-frog at the first objective varied—sometimes such battalions were 400 yards in rear of the leading battalions, sometimes as little as 200. When our counter-battery work is effective, the enemy's barrage can in most cases be disregarded.

" The disadvantage of forming up in too close a formation is that there is a great probability of organisation being lost too early in the fight, and of not only rear waves telescoping rapidly into forward waves, but of battalions detailed to go through telescoping into battalions detailed for the first objective. I do not consider it feasible to gain normal distance on the move. . . . It is better to maintain distances between waves and battalions, even if this entails going through an enemy barrage, rather than risk the chance of telescoping and the consequent breaking-up of formations early in a fight. There is no doubt that in several instances objectives were taken by practically a mob of men, which undoubtedly follows from close forming-up, but I am certain it would be false teaching if we adopted the policy of close forming-up as a general practice."

General Shoubridge did not consider that a company reserve could be kept in hand with the actual assaulting companies, but a battalion reserve should be maintained, and move forward with the assaulting battalion to act on general instructions rather than direct orders from the battalion commander.

" The capture of strong-points, particularly those of concrete, entirely depends on the closeness with which the infantry follow the barrage. In every case where this was feasible, such strong-points fell without difficulty. When, however, the state of the ground was such that the infantry could not pass over the intervening 50 yards after the barrage lifted, the capture of the concrete strong-point presented greater difficulties. In one case a pill-box was subjected to direct Lewis-gun fire and then rushed from both flanks. In another case a strong-point which had given considerable trouble was captured later in the fight by an enveloping movement without artillery support during the hours of darkness.

" The practice of this division is for the leading line only to be extended, the whole of the remainder of the lines and waves moving in either section or platoon columns in file. It was found, however, that the leading line soon formed itself into small columns when advancing over shelled ground. If the enemy is going back to his old methods of holding his front line more thickly, and also to retaining a larger number of machine guns in his forward positions, the question of formations will again require consideration, as extended lines are probably the best method of dealing with machine-gun fire. I would not, however, be prepared to express a definite opinion on the subject until I have had a further opportunity of considering the matter."

The tactical problem of assault and defence was, then, no easy one. With the situation in Italy in his mind, and " in view of other projects " (Cambrai), Sir Douglas Haig continued to smash at Passchendaele with the Canadian Corps. " The fifth act of the great drama in Flanders opened on the 22nd October. Enormous masses of ammunition, such as the human mind had never imagined before the war, were hurled upon the bodies of men who passed a miserable existence scattered about in mud-filled shell-holes. The horror of the shell-hole area of Verdun was surpassed. It was no longer life at all. It was mere unspeakable suffering. And through this world of mud the attackers dragged themselves, slowly but steadily, and in dense masses. Caught in the advanced zone by our hail of fire, they often collapsed, and the lonely man in the shell-hole breathed again. Then the mass came on again. Rifle and machine gun jammed with mud. Man fought against man, and only too often the mass was successful. What the German soldier experienced, achieved, and suffered in the Flanders battle will be his everlasting monument of bronze, erected by himself in the enemy's land." (Ludendorff.)

And when one considers that the world of mud was more extensive on our side, and was being added to by each successful attack, the renown and terrible fame of the Ypres Salient are not surprising.

.   .   .   .

Our 1st Battalion was relieved on the 28th October and went back to Sercus—one train (containing Headquarters and the greater part of B and C Companies) was sent on to Boulogne by mistake and did not return until the 31st. The order was for training. On the 8th November the 7th Division was inspected by the King of the Belgians. All seemed quiet in that part of the country, but rumours were busy. The Italian disaster was spoken of ; Lord Cavan's name was mentioned ; and then the announcement that the Division was to move to Italy.

On the 18th the battalion moved by bus to entrain at Hesdin. There followed a long journey with many halts. The first train stopped at Mesgrigny and Darcey on the 19th ; Villefranche and Marseilles on the 20th ; Toulon on the 21st ; Cannes and Ventimille on the 22nd, the journey through the Riviera being made by day and under good weather conditions ; Borgo San Domino on the 23rd ; Cerea and Legnano on the 24th ; and here the first half-battalion detrained and went into billets at Bonavigo, marching to Sossano on the 25th.

The second train halted at Mesgrigny on the 19th ; Lyon Vaise on the 20th ; Marseilles on the 21st ; Toulon and Ventimille on the 22nd ; Savona on the 23rd ; Cremona and Mantua on the 24th ; and on the 25th the second half-battalion detrained at Cerea and went into billets at Bonavigo, marching to Sossano on the 26th.

.   .   .   .

Our 10th Battalion, relieved on the 29th September, marched back to Ypres and Winnezeele. They entrained at Wizernes on the 5th October for Bapaume. Thence to Barastre and Mory, and into the line at Ecoust on the 19th.

The 13th, 14th, 15th, 16th, and 17th Battalions moved down to the Armentières—Laventie sector with the 38th Division between the 13th and 15th September.

The 2nd and 9th Battalions remained, for the time being, in the Ypres sector. The battle did not die down for some time, but nothing can be learned from the laconic entries in the official diaries of that strenuous period beyond dates. The state of the battle-front may be imagined from the account of the 2nd Battalion.

They left Dickebusch and embussed for Blaringhem on the 28th September. " At 6 a.m. on the 5th October the battalion marched via Arques, Lonhuesse, and Wisques (Whiskers), all in pleasant hilly country, to dirty billets in the dirty village of Acquin. We expected to be there a week, but in the evening we were warned for the line again. On the 6th companies marched in rain to Wizerne, thence by train to La Courte Pipe Camp, near Bailleul, arriving there just on midnight, when summer time changed to winter time. Winter came in the night—it was very cold. This year, as last year, I felt there had been no autumn. We were in a war-wasted country, where no flowers bloomed, where there was no harvest ; there were no autumn tints or fallen leaves, for all trees were leafless, branchless stumps.

" On the afternoon of the 8th the battalion marched through Neuve Eglise in the pouring rain, so it scarcely mattered that many of the men slipped on the greasy path and duckboards, and fell into brimful shell-holes as we moved in the inky darkness to the support position on the forward slope of Messines Ridge. Of the village to the right rear there remained but the foundations and some loose bricks. It was a dismal district, but the weather remained fine until the night of the 12th, when the battalion relieved the 5th Scottish Rifles in front. It poured, and the communication trenches were shelled, causing a tedious and confused relief.

" Enemy patrols were aggressive on the divisional front, seeking identification, but the battalion escaped the raids that were attempted and brought off on other units. A most unpleasant feature of these trenches was the number of decomposed Germans built into the parapet. The relief on the night of the 14th was without incident, and the battalion went back to billets at Neuve Eglise, a dull village.

" On the 18th the battalion was conveyed by bus via Dranoutre and Vlamertinghe, past the Asylum and the remains of the Cloth Hall at Ypres, to just outside the Menin Gate, to be employed as pioneers in the Australian Corps area.

" Engineers were directing the labour of thousands of men repairing roads, constructing miles of railway-sleeper corduroy, and raised duck-board tracks across a couple of miles of shell-holes full of noisome water. Until 25th October the strongest possible numbers were sent at daylight each morning to work on the Menin road. Though there was still active movement along the front, the heaviest casualties were incurred in the back areas. On our arrival the Germans were having too much of their own way. On the 19th October B Company alone had 12 killed and wounded. After the 22nd and 23rd, when the counter-battery guns had been moved forward, the German artillery was kept under control.

" On the 25th the battalion was relieved. After marching through Ypres, it was carried in buses to Bulford Camp, near Neuve Eglise.

" Bulford was a comfortable hutted camp. On the 30th the battalion went into support, relieving the Argyll and Sutherland, on the left of its former position. Between the support and front positions eight days were spent before returning to Bulford Camp. Nothing noteworthy happened on the battalion front. The enemy's patrols were still active by night and his artillery by day. The sigh of our heavy shells passing over us to the German back areas could be heard all night long, save when it was drowned by the eldritch shrieks raised by the village cats that made love on the bare ground where their houses had once stood. Their persistence in the neighbourhood was strange—strange, too, the flocks of sparrows that chirruped about the pill-boxes.

" Back in Bulford Camp on the 8th November, a draft of about 200 joined the battalion. All but a score of them were eighteen-year-old boys, for the age of drafts had just been reduced from nineteen. Seventy eighteen-year-old boys had joined ten days previously. They were no better trained than their predecessors of the past fifteen months, but for their age their physical standard was good. I viewed with grave misgiving the sending of these youths to the forward areas at the beginning of the winter. In April 1918 I learned from the Orderly Room that of the 60 or so per company, 9 was the highest company residue, though the battalion had not been in action." (Dunn.)

On the 14th the battalion moved to Strazelle, and on the 19th sent working parties to Potijze.

" On the 24th the battalion paraded in Ypres and marched with intervals between platoons via the Menin Gate and the Hooge Road to an elevated track which led eventually to Boethoek and Abraham's Heights. There were a few casualties on the way, for the track was being shelled. There was safety in numbers in that corpse-strewn area—there were rescuers for the wounded ; but a wounded individual might perish in a shell-hole or in the mud beside the track before help came. The constant shelling of the tracks necessitated the employment of breakdown gangs to keep them in repair. As destructive of the tracks as the enemy guns was the pilfering by the troops of the wood for fuel and the making of shacks. There was no real cover in this support position, only a few badly constructed dugouts. Headquarters pill-box was an unsavoury place, in which one was bent double, for the weight of concrete had sunk into the boggy ground.

" On the 27th the battalion moved forward. It was to the apex of the salient at Passchendaele. Short though the road was across country to the *pavé* of the Broodseinde-Passchendaele road—it was still in a state to be a godsend in that water-logged country of shell-craters—it was a toilsome journey and the isolated posts were not easy to find. The system of defence was small posts distributed in depth. A and C Companies were in front, in the debris of the village where they occupied shell-holes that were always wet or cellars with shattered floors over them, into which mud oozed. B Company was in support at Crest Farm, and D in reserve. Where the position was overlooked, the men were immobile by day, and numbed by day and night ; but there were posts—as behind Crest Farm—where great freedom was possible, and was apt to be exercised imprudently. Crest Farm was the highest point there, and its retention a matter of anxiety to the High Command, so the intermediate commands lived in an atmosphere of expected counter-attack, of which they kept warning the battalion. But on the battalion front German Moorslede was separated from Passchendaele by a hollow that was an almost impassable sea of mud and flood-water from a meandering stream. In that hollow, however, a few German posts contrived to exist. Until the ground dried or froze, neither side could advance." (Dunn.)

Moody writes : " I joined the battalion when it was at Ypres, before going up to Passchendaele, where it was my lot to command C Company. Three days there were the worst three days I experienced during the whole of the war. C Company occupied a freshly dug strong-point, very narrowly cut. We had orders that on no account was anyone to move by day, for the position was not to be given away. The strong-point was near Passchendaele Church, a well-known range-mark. The outgoing company commander told me he had been heavily and repeatedly shelled for hours at a time. The shelling to which the enemy treated us was at times like the bombardment previous to an attack. Under this ordeal one of my officers lost his nerve and had to be sent away. The draft of young soldiers who had just joined were naturally very nervy, for this was their first experience of war conditions. Standing up hour after hour under heavy shell fire, unable to move about, all in extremely unpleasant weather conditions, is a severe test of anyone's *moral*. Ration parties were not regular and most of the food arrived sodden with mud-water.

" The pathetic part was dealing with casualties. Stretcher cases had to remain until night, and four bearers were required for each stretcher. In that part of the salient during that season hundreds of wounded, who would have been evacuated under better conditions, must have been left owing to the difficulty in getting them away. In many cases they died from exposure and inattention.

" The second morning the company had casualties from two aeroplanes that flew over less than 100 feet up. On the afternoon of the third day, during one of the usual heavy shellings, Company Sergeant-Major Cumberland and I, who shared a hole covered with a waterproof sheet, were buried —we had had a minor experience of the kind the day before—and were dug out little the worse ; but the same shell killed and wounded some of the company. Later in the day Radford, who was Adjutant at the time, came up to say we would be relieved. He was the first representative of Headquarters we had seen for three days (he had been to other parts of the front that morning). To approach Company Headquarters in daylight was forbidden, to find a Company Headquarters in the dark was not easy—

a wire fixed on stakes had to be found and followed, and it was easy to be lost. The relief took place about midnight ; it was a quick one, for there was nothing to hand over except a few boxes of ammunition and the battered trenches."

On the 11th December the battalion went back to the Waton back area.

CAMBRAI, 1917.

The 19th Battalion had remained in the sector about Gouzeaucourt. After the affair in front of Gonnelieu on the 21st April, they took part in a raid on La Vacquerie village, which turned out to be quite a hot little battle.

The raid was undertaken by the 17th Welch and 12th South Wales Borderers, and our 19th Battalion provided a party of 200 to act as moppers-up—they were armed with bombs and sticks. Masses of unexpected wire were encountered in the village, and the moppers, telescoping with the assaulting troops, found themselves in the very front of the battle. Two of our men, J. Trodden and Cullen, got through the wire at one point, and, unsupported by armed troops—they had already got rid of their bombs—attacked, and put to flight a party of the enemy with their sticks.

The raid was not entirely successful, but a good deal of damage was done and identity secured.

Major A. C. White (King's Own Yorkshire Light Infantry) assumed command on the 14th May, Lieutenant-Colonel Downes-Powell being on the sick-list.

This part of the front was fairly quiet, with the battles of Arras and Ypres going on to the north, but raids were frequent. The German line being strongly protected by belts of wire, the Bangalore torpedo was much favoured. On the 12th August our battalion attempted a raid, but failed to get the torpedo in place before zero hour and the enterprise was cancelled—but the torpedo was exploded.

The next day was stormy and wet, but favourable to the reconnaissance that was made in the evening. It was found that the enemy had repaired the inner belt of wire, which had been slightly damaged, but had left the gap in the outer belt. It was decided to carry out the raid at 2.30 a.m. (14th).

The raid which had been arranged was to be made by thirty-three all ranks, divided into two parties, the one led by 2nd Lieutenant Mullens, the other by 2nd Lieutenant E. T. Roche, the whole party under the command of Captain G. H. Morgan. This party left our lines with the Bangalore torpedo at 10.30 p.m., but after a little more than two hours had passed Captain Morgan reported that the enemy was lining his parapet and the torpedo could not be placed.

There was the gap in the outer belt of enemy wire, and further reconnaissance showed that there were two gaps in the inner belt—though not opposite the outer gap—through which it was thought troops might enter the German line. But the raiding party asked that the artillery barrage should be cancelled and that the gunners should support them by five minutes' intensive fire on Barrier Trench, as it was called. This was done at 2.30 a.m.

The whole party got through the gaps in the inner belt, and 2nd Lieutenant Roche took his men to the right, while 2nd Lieutenant Mullens went to the left.

It had seemed, at first, that the raid was bound to be a failure, but they turned it into a success. They inflicted heavy casualties, destroyed all the shelters they found, and returned with two unwounded prisoners of the 6th Bavarian Reserve Regiment.

A few days later, on the 28th/29th, another party, under Captain P. E. Williams, with 2nd Lieutenants E. O. Hill and W. F. Cooke as section leaders, blew a gap in the enemy wire and brought off a silent raid, that is, without artillery support. They killed fourteen Germans, blew up a dugout, in which there were some men who refused to come out, and returned with one prisoner of the 6th Bavarian Reserve Regiment. In both these raids our casualties were insignificant.

Other raids were made with varying success.

On the night 7th/8th October the battalion was relieved and proceeded to Hendecourt, thence to Doingt, and commenced training on the 10th at Simencourt. On the 29th they moved to Couturelle, and on the 16th November commenced to march towards the Cambrai front, " in view of other projects " !

.   .   .   .

The Battle of Cambrai is one of the two most interesting battles fought on the Western Front. At the close of it we were humbled to the dust, but it accomplished one convincing demonstration : up to that moment tanks were not considered serious or successful engines of war, and it opened the eyes of the Higher Command to their value and to their tactical handling.

The credit of first conversion appears to lie with General Byng, who listened to the tale of the tank, and saw the vision conjured up by enthusiasts commanding the new arm. Our General Headquarters seem to have given a grudging consent to the experiment. True, the situation was not happy—they had before them the Salient, heaped high with dead, the unbroken enemy line, and, on the Italian front, a rout! Before the unveiled mysteries of 1918, an insistent thought in their minds, they may be excused a shiver of apprehension. That fearful cry of the struggling commander, " If I had only more men! " had already been uttered.

The decision was, however, taken on the grounds that enough troops were available to win a preliminary success, and the plan having been communicated to the French Commander-in-Chief, he " most readily agreed to afford me every assistance. In addition to the steps taken by him to engage the enemy's attention elsewhere, he arranged for a strong force of French infantry and cavalry to be in a position whence they could be moved forward rapidly to take part in the exploitation of our success, if the situation should render it possible to bring them into action. On the 20th November certain of these French units were actually put in motion. The course of events, however, did not open out the required opportunity for their employment, but the French forces were held in readiness and within easy reach so long as there appeared to be any hope of it. Had the situation on the 20th November developed somewhat more favourably in certain directions, the nature of which will become apparent in the course of this report, the presence and co-operation of French troops would have been of the greatest value." (Despatch.)

Briefly the scheme was that tanks, followed by infantry, should break through the German line between Gonnelieu and Hermies, seize the crossings of the Canal de l'Escaut at Masnières and Marcoing, cut the last of the enemy's defences on the Beaurevoir–Masnières line, and that the cavalry should pass through the gap made.

The cavalry would then capture Cambrai and Bourlon Wood, cut all railway communications into Cambrai, and occupy the crossings of the Sensée north of Cambrai. They were to go up from Gouzeaucourt and Metz-en-Couture.

The III Corps were to capture the canal crossings at Marcoing and Masnières, and form a flank to the IV Corps, attacking through Flesquières and Graincourt.

The opening of the attack on the 20th November was full of promise: the III Corps carried out its task and secured the bridge intact at Marcoing, but at Masnières a tank, trying to cross, completed the partial destruction of the bridge the Germans had been able to carry out.

The IV Corps broke through the Hindenburg Line. It was a moment for swift decision and determined action, such as General de Lisle had shown in moving his 29th Division on the report of his observers rather than wait for the order from III Corps, but the Cavalry Divisions were cautious, and the 51st Division, after severe fighting about Flesquières, reported they were held up. One squadron of Fort Garry Horse (Canadian) crossed the canal by a lock near Masnières, and a patrol of King Edward's Horse rode into Flesquières soon after midday, from Graincourt, but nobody else moved. Darkness fell, and the opportunity passed.

The Germans were favoured by one stroke of good luck in this attack : the 107th Division, a strong division from the Eastern Front, arrived, in the ordinary course of relief, as the battle broke out. They were not in time to be cut up by the first attack, but were a reinforcement ahead of the time calculated by our Staff.

Flesquières was found to be empty on the morning of the 21st, and the 51st Division advanced and captured La Fontaine, but lost it on the 22nd. The 62nd Division meanwhile stood on the ground won on the first day up to Anneux, on the left of the 51st.

. . . .

Moving through Simencourt and Gommiecourt, and marching by night, the 40th Division arrived in the Barastre area in the night 19th/20th. On the 21st they moved to Doignes, Beaumetz, and Lebucquière.

General Ponsonby then received orders from IV Corps to send the Brigadier and Commanding Officers of the most advanced brigade, which was the 119th, to reconnoitre Bourlon Wood from the south.

The situation was that the 62nd Division held as far as Anneux, and the 51st Division were in La Fontaine. But when the 40th Division relieved the 62nd during the night 22nd/23rd, La Fontaine had been lost and the difficulties of their task increased.

The 119th Brigade was given the right, that is to say the whole of Bourlon Wood, and the 121st Brigade the left, which included the village of Bourlon. The attack was to be launched at 10.30 a.m. on the 23rd.

Twelve tanks were allotted to the 119th Brigade, twenty to the 121st. There was a period of anxiety when, owing to the congestion on the road, petrol did not arrive at the expected time. The tanks were filled, but the time was cut so close that their move from Graincourt became without pause the advance with the infantry.

Visibility, however, was not good, and the advance of the tanks was unobserved by the enemy.

Our 19th Battalion had relieved the 14th West Yorkshire at Anneux, and at 10.30 our artillery opened fire on the south edge of the wood as the tanks were going through our line. The infantry advanced about 200 yards behind the tanks, and our battalion, on the extreme right, entered the wood at 10.45 a.m.

On the left of our 19th Battalion was the 12th South Wales Borderers, while echeloned on our right rear were three sections of the 119th Machine-gun Company, one with the infantry, the others to move forward with the advance and cover the right flank.

Machine-gun fire from the wood was slight. About 100 yards beyond the edge of the wood the battalion halted, reorganised, and checked positions, for the undergrowth was fairly thick. Aligned and in good order the battalion continued the advance.

The enemy held a series of posts, and were undoubtedly shaken by the tanks ploughing slowly through the undergrowth and ponderously threading their way between the trees. It was, however, a bad place for tanks. Gradually they dropped out.

The German posts were rounded up by our men and batches of prisoners began to arrive at Battalion Headquarters in Anneux. At 11.30 a.m. the first stage of the advance, to the sunken road in the centre of the wood, was accomplished. Here the battalion reorganised once more.

It is not easy to determine what part the tanks played in this action. General Ponsonby, to whom, of course, all reports were forwarded, says : " It is difficult to discover where the tanks allotted to the 119th Brigade were at this time, but apparently at least five of them had arrived at the sunken road with the infantry, and it is probable that all these, and more, moved forward with the infantry during the advance of the latter. . . . No reports were received from tank commanders throughout the action, and, though reports were received from the infantry from time to time that the tanks were doing well, it is not possible to give any clear account of them."

From the sunken road our battalion advanced with dash and by 12.30 p.m. emerged from the northern edge of the wood. Lieutenant-Colonel Plunkett [1] now went forward to study the situation himself.

Naturally enough in the confusion of wood fighting, the battalion wanted reorganising after each advance. The Commanding Officer found about sixty men outside the wood and placed them in position on the northern edge of it, continuing the line round the eastern corner as more men came up. The 17th Welch, who were following in support, carried on this line, forming, with the machine guns, a flank facing east.

---

[1] Lieutenant-Colonel B. J. Jones, who had been wounded earlier in the year, returned to command on the 2nd June. He relinquished command on the 6th August and handed over to Major T. F. Plunkett.

III—24

At this time small bodies of the enemy were observed retiring in a north-easterly direction.

Meanwhile the South Wales Borderers had advanced more slowly, but their left company got through the right fringe of the village and almost to the railway, and their right company came up and gained touch with our left.

The 18th Welch, who had been in reserve at Anneux, were now moved up and reinforced the front line, two companies to each of the assaulting battalions.

The situation presented to General Ponsonby at this stage was that his 119th Brigade was short of its final objective, but the attack of the 51st Division on the right had failed, and the state of affairs on the 121st Brigade front was obscure—resistance on the west of the wood was very strong. The support battalion of the 119th Brigade, the 17th Welch, was split in two, on either brigade flank ; the reserve battalion was in the front line.

Enemy artillery fire was heavy, and at 3.10 p.m. a counter-attack, coming through the village, forced the left of the 119th Brigade back to the central cross ride in the wood ; but the 18th Welch, reattacking, drove the enemy back once more and re-established our line. " The tanks," General Ponsonby states, " materially assisted in repelling this first counter-attack."

Lieutenant-Colonel Plunkett was now given command of the whole of the 119th Brigade line, and moved his Headquarters to the red brick chalet in the centre of the wood—a most unpleasant place on which the German artillerymen ranged their guns. He ordered the battalions to dig in on the 100-metre contour line, and put outposts on the northern edge of the wood.

During the evening the 14th Argyll and Sutherland Highlanders, the 15th Hussars (dismounted) Battalion, and eight machine guns from the 244th Machine-gun Company were placed under the orders of Lieutenant-Colonel Plunkett.

Although the South Wales Borderers had gone through the eastern outskirts of the village, Bourlon itself had not been taken, and General Ponsonby decided that the 121st Brigade, reinforced by the 9th Cavalry (dismounted) Battalion and the 14th Highland Light Infantry, and assisted by twelve tanks, should attack the village on the 24th. Orders were accordingly issued. Zero hour was fixed at 3 p.m.

The night 23rd/24th was a disturbing one. Strong parties of the enemy advanced several times against our battalion posts, with the object, no doubt, of placing our line, and at daybreak, when it was light enough to see some distance, the enemy was observed to be massing near La Fontaine and on the left flank about Bourlon village.

At 8.45 a.m. the enemy advanced against both our flanks, but the minor successes he gained were immediately lost by him before prompt counter-blows. He repeated his effort, however, about 11 o'clock, and this time drove back our battalion and supporting troops on the right flank of the brigade.

While all this fighting was going on—and it was a matter of some hours—the Corps Commander had visited Divisional Headquarters, and had decided that twelve tanks were not sufficient to enable the 121st Brigade to capture Bourlon : the attack was therefore countermanded. But the message never reached the 121st Brigade, and the attack was launched as arranged.

During the whole of the afternoon the wildest rumours were flying about, and the wood, especially about the chalet, assumed the appearance of a shambles.

The two counter-attacks against our battalion front—now held by mixed troops—had resulted in small gains by the enemy, but fighting was really continuous in the north-east corner of the wood. Now, at 3 p.m., the Germans launched a strong attack from the north and east, and succeeded in driving the 119th Brigade back to the sunken road line in the centre of the wood—and this as the 121st Brigade launched their attack against the village.

Lieutenant-Colonel Plunkett hurriedly reorganised his force. He placed the officers of his Headquarters in command of various parts of the line, himself taking the centre, and once more drove the enemy right out of the wood, re-establishing his former line.

On the left, the 121st Brigade, assisted by the tanks, went through the village, but in the confusion of village fighting—and the Germans held on stoutly—touch was lost between the two assaulting battalions. The Highland Light Infantry on the right reached the railway and started to consolidate their gains ; but the Suffolk on the left, never firmly established, half of them still fighting in the village while the rest went through, were promptly counter-attacked, and driven back to the confusion in the village. The Highlanders were then with both flanks in the air, and the situation in Bourlon was obscure.

Meanwhile, on the 119th Brigade front the Germans kept the wood under heavy shell fire, and made small and repeated efforts to dislodge our troops. To some extent they succeeded about the north-east corner of the wood.

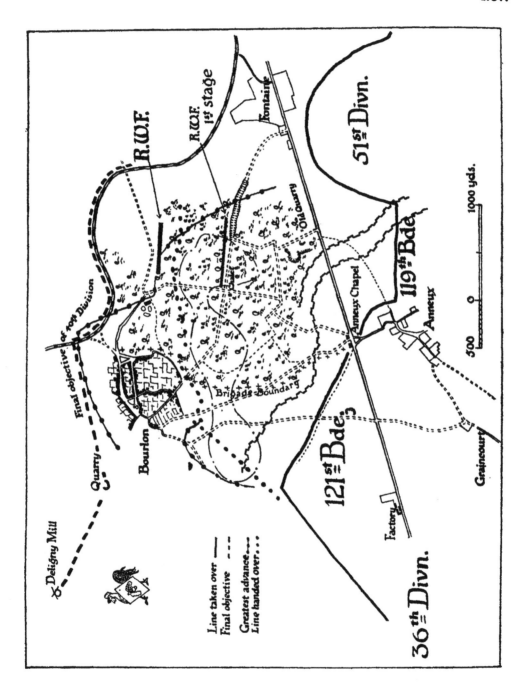

R.W.F.

R.W.F.
1st stage

Fontaine

51st Divn.

Old Quarry

119th Bde.

Anneux Chapel

Anneux

Graincourt

Brigade Boundary

121st Bde.

Factory

36th Divn.

Final objective of 107th Division

Quarry

Bourlon

Delisgny Mill

Line taken over ————
Final objective – – – –
Greatest advance – · – · –
Line handed over · · · ·

1000 yds.

500

General Ponsonby then set about organising an attack for the morning of the 25th, with the object of clearing the wood once and for all, and taking Bourlon village. It was arranged with the IV Corps that twelve tanks should co-operate.

The 119th Brigade was reinforced by the 2nd Scots Guards, and the capture of the village was entrusted to the 13th East Surrey and 11th King's Own. But no tanks arrived at zero hour, 6 a.m., on the 25th, " nor did any turn up during the day " ! The East Surrey and King's Own were not strong enough to mop up the village. Fighting proceeded all through the day, and at night the situation was that the 119th Brigade had re-established their line on the high ground, but the 121st Brigade had lost their hold on the village.

One can only indicate approximately the positions of battalions, as all were hopelessly mixed up. Our 19th battalion remained on the right flank with the Argyll and Sutherland Highlanders and Hussars. Casualties had been heavy. Captains P. E. Williams, J. H. Fletcher, G. H. Morgan, A. C. Janes, T. I. Hope Evans, Lieutenants L. ap T. Shankland, T. G. Daniel, 2nd Lieutenants W. S. James, T. Thomas, were killed, with 30 other ranks ; Major H. P. Coles, Captain Lloyd Roberts, Lieutenants G. H. Mills, D. D. Phillips, 2nd Lieutenants W. F. Coke, D. J. Janes, H. M. P. Dennis, G. T. Board, E. G. Rees, and 237 other ranks were wounded ; 85 other ranks were missing.

The 40th Division was relieved by the 32nd Division on the night of the 25th, and our battalion marched back to the Hindenburg Line, moved on the 26th to Lechelle, and on the 27th entrained at Ytres for Beaumetz.

It had been a desperate battle and the congratulatory messages received by the 19th Battalion were merited. Their right flank was always exposed—La Fontaine was never held, although a brigade of the Guards Division entered it—and on the left the village of Bourlon was defended with the greatest valour by the enemy : no doubt if some of the tanks could have remained to picket the village while the mopping-up was proceeding we might have tightened our grip and held on to it ; but the tanks had to return through lack of petrol, and the infantry, by themselves, were not strong enough to hold on. But the capture of the wood was a great achievement for the Bantam Battalion, under such adverse conditions.

. . . .

Meanwhile, our 4th Battalion had been working in the comparative quiet of the Arras sector. Rumour had been busy, and the 47th Division, when relieved in the line on the 19th November, commenced a march which, it was thought, would end in Italy.   The 4th Battalion concentrated at Roclincourt, and after passing through Acq and back to Dainville found themselves at Courcelles, in the devastated and depressing area of the Somme battlefield.   They passed through Bapaume to Beaulencourt. It was frightfully cold, and the sound of continuous artillery fire could be heard in the distance.   On the 26th, the day after the 19th Battalion had left Bourlon Wood, the 4th Battalion moved to Bertincourt, after sending a detachment of 100 to Mailly Maillet.   Here they waited until the 30th, when they had orders to move through Metz to Trescault.   The 47th Division had taken over Bourlon Wood during the night 28th/29th.

It is always as well to remember, when considering regimental, or general, action, that we were fighting the most highly trained military Power in the world—a trite remark, perhaps, but it does seem to have been lost sight of by the Third Army.   All calculations prior to the battle had shown that German reinforcements would commence to arrive within forty-eight hours of the opening of our attack—by pure luck one division had commenced to detrain in the ordinary course of relief in the Cambrai sector.   And the battle had been raging for ten days !   We had failed to exploit the success we had gained on the first day—we were held at Bourlon and La Fontaine.   By the 29th the German Commander, General von der Marwitz, had assembled troops for a serious counter-attack, and struck on both sides of the salient we had made.   The southern attack, in the direction of Banteux and Gouzeaucourt, was the main effort, at the junction of our VII and III Corps.   The blow fell on the morning of the 30th, and was successful.

Our 4th Battalion set out to march to Metz.   " We came to the conclusion, long before we reached Metz, that the Boche had sprung an unpleasant surprise upon some part of the salient.   The roads were thick with transport, all moving backwards, Metz was being heavily shelled, and Boche aeroplanes were flying about as they pleased. . . . Once clear of Metz we made better progress, but the sights which greeted us as we marched along towards Trescault were enough to dishearten the stoutest.   Gunners carrying their dial-sights, infantry in stray groups, some in the very act of throwing away their Lewis guns, others without rifles, all wearing a hunted look, and all hurrying back towards Metz. . . . We now understood why the Guards had been ordered forward." (*4th Royal Welch Fusiliers in the Great War*, Ellis.)

The 4th Battalion also realised that they stood a very good chance of being rounded up and ending their march in Berlin !   As they moved forward they found that " pandemonium was now raging to our immediate front, as well as to the south "—the 47th Division was in the thick of the northern fight.

Following fresh orders, the battalion passed on through Havrincourt and occupied the Hindenburg Support Line on the left of Flesquières.

Fortunately the artillery in general did not obey the somewhat panicky orders issued for withdrawal, and batteries of field guns stood in the open giving invaluable assistance to the 47th and 2nd Divisions in their gallant resistance against the attack through Bourlon and La Fontaine. On this side of the salient the enemy was held—he gained a little ground. On the southern side he made large captures of men and guns, but was eventually checked and held about Gonnelieu.

The 4th Battalion was kept busy. As darkness fell on the 1st December they were up in Bourlon Wood digging trenches in place of the line of shell-holes now occupied by front-line battalions. The latter were reduced to about a fourth of their strength, and our battalion also provided carrying parties to bring back the wounded and to carry up ammunition.

The work was repeated on the night of the 2nd. The 7th and 8th London Regiment had attacked and recovered ground lost on the 30th November, but the old trenches were battered to pieces ; A and B Companies dug 450 yards of trench for them, while C and D, on the right, dug 175 yards of trench under appalling shell fire, a large portion of which was gas. " As dawn was breaking, the 4th, laden once more with scores of wounded from the forward aid-posts, staggered back to the Hindenburg Support Line, having completed as fine a night's work as they had ever achieved."

Orders for further work in Bourlon Wood were then cancelled, and the battalion put every man on to the wiring and fire-stepping of the Hindenburg Support Line. The 47th Division were ordered to withdraw on the 4th/5th December, and the 4th Battalion were to make four strong-posts about 700 yards in front of the Hindenburg Support, which posts were, later, to be joined into one forward trench. The work was completed up to time, and the battalion, holding the posts they had made, watched the enemy advancing cautiously on the 5th December. The whole of Bourlon Wood was now in German hands.

That night, at dusk, four platoons went forward to the outpost line held by the 15th London Regiment, and dug trenches for them in place of the shell-holes they occupied. Before dawn the enemy was making vigorous thrusts on the right, and soon after midday on the 6th the out-posts were falling back on the Hindenburg Support Line. By 4 p.m. our 4th Battalion held the advanced positions.

The Germans evidently thought our withdrawal to the Hindenburg Line was completed, for they advanced confidently, and D Company, commanded by Captain T. R. Williams, holding the right strong-point which commanded the approach on Flesquières, were suddenly surprised by the unusual spectacle of a column of Germans marching along the road to that village. It was late in the day, the sun was setting, and the enemy was approaching a stretch of road that ran straight towards the strong-point, now manned, with every rifle and Lewis gun on the parapet. With heads below the parapet, motionless, the men waited for the word from Captain Williams, who watched patiently the advance of the foolhardy Germans. When the whole column was on that straight bit of road, he gave the order to fire.

In a few minutes the enemy had disappeared, leaving the road littered with their dead.

The battalion handed over the strong-points and the length of the Hindenburg Support they were holding to the 142nd Brigade, and continued their work on the support line (which was to be our front line) from a base which they established in the old British front line, south of Havrincourt.

The Battle of Cambrai, so well planned in the early stages, was over, and the enemy had once more successfully countered. Although north of Havrincourt we occupied his support line, south of that place we had not re-established ourselves in our former front line. There had been a fairly equal exchange of prisoners and guns.

Our 4th Battalion was out of the line for Christmas Day, which was spent in a village called Senlis : it was a roaring day of feasting.

.   .   .   .

As was generally the case, the opening of the Battle of Cambrai was marked by minor and subsidiary operations. Our 10th Battalion had entrained on the 5th October at Wizerne for the Third Army area about Barastre ; thence, on the 13th, into the line at Bullecourt.

On the 17th October orders were received from the VI Corps that the 3rd and 16th Divisions were to prepare plans for the capture of Bossie and Tunnel Trenches, and Tunnel Support, points already well known to the regiment. The date originally fixed for this operation was the 14th November, but it was subsequently decided to carry out the attack on the 20th November.

Our 10th Battalion took no part in the operation, which was moderately successful.

Our 19th Battalion, after Bourlon Wood, went to Beaumetz, thence to

Bienvillers, and on the 2nd December to Ervillers, and relieved the Munster Fusiliers at Bullecourt.

On the 15th December the 19th Battalion was ordered to carry out a minor operation with the object of (*a*) clearing the enemy from Neptune Trench and taking prisoners, (*b*) destroying dugouts or tunnels, (*c*) establishing blocks in Trident and Vulcan Trenches until permanent posts were established at the junction of these trenches with Neptune.

General Haldane, commanding IV Corps, describes this affair as " the

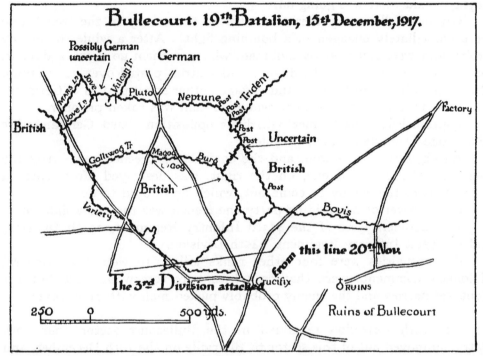

complement to the attack made by the 3rd and 16th Divisions on the 20th November."

In support of this attack were two machine-gun companies, the 119th and 244th, and two light trench-mortar batteries, 119th and 121st; also the divisional artillery and medium trench mortars.

These various batteries were to place the whole objective under an intense bombardment for three minutes: at zero the flank batteries and all trench mortars were to lift; at zero plus twelve minutes the centre batteries would lift. The artillery and machine guns would then open fire on Fontaine-les-Croisilles with the hope of leading the enemy to suppose that the attack would be directed on the trenches about those ruins.

The battalion provided a right attacking party, under Captain E. O. Hill and 2nd Lieutenant C. P. Crabtree, consisting of 54 other ranks ; and a left attacking party, under Captain C. F. Ellis and 2nd Lieutenant Harland, consisting of 46 other ranks.

A party of one officer and 24 sappers, Royal Engineers, was to follow the assaulting troops and destroy dugouts.

At three minutes before zero (3 p.m.) the bombardment opened, and on the hour the assaulting troops advanced. Everyone could see in this daylight raid what was going on.

Captain Hill's party met a number of the enemy in the trench and were immediately engaged in a bombing fight. After a while the enemy broke, and were followed by our men, who saw them go down a dugout. Bombs were thrown into the dugout and sentries posted over it. Captain Hill then led his men forward and engaged other small parties of Germans, who were rapidly dispersed : one wounded man was taken prisoner.

Captain Ellis's party met with little opposition : two Germans were killed, one (wounded) taken prisoner.

All objectives were won, and the engineers proceeded to destroy the dugouts : the occupied one, on the right, was destroyed after repeated invitations to the enemy to come out, which he refused to do.

Under cover of our raiding party the trench was then consolidated.

The prisoners were of the 453rd Infantry Regiment, 234th Division, and the 471st Infantry Regiment, 240th Division.

Our casualties were four other ranks killed, 16 wounded. General Haldane's comments were that casualties were somewhat high, but the front was narrow and the enemy probably picked men with good cover.

.   .   .   .

The 19th Battalion remained in the Bullecourt sector ; our 10th Battalion moved out of this sector to Blairville on the 19th December, and went into the line again on the 30th January rather to the left, near Guémappe. Great changes were then taking place ; brigades were being reduced to three battalions. These two gallant battalions were marked for disbandment, having upheld the honour of the regiment to the last day of their existence. Drafts were sent to other battalions of the regiment, and the remainder were amalgamated and became the 8th Entrenching Battalion under Lieutenant-Colonel James.

VI

DEFENSIVE OPERATIONS

DEFENSIVE OPERATIONS

THE GREAT GERMAN OFFENSIVE, 1918.

OVER three years of war, and the end not in sight !

The year 1917 opened with a monthly casualty return of 4,592 killed and 15,289 wounded ; in the month of April it jumped up to 32,131 killed, 120,070 wounded. The latter figure is almost equalled in October by 28,628 killed and 119,808 wounded.[1] No month equalled that of July 1916, when the return was 41,338 killed and 196,081 wounded, but after three months of heavy casualties on the Somme the returns dropped to about 40,000, whereas in 1917 they remained over the 70,000 mark for eight months.

The strength of the Armies in France had risen steadily to 2,038,105 in October 1917. But on the 1st January 1918 Sir Douglas Haig had, under his command, Armies amounting to 1,828,616 men.

The winter of 1917–18 is remarkable for a curious psychological change arising from causes both political and military.

Up to the end of the third series of Ypres battles General Headquarters in France, and Sir William Robertson, Chief of the Imperial General Staff in London, had been full of confidence. The 1916 offensive saw, in a general sense, the end of the volunteers ; the 1917 offensives had, also in a general sense, smashed the manhood of the Empire—that is to say, there was neither quality nor quantity to draw from. On the other hand, the French had, after the Nivelle catastrophe, to deal with mutiny during 1917. And one predominant fact stood out : Germany had an overwhelming number of divisions freed by the Russian débâcle.

---

[1] The intervening months are :

> May, 18,402 killed ; 76,040 wounded.
> June, 16,142 killed ; 75,173 wounded.
> July, 15,676 killed ; 84,695 wounded.
> August, 19,741 killed ; 81,080 wounded.
> September, 18,850 killed ; 81,249 wounded.
> October, 28,628 killed ; 119,808 wounded.
> November 15,048 killed ; 73,888 wounded.

There came the inevitable clash between soldier and politician. But in the study of war strategy and policy one must be fair to the politician : it will not do to throw the blame for the events of 1918 on to the " black coats." The regiment was deeply involved in the fighting ; the attitude of the Staff, as winter approached, stimulated discussion on the conduct of the war, and our soldiers in the front line very naturally supported the Army argument ; but the weight of responsibility for success or failure rested on the shoulders of the King's Ministers, and some of them, not unnaturally, were dissatisfied with the military results.

It was the most critical stage of the war, when doubt was lodged in the hearts and minds of many leaders. As early as August 1917, in the midst of the Ypres battles, the appalling list of the year's casualties provided a total which, corrected daily, appeared in letters of crimson before the Prime Minister's eyes. With the fate of Russia decided, all thoughts of victory were indefinitely postponed, and reserve man-power became a vital question. There was a limit—and not far distant. The Army in France— the main theatre—had not been starved in men or munitions ; both had been poured without stint on to the battlefield. And what was there to show ? With a free hand Robertson and Haig had won Bullecourt, Messines, and the slopes of Passchendaele on the Western Front, where the war, they declared, was to be won, but, as Sir Henry Wilson points out, on a larger map of the battle-front we had to mark Rumania, Russia, and apparently Italy as lost !

Sir William Robertson expressed himself satisfied with the conduct of the war under his direction : it is not surprising that Lloyd George thought his ideas parochial.

The critical situation had not been brought about by intrigue. There had been no interference with military plans—questions had been asked, suggestions made, by the Prime Minister, but that was not incorrect. Now the situation itself gave birth to intrigue, indecision, and the resultant bitterness. Even the power of change, which was in the Prime Minister's hands, could not be used in such circumstances without caution : forces ranged themselves for and against the Chief of the Imperial Staff. Sir Henry Wilson's name came once more to the front.

With all this discussion going on at the fountain-head, echoing through General Headquarters to lesser formations, though it did not reach the lowest, and with the pressing need for immediate and vast preparation for the coming German onslaught, the Staff mind vacillated and dithered. Considered apart from climatic conditions, this winter was the most trying for the regimental officer.

The order was to prepare for defence, but, judged by the nature of the instructions which came pouring into Battalion Headquarters, the moral ascendancy which General Headquarters had always claimed over the enemy had suddenly deserted them—and Army, Corps, perhaps also Divisional Staffs as well.

We had never, even in the worst days of the Ypres Salient, constructed successive lines of defence to any depth. Now the harassed regimental officer was confronted with orders about blue, green, red, black, and purple lines behind him, with plans, in the event of his battalion being out of the front line when the blow fell, for counter-attacking peaceful villages where billets were good, civilians traded, and active warfare could for a while be forgotten. A mass of detail—posts for the collection of stragglers, medical aid, points of supply, immediate action on " the Word," with movement always to the rear. Even Battalion, Brigade, and Divisional Headquarters were in many cases moved farther back in anticipation. And warnings of vast enemy preparation, of accumulation of ammunition, of tanks ! The front line must fight to the last—it would be wiped out : that was generally agreed. The fight would be carried on by supports and reserves, falling back on successive zones of defence.

All these preparations were, of course, very necessary, and time was, comparatively, short, but the conditions which prevailed, from London to the front-line sentry-post, conspired to create excitement, to fan it to fever pitch, and, with everyone tense, give them orders for ever pointing to the rear. It was, perhaps, inevitable. It had least effect on the soldiers in the fighting formations, but it seems to have accelerated, in some places, the rapid withdrawal of Staff and Supply.

Whatever the criticisms of Sir William Robertson's strategy may be, it was evident that the opportunity of bringing the war to a decision on some front other than the Western was gone. The initiative was in the hands of the enemy, who selected the Western Front for his final effort, and to meet it, and repair, as far as was possible, the damage sustained in our offensives by our divisions, other fronts were reduced in strength. The various expeditionary forces were rearranged. Indian troops commenced to move in substitution for white battalions who were to shift to France.

On the other hand, divisions in France were reduced in strength. Under date 26th January 1918, the 38th Division issued the order : " It has been decided by G.H.Q. to disband three battalions per division serving with the British Armies in France. The battalions to be disbanded in the 38th Division are as follows :

15th Royal Welch Fusiliers (113th Brigade), 10th Welch Regiment (114th Brigade), 16th Welch Regiment and 11th S.W.B. (115th Brigade).

" The 2nd Battalion Royal Welch Fusiliers, from the 33rd Division, will join the 38th Division at a date to be notified later.

" Order of Battle on completion of the above readjustments will read as follows :

113th BRIGADE.	114th BRIGADE.	115th BRIGADE.
13th R.W.F.	13th Welch Regiment.	2nd R.W.F.
14th R.W.F.	14th Welch Regiment.	17th R.W.F.
16th R.W.F.	15th Welch Regiment.	10th S.W.B."

Without this general sense of uneasiness the winter would not have been too bad. In the worst part of the line, the Ypres Salient, our 2nd Battalion, after their Passchendaele tour of duty, remained out of the line for five weeks. From St. Jean the battalion marched to Eric Camp, at Brandhoek, near Poperinghe, on the 1st December. " Six slack days were spent there, while the ground was icebound under a powdering of snow. On the 7th the battalion returned to a camp of sorts on the Menin road, between the Cemetery and the White Château. It was curious to see a Canadian polling-booth in Ypres as we passed through. At this election the Canadians adopted conscription—at a plebiscite soon afterwards Australia adhered to the voluntary system. Four days were spent working in the forward area in conditions of thaw and rain. The German artillery was still doing good work for its side. A high-velocity gun, ' Slippery Dick,' fired at frequent irregular intervals on the Menin Gate. German aeroplanes bombed the town and the surrounding camps with little check. For several months there were many complaints by the Army at the failure of the Royal Air Force to assist and protect them. The flying men were accused of devoting themselves to decoration-hunting stunts instead of co-operation and intelligence. Whatever the facts, the High Command thought it necessary to bring about an entente, and introduced a system of sending infantry brigadiers and commanding officers to spend a few days at aerodromes dining, wining, and ' joy-riding ! ' Major Kearsley went on such a course in January and was thrown out on his head. Other guests of the Royal Air Force fared worse." (Dunn.)

The Rev. P. B. Clayton, sometime Garrison Chaplain at Poperinghe, writes of the winter 1917–18 as " supremely wretched." It is difficult to separate, in this question of wretchedness, the effect of climatic conditions and the depression arising from a sense of failure. Occupying at Talbot

ROYAL WELCH FUSILIERS MOVING TO FORWARD AREA BY LIGHT RAILWAY, PILCKEM RIDGE, SEPTEMBER 1917.

Imperial War Museum photograph, Crown copyright.

384]

House, in Poperinghe, a favourable position for observation, he states that
" an evil spirit for the first time troubled both officers and men ; and in the
inevitable stagnation the phantom of failure, ridiculed before, walked
grimly abroad, and was not always challenged." He saw rancour and ill-
feeling growing between officers and men. He started what were called
" grousing circles," where men with grievances could go and air them, and
notes that the chief causes of complaint were the injustice of the distribution
of leave, the inequitable distribution of the bread and biscuit ration, in
which the infantry, as usual, came out the losers, the absence of restaurant
accommodation for men, the grotesque inequalities of pay, and so on.
The bulk of the men he saw were, of course, engaged on transport and
kindred services, and he admits, what was more evident in more distant
back areas, that in this " suburb " of the war the spirit of fraternity which
existed up to the end in the infantry units of the front line was absent in
the transport and supply services.

Nevertheless this feeling was reflected in the general behaviour of
infantry battalions. Major Dunn's notes on our 2nd Battalion show a
slackening of discipline in the ranks, which were now filled with " duration-
of-the-war " soldiers.

" On the 11th December the battalion entrained at St. Jean for
Abeille, and marched to billets in farms between Steenvoorde and Watten.
Ten uneventful working days were passed there. The wet and frosty
weather was so cold that for want of other fuel the men were burning farm
utensils, latrine seats, and any other combustible they could find. Since
the beginning of the severe cold a like burning of equipment had been
going on in the camps round Ypres ; in the White Château district, ablution
benches, latrines, and 1,100 floor-boards were said later to have been burned,
with the consequence that there was deep mud within the tents when the
thaw came. The fuel ration was so small that officers' messes were allowed
to buy coal within limits, at 3 francs a bag, but the scheme was not working
until the New Year was in.

" On the 21st December the hoped-for chance of spending Christmas
in Poperinghe came. Thence the companies started out each morning in
the dark to start work at daylight on another light railway to supply the
Salient. The convent with the blown-in gable, off the Rue de Cassel,
in which the entire battalion found itself, had to be endured. Its spacious-
ness increased the chill of large broken windows, ill-fitting doors, diminutive
fireplaces, and a lamentable short supply of fuel. A corps telegram that
would have assured us an undisturbed day and a Christmas dinner was not
delivered until so late on Christmas Eve that there was no time to make

arrangements.   A pay-out helped matters, and the estaminets were allowed to remain open for an extra hour. . . .

" The shops in this piece of Belgian salvage were stocked with provisions that could be bought in pounds and dozens (sugar, butter, meat, poultry, oranges, and preserved fruit) that were doled out by the half-ounce by permit to waiting queues in England.   Officers and men took joints and quantities of sugar with them when they went on leave, until the practice was forbidden.

" On the 29th December the battalion marched back to the Watten area through a snow-clad country.

" New Year's Day was a holiday.   It was a fine, frosty day.   The companies had their deferred Christmas dinners.   Each company made its own arrangements, one of them with indifferent success.   The billets were too scattered, and none too comfortable for a battalion dinner, though the purchases were made at St. Omer from a battalion fund.   An interesting light was shed on the drinking habits of the men.   No less than 40 per cent. of D Company preferred coffee to beer ; two other companies were 25 per cent. and one was 30 per cent. coffee-drinking.   The number of Old Army men in the companies was negligible.   The transport, Old Army almost to a man, were all beer-drinking ; so were the drums.

" While referring to social habits, it is worth recording that down to the Somme period only defaulters detailed to make a congregation attended a voluntary Church service ; at Airaines in midsummer 1917 a real voluntary congregation of thirty would assemble.

" On the 3rd January the battalion entrained at Abeille.   A poor camp, Toronto East, at Brandhoek, was occupied for one night.   On the 4th, after conveyance by bus to Ypres, a short march was made to Alnwick Camp, at Potijze.   Everywhere there was great activity in preparing defences.   At nightfall a move was made to support trenches, and on the 5th to the front line at Passchendaele, with Major Kearsley in command. The line had become stabilised ; a non-provocative policy was reciprocated by the Germans—the outgoing battalion had no casualties.   The battalion was to have upwards of a dozen from shelling.

" Apart from the abatement of gunfire, all the conditions at Passchendaele were much more tolerable than in November : duck-board tracks had been carried far forward, and a Decauville railway was well up.   The company at Crest Farm found spacious dugouts, which it shared with rats and standing water.   The front line was still nebulous.   On the early morning of the 7th, Moody (now Adjutant) and the Medical Officer were 100 yards in front of an advanced post of the battalion on the right when a shout recalled them as they were walking into the German lines. Relief on the night of the 9th was long held up because two posts could not be found in the snow. Relief in the salient had a character of its own. On other fronts relief was welcomed, but men would delay to tell or listen to a yarn, to have a drink, or they might dawdle. In the salient men had no smile until the moment of relief, when they stood not on the order of their going, but went with all the speed they could make.

" By the time Ypres was reached the snow had become sleet. The night was spent in chilly cellars in the Rue de la Bouche.

" Having travelled by light railway to St. Lawrence Camp, Brandhoek, on the 10th, the battalion returned by the same conveyance on the 13th and went to Whitley Camp, close to St. Jean. We were regretting the impending departure of Major Kearsley, who had been appointed to command the 11th South Wales Borderers, when on the 19th January his horse fell on him and broke his leg.

" Parties of men were employed on various fatigues, most on the construction of a second Decauville railway. The period of pioneering lasted two weeks.

" Political considerations were modifying the military situation, which was changing rapidly. Germany and Russia were negotiating peace. A peace by negotiation had influential advocates in England. Government control of everything had exasperated everybody ; there were so many authentic stories of folly, waste, and scandal. Officers and men rejoining off leave announced that ' fighting was over ' : that was the opinion of the moment on the ' home front.' More real to the troops was a reduced, though still sufficient, scale of rations. Bacon was as formerly ; bread was 1 lb. or biscuits 10 oz. ; fresh meat was down to 12 oz., and in practice it not infrequently fell to 200 lb. among 800 men ; from 3 oz. of sugar a half-ounce was deducted if the tinned-milk issue was sweetened ; potatoes had become so scarce that rice (2 oz.), oatmeal, carrots, etc., were given instead.

" Fantastic stories were circulated, in circumstantial detail, that the German dead were collected so that the fat and other useful derivations could be extracted for the manufacture of munitions, and even nutriment (proving conditions on their side worse).

" Rumours of impending reductions in establishment got into circulation quickly. The discussions and distractions caused by these matters of high policy deepened the gloom, without relieving the monotony of this tour of disgustingly uncongenial navvy work."

On the 27th January the battalion moved from St. Jean by train to

St. Omer, and marched by moonlight to Longuenesse.   On the 3rd February came the order transferring the battalion to the 38th Division.   On the 4th the battalion were played out of the 19th Brigade area by the pipes of the Cameronians and 5th Scottish Rifles.   The march was via Arques to billets in farms near Renescure ; on the 5th to Thiennes ; on the 6th the band of our 17th Battalion and the 10th South Wales Borderers played the incoming Battalion through Merville, and so to Robertmetz.

On the 13th February the battalion moved to Erquinghem, west of Armentières, the 38th Division having taken over the front line on the left of the Portuguese Corps.   And on the 18th a further move was made into the farms—Artillery, Gris-Pot, and Rolanderie—around Bois Grenier.

A few remembered their former visit to this place.   Captain Moody says : " I remember guiding the M.O., Captain Dunn, over the ground I had known so well in 1915.   It was interesting to note the difference in the general aspect of the country since then.   Streaky Bacon Farm and Artillery Farm were still occupied, although severely damaged by fire, especially Streaky Bacon, the roof of which was practically demolished. Armentières and the suburbs, l'Armée and Chapelle d'Armentières, were only skeletons of villages.   Most of the civilians had left, and the once gay town was now a desolate wreck, reeking with gas and filth.   The well-known church, the shops, and the regimental rest-house were only masses of debris.   I guided the Doctor through these places on to Bois Grenier, whose church tower had entirely disappeared.   Dead Cow and Moat Farms could still be located, but only by a mass of ruins.   Strange to relate, on coming to the entrance of the communication trench built by Stanway so long ago, it still remained in fair condition, and even the tubs containing the orange trees were still in position, although the plants were dead."

The front line was in a bad condition.   It was held by posts of seven or eight men at intervals of 200 yards ; the support line, about 200 yards in rear, was similarly held.   Battalions were expected to put out 1,000 yards of wire a night in their areas.   Work was concentrated on a new reserve line, but many had the uneasy feeling that the posts in the front line would be overwhelmed and the enemy attacking the new reserve line before it was known that an assault had been launched.   Nervous apprehension spread.   The civilian population that remained was being evacuated.   Every enemy shell and trench-mortar bomb was noted and reported.   March 1st was given as the date of the German attack.

St. David's Day was never celebrated in such strange surroundings and nervous tension.   The 2nd Battalion was relieved in time for dinner, and officers found a splendid meal prepared by the invaluable mess cook,

Parry. It was laid in the only available hut, near La Rolanderie Farm, which had been occupied until after dark by Englishmen who had probably never heard of St. David. The pioneer sergeant did wonders, but only the largest of the apertures, through which a raw and bitter night wind blew, could be closed in the time. At 8.30 p.m. it was not known where plates, glasses, cutlery, etc., could be got, and then one of the remaining estaminets, outside Erquinghem, was persuaded to lend what had been packed for removal, and clean bed-linen served as table-cloths. It was midnight when the Commanding Officer (Lieutenant-Colonel Garnett) invited the Brigadier to be seated. Only port was lacking ; " even the Portuguese canteen could not supply any ! " Of the thirty-one at table, twenty-three ate the leek in the odour of the goat and to the roll of the drum. The toasts were proposed by the Commanding Officer (St. David, the King, other Battalions), Cuthbert (Toby Purcell and his spurs), Moody (Shenken ap Morgan), French (the Ladies), Radford (the Guests).

The Doctor, returning from leave on the 20th, says : " I passed through the back of the front. Steenwerk, Estaires, and Merville were being shelled with big stuff ; a lot of damage was done round Merville station. Large numbers of civilians were on the roads moving to the rear, each family had a cart or hand-cart load, no more, of personal property and utensils, and the women mostly carried some cherished article.

" On 21st March I awoke at 4 a.m. There was a dispersed shelling of our area and the rumble and dull thudding of very heavy gun fire in the distance. Opening the door of the hut, I saw our working parties starting out, and could locate the gun fire in the south, beyond Arras. There was a trace of bromine in the outside air. It was an ideal morning for gas shelling, windless with a damp, moist mist. As it was plain that there would be no infantry attack on our front, I went back to bed."

.   .   .   .

The 9th Battalion—temporarily under the command of Lord Howard de Walden—after playing its part in the initial stages of the battle for the Passchendaele Ridge, when Colonel Smeathman was wounded, was employed in November and December 1917 in minor operations in the immediate south of Ypres. The main battle was still in progress, but the old salient and the ground about Hill 60 and Messines was comparatively quiet though unpleasantly boggy. Canvas camps and hutments were erected at every possible spot. The battalion was mainly occupied with con-solidating the line and providing large working parties—with occasional rests at Spoil Bank, Beggers' Rest-camp (on the Vierstraat–Kemmel road), Kemmel Shelters, and Tournai Camp (Vierstraat). It finally moved to the back areas about Strazeele and Ebblinghem and Blaringhem in the vicinity of Hazebroucke.

Suddenly on the 4th December came the order to entrain for the Cambrai–Flesquières Salient—where the victory which had set church bells ringing in London had been followed by disaster.

The 9th Battalion (Colonel Smeathman having returned to his command) entrained on the 7th December at Arques, detrained at Beaumetz and marched viâ Blairville to Gommiecourt, to Etricourt, thence on the 11th December into the front line about Marcoing and Ribecourt. It was truly a forced march under the most severe winter conditions.

The 19th Division was in the V Corps, and the 9th Battalion was in close vicinity to the 4th Battalion.

The battalion continued to occupy this part of the front, sometimes the left sector about Ribecourt and Marcoing, sometimes the right sector on Welsh Ridge, with supporting positions in the Hindenburg Line and at Trescault, and with brigade and divisional reserve positions at Havrincourt Wood and Lechelle respectively.

At that time the portion of the front on which the first German blow would fall was uncertain. But if we were to be driven back, the country behind the Flesquières salient, the old Somme battlefield and devastated area, was the one we could best afford to vacate.

Ludendorff tells us he found it very difficult to decide where to attack. He considered three sectors. First, between Ypres and Lens. Here he thought the ground difficult and that success would depend too much on the season and the weather. Sir Douglas Haig and his Staff, with the same ground under consideration, had decided that they could not afford to give up anything on this front, and that the necessary reserves must be kept in close proximity ; they, too, considered that an attack could·not be launched early in the year in that sector, but the weather was exceptionally dry, and they were by no means convinced.

The second sector considered by Ludendorff was between Arras and St. Quentin, or La Fère. The weakest part of our line was, he knew, in the neighbourhood of St. Quentin, but progress would be hampered by the crater-areas of the Somme battle. And here, Haig said, " ground could be given up under great pressure without serious consequences."

The third sector, on both sides of Verdun, would lead the Germans into very hilly country.

Ludendorff favoured the centre attack, the second sector, where the strategic results " might indeed be enormous, if we should separate the bulk of the English Army from the French and crowd it up with its back to the sea." He was influenced, he says, by the time factor and by tactical considerations, " first among them being the weakness of the enemy." He says : " A strategic plan which ignores the tactical factor is foredoomed to failure. Of this the Entente's attacks during the first three years of the war afford numerous examples."

He regrouped his forces. The Seventeenth Army, under Otto von Below, was slipped in between the Sixth and Second, opposite Arras ; the Eighteenth, under von Hutier, between the Second and Seventh, opposite St. Quentin ; the whole front was fed by fresh divisions from the east.

If our preparations were of an alarmist nature, those of the German Armies were optimistic : training for an advance is so much more cheerful than preparing for retreat ! We heard of our Royal Engineers laying gun-cotton charges beneath cross-roads and bridges which would be fired when our troops were wiped out, or even before ; but away in Rumania selected German officers trained fresh troops in western principles, and practised the advance behind a barrage with live shell.

It must not be thought that everything in Germany was easy. Some of the more alarmist instructions issued to our troops suggested that the Germans were supermen ; actually the nation was showing itself to be of ordinary human clay. " The nation could no longer brace the nerves of the Army ; it was already devouring its marrow. How far the secret agitation of the Independent Socialists had extended we were unable to determine. The strikes at the end of January 1918 had thrown another lurid light on their activities." (Ludendorff.) We, too, had strikes in England—strikes for more pay, not for the end of the war.

After all, the chances were equal : at the end of the war it was as at the beginning, a matter of nerves. The strain was felt in every country, nerve was giving way in every country—there are no supermen. Ludendorff says he had only " a kind of militia with much experience of war," and adds, " the enemy was no better " : he was right. He had reduced the battalions in his regiments, we had reduced the battalions in our brigades ; he was scraping men together from all theatres, so were we. He admits Germany had never been so strong on the Western Front, but we had the forlorn hope of America approaching. Ludendorff did not underrate the magnitude of his task.

Having selected the front of attack, his plan was to pinch off the Flesquières Salient, the Seventeenth Army, of twenty-four divisions, to attack north of Cambrai ; the Second Army, of 17 divisions, south ; on the left of the latter the Eighteenth Army, of 27 divisions, was to carry the attack down to La Fère.   Preparations were so far advanced that at the beginning of February the date for the opening of the great offensive was given—the 21st March.

Sir Douglas Haig was still uncertain of the point of attack.   Enemy rail and road communications were being improved and ammunition dumps increased from Flanders to the Oise !   But by the end of February preparation in front of the Fifth and Third Armies became marked.   He was not aware of the date selected by the enemy for the opening of their offensive until the 19th March.

. . . .

Our 4th Battalion, after spending Christmas at Senlis, commenced two months of most " acute wind-up " in this area, which they had not left since the Battle of Cambrai.   " The phrase ' in the event of enemy attack ' was now constantly recurring in the orders we received, and gave us the impression that the scores of German divisions released by the Russian débâcle were concentrated upon our immediate front."   February was a month of " panic orders and wild rumours " (C. Ellis, *History*).   February also saw the Battalion conform to the new Brigade organisation and become three companies.   There was no divisional rest.   The whole battalion was employed on the Third System of the battle-zone, but the need for speed was not fully recognised until the beginning of March.   They were now working on the defences of Metz-en-Couture and the second system of the battle-zone, digging and wiring a new reserve line in front of Trescault.   " Every day there came urgent warnings bidding us be ready to move to a destination unknown, in fighting order.   The ' Bab ' [1] code words were changed with bewildering rapidity and the atmosphere became generally electric."   Orders to " stand to," orders to " stand down."   Every man—cooks, officers' servants, signallers—was pressed into service, digging and wiring with all speed.

. . . .

THE FIRST BATTLES OF THE SOMME, 1918 : THE BATTLE OF ST. QUENTIN.[2]

At the end of February the 19th Division was withdrawn into Corps Reserve and the 9th Battalion was billeted in Herrick Camp on the Haplincourt–Bertincourt road.

[1] A code book issued to all battalions.
[2] Date: 21st–23rd March.   Area: the River Oise to Chauny ; thence road to Guiscard—Ham—Peronne—Bapaume—Boyelles ; thence the River Cojeul.

The 19th Division should have relieved the 17th Division in the left sector on the 8th March ; but in view of the scare of an immediate attack, all reliefs were cancelled. The 47th Division was in a like case ; they should have relieved the 2nd Division on the right of the corps front. So the V Corps (Fanshawe) stood, 2nd Division on the right, 63rd in the centre, 17th on the left, and the 47th Division right reserve, 19th Division left reserve.

The V Corps was the right of the Third Army, with the VII Corps (Fifth Army) on its right and the IV Corps on its left. The left division of the VII Corps was the 9th, the right division of the IV Corps was the 51st.

The divisional " rest " was, on this occasion, no rest at all. Digging and wiring were carried out in the battle-zone and the rear defences, and officers were made to reconnoitre and become thoroughly familiar with schemes for the defence and the recapture of Havrincourt, Hermies, Doignes, Louverval, and Beaumetz. Practice assemblies along the whole of the V Corps area were rehearsed under the supervision of the Corps and Divisional Commanders. The orders were that on the word " stand by " all units must be prepared to move at half-an-hour's notice ; and on the word to move each brigade was to march forthwith to its assembly position—the 58th Brigade to Gaika Copse, west of Velu Wood.

The 19th Division was again ordered to relieve the 17th on the 14th March, but another scare caused the order to be once more cancelled. It was, however, clear that the enemy attack was imminent : no less than 120 new battery positions had been counted on the IV Corps front. Ludendorff had assembled guns on the front to be attacked at the ratio of one to every 11 yards, and had massed trench mortars in the front-line system as well. Still, something had to be done—the front-line divisions could not stay there indefinitely—and the 47th Division was ordered to relieve the 2nd by the 22nd March.

Although this period of waiting was " jumpy," it was not tame. Our artillery carried out vigorous counter-preparation in the form of bursts of fire for short periods during the night, and more sustained fire for half an hour before dawn until it was evident that no attack was about to be launched. This was the commencement of artillery " crashes " which were found to be effective : every gun, within a definite area, was ordered to fire at a given time on a given target, and the " crash," the concentration of a great number of shells on one spot, came as a surprise, and was over—it might be repeated after a pause of a few minutes. Our artillery activity increased as the days passed, but the enemy tactics showed no change, except that on two nights Trescault was heavily bombarded with mustard-gas shells.

The details of what happened during the first days of the great German onslaught are in the main correct, but the fact is that Lieutenant-Colonel L. F. Smeathman and his staff were at one period practically cut off and surrounded, and in those circumstances he carefully burned all maps, notes, and papers.

Details with regard to times and incidents, recorded subsequently from memory, must be taken as approximate ; some no doubt have not been recorded at all.

It was 4.40 a.m. on the 21st March. There was no glimmer of dawn—the night was misty—and our artillery, busy since dusk the previous day with harassing fire, commenced their more sustained fire in counter-preparation on the forward enemy trench system. Ten minutes later the whole world seemed to be falling to pieces before the roar and shock of drum fire from a continuous line of German guns covering fifty miles, and the massed trench mortars in front of them : Germany had opened her attack.

There could be no mistake about it ; before the order to " stand to " could be circulated through corps, division, and brigade, the battalion was ready to move. The German bombardment increased in depth, and at 7 a.m. the transport lines, west of Bertincourt, were heavily shelled—mules were killed and the quartermaster's stores were hit several times.

The drum fire continued unabated, but no report of infantry action was received by General Jeffreys at 19th Divisional Headquarters until 10.25 a.m., when the liaison officer with the 51st Division reported that a message timed 9.45 a.m. stated that S.O.S. signals had been seen on the left brigade front and the enemy was attacking. Half an hour later the 51st Division reported the enemy in possession of the front-line system held by their centre and left brigades, and that it was their intention to hold the Beaumetz–Morchies system.

About the same time news came in that the enemy was advancing on the VII Corps front, between St. Quentin Redoubt and Gauche Wood.

The German plan was now revealed. The German Seventeenth Army was advancing between Croisilles and Mœuvres ; the Second and Eighteenth between Villers Guislain and La Fère. " In this operation," says Ludendorff, " the Seventeenth and Second were to take the weight off each other in turn, and with their inner wings cut off the enemy holding the Cambrai re-entrant, afterwards pushing through between Croisilles and Peronne. This operation was to be protected on the south flank by the Eighteenth

Army, in combination with the extreme left wing of the Second." The V Corps was, for the moment, not being assaulted, but the corps on either flank were being pushed back.

Our 9th Battalion received the order, soon after eleven o'clock, to move to the assembly position, Gaika Copse. They arrived to find the area under shell fire—in fact there were few places where troops could assemble that were not being shelled.

Meanwhile, the enemy had driven the 51st Division out of the Second-line system about Louverval and Lagnicourt, and a company of the 6th Wiltshire, of the 58th Brigade, was sent to the high ground between Beugny and Lebucquière to establish observation posts and keep the division informed.

It was anxious work, waiting at Gaika Copse with the thunder of battle in the air, and the struggle too far distant to be seen. The first order to our battalion to move came at 4.30 p.m. : they were to dig a new line on the Beaumetz–Hermies Ridge. The three battalions, 9th Welch on the right, 9th Royal Welch Fusiliers on the left, and Wiltshire in support, less a company, had almost finished this line by 9.30 p.m., when fresh orders came in to rest the men as much as possible, to move back behind the crest on which the trenches had been dug, and await further orders.

At midnight 21st/22nd March the battalion was ordered to a hut camp near Lebucquière. They arrived there about 4 a.m. At 9.30 a.m. they were on the move again to dig a new line covering the ridge south-west of Morchies. Our battalion faced north and north-east ; the 6th Wiltshire dug a line on the road from Morchies to the Beetroot Factory, on the Cambrai–Bapaume road facing east. A battalion of the Cheshire Regiment from the 25th Division had dug in behind the Royal Welch Fusiliers, and the three commanding officers had their headquarters together in the sunken road running from Beugny in a north-easterly direction. The 9th Welch Regiment were detailed to garrison and hold the village of Beugny at all costs.

No troops could be found on the left, but some of our troops were obviously to the north and north-west of Morchies, where firing was going on, and subsequently the 1st Leicestershire retired through our battalion lines. One company (A) of the 9th Welch was moved up to the left of our battalion and dug in about the Beugny–Vaulx road.

About 2.30 p.m. the enemy could be seen massing in great numbers on the high ground between Morchies and Vaulx. An hour later he advanced against the front held by the 58th Brigade. He had moved his guns forward during the night and the barrage in front of his troops was severe ; but the assault was broken up and thrown back by our Lewis-gun and rifle fire.

This attack by the Germans coincided with a message from IV Corps (to which the 19th Division had been moved on the 21st) to the 58th Brigade, that the enemy had broken through between Morchies and Vaulx, and that the brigade was to form a flank joining the third system with the Green line. Tanks were to co-operate in establishing this flank, and any available infantry were to follow and occupy the ground cleared by the tanks.

The first order issued by Colonel Parker, commanding the 2nd Tank Brigade, was to the Officer Commanding 2nd Tank Battalion, and was based on the bare information from IV Corps that the enemy had broken through. " I telephoned to Colonel Bryce (2nd Tank Battalion), explained the situation, and ordered him to move immediately on both sides of Beugny to meet the enemy and drive them back beyond the line Vaulx—Vraucourt— Morchies. I told him to get into touch with G.O.C. 58th Brigade, south of Beugny, who would give him as many troops as available to counter-attack with the tanks."

Colonel Bryce says that the G.O.C. 58th Brigade " explained that he had one battalion Royal Welch Fusiliers in Beugny, and a battalion of the Welch Regiment in posts to the north of Beugny. He told me that it was of the utmost urgency that the tanks should be got into action at the earliest possible moment, as he had just received information that the enemy were massing in great strength to the north of Beugny for an attack on that village and the Army line.

" The distance to Beugny being about three miles, it was calculated that the tanks would take about three hours to get into action from the time they started . . . .

" After leaving Brigade H.Q., I proceeded . . . to the hill to the west of Beugny, and found that the tanks were already arriving.

" The tanks of B Company proceeded round to the east of the village, and got into action about 4.30 p.m.

" The tanks of the other two companies were delayed through a difficult crossing and owing to the fact that the Officer Commanding the Welch Fusiliers sent for Major Lasky, and told him that he could not send the two companies in support, as had been arranged, because it would leave him with too weak a force to defend the village. Major Lasky told him he had been warned that tanks might have to operate without infantry assistance, and that he must carry out his orders and get his tanks into action without delay."

Colonel Bryce's report confuses the 9th Welch and the 9th Royal Welch Fusiliers. The 9th Welch were in Beugny and the Royal Welch Fusiliers in posts on the north and north-east of Beugny. Lieutenant-Colonel Smeathman, having received orders to entrench on the ridge between Morchies and Vaulx, had done so and was occupying the line about 500 yards south-west of Morchies. Also his battalion had just repulsed a strong attack. He says in his account that two companies of the 9th Welch which should have supported the tanks could not get there, and that one company of the Cheshire Regiment eventually supported the tanks. It is all rather a jumble. Actually the Commanding Officer of the 9th Welch, Lieutenant-Colonel King, had orders to hold Beugny and not to counter-attack under any circumstances, and his position fulfilled the corps order to form a flank connecting the third system and Green line. Indeed the three battalion commanders were unpleasantly situated : information was scant, orders were many and contradictory, rumour was wild, and they knew nothing of what was taking place on their left.

The tank commander decided to meet the German attack, then in progress, without infantry support.

" A tremendous concentration of machine-gun fire was opened on the tanks of B Company (east of Beugny) as soon as they were perceived by the enemy, and shortly after a barrage was put down which accounted for a number of tanks.

" The appearance of the tanks of the other two companies round the ridge from the west seems to have taken the enemy by surprise, and these tanks did great execution. One male tank dealt successfully with the personnel of a field gun which was firing on the tanks of B Company."

Casualties were heavy. " Of the 25 crews, or 175 men, who went into action, 108, or about 70 per cent., became casualties ; and of the 25 officers, 19 became casualties. During the action there was a considerable concentration of aircraft, and about twenty enemy planes swooped down over the tanks, firing at them. . . . The enemy was eventually pushed right back in the direction of Morchies.

" According to some infantry on the spot, the enemy had occupied Vaulx that afternoon, but retired from it when the tanks of C Company appeared over the ridge.

" During the course of the action the following message was sent back to their Brigade H.Q. by the Welch Regiment, who were occupying posts in front of Beugny : ' Two companies of the Welch are going forward to consolidate ground won by tanks.' " This was done at the request of Colonel Smeathman, but later they were withdrawn into Beugny on relief by the Royal West Kent.

How the battle appeared from the air is contained in a message sent at 6.30 p.m. Our troops were said to be holding Vaulx and the enemy the Bois de Vaulx. The tanks could be seen advancing, and some of our infantry was thought to be going through Morchies. All this may have been so : some battalions had been split up, and no one could be sure where British troops stood. These messages support Lieutenant-Colonel Smeathman's report that " the enemy was driven back over the line of the Morchies —Vaulx road by this counter-attack, and could be seen fleeing up the high ground north of the road," but, he says, the enemy again crossed the road soon after dusk.

A battalion of the Royal West Kent and a battalion of the Queen's came up soon after dark—they were of the 41st Division—and the line was then reorganised.

The Royal West Kent were placed on the left of our battalion, relieving the two companies of the 9th Welch who had been fighting there all day, and also one of our companies ; the former rejoined their battalion at Beugny, the latter was held in support. On the right of our battalion the 6th Wiltshire carried the line down to the Factory. The Queen's relieved the Cheshire Battalion, who dug a new line on the right flank.

Another brigade of the 41st Division was to have continued the line on the left, but it was reported to have lost its way ; the left flank of the Royal West Kent was open.

During the night six prisoners and a machine gun were captured by our battalion patrols.

Up to this point the enemy had made no great headway, but the proper perspective can only be obtained by glancing at the events on the right of the Flesquières salient.

The 47th Division had taken over the line from the 2nd Division, as ordered, when the storm broke. Our 4th Battalion was sleeping in camp at Lechelle. With the opening of drum fire on the 21st March came the crash of shells in the camp itself. At 9 a.m. the battalion was ordered up to man the inner defences of Metz-en-Couture. It was an unpleasant march in the thick mist, and with shells falling round them throughout the entire journey. The three companies of the battalion were quickly placed, A and B in the trenches before the village, C in cellars and cupolas in Metz. And there they remained, listening to the bombardment which continued unabated through the day and night.

At dawn on the 22nd no one had any idea of the situation in the front battle-zone until, during the morning, eight guns from the 47th Machine-gun Company reported to Lieutenant-Colonel Marshall that they had been ordered to place themselves at his disposal (he returned from leave at midday).

At 1.30 p.m. the battalion was ordered to move forward on to Dessart Ridge to form a flank on the right of the 47th Division : the 9th Division had been driven back.

The Germans worked their way round the flank of our 4th Battalion —there was no one to stop them, as the whole of the Fifth Army was retreating rapidly—and by 10 p.m. were in Fins, behind our right flank.

During the night of the 22nd/23rd the 47th Division fell back on the Metz line, and our 4th Battalion found itself mixed up with troops of the 140th and 142nd Brigades. At dawn the enemy proceeded to exploit the success he had gained and pressed the 47th Division closely. He subjected the front line to a heavy bombardment, and his machine gunners, having again worked round the right flank, opened fire and took the whole line in enfilade.

Our battalion was ordered to withdraw to the Green line at 10 a.m., but the fire was so hot and they were so closely pressed by the Germans that the battalion split in two, some going with Lieutenant-Colonel Marshall and the main portion with Major Langton. The latter succeeded in getting back, as ordered, to the Rocquigny area, but the party under Lieutenant-Colonel Marshall had the greatest difficulty in avoiding capture—they joined the 142nd Brigade and spent the night 23rd/24th marching through Ytres and Bertincourt, both of which they found deserted, and then, to avoid Bus, which was reported in enemy hands, to Barastre, and so to the Rocquigny area.

Briefly, the crumbling of the Fifth Army front had brought the 47th Division back with a rush, which commenced on the morning of the 23rd, when they found the Germans behind them. The 63rd Division had to go as well.

Now we come to the situation of our 9th Battalion on the morning of the 23rd. The enemy was finding resistance stubborn on this flank and progress was not being made according to plan. " On the 22nd March," says Ludendorff, " there was little change on the Seventeenth Army front. . . . The Seventeenth appeared to give its various tactical groups too much latitude ; but for this the action of the different units was too inter-dependent. G.H.Q. took steps to get the general direction of the fighting under a single control."

Whether the result was due to the intervention of the German Higher

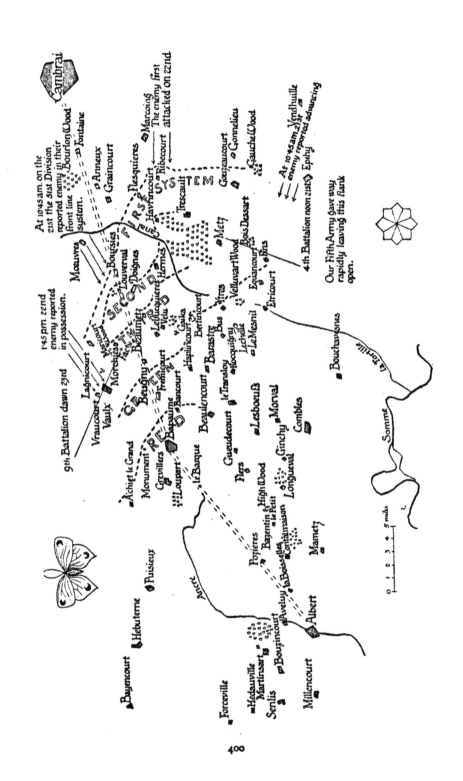

Command or not, a change took place on the morning of the 23rd. At 7 a.m. a bombardment, such as had not been experienced since the first day of the battle, opened on the front held by the 58th Brigade. All communication was cut—excepting by runner, and only a small percentage of these brave men won through. Small groups of men commenced to dribble back from the front line to " Battalion " Headquarters, which was now a conference of five commanding officers. On the high ground in front of our battalion the enemy could be seen massing for the assault.

The situation was bad enough, but it was made impossible by the state of affairs on the right of the brigade front. The whole of the V Corps was sliding away, out of the jaws of the trap, from the right ; the enemy was already behind the 47th Division on the extreme right, and one might well say that the British front was in a fluid state.

The messages which reached General Jeffreys at Divisional Headquarters were alarming. The S.O.S. signal had been fired at Lebucquière at 7.15 a.m. ; the enemy was at the Beetroot Factory at 8.30 a.m. ; and at midday he had broken through the front of the 51st Division, on the left.

But at noon this group of five battalions still stood on their original ground. The 6th Wiltshire reported their right flank in the air. The commanding officers decided to send two companies of the 11th Cheshire to prolong the flank from the Factory in a south-westerly direction, but soon found that the enemy had worked round behind them.

At about 3.15 p.m. an order got through from the 58th Brigade Headquarters for the brigade to withdraw in small groups to the Green line. This placed the commanding officers in a difficulty : the two from the 41st Division had received no orders to withdraw, and it was obvious that the 58th Brigade could not withdraw without involving them. But the left flank seemed as much in the air as the right, and so they all decided to go. Lieutenant-Colonel Smeathman says : " The shelling by this time had become most intense on the Battalion Headquarters, and it subsequently transpired that no runner got through to companies with this message. Various attempts were made with Battalion Headquarter Staff to form a defensive flank, but all these attempts were completely wiped out by the enemy barrage. The remaining two companies of the Cheshires were also practically wiped out."

Lieutenant-Colonel Smeathman, with the Commanding Officers of the 6th Wiltshire and the Cheshire Regiment, came away about 5 p.m., " when it became evident that companies were endeavouring to withdraw."

The enemy was well round their right flank, and there is no doubt that the entire brigade, together with the Queen's and Cheshire, would have

III—26

been surrounded had it not been for the gallant stand of the 9th Welch. They had met the enemy advancing between Lebucquière and Beugny, behind the Wiltshire, and held him until after 5 p.m.   The remnants of our battalion, the Wiltshire and Cheshire, managed to extricate themselves. It was during this fighting that all papers, notes, anything that might be of use to the enemy, were burned.

Captain W. Davies, commanding D Company, gives a graphic account of the events on his part of the front on the 23rd March.

" The early morning was quiet enough.   The enemy could be seen quite clearly in great numbers, and further away to the left one could observe large units complete with transport on the march.   At first we were troubled only by shells and aeroplanes, but as the day advanced their machine guns began to get very active.   I got in touch with C Company and also discovered a platoon of the Queen's on my right.   Presently several enemy planes appeared and, flying very low, seemed to be making a careful reconnaissance.   Then there was a lull, disturbed only by bursts of machine-gun fire from our right rear : this we thought to come from some of our own troops.   We were later to discover our error.

" In the afternoon I endeavoured to find C Company again and the platoon of the Queen's, but instead found the enemy all around us.   I then took steps to get my men and officers together from their isolated posts and sent for Lieutenant Beddow, who was watching my extreme left some 500 yards away.   He reported that there was nothing but enemy troops on his left.   We could find no British troops at all and could not communicate with Battalion H.Q.   Soon the enemy concentrated a fierce shelling with whizz-bangs [*field guns*] on our posts ; the machine-gun fire from our right rear became more and more intense, and then the ' flying circus ' came down on us.   A few minutes later ' Jerry ' [*Germans*] came at us at the double, bayonets fixed, and looking like a cup-final crowd (they were in good form in those days).   I then gave orders to ' hop it,' and the few of us did the 100 yards inside evens, chased by the multitude on the ground and aeroplanes overhead.   These flew so low that they were almost able to take our tin hats off our heads.   We suddenly pulled up short when we found ourselves looking down the barrels of some enemy machine guns and rifles.   These it was who had been shooting at us all the time from our right rear.   However, we gave them the dummy [*bayonet*], and by some means or other found ourselves, after a run of a half-mile or so (it seemed more like seven miles), among some of our C Company, who were holding up the Boches who were pursuing us.   There we stayed and returned the compliment to our pursuers with such effect that they decided to pack up for the night. Then there was peace for a time, and later the remnant of us received the order to withdraw behind Beugny."

When the battalion was reorganised during the night 23rd/24th March behind Beugny, it consisted of 9 officers and 60 other ranks.

THE FIRST BATTLE OF BAPAUME.[1]

The attenuated units of the brigade were still together, our battalion and the South Wales Borderers being in support. No further attacks were delivered by the Germans that night, but in the morning they attempted to assault the Green line held by the 9th Cheshire and 9th Welch and were dispersed. Pressure, however, increased : weak though it was, the 58th Brigade retained cohesion, but on their right units were mixed and uncertain in their purpose. At about 2.30 p.m. the line on the right of the 19th Division began to give way and it was decided to withdraw the Welch Regiment.

This retirement was covered by our 9th Battalion and a detachment of 5th South Wales Borderers—a delicate and difficult operation with the enemy pressing hard on the heels of the Welch. Major Lloyd Williams, who came up to relieve Colonel Smeathman, the latter being required at Brigade H.Q., was in charge of these operations. He directed Captain Malcolm Lewis with Lieutenants Nash and G. F. Lewis to form a defensive flank on the right around Frémicourt and to hold on until ordered to withdraw along specified lines. The purpose was to ensure the complete withdrawal of the Welch and two companies of the K.R.R. on the left, who were finding difficulty in extricating themselves from the Green line. With great stubbornness the Royal Welch Fusiliers and South Wales Borderers hung on to their ground, and when hard pressed actually launched a series of local counter-attacks up the slopes and succeeded not only in holding up the enemy and so accomplishing their purpose, but in putting the enemy to flight on this part of the front. When the troops on the Green line had been extricated, they withdrew in complete order to the positions previously determined. A great, gallant, and skilful effort this on a stricken field.

At 4 p.m. all troops of the 58th Brigade were ordered to withdraw, under the cover of troops of the 51st Division, to the Red line running immediately in front of Bapaume, and there General Glasgow, Colonel Smeathman, and Colonel King (Welch Regiment) collected and organised

[1] Date : 24th–25th March. Area : the River Somme to Bray ; thence road to Albert—Martinsart—Sailly au Bois—Monchy au Bois—Arras ; thence the River Scarpe.

the remnants of units as they fell back, and prepared for another desperate resistance to the enemy attack, which, it was expected, would be resumed when light appeared. On the right was the 56th Brigade, on the left the 57th. Here they remained from 6.30 p.m. till 10 p.m., when a further retirement was ordered to the Bapaume–Albert road, where a welcome reinforcement met the units of the 58th Brigade, consisting of all men that could be collected from the Transport and Brigade Headquarters, a corporal and three men who had been left as guard to a blanket dump at Grévillers, bands, cooks, anyone who could be found : our battalion received 60, which brought its strength up to approximately 80 rifles.

Meanwhile our 4th Battalion with the 47th Division, having escaped from their precarious situation during the night 23rd/24th March, and still in two portions, fell back, the one under Lieutenant-Colonel Marshall through Rocquigny to Le Transloy, the other under Major Langton to the Les Bœufs–Ginchy road. The latter put in some good work on this line, in conjunction with the 47th Divisional Royal Engineers, holding up the German advance with rifle fire, and falling back swiftly during the afternoon of the 24th to a line east of Delville Wood.

It was as well that men were there who remembered the old Somme battlefield ; with the Fifth Army still moving rapidly back, this flank of the Third Army was bound to be in a ragged condition. The difficulty was to keep in touch with their left, and with news of Germans in Flers the 47th Division made a final stand that night behind High Wood.

Here troops of that division saw a memorial cross " To the Glorious Memory of the gallant Officers, Non-commissioned Officers, and Men of the 47th Division who lost their lives in the capture of High Wood, 15th September 1916 "—a strange twist of Fortune's wheel. The enemy was actually in possession of High Wood that night, and was amusing himself in a strange fashion. " His Verey lights seemed uncomfortably close and his presence in High Wood was proclaimed by an occasional shout. Much of this shouting was in English, but the accents were too guttural to be deceptive. We were amazed to hear phrases culled from the soldiers' game of 'House,' such as ' Kelly's eye,' ' Legs eleven,' ' Clickety-click,' ' Top of the House.' No other expressions could have been more convincingly English. Nevertheless Lieutenant O. P. Blake and three men, patrolling near the spot whence issued these reassuring sounds, were captured." (C. Ellis, *The 4th Royal Welch Fusiliers*.)

The uncomfortable feeling of being out of touch, and of scrambling to gain touch, which had prevailed throughout these days was somewhat allayed on the 25th by the knowledge that the 17th Division had come into the battle on the right of the 47th.   The retreat continued to Contalmaison, and then came the cheering news of relief by the 12th Division.

" We held on to the Contalmaison position until 2.30 a.m. (26th), by which time the 12th Division had taken over the line.   Our share in the great retreat was over at last.   Back we trudged through La Boiselles-Aveluy, and across the Ancre to Bouzincourt, done to the world and practically walking in our sleep, yet conscious of a great contentment. The sky behind us glared with the blaze of the burning ammunition-dumps of Pozières—now abandoned to the enemy."

The presence of fresh troops on the 25th was encouraging, but the retreat was not yet ended, and the time was still anxious.   The 58th Brigade had at 10 p.m. on the night of the 24th been withdrawn through Bapaume and was holding positions between that town and Grévillers. From early morning, heavy machine-gun fire from the south-east was making the position extremely uncomfortable, and at 9 a.m. it was found that the troops on the right of the 58th Brigade had begun to fall back.

An hour later the 57th Brigade on the left was forced on to Grévillers, and the 58th found themselves in a dangerous salient, and so withdrew to the edge of Loupart Wood ; but they had to fight.   The enemy attacked several times and the decision to move had to be postponed until 1.30 p.m., when once more they retired through the 51st Division.

The skimpy details of this period of the battle are due to the fact that the whole of the 58th Brigade was now reduced to a fighting force of some 30 men and 4 officers : our 9th Battalion was represented by 8 men and 1 officer—Lieutenant-Colonel Smeathman.

Lieutenant-Colonel Smeathman rallied and reorganised the mixed units and inspired them with energy.   Every man was weary ; it was impossible to keep the troops in their units ; the 51st (Scottish) Division had lost its officers, and the men without leaders were uncertain what to do.   When Lieutenant-Colonel Smeathman appeared, they at once responded and, hammered though they had been during the past four or five days, put up a great resistance, which enabled the remnant of the 58th Brigade, who had been stranded on the edge of Loupart Wood, to extricate themselves.   The fight continued for several hours : the enemy attacked ; our troops re-formed and counter-attacked and yielded their ground reluctantly.   Other units began to arrive, and at 5 p.m. the 58th Brigade was withdrawn to Puisieux and there took up a line of outposts.   There were no troops on the right or left, and only a few stray units to their front. At 10.30 p.m. orders were received to fall back to Hebuterne, which was reached at 2 a.m.

The condition of affairs may be gauged from the fact that since the last contact with the enemy, about 1.30 p.m. to the early morning of the 26th March, when it was decided to organise the 58th Brigade as a battalion, the strength of our 9th Battalion had again risen to about 90 men and 3 officers. Split into small parties, separated, lost, they plodded on through the day, by chance in the same direction, and came together again. They were organised into three platoons.

At about 10 a.m. on the 26th, when practically the whole of the remnant of the 58th Brigade and other units were in Hebuterne, the enemy appeared in force on the south-eastern edge. The composite battalion withdrew to the north-western outskirts, taking up a defensive position until the situation could be more accurately gauged. The 57th Brigade was in touch on the left and the 56th in reserve, but there were no troops on the right. Fighting and reconnoitring patrols were pushed out and through Hebuterne, some of them actually led by the Brigadiers of the 58th and 57th Brigades—Generals Glasgow and T. A. Cubitt. The enemy had seized various positions and houses, and his concealed machine guns proved very troublesome. There was street fighting with many casualties, but by dusk the village was cleared and some prisoners and a machine gun were taken. A line of outposts along the south and east of the village was then established and a continuous line of defence organised. At 10 p.m. the battalion was unexpectedly relieved by a battalion of Australians, who marched up boldly in fours and took over a well-defined and organised line of defence which only the persistent and gallant determination of the weary troops of the 58th Brigade had made possible. The 58th Brigade was thereupon withdrawn into billets at Bayencourt, and on the 28th March moved to Famechon. On the 30th the whole brigade entrained at Cardas and Doullens for the Second Army area, under General Plumer.

Our 9th Battalion casualties were returned as 6 officers killed (Captain F. M. Arnold, Lieutenants Nash, W. J. Ellis, H. F. Owen, W. Handley, E. T. Llewelyn), 5 officers wounded, 3 officers wounded and missing, 3 officers missing ; other ranks were lumped together under the figure 443.

Our 4th Battalion, after staying at Louvencourt and Harponville, finally rested at Senlis. Their casualties included Captain T. C. W. Minshall, Lieutenant Chettle, 2nd Lieutenants J. W. Roberts, Quicke, and 56 other ranks killed or missing ; Captain C. B. Christopherson, 2nd Lieutenant R. A. Williams, and 115 other ranks wounded. The 47th Division was not withdrawn from this front.

.   .   .   .

The V Corps was now behind the Ancre, and from the 25th March was no longer the flank corps of the Third Army, under which command all troops north of the Somme had been placed. It was hoped that the right of the Third Army would remain on the Bray-sur-Somme line, more or less in touch with the left of the Fifth Army, but on the 26th the retreat was continued and Albert was abandoned to the enemy, who also obtained a hold on Aveluy Wood.

The situation was, however, a little brighter : fresh British divisions had been thrown into the line. The 38th Division, with our 2nd, 13th, 14th, 16th, and 17th Battalions, was moved down from the Laventie—Givenchy sector, Divisional Headquarters closing at Merville and opening at Toutencourt on the 1st April. The division was ordered to relieve the 2nd and 47th Divisions in due course, but for some days it stood behind them.

Our Third Army, being in greater strength than the Fifth, had retired before the onslaught more slowly, and by so doing caused the enemy to modify his plan. The German Higher Command found that their Seventeenth Army was exhausted on the 25th, and the Second was in little better case. Farther south, where their task had been easier, their Eighteenth Army was comparatively vigorous, and was still gaining ground.

On the 4th April the German commanders made a last effort to capture Amiens, and attacked with their Second and Eighteenth Armies. This brought in the front held by the weakened 47th Division, about Aveluy Wood.

Our 4th Battalion, still billeted at Senlis, had been doing pioneer work in the Bouzincourt line, and in common with the infantry brigades of the division were warned that the enemy was expected to attack in the early morning of the 5th. They were also warned that they would, in any case, be called upon for trench duty by relieving the 142nd Brigade about Aveluy Wood.

The Brigades of the 47th Division were, naturally enough, much below establishment, all ranks were in a state of exhaustion, and the organisation in the line was not normal—battalions were not under the command of their own brigadiers.

The line ran well into Aveluy Wood on the left, and at 6.30 a.m. on the 5th April a heavy barrage was opened on the left brigade, the 142nd. The shelling spread from the north to the south along the divisional front, and by seven o'clock had become general.

The enemy commenced his attacks about 8 a.m., and by 11.40 a.m. the right battalion of the 142nd Brigade had fallen back out of the wood on to the line of Battalion Headquarters. A curious and uncertain front was then presented to the enemy, which he exploited, and by evening all but the extreme left of the brigade line was out of the wood.

Orders were then sent from Divisional Headquarters, in confirmation of verbal orders given on the telephone to the Brigadier, that a counter-attack would be delivered by the remaining troops of the 22nd London Regiment, supported by our 4th Battalion. Our battalion had moved up from Senlis early in the afternoon, under heavy shell fire, which had caused many casualties, and had taken the position of the reserve battalion sent forward to reinforce the line. The counter-attack was to be in a southerly direction, and was to be launched as soon as the artillery and machine-gun observers could see the objective clearly. On the morning of the 6th, the written order was not received at the 142nd Brigade Headquarters until 12.40 a.m., by which time the Brigadier had already discussed the arrangements for the counter-attack with the artillery and machine-gun officers and Major Marshall, and had decided to form up on the line of the railway and advance in an easterly direction, his reasons being that the Royal Welch Fusiliers had no knowledge of the country, which they had never seen in daylight, and that the railway line was the simplest forming-up position.

It was then too late to alter the arrangements, and at 6 a.m. A and B Companies advanced on the edge of the wood.

The enemy held the whole of the southern portion of the wood as well as part of the northern. He had had a number of machine guns on his right, but he had massed them mostly at the south-western corner of the wood. Our A and B Companies advanced with a screen of scouts, each company attacking in two waves on a two-platoon frontage. The artillery barrage was feeble and left the German machine gunners in the corner of the wood on our right untouched. The attack failed.

The deployment and steady advance of our two companies under heavy machine-gun fire received special commendation, but it was hopeless to press the attack and matters were left as they were.

These two companies lost Captain J. B. Howard, Lieutenants N. I. Wilson, W. G. Jones, J. Walsh, H. S. Axton, R. C. Evans, T. E. Jones, 2nd Lieutenants G. H. Woodcock, and 65 other ranks killed ; Lieutenants S. A. Alexander, V. A. Clappen, and 81 other ranks wounded.

The whole division was relieved that evening by the 35th Division, and our battalion marched back to Senlis. During the night 7th/8th April, Senlis was bombarded with mustard-gas shells ; nothing was thought of it at the time, and in the morning the battalion started for Puchvillers. It was raining, and the men's great-coats were saturated with liquid from the shells during the overnight bombardment. The result was that 8 officers and 130 other ranks were sent to hospital.

The remnants of the battalion continued their journey into Third Army reserve area, and rested finally at Froyelles and Fontaine-sur-Maye, where large drafts soon brought them up to strength.

THE BATTLES OF THE LYS.

Many hard words have been said about the retreat of the Fifth Army and the right wing of the Third Army, and some of the charges are, no doubt, justified. But the Germans did not find it as easy to carve a way through their defence as through a lump of butter : there was a hardness here and there that pushed Hindenburg's troops off their course, narrowed their thrust, and brought it into a point ; they found it difficult to move ; they wanted elbow-room, and tried to obtain it by attacking at Arras. They failed.

Their success had, however, been great, and the chief danger lay in Ludendorff's appreciation of the situation. He was not going to be tempted into battering his head against a wall, and he broke off the battle.

On our side the wordy warfare and manœuvres of intrigue came to an abrupt end with the first shock of catastrophe. On the 18th February General Sir William Robertson had been relieved of his appointment as Chief of the Imperial General Staff, which he had held since December 1915, and replaced by General Sir Henry Wilson, but dissatisfaction with the conduct of the war had gone beyond mere change of individuals and the question of single command was acute and delicate. On the 26th March the Doullens Agreement was concluded, and a decision to appoint General Foch to co-ordinate the efforts of the British and French Armies was arrived at. General Foch's appointment as the Commander-in-Chief of the Allied Armies in France followed on the 14th April. Before he got into the saddle a second enemy thrust was delivered.

Although the strategic result of the first great German effort was to them a disappointment, their tactics were sound, and they decided to launch an attack on the same plan as that of the 21st March against the Portuguese on the Armentières—Laventie—Givenchy front. It was one of the original points of attack contemplated by the Higher Command, and all arrangements had been made. The condition of the ground, the principal objection, was now good, and it was known that Haig had weakened his front there and at Ypres by sending divisions south. The artillery officer of the

Eighteenth German Army, Colonel Bruchmüller, who originated the artillery plans on which the attack on the 21st March had been based, was sent to the German Sixth Army to check and supervise their arrangements, and " reported that all was in order." The attack was launched on the 9th April ; the Kaiser went to Avesnes to hear the news, and stayed to lunch. He gave an iron statuette of himself to Ludendorff.

Sir Douglas Haig was only too well aware of the dangerous situation which had now arisen on the fronts of his northern armies. " The bulk of the divisions in front line in the northern battle, and in particular the 40th, 34th, 25th, 19th, and 9th Divisions, which on the 9th April held the portion of my front between the Portuguese sector and the Ypres—Comines Canal, had already taken part in the southern battle. It must be remembered that before the northern battle commenced, forty-six out of my total force of fifty-eight divisions had been engaged in the southern area." (Despatches.) And, although the battle had died down in the south, there was still a mass of German divisions concentrated there, ready to take advantage of any weakening of the front. The German arrangements were excellent.

Our 9th Battalion entrained at Doullens for the Second Army area on the 30th March and detrained at Strazeele on the 31st. They were conveyed by lorries to Wakefield huts, near Locre and Danoutre. Some 400 reinforcements arrived. A very small proportion of these were N.C.O.s and very few had any experience of war. The battalion was hastily reorganised into what was scarcely a trained fighting machine.

The 19th Division was posted to the IX Corps and was allotted a front on the east of Messines and Wytschaete, from the River Douve to Charity Farm, a front of about 6,000 yards. The 58th Brigade was on the left of the Wambeke, the 57th on the right, and the 56th in reserve. The flank divisions were the 9th on the left and the 25th on the right.

On the 3rd April the battalion moved to Neuve Eglise, and on the 7th relieved the 2nd Lincolnshire in brigade support about Onraet Wood. On the 9th the battalion took over the front line from the 9th Welch, across the front of Green Wood and Ravine Wood. Two companies (A and B) occupied the front and support lines, the other two being in reserve about Denys Wood and Rose Wood.

Although General Headquarters was aware that an attack was imminent somewhere on this northern front, no special warning was received by the 19th Division.

THE BATTLE OF MESSINES, 1918.[1]

The Portuguese, between Sailly and Festubert, had been in the line for a long time and were in need of rest ; relief was due. The Germans anticipated this relief and attacked on the 9th April at 7 a.m. The Portuguese were driven in, and the enemy reached the line of the River Lys. The flank divisions bent back ; the attack spread. The situation was sufficiently alarming, although from the German point of view the progress made during the afternoon of the 9th was not what they had expected : they were held at Givenchy and Festubert by the 55th Division, in which Brigadier-General Stockwell commanded a brigade. They made little progress in the direction of Bethune, but in the evening were approaching Armentières. They employed tanks, which they considered a hindrance. Still, they advanced on a wide front, and it was evident by nightfall that an attack on the positions held by the 19th Division was more than probable. The relief of the 57th Brigade was cancelled.

On the 58th Brigade front the 6th Wiltshire held the right and our 9th Battalion the left. At 5.30 a.m. on the 10th April the enemy opened a heavy bombardment, mainly south of the River Wambeke, on the 57th Brigade front, and, in accordance with the tactics they adopted in these great efforts, assaulted shortly after. No attack was delivered on our battalion front until somewhere between 9 and 10 a.m. ; but at 7 a.m. Messines was reported in enemy hands, and by 9 o'clock it was apparent that the 57th Brigade had been driven back. The 6th Wiltshire were ordered to form a flank along the ridge north of the Wambeke to Pick House, where the nearest troops, some of the Warwickshire, were to be found.

The storm burst on our front, and at noon a message was received by Lieutenant-Colonel Smeathman that our front-line posts had been overwhelmed ; the bombardment had become exceedingly heavy, especially on the left in Ravine Wood, where all the posts were blown in, leaving a gap through which the enemy trickled.

About 3 p.m. touch was lost with the Wiltshire on the right, and our right company was withdrawn to the reserve line, as were also our posts in Rose Wood. From 4 to 7 p.m. all companies were in the reserve line, and the enemy was successfully held ; and then the enemy was found behind our right flank in Oosttaverne Wood.

The long flank held by the 6th Wiltshire, some 2,000 yards, was from

---

[1] Date: 10th–11th April. Area: road Armentières—Bailleul—Locre—Dickebusch—Voormezeele ; thence the Ypres—Comines Canal.

the first a weakness, but they clung on until about 7 p.m., when a runner got through to Brigade Headquarters with the information that his Battalion Headquarters had been driven out of their dugout by the enemy advancing from the Pick House–Torreken Farm direction.

The situation of the brigade was precarious. At 4 p.m. it had been placed under the command of the 9th Division, and our battalion had then reported that their left, north of Denys Wood, was not in touch with any troops of the 9th Division. A company of the 9th Welch Regiment was then sent forward to try to fill this gap. Later two battalions from the 9th Division were sent up to help fill the gap.

The experience of the German attack in March was repeated : companies were being separated. Lieutenant-Colonel Smeathman had to send out patrols to ascertain the position of his battalion. At 7.30 p.m. he found he had one company holding the reserve line in Denys Wood, one company near Goudezeune Farm, but the front- and support-line companies, A and D, had lost heavily and he could learn nothing more than vague rumours of small parties holding out. At that time the 9th Welch had two companies and a portion of a third in the cutting southeast of Wytschaete, and a fourth company about Pheasant Wood.

But nothing was stable, and reports not always trustworthy. A few men from D Company reported that the whole company had been surrounded—this proved to be true ; they fought to the last and ceased to exist. About 9 p.m. B Company, on the left, reported that touch had been lost with C Company, which was no longer in position at Goudezeune Farm ; this, however, was incorrect, as C Company remained in position until the early morning of the 11th, when, finding no troops on either flank, the company fell back. But at the moment Lieutenant-Colonel Smeathman's command seemed small. He was ordered to place the one company he knew of, B Company, under the 9th Division, and they were instructed to dig in on the Dammstrasse line, while he and his Headquarters with a few men of A and D Companies moved to Parma Dump on the Western Edge of Grand-Bois. Although it was nearly midnight, they were soon shelled out of Parma Dump and shifted to a position behind Vierstraat.

The enemy did not press his attack during the night, and two battalions of the 62nd Brigade took over the line on the left of the 9th Welch Regiment who were in the cutting in front of Wytschaete. B Company of our battalion remained with the 9th Division ; efforts were made to collect what remained of the other three companies at Tournai Camp ; C Company appeared during the morning.

By midday (11th) the enemy effort to the south had developed against

Ploegsteert and Hill 63, which would enable him, if he succeeded, to take the Messines Ridge in reverse. General Jeffreys decided that the policy of the 19th Division should be to hold on at all costs, throwing back a defensive flank along the Wulverghem–Messines road. He had under his command the remnants of the gallant South African Brigade, who had

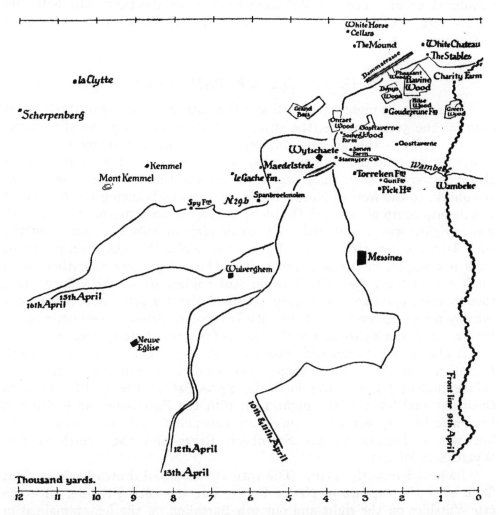

counter-attacked on the 10th, and the 108th Brigade ; and Hill 63 having definitely fallen into the hands of the enemy towards evening, these two units formed the defensive flank while the elements of the 57th and 58th Brigades were withdrawn.

Our B Company was relieved and left the 9th Division on the morning of the 12th to rejoin the battalion at Tournai Camp. The whole battalion moved in the evening to De Zon Camp, near Scherpenberg. Command of the 58th Brigade, however, remained with the 9th Division until the 13th, when, about midday, they came once more under the 19th Division, and were ordered to relieve the South African Brigade from Spy Farm to Spanbroekmolen. The 6th Wiltshire went in on the right, our battalion on the left taking over from the 4th and 2nd South African Infantry Battalions.

THE BATTLE OF BAILLEUL.[1]

Although the night 13th/14th and the 14th was a comparatively quiet time for the 58th Brigade, the situation to the south continued to cause General Jeffreys the gravest anxiety. Not once but many times was Neuve Eglise reported to have fallen to the enemy; the 25th Division also reported that their right was in the air and that the Germans were in Nordhoek, to the west of Neuve Eglise, and were advancing north. There was no grip south of the 19th Division, and in the early morning of the 14th Neuve Eglise was abandoned. Up to midday patrols sent out from the 19th Division reported Neuve Eglise unoccupied by the enemy, except for a few snipers in the southern part of the village, and that there were small parties from the 25th Division still holding on in the village itself, though unsupported. The enemy attacked about 2 p.m., and throughout the day troops on the right of the 19th Division continued to straggle back : the line at Neuve Eglise and to the north of it was definitely broken.

A glance at the map will show the rôle played throughout by our 9th Battalion and the 19th Division. The whole line swung back from the White Château ; but to the north the Ypres Salient stood, although from the night 12th/13th to the night 15th/16th the Passchendaele Ridge had been held by outposts only. Obviously this point would have to go. The line was withdrawn to the Steenbeek River and the Westhoek and Wytschaete Ridges.

Bailleul fell on the 15th. The 19th Division had drawn back its right flank after the capture of Neuve Eglise, but the 58th Brigade, with the 6th Wiltshire on the right and our 9th Battalion on the left, remained in position. On this day the enemy made full use of his territorial gains on the 14th and shelled our battalion lines and the whole divisional front accurately ; early in the morning the 108th Brigade, on the right of the

---

[1] Date: 13th–15th April. Area: road Meteren—Mont des Cats—Boeschepe—Reninghelst—Ouderdom—Vierstraat—Wytschaete.

58th, was attacked and lost some ground, but nothing of consequence. Later orders were issued that the 62nd Brigade (21st Division attached to the 9th Division) would take over the line to Spanbroekmolen, inclusive, and that the 19th Division line would be withdrawn· at 2 a.m. (16th). Our 9th Battalion was duly relieved and went into left support with the Wiltshire in right support.

In spite of heavy losses, the strength of our battalion, thanks to drafts, was not inconsiderable. Lieutenant-Colonel Smeathman gives his strength as 400. He was relieved by one company of the 7th West Yorkshire, 130 strong. On the right of the 19th Division there had been a further withdrawal to what was known as the Meteren—Kemmel line.

At 5 a.m. on the 16th the rearrangement was completed. The enemy was not vigorous in following up the withdrawal. There was a heavy morning mist, and patrols and outposts on the 19th Division front were able to operate freely. But at 6 a.m. a heavy barrage was put down on the 62nd Brigade front, followed by an attack which drove the one company of West Yorkshire from the line previously held by our battalion. The enemy gained possession of Spanbroekmolen. Our A, B, and C Companies were sent up to form a line about La Gache Farm, with D Company in support.

French reinforcements now commenced to arrive on this portion of the front. During the afternoon news was received that the French would attack from the general line Wulverghem—Wytschaete at 6 p.m. Heavy barrages were put down, but the French were late and the attack did not develop. One French battalion came up, however, into the 58th Brigade lines.

French troops continued to arrive on the 17th, and during the night 18th/19th our battalion was relieved and marched back to bivouac in a field on the main road between Reninghelst and Abeele.

THE SECOND BATTLE OF KEMMEL RIDGE[1] AND THE BATTLE OF THE SHERPENBERG.[2]

The whole division moved back to the Proven area on the 21st and so took no part in the battle of the 25th, when Mont Kemmel was lost, in the course of a terrific gas attack. The capture of this commanding position from the French marks the climax of the German advance over the River

---

[1] Date: 25th–26th April. Area: road Meteren—Mont des Cats—Boeschepe—Reninghelst—Vlamertinghe—Ypres (exc.) ; thence the Comines Canal.

[2] Date: 29th April. Area: road St. Jans Cappel—Boeschepe—Reninghelst—Vlamertinghe—Ypres (exc.) ; thence the Comines Canal.

Lys. It was a deep penetration, and had drawn from Sir Douglas Haig one of the few documents—there is, perhaps, only one other—of an arresting nature issued during the war.

" Three weeks ago to-day the enemy began his terrific attacks against us on a fifty-mile front. His objects are to separate us from the French, to take the Channel Ports, and destroy the British Army.

" In spite of throwing already 106 divisions into the battle, and enduring the most reckless sacrifice of human life, he has, as yet, made little progress towards his goals. We owe this to the determined fighting and self-sacrifice of our troops.

" Words fail me to express the admiration which I feel for the splendid resistance offered by all ranks of our Army under the most trying circumstances.

" Many amongst us are now tired. To these I would say that victory will belong to the side which holds out the longest.

" The French Army is moving rapidly and in great force to our support.

" There is no other course open to us but to fight it out. Every position must be held to the last man : there must be no retirement. With our backs to the wall, and believing in the justice of our cause, each one of us must fight to the end.

" The safety of our homes and the freedom of mankind depend alike upon the conduct of each one of us at this critical moment."

The objective of the enemy on this northern side was the high ground from Mont Kemmel to Cassel, and to force the evacuation of the Yser positions : he imposed a gradual withdrawal until our line rested on the ramparts of Ypres, and there it held.

Hammered and battered though they were, the stout spirit of the 9th Royal Welch Fusiliers remained. The command had, on the 25th April, been taken over by Major Lloyd Williams, and many reinforcements had arrived.

During the fighting on the 25th the 19th Division moved from Proven, the 58th Brigade to the Busseboom area as divisional reserve. The whole division was engaged in digging further defensive lines—the Poperinghe line and the Vlamertinghe–Hallebast line—until the 30th, when they took over the front line from the 21st Division nearer to Ypres, in the Dickebusch sector, from a point just west of Vierstraat to a point about 1,000 yards south-west of Zillebeke Lake. The 58th Brigade was on the right, the 56th on the left. Our battalion relieved the 6th Leicestershire on a front extending from the Canal to a point some 1,500 yards west of Hollebeke. Gradually they pushed posts forward until on the 7th/8th of May a continuous line of posts was held, marking an advance on the position taken over of some 1,000 yards. They were relieved on the 10th by the 1/4th King's Shropshire Light Infantry, 56th Brigade, and proceeded by train to bivouacs at St. Jan-ter-Biezen.

The division was relieved during the night 11th/12th by the 6th Division, and on the 16th entrained for a quiet sector in the south.

Convinced that nothing more could be done in that part of the field, the Germans broke off the attack. It was only a partial triumph. One need not dwell on the superiority of numbers concentrated against us on the front attacked—without such superiority no attack of this nature would have been possible, and they were not greater than we had frequently succeeded in concentrating against the Germans. One sees, however, a determination not to become involved in a battle of attrition ; when the advance slackened, the German Higher Command called a halt, and transferred its attention and troops to another quarter. But there remain to the credit of the German commanders these very deep indentations. We had not the trained riflemen of 1914, but we had the machine-gun corps, a skilled and well-fought corps ; we had, also, artillery, and ammunition in sufficient quantities. What, then, had the Germans demonstrated ?

Colonel Bruchmüller's artillery arrangements strike out definitely the lengthy preparation which had become an obsession with our General Headquarters. Once only, on the 14th July 1916, had we attempted anything of the sort ; it was successful in spite of the firm hold retained by the Higher Command on subordinate commanders (we never tried it again ; the Battle of Cambrai was a different plan altogether). Each German attack was a " surprise." No time was allowed the defenders to move reserves ; and subordinate attacking commanders, pressing forward where they could, without that eternal fear of their own flanks, came through small gaps and turned our flanks : these tactics, sensible, and advocated by General Haking before the Battle of Loos, gave a new catchword to our Staff—" infiltration."

But the Germans never succeeded in " routing " the troops before them ; there was always a thin line straggling across their front, imposing fatal delay. A real " break-through " might have been accomplished by masses of cavalry, but the problem of how to get them on the ground was not solved.

Still, repeated thrusts as on the 21st March and the 9th April would in time drive the whole Allied forces across France. On the other hand, there was no escape from the *war* of attrition, no matter how the German

Higher Command might wriggle out of a *battle* of attrition.   The axiom of loss to the attackers held good.   Our losses were heavy ; the German losses were heavier.   They paid a fearful toll for each advance.   The hurricane fire from their massed artillery stunned and destroyed our advanced troops, but the protective barrages of our artillery fell on their assaulting units, of necessity massed for the charge.   Our machine gunners gave them trouble ; they were stung by groups of determined riflemen.   And the farther they advanced, the more difficult their position became : the men became weary, communications became bad, the power of thrust was exhausted.   " The fact that certain divisions had obviously failed to show any inclination to attack in the Plain of the Lys gave food for thought." (Ludendorff.)

General Foch remained imperturbable.

THE VIRGIN AT ALBERT.

The 38th Division, by moving south, had escaped the Lys attack.   They had been relieved on this Armentières front by the 34th Division, which had come up from the Somme area to rest.   The relief was slow, and "parties were still straggling into Croix du Bac at 5.30 a.m. on the 30th March."

The account of the march south given by the Medical Officer of our 2nd Battalion, Major Dunn, throws light on the condition of the back areas during this exciting period.

" At 10 a.m. (30th) the battalion marched via Estaires and Merville to Le Sart.   The population of the country-side had gone, or was packing up [*note that this was before the Lys attack*].   Billets at Le Sart were hard to find, so crowded was the village with refugees ; it had been the same at Croix du Bac.   It was Easter Day.   The church was crowded with civilians, who gossiped and drank much beer after the service.   The battalion's voluntary morning services were quite unattended, to the embarrassment of the Padres.

" On 1st April the battalion entrained at Calonne, travelled via St. Pol —evidently a haunt of enemy bombers—to Doullens, which was reached at 3 p.m.   Proceeding by road, there was a halt for tea at Beauval, where the Divisional Canteen distributed cigarettes, chocolate, and biscuits— they had done so at Calonne, too.   As the transport had travelled by road, the men carried a blanket each, and dixies, and extra ammunition, besides packs and equipment, but they marched well ; when Villers Bocage was reached at 12.30 a.m. on the 2nd, only a dozen had fallen out, and two of these had influenza.   The march, which was resumed at noon, was, however, too much for many who had stuck it in the cool of the previous night.

The air was warm on the downs of this Somme country. Sixty had fallen out before Hedonville was reached.

" Again many refugees were passed on the road. On the morning of the 3rd, Headquarters witnessed one of these sudden departures. Our breakfast was cooking and the table was laid in our billets, when stove and table were taken and put on the farm-cart. A sack or two of potatoes were taken, but a cellarful was left. The daughter of the house held the fowl-house door while the mother went in and tied the fowls by the legs in threes, in which bundles they were put in baskets and loaded on top of the furniture ; a few single fowls were tied to various articles on which they squatted. Then a heifer calf was tied behind and, struggling violently, was belaboured out of the yard by the grandmother, who had been wailing all the morning, ' No bon, la guerre ! '

" These simple villagers were pleasant people to deal with. It was quite otherwise with the tradespeople of Doullens, who ascribed the German success to the culpable failure of the British Expeditionary Force to resist. Not infrequently the men were refused service in the shops : ' Anglais, no bon ! ' they were told scornfully.

" For four days the battalion remained at Hedonville. From midnight on the 4th the 115th Brigade was on an hour's notice to move to Aveluy Wood, but no one slept less soundly on that account, and no move was made until the 7th, when the battalion marched back through Warloy on muddy roads to Herissart, a dirty village where it remained for four days digging a new line."

The statue of the Virgin that surmounted the spire of Albert Cathedral was one of the curious sights on the British front. Damaged by German shells, the masonry had given way beneath the figure, and it hung out over the side of the spire, horizontally, retained by iron bars embedded in the base of it which had bent under the force of the high explosive, but were still strong enough to hold the weight of the stone statue.

The 38th Division was at Toutencourt, and our 13th, 14th, and 16th Battalions went into the front line above Albert, and to the right of Aveluy Wood, on the 11th April. The 114th Brigade were on their right, and the 115th Brigade, with our 2nd and 17th Battalions, in reserve.

On the 16th April a direct hit from one of our guns brought the Virgin crashing to the ground ; the time is noted as 3.45 p.m. It had hung there so long, through so many bombardments, that the men prophesied the war would not end until the Virgin fell. There was still a period of trial, but the tide had almost turned.

Captain Moody, of our 2nd Battalion, writes : " The outstanding event of the six days at Henencourt occurred on 16th April during an extra-active shelling of Albert. I saw a direct hit on the already damaged tower of the cathedral, which brought the leaning Madonna crashing to the ground. It happened about four in the afternoon. The incident caused a certain amount of gloom among those who believed the well-known prophecy that when the Madonna fell the war would soon end, and the nation that perpetrated the deed would suffer a severe defeat. There is no doubt that the Madonna was brought to the ground by a British shell. We wondered what the French reservists behind us would say when they heard of it."

The strain on our resources was obvious in so many ways at this period. Besides the cutting down of brigades to three battalions, battalions were suffering from lack of reinforcements. The trench organisation had been the subject of a number of pamphlets and instructions ; ever since the Somme battles of 1916 certain officers were left out of the " trench strength," to amuse themselves at the transport lines or some camp. At first it was either the commanding officer or the second-in-command from Headquarters ; the company commander or his second-in-command. At one time not more than twenty officers, including the medical officer, were allowed in the line. Warrant officers and senior non-commissioned officers became precious, as did Lewis gunners, scouts, signallers, snipers : a third of these were ordered to remain out of the line.

In minor details the instructions may have varied in different divisions, but the basic principle was to preserve a third of the battalion specialists, and to work on a platoon strength of twenty-eight. Sometimes this minimum figure of twenty-eight was hard to find ; at others the number of " details " left out of the line was swollen to a respectable figure.

It is curious to find that at this time, while the Higher Command was dithering with fear that the enemy might break through, a certain amount of fraternisation went on at Aveluy Wood. " Where the lines approached, there was an exchange of messages, cigarettes, visits. By May the whole division was fraternising, until a peremptory order from the G.O.C. stopped the practice." (Dunn.)

On the 21st April the 113th Brigade took over a new stretch of line from the 35th Division, on the left of the 38th Division, in preparation for a minor affair on the 22nd April. The object was to secure observation into the Ancre Valley, and the operation was carried out in conjunction with the 35th Division.

There is not much to be said for this affair, except that it was gallantly carried out by the 13th Battalion on the right, the 16th, supported by two companies of the 14th, in the centre, and two companies of the 14th Battalion on the left ; the 2nd Battalion had two companies attached to the 113th Brigade as reserve.

There was no preliminary bombardment, and troops left the trenches with an ineffective barrage in front of them. The brigade suffered heavy casualties, but won a position from which the desired observation could be obtained. Eighty-six Germans were captured, and six machine guns.

Our 13th Battalion, at a tremendous sacrifice, reached the objective given, the shell-hole position, thanks to the gallant leadership of Captain C. B. Williams. But 2nd Lieutenants B. T. Evans, H. S. Heaton, F. C. Hutchins, J. F. Samuel, T. B. Winter, and D. J. Thomas (attached from

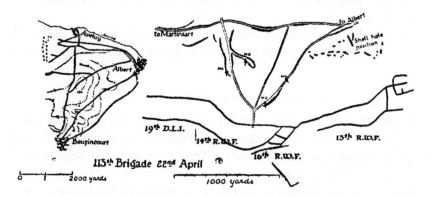

the 15th Battalion) were killed, together with 62 other ranks ; and 3 officers and 201 other ranks were wounded ; 2 other ranks were missing.

The 16th Battalion, in the centre, only succeeded in advancing some 250 yards. All the officers of A, B, and C Companies were casualties. Lieutenants F. T. Linton, W. S. Goff, V. P. Williams, H. Bennet, S. E. Jenkins, and 46 other ranks were killed ; 2nd Lieutenants B. O. Davies, A. O. Owens, and 20 other ranks were missing ; 2nd Lieutenants A. B. Brodin, S. C. Skuse, and 159 other ranks were wounded.

With two companies assaulting, the 14th Battalion made no appreciable advance and lost Lieutenant J. G. Webb, 2nd Lieutenants J. Huxley, G. O. Richards, and 5 other ranks killed ; 14 other ranks missing ; and 95 other ranks wounded.

Counter-attacks on the 23rd and 24th April were beaten off.

The position was slightly improved by the 17th Battalion on the 1st May, the enterprise being carried out by Captain J. C. Gledhill with two platoons.   But although we had only secured a part of the line we wanted and a small patch for observation into the Ancre Valley, we were so close to the top of the ridge that we had robbed the Germans of the observation they had enjoyed.   And so, on the 9th May, they made a determined attack on our new position.

There had been a general side-slipping to the left, and the right of the 38th Division was taken over by the Australians, leaving the 115th Brigade to hold the gains made by our 13th Battalion.   The German attack drove the Australians back, but our 17th Battalion, holding the right of the brigade front with C and D Companies, refused to budge.   They repulsed all attacks until the following day, when the Australians restored the situation on their front.

The next day (10th May) was also the occasion of an abortive attack by the 114th Brigade on Aveluy Wood, which our 4th Battalion had attempted to capture.

This was also the date on which our 9th Battalion was relieved in the front line south of Ypres, preparatory to a quiet time of recuperation in the south.

The Offensive in Champagne.

Ludendorff never pinned his faith on a break-through at one point : if it came, well and good ; if not, he was prepared to attack elsewhere, and by repeated blows shatter the entire front.   Early in April the German Crown Prince was directed to submit a plan for an attack between Pinon and Reims.   The operations decided upon, as given by Ludendorff, were :

" Attack by the 7th and 1st Armies from the line Anizy (south-west of Laon)—south of Berry-au-Bac, in the direction of Soissons—Fismes—Reims.

" Prolongation of the attacks, to the right across the Ailette towards the Oise, and to the left as far as Reims.

" Attack by the 18th Army west of the Oise, with its principal effort towards Compiègne."

The artillery arrangements, still under Bruchmüller, did not permit a simultaneous attack on so broad a front ; it was taken, therefore, in " phases."   " I hoped it would lead to such heavy drain on the reserves of the enemy as would enable us to resume the attack in Flanders."

The country was difficult, but the Germans knew that the front was weakly held, and that it had been selected as a resting-place for the exhausted divisions from the north.

By the beginning of May eight British divisions had been reduced to cadres and were written off temporarily as fighting units, and a further five divisions—four of which had taken part in both German attacks, and one much cut up in the March defence—with their ranks filled with young recruits had been handed over to Marshal Foch for employment on a quiet part of the French front, where they could rest and train. The latter divisions, the 19th, 21st, 25th, 50th, and 8th, constituted the IX British Corps, under Lieutenant-General Sir A. Hamilton Gordon, and were sent by Marshal Foch to the French Sixth Army.

All this sounded extremely pleasant to the weary survivors, from the two fierce battles, who were still in our 9th Battalion. From their bivouacs at St. Jan-ter-Biezen our battalion marched to billets at Herzeele on the 12th May; entrained at Rexpoede Station on the 16th, and arrived at Coulus, near Epernay, on the 18th. They were billeted in extreme comfort in the village of Chepy, on one of the tributaries of the River Marne, where they " revelled in the beauties of the country." They were inspected by the celebrated General Gouraud (" Le Lion d'Argonne ") on the 23rd May.

The 19th Division was a late arrival in the IX Corps. The 8th, 21st, and 50th Divisions had already taken over a front of about 15 miles between Bermicourt and Bouconville, to the north-west of Reims. In the middle of May the German concentration commenced, and on the 27th they opened their attack against the French Sixth Army between Vauxaillon and Sapigneul. The first information the French had of the impending attack was from prisoners captured by them on the 26th May.

The Germans were jubilant over the progress they made. Ludendorff says he thought they might reach the neighbourhood of Soissons and Fismes, but by the second and third days these objectives had " in places " been left far behind.

The preliminary attack is shortly described in the Despatches :

" Preceded by an artillery and trench-mortar bombardment of great intensity, the German infantry broke into the battle positions of the Allied divisions. The enemy gained a footing on the Chemin des Dames at an early hour, and pressing on in the centre of his attack in overwhelming strength, forced the line of the Aisne on a wide front. By nightfall he had crossed the Vesle west of Fismes, and in the British sector, after very heavy and determined fighting, had compelled the left and centre of the IX Corps, now reinforced by the 25th Division, to swing back to a position facing west and north-west between the Aisne and the Vesle.

" On the 28th May and following days the enemy launched fresh attacks in great force, pressing back our Allies to the west of Soissons and south of Fère-en-Tardenois. The IX British Corps, greatly reduced in numbers by severe and incessant fighting, was forced to withdraw across the Vesle, and thence gradually pressed back in a south-easterly direction between the Vesle and the Ardre. During the nights of the 28th/29th May the 19th Division was brought up in buses."

The intention had been that the 19th Division should take over a quiet sector in the Tahure area, on the front between Reims and Verdun, after a period in the Chalon area for training the new drafts.

BATTLE OF THE AISNE, 1918.[1]

When, at 4 p.m. on the 27th May, the official information was received of the German attack, with the news that they had penetrated the front between Reims and Soissons to some considerable depth, an order was issued to the infantry to hold themselves in readiness to embus, and to the artillery and all mounted personnel and transport to prepare to proceed to the front line by road under the command of the C.R.A.

The order was soon given effect. At nightfall on the 28th our 9th Battalion left Chepy by buses, and arrived at Chaumuzy at 3.30 a.m. on the 29th. They marched to billets at Bligny, where they stayed a very short time.

The leading brigade, the 57th, had debussed at Chambrecy by 3.50 a.m. ; the 58th Brigade was not present until 5 a.m. Assembled in the Bligny area, the 2nd Wiltshire[2] took up an outpost position on the high ground north and north-west of Bligny.

The situation was a repetition of that in which the division found itself in March—confusion and alarm reigned everywhere. General Jeffreys learned from the IX Corps and from the General Officer Commanding the French 154th Division that the enemy had continued to gain ground rapidly after his initial success, and had reached an approximate line Branscourt—Crugny Wood north-west of Brouillet—Bois des 5 Piles.

The enemy attack between Reims and Soissons was in a general southerly direction ; our troops were on the right of the salient he had

---

[1] Date : 27th May–6th June. Area : between the Chemin des Dames and the Montagne de Reims, east of the line Bouconville—Fismes—Vermeuil.

[2] The 2nd Battalion Wiltshire Regiment went out to France with the 7th Division, in the 21st Brigade. The brigade was transferred to the 30th Division on the 20th December 1915. The 6th Battalion had absorbed the Wiltshire Yeomanry on the 20th September 1917, and, after the Lys battles, was itself drafted to the 2nd Battalion, which joined the 19th Division on the 14th May. But on the 19th the 6th Battalion was posted as a training cadre to the 30th Division. This battalion returned to England with the 14th Division in June, and was back again in France with the 42nd Brigade, 14th Division, on the 1st July 1918.

created, and were therefore facing north-west—a direction not usually associated in the British mind with attack.

But considerable uncertainty existed as to the exact position of the Allied troops : British and French were mixed and disorganised ; all were tired and had lost heavily.

General Le Breton, commanding the French 154th Division, stated that the situation on his front was distinctly critical, and that a gap existed between Brouillet and Sercy. General Jeffreys was ordered by the IX Corps to occupy this gap. He had only the 57th and 58th Brigades with him, the divisional artillery was far away, and owing to the loss of guns there was little artillery on the spot to cover the Allied troops. However, the General issued his orders to brigadiers in person : the 58th Brigade on the right and the 57th on the left were to take up and hold a line Faverolles—Coemy—Lhery. The 58th Brigade would get into touch with the French 154th Division on their right, and the 57th Brigade with the French 13th Division on their left. The brigadiers were further instructed that as soon as they had occupied that line every effort would be made to push forward to a further line, Savigny—Prin—Brouillet, provided Brouillet and Savigny were held by any of the Allied troops.

The brigadiers in turn gave verbal orders to the battalion commanders, and by 9.30 a.m. troops were moving in accordance with these orders, the battalion commanders having gone ahead to reconnoitre and determine the positions on which they proposed to place their men. Our battalion held the front line of the 58th Brigade and took up an outpost position extending from a point a quarter of a mile south of Coemy to Faverolles ; the 9th Welch Regiment were in support about Tramery, and the 2nd Wiltshire in reserve about Sarcy. Touch was obtained on the right with the 154th French Division and remnants of the British 25th Division ; and on the left with the Gloucestershire of the 57th Brigade.

The 10th Worcestershire were on the left of the 57th Brigade front, and the 10th Royal Warwickshire were in support.

Officer patrols and patrols from the IX Corps Cyclist Battalion, which had been attached to the 19th Division, discovered that there were disorganised elements of French and British troops to the north-west of the Faverolles—Lhery line, but the villages of Savigny and Brouillet were strongly held by the enemy. Consequently the second forward move was not attempted.

Although touch had been obtained with troops on the right of our battalion, the situation there was not satisfactory—there were few of them with no cohesion—so the 2nd Wiltshire were moved up on our right flank.

The mist of uncertainty which covered the country in front of the division began to lift. An organised but tired body of troops appeared between Lhery and Coemy, made up of elements from the 8th, 25th, and 50th British Divisions, and under the command of Brigadier-General Craigie-Halkett, and designated by him the 74th Brigade. This body of troops must not be confused with the scattered parties of the same three British divisions who were mixed up with the 154th French Division on the right of our battalion.

A welcome support arrived during the morning in the shape of the 19th Division Machine-gun Battalion, but no artillery as yet. One company was sent to the 58th Brigade and one to the 57th Brigade. The 56th Brigade also arrived.

The 8th Division Headquarters was still operating on the right of the 19th Division line, and informed General Jeffreys, early in the afternoon, first that the enemy had taken the high ground north-west of Savigny, then that he had reached Faverolles, and finally that the French and British troops were retiring.

Fighting was in progress on the ridge immediately north of the Bouleuse Spur and in the neighbourhood of Treslon and Germigny. Soon messages from the Wiltshire stated that parties of the 8th and 25th British Divisions and 154th French Division were retiring through their line, which now became the front line.

Much the same thing happened on the left, the 57th Brigade front, and about 4.30 p.m. the enemy was seen advancing from Prin Château, and down the slopes of the high ground north of Treslon.

The waiting and preparation for development, the slow appearance of the enemy, created an atmosphere of tension.

That evening there was a rearrangement of the line. The 56th Brigade, less the 9th Cheshire, was placed under the command of the 8th Division, as also were the 2nd Wiltshire ; the 9th Cheshire were attached to the 58th Brigade. At dawn on the 30th May the line ran : 8th North Staffordshire on the right, 1/4th King's Shropshire Light Infantry, 2nd Wiltshire ; then a body of French Senegalese Tirailleurs, our 9th Battalion (with the 9th Welch Regiment in support and the 9th Cheshire in reserve) in touch on their left with the 57th Brigade, who had the 10th Gloucestershire on the right and the 10th Worcestershire on the left ; the 10th Royal Warwickshire were in brigade reserve. All units of the 19th Division had absorbed small parties of men fron the 8th, 25th, and 50th British Divisions, about 500 in all.

Early in the morning of the 30th the enemy commenced to move.

In the uncertain light of dawn listening-posts from our battalion heard and saw patrols advancing—the process of " infiltration " was being pursued. The first enemy patrol was allowed to filter no farther than the first group of listening Royal Welch Fusiliers—they were rounded up and brought in as prisoners.

But by 3.30 a.m. it was apparent to General Jeffreys, from reports coming from all parts of his front, that the Germans were on the point of delivering an attack in strength. The enemy was seen massing on the forward edges of woods, and in the vicinity of Largery. A message from our battalion, timed 3 a.m., reported that they were already in action. The weak spot was found in the French Senegalese, who were driven back, and the right of our battalion was soon seriously engaged on the south-east outskirts of Faverolles ; repeated efforts were made to get in touch with the Wiltshire.

Meanwhile, on the left, a similar experience had befallen the 57th Brigade : by 6 a.m. the enemy was round their left flank and entering Lhery. And then a strong enemy attack was launched against the whole of the 19th Division front.

The Germans had not been idle during the night : their heavy artillery had moved forward, and they had brought up numbers of trench mortars. The trench mortars were particularly effective, and a shower of their small but unpleasant missiles descended from the sky, in some cases with great accuracy. And with the bombardment came the Germans, in eight lines. The weak spots, already probed by strong patrols, were pierced ; the assaulting lines pressed through the gap between our battalion and the Wiltshire, left by the retreat of the French Senegalese. They curled round the flank of our battalion and the right platoon was wiped out. The left flank of the Wiltshire was pushed away.

The 57th Brigade, in an endeavour to rectify the outflanking movement to their left, had fallen back on their support line, and General Jeffreys ordered the 58th Brigade (our battalion was alone in the front line) to do the same. To some extent this was done—that is to say, junction was established with the Welch Regiment—but the enemy was pressing strongly and a retirement to definite positions under such conditions was impossible.

The situation became worse. The Wiltshire were fighting strongly, and maintaining themselves on high ground north of Bouleuse, but they were some way off. In spite of that our battalion and the Welch Regiment held the enemy on their right ; and then the line on the left became loose under the retirement ; Aulnay Wood fell into the hands of the Germans, who appeared behind the left flank of our battalion. It was at this moment that Major Lloyd Williams received the order to fall back on the Poilly—Bois d'Aulnay line.

A rearguard action commenced that was like a nightmare. The truth

Battle of the Aisne 1918.

was that both battalions, 9th Royal Welch Fusiliers and 9th Welch Regiment were by this time completely surrounded. Hand-to-hand fighting took place as remnants of companies tried to charge through. In the end it was a mere handful of our battalion and less than a company of the Welch

Regiment formed up on the Poilly—Bois d'Aulnay line, only to fall back later on a position held by the 9th Cheshire to the north and north-west of Sarcy.

The situation on the left of the division was critical. The 10th Worcestershire and the 74th Composite Brigade, under repeated attacks, and with no French troops on their left, had practically ceased to exist as organised units ; the 10th Royal Warwickshire, who had been in brigade reserve, were now the left battalion of the 57th Brigade, and there was a gap of some 1,200 to 1,500 yards between them and the remaining elements of the 74th Brigade. A mixed force of weary stragglers and details of the 8th, 25th, and 50th Divisions was hurriedly organised, and, with an officer and four machine guns from the 19th Machine-gun Battalion, were moved to a position north of Ville-en-Tardenois. Farther to the left the 5th South Wales Borderers, the Pioneer Battalion, put up a stout fight and held the enemy, enabling a certain amount of reorganisation to be done.

The reorganisation took place between 11 a.m. and 1 p.m. The 58th Brigade line, from just west of Sarcy to the river, was held by the 9th Cheshire on the left, the remnants of our battalion, the 9th Welch Regiment, and the 58th Trench-mortar Battery (acting as infantry). The 56th Brigade, bent back over the ridge on the right, were in touch with the 28th French Division, who were then relieving the 154th French Division : the 57th Brigade, on the left, stretched away indefinitely, in vain endeavour to find the 13th French Division, which had entirely disappeared ; but it was known that the 40th French Division was on its way to relieve the absent 13th.

During the afternoon Brigadier-General Glasgow was wounded, and the 58th Brigade was placed under Brigadier-General Heath (56th Brigade). Earlier in the day the Headquarters of the British IX Corps were withdrawn, and the 19th Division was placed under the orders of the V French Corps. It was laid down by the French Corps that from midnight General Officers Commanding Divisions would take command of all troops, of whatever nationality, within their divisional boundaries. Before this order came into force General Jeffreys was commanding troops outside his Divisional boundaries ; they were spread over 12,000 yards of front. In view of the fact that troops of the 8th, 25th, and 50th Divisions were absolutely exhausted, General Jeffreys sought to have them relieved. This, however, the Commander of the left French Corps would not agree to, until General Pellé, commanding the French V Corps, had applied to the French Army. The South Wales Borderers and 74th Composite Brigade were then released. On the right there had been no difficulty, and the 28th

French Division had taken over most of the positions held by the 1/4th King's Shropshire Light Infantry and the 8th North Staffordshire.

The situation on the 19th Division front was slightly better, but at the same time all units had lost heavily.

In the course of the reorganisation the remains of our 9th Battalion and the Welch Regiment were formed into a composite company, and put under Lieutenant-Colonel W. W. S. Cunninghame (2nd Life Guards), commanding the 9th Cheshire Regiment, and went into the line as a company of the 9th Cheshire.   For the moment they lose their identity, and can only be followed through the account of the 9th Cheshire.

Throughout the morning of the 31st May the enemy shelled the thin line of the 19th Division.   At 1 p.m. they massed for attack, and at 1.45 p.m. commenced to advance from the direction of Romigny.   Here they met some of the gallant but sorely tried 74th Composite Brigade, turned the flank of the 10th Royal Warwickshire, and entered Ville-en-Tardenois. The greatly reduced 10th Worcestershire were sent up from reserve.

By 3 p.m. the attack had been taken up by the enemy on the right of the division, and the French 28th Division was being driven off the Aubilly Ridge.   Heavy fighting developed on the front of the 9th Cheshire and the right of the 8th Gloucestershire, both battalions having to give ground.

It looked as though the whole division would have to go.   General Jeffreys ordered the 2nd Wiltshire to counter-attack.   At 5 p.m., however, it was reported that the French were advancing again, and that a local counter-attack was already in progress.   This effort was led by Lieutenant-Colonel Cunninghame.

Words cannot describe such actions.   These tired men, remnants of units, having been driven off their position, responded to Lieutenant-Colonel Cunninghame's call.   He, mounted, formed up the " battalion " in the midst of heavy artillery, machine-gun and rifle fire ; his horse was shot, and he led the counter-attack on foot.   The position of the morning was practically restored, the advance of the 2nd Wiltshire coming upon the heels of the Cheshire " Battalion," and driving the enemy off the high ground on the left so that they then stood between the Cheshire and the Gloucestershire.

The enemy was also held on the Ville-en-Tardenois—Chambrecy road, the artillery and machine gunners doing fine work.

No further action ensued on the 31st, and once more the division was reorganised.   The 1/4th King's Shropshire Light Infantry were astride the River Ardre, in touch with the 28th French Division ; the 8th North Staffordshire and 9th Cheshire came next on the 56th Brigade front.

The 2nd Wiltshire, the 8th Gloucestershire, 10th Worcestershire, and 10th Royal Warwickshire, with their left in touch with the 40th French Division about half a mile south of Ville-en-Tardenois. The approximate strength of brigades was 56th, 900 ; 57th, 750 ; 58th, 350 ; Pioneers, 500.

Great efforts were being made behind the line to collect reinforcements. Employed men were assembled, and men who had been lost amongst the French, and further composite battalions of the 8th, 25th, and 50th Divisions were being organised. In course of time these scratch formations were sent up, but as yet General Jeffreys had the 74th Composite Brigade, the Pioneer Battalion, and the French 2nd Battalion of the 22nd Regiment (Commandant A. de Lasbourde) in reserve.

The morning of the 1st June passed as the previous morning—the enemy was seen preparing to attack, and our artillery did what it could to break up his assembling. But he launched his attack about 4 p.m., first against the 40th French Division, which was forced back, although maintaining touch with the Warwickshire ; and then against the Gloucestershire and Wiltshire Battalions. The latter were driven from their positions and the situation was critical for a while. The Gloucestershire rallied, under Captain E. B. Pope, and the French battalion, not waiting for orders (although they were on the way), counter-attacked with the remnants of the Gloucestershire and restored the original situation.

The enemy, however, retained the country he had won from the 40th French Division, where he was in complete possession of the Bois de Courmont. North-east of Chambrecy, between that village and Bligny, was a hill known as the Montagne de Bligny. It was a most important feature, masking the Valley of the Ardre that remained in our possession, and—if lost to the enemy—affording direct observation up the valley where the greater part of our batteries were in position. General Jeffreys ordered a retirement to positions which bent round this hill and connected with the French on either flank.

In this retirement the 9th Cheshire again lost heavily from shell and machine-gun fire. There was no longer any distinction in companies : the battalion was made up of Royal Welch Fusiliers, Welch Regiment, 58th Trench-mortar Battery, and a handful of its own men.

The line of battle that night ran : 28th French Division, 1/4th King's Shropshire Light Infantry, 8th North Staffordshire, 9th Cheshire, 2nd Wiltshire and elements of the 3rd Worcestershire (25th Division), 8th Gloucestershire, 10th Worcestershire, and 10th Royal Warwickshire to the 40th French Division.

The 74th Composite Brigade, and the 5th South Wales Borderers (Pioneers), the 2/22nd French Regiment, and the three Field Companies Royal Engineers were held in support.

The 2nd June passed quietly. The French 154th Infantry Group composed of remnants of the 154th Division, was given to General Jeffreys for counter-attack purposes, and was sent to the Nappes—Espilly area ; the IX Corps, busy reorganising stragglers and elements of the 8th, 25th, and 50th Divisions, sent up a composite battalion, of about 750 all ranks, from the 8th Division, which was posted to the 74th Brigade ; from the latter composite brigade the 1/6th Cheshire and 50th Division Composite Battalion were put at the disposal of the 57th Brigade and sent to relieve the 2/22nd French Regiment in the Bois d'Eclisse. In addition a composite machine-gun company, from the 8th and 50th Divisions, was given to the 74th Brigade.

The enemy remained quiet for several days. There were more changes in the 19th Division, as the IX Corps succeeded in sending up formed bodies of troops. There was reorganisation, too, and, as affecting our battalion, the 58th (Brigade) Composite Battalion was formed of one company of Royal Welch Fusiliers, one company of Welch Regiment and 58th Trench-mortar Battery, and two companies of 2nd Wiltshire Regiment, a total strength of 14 officers and about 460 other ranks. The 74th Composite Brigade became, with a number of new formations, the 7th Composite Brigade. Briefly, on the night 5th/6th June the line of battle ran :

28th French Division ; 56th Brigade, with 8th North Staffordshire and 58th Brigade Composite Battalion in the line, 1/4th King's Shropshire Light Infantry in support ; 57th Brigade, 8th Gloucestershire, 10th Worcestershire, and 10th Royal Warwickshire in line with the 50th Division Composite Battalion, 1/6th Cheshire (25th Division) and 5th South Wales Borderers in support ; 8th Division Composite Battalion, with a composite battalion (25th Division) in support ; 161st Regiment of the 40th French Division.

On the morning of the 5th June the enemy increased his artillery fire, and had obviously brought up his heavy artillery. Our artillery opened vigorous counter-preparation every morning, and this was carried out on the morning of the 6th June from 2 to 3 a.m.—it was the usual hour. As our fire slackened, the enemy opened an hour's bombardment of some intensity on the 19th Division and the 28th French Division, a great proportion of gas shell being used on battery positions.

At 4 a.m. the Germans launched the attack we had been expecting for three days. It was directed against the north-west edge of the Bois d'Eclisse and the Montagne de Bligny, that is, the front held by the 57th Brigade, the 58th Brigade Composite Battalion, and the 56th Brigade.

The 58th Composite Battalion, with its companies of Royal Welch Fusiliers, Welch Regiment, and Wiltshire, did not wait for the enemy, but climbing out of their trenches charged down on him with the bayonet. It was soon over : the Germans, of a quality which caused Ludendorff to sigh, could not meet the bayonet—they turned and fled, but many casualties were inflicted.

On the remainder of the 57th Brigade front the enemy attack was less severe. Two bodies of infantry approached the 10th Worcestershire and 8th Gloucestershire, who held their fire until the last moment. Practically all of the enemy were killed ; a few who escaped had to lie in the long grass under fire all day.

Everywhere on the 19th Division front the enemy was repulsed, and by 8 a.m. fighting had died down and all was quiet.

On the right, however, the Germans succeeded in driving the 28th French Division back until the 8th North Staffordshire, refusing their right to maintain touch, rested this flank on Chaumuzy Hill. The French prepared to counter-attack.

At 11 a.m., before the French troops were in a position to advance, the enemy made a second attempt on the Montagne de Bligny, and this time succeeded in gaining the summit of the hill. The 9th Cheshire promptly counter-attacked, pressing forward with great gallantry. General Jeffreys ordered the King's Shropshire Light Infantry, in reserve, to complete and make good the success of this counter-attack, an operation which was most brilliantly accomplished. By 12.15 p.m. the Montagne de Bligny was again in our hands with one German officer and 33 men prisoners. The enemy was taken completely by surprise and many were killed.

With the hill in our hands, the French counter-attack, delivered later in the afternoon, was happily launched and Bligny regained.

During the night 6th/7th June the 56th Brigade, with the 58th Composite Battalion, was relieved by the 50th Division Composite Brigade, and went into Divisional reserve about the Bois de Courton.

As already indicated, the 9th Battalion had suffered very severely in this series of battles in Champagne in May and June. Many had probably been taken prisoners, but many were killed in the hand-to-hand fighting, and these included three gallant officers, viz. Captain Cowie, Lieutenant Dobell, and Major Ian Baxter, the Adjutant. The last-named had been with the 9th Battalion continuously since 1915.

No further operations were undertaken by the enemy. The 19th

Division was reorganised for the last time as one composite brigade, which, with the 7th and 50th Division as composite brigades, formed the division now commanded by General Jeffreys. They were relieved on the 19th June by the 8th Italian Division.

.   .   .   .

Comments made immediately after a battle of this description are sometimes illuminating, and throw light on some of the difficulties, and even the incidents of fighting. Thus :

" The extreme difficulties experienced when the forces of two allied nations speaking different languages and with different national characteristics and methods of fighting are alongside one another, and particularly in the circumstances of a retreat, when the troops become unavoidably intermingled, were fully emphasised by these operations.

" In such circumstances there is always a certain amount of mutual suspicion that the troops of one nation will ' let down ' the troops of the other. On at least one occasion, when a party of British were being deliberately withdrawn in accordance with the orders of superior authority, a neighbouring French commander also at once withdrew his troops, thinking that we were leaving him in the lurch, and owing to the fact that the British officer in command on the spot was not able to explain clearly in French the reason for his action. The result was that a certain portion of valuable ground was evacuated quite unnecessarily.

" As the troops of the 19th Division and the neighbouring French units got to know one another, such incidents no longer occurred and mutual co-operation was excellent. . . .

" When a withdrawal is ordered by higher authority, officers on the spot (platoon and company commanders) must arrange that men know where to withdraw to. . . .

" Junior officers and N.C.O.s do not understand sufficiently the necessity of keeping a sharp look-out. The German system is for his forward parties to trickle forward covered by machine-gun fire, with the express object of making our men keep their heads down. On occasions he has done this so successfully that parties of considerable strength have got through on to the flank, and even in rear of our men without being seen at all. It should be realised that the heavier the fire on our trenches the more important it is to have a good look-out.

" Young officers, N.C.O.s, and men do not appear to realise the enormity of the crime of ' straggling,' or even that it is a crime to straggle. If they become detached from their own unit, there is often a tendency to retire from the battlefield instead of attaching themselves to the nearest British formation until such time as they can regain their unit.

" All cases of deliberate straggling should be ruthlessly dealt with by summary court-martial, and infliction of the death penalty as early as possible as a deterrent to others. . . .

" It is not too much to say that ' concealment discipline ' amongst British troops is almost non-existent. Quite unnecessary movement in the daylight is continually carried on and no attempt whatever is made by troops on the move to take what cover is available. Headquarters of infantry brigades, artillery groups, etc., are frequently concentrated together without any attempt to conceal themselves, or to minimise the continuous movement which usually takes place in the vicinity of Headquarters."

General Jeffreys was a little rigid, but his qualities as commander drew from the French the highest praise—the men, they said, seemed to have the most absolute confidence in the leaders, and the leaders in their superiors. But one must not forget that his just criticisms were on units which had been through three desperate battles, " with their backs to the wall " ; and the condition of the division before this last German onslaught should be remembered. His comments are interesting in conjunction with the actual record of the resistance, so determined, so gallant, offered by the units of this division—they were of the bravest that stood.

The Albert Front.

These disasters brought about a strange state of affairs. At times there is but the finest line between victory and defeat. A queer sort of " horse sense " in the British rank and file protected them from prolonged panic, but there is no doubt their spirits were depressed.

We know now that at the moment of their greatest triumph the German soldiers were as weary of war as our own and that the rot set in shortly afterwards ; but at that time the signs, if read at all, were understood by very few. With us the men would still respond to leadership, but were not too willing to have responsibilities unloaded on their backs. The same applies to regimental officers. But the Staff was still thinking of retreat and the saving of indispensables. A note from the 38th Division gives the general feeling throughout the Army in few words :

" At the beginning of May the G.S.O.1 came and expounded the view that once a battalion commander had placed his platoons on the ground, he had discharged his duties ; even the company commanders became passive spectators of their subaltern's battles. At least one subaltern listened to an account of this latest order of defensive battle with rising indignation ; then he summarised the situation : ' I'm to stand and fight to the last while the S.A.A. limbers and everybody else is legging it to the transports off the coast ?   No b—— fear ! ' "

The young officer's appreciation of the situation was to some extent confirmed on the 24th April, when two parties of Germans in full marching order suddenly left their trenches and advanced on ours. They were unsupported by artillery or small-arm fire, and may have been deserters, but they were fired on by our troops and dispersed. The S.O.S. had, however, been sent up promptly and created alarm and despondency in rear of our lines.   The transport received orders to stand-to, ready to move at a moment's notice, to Herissart in the first instance : it was not to be captured on any account ; ammunition limbers were also to go.

And with these orders for commanders to scamper away from their men came continuous demands for fatigue parties to dig, so that the men had little rest.   And they had little warmth.   When the 38th Division moved south, great-coats had been withdrawn, and were not reissued until the weather was so mild that all were longing for a chance to get into lighter clothing ; this was not until the early summer.   Opportunities for giving the men baths were rare ; there was no change of underclothing available ; verminous sores were common ; the health standard of the division was low.

Under these circumstances discipline suffered. At the beginning of May a company was found not wearing equipment in the front line ; another company had no sentries at their posts, and no officer on duty : in yet another company area everyone was found asleep at seven out of twelve sentry posts.

Subject to minor alterations and modifications of the front held, the 38th Division remained in the neighbourhood of Aveluy Wood, while the artillery on both sides pounded away, with harassing fire and " crashes " day and night, week after week.   The monotony of this kind of trench warfare, in which the infantry played the part of target, was relieved by occasional raids : they were not always well thought out.   One such took place in June and is well described, with pungent comments, by Captain Radford, of our 2nd Battalion.   It has its place in contributing to the general state of depression.

" The battalion was warned that it would participate in a big raid on the enemy occupying the Valley of the Ancre.   The area to be raided stretched from the southern outskirts of the village of Hamel to the northern edge of Aveluy Wood. Part of Aveluy Wood was in our occupation, but the wood ran down to the river in a north-easterly direction and met the Albert—Hamel road in the valley, and in this north-eastern corner there had been a prisoner-of-war cage which was now converted into a German strong-point.

" The raid was to be a two-battalion one, and the battalion was allotted the right hand or southern half.

" For more than a week both battalions practised over ground near Caterpillar Wood. B, D, and C Companies were to attack, and A Company was responsible for putting out tapes and acting as a covering party while the remainder of the battalion assembled.

" From the point of view of the company commanders and their subordinates the whole raid from its inception appeared farcical. It was a recognised fact that whereas the Germans held one or two isolated posts by day, on the west side of the Ancre, these posts were withdrawn at night-time to the east bank, and therefore, apart from the posts in Aveluy Wood, there was nothing to raid.

" Towards the appointed day the weather turned wet, and on the afternoon of the day itself there was a colossal thunderstorm with torrential rain. Everybody was of the opinion that the raid would be washed out, in more senses than one ; but no orders came through that the operation was to be cancelled or postponed.

" Zero was somewhere between 1 and 2 in the morning, and the battalion, which was in reserve miles behind the line, marched off at about 9 p.m. Everything was soaking wet, and a cold drizzle fell throughout the night. The communication trenches were in places up to one's fork in water. Every rifle got caked and plastered with mud, and all bombs, Lewis-gun equipment, etc., were inches deep in mud and slime.

" Overnight the Germans sent out a strong patrol, which captured a listening-post of the battalion holding the line. Even after reaching the assembly-point the company commanders were convinced that the operation would be cancelled as the conditions were so appalling, but no word came through, and about two hours were spent by the officers and men huddled in the front line shivering with cold and wet.

" During the practice raids all that the men had been told was that the raid was to last about forty-five minutes, and the signal for withdrawal was to be a large luminous shell or light of some description fired by a trench mortar. No actual sight of such shell or light had been given, and the matter was left to the men's imagination.

" A Company parties went out as covering parties and to put out tapes about three-quarters of an hour before zero.   About a minute before zero the trench mortars began their barrage, and when the artillery opened the German artillery were quite ready and replied instantly.   Incidentally their barrage fell just in front of the right company's jumping-off ground.

" As soon as our artillery started, A Company's covering parties, apparently thinking their job was over, got up, ran back, and fell into the already overcrowded front line.   To crown everything, almost immediately after the artillery commenced, a large phosphorous-like bomb exploded in the air, high over our heads, and most people, quite naturally, took it to be the much-discussed signal for withdrawal, fired at this time to signify that the operation was cancelled.

" The battalion, however, started out, and the two left companies walked down to the river, found nothing, as they had expected, and walked back again.   The right company was first of all delayed by A Company's covering party rushing back, and then, on emerging (from the trench), walked into the German barrage, hesitated, then saw the phosphorous bomb and returned.   A few, including the company commander, got down the slope (the position was high up, above the river), but finding themselves alone returned after waiting about and seeing no enemy.

" It was a thoroughly bad show from start to finish.   Its object was futile, the organisation was bad, and the men were left too much in doubt and were therefore very ' windy,' with the result that they took the first opportunity of coming back.

" The battalion on the left walked down to the river, found no opposition but a rusty old machine gun, which they brought back.

" It is true that the *moral* of the battalion was none too good at the time, but things were not improved next day when the Divisional Commander [1] came and, after sending the men away—" I don't want them " —proceeded to slang the officers for their failure.   The net result was that the battalion was told that it had to go on raiding until a prisoner had been captured.   Night after night the companies in turn sent out parties without result.   The matter became a joke in the brigade and division.   If one met an R.E. officer, one was greeted with the remark, ' Caught your prisoner yet ? ' "

Annoying, no doubt.   But a weekly report, dated 17th July, and typical of this period, put an end to the joke.

" At 11 p.m., 11th July, the 2nd Battalion Royal Welch Fusiliers raided the village of Hamel and the trenches round it.   The troops were

---

[1] Major-General T. Astley Cubitt, who succeeded Major-General C. G. Blackader in May.   (See page 406.)

formed up in front of Hamel outposts by 10.45 p.m. and advanced at 11 p.m. under cover of an accurate artillery and machine-gun barrage. The objective, which was a line drawn from Q.24.a.0.2 to Q.23.a.9.8, was reached at all points. Several dugouts were bombed and blown up. One wounded and eighteen unwounded prisoners were captured, all belonging to the 29th R.I.R., 16th Reserve Division. In addition a large number of the enemy were killed and one machine gun brought back.

" Our patrols have been active nightly along the whole division front.

" 13th/14th.—Four enemy sentries were shot, and on the night 14th/15th an enemy patrol was dispersed and the leader shot.

" Our artillery fire has been normal. All guns co-operated in the raid on Hamel on the night 11th/12th. The Ancre crossings have been successfully engaged on several occasions with good results, particularly the new bridges. All guns fired concentrations on road Q.18.c, where enemy cookers were reported to stop. The enemy trench mortars in Hamel and Railway Q.35.b have been silenced.

" Hostile artillery has been generally quiet, light harassing fire on forward areas predominating. Reply to our raid on Hamel was weak. During the night 12th/13th a concentration of 400 green cross and high explosive [shells] was fired on a battery position, and night 14th/15th, 1,500 rounds of yellow and green cross were fired on Englebelmer. Night 16th/17th there was a heavy shoot with 15 cm.

" Hostile machine guns and trench mortars have been normal.

" Only two enemy patrols have been encountered. Both were dispersed ; these were on the night 10th/11th and evening 14th respectively.

" Hostile activity in the air has increased somewhat. Low-flying planes have been active over our forward system, and four of our balloons have been brought down.

" The enemy's attitude remains purely defensive, and no work of any importance has been observed."

The raid of the 2nd Battalion was a pretty little movement. The village of Hamel lay in a small salient, with the River Ancre behind it—it was more marsh than river—and although a ruin the hedgerows of gardens and orchards remained. A railway ran between the village and the marsh —on the eastern side of the village—and the main streets east and west.

Patrols from various units had discovered that the Germans altered their dispositions every night, and never held the line of the railway in strength.

The problem was to attack a village (ruins) with no definite defensive trench system ; which, on a dark night, presented opportunities for disastrous confusion. The salient gave alternate directions for attack ; from the west, which would give the raiders the main roads as a guide for direction —and not a very sure one ; or from the south-west, which would give the right flank the line of the railway for direction.

Careful observation of enemy works, movement, and fire had revealed that there was strong wire in front of the village, i.e. facing west, on the longest side of the salient ; that the hedgerows, which generally concealed posts, ran north and south ; and that the protective barrage line was on a north and south line to the west of the village. To raid the village from the west would, therefore, subject the raiders to frontal fire from artillery and infantry, and to flank fire from the left as well ; also give them the hedgerows as obstacles across their front.

It was decided to raid from the southern position, with the railway

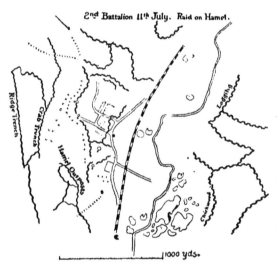

2nd Battalion 11th July. Raid on Hamel.

1000 yds.

on the right flank, using the hedgerows for direction and the roads as stages, and take the defensive lines of artillery and infantry (to a great extent) in flank.

Early in the morning the battalion moved into the support line, already occupied by our 17th Battalion, and before zero hour formed up in front of the Hamel outpost line. The right company was in column of platoons, and had the task of forming a flank along the railway : the other three companies attacked in three lines—two platoons in the front line, one in the second and third, per company—with 20 yards' interval between first and second lines, and 30 yards between second and third.

The " lines," it is interesting to note, were composed of small columns in single file, and each column, from five to seven men, had its definite task. This single-file or " worm " formation was found to be an excellent one for the purpose.

A bad storm towards the evening had made the ground slippery, but everything worked " according to plan." The three assaulting companies, C, D, and B, worked their way down the length of the hedgerows, while A Company posted itself along the railway line, guarding the flank. The German barrage went over the heads of the raiders, and there was little flank fire from across the river. Casualties would have been exceedingly small but for one of the Royal Engineers, who accompanied companies with " mobile charges," bungling his slabs of gun-cotton as he was trying to destroy a dugout, so that he blew himself and several of C Company into the air. Also, in spite of elaborate artillery arrangements—which included the field guns of neighbouring divisions and the heavy guns controlled by the corps—some trench mortars to the east of the river were missed out and commenced to fire on the centre of the village when the raiders had been in it for about thirty minutes. 2nd Lieutenant W. R. Lloyd and 10 men were killed ; Lieutenant R. D. Briercliffe, 2nd Lieutenant J. Sneddon, Thomas Smith, C. C. Davies, and 47 men were wounded.

In this cleverly executed enterprise Lieutenant Briercliffe commanded A Company ; Lieutenant S. E. Montgomerie, B ; Captain M. Radford, C ; and Captain S. H. Charlton, D.

Captain Radford says : " So far as the right company (C) was concerned, I attribute its success very largely to Lieutenant-Colonel Cockburn,[1] because as they emerged from the front line they met him accompanied by a runner in No Man's Land. His remark, ' You're a bit late ! I've been down to have a look—there aren't any Germans near this part,' acted as a magnificent tonic, and when the barrage started, the men went forward well and light-heartedly."

On the 19th July the Division was relieved, and on the 2nd August, being due to return to the line in a few days, General Cubitt was called to a Corps conference to discuss what action should be taken—the enemy having retired to the far side of the Ancre.

NEW BATTALIONS OF THE REGIMENT IN THE FRONT LINE. THE 26TH BATTALION.

Ever since June 1916 there had been, in France, a battalion of the regiment which had been raised on the 15th April of that year at Bebington, under the designation of the 4th Garrison Battalion Royal Welch Fusiliers.

Colonel G. W. Priestley was the first commanding officer, appointed on the 1st May, and he proceeded, under War Office authority of 15th April, to shake together drafts of men from all the Welsh regiments and from the county regiments of Lancashire, Cheshire, and Shropshire—no less than sixteen regiments altogether. They left Bebington on the 6th June,

---

[1] Lieutenant-Colonel Garnett left the battalion to command the 121st Brigade, 40th Division, on the 6th May, when Major de Miremont assumed command. Lieutenant-Colonel Cockburn took over in July.

sailing from Southampton. A few days prior to sailing for France, Lieutenant-Colonel E. H. Thruston assumed command.

On arrival at Le Havre they were immediately split up—A Company going to Dieppe, B Company to Abancourt, C Company to Rouen, while D Company and Battalion Headquarters remained at Le Havre at what was known as the Cinder City.

They were called upon to furnish parties for various duties, " fatigues " and guards ; to conduct batches of prisoners to England, and to mount guards over " cages," which meant that smaller detachments went farther afield, to Achiet le Grand, to Peronne, to Adinkerke, etc. Many gained the experience of being attacked from the air, and by long-range gun fire.

When the great German offensive started, the imperative need for men caused a general combing out of troops employed in the back areas, and the garrison battalions were ordered forward.

Exactly two years after the battalion had been raised, on 15th April 1918, Lieutenant-Colonel Thruston received instructions to assemble his battalion at Lattre St. Quentin, from 10 to 11 kilometres west of Arras. All companies were present on the 19th.

The battalion was at first under Brigadier-General C. C. Williams, commanding 199th Brigade ; they " manned " rear defences in the neighbourhood, improved them, and trained. On the 16th May they were posted to the 176th Brigade, 59th Division, and started, on the 19th, to march to Laires, arriving on the 16th June, with the object of commencing a period of intensive training to last two months.

The 59th Division, which had been in France since February 1917, had been reduced to a training cadre, and was now reconstructed with garrison battalions ; but the designation " garrison " was no longer correct and was abolished. In the case of our garrison battalion, however, there was already a 4th Battalion in the regiment, so they were given the number 26. Command of the new Service battalion was given to Lieutenant-Colonel H. H. Lee (23rd July), and the battalion moved to the Bretincourt area, relieving the 9th Canadian Brigade in reserve.

The battalion was billeted at Wailly ; the weather was wet. On the 24th July company commanders and officers commanding " specialists " visited the front line near Mercatel, and the next day the battalion took over portion of the front line held by the 49th Canadian Battalion, 7th Canadian Brigade.

.   .   .   .

THE 24TH BATTALION.

Troops were also drawn from other theatres of war. The 74th Division, from Palestine, arrived at Marseilles on the 7th May, and proceeded by train to Noyelles. In this division were the 24th and 25th Battalions of the regiment.

The 24th Battalion was billeted at Hauteville, close to Lattre St. Quentin.

The 31st Division, reduced to cadre, was being re-formed at the same time as the 59th. The training cadres of the 2nd Royal Munster and 2nd Royal Dublin Fusiliers had absorbed the 6th Battalions of their respective regiments, who had come from Palestine with the 74th Division (they had also been at Gallipoli and Salonika). These two battalions were in the 94th Brigade, 31st Division, and under orders to move forward to the fighting line, when it was discovered that neither battalion was in a fit state for service : there was a daily sick-list of from 75 to 100 officers and men suffering from recurrent malaria. The whole brigade was, therefore, reconstructed, and three battalions—12th Royal Scots Fusiliers (Ayr and Lanark Yeomanry), 12th Norfolk (Norfolk Yeomanry), and 24th Royal Welch Fusiliers (Denbighshire Yeomanry)—were taken from the 74th Division, whose brigades arrived in France with four battalions.

In the reconstructed 31st Division the 92nd Brigade was commanded by Brigadier-General O. de L. Williams, Royal Welch Fusiliers.

The transfer of our battalion took place on the 21st June, when the battalion entrained at Tinques and detrained at Blaringham to be billeted at Lynde. The 31st Division was already under orders to move, and had done so. On the 25th June our battalion moved forward into reserve billets, and on the 28th the 31st Division delivered an attack, with the 92nd Brigade, the object being to get a bit more elbow-room east of the Forêt de Nieppe by advancing the line to the banks of the Becque.

Our 24th Battalion was detailed to carry wire, etc., and went up with the fourth attacking wave. " It is reported," says the Brigade Diary, " that carrying parties of the 24th Royal Welch Fusiliers, starting behind the fourth wave, were first to reach the objective." These battalions of the 74th Division were still composed of original yeomen, hardened by their war experience in Palestine.

On the 30th June the 94th Brigade relieved the 92nd Brigade in the front line. The attack had been successful : some 250 prisoners had been taken, together with 3 field guns and 32 machine guns.

A great deal of aggressive patrolling was carried out, at first with success ; but soon after our battalion had taken over the front line, the Germans relieved the division that was holding their line, and a stouter lot of troops took over : they shifted their main line of defence forward and were extremely vigilant. During the month of July the enemy's line was thoroughly tested, his posts located. Sometimes a patrol would meet with a small success in the way of identification ; but the outstanding deeds were performed by 2nd Lieutenant D. R. Miles—a great night for him was the 5th/6th August.

Miles left our lines at 11.30 p.m., accompanied by one man, with the object of examining a suspected new post. He found it partly protected by a belt of wire, but saw no enemy. He did not venture into the post, but returned to our lines. He then went out again, this time with two men, and crawled up to the post to find it occupied. Having reached a favourable position unobserved, he and the two men rushed the post, and captured a machine gun with its crew of five men. He conducted his prisoners back to our line.

Again he left our lines, with three men, to work from the post originally entered along the enemy line. He soon came upon a second post, rushed it, and took the machine gun and crew of five men. This time he sent his prisoners back under escort of two of his men, while he, with the one that remained, crawled along to the right, some 200 yards. Another post ! Occupied ! Whispered instructions ; a few moments of anxious crawling ; a rush in the dark ; and he returned with a third machine gun and four men.

In the history of patrolling it is probably unique, and must stand high in the record.

That same night Lieutenant J. I. J. Edwards with two men went out and returned with a machine gun which had been left unguarded by its crew. Four machine guns and fourteen prisoners in one night was, under the conditions of their capture, a great bit of work.

The next night Miles brought back a Lewis gun and four magazines placed in position by the enemy in their line but left unguarded ; and on the 7th he again, with only two men, pounced on a machine gun and crew of five, and brought them all back.

During the month of August small advances were made on the divisional front, our battalion moving forward from 250 to 300 yards on two occasions. The tide had already turned down south. At the end of the month the division was relieved, and our battalion spent some days repairing the roads at Bailleul (once more in our hands). They moved up to the line in Flanders on the 5th September, relieving the 1st Leinster on Hill 63, with Messines and Wytschaete in front of them.

. . . .

THE 25TH BATTALION.

After concentration at Noyelles, the 74th Division had moved, on the 21st May, to Roellecourt, and on the 25th to Le Cauroy : it was from this area that the 24th Battalion had left them. The division trained. On the 26th June a move was made to Norent Fontes, where work was carried on on rear defences until the 10th July, when the division started to relieve the 61st Division between the La Bassée Canal and the River Lys, with their left on the small village of Corbie. The town of Merville, some 3,000 yards away, was in enemy hands.

Our 25th Battalion relieved the 1st East Lancashire in the right sub-sector of the line, covering St. Venant.

Ever since they had landed in France, these battalions from Palestine had been training in the methods of " Western Front " warfare ; but their previous experience had made them adepts at patrolling, and the " top," the open country in face of the enemy, had no terrors for them. The Diary notes on the 14th July : " The day was quiet, and our patrols succeeded in getting well afield by daylight. Vigorous patrolling is being carried out every night and all night, with the result that the enemy rarely ventures out of his trenches."

The word " trench " is not, however, always applicable. The British line had been driven back beyond Merville, but we were still in the flat plain of the Lys Valley, and the greater part of the defences were breast-works. They were constructed in the midst of what had been a quiet back area, where peasants worked their land, and one of the first duties of the 25th Battalion, on taking over the line, was to cut the crops and clear two wide belts on either side of the wire.

On the 17th July Sergeant Varley, patrolling with two men, entered the German line by himself, and while a sentry's back was turned, quietly removed a machine gun and brought it away.

The next day, the 18th, 2nd Lieutenant Jowett, one sergeant, and ten men raided a post and captured the machine gun and crew of five. These were the first prisoners captured by the 74th Division in France.

. . . .

THE 9TH BATTALION REFITTED AND UP TO STRENGTH.

On the 1st July the 19th Division, with our 9th Battalion, was centred at Fauquembergues, in General Headquarters Reserve, under the Fifth Army, with instructions to assist either the XI or XIII Corps if necessary. The division moved slightly forward to Bomy on the 11th July.

The battalion was first at Happe, and then at Ligny-les-Aire. Reinforcements arrived in batches of fifty and a hundred, and companies soon began to swell out to normal size. On the 7th August they moved to Choques, and on the 11th in support to the front line before Hinges. They were now in the XIII Corps in the La Bassée area.

VII

PURSUIT OF THE ENEMY

PURSUIT OF THE ENEMY

REPULSE OF THE GREAT GERMAN ONSLAUGHT.

THE blows delivered by the Germans were spectacular in effect, but the German Higher Command was amazed to find resistance was still strong and active before them : Ludendorff writes of disillusionment.

The month of July was the turning-point. Marshal Foch out-generalled the enemy. He had to forestall the next move, make a fateful decision.

On the British front there was still nervous tension. " It was known," the Despatches state, " that Prince Rupprecht's reserve group of divisions about Douai and Valenciennes were still intact and opposite the British front." There was every reason to believe that an attack on the British front was imminent, and so it was. The German plan for the middle of July was to attack on both sides of Reims, and on completion of this operation to concentrate swiftly on the Flanders front. Marshal Foch, however, disregarded the northern threat and withdrew the whole of the French forces from Flanders, and further requested Sir Douglas Haig to place four divisions unreservedly at his disposal and move four others to the south of and astride the Somme. This was done, and the 15th, 34th, 51st, and 62nd Divisions, constituting the XXII Corps, were sent to the Marshal.

The drama opened on the 15th July, and it is interesting to find that secrecy was not preserved by either side. A deserter from the French Army brought news to the Germans of the preparation of a tank offensive from the Forest of Villers Cotterets, but he was wrong in his date—or rather, the date was altered by Marshal Foch. On the other hand, the French captured German officers and men who confirmed the Marshal's belief that the next enemy offensive was to be launched on that front.

Ludendorff admits, grudgingly, that he was outmanœuvred. " Our crossing of the Marne was a remarkable achievement which succeeded, although the enemy were fully prepared for it. . . . About five kilometres south of the Marne the attacking troops came upon an enemy force so strong that it could only be overcome by bringing a large number of batteries over the river. . . . According to plan, the enemy had withdrawn in front of the 1st and 3rd Armies to their second position, and held us firmly all along the line." [1]

The Germans had fallen into a trap. But the Army could not spring back like a frightened cat. Orders were issued on the 16th to retire on the night 20th/21st, and meanwhile the offensive was to be pushed round Reims. The precise nature of Marshal Foch's trap was not apparent to the German Command. The crossing of the Marne was a disappointment, but Reims was a plum to be plucked, and " G.H.Q. still clung to the idea of an attack in Flanders by the Army Group of Crown Prince Rupprecht . . . . The railway transport of artillery, trench mortars, and planes from the Reims district had begun according to plan on the 16th." The attention of the German Higher Command was turned to the north. The Fourth and Sixth German Armies were to be launched, with the heights between Poperinghe and Bailleul and round Hazebrouck as their objectives. Ludendorff, Prince Rupprecht, and the Army Group Staff were deep in the discussion of final arrangements on the morning of the 18th July, with maps scored by coloured pencils to mark the movements and bounds of assaulting troops in the projected offensive. The last thing they thought of was the French deserter who had told them of the tanks in the Forest of Villers Cotterets ; Ludendorff had at most experienced a hope during the morning that the German Crown Prince would speed his arrangements for surrounding Reims.

The German thrust west of Reims had gone deep, surprising the Germans themselves : they had crossed the Marne ; a great salient was shown on the map, with extended flanks, and on the western flank the patch marking the forest. Out of the forest came the massed tanks, some of them the low and, at that period, fast tanks called " whippets." The German line was pierced.

Marshal Foch, of course, launched troops on other parts of this front ; the British XXII Corps pushed up the Ardre Valley, and retook the Montagne de Bligny.[2] The whole German line was hurled back, fighting desperately. They left over 30,000 prisoners, 900 guns, and 6,000 machine guns in the hands of the Allies, which they could ill afford to do, but they claim that after the first surprise they dealt successfully with the counterstroke. On the ground this is to some extent true, but, as a direct result of the attack, orders were issued for the suspension of all offensive plans

---

[1] This was the local French commander's act, an interesting decision.
[2] Bligny had been lost in June after the departure of the 19th Division.

on the whole German front. Ingenuously Ludendorff explains that " a pause in the operations was nothing extraordinary. . . . It had occurred after . . . the great offensive of the 21st March. . . . The desire for rest was as legitimate now as it had been then." Meanwhile ten German divisions had been broken up.

The Germans had been staggered by the battle which commenced on the 18th July—the Second Battle of the Marne—and our battalions, at some distance from the battlefield, saw the line in front of them rock under the force of the blow. We find on the 2nd August—the 38th Division being out of the line—a conference taking place at Corps Headquarters on the action to be taken owing to the enemy retirement across the Ancre. The 115th Brigade relieved the 50th Brigade on the 5th August, our 2nd Battalion being in the front line, and found the whole of the ridge south of Aveluy Wood, for which the 113th Brigade had fought and lost so heavily on the 22nd April, free of the enemy ; the 2nd Battalion held, as a line of resistance, Rejection Trench, the former German support trench ; and the line of the railway, down by the Ancre, was held by patrols. Patrols examined the crossings of the Ancre on the night of the 6th.

Further north, while the 19th Division was moving up to take over the line as the centre division of the XIII Corps, opposite Hinges (north of Bethune), the 4th Division, on the left, reported the enemy retiring ; the 58th Brigade, with our 9th Battalion, moved forward from the original line that day. And on the 8th August the whole Corps, 46th, 19th, and 4th Divisions, went forward, although severe opposition was met at a place called Vertbois Farm.

All this as a direct result of Foch's attack on the 18th July. " Knowing that the next measures must be purely defensive," Hindenburg and Ludendorff had already ordered a withdrawal in the Plain of the Lys and the evacuation of the bridgeheads on the Ancre and Avre, when a second blow fell. The 8th August was " the black day of the German Army in the history of this war," says Ludendorff. " This was the worst experience that I had to go through, except for the events that, from September 15th onwards, took place on the Bulgarian Front and sealed the fate of the Quadruple Alliance."

Marshal Foch's order for August was :

" The British IV Army and the French I Army will advance on the 8th, under the command of Field-Marshal Sir D. Haig, the former north and the latter south of the Amiens—Roye road. The offensive, covered by the Somme, will be pushed as far as possible towards Roye. The French III Army will attack the left flank of the Montdidier Salient on the 10th inst. The French X Army, in the Oise Valley (on the left bank), will continue to advance eastwards.''

On the 8th August the Battle of Amiens commenced, yielding the visible military gain of some 22,000 prisoners, 400 guns, and all the country between Amiens and the old German position before the Battle of the Somme,

1916. Actually it was a great deal more. The German High Command acknowledged itself beaten. " I had no hope of finding a strategic expedient whereby to turn the situation to our advantage " (Ludendorff). Hurried meetings were held, and the decision arrived at that the war must be ended.

Then commenced a gigantic movement, the advance of Armies on distant objectives, the French and American towards Mezières, and the British to cut the communications through Maubeuge to Hirson. Our battalions were scattered over the entire British front—the 4th Battalion behind the 47th Division, about the Bois des Tailles, ready to make roads as the III Corps advanced on the right of Albert ; the 2nd, 13th, 14th, 16th, and 17th, with the 38th Division, in the V Corps on the immediate left of Albert ; the 26th at Mercatel in VI Corps ; the 9th Battalion, with the 19th Division, on the XIII Corps front, at Hinges, slightly north of Bethune, on the south of the great German advance over the Lys Plain ; the 25th Battalion with the 74th Division about St. Floris, on the XI Corps front, in touch with the XIII Corps ; the 24th Battalion with the 31st Division, in the XV Corps front, east of the Forêt de Nieppe.

To complicate matters, there is an immediate move, as operations in which the regiment is concerned commenced on the 23rd August, of the 26th Battalion to the north, into the XI Corps, when the 59th Division relieved the 74th Division ; our 26th Battalion watched the 52nd Division " go over the top " at Mercatel, and marched that evening, the 23rd, out of the line, to arrive at La Pierrière on the 26th. The 25th Battalion moved with the 74th Division to the III Corps front, and went into the line north of Peronne. Also the 24th Battalion moved north, to Hill 63, about Neuve Eglise, on the Belgian Front.

THE BATTLE OF ALBERT.[1]

Our 2nd and 17th Battalions had on several occasions attempted to cross the Ancre before the battle opened on the 21st. The difficulties were great, owing to the marsh through which the river meandered, and the known crossings being covered from the eastern bank by the enemy. Albert was still held by the Germans ; but on the 38th Division front the Ancre was the dividing-line between them and the enemy.

The battle opened on the left of the division (V Corps) with an attack by the IV and VI Corps which drove the enemy back through Bucquoy to the line of the railway north of the point on which the 38th Division stood ; this railway, the Arras—Albert line, after passing between Aveluy Wood and the Ancre, takes a sharp turn east to Achiet le Grand, whence it runs straight to Arras. It is important to note this preliminary movement to the drive across the old Somme battlefield, for it determines the direction of the attack, south-east, and turns all the old German positions of 1916. Our battalions in the 38th Division revisited all the scenes of 1916 slaughter, but approached them from a different angle.

On the right of the V Corps the III Corps attacked on the 22nd August, the 47th Division taking part in the action, while our 4th Battalion waited in trenches behind the Bois des Tailles ready " to undertake any work which the tactical situation demanded "—as it turned out, none was required that day. The attack of the III Corps cleared Albert of the enemy and, to the south of it, pushed well to the east of the Albert—Bray road.

The situation then was that the line on either side of the V Corps was well forward.

---

[1] Date: 21st–23rd August 1918. Area: road Chaulnes—Lamotte—Corbie—Warloy—Acheux —Souastre—Berles-au-Bois—Bretencourt—Heninel.

The conditions on the river-bank were a little easier, and our 17th Battalion succeeded in establishing a post on the eastern side.

A preliminary movement to a more general attack was ordered for the morning of the 23rd : a supporting operation to complete the III Corps jump of the previous day, which was entrusted to the 113th Brigade. The instructions were to attack at the same time as the III Corps and seize Rubber Lane ; also clear Crucifix Corner, the site of a strong-point. The direction of the attack was on La Boisselle, the scene in 1916 of the 9th Battalion attack.

The brigade was in reserve, and assembled on the 22nd north of Henencourt, and at 9.30 p.m. marched through Albert to the assembly positions, held by troops of the 18th Division. The 13th Battalion led the attack, supported by the 14th ; the 16th was in reserve.

Covered by an artillery barrage, the assault commenced at 4.55 a.m., on a wide front of some 2,000 yards, and penetrated to a depth of 1,800 yards. It was not child's play, although all objectives were taken by 9.45 a.m. Portions of our 14th Battalion, advancing in close support, frequently found themselves in the forefront of the fight—A Company was sent by Lieutenant-Colonel Collier to the right, on Usna Hill, where there was heavy fighting, B Company on the left to help the 13th against two pill-boxes which were eventually rushed.

The 13th lost 2nd Lieutenant Davies and 20 other ranks killed, Captains Vaughan, C. B. Williams, Lieutenant H. Lewis, 2nd Lieutenants R. B. Morgan, and A. G. Page wounded, with 117 other ranks ; 19 other ranks were missing. The losses of the 14th Battalion were lighter : Captain Humphreys Owen, second-in-command, was wounded while Rubber Lane was being consolidated ; Lieutenants K. O. Parsons and D. D. Roberts were also hit.

But the booty was considerable. Prisoners numbered 194, and heading the list of material captures were 2 field guns and 16 machine guns.

The 115th Brigade took over a part of the captured line, from Crucifix Corner to the Chalk Pit, and orders were issued for a further advance : the 113th and 115th Brigades in the direction of La Boisselle and Ovillers, the 114th Brigade on the high ground south-east of Thiepval. The 114th Brigade had also been engaged in hard fighting on the 23rd—the men had to wade and swim the Ancre, but they established themselves on the eastern bank.

Under the official arrangement of battles the Battle of Albert comes to an end on the 23rd August ; so far as the 38th Division is concerned it had only just started and was continued with vigour on the 24th. The instructions were for a converging attack by the 113th and 114th Brigades on a point well to the east of Aveluy Wood ; the 115th Brigade would then mop up the triangle containing the wood, and the three brigades would proceed to the further objectives, as above.

The attack started at 1 a.m.   On the 113th Brigade front our 16th and 14th Battalions attacked, with the 13th in reserve.   On the 115th

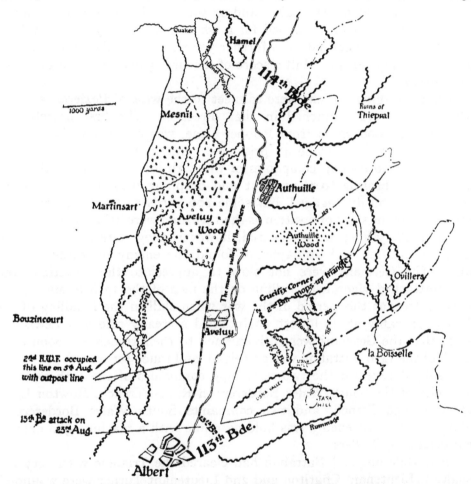

Brigade front the mopping-up of the Triangle was given to our 2nd Battalion, while our 17th advanced on the left of the 14th.   The 114th Brigade drove down in a south-easterly direction from the north of Aveluy Wood.

The 113th Brigade, having taken Usna Hill on the previous day, were on the crest line of a spur which comes slanting down from the north-east to the Ancre.   The 16th and 14th Battalions advanced into the curling valley on the far side, meeting with little opposition until they came to the craters of the original 1916 line, in front of La Boisselle—a favourable spot, this, for the concealment of machine guns, resulting in what was described as a "general mix-up of battalions." But the position was overrun, B Company of the 16th secured La Boisselle, and, after a pause for reorganisation, A, C, and D Companies of the 16th advanced to the second objective, across the valley and on the crest line of the next spur.

The 14th Battalion remained for a while in the valley to throw back a counter-attack, which added a further 30 prisoners to the hundred or so they had already taken. Half a score of machine guns were also found on this position.

The converging attacks were to meet to the west of Pozières, and our 17th Battalion was launched in that direction. The first objective, a trench about 1,000 yards from Rubber Lane, was reached without much difficulty, and yielded some 40 prisoners. But in the darkness of early morning the two leading companies of the 17th lost direction in the next leap forward, bearing to their right and dropping into the valley where the 14th were busily engaged, but some 800 yards to the north of them. Here they met the same opposition as the 14th, and were held up by machine-gun and artillery fire; being isolated, however, they were in a somewhat precarious position and at daybreak found the enemy on three sides of them. The Germans were not slow to appreciate the situation, and counter-attacked vigorously, calling on the men of the 17th to surrender; but the latter, at this period of the war when skill in the handling of the rifle was probably at its lowest, maintained a steady rifle and Lewis-gun fire, so that the Germans were driven back to their trenches. Soon after the left of the 14th Battalion was perceived, and touch secured.

Daylight revealed the two remaining companies of the 17th and two companies of the South Wales Borderers in Ranch Trench, Rowton Lane, and Rummage Trench, and two companies South Wales Borderers in Rubber Lane. The enemy was holding a line with a machine-gun detachment defending Ovillers.

Meanwhile our 2nd Battalion had cleared the Triangle with very few casualties (Lieutenant Charlton and 2nd Lieutenant Turner were wounded, and between 20 and 30 other ranks), and had secured over 200 prisoners and 17 machine guns.

The advance had ceased before midday. During the afternoon the whole division was ordered to move forward at 4.30 p.m. The situation on the extreme left (114th Brigade) was not clear, and the 115th Brigade was wrongly informed that our troops were in Pozières.

On the right of the 113th Brigade, the 16th Battalion, already on the slopes above La Boisselle, pushed forward in the direction of Contalmaison until checked on the western outskirts of that village by machine-gun posts. The 14th Battalion, after clearing the lower trenches, left the valley and moved up the slope to get in touch with the 16th. Lieutenant Farrell was wounded while trying to find the 16th. They too were checked by the enemy, who had all the advantage which the old, churned-up battlefield offered for rearguard tactics. The 14th took up a shell-hole position on the left of the Albert—Bapaume road, which runs through Pozières, with the enemy, in force on their left flank, trying to work round them ; they had to refuse their flank, B Company moving to the left.

In order to overcome the resistance at Ovillers, the 17th Battalion and 10th South Wales Borderers were ordered, about 4 p.m., to attack, but this order was countermanded, and the 115th Brigade was directed to pass by the site of the village, leaving it on their right, and make for Pozières. So at 4 p.m. the 2nd Battalion, having completed the mopping-up of the Triangle, led the 115th Brigade ; but, contrary to expectations, for they had been told that Pozières was in our hands, they were held up by machine-gun fire to the west of the village, at the head of the valley, and slightly in advance of the line held by the 14th Battalion. Here they remained through the night until about 1.30 a.m., when fresh orders were received to be on a line south-east of Bazentin le Petit Wood and north-west of Mametz Wood by 6.30 a.m. This line was occupied by our 2nd Battalion on the right and the 10th South Wales Borderers on the left ; our 17th Battalion was in support. A few prisoners were taken, but very slight opposition was met with.

The move of the 115th Brigade was made simultaneously with an attack, behind a barrage, delivered by the 16th Battalion on the extreme right, through Contalmaison ; the 14th Battalion filled the gap between the 16th and South Wales Borderers. The morning found the 38th Division to the west of Mametz Wood, the line running roughly in a north-east and south-west direction.

The 113th Brigade spent the day (25th) looking across the valley at Mametz Wood. At 5 p.m. fighting patrols from the 16th Battalion advanced and cleared the wood, which was only lightly held.

The position occupied at 11 p.m. by the 113th and 115th Brigades was east edge of Mametz Wood to Bazentin le Petit Wood ; and the 114th Brigade, on the left, about 1,000 yards to the west of High Wood. There had been few incidents during the day. C Company of the 2nd Battalion had bumped into a strong-point while advancing on Bazentin le Petit Wood, and had suffered several casualties, amongst them being Lieutenant

C. Jones and 2nd Lieutenant Ledbury, both wounded.   Otherwise casualties had been light, although there was much machine-gun fire from the high ground about High Wood and Montauban.   In the evening the 113th Brigade was ordered to advance next day at 4 a.m. on Longueval, with the idea of forcing the enemy from High Wood, in front of the 114th Brigade.

The 26th August was a day of heavy fighting for the 113th Brigade. The 13th Battalion led, with the 16th and 14th in support, and the 2nd Battalion, attached, in reserve.

From the commencement of the advance the 13th Battalion were badly hammered, although there is no record of their casualties on that day.   The supporting battalions came into the fight at once.   Machine-gun fire was severe, and the ground, over which the 1st Battalion had fought on the celebrated 16th July 1916, was difficult.   In 1916 the advance had been from the south, a frontal attack on the ridges ; this time it was from the west.   Flank fire was the trouble.   As troops worked their way up the centre ridge towards Longueval they were raked from the high ground on the right about Montauban, and on the left about High Wood.   The 13th Battalion was checked—companies had strayed a little to the right— and B Company of the 14th Battalion moved up on the left of the 13th and entered Bazentin le Grand village.   All battalions were engaged at this time—it was about 9 a.m. : the 16th, on the right, was held up by fire from Caterpillar Wood ; the 2nd Battalion sent B and D Companies as a guard to the right flank.

Lieutenant Llewellyn Evans, at that time adjutant of our 2nd Battalion, gives a personal experience which helps to " paint the picture."   " The 2nd Battalion was to follow the advance, two companies to drop posts facing outwards—the division on the right were not attacking until next day.

" It was a very misty morning when zero came and the attack commenced.   Colonel Cockburn followed the advance and detailed me to proceed along the defensive flank and see that each post had been rightly placed, and then rejoin him when I caught up with the advance.

" Pierpoint, hereditary adjutant's runner, and whilom professional golfer, accompanied me on the job, and we found Post No. 1 quite all right. But owing to the mist and early morning darkness we veered out of line in the direction of Caterpillar Wood, and this we realised and feared we were outside our posts, and began to work in gradually to our left.

" Ruined buildings——!   Recently killed and some wounded Germans——!   Noise of firing——!   Ghostly figures looming in the mist——!

" We realised we were watching our own men advancing, but they, of course, knew nothing of us and had, in the previous moment, dealt with a party of Germans. When they sighted us there was a tense pause. Everything was still, etherially vague ! And our relief was great when a voice was heard, ' Let's take the —— prisoners ! Come on, Jerry ! '—and to them we went with our hands up in true ' Kamerad ' fashion. ' Good God ! it's the adjutant ! ' said our captor, a diminutive lance-corporal, Perkes, who, I regret to say, was killed later in the day.

" I kept inside our line from then on, and caught up the advance in a little copse, Bazentin le Grand. Here there was vigorous ' mopping up ' proceeding, as this copse was strongly held. I rejoined the C.O., who then sent me to catch the advancing front wave and order it not to proceed beyond the road which ran parallel to our front through Bazentin le Grand. I got there before them, however, to find the road (it was sunken) empty, save for a cubby hole in its western bank, with a door which opened and gave up to Pierpoint and myself some eleven very scared ' Jerries,' one after another, coming out in single file to see what the Fates had in store for them. Fortunately at that moment the front wave of the 113th Brigade dropped into the road and relieved us of our embarrassing charges. I gave them their orders just as a beautifully placed barrage fell on the road ; but thanks to a deep ditch on the eastern side of the sunken road the whole line lay snug.

" We then returned to the spot where I had last seen the C.O., only to find him on a stretcher. We had lost heavily during the day, but this was the culminating blow !

" It appeared that Cocky (Lieutenant-Colonel Cockburn), accompanied by Lance-Corporal W. Evans, an excellent fellow, had come suddenly upon a German machine-gun post which fired on them at point-blank range. The C.O. was shot in the leg and fell. Evans ran forward unhesitatingly, shot and bayoneted several, and captured the remainder with their gun. He then marched them back, with gun, and made them help with the colonel, and rejoined in that fashion."

The first obstruction was moving. B Company of the 14th Battalion, having turned the enemy out of Bazentin le Grand village, followed him to the main Longueval—Contalmaison road, only to be driven back themselves to Bazentin le Grand. C Company was sent to clear the enemy from the left flank, and, aided by the South Wales Borderers, who were moving up on the left of the 113th Brigade, captured some thirty prisoners and two machine guns.

About this time, 10 a.m., our 17th Battalion was ordered to move east, north of Bazentin le Petit Wood, but to avoid High Wood if it was strongly held. The battalion, advancing in artillery formation, found little opposition and took possession of High Wood, with five prisoners and a machine gun. They found the enemy established in some strength farther to the east.

Meanwhile, with the 16th and 13th Battalions at a standstill, the 14th Battalion had pushed forward on the left of the 113th Brigade. They were on the old Windmill position, and advanced towards the shoulder of the centre ridge from the north-west : A Company on the right, D Company and two platoons of C on the left. They turned the flank of the enemy who were holding up the 13th Battalion, captured over 100 prisoners and 8 machine guns, and took up a position across the ridge scarcely 1,000 yards west of Longueval.

Officers and men of the 14th Battalion had done well, showing wonderful dash. Conspicuous was Lance-Corporal Henry Weale (No. 5046) (Shotton Cheshire), who was afterwards awarded the Victoria Cross. The *Gazette* reads : " The adjacent battalion having been held up by enemy machine guns, Lance-Corporal Weale was ordered to deal with the hostile posts. When his Lewis gun failed him, on his own initiative he rushed the nearest posts and killed the crew, then went for the others, the crews of which fled on his approach, this gallant non-commissioned officer pursuing them. His very dashing deed cleared the way for the advance, inspired his comrades, and resulted in the capture of all the machine guns." Captain J. Jack, Lieutenant G. Jones, and 2nd Lieutenant W. G. Evans were wounded in this movement.

The 14th Battalion remained somewhat isolated, about 1,000 yards in advance of the rest of the 113th Brigade, and with their flanks in the air. An attempt was made by the division to use the mounted troops, and patrols of the 6th Dragoon Guards (Carabineers) were ordered to clear Longueval : they lost heavily, only a few men getting back. At 5 p.m. the enemy launched a counter-attack from Delville Wood, and farther to the right, from Trones Wood—a determined effort. He failed, however. But the Commanding Officer of the 14th Battalion (Lieutenant-Colonel Collier) decided he must withdraw slightly and secure his flanks by conforming with the general line. Lieutenant Haycock was killed during the counter-attack, and Captain Murray wounded. It was viewed by Llewellyn Evans, who states that a rumour reached Battalion Headquarters " that the 2nd Battalion was falling back. I took Lance-Corporal Evans with me and visited the whole of the line to find everything normal, and nothing at all in the scare, but in time to observe preparations for an enemy counter-attack slightly to the right of our front. The Germans had assembled in

Trones Wood and were now streaming out of it, exactly like a crowd leaving a theatre, and moved parallel to our front and towards the left. They turned to attack down the road from Longueval towards a section held by the 13th Battalion, who went forward to meet them with the bayonet, formed an opening in their line and let the Hussars (?) through. At that time cavalry was operating freely in the attack, but practically wholly as liaison units and gallopers, but this party had a rare gallop, and an exciting dash at the counter-attacking Germans, who feathered away in very quick time.

" The remainder of that night passed without incident and the following day the 2nd Battalion was relieved and rejoined the 115th Brigade, well to the left of the 113th Brigade front."

The line that night ran from the left of the 18th Division, who held the north edge of Bernafay Wood, through a point 1,000 yards west of Longueval, and through a point 1,000 yards east of High Wood. The 113th Brigade was directed to attack towards Ginchy at 4 a.m., and the 114th Brigade towards Morval ; the 115th Brigade would fall back into reserve.

On the 27th the 113th Brigade, with the 13th Battalion as advance guard, moved once more on Longueval, but it was evident that Longueval, that is to say Delville Wood, was held by the enemy in strength, as was Trones Wood on the right of it, in front of the 18th Division. The artillery barrage, which started at 4 a.m., failed to dislodge the machine guns which swept the approach to the wood. The 13th Battalion estimated their casualties at 100, amongst them Lieutenant Allison. It was decided not to press the attack, and the 13th Battalion was withdrawn. The site of the village and Delville Wood were then subjected to an intense bombardment by the artillery, which commenced at 6.30 p.m.

This same kind of fighting was being carried on from the Somme to Arras by the Fourth and Third Armies. On the left, troops were approaching Bapaume ; on the right, Peronne. It was expected that the fall of the former town, which was almost surrounded, would cause a further hasty retirement by the enemy.

The night passed fairly quietly, and in the morning of the 28th the artillery recommenced the bombardment of Longueval and Delville Wood. The outpost line was held by the 16th and 14th Battalions of the 113th Brigade, and the 114th Brigade was on their left ; the 115th Brigade was in reserve, and spent the day about High Wood. In the afternoon Lieutenant Seel with three other ranks of the 14th Battalion reconnoitred Longueval and found the enemy had gone ; Lieutenant Pringle then advanced with C Company and took up a position 200 yards in advance of the Longueval—Flers road. The 16th Battalion also sent patrols forward and advanced their line.

In the orders for the next day, Major-General Cubitt gives the information that " there is little change on the Third Army front. The 12th Division are reported this morning as approaching Maurepas. The 18th Division hold the south-east corner of Bernafay Wood and the east edge of Trones Wood." The 113th Brigade were ordered to move on Ginchy, passing south of Delville Wood, while the 115th Brigade, passing to the north, would occupy the high ground above Ginchy. The 114th Brigade would " mop up " Delville Wood.

On the right the attack was made by the 16th and 14th Battalions. The artillery barrage opened at 5.15 a.m., and a quarter of an hour later the two battalions advanced. There was practically no opposition—the enemy had fallen back during the night to the Morval Ridge. The 115th Brigade, attacking with our 17th Battalion and the 10th South Wales Borderers, had the same experience : during the evening the South Wales Borderers occupied Les Bœufs.

The line then ran west of Morval and east of Les Bœufs. It was thought that the enemy would withdraw during the night—the New Zealand Division had entered Bapaume during the night of the 29th, and on the immediate right the 18th Division was in Combles—but he did not do so, and the 114th Brigade, taking up the advance on the 30th, was held up in front of Morval. Patrols trying to enter the ruins the next day found them strongly held ; it was even thought that the enemy had reinforced the position. Orders were issued to attack at 4.45 a.m. on the 1st September, under a field artillery and machine-gun barrage, the 114th Brigade being directed on trenches to the east of Morval, when they would be relieved by the 113th Brigade, who would take up the advance with the 115th Brigade on the left. The final objective was on the line Sailly-Saillisel.

THE SECOND BATTLE OF BAPAUME.[1]

Sir Douglas Haig, in his despatch, treats these operations as one great battle, which he calls the Battle of Bapaume, starting from the 21st August and ending on the 1st September ; indeed, it is one wide movement which commenced with the Fourth Army attack on the 8th August and ended at the Canal du Nord. But no matter how the advance is split up into

---

[1] Date : 31st August—3rd September. Area : road Athies—Chaulnes—Rosières—Bray—Miraumont—Hamelincourt—St. Leger—thence a line to Noreuil—Mœuvres.

battles, fighting was incessant ; between prepared engagements the front line battalions were always pushing fighting patrols forward to test the enemy positions and take advantage of any weak spot or retirement of his line.

The engagement fought on the 1st September was a severe one for the regiment. The 114th Brigade attack on Morval was timed to commence at 4.45 a.m., and the 113th Brigade was to relieve them east of Morval by 6 a.m. The latter time coincided, within a few minutes, with the advance of the 115th Brigade from their position east of Les Bœufs, and as this brigade attacked with the 17th Battalion on the right and the 2nd Battalion on the left, the advance, after the capture of Morval, was to be made by four battalions of Royal Welch Fusiliers in line.

The 114th Brigade attacked Morval, where they met some opposition, but captured the position up to time. They were duly relieved by our 16th and 13th Battalions.

On the 115th Brigade front the attack was already in progress—the barrage had started at 5.45 a.m. From Les Bœufs (on the falling slope of the ridge) a roll in the ground, or small spur, intervened between the assembly position and Sailly-Saillisel, and the first objective of the 17th and 2nd Battalions was a road on this spur. The two battalions had been lying under shell fire since the 114th Brigade attacked, and when they rose to advance met with immediate opposition. They pressed forward without a pause and reached the road, capturing some fifty prisoners and machine guns. This advance was to have been supported by a battalion of the 17th Division on the left, but meeting with stout opposition, the support faded away. Our 17th and 2nd Battalions attacked on a two-company front, and the support companies were to pass through the leading companies on the first objective ; the latter had orders to remain on the position until the success of the advance on Sailly-Saillisel was assured.

There was, then, no support on the left of our 2nd Battalion, and B and A Companies passed through C and D on the first objective and commenced to drop down into the valley in front of the village ; on their left was Le Transloy. As they advanced, their line of march soon placed Le Transloy on their left rear ; and they found the enemy well entrenched in the uneven corrugations of the hollow in front of Sailly-Saillisel. They were met by machine-gun and rifle fire, which was reinforced by trench-mortar and rifle-grenade discharges, and as their advance was checked the enemy issued from the Le Transloy defences.

The German attack developed first against the two leading companies of the 2nd Battalion, then against the support companies on the spur, and finally Battalion Headquarters had to defend itself.

Llewellyn Evans describes the ground as rising gradually " in front of the village, and at zero the battalion disappeared over the crest, in a bee-line for its objective, a railway parallel to its front.

" We, Headquarters, moved after it—Greaves, Hughes and I, a few runners and a signaller or two. I believe, at the moment, the C.O. (de Miremont) had gone, or been called to Brigade Headquarters. Our first surprise was experiencing that uncomfortable sensation of being fired at from behind—our left rear, as a matter of fact. Some 80 yards in that direction was a shell hole with Germans in it; suspecting them, I went over to their shell hole, but found them unarmed, wounded, and some were stretcher-bearers, so they were proved ' not guilty.'

" Very shortly afterwards some of our men on the left—the defensive flank merchants—were seen falling back rather hurriedly to our ' kicking off ' point, so we linked up with them, and formed a post in some ragged trenches just as a strong enemy machine-gun force appeared on the crest at the point our men had come from, and about 400 yards away. They settled down without delay to get their light machine guns at work, while we in our trench got equally busy with rifles and a providential machine-gun team, which at this stage was attached to infantry battalions.

" Some details, a few men only, of the 17th were somehow in this trench, and one of them, at my elbow, was shot through the head early. Our padre (Rev. E. R. Jones) had got here—I don't know how—and he assisted us by going back to the village, where some of our Headquarter details still were, for their ammunition, and with a message to the Brigade to push out the supporting troops to deal with the menace to our exposed flank.

" Very shortly two companies of the South Wales Borderers were seen advancing on our left rear towards this German stronghold, and soon after that they returned, and passed our post with a good bag of prisoners —and that menace was over.

" By this time de Miremont had joined us, but there was no news of the companies. Later in the morning a runner came from Chick (A Company) asking for help and reporting himself in difficulties.

" The C.O. looked round his staff and said to me, ' I think, Yanto, you had better go and see what has happened,' and off I went with the faithful and phlegmatic Pierpoint.

" We found Chick in some trenched ruins mixed up with elements of the 17th Battalion and in a bad state. He had lost a number of men, and he himself was hanging on his nerves only, had been wounded, and was

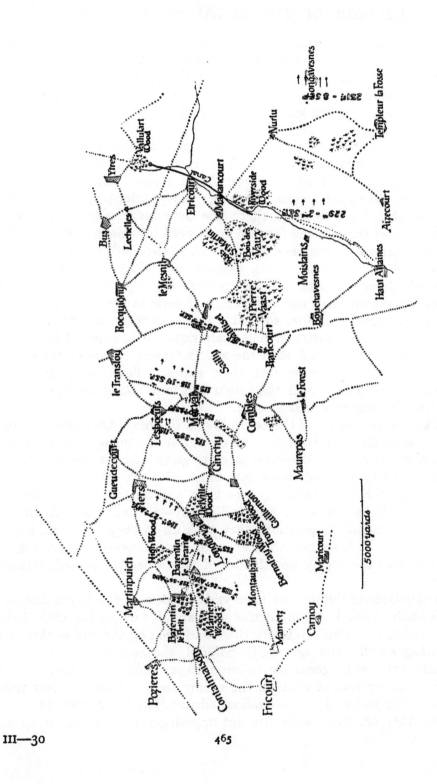

altogether quite unfit to continue any longer. He was relieved during the day, Hughes taking over what there was of the company.

"Going forward again, across the railway, we came across elements of D Company—a few men. The officer commanding, 2nd Lieutenant F. L. C. Jones, had been killed and the company almost surrounded, having had to fight their way back to the railway. Crabtree and Jones and some men had been overwhelmed (Crabtree was wounded then) by Germans breaking through the centre as well as round our left flank, but Crabtree had managed to send back his orderly to report what he could, much against the man's inclination. Another party belonging to D Company told me, when I got to them, that some Germans who had ' Kameraded ' as they passed them in the forward rush, fired into them from behind and did much damage as well as escaping back to their side of the 'fence.' "

The whole line of the 115th Brigade had fallen back. On the right the 113th Brigade had taken over trenches scarcely more than 500 yards east of Morval, and had not had time, and perhaps were not able, as they were under heavy shell fire, to deal with the country on the right ; consequently the 17th Battalion had their right flank exposed to a galling fire and were no better off than the 2nd Battalion. Indeed, the Germans commenced to advance against their exposed flank, and the support companies had to draw back their right and form facing south, even as the 2nd Battalion was now facing north.

The two companies of the South Wales Borderers who were sent to the assistance of the 2nd Battalion succeeded in capturing about 70 of the venturesome Germans and several machine guns. About the same time, on the right, the 13th Battalion got into touch with the 17th and secured this flank. But all these movements took time, and the two leading companies of the 2nd Battalion were practically lost—38 dead were found lying together on one of the positions they took up as they fell back, and 2nd Lieutenant D. A. I. Ainger, with 25 men, was afterwards relieved, having held out, with the enemy on all sides of him, when the brigade retired on Morval.

Major-General Cubitt now gave verbal orders to the 113th Brigade to attack Sailly-Saillisel, in conjunction with an advance by the 18th Division on the right, at 6 p.m. Actually there had been on the site of these ruins two villages : the first one Sailly-Saillisel, the second, or eastern one, Saillisel ; they were generally referred to as Sailly and Saillisel. The pause in the operations enabled the enemy to withdraw his near troops, and when the 16th and 13th Battalions advanced at 6 p.m., behind a rolling barrage, they occupied Sailly without opposition, the line taken up being just east of the road to Le Transloy. The latter village was still in the hands of the enemy, but the 115th Brigade was able to advance and passed the night echeloned to the left rear of the 113th Brigade.

In this hard fighting Lieutenant Christopherson, the Medical Officer, proved a gallant successor to Major Dunn, going out himself to see to the wounded who were not being brought in fast enough by the stretcher-bearers. Several owed their lives to his fearless energy.[1]

The action of the enemy all along the front of the British Fourth and Third Armies was the same : he retired, here rapidly and in some confusion, there steadily, pausing to fight, sometimes successful in checking the pursuing troops, sometimes being overrun. For one more day he stood in front of the 38th Division.

The orders for the 2nd September were that the 115th Brigade should re-form behind the 113th Brigade and advance at 5 p.m. on the high ground east of Mesnil-en-Arrouaise. The 2nd Battalion, organised as two companies, was ordered to attack on the right, the 10th South Wales Borderers on the left ; the 14th Battalion of the 113th Brigade were to make good Loon Copse, on the left of the attack.

All troops remained in their overnight positions until the afternoon, when they moved forward to take up the assembly positions allotted to them on the east of Sailly. The artillery and machine-gun barrage came down punctually at 5 p.m., but too far ahead of the troops, leaving out the village of Saillisel, which was found to be still occupied by the enemy. Before they reached the assembly positions our 2nd Battalion and the 10th South Wales Borderers came under machine-gun fire, and when darkness fell were still fighting amongst the flattened ruins of Saillisel. Our 14th Battalion had the same experience in their attempt on Loon Copse. But the ruins of the village were cleared and a defensive line established for the night to the east.

The 113th Brigade were under orders to advance in a north-easterly direction on the 3rd September, in conjunction with the 17th Division on the left, but at 6 a.m. patrols failed to get into touch with the enemy— he was not to be found. Orders were cancelled, and the 115th Brigade on the right and 113th on the left were directed to advance on the trench

---

[1] Major Dunn had been gassed on 21st May. Llewellyn Evans notes seeing " pitiful rows of gas-blinded men lying in the shade of the trees (near Herissart) and Dr. Dunn, with tinted glasses and a parasol, striving to convince himself that it was nothing much and would soon pass ! . . . Anyhow, I must say how fortunate was the battalion in Dunn's successor, one Christopherson, of the U.S. Medical services. We had had, for years, a Medical Officer who was a legend almost, and this Yankee came and took his place, not unworthily, but with distinction, for he knew and did his job. He was of the battalion and not attached, and he honoured us and himself with as well won a Military Cross as there could have been."

line Martin Wood—Mesnil as rapidly as possible, while the 114th Brigade prepared to become advance guard from that position. The move forward commenced, no Germans were seen, and at 2.15 p.m. the 114th Infantry Brigade, 122nd Brigade R.F.A., 123rd Field Company R.E., 1 Bearer Sub-division R.A.M.C., 1 troop Carabineers and Cyclist Squadron, and 1 section 60-pounders, constituting the advance-guard, passed through the 115th and 113th Brigades on the line Martin Wood—Mesnil, and pushed battle patrols along the high ground down to the west bank of the Canal du Nord. The line for the night remained on the west side of the canal.

Two companies of the advance-guard crossed the canal on the 4th. A warning order was sent round that the division would be relieved by the 21st Division. On the 5th the relief took place.

In this advance, commencing on the 23rd August, our 2nd Battalion had suffered the most severely of all; their casualties are returned as 357, and at the end they were organised as a company, with a strength of about 90 rifles.

.   .   .   .

The III Corps was on the right of the 38th Division, and on the 31st August the 74th Division, having moved south from the Lys, relieved the 58th Division about three miles north of Peronne, on the right of the corps and next to the 3rd Australian Division (the 47th Division was in the centre of the corps front, and the 18th Division on the left).

The 229th Brigade advanced on the 2nd September south of Moislains, with the object of carrying the advance beyond the Canal du Nord; they met with stout opposition and the canal was not crossed until the 4th September.

The 231st Brigade was in reserve, and our 25th Battalion was bivouacked in Trigger Wood, where they had their first heavy dose of gas; the number of gas shells fired by the enemy at Trigger Wood was estimated at 1,000.

On the night of the 4th September the divisional front was readjusted; the 230th Brigade relieved the 229th, and the 231st took over a portion of the line held by the Australian Division (2nd). Our battalion relieved the 25th and 27th Battalions Australian Infantry.

The advance was continued by the 230th Brigade, meeting with little opposition, and our battalion moved in rear of the right flank.

On the 6th a check was met with just east of Longavesnes about 3 p.m. The Australians had come to a standstill slightly in rear. A and B Companies of our battalion formed a defensive flank, connecting with the Australian troops.

On the 7th the 231st Brigade passed through the 230th, the 24th Welch

Regiment and 10th Shropshire Light Infantry leading, our battalion in support. Villers-Faucon was occupied, and the enemy pursued to the east of the railway. The 74th Division was now in advance of both flank divisions, and our battalion had again to form a flank, in touch with the Australians on the right.

At 12.30 a.m. on the 8th the battalion was ordered to advance on the left of the divisional front, through the 58th Division lines (the 47th Division had been relieved) and attack some trenches north-east of Hargicourt at 7 a.m. The enemy, well posted in front of Epehy, saw our battalion moving up at dawn, and opened on them with machine guns. The whole battalion was forced to take cover in trenches in rear of the outpost line, and failed throughout the day to advance. Patrols were pushed out, but could make no substantial headway, and a heavy bombardment by our guns failed to shake the enemy. Lieutenant G. S. Williams and 2nd Lieutenant G. H. Elliot were killed with 5 other ranks, and 45 other ranks wounded. No advance was made that day either by the 74th Division or the flank divisions. The 231st Brigade was relieved by the 229th during the night, and our battalion withdrew to Longavesnes.

There followed a period of heavy rain and stormy weather for some days.

The Lys Salient.

The Lys Salient ran in front of Givenchy and Festubert (where, it will be remembered, troops stood fast against violent German attacks in the spring) and back almost to the Forêt de Nieppe; it then curled round to the east, giving the Germans Meteren, Bailleul, and Kemmel, to about St. Eloi.

This front had already commenced to move—the enemy were making preparations in July—but in September the movement was hastened. Already on the 27th August the Royal Air Force had reported fires and explosions at Laventie, Armentières, La Bassée, Aubers, and Fromelles, and at 7 a.m. on the 28th an officer patrol, under Captain Harris, from our 9th Battalion reached the Lestrem road without encountering any of the enemy. A general advance, however, soon came into contact with strong and alert rearguards.[1] Captain Harris and Lieutenant Shereff-Roberts, whose courage and enterprise had been conspicuous in driving forward, were killed.

On the 29th the Germans fired Estaires shortly after dark, and our

---

[1] Ludendorff gives the 3rd September as the date on which the evacuation of the salient was ordered.

patrols reached the banks of the Lawe River. The battalion was then relieved and went back to Hinges on the 31st August. It returned to the line on the 2nd September and continued the task of pushing the line forward.

To the north our 26th Battalion was in reserve at La Pierrière, but moved on the 31st August to the Asylum at St. Venant, and followed the advance in support to the 176th Brigade on the 3rd September.

Still farther north the 24th Battalion received orders to move from Bailleul. The 31st Division commenced to relieve the 29th in the neighbourhood of Hill 63 on the 3rd September. The 92nd Brigade was already in line on the morning of the 4th September, when the 29th Division, on their left, captured Hill 63. After dark the support battalions of the 86th and 88th Brigades were relieved by the 94th Brigade.

Our 24th Battalion found the line receiving considerable attention from the enemy's artillery. Prisoners stated that the Germans intended to hold the line they then occupied, west of the Lys and including the Pont de Nieppe, but their artillery activity suggested that they were emptying the ammunition dumps—as they had done on the first day of their retirement. Our battalion took over the line held by the 1st Leinster on Hill 63.

Considerable fighting had taken place at Ploegsteert, which was now in British hands. In the dugouts, beneath the foundations of that village, and generally along the captured enemy lines, care had to be exercised in order to avoid " booby traps," rough contrivances to explode bombs when, for example, the door of a dugout was opened, or a man sat on a bench, or even kicked a tempting-looking tin lying on the duck-boards. There were also timed mines. There was a general order that no dugouts were to be entered until the 3rd Canadian Tunnelling Company had first examined them.

Our 24th battalion was on the left of the 31st Division front, and on the 6th September the 36th Division, on their left, attacked successfully : the left company of the 24th Battalion, under Captain W. Mayhew, advanced with the 36th Division, and gained some 1,500 yards of ground. On the 8th the battalion was relieved by the 1st Royal Irish Rifles.

The enemy then made a stand, and considerable fighting took place in Ploegsteert Wood, culminating in a big attack on the 29th and 30th September, but our battalion took no part beyond a nominal attachment of B Company to the 12th Norfolk.

On both the 59th and 19th Division fronts much the same thing happened : the advance slowed down. Our 26th Battalion relieved the

Northumberland Fusiliers in the front line at Picartin and repulsed an
enemy raid on the 9th September. Our 9th Battalion had advanced persistently from its original line along the canal in front of Hinges, and
throughout August and September continued to gain ground, mainly by
means of fighting patrols.

On the 3rd September the 58th Brigade made an organised attack
along its whole front and advanced beyond the River Lawe, capturing
some 200 prisoners and some batteries of field guns. Within less than
seven days the 9th Battalion had arrived at the old British front line at

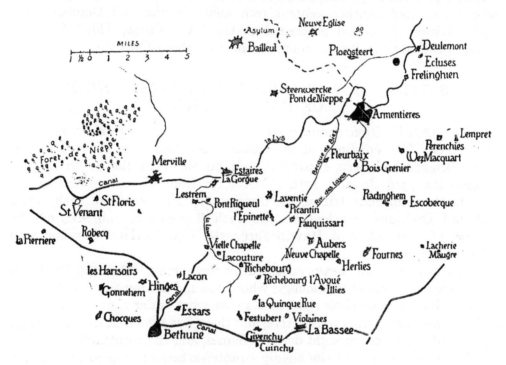

Neuve Chapelle, having assisted in driving the enemy out of Richebourg
and Lacouture—places with which the battalion had been very familiar in
the latter months of 1915 and the early part of 1916.

The next operation of consequence on this part of the front took place
on the 30th September, when a footing was obtained on the Aubers Ridge.
This operation proved to be the last stand made by the enemy before
finally withdrawing from his long occupation of that commanding position
over which so much blood had been spilt in 1915.

The battalion met with obstinate resistance. Fighting patrols attacked
enemy strong-points and seized intervening trenches, such as Biezer

Trench. By noon they had secured an advantageous position on the slopes of the ridge. Shepherd's Redoubt and the Distillery were now in our hands. The remainder of the day was spent in dealing with troublesome enemy machine-gun posts lurking in the wooded parts.

The casualties sustained were : Lieutenant Jagger and 6 other ranks killed, 3 officers and 27 other ranks wounded.

The Aubers Ridge was now virtually in our hands, and when the 74th Division came up to take over, they were fortunate enough to be able to advance over the ridge unopposed and to continue in pursuit of the enemy, who commenced another general retirement on the 2nd October. The 19th Division thereupon proceeded to the XVII Corps, Third Army, to assist in the advance farther south in the area about Cambrai.

THE BATTLES OF THE HINDENBURG LINE : THE BATTLE OF HAVRINCOURT.[1]

The 38th Division commenced to march forward again on the 10th September. The crossings of the canal which had been secured by the 114th Brigade had been expanded, and on the 11th the 115th Brigade relieved the 53rd Brigade, 17th Division, in front of Gouzeaucourt.

On the immediate left of the division the New Zealand, 37th, 62nd, and 2nd Divisions attacked on the 12th September, and secured the villages of Trescault and Havrincourt ; the New Zealand Division won African Trench.

The front line was heavily shelled by the enemy. Our 2nd Battalion suffered some 20 casualties, amongst whom was 2nd Lieutenant T. Parkinson; our 17th Battalion on their right had a somewhat easier time. During the night German aeroplanes were active, and there was a good deal of bombing ; but four of them were brought down in flames, and the air attacks ceased.

The next day (13th) the enemy counter-attacked at 9.30 a.m. and a few entered the left of the trench held by our 2nd Battalion ; they were speedily ejected, leaving 13 dead. The main battle, however, and the counter-attack were on the left of the 38th Division, and our battalions only came in for the fringe of them.

The great sweeping movements which had driven the enemy back to the Hindenburg Line had not cowed him, and the pause which occurred in front of those celebrated works was devoted to an artillery battle of great intensity. Not only were the front and support lines continually

---

[1] Date : 12th September. Area : road Gouzeaucourt—Fins—Ytres—Beaumetz—Morchies— thence a line to Mœuvres.

bombarded, but the back areas as well ; and there was, during this period, a considerable amount of gas shelling. Our 14th Battalion, back at Dessart Wood, lost 5 officers and 76 men through gas shelling.

On the 16th September the 113th and 114th Brigades relieved the 115th in the line ; the divisional front was slightly extended to the left.

THE BATTLE OF EPEHY.[1]

On the 18th September the First French Army and the Fourth and Third British Armies attacked, the regiment taking part in the battle south of Epehy with the 25th Battalion, and north of it with the 13th, 14th, and 16th Battalions.

On the 74th Division front the line had been advanced beyond Templeux-le-Guerard and Ronssoy. In front of them was a considerable trench system, on favourable ground, and with what was known as a " sticky patch " on the left, where the enemy, while holding the attacking divisions, could enfilade the 74th Division. The final objective did not appear to be, when compared to the advances in Palestine, at an ambitious distance—a little over a mile. The 230th Brigade were given the right of the attack and the 231st the left : battalions were to " leap-frog " on a two-battalion front. There were three objectives—Green, Red, and Blue lines.

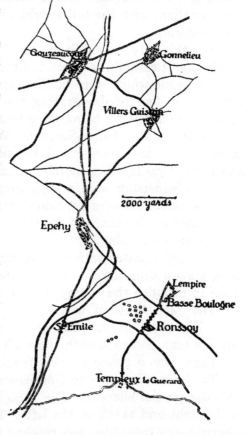

In the early morning of the 18th troops formed up for the attack in a downpour of rain through which it was impossible to see farther than a few dozen yards. The attack of the 230th Brigade on the right made good progress all day, although they could not hold on to the final objective. On the left the 231st Brigade met with fierce opposition after the first

[1] Date : 18th September. Area : St. Quentin (exc.)—Beauvois—Cartigny—Manancourt— thence by the southern edge of Havrincourt Wood to Villers Pouich.

objective had fallen. The Shropshires and our 25th Battalion passed through the Devons and Welch Regiment, but their advance, with right shoulders up, should have coincided with the advance of the 18th Division : the 18th Division had, however, met with stout resistance at the commencement of the battle and could not move. On the boundary line between the two divisions was a formidable quadrilateral work which held the two battalions at 500 yards from the second objective, the Red line. The Shropshire and our 25th Battalion occupied an intermediate trench by the side of the Ronssoy road.

A further bombardment of the Red line was ordered during the afternoon, and the 10th Shropshire succeeded in making a short advance, but our battalion, with the full weight of the quadrilateral against them, could not conform.

On this day Lance-Sergeant William Waring (No. 355014 Corporal (Welshpool)) earned the Victoria Cross. " He led an attack against enemy machine guns which were holding up the advance of neighbouring troops, and, in the face of devastating fire from flank and front, single-handed rushed a strong point, bayoneting four of the garrison and capturing twenty with their guns. Lance-Sergeant Waring then, under heavy shell and machine-gun fire, reorganised his men, and led and inspired them for another 400 yards, when he fell mortally wounded. His valour, determination, and leadership were conspicuous throughout."

Our casualties were Captain Charlesworth, Lieutenant Dudley Thomas, 2nd Lieutenant Penson, and 10 other ranks killed ; 44 other ranks wounded ; 5 other ranks missing.

The night passed with intermittent shelling on both sides, the Germans using a good deal of gas. During the afternoon of the 19th an effort was made to dislodge the enemy, but it was too small, and failed.

The 74th Division was then in touch with the Australians on the right, just short of the final objective, but on the left were some 1,500 yards in rear, in touch with the 18th Division.

There was a pause on this front.

To the north, opposite Gouzeaucourt, the 38th Division had met with a similar partial success. The attack was made with the 114th Brigade on the right and 113th on the left. The 114th had some stiff fighting and suffered many casualties, but reached their objectives. The 113th attacked with our 14th Battalion on the right, 16th on the left, 13th in support.

The 14th Battalion advanced on the three-company front—D, A, and B, with C in support. A and D Companies reached the second objective, the Green line, but B Company was held up by a machine gun in African Trench.

The 16th Battalion on the left attacked with D, half A and C Companies in line, one platoon of A in support, and B in reserve. There was a platoon of A in liaison with the 5th Division, and a platoon of D performed the same office on the right towards the 14th Battalion. Only D Company (three platoons) succeeded in reaching African Trench, and was ordered to send bombing parties to the left ; B Company was sent to assist D, but did not succeed in reaching the trench.

Both the 14th and 16th Battalions had reached the enemy trench with their right companies. To deal with the pocket of Germans between them and the 16th, the 14th Battalion sent their C Company to assist B, but both companies had to fall back to African Support. Soon after the whole of the 16th Battalion were back in African Support.

The messages that came through to Brigade and Division Head-quarters were of a confusing nature. The 5th Division had not advanced, and the exact position of the 113th Brigade was uncertain throughout the day. In the evening, however, it became clear that two companies of the 14th Battalion were in African Trench. These two companies were counter-attacked at 6.30 a.m. on the 19th and driven back to African Support. They again won a footing in the

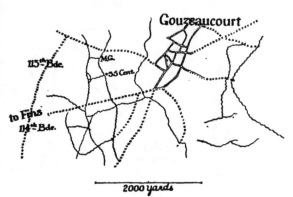

AFRICAN TRENCH WITH MACHINE-GUN POST AND PT. 35 CENT.

trench by bombing up a communication trench (35 Cent.), assisted by the 13th Battalion. Later in the day the 13th Battalion got into African Trench in touch with the 114th Brigade.

It was hard fighting and nothing much to show for it. Our 2nd Battalion and the 10th South Wales Borderers relieved the 113th Brigade on the evening of the 19th, and the next day the division was relieved by the 17th Division, and went back—the 113th Brigade to the Rocquigny area, the 114th to Equancourt, the 115th to Le Transloy.

In the 14th Battalion 2nd Lieutenants Parker and T. W. Darwell had been killed ; 2nd Lieutenants J. O. Roberts, J. Evans, and H. Handcock were missing ; 2nd Lieutenants G. F. Gates, W. Beveridge, and E. Roberts were wounded.

In the 16th Battalion 2nd Lieutenants T. W. Holland, J. Richards,

G. E. Saunders, and J. E. Young were killed ; Captain I. Griffith, Lieutenants V. B. Hughes, S. G. Young, 2nd Lieutenants C. Mack, T. B. Price
and D. Edwin were wounded.

All this left part of the attack, between the 74th and 38th Divisions,
had been " sticky." Our 25th Battalion remained in the line on the left
of the 74th Division and the whole division, with the 18th Division on the
left and one battalion of Australians on the right, attempted on the 21st
to establish the line on the final objective of the 18th—the Blue line.

The plan of the 231st Brigade was that our 25th Battalion, with four
tanks, would advance in a north-easterly direction on the quadrilateral
system of enemy trenches ; the 24th Welch Regiment would then carry

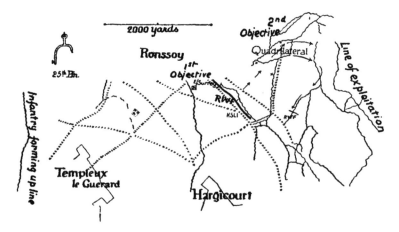

on to Gillimont Farm, while our battalion turned east and entered the
Blue line (2nd Objective).

The battalion advanced at 5.40 a.m. behind a heavy barrage and
swept over the quadrilateral system. All seemed to be going according to
plan. The battalion re-formed and entered the Blue line, capturing about
150 prisoners and some 30 machine guns. They then found themselves
with an exposed left flank : the Welch Regiment lost direction, and instead
of going to Gillimont Farm (Line of Exploitation) followed our battalion,
while further on the left the 18th Division did not advance at all. The
quadrilateral system of trenches in rear of our battalion had thus been left
open for the enemy to reoccupy, which he promptly did. The enemy then
began to close in.

Where were the tanks ? They never arrived. The situation was not
clear even to the battalion officers. They were being heavily shelled and
movement was difficult : patrols sent out to gain touch with troops supposed

to be on the flanks either failed to return or were turned back by enemy fire. The absence of news was in itself serious.

At midday their precarious position became apparent to all ranks of the battalion. The enemy attacked *from the rear*, from the quadrilateral system ; also on the battalion front ; and finally commenced to bomb down the trenches from the north. The Germans were trying to advance on three sides.

The 230th Brigade had attacked on the right with the Buffs and Sussex, and although our 25th Battalion was not in touch with the 230th Brigade, the remnants of two platoons of the Sussex had found their way to the uncertain position that was being held ; also the 24th Welch Regiment, but not the whole of that battalion—rather more than one company. These troops, Welch and Sussex, were ordered to withdraw down some trenches running in a southerly direction in the hope of gaining touch with the main body of the 230th Brigade. While this was taking place, the Lewis guns of our battalion were firing over opposite sides of the trench at parties of the enemy who were obstinately, but not very swiftly, advancing. The fire from the automatic weapons was effective, but ammunition soon ran out and the orderly retirement became a rapid evacuation, covered by bombers under 2nd Lieutenant 'Richards, and small parties of riflemen. A few of the wounded were taken out, but many were left in enemy hands. The battalion took up a position in the 230th Brigade area, which they held until relieved about 6 p.m. The strength of the battalion was then 6 officers and 189 other ranks.

At midnight the Shropshire Light Infantry cleared the quadrangle system, and our battalion, which had spent the time in brigade support at Hussar Road reorganising and resting, moved up in close support to the Shropshire. They were finally relieved by the 16th Devons during the night 22nd/23rd and marched back to Templeur-la-Fosse.

On the 25th they entrained at Peronne for Villers Bretonneux ; and on the 28th entrained at Corbie for Chocques, with the enemy evacuating the Lys Salient in front of them.

THE BATTLES OF THE ST. QUENTIN CANAL,[1] AND OF THE BEAUREVOIR LINE.[2]

The Canal de l'Escaut was a considerable work, and was not embodied in the Hindenburg defences as a trench—it was far too deep and wide—

---

[1] Date : 29th September—1st October. Area : road St. Quentin (exc.)—Vermand—Roisel—Villers Faucon—Fins—Gouzeaucourt—Banteau (exc.).

[2] Date : 3rd–5th October. Area : road Sequehart—Bellenglise—Pontru—Epehy—Vendhuille—Villers Outreux.

but as a place for sheltering troops. The actual fire trenches lay on either side of the canal, according to the configuration of the ground. Between Bellecourt and Vendhuille the canal ran through a hill, the tunnel being some 6,000 yards in length, with, of course, a deep cutting at the entrance.

The big battle which swept the enemy from this line started on the 27th September, and continued, as dealt with in Sir Douglas Haig's Despatches, until the 5th October ; but it has been split for naming purposes into a series of battles, the regiment having, under the general title of " The Battles of the Hindenburg Line," Havrincourt, Epehy, St. Quentin Canal, and Beaurevoir. St. Quentin Canal and Beaurevoir are best dealt with as one.

On the 27th September the Third and First Armies attacked on a 13-mile front, while on the Fourth Army front a bombardment was started which continued for two days. At 5.50 a.m. on the 29th September the French First Army, the British Fourth Army (consisting of the IX Corps, II American Corps, and III Corps), and the V and IV Corps of the British Third Army attacked.

In the orders for this attack the American Corps, on the right of the 18th Division, were to occupy a line from Pienne to the canal. The 38th Division stood at one hour's notice " to move and fulfil one of the following rôles : (*a*) relieve the 105th American Regiment east of the Canal de l'Escaut ; (*b*) take up assembly positions between Vendhuille and Hendecourt ; (*c*) relieve the 18th Division in bridgeheads at Vendhuille.

On the southern side of the tunnel, about Bellecourt, Nauroy, and Gillimont Farm, the American troops overran a large number of Germans, and there was, for a while, a good deal of confusion. But " these points of resistance were gradually overcome, either by the support troops of the American Divisions, or by the 5th and 3rd Australian Divisions, which, moving up close behind the American troops, were soon heavily engaged." (Despatches.)

The result of it all was that the 38th Division did not move until the 3rd October, when the 115th Brigade (2nd and 17th Battalions) moved from some old trenches near Sorel-le-Grand and Hendicourt to positions north-west of Ronssoy, and the next day to the Hindenburg Line near Bony.

The intention had been to move the division through Vendhuille and operate north-east, crossing the front of the 33rd Division, who were along the Canal de l'Escaut, when the latter division would follow in support ; but during the night 4th/5th October the enemy retired. On the morning of the 5th the situation was : 115th Brigade on a line from La Pannerie to Hargival Farm, facing north, and astride the Hindenburg Line which faces west; the 113th Brigade was at Bony; the 114th Brigade east of Epéhy.

The 115th Brigade Group was then directed on Aubencheul, while the 113th Brigade, passing through Vendhuille, was directed on Mortho Wood, on the left of the 115th.

The enemy rearguards gave little trouble. The 14th Battalion, march-ing as advance-guard to the 113th Brigade, detached A Company, under Lieutenant Pringle, to deal with a pocket of the enemy in the Hindenburg Line, and he reported, sor-rowfully, that there were only eight of them who surrendered. West of Mortho Wood, however, the battalion was held up by machine-gun fire. At dusk the 38th Division was on the line Vaux-hall Quarry—east edge of Aubencheul—west edge of Mortho Wood, in touch with the 50th Division on the right and the 21st on the left.

The divisional artillery had crossed l'Escaut over a temporary bridge at Ossus, and with an artillery brigade of the 18th Division assisted the advance.

The 38th Division was now facing a strong position west of Villers-Outreux called the Beaurevoir line. It was heavily wired, and machine guns at Villers Farm were well sited on a commanding position; indeed, the whole line was strongly held by machine guns. Attempts were made by patrols to cut the wire, but this was found impossible in daylight. There followed a pause of two days while artillery was brought up for a frontal attack on the Fourth and Third Army fronts.

The 38th Division opened the battle on the 8th at 1 a.m.—theirs being a preliminary attack to the main operation—and were soon involved in an anxious and difficult situation. The 115th Brigade attacked on the right with the 10th South Wales Borderers and the 17th Royal Welch Fusiliers. In front of them was the village of Villers Outreux. The line of the advance was in a north-easterly direction, and the South Wales Borderers were to pass to the east and our 17th Battalion to the west of the village. When the village had been enveloped, our 2nd Battalion was to pass through it and clear it of the enemy with the aid of two tanks.

The 113th Brigade, on the left, attacked with our 16th Battalion and 13th Battalion through Mortho Wood.

Following the battle from the right, the 10th South Wales Borderers and our 17th Battalion came on belts of wire which had been considerably strengthened by the enemy and were very little damaged by our artillery. Heavy machine-gun fire was opened by the enemy and troops were thrown into confusion. It seemed as though the attack had failed at the very commencement. It was extremely dark and it was raining. Communication was not easy.

Our battalion had suffered heavy casualties, but officers and non-commissioned officers proceeded to reorganise for a second attempt.

Meanwhile, our 2nd Battalion was marching up, unaware of the situation in front of them. When close up to Villers Outreux, Lieutenant-Colonel Norman received news of the true state of affairs, and found the attacking battalions of the brigade were still on their original line. He hastily issued fresh orders. The tanks (six) were present, and he directed them on the village, while B Company attacked east and A Company west of the village ; the remaining two companies he sent to co-operate with the tanks. Our 17th Battalion, led by Lieutenant-Colonel Beasley, assisted on the left—they lost 10 officers and 120 other ranks during the morning. One battery commander had brought a telephone wire up to the front line and was able to give invaluable assistance.

The attack was proceeding when the 114th Brigade arrived on the scene. Orders had been issued by Division postponing their advance, but did not reach Brigadier-General Rose Price, who had already moved.

B Company of our 2nd Battalion, under Captain Kirkby, succeeded in breaking through the enemy line, and was followed by C Company. The gap was widened, and as the battalion, with the tanks, proceeded to clear the village, two battalions of the 114th Brigade came in on the extreme left and drove the enemy from Château des Angles, from which the Germans had been pouring heavy fire.

LANCE-CORPORAL H. WEALD, V.C., 14TH BATTALION.

CORPORAL (LANCE-SERGEANT) W. H. WARING, V.C. 25TH BATTALION.

480]

Up to 10 a.m. the situation had been so obscure the artillery had not been allowed to move forward,[1] but by 11 o'clock the action of our 2nd Battalion and tanks had secured the line from which the 114th Brigade had been ordered to advance. Three-quarters of an hour later all the guns were in action near Villers Outreux, and the attack was resumed.

The attack of the 113th Brigade was also greatly impeded by troops running into belts of wire in the darkness of the night. Our 16th Battalion were unable to get further than Angelus Orchard, but Captain Wynne Edwards, of our 13th Battalion, had marked down two gaps in the wire the previous day, and the battalion worked their way through them. Progress was, however, slow, and as the light improved, the 13th Battalion suffered from fire from Villers Outreux and Château des Angles ; also from an enemy field gun firing over open sights. Two tanks allotted to the brigade commenced operations and cleared some pockets of enemy troops in the centre of the brigade front ; the final objective was reached at 11.15 a.m. in conjunction with the advance of the 115th Brigade on the right, and everywhere the situation was clear for the advance of the 114th Brigade.

The next day (9th) the 33rd Division passed through the 38th, the latter remaining in support at Clary.

This hard-fought battle is a memorable one, inasmuch as it brought our battalions through the entire system of fortifications constructed by the enemy into the civilian-inhabited country beyond. The people of Clary gave them a great reception, and the tricolour flag flew from every house.

The 2nd Battalion lost Lieutenant A. C. F. Griffiths and the Rev. W. E. Jones, killed ; the 16th Battalion had 158 casualties, with 2nd Lieutenants J. M. Davies and A. Palfreyman amongst the killed.

The pursuit of the enemy continued to the River Selle. On the 11th the 113th Brigade moved to Bertry, the 115th to Troisville. On the 13th October the 115th Brigade relieved the front brigade of the 33rd Division in the front line, the 114th Brigade being in support and the 113th in reserve.

THE ENEMY RETREAT IN FLANDERS.

Our 24th Battalion was the most northern of the regiment. The big battles fought by the First, Third, and Fourth Armies had an effect, while they were in progress, on the enemy in the north.

At a conference held by Marshal Foch at Cassel on the 9th September, the Second Army, with some French Divisions, was placed under the orders

---

[1] Lieutenant-Colonel J. E. Munby, *A History of the 38th (Welsh) Division.*

of the King of the Belgians, with instructions to press the enemy. A big attack was opened on the 28th September which drove the Germans beyond the high ground we had fought for in 1917. Ploegsteert Wood, Messines, the whole of the left bank of the River Lys as far as Comines, fell into our hands. In this first movement the 24th Battalion took no part, remaining in camp near Bailleul.

The 26th Battalion, in the Fifth Army, was repairing roads at Pont Riquel from the 14th to the 28th September, when they took over the left of the 59th Divisional front, relieving the 36th Northumberland Fusiliers, still about Picantin. They were themselves relieved by the 25th King's Liverpool Regiment and the 17th Sussex the next night, and went back to billets.

The general retreat of the enemy commenced on the 2nd October, influenced by blows from north and south—principally the latter ; and on that day the battalion passed under the orders of the 178th Brigade, and moved forward by bus to take over the left centre of the 61st Division front, relieving the 2/8th Worcestershire. The new front was about Bois Grenier (well known to the 2nd Battalion), and the whole of the 59th Division side-slipped, their old front, about l'Epinette, being taken over by the 47th Division (our 4th Battalion left the Hindenburg Line front on the 8th September, and spent most of the time at Camblain-Châtelain, near Chocques).

The 59th Division followed the slow and deliberate retirement of the enemy, our 26th Battalion being directed on the village of Wez Macquart. They were close to this village when they were relieved by the 17th Sussex on the 6th October and went into billets on the Fleurbaix—Armentières road.

Lieutenant-Colonel W. W. Gardner took over command on the 8th.

Meanwhile prisoners gave information that a retreat from Lille was imminent. Our battalion returned to the line, relieving the Sussex on the 11th, and on the 16th October a general advance was made by the whole division to a depth of some 3,000 yards. The next morning the battalion moved forward without opposition and reached the line of the Lille Canal at Marquette, north of Lille.

The 47th Division had been advancing on the line of Lille, but were relieved by the 57th Division on the 15th. Our 4th Battalion then marched back to Estaires, where they entrained for Aire. But they took part in the official entry into Lille on the 26th.

The 74th Division moved up to the Fifth Army front, commencing on the 25th, when they marched to Peronne to entrain for Villers Bretoneux.

They marched to Corbie on the 27th, thence by train to Norrent Fontes ; our 25th Battalion was at Hinges. The arrival of this division coincided with the retirement of the enemy. The 58th Brigade of the 19th Division had been relieved by the 230th Brigade, and other reliefs were in progress when it was discovered, on the morning of the 2nd October, that the enemy had gone ! The 56th Brigade therefore did not wait for relief, but pursued the enemy until the afternoon, when the 231st Brigade took over, our 25th Battalion being in reserve. The 74th Division went forward, without opposition. The enemy was eventually found east of Wavrin and Lattres. The division was relieved on the 10th, and our battalion marched to billets at Herlies.

Back again in the line on the 17th, to relieve the 230th Brigade, the enemy " had vanished " ! and the pursuit was in full cry before the relief took place. The 25th Battalion marched forward to Lacherie, and then via Maugre, Ancoisine, Noyelles, to Wattignies. That evening the battalion took over the outpost line from the 10th Buffs.

At 8.30 a.m. the next day the battalion moved as advance-guard to the brigade, and was accompanied by a battery of the 44th Brigade Royal Field Artillery and a section of machine guns. The vanguard, under Lieutenant Woosman, found the enemy at Sainghin—some cyclists and a machine gun. Farther on a light screen of troops was driven through a wood and across the River Marcq, where the enemy had established a strong position on the high ground east of and commanding the crossings ; all the bridges had been destroyed. Efforts to get patrols across the river failed. When night fell, a line was held on the high ground across the face of Sainghin Wood.

Lille was found clear of the enemy.

It was on the 17th that our 24th Battalion commenced to move forward, moving to the junction of the Ploegsteert and Pont-Rouge—Warneton roads. They crossed the Lys on the 20th and marched to Lannoy, southeast of Roubaix.

All these battalions (the 4th resting but ready to come forward) were now gathered together on a 6-mile front, to the east of Lille. The 24th commenced to move north, marching to Mouscron on the 25th, Staceghen on the 26th, Deerlyck on the 27th, and Veerke on the 29th.

Meanwhile the 26th Battalion had moved on the 18th October to Annapes and on to Hemponpont, being relieved the next day on the line of the Lannoy—Forest—Lille railway. The battalion went into billets at Sailly-les-Lannoy, within a couple of miles of the 24th Battalion. On the 20th they moved to Mulans, and on the 22nd back to Toufflers.

To the south, on the 74th Division front, our 25th Battalion found they had lost touch with the enemy on the morning of the 19th, and advanced through Camphin to Haudion before they found him again. The next day the 229th Brigade and 55th Division carried on the advance, and our battalion went into billets at Hertain. The end of the month saw the 231st Brigade in the front line again, with our 25th Battalion in reserve and billeted in Marquin, but the whole advance was held up on the west bank of the Scheldt.

THE BATTLE OF THE SELLE.

The 38th Division had reached Clary on the 9th October.

On the 3rd the 19th Division, having handed over to the 74th Division on the Lys front, commenced to move south. Our 9th Battalion marched back to its billets at Sachin, and on the 4th entrained at Pernes, to detrain at Saulty Labret on the 5th, when they marched to billets at Sombrin.

The concentration of the division in the XVII Corps area, Third Army front, was complete, and they were held in corps reserve, Major-General Jeffreys having command of the support group. They were then at no great distance from the 38th Division, ready to take part in the thrust which was causing the enemy to retire with such speed in the north.

The division then followed up behind the advance. On the 7th our battalion embussed for Graincourt, and there occupied bivouacs and dug-outs. The following day to Cantaing; on the 10th into billets at Pronville, a suburb of Cambrai; to Cagnoncles on the 12th; to Rieux on the 16th.

On the 18th came the turn of the division to take up the running, and the 9th Battalion went into positions of assembly in front of St. Aubert and about Saulzoir and Montrecourt.

Sir Douglas Haig's Despatch divides the fighting which followed the breaking of the Hindenburg Line into three stages, " the breaks between the different battles being due chiefly to the depth of our advances and the difficulties of re-establishing communications."

The first stage is under the heading of the Battle of Le Cateau, a name which recalls the first days of the war, and fixes in our minds the fact that we were traversing the same ground, the Fate Line of the war. The result of this battle, which includes the capture of Villers Outreux by the 38th Division, was that the enemy was compelled to evacuate Cambrai and fall back to the River Selle. The 19th Division was warned on the 16th October that they would be required to attack the high ground east of the Selle on the 20th : the 24th Division had, on that day, captured Haussy, but the village had been recaptured and our troops driven back across the river.

The 38th Division also moved forward : on the 11th October the 115th Brigade moved to Troisvilles, and the 113th to Bertry to become support and reserve to the 33rd Division.

On this part of the front there was, on the enemy side of the river, a railway embankment which proved to be a greater obstacle than the river. The 115th Brigade took over the front line on the 13th and attempted to establish posts on the far side of the Selle, but failed. It was decided to cross by foot-bridges, which would be launched on the night of the attack.

The Battle of the Selle was the second phase mentioned by Haig. The 38th Division with five of our battalions being on the right of the Third Army, and the 19th Division, with our 9th Battalion, on the left, the 4th Division of the First Army attacked on the left of the latter battalion, otherwise it was a Third Army Battle.

On the 18th the 115th Brigade was relieved by the 113th and 114th, the former returning to Troisvilles ; but our 17th Battalion did good work prior to the attack in carrying up foot-bridges : twenty-four bridges were placed over the river on the division front.

The concentration of guns assisting in the attack on this formidable position consisted of the Field Artillery of the 38th and 33rd Divisions, the 13th Brigade Garrison Artillery, and all the available light and medium trench-mortar batteries ; and the barrage was thickened by the 38th Battalion Machine-gun Corps, and two companies of the 33rd Battalion. Two tanks were also detailed to assist on the division front, but, as it turned out, could do nothing owing to the soft ground and steep embankment.

On the left of the 19th Divisional front was our 9th Battalion, with forward Battalion H.Q. under Colonel Lloyd Williams at Montrecourt. During the afternoon of the 19th October the companies were directed to send out patrols with a view to securing a foothold across the River Selle and on the railway embankment, which, it was expected, would make the initial stage of the advance very difficult. Captain C. G. N. Morgan, of the left front company, thereupon detailed Lieutenant C. C. Marsden with a strong patrol to endeavour to cross the river at Saulzoir and to enfilade the enemy machine guns located in the embankment opposite the battalion front. This patrol succeeded in penetrating into Saulzoir, driving out the enemy who were there. It also met with bands of civilians who furnished useful information as to the positions and intentions of the enemy. Having secured an advantageous position, the patrol set about clearing the embankment of the enemy machine-gun posts by enfilading them from

Saulzoir. This enabled the remainder of the companies to cross the river and take up positions on the embankment from which to launch the main attack. There was, however, great difficulty in inducing the artillery commanders to make the necessary adjustments in their barrage plans, which had fixed the river as the first line of the barrage.

The enterprise of this patrol saved many casualties and rendered the task of the battalion, when the hour of battle arrived, a comparatively easy one. Other battalions who were not so fortunate sustained their heaviest casualties when they were crossing the river and the embankment in the course of the battle.

Following events from the right of the Army our 13th, 14th, and 16th Battalions left their billets at Bertry after dark on the 19th and marched across country to their assembly positions on the west bank of the river. Rain was falling and the ground was very heavy. The assembly, however, was carried out without a hitch, tapes were laid to the bridges, and at 2 a.m. the barrage opened.

The position they had to attack was not easy. After crossing the river they had to advance up a glacis to the precipitous railway embankment, some 50 feet high. But the artillery arrangements, covering a portion of the glacis slope and the embankment, were admirable : battalions crossed over the bridges, formed up on the enemy side of the river, and advanced on the railway. All our battalions attacked on a two-company front, the rear companies passing through on the first objective, about 100 yards beyond the railway.

The final objective, 1,000 yards or so beyond the railway, was won ; great execution was done by our artillery amongst the German machine gunners on the embankment, and those that survived were overcome by a smart outflanking move of the 16th Battalion, under Major Dale : they were on the right.

The 16th Battalion had 3 other ranks killed and 19 wounded ; the 13th Battalion had 8 other ranks killed and 47 wounded—one officer, 2nd Lieutenant E. J. Hughes, was killed ; the 14th Battalion had 7 other ranks killed and 27 wounded—2nd Lieutenant A. H. Roberts was killed in this action. In view of the strength of the position, which had already resisted an attack by the 33rd Division, the casualties were not excessive.

The 16th Battalion formed a defensive flank on the Montay—Forest road. Patrols sent out by the 14th Battalion found that the village of Forest was held in strength.

Meanwhile, on the 19th Division front, the 9th Battalion having crossed the River Selle on the previous evening and being already on the embankment when zero hour (2 a.m.) arrived, advanced to its appointed objectives

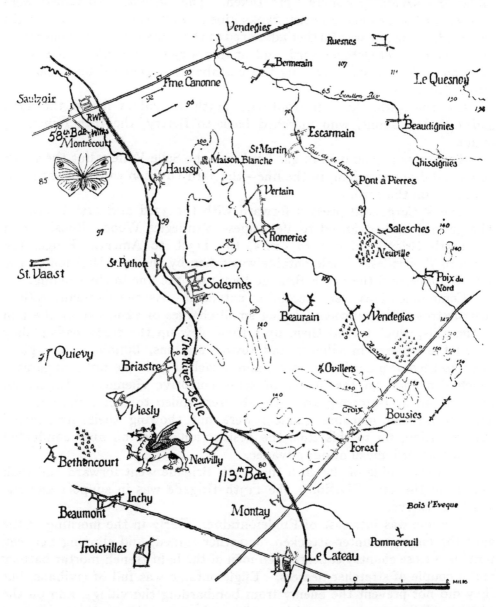

with little opposition. There was some confusion at first, due to the short-shooting of our artillery, which had not entirely adjusted its barrage line to meet the new situation created by the battalion using its first objective as its jumping-off line. However, the energy of Lieutenant Dealing soon put matters right ; the advance was continued according to the time-table, and several prisoners were taken. The casualties sustained were Lieutenant Pickard and 19 other ranks killed ; 2 officers and 61 other ranks wounded. The line was further advanced in the course of a minor operation on the morning of October 23rd, and at that stage it ran along the River Ecaillon. On the same evening the battalion was relieved and marched into billets at Rieux.

On the 38th Division front the 115th Brigade relieved the 13th and 14th Battalions, who marched back to Bertry, the 16th remaining in line.

There was a good deal of gas fired into the Selle Valley, but the 115th Brigade did not stay long in the line—the 33rd Division came forward and took over on the 23rd.

The V Corps still pressed forward with the 33rd and 21st Divisions. The general line advanced to Vendegies—Vendegies Wood—Bousies, and the 115th Brigade moved to Croix, the 113th to Amerval Ridge, the 114th to Troisvilles. Englefontaine was taken by the 33rd Division on the 26th October, and the 115th Brigade took over the line in the evening.

Communications were becoming extended. As the Germans retired they destroyed the railways, placing small charges of explosive at the join of the rails, which turned them up ; they blew up the cross-roads ; they mined the squares in villages and towns, stations, buildings, any place likely to become a depôt for stores, and attached a simple firing apparatus which depended on the action of some corrosive chemical. Engineers, pioneers, an ever-growing army of labourers toiled to repair the damage. Though German machine gunners were not showing their accustomed determination, up to this time the destruction under an ably conducted retreat was well ahead of our advance.

On the evening of the 26th the 115th Brigade went forward and took over from the 33rd Division ; the 113th Brigade was in support and the 114th in reserve.

The line was just east of Englefontaine. Early in the morning of the 27th the enemy counter-attacked, or rather raided, and slipping between posts in a close country captured ten men of the light trench-mortar battery and a couple of stretcher-bearers. Englefontaine was full of civilians, but they did not prevent the enemy from bombarding the village, and on the 28th the civilians were ordered from this and other villages.

The Armies were preparing for the next advance, but as a reply to the German raid our 17th Battalion raided them on the 29th, and secured

Arm.-Sergt. J. Belfield.   Sgt. Childs.   Cpl. Davies.   Driver Swift.

Capt. W. H. Fox,   Lt. D. Roberts-Morgan,   Sgt.-Driver Dyer,   R.Q.-M.S. J. Hughes,   Driver   Capt. H. Yates,
M.C.   D.C.M., M.M.   M.M.   D.C.M.   Lloyd.   M.C.

2ND BATTALION GROUP OF THOSE WHO SERVED IN FRANCE THROUGHOUT THE WAR.

488]

a batch of between thirty and forty prisoners. It was a sharp little engagement, complicated by the presence of a lot of civilians who were being evacuated from Englefontaine while the raid was in progress.

THE BATTLE OF VALENCIENNES[1] AND THE BATTLE OF THE SAMBRE.[2]

(2ND, 9TH, 13TH, 14TH, 16TH, AND 17TH BATTALIONS.)

Weak in numbers, but no weaker than the enemy, who, in addition to the heavy casualties inflicted on him, was losing heavily by capture, the Fourth, Third, and First Armies prepared for a general advance on the 4th November. Valenciennes had fallen to the Canadians on the 3rd.

The enemy was in bad case. Ludendorff had resigned on the 26th October, and in the epilogue of his book he puts the case briefly : " From the end of October events followed one another at an increasing pace. In the west, on the 4th November, the German Army was withdrawn in good order to the Antwerp—Meuse line under the pressure of the enemy from Verdun upwards. The Alsace-Lorraine front, well organised, awaited an enemy attack.

" The Austro-Hungarian Army had completely dissolved as a result of the fighting in Upper Italy between the 24th October and the 4th November.

" Hostile forces were moving on Innsbrück. G.H.Q. took comprehensive measures for the protection of the southern frontier of Bavaria. In the Balkan theatre we held the Danube.

" We stood alone in the world."

Turkey and Bulgaria had already thrown up the sponge.

But there is no object in burking the fact that our Army was strained to the limit. It was becoming increasingly difficult to maintain communications. From the moment the advance commenced in August we had not been able to use any railway line beyond the then railhead unless laid by ourselves. The engineers were performing marvels, but they could not keep pace, and the roads, even in the clear country east of the devastated area, that wide belt that had been churned up by shell fire for four years, were in a dreadful state.

---

[1] Date: 1st–2nd November. Area : the Bavai—Cambrai road as far as Vendegies ; thence the stream to its junction with the River Escaut ; thence a line to Wallers ; thence along the southern edge of the Forests of Vicoigne and Raismes.

[2] Date: 4th November. Area : the railway Boué—Le Cateau (exc.) ; thence the road to Romeries—Famars—Onnaing—thence the railway to Mons.

German units were offering less resistance; they would not stand, but the retreat was well carried out. Our pursuit was bound to get slower. And there was difficult country ahead. This on the British front, where the main blows were still falling. Ludendorff, however, saw the danger. " Owing to the destruction of the railways, the enemy attacks in the north would be bound to lose impetus. It was to be expected that they would now attack in Lorraine." And with his troops in a depressed and sullen mood, what could he expect ?

Up to this point, however, the artillery ammunition supply was well maintained.

In front of the 38th Division lay the Forêt de Morval, much depleted by German wood-cutting, but still a formidable obstacle. The plan was to go through it on the " leap-frog " principle. The 115th Brigade had the first task, to what was called the Blue line ; the 113th had to jump over them to the Jolimetz—Landrecies road (Red line) ; the 114th over them to the roads running north-east and south-east from Les Grandes Pâtures (Green line). Brigade units also attacked in the leap-frog manner.

Our 2nd Battalion practised the attack in Vendecies Wood on the 1st November, and took over the line on the 2nd. The order of battle was : 2nd Royal Welch Fusiliers, 10th South Wales Borderers, 17th Royal Welch Fusiliers. A tank was allotted to each battalion.

The 38th Division was ahead of the 18th on the right, and the 17th on the left, and the big attack opened at 5.30 a.m. on the 4th November. But for the 38th Division zero hour was 6.15 a.m.

About 5 a.m. the brigade was formed up for attack. On the right C and D Companies of our 2nd Battalion led, B and A in support, and to leap-frog in due course. But it was not a simple movement. The flank of C Company rested on the Ruisseau des Eclusettes, a meandering stream, now contracting the battalion front to 300 yards, now opening out to 800 and more ; on the forming-up line the two leading companies were on a 500-yards front, and their final objective was 1,200 yards of front. So it was not plain leap-frogging. C Company had to remain in position and advance from the leap-frog line while B Company moved up from support and became the right company in the further advance ; but on the left A Company jumped over D. In the course of the advance there was also a change of direction.

There was a heavy morning mist when the rolling barrage opened in front of the 2nd Battalion. The tank allotted to them failed to arrive, but it was replaced by one that should have gone to the 18th Division front, but had missed the road. The advance was made in columns of platoons at wide intervals.

The advance of the 115th Brigade was met by considerable machine-gun fire. The tanks did useful work, and the formation adopted by the infantry enabled platoons to pass between enemy posts and take them in reverse. Also the morning mist embarrassed the Germans far more than it did the attacking troops, who kept direction well.

On the 2nd Battalion front there were scattered houses which required mopping up, and companies were so weak that this task was given to Battalion Headquarters. A good many casualties were caused during the advance to the Blue line by a gap between the right company and the 18th Division, in which enemy machine guns, on the far side of the river, remained undisturbed and were able to enfilade the advancing troops. D Company cleared up this space.

In the 2nd Battalion 2nd Lieutenant W. R. C. Keepfer and 10 other ranks were killed, 67 other ranks wounded. In the 17th Battalion 2nd Lieutenant N. E. Evans and 7 other ranks were killed, 3 officers and 41 other ranks wounded.

The 113th Brigade had meanwhile formed up east and south-east of Englefontaine, and when the 115th had taken the Blue line, advanced through them to the Red line.

There had been little sleep for the men of the 113th Brigade. Réveillé had been at 2 a.m.; hot breakfasts had been served immediately, and battalions were on the move at 3 a.m. Arriving at Englefontaine, they were under fire at 5.30 a.m., when the barrage opened for the 17th Division on their left and drew enemy retaliation on the village. Casualties occurred in all battalions, but most in the 16th. Major W. P. Weldon, commanding the 14th, was wounded, but carried on until Lieutenant-Colonel Collier came up, later in the day, from the reserve details.

The enemy resistance broke down after the 115th Brigade attack, and apart from the early-morning shelling, little opposition was met with by the 113th Brigade. There was a pause for two hours on the Red line to enable the 114th Brigade to come up, and also the artillery to move forward. The final objective was won before dark, and the advance was continued through the night, beyond the edge of the forest to the village of Berlaimont—the first objective of the 33rd Division, which passed through the 38th in the morning.

The 13th Battalion lost Captain Jones Maitland and 14 other ranks killed, 64 other ranks wounded ; the 14th, Lieutenant W. B. C. Hunkin,

2nd Lieutenant V. Llewellyn killed [1]; the 16th 23 other ranks killed, 85 wounded.

THE 9TH BATTALION.

The objectives of the 19th Division in the Battle of the Sambre were the high ground west of and overlooking Jenlain, and the spur west of and overlooking the villages of Eth and Bry. If the situation allowed, patrols were to be pushed forward across the river and on to the high ground north-east of the villages.

The first objective was to be carried by the 56th Brigade ; the second by the 56th on the right and the 58th on the left.

The 56th Brigade was in the front line on the night 2nd/3rd November, and the 58th Brigade concentrated in Vendegies and Sommaing.

The 56th Brigade had just taken over the front line when they heard, early in the morning, that patrols of the 11th Division, on their left, had failed to find the enemy, and that forward brigades were advancing. Patrols were at once sent out from the 56th Brigade, and found the enemy at Jenlain, and at the Château d'en Haut Farm, and on the Villers Pol—Jenlain road. Patrols from the 24th Division, on the right, were fired on from Villers Pol and could not advance. After some sharp encounters the 56th Brigade secured the line of the first objective given for the next day, the 4th.

All this necessitated a considerable modification of plan. It was decided to start the attack next morning from the line of the Le Quesnoy—Valenciennes road, and battalions of the 58th Brigade were ordered up in position.

Our battalion was in support to the 9th Welch and 2nd Wiltshire, and took up assembly positions in the vicinity of Artres. The night was exceedingly dark, rain was falling steadily, and there were no guides to lead troops through the totally unknown country. Lieutenant-Colonel Smeathman, who had returned and resumed command, states, however, that his battalion found no difficulty in reaching the assembly position ; other units passed an anxious night, more especially the artillery, who had to move up guns.

A heavy mist lay in the valleys at dawn. Zero hour had been fixed for 6 a.m. The Welch and Wiltshire, starting on a 500-yards front, had to fan out to 2,000 yards, but they went away well, and crossed the Petit

---

[1] Previous to this battle, the battalion was quartered at Pont du Nord. A shell struck the joint mess of C and D Companies and killed Lieutenant O. M. Jones, 2nd Lieutenants H. D. Roberts, J. Bartley, G. H. Charles, and wounded two others.

Aunelle River, which was found to be a deep stream with high banks. Opposition was encountered east of the river, but all objectives were taken and patrols were sent forward to secure the high ground east of Eth and Bry.

Our battalion, in support, was not greatly troubled by the enemy reply to the barrage. In some places shells fell thickly, such as the Ferme de Wult, but Battalion Headquarters, which had been in the farm, had moved to a copse and was not fired at. The chief trouble encountered was gas, of which there was a sufficient concentration in certain areas to necessitate the wearing of masks. At midday the battalion was ordered forward to the west bank of the Petit Aunelle, and later to the west of Eth and Bry on the ground occupied by the attacking battalions, who were to advance under a barrage on the high ground east of the villages. The country was full of deep, steep valleys with small streams, and would have been difficult had the enemy's appetite for fighting been keen.

The attacking battalions had some stiff fighting. The 2nd Wiltshire had captured Eth and were on the slopes to the east of it, but were unable to win the crest of the spur ; the 9th Welch had gone forward, refusing their left flank to keep in touch. A lot of machine-gun fire came from the left, where the 11th Division attack had not materialised.

The night passed in comparative quiet, and at 6.26 a.m. on the 5th the advance was continued under a light barrage. The enemy had moved back—very little opposition was encountered—and the forward line was established on the Wargnies—La Marlière road.

At 11 a.m. Lieutenant-Colonel Smeathman received verbal orders to march forward, pass through the two attacking battalions, who should by that time have reached a road running north and south just below Roisin : his objective was unlimited, but he gave his company commanders three bounds to Bettrechies.

Our battalion was in position and moved through the advanced troops at 1 p.m. Lieutenant-Colonel Smeathman says : " Two sections of field guns were placed at my disposal, and 8 machine guns. Only one liaison officer (R.A.) arrived. He belonged to one section only, and as it appeared that his guns were 3,000 yards away and he had no means of communication with them, and he did not report till one o'clock, the guns were of no use. The machine gunner failed to report at all."

Without this support our battalion moved forward and encountered little opposition until they reached the high ground west of Bettrechies : here they met heavy machine-gun fire and progress was arrested.

The whole of this advance, and the march to the jumping-off line, had taken place in the pouring rain. The men were tired and night was falling. On the left the West Yorkshire (11th Division) had come up, while on the right our battalion was in touch with the North Staffordshire. It was decided to try to occupy the high ground with patrols during the night.

But patrols failed to gain the crest, and so, at 6 a.m. on the 6th November, the battalion, in conjunction with the 56th Brigade on their right, advanced under a barrage and occupied the village of Bettrechies ; but although two of our patrols succeeded in crossing the River Hogneau,

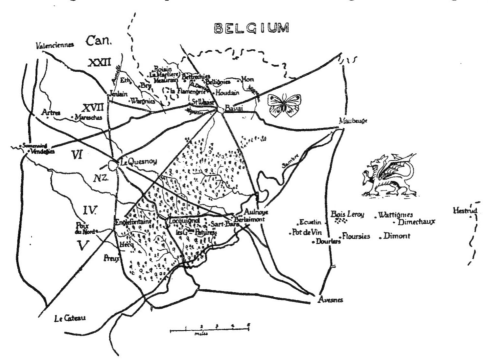

the battalion could not do so, and the patrols had to fall back. The enemy opened heavy shell fire on the forward troops and the village of Bettrechies, which was full of civilians, and continued to do so until darkness set in.

On our front the point of resistance was the Bois Dancade, and orders were issued to the 57th Brigade to attack on our right at 6 a.m. on the 7th, while our battalion kept the wood under heavy rifle and machine-gun fire —twelve more machine guns had been sent up to reinforce the original eight.

The orders arrived in the night, and at 6 a.m. the attack opened. It soon became evident, however, that the enemy had retired on our battalion front, and patrols, followed by two companies, were sent forward to occupy the high ground and the village of Bellignies, on the south bank of the northern branch of the Hogneau River. This was done, the only opposition being artillery fire. Two companies held the line ; the remainder of the battalion sought shelter in the cellars of Bellignies.

The course of the river, which was the divisional boundary, now caused the front to contract, and the 57th Brigade took over the advance ; but our battalion was ordered to protect their left flank, as troops on the left were some way behind, and the line we held was eventually extended to the village of Houdain.

" All troops," says Lieutenant-Colonel Smeathman, " were sopped to the skin and tired out, having come approximately 14 miles since the 3rd November. They had consolidated no less than eight different lines, and had practically no hot food during the entire period."

The casualties in these operations were 8 killed and 51 wounded.

Subsequently the 11th Division came up on the left, and our battalion was withdrawn and billeted in Houdain. On the 9th they moved back to Eth.

Across the Scheldt.

Our 25th Battalion remained in billets in Marquin until the 5th November, when they took over the outpost line in front of Tournai from the 10th Shropshire. The relief was carried out in pouring rain.

Rumour was busy. It was said that the enemy had withdrawn, but patrols found him in normal strength. The line was tested every night at all points, and finally, in the early morning of the 8th November, patrols from our battalion found that the Germans had really gone and entered the outskirts of Tournai ; before their report came in a Belgian lady walked into our outpost line with the information that the enemy had left at 3 a.m. Our patrols, however, found him on the east side of the river which runs through the town. All the bridges had been blown up. The battalion was relieved that night and went into billets at Orcq.

By the next morning the engineers had thrown a bridge across the river, and at 11 a.m. our battalion crossed over and became the advance-guard to the 74th Division, together with a troop of 19th Hussars, 2 sections of machine guns, and a battery of the 44th Royal Field Artillery, the force being commanded by Major W. N. Stable. A few shots were fired at them before reaching Rumillies, at 12.30 p.m., but beyond that village the enemy had vanished. Thimougies was entered at 6.45 p.m., the inhabitants stating that the Germans had left at 4 p.m.

The next day the battalion reached Cocquereaumont. The roads to the east were all mined, but had not been fired. No contact was obtained with the enemy.

On the left of the 74th Division was the 47th. Our 4th Battalion, after marching past the Army Commander, the Secretary of State for War (Mr. Winston Churchill), and the Mayor and Corporation of Lille, remained in the city until the 31st October. The 47th Division then went into the line north of Tournai, and the 4th Battalion was employed from 2nd November to the 6th in digging a new support line. When the enemy moved, they had a more congenial task of making roads up to the bridges the engineers had built—mud roads.

The whole Second Army (and the Fifth) was advancing without opposition. Our 26th Battalion left Toufflers on the 9th November, and crossed the Scheldt at Pecq, in support to the 178th Brigade. They billeted that night in Grand Rejet, and on the night of the 10th at Delpre, just north of Velaines.

Still farther north, level with Courtrai, our 24th Battalion had some stiff fighting before the 31st Division reached the Scheldt on the 31st October. The 35th Division attacked on the right, and the 34th and 41st French Divisions on the left. Our battalion attacked with the 12th Royal Scots Fusiliers, and the notable feature of the battle was the fierce hand-to-hand fighting that occurred in the farmhouses and hedges of this close country. The 24th Battalion swept forward irresistibly, and captured over 200 prisoners, many machine guns, and four field guns. Starting at 5.25 a.m., the battalion took the final objective east of Caster at 10.15 a.m. They were relieved by the 3rd Battalion, 23rd French Regiment, on the 2nd November, and marched back to Laaten, thence to Lauwe.

Their fighting was over. On the 10th they marched to Avelghem and on the 11th to Renaix.

The enemy was streaming out of Belgium. On the Third Army front the 33rd Division was marching towards the Sambre, which they crossed on the 6th November. The 113th Brigade moved from the forest to the Sart Bara—Ribaumont area ; the 115th to the ground vacated by the 113th at Les Grandes-Pâtures ; the 114th remained in the forest. The next day the 114th Brigade moved up to Ecuelin, in support to the 113th, who passed through the 33rd Division to become advance-guard to the 38th Division. The march up to the outpost line, at Dourlers Wood, was far from pleasant, as the enemy shelled the roads ; the 13th Battalion had 14 casualties.

In the early morning of the 8th the 14th and 16th Battalions were on

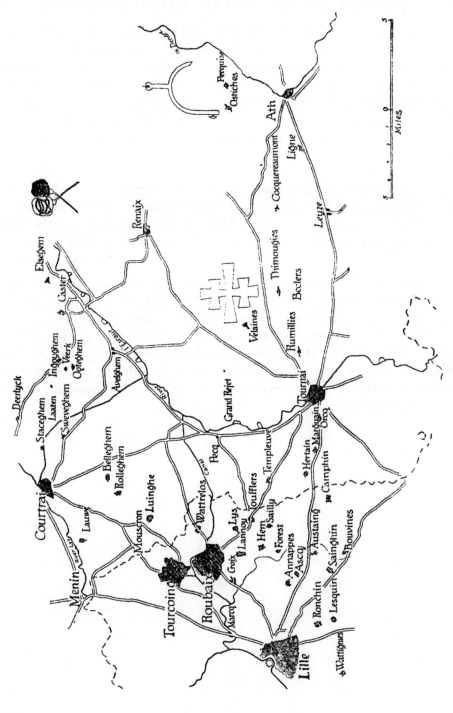

the Avesnes—Maubeuge road.   At noon one company of the 13th attacked La Belle-Hôtesse Farm, from which fire had been opened ; but on the approach of our troops the enemy fled.   No signs of the enemy were seen after this.   On the 9th the 13th Battalion entered Wattignies, while the Oxfordshire Hussars reported Hestrud, on the Belgian frontier, clear of the enemy.   The 113th Brigade went into billets at Wattignies, and the Corps Cyclists, with C Squadron Oxfordshire Hussars, patrolled the forward area.

On the 11th November the famous Army Order was sent out to all units : " Hostilities will cease on the whole front as from November 11th at 11 o'clock (French time).   The Allied troops will not, until a further order, go beyond the line reached on that date and at that hour.

" Marshal Foch."

At that hour the 13th Battalion was at Wattignies ; the 14th at Dimont ; the 16th at Dimechaux ; the 2nd Battalion at Aulnoye ; the 17th at Dimechaux ; the 9th at Eth ; the 25th was on the march and did not get the order until 3 p.m., when the advance-guard was halted at the village of Perquise ; the 26th was at Delpre ; the 24th was marching from Avelghem to Renaix.   At one place only on the whole British front was there any resistance—at Mons, which was captured by the 3rd Canadian Division during the morning.

INDEX

FRANCE AND FLANDERS

III—32*

INDEX

INDEX

INDEX

INDEX

INDEX

INDEX

INDEX

INDEX

INDEX

INDEX

INDEX·

INDEX

INDEX

INDEX

INDEX

Lightning Source UK Ltd.
Milton Keynes UK
UKHW032233171218
334167UK00006B/670/P